LEGAL ASPECTS OF CONTRACTS AND THIRD PARTIES

Common Core of European Private Law

1. *Interpretation of Commercial Contracts in European Private Law*, C.J.W. Baaij, D. Cabrelli and L. Macgregor (eds.)
2. *Immoral Contracts in Europe*, A. Colombi Ciacchi, C. Mak and Z. Mansoor (eds.)
3. *The Acquisition of Immovables through Long-Term Use*, B. Hoops and E.J. Marais (eds.)
4. *Boundaries of Information Property*, C. Godt, G. Van Overwalle, L. Guibault and D. Beyleveld (eds.)
5. *Mass Harm in Europe*, T. Arons and R. Rijnhout (eds.)

LEGAL ASPECTS OF CONTRACTS AND THIRD PARTIES

On Third-Party Rights, Transfer of Rights, Agency and Contracts

Edited by
Jan BIEMANS
Lorna RICHARDSON

INTERSENTIA
Cambridge – Antwerp – Chicago

Intersentia Ltd
8 Wellington Mews
Wellington Street | Cambridge
CB1 1HW | United Kingdom
Tel: +44 1223 736 170
Email: contact@larcier-intersentia.com
www.larcier-intersentia.com

Distribution for the UK and
Rest of the World (incl. Eastern Europe)
NBN International
1 Deltic Avenue, Rooksley
Milton Keynes MK13 8LD
United Kingdom
Tel: +44 1752 202 301 | Fax: +44 1752 202 331
Email: orders@nbninternational.com

Distribution for Europe
Lefebvre Sarrut Belgium NV
Hoogstraat 139/6
1000 Brussels
Belgium
Tel: +32 (0)2 548 07 13
Email: contact@larcier-intersentia.com

Distribution for the USA and Canada
Independent Publishers Group
Order Department
814 North Franklin Street
Chicago, IL 60610
USA
Tel: +1 800 888 4741 (toll free) | Fax: +1 312 337 5985
Email: orders@ipgbook.com

Legal Aspects of Contracts and Third Parties. On Third-Party Rights, Transfer of Rights, Agency and Contracts

Artwork on cover: djero.adlibeshe / Shutterstock

ISBN 978-1-83970-541-0
D/2024/7849/98
NUR 822

British Library Cataloguing in Publication Data. A catalogue record for this book is available from the British Library.

GENERAL EDITORS' PREFACE

It is a special pleasure to welcome the 23rd book in the series The Common Core of European Private Law. This book is edited by two scholars, who together represent two different legal cultures: the Dutch and the Scottish. Their works are already renowned and appreciated well beyond the 'Common Core' circles.

The Common Core project was launched in 1993 at the University of Trento under the auspices of the late Professor Rudolf B. Schlesinger. The methodology used in the Common Core project, then novel, is now a classic. By making use of case studies, it goes beyond mere description to detailed inquiry into how most European Union legal systems resolve specific legal questions in practice, and to thorough comparisons between those systems. It is our hope that these volumes will provide scholars with a valuable tool for research in comparative law and in their own national legal systems. The collection of materials that the Common Core project is offering to the scholarly community is already quite extensive and will become even more so as more volumes are published. The availability of materials attempting a genuine analysis of how things seem to be is, in our opinion, a prerequisite for an intelligent and critical discussion on how they should be. Perhaps in the future European private law will be authoritatively restated or even codified. As of today, the Common Core project is the longest-running scholarly enterprise in the field. The analytical work carried out by the more than 300 scholars that have so far joined us in the Common Core project is also a precious asset of knowledge and legitimisation for any such a normative enterprise.

We must thank the editors and contributors for their work. With a sense of deep gratitude, we also wish to recall our late Honorary Editors, Professors Rudolf B. Schlesinger and Rodolfo Sacco.

No scholarly project can survive without committed sponsors. The International University College of Turin allows us to organise the General Meetings together with the Centro Studi di Diritto Comparato of Trieste. The European Commission has partially sponsored some of our past General Meetings, having included them in their High Level Conferences Program. The Italian Ministry of Scientific Research, the University of Turin, the University of Trieste, the University of Salento, the University of Gothenburg, the University of Stockholm, the University of Groningen, the Fromm Chair in International and Comparative Law at the University of California and the Hastings College of the Law, the University of Trento, the Collegio Carlo Alberto and the Consiglio

Nazionale del Notariato all contributed to, or are still contributing to, the funding of this Project. Last but not least, we must thank all those involved in our ongoing Common Core projects in contract law, property, tort and other areas, whose results will be the subject of future published volumes.

Our website home page can be found at www.common-core.org. There you can follow our progress in mapping the common core of European private law.

General Editors

Mauro Bussani, University of Trieste – University of Macao
Ugo Mattei, University of Turin – University of California, Hastings College of the Law

Late Honorary Editors

Rudolf B. Schlesinger, Cornell University – University of California, Hastings College of the Law
Rodolfo Sacco, Emeritus, University of Turin

ACKNOWLEDGEMENTS

The idea for this work was first discussed at a Common Core of European Private Law conference in 2016. Much has happened since then! The editors wish to thank a number of people without whose work and commitment this volume would not have been possible. Firstly, our thanks go to the national reporters for agreeing to be a part of this project, and for their efforts and commitment to it throughout. A real community of scholars has come together and faced significant challenges, not least the COVID-19 pandemic, with national lockdowns and precautions, resulting in libraries being closed and colleagues moving to online working, to bring this project to fruition. We also wish to thank Dr Michael Milo and Professor Miquel Martín-Casals for their chapters, which significantly enhance our understanding of contracts and third parties and help set the context for the national reports which follow. Our thanks also go to Professor Aurelia Colombi Ciacchi, Head of the Contract Group of the Common Core project, for her advice, encouragement and good humour from the inception of the project. We are indebted to Irma Langeveld, Femke van Leeuwen, Michelle Maessen and Oksana Tovstopyat for their tremendous assistance in indexing the book. Finally, we are grateful to Rebecca Bryan and the team at Intersentia for their perceptive comments during editing and in bringing the book to publication.

We hope that this book provides a useful guide to the area for those interested in comparative law, whether students, academics or practitioners.

CONTENTS

LIST OF ABBREVIATIONS

AB	Allmänna bestämmelser för entreprenader (Swedish General Provisions for Construction Contracts)
AnfG	Anfechtungsgesetz
Arr.Cass.	Arresten van het Hof van Cassatie
AT	Allgemeiner Teil
Bankruptcy Act 2003	Ustawa z dnia 28 lutego 2003 r. – Prawo upadłościowe (Polish Act of 28 February 2003 – Law of Bankruptcy)
BCC	Belgian Civil Code
BGB	Bürgerliches Gesetzbuch (German Civil Code)
BGH	Bundesgerichtshof (German Federal Court)
BGHZ	Entscheidungen des Bundesgerichtshofes in Zivilsachen (Collection of Judgments of the Federal Court in Civil Matters)
BSC	Bulgarian Supreme Court
BSCC	Bulgarian Supreme Court of Cassation
CA	Bulgarian Commerce Act
Cass.	Belgian Court of Cassation (Cour de cassation/ Hof van cassatie)
c.c.	Italian Civil Code
CC	Czech Civil Code, Act No. 89/2012 Coll., as amended
CC 1964	Czech Civil Code, Act No. 40/1964 Coll., as amended
cf.	confer/conferatur (compare)
Com.	Belgian Tribunal of Commerce (tribunal de commerce/ rechtbank van koophandel)
CommC	Czech Commercial Code, Act No. 513/1991 Coll., as amended
CRTPA	Contract (Rights of Third Parties) Act 1999

DCC	Dutch Civil Code
Draft Statute Tort Law	Draft Statute of 8 March 2023 on introduction of Book 6 'Tort Law', *Parl.St.* 2022–23, 3213/1
e.g.	exempli gratia (for example)
Explanatory Memorandum	Explanatory Memorandum to the Draft Statute of 24 February 2021 on introduction of Book 5 'Obligations', *Parl.St.* 2020–21, 1806/1
Explanatory Memorandum Tort Law	Explanatory Memorandum to the Draft Statute of 8 March 2023 on introduction of Book 6 'Tort Law', *Parl.St.* 2022–23, 3213/1
ff.	and the following
FCC	French Civil Code
GACC	General Assembly of Civil College
HD	Högsta domstolen (Swedish Supreme Court)
HGB	Handelsgesetzbuch (German Commercial Code)
IC	Bulgarian Insurance Code
i.e.	id est (that is)
InsO	Insolvenzordnung (German Insolvency Code)
JLMB	Revue de jurisprudence de Liège, Mons et Bruxelles
Judicial Code	Belgian Judicial Code of 10 October 1967 (Gerechtelijk Wetboek/Code Judiciaire)
JZ	Juristenzeitung
KG	Kammergericht
KPP	Kwartalnik Prawa Prywatnego
LMK	Lindenmaier-Möhring – Kommentierte BGH-Rechtsprechung
LMR Act	Ustawa z dnia 6 lipca 1982 r. o księgach wieczystych i hipotece (Polish Act of 6 July 1982 on Land and Mortgage Register and on Mortgage)
LOC	Bulgarian Law on Obligations and Contracts
LPA	Law of Property Act 1925
LRA	Land Registration Act 2002
LTCA	Landlord and Tenant (Covenants) Act 1995

NJA	Nytt juridiskt arkiv (New Legal Archive)[1]
NJA II	Nytt juridiskt arkiv avdelning II (New Legal Archive Section II)[2]
NJW	Neue Juristische Wochenschrift
NJW-RR	NJW Rechtsprechungs-Report Zivilrecht
NJW	Nieuw Juridisch Weekblad
NP	Nowe Prawo
old BCC	Old Belgian Civil Code
OLG	Oberlandesgericht (German Court of Appeal)
Pas.	Pasicrisie belge
PCC	Polish Civil Code, ustawa z dnia 23 kwietnia 1964 r. – Kodeks cywilny (Act of 23 April 1964 – Civil Code)
RABG	Rechtspraak Antwerpen Brussel Gent
RCJB	Revue critique de jurisprudence belge
RGAR	Revue générale des assurances et des responsabilités
RGDC	Revue générale de droit civil belge
RGZ	Entscheidungen des Reichsgerichts in Zivilsachen (Collection of Judgments of the Imperial Court in Civil Matters)
Ruch PES	Ruch Prawniczy Ekonomiczny i Socjologiczny
RW	Rechtskundig Weekblad
SA	Sąd Apelacyjny (Polish Court of Appeal)
SCommC	Slovak Commercial Code
SCC	Slovak Civil Code
SG	State Gazette
SN	Sąd Najwyższy (Polish Supreme Court)
SOGA	Sale of Goods Act 1979

1 A semi-official collection of and the standard source for Swedish Supreme Court case law.

2 A semi-official collection of mainly preparatory works for different statutory acts. In Swedish law preparatory works are considered a source of law.

SOU	Statens offentliga utredningar (Official investigations of the State)[3]
SPE	Studia Prawno-Ekonomiczne
SRC	Sofia Regional Court
SSC	Slovak Supreme Court
Staudinger	J. von Staudingers Kommentar zum Bürgerlichen Gesetzbuch (commentary on the Civil Code)
T.App.	Tijdschrift voor appartements- en immorecht
TBH	Tijdschrift Belgisch Handelsrecht
TBO	Tijdschrift voor bouwrecht en onroerend goed
TPP	Transformacje Prawa Prywatnego
Trib.	Tribunal of first instance (tribunal de première instance/ rechtbank van eerste aanleg)
VersR	Versicherungsrecht
vol.	volume
VVG	Versicherungsvertragsgesetz (German Law on Insurance Contracts)
WER	Wetboek Economisch Recht/Code de droit économique (Belgian Code of Economic Law of 28 February 2013)
WM	Wertpapier-Mitteilungen: Zeitschrift für Wirtschafts- und Bankrecht
ZIP	Zeitschrift für Wirtschaftsrecht
ZMR	Zeitschrift für Miet- und Raumrecht
ZPO	Zivilprozessordnung (German Code of Civil Procedure)
ZVG	Zwangsversteigerungsgesetz (German Law of Forced Execution into Land)

[3] A collection of official investigations, and most importantly preparatory works for different Swedish statutory acts.

LIST OF CONTRIBUTORS

Claudia Amodio is associate professor of comparative law at the University of Ferrara. She holds a PhD in comparative law from the University of Florence. Her research deals with comparative law theory and method, French law, constitutional comparative law, European private law and digital vulnerabilities.

T.T. Arvind is professor of law and head of department at York Law School. He teaches and writes across contract law and other areas of private law, and on legal history. His recent publications include *Contract Law and the Legislature: Autonomy, Expectations, and the Making of Legal Doctrine* as well as a textbook on English Contract Law.

Jan Biemans is a professor of law at Utrecht University. He is chair and member of various (editorial) boards, committees and supervisory boards. He lectures and publishes on financial (private) law, (European) contract law, property law, insolvency law and succession law. He studied at the University of Groningen (law, philosophy) and Harvard Law School (LLM programme) and obtained his doctorate at Radboud University Nijmegen, on the legal effects of undisclosed assignment. His recent publications include the *Handbook on Dutch and European (Consumer) Credit Law*, in the renowned Asser series. Jan practised as a lawyer for six years with two large commercial law firms, including Supreme Court litigation.

Camilla Crea is associate professor of private law at the University of Sannio (Benevento, Italy), where she teaches private law and European contract law. She is the author of various books, and many articles published in Italian and international journals and volumes, on issues of private law, business law and comparative law. Furthermore, she is a founding member and co-editor-in-chief of the *Italian Law Journal*.

Kristián Csach is an associate professor in commercial law at the Faculty of Law, Trnava University, Slovakia. His fields of expertise are company law, contract law and private international law.

Dr Siel Demeyere is a senior attorney with the Belgian law firm Eubelius, and a voluntary assistant at the Institute for Property Law within KU Leuven. Siel practises mainly as a real estate contract lawyer. She has received several prizes for her academic work, including the Ius Commune Prize.

Pasquale Femia is full professor of private law at the University of Salerno, and a founder and co-editor-in-chief of *the Italian Law Journal* and *Tecnologie e diritto*. He deals with contract law, and the theory and history of private law.

Monika Jagielska is professor at the Institute of Legal Sciences, Faculty of Law, University of Silesia in Katowice; author of several books and articles on EU private law, sales law, consumer protection, product liability and private international law; expert and reviewer in EU and international projects; and chairwoman of the Ethics Committee at the University of Silesia.

Monika Jurčová is a professor of civil law at the Faculty of Law, Trnava University, Slovakia. She publishes regularly in the fields of contract law, consumer law and travel law.

Agata Kozioł is doctor of law and assistant professor at the Faculty of Law and Administration at the University of Silesia in Katowice, specialising in substantive and private international law issues of family and property law, as well as the law of securities over tangible and intangible assets.

Bartosz Kucia is doctor of law *(cum laude)* and assistant professor at the Faculty of Law and Administration at the University of Silesia in Katowice, attorney-at-law specialising in commercial and inheritance law, and author of publications on domestic, comparative and international succession law, including the administration of estate and succession law in common law countries.

Lorna MacFarlane is currently an associate in the litigation team at Dentons UK & Middle East LLP. She previously wrote an LLM by Research and PhD at the University of Edinburgh, which focused respectively on third-party rights and the privity doctrine in Scots contract law. Prior to her postgraduate research, she was a legal assistant at the Scottish Law Commission.

Miquel Martín-Casals is professor of Civil Law at the University of Girona (Spain) and director of the Institute of European and Comparative Private Law of the same university. He is an elected member of the International Academy of Comparative Law (IACL/AIDC), and of the American Law Institute (ALI). He is a member of the European Group on Tort Law (EGTL), the European Centre of Tort and Insurance Law (ECTIL) and the Pan-European Personal Injury Lawyers Association (PEOPIL). His research interests are in comparative law, tort law, contract law and legislative drafting.

Sonja Meier is professor of German and comparative private law and director of the Institute for Comparative Legal History, University of Cologne, and has been since 2022. Prior to this, she was professor of German, European and comparative law, University of Freiburg (2012–22). She has also been a senior research fellow at the Max Planck Institute for Foreign and International Private Law, Hamburg (2002–09) and professor of private law and legal history, University of Marburg (2009–12).

Peter Mészáros is an associate professor at the Faculty of Law, Trnava University, Slovakia. His professional interests include civil law, commercial law, civil procedure and consumer law.

J.M. (Michael) Milo is associate professor of law at the University of Utrecht. He read law at the University of Groningen and obtained his PhD at the University of Maastricht (1997). Property law, legal history and comparative law are his areas of interest. He is on the board of editors of the legal history review of the Netherlands *(Pro Memorie)* and chair of the Netherlands Association of Comparative Law.

Oskar Mossberg is associate professor in private law at Uppsala University. He teaches on a range of private law subjects and legal theory, with a particular focus on contract law. He does interdisciplinary research at the intersection of law, rhetoric and sustainability, and has published on a variety of subjects, including third-party effects of contract, which was the subject of his doctoral dissertation.

Luca Ettore Perriello is associate professor of private law at Marche Polytechnic University in Ancona, Italy, where he teaches commercial law, insolvency law and international contract law. He is the author of three books, and many articles published in Italian and international journals and volumes, on issues of private law, international law and comparative law.

Sylvain Ravenne joined the University of Tours in 2010. He has been co-director of the Biotechnologies and Law Master's programme since 2021. His research focuses on the reciprocal influence of civil law and business law, and on legal theory.

Lorna Richardson is a senior lecturer in commercial law at the University of Edinburgh. She teaches on a variety of private law and commercial law subjects, including (European) contract law and commercial leasing. She has published extensively in these areas, with a particular focus on interpretation of contracts and remedies for breach of contract. Prior to becoming an academic, Lorna practised as a solicitor for ten years with large commercial law firms. She is currently analysis editor of the *Edinburgh Law Review*.

Tomáš Richter practices law at JŠK, advokátní kancelář in Prague. He earned his PhD in 2002. Between 2011 and 2014, he held the Chair in Cross-border Corporate Insolvency Law at the Radboud University Nijmegen Law School. In 2018, he completed habilitation proceedings at the Prague School of Economics.

Vincent Sagaert is a professor at KU Leuven, KULAK and the University of Antwerp. He is co-director of the *Journal of Private Law* and a member of the core editorial board of the *Rechtskundig Weekblad*. He is also an editorial board member of the *Journal of Belgian Civil Law*, the *Journal of Justice of the Peace*, the

European Property Law Journal and the Civil Law Library Series. He is co-editor of the *International Encyclopaedia on Property and Trust Law*, chairman of the editorial committee of the Property Law Series and member of the advisory board of the General Practical Law Collection. Vincent has worked as of counsel at the Brussels Bar since 2003. He is part of the law firm Eubelius, where he focuses on real estate and securities law.

Dariusz Szostek is professor of the Faculty of Law and Administration at the University of Silesia, partner and founder of the law firm Szostek-Bar and Partners, expert in the European Parliament's AI Observatory, director of the Silesian Centre for Law Engineering, and digital competence technologies expert in new technologies.

Petar Stefanov Topurov is a PhD in Law (2023) and an assistant at the Civil Law Section of the Institute for the State and the Law at the Bulgarian Academy of Sciences (2019–present). He also practises as an advocate at the Sofia Bar Association (2018–present). Since 2021, he has been teaching as a part-time lecturer at the Faculty of Law of Sofia University 'St Kliment Ohridski' in the disciplines family and succession law (2021–present) and law of obligations (2023–present).

Carles Vendrell has been a partner of the Spanish firm Uría Menéndez since 2019. He is also a civil law lecturer at the School of Law of the Universidad Autónoma de Madrid. He holds a PhD in law from the University of Barcelona (special distinction), and was recipient of the XIII Francisco de Asís Sancho Rebullida Award for the best doctoral thesis in civil law (Universidad de Navarra, 2012).

Flora Vern holds a PhD in French private law from Sciences Po Paris, and is currently a senior lecturer in property law at the University of Glasgow. Her research interests span from complex land rights to private law theory more generally, including comparative aspects thereof.

Veronika Zoričáková is a researcher at the Faculty of Law, Trnava University, Slovakia, focusing on unjustified enrichment and tort law.

INTRODUCTION

Jan BIEMANS and Lorna RICHARDSON

The subject of this volume is 'contracts and third parties'. Although the reader could infer from the title that the scope of the project is restricted to contract law only, that has not been the case. While going through the project and drafting the cases, the editors had some difficulty in identifying the scope of the project.

Narrowly defined, the project 'contracts and third parties' could be limited to third-party clauses in contracts, restricting the project to contract law alone. In this case, the contractual parties may, for example, grant a right to a third person in their contract. However, 'contracts and third parties' could also encompass cases where a third party may indirectly rely on a contract to which they are not a party, such as a limitation of liability clause in a related contract. In such cases, third-party rights and contract law are very much related to delictual law (unlawful acts, tort law), already expanding outside the field of contract law.

From a broader perspective, 'contracts and third parties' will also deal with several separate doctrines, such as agency or representation, tort law (again), property law, assignment, commercial law, insolvency law, general rules of patrimonial law and other parts of the law of obligations. This broader perspective readily appears if a third party is involved in the conclusion or execution of a contract. This party may conclude a contract in their own name for the benefit of the principal, or may collect claims arising out of a contract for the principal, receiving money or property for the benefit of the principal as a contractual party. From another perspective, a third party may acquire contractual rights from one of the contractual parties. This may happen not only through assignment of a claim, but also by a transfer by operation of law (or otherwise) of a contract or contractual rights, if property is transferred to which that contract or those contractual rights are closely linked. In such cases, a third party may acquire contractual rights without having asked for them. From another, third, perspective, a third party who is a creditor of one of the contracting parties may be directly harmed by their contract, in seeking recourse for their own claim against one of the contractual parties.

In taking up this project, the editors have decided to take the broader approach described above. Focusing only on third-party clauses and/or the position of a third party in relation to the contract, without considering those third parties who may acquire or exercise rights out of the contract, seemed too limited.

This is especially true as many of the subjects identified are unlikely to be dealt with in other projects, as they are so much at the intersection of various disciplines, as described above. The editors were keen to create a book that was as useful as possible in considering the very many ways in which third parties can have or acquire rights deriving from the contracts of others. Looking at the sometimes very different answers to the cases, it also turned out that, in some jurisdictions, some cases are framed/answered according to different areas of law (property law, commercial law, insolvency law), as opposed to other jurisdictions where general rules of contract law are used.

Having chosen a broader approach, the editors have, at the same time, limited the scope of the project to general aspects of third-party rights and contracts, and have not gone into highly specialised areas of law, such as life insurance law, succession law or civil procedural law. In light of initial discussions with national reporters, it became clear that, in those areas of law, more specific rules generally applied, such that the discussion would not be related to contracts at all, and also that there was a high degree of particularity such that comparisons across jurisdictions would produce less fruitful insights. Although some legal institutions are very much related to third-party clauses – for example, beneficiary clauses in life insurance policies and bequests in wills – these seemed too far removed from the general rules of private law to include in the project. Also, more technical aspects of a third party collecting a claim for a principal in court, or acquiring rights of a contractual party during litigation before a court, seemed too specialised to include in a project dealing with substantive private law. Choosing to include these topics would have taken the project (deliberately) outside the scope of general contract law.

In addition, although the subject of debt and liability appears from time to time in the cases, as it is related to contractual rights, the editors have not focused on 'third-party debt' or 'third-party liability' and contracts as such (for example, by adding a case on transferring liability or debt, the passive side of a right or claim). The editors have only done so in the case of the exclusion or limitation of liability of a third party in a contract, which exclusion or limitation can, to some extent (in an abstract sense), also be considered a third-party 'right'. The topic is also addressed indirectly in searching for the limits of third-party clauses granting only rights but never burdening the third party with liabilities.

The aforementioned choices in defining the scope of the project have resulted in 11 cases in which various topics revolving around the general theme of 'third-party rights and contracts' have been addressed. Although the cases may seem very diverse at first sight, they can be reduced to four main aspects of third-party rights and contracts:

- Cases 1, 3, 8 and 9 focus on the limits of defining the third party's rights and obligations in the contract between the two other (contractual) parties, including limitation of liability, and granting benefits and/or negative rights.

- Case 11 (which is related to the previous item) addresses the limits of contractual freedom where the position of a creditor (as a third party) is harmed by that freedom.
- Cases 2, 5, 7 and 10 all essentially deal with the following question: if you transfer (property, contract and/or contractual) rights, what (in terms of the contractual relationship between the transferring party and its counterparty) remains with one party, and what passes on to the acquiring party?
- Cases 4 and 6 are concerned with the friction between 'powers' (of the contractual party and/or the person exercising contractual rights), on the one hand, and 'interests' (in terms of potential loss by the principal, and acquisition of money and property/things) in the conclusion and execution of contracts, which cases are related to the areas of agency and property law, and in which the concept of a third party in relation to the contract is more fluid (as the third party can either be the principal or the agent).

In creating the questionnaire, the editors have used the methodology of the Common Core of European Private Law project. This method is 'factual'; what are being compared are not doctrinal systems but, rather, the most likely outcomes that would be reached, in the various legal systems, in specific hypothetical cases. This analysis is based not merely on legal rules ('operative rules'), but on any elements in the legal system ('legal formants') that may determine or influence the legal outcomes of the questions asked. As with all other Common Core projects, this project made use of questionnaires containing hypothetical problems, on the basis of which the most likely solutions in the respective national legal systems are compared.[1]

In order to support the notion of third-party rights and contract in a broader perspective, two chapters have been added to this volume. The first chapter was written by Michael Milo, and deals with the legal-historical aspects of third-party rights and contract law, showing a shifting perspective on third-party rights during the course of history. The second chapter was written by Miquel Martín-Casals, and addresses the concurrence between contract law and tort law in the protection of third parties; of all areas of law, most notably tort law is the area that generally comes up most often in discussing the positions of third parties in relation to contracts. We are very grateful to both authors for their insightful contributions.

The editors are enormously grateful to the contributors of the national reports. As for the method of comparative law, there has been input from the following jurisdictions (in alphabetical order): Belgium, Bulgaria, the Czech Republic,

1 Further details on the methodology of the Common Core of Private Law project can be found in M. Bussani, 'Current Trends in European Comparative Law: The Common Core Approach' (1998) 21(4) *Hastings International and Comparative Law Review* 785 (available at https://repository.uclawsf.edu/hastings_international_comparative_law_review/vol21/iss4/3/).

England, France, Germany, Italy, the Netherlands, Poland, Scotland, Slovakia, Spain and Sweden. As is shown by this list, the jurisdictions are very diverse and range from common law, mixed legal, and traditional civil law jurisdictions, to Scandinavian and former East European jurisdictions. In some of the jurisdictions the reigning codes are more than 150 years old, whereas in others, such as Belgium and the Czech Republic, new legislation in the field of contract law has recently been adopted. The editors hope that the wide variety of jurisdictions has contributed to the strength of this volume.

PART I

GENERAL PART

COMMON TRADITIONS IN THIRD-PARTY RIGHTS

J.M. Milo

1. INTRODUCTION

The third party is omnipresent, yet hard to define in law.[1] There is one foundational principle which has set the stage throughout legal history: *alteri stipulari nemo potest* – no-one may stipulate for another.[2] Third persons find themselves, thereby, principally placed outside another's obligation – this *vinculum iuris* (chain of law) which binds debtor to creditor. Justinian's metaphor[3] characterises the obligation between the parties, and also signifies its exclusionary force towards third parties. It is not just a principle from civil law, but is similarly strongly present in common law traditions of privity of contract:

> in the law of England certain principles are fundamental. One is that only a person who is a party to a contract can sue on it. Our law knows nothing of a jus quaesitum tertio arising by way of contract.[4]

Yet contracts and obligations not only appear in *juridicial vitro* – in the books – but also *in vivo* – in practice. Hence, third parties have quite commonly appeared in the actual world of transactional practice throughout history.

---

1 In contemporary scholarship, it has been concluded that it is difficult to come up with a sensible unifying theory. 'Third party' is, as a term, an antinomy, and presupposes a first and a second party; it is a relative concept and depends on the position of the observer, and is, furthermore, ambiguous. See E. Dirix, *Obligatoire verhoudingen tussen contractanten en derden*, Maklu, Antwerp 1984, p. 21. Likewise, E. du Perron, *Overeenkomst en derden*, Kluwer, Deventer 1999, p. 1.

2 Institutiones (Inst.) 3.19.4 and Digesta (D.) 45.1.38.17.

3 Inst. 3.13.

4 *Dunlop Pneumatic Tyre Co Ltd v. Selfridge & Co Ltd* [1915] AC 847 per Lord Haldane at 853, following *Tweddle v. Atkinson* [1861] EWHC J57 (QB), (1861) 1 B&S 393, and establishing the privity of contract doctrine.

The third party found its bond as a debtor or creditor only with difficulty, established in the variety of legal formants over time, whereby schools of legal thought, sources of law, means of reasoning, as well as substantive concepts provided the building blocks making or breaking the third parties' position. The factual variety in social reality adds to the picture. Third parties may appear where, for example, a donation is to be made within a family relation; a transfer is to be made to a third party in a commercial setting; a debt is to be paid to a third party; or a debt is to be paid resulting from entitlement to land, or a creditor's claim on a third party based on a fraudulent act.

Recent legislation and judicial developments appear to allow third parties, perhaps relatively easily, to establish their positions under other persons' contracts. Contemporary national stances have not been carved out in a single line of tradition, nor did the acceptance of the third party appear for the first time in the nineteenth century.[5] Earlier, third parties saw their positions recognised with or without ease. This all came to be established on the playing fields of inductive common law and deductive civil law, between the conceptual strongholds of persons, property, obligation and actions, and was first and foremost induced by a practical necessity, the rise of the person's free will, and contractual and proprietary freedom, backed by natural or canonical *aequitas*, customary rules and local statutes – the latter definitely not in the last place. The debate on a third party's position has been a continuing sfumato between various opposing views over time, until our contemporary days, in which influences of a new *ius commune* in principles, paradigm or common core, as well as positive national laws, have provided the third party with strongholds in frameworks that remain traditional.

In the following sections, some of the seminal situations in which the third party saw its position debated will be historically analysed. The third party may be seen as a creditor or debtor bound to another party's contract (section 2); the third party may likewise be bound on the basis of agency, though as a general concept this emerged only in early modern times (section 3); the third party may be made into a creditor by the transfer of a claim, though this faced a similar principle of untransferability (section 4); the third party may experience being bound to another on the basis of property acquired (section 5); and the third party may be held liable under a revocatory action, the *actio Pauliana*, which has been ever-present from Roman times (section 6). The chapter ends with some concluding remarks (section 7).

---

5 As could be inferred from H. Kötz, 'Third party consequences' in H. Beale (ed), *Cases, Materials and Texts on Contract Law*, Hart, Oxford 2002, p. 881.

2. *IUS QUAESITUM TERTIO*

2.1. ROMAN FOUNDATIONS

The concept of obligation is, in its civilian origin, by definition a personal bond: only debtor and creditor are bound.[6] An obligation is, in Justinian's *Institutes*, 'a bond of law by which we are reduced to the necessity of paying something in compliance with the laws of our state'.[7]

This definition of an obligation is a corollary of *alteri stipulari nemo potest*, an influential principle in the civilian tradition which is even explicitly included in Justinian's *Institutes*.[8] A key fragment is Ulpian's:

> No one can stipulate for another except a slave for his master, and a son for his father, as obligations of this description have been contrived in order that everyone may acquire for himself anything in which he may be interested, but I have no interest in what is given to another.[9]

Stipulations were highly formalised contracts, and only came into existence through the force of precise prescribed words: 'Do you promise? I do promise!' was only one of the possible formulations which had to be reciprocally spoken.[10] It was not just this principled rule which caused the prohibition on third parties being bound. The formalities of the *stipulatio*, as well as the procedure to be followed, are seen as the real causes. A decision in a court procedure needed to be in a sum of money, as the value of the third party's interest, yet this could not be claimed by the stipulator.[11] The stipulator needed to have an interest in the promisor's performance towards a third party, and the need to ensure that a *stipulatio alteri* had effect led to the standard of inserting a penalty clause to construct such an interest. This caused the promisor to

---

6 Instructive in particular are R. Zimmermann, *The Law of Obligations: Roman Foundations of the Civilian Tradition*, Juta, Cape Town 1990, pp. 34–45; J. Hallebeek, 'Ius Quaesitum Tertio in Medieval Roman Law' in E.J.H. Schrage, *Ius Quaesitum Tertio*, Duncker & Humblot, Berlin 2008, pp. 61–107; G. Wesenberg, *Verträge zugunsten Dritter*, Böhlau, Weimar 1949.

7 Inst. 3.13.pr.

8 Inst. 3.19.19.

9 D. 45.1.38.17.

10 Gaius (G.) Inst. 3.92 provides a catalogue. The *stipulatio* is perceived as an original and highly practical development of Roman law. As the actions based on other contracts were limited, the stipulation made it possible to create an action that other contracts were not offering. See M. Kaser, *Das Römische Privatrecht I*, C.H. Beck, München 1971, §128.

11 J.A. Ankum, *Une nouvelle hypothese sur l'origine de la regle Alteri dari stipulari nemo potest, Etudes offertes a Jean Macqueron*, Faculté de Droit et des Sciences Économiques, Aix-en-Provence 1970, pp. 21 ff.

forfeit a specific sum of money as the stipulator's interest. Ulpian's fragment continues with this option:

> It is clear that if I wish to do this, a penalty should be included in the stipulation, in order that, if what has been agreed upon should not be done, the stipulation will become operative, even in favour of a person who has no interest in the transaction. For when anyone stipulates for a penalty, his interest is not taken into account, but only the quantity and difference of the stipulation, whatever that may be.

Formalities gradually disappeared over the course of Roman law's development, but the prohibition remained as a principle, and found its way into the Justinian *Corpus Iuris Civilis*. A more general application of this principle in other contracts can be inferred from other excerpts, such as 'no one can benefit another to the detriment of a third party, either by an agreement, by prescribing a condition, or by entering into a stipulation'.[12] Exceptions to the principle, up to the Justinian codification, illustrate the need to accommodate third parties and illustrate flexibility in the law as well. Thus, the following examples may be found: an agreement favouring the pledgor and debtor, accompanying the sale of a pledged object;[13] an agreement to return a deposited thing to its owner;[14] a donation which should be handed to a third party – the *donatio sub modo*, considered to be the most important exception;[15] a *fiducia cum amico* between parents, favouring their son;[16] an agreement between the seller and buyer of an immoveable property, favouring the tenant;[17] a stipulation concerning a *dos* (dowry);[18] and a stipulation favouring one's own heirs;[19] as well as many other examples found or constructed in ancient sources.[20]

The response of Roman law was particularly accommodating to third parties, allowing them to demand performance through an *actio utilis* (an action based on fairness or utility), through praetorian as well as imperial edicts, as the formalities in the law of contract, as well as in the law of procedure, decreased. But this leniency in Justinian law is not what came to be received.

---

12 D. 50.17.73.4 (Q. Mucius Scaevola); and likewise broad in its application is D. 44.7.11 (Paulus).

13 D. 13.7.13.pr.

14 C. 3.42.8 (293).

15 C. 8.54 (55).3 (290). See J. Hallebeek, above n. 6, p. 72; J.A. Ankum, *De voorouders van een tweehoofdig twistziek monster*, Tjeenk Willink, Zwolle 1967, p. 17.

16 D. 24.1.49.

17 D. 19.2.25.1; C. 4.65.9 (234); D. 19.1.13.30.

18 C. 5.13.

19 C. 8.37 (38).11 (258); C. 4.11.1 (531); G. 3.100.

20 C. 8.54(55).3 (Diocl. et Max.), containing the *donatio sub modo* – the acquirer has received under condition to give to a third party – *quod donatum est alii restituatur*. See also I.3.19.4 and 3.19.19. For an extensive exposition, see G. Wesenberg, above n. 6, pp. 23–93; see also J. Hallebeek, above n. 6, pp. 61–107 – the exceptions are listed at pp. 69–73.

2.2. THE RECEPTION OF ROMAN LAW

When Roman law came to be received half a millennium later, the principled approach was having a scholarly, learned 'high tide'. Irnerius' *glossa 'Danda'* sets the scene: in general, from another's stipulation, one acquires no action – *generale est, ex alterius stipulatione alteri accionem non queri*.[21] Other glossators likewise took this approach, as did three of the four *quattuor doctores*: Bulgarus, Jacobus and Hugo. But famously the fourth, Martinus, built on natural fairness – *aequitas* – present in the civilian framework,[22] to provide any third party with an *actio utilis*. This difference in stances survived the ages, in the description of Hugolinus:

> Whether from another contract an actio utilis will be given to him, in whose person it is agreed upon? Thus said Martinus, that from another contract an actio utilis is given to him, in whose person it is agreed upon, and thus for example in C.3.42.8 and C.8.54.3. But in truth, Bulgarus, Hugo and Jacobus said it will not be given, because the legal rule is that from another contract no action will be given.[23]

Martinus took an exceptionally lenient stance. Other glossators were also less accommodating than Martinus in awarding an action to the third party:[24] there needed to be an interest on the side of the stipulator, who promised in favour of a third party, in order to have the obligation present and enforceable. But in case this interest was absent, Accursius did, however, concede the presence of a natural obligation,[25] as well as an *actio utilis*, in extensive interpretations of texts concerning exceptions.[26] This certainly becomes visible in the works of the commentators. Bartolus may be seen to do likewise, and to argue that the interest of the stipulator is already present on the basis of the conclusion of the contract as such.[27]

---

21 Irnerius, Glossa ad D. 3.3.27.1, as cited in U. Müller, *Der Entwicklung der direkten Stellvertretung und des Vertrages zugunsten Dritter*, Stuttgart 1969, p. 30.

22 Inst. 1.2; D. 1.1.1.3.

23 Hugolinus, in G. Haenel (ed), *Dissensiones Dominorum* (1834, repr. Aalen 1964), para. 256, p. 429: *'An ex alieno pacto utilis actio ei d[a]tur, in cuius persona conceptum est? Item dicit M. (Martinus), quod ex alieno pacto utilis actio datur ei, in cuius persona conceptum est, et hoc exemplo C.3.42.8. [et] C.8.54.3. Bulgarus vero et Hugo et Jacobus dicunt, non dari, nisi expressim dixit, quum iuris regula sit, ex alieno pacto actionem non dari.'*

24 E.g. Bassianus, Azo and Accursius, as mentioned in J.A. Ankum, *De voorouders van een tweehoofdig twistziek monster*, above n. 15, p. 19; and in J. Hallebeek, above n. 6, pp. 77–79.

25 Accursius, glossa nihil interest ad D. 45.1.38.17; J.A. Ankum, *De voorouders van een tweehoofdig twistziek monster*, above n. 15, p. 20.

26 J. Hallebeek, above n. 6, pp. 80–81.

27 Bartolus, ad D. 46.1.56. no. 12: '*quia ex tali conventione oritur obligatio naturalis: ut ibi notavi*' ('because from such a contract a natural obligation is born: as I have noted there'). It may be found elsewhere, e.g. Bartolus ad D. 45.1.38.17.

> Canonists were arguing, on the basis of natural law, in favour of the binding force of a promise.[28] A simple promise would already give rise to a natural obligation, according to Aquinas.[29] A subsequent oath could convert the natural obligation into an enforceable civil obligation; thus, canon law set a distinct difference from Roman law: *sed credo iure canonico me teneri si ego promitto tibi me daturum Titio decem. … maxime ubi intervenit sacramentum* (I believe I am bound according to canon law, if I promise you that I shall give Titius ten, especially when I promise under oath).[30]

This argument was well received. Among others, Diego de Covarruvias (1512–77), Luis de Molina (1536–1600) and Leonardus Lessius (1554–1623) argued in line with this, and had an important influence on Grotius.[31] Court decisions,[32] regional[33] and local municipal statutes, and customary law appeared, which did allow the third party a stance.[34] Wherever municipal laws were established, giving the third party a stance, civil law followed, Iason de Mayno noticed.[35]

2.3. EARLY MODERN ACCEPTANCE

Grotius (1583–1645) is considered to have been the first to 'frontally attack' the principle of *alteri stipulari nemo potest*,[36] but he was fuelled by what had already been established in paving the way towards the acceptance of the third-party right. Natural law and local statutory law, as well as customary law, were incorporated in Grotius' analysis – in *De Iure Belli ac Pacis* (1625) and, prior

---

28 X. 1.35.3 – Pacta quantumque nuda, servanda sunt; J.H. Dondorp, '"Ius Quaesitum Tertio" in Medieval Canon Law' in E.J.H. Schrage (ed), above n. 6, pp. 109–33, p. 110.

29 On promise, see *Summa Theologica*, II – II, q. 110, a.3 ad 5. On which, see, in particular, J. Gordley, *The Philosophical Origins of Modern Contract Doctrine*, OUP, Oxford 1991, pp. 11–12 and 45–49; J.H. Dondorp, above n. 28, p. 114.

30 J.H. Dondorp, above n. 28, pp. 113–14.

31 L. Waelkens, 'Ius Quaesitum Tertio, Dutch Influences on Grotius', pp. 175–77, and D.J. Ibbetson and E.J.H. Schrage, 'Ius Quaesitum Tertio', pp. 19–20, both in E.J.H. Schrage (ed), above n. 6.

32 An early modern synthesis of theory and practice, Ibbetson and Schrage qualify (D.J. Ibbetson and E.J.H. Schrage, above n. 31, p. 14; see p. 21 as well). Case law rarely, if at all, contributed directly as an argument in scholarly reasoning, for courts decide cases, and were not seen as making the law, on the basis of an influential Codex text, 7.45.13 – *non exemplis sed legibus iudicandum est* – not by cases, but by law judgments need to be given.

33 The Castilian 'ley paresciendo' of 1348 removed all Roman formalities, which 'may have prompted the commentators … to develop within the civilian tradition … possibilities to stipulate effectively in favour of a third party': J. Hallebeek, above n. 6, p. 85.

34 U. Müller, above n. 21, pp. 55–72; J. Hallebeek, above n. 6, p. 77; J. Brissaud, *Manuel d'Histoire du Droit Privé*, 1907, p. 494. A.S. de Blecourt and H.F.W.D. Fischer, *Kort begrip van het oud-vaderlands burgerlijk recht*, Wolters-Noordhoff, Groningen 1969, no. 202.

35 C. Dumoulin, *Opera IV*, c.138: *'sed hodie in praxi, hae et omnes leges et theoriae de formulis stipulationum supervacuae sunt'.*

36 R. Zimmermann, above n. 6, p. 43.

to this, his *Inleidinge* or *Jurisprudence of the Law of Holland* (1619). Stipulation for a third party, agency and cession are distinguished, in a systematisation inspired by Justinian's *Institutes*.

Natural law provided Grotius with a line of reasoning to admit the third party to the contract. *Inleidinge* III.1.28 provides the still-existing principle (repeated at II.1.36) that, 'generally speaking, no one can bind another, because an obligation comes from the power which each man has over his own acts'.[37] This principle is founded explicitly on the person's individual autonomy. In the event that a person's 'free exercise of the will' is hindered by an incapability in understanding, no obligations will arise. But 'in the general interest', Grotius resumes, 'the laws have enacted ... that certain persons are bound by others'.[38] Here, representation is clearly and systematically distinctly inserted. Guardians bind their wards (whether minors or the insane).[39] And the second exception concerns merchants and shopkeepers, as 'both are bound by the administrators of their business by sea and by land, that is to say, within the scope of their authority, and not beyond, and not if their authority is revoked'.[40] These are clearly examples of agency, but as Grotius' further exposition shows, are related to, but separated from, third parties' relation to other's contracts.

Inleidinge III.3.37 and 38 provide the turn to the acceptance of the third parties' stance under another contract, with the principled approach:

> a person may also stipulate for or accept a promise to give something to him or a third person, in which case the promisor has the choice of paying to either, though the third person may not demand payment, since in general, *no one acquires a right through another*.[41]

Yet in just the next fragment, the exception to the principle takes the lead, fuelled by the force of practical needs as well as natural law:

> a stipulation or acceptance for a third person merely (except in the cases mentioned above in which one person acquires a right through another's act) is without effect, unless it be made in God's service, or for the poor, or unless the acceptor himself has an interest in the performance of the contract, or a penalty is annexed which the

37 Grotius, *Inleidinge*, III.1.28, translated by R.W. Lee, in Grotius, *The Jurisprudence of Holland I*, Clarendon Press, Oxford 1926; II.1.36 repeats, without giving a reason, but with the option of transfer, using the concept of cession: 'Again, no one can acquire a personal right through another without cession.'

38 Grotius, *Inleidinge*, III.1.19 and 29.

39 Ibid., III.1.30.

40 Ibid., III.1.31. Grotius distinguishes further between the Roman law *in solidum* liability of the individual merchant in the case of co-ownership of ships or joint trade operations (D. 14.1.1.25), which is, 'with us' (*'by ons'*, in the province of Holland), not admitted as being harmful to business. Liability follows only for the merchant's pro rata share in the business.

41 Ibid., III.3.37; emphasis added.

promisor will incur, if he fails to perform; but since with us more attention is paid to equity than to legal subtlety, even apart from these exceptions, a third party may accept a promise, and thereby acquire a right, unless the promisor has revoked his promise before the third party has accepted it.[42]

This stance, deviating from Roman law, and founded in natural law, is also given in *De Iure Belli ac Pacis*, where Grotius distinguishes sharply between stipulation in favour of a third party and agency:

if a promise is made to me, without considering whether I have any interest, as Roman law has introduced, it appears to me that by the law of nature I acquire a right to accept that thereby the right to demand performance will pass to another, and if he accepts that the promissor may not revoke the promise; but I to whom the promise was made, may remit it. For this meaning is not against the law of nature, and corresponds to the words of the promise. It is to some extent in my interest if another through me acquires a benefit.[43]

Groenewegen, in general terms, recognised the third-party stance:

hinc moribus hodiernis ex nudo pacto datur actio et stipulando alteri obligatio acquiritur – here according to contemporary custom mere pacts give an action and an obligation is acquired by a stipulation for a third party.[44]

Voet remarked, likewise, '*moribus hodiernis obtinuit unumquemque alteri aeque ac sibi posse stipulari*'.[45] Other writers concurred,[46] or even went further. Indeed, Stair unequivocally accepted without hesitation, on the basis of natural law,

42 Ibid., III.3.38. Grotius, *De Iure Belli ac Pacis* (1625, ed. Molhuysen 1919), 2.11.18.1 and 19; see also J.A. Ankum, *De voorouders van een tweehoofdig twistziek monster*, above n. 15, pp. 27–28; R. Zimmermann, above n. 6 (repr. 1992), p. 43, who sees the first acceptance of the third-party rights in *De Iure Belli ac Pacis*, II.11.18 – a 'frontal attack'. The third party's will and consensus is a necessary ingredient.

43 Grotius, *De Iure Belli ac Pacis* (1625, ed. Molhuysen 1919) II, 11.18.1: '*Si mihi facta est promissio, omissa inspectione an mea privatim intersit, quam introduxit ius Romanum, naturaliter videtur mihi acceptan[d]i ius dari efficiendi, ut ad alterum ius perveniat, si et is acceptet; ita ut medio tempore a promissore promissio revocare non possit; sed ego cui facta est promissio eam possim remittere. Nam is sensus iuri naturae non repugnat, et verbis talis promissionis maxime congruit. Neque nihil mea interest si per me alter beneficium acquirat.*' Translation by the author.

44 Groenewegen, *De Legibus abrogatis et inusitatis* (ed. 1649), Ad Inst. 3.20.19.5. (p. 48). Translation by the author.

45 J. Voet, *Commentarius ad Pandectas II* (ed. Van Dole, Hagae-Comitum 1734) ad D. 45.1, no. 3 – 'according to contemporary custom every one may acquire for another just as he can stipulate for himself'. Translation by the author.

46 A. Vinnius, *In quattor libros Institutionum Imperialium Commentarius* 3.19.4.3; S. van Leeuwen, *Het Rooms Hollands Regt* (1664), 4.2.5; D.G. van der Keessel, *Theses selectae* 510; J. van der Linden, *Rechtsgeleerd, practicaal en koopmanshandboek*, J. Allart, Amsterdam 1806, p. 119.

the presence of third parties' entitlements to stipulations in others' contracts.[47] He went further even than Grotius – 'in this Grotius differeth' – based on canon law, as well as *ius gentium* ('the common custom of nations'), referring to Luis de Molina's *De Iustitia et de Iure*, and accepting the binding force of a promise favouring a third party.[48] It was the will which brought forth the binding force of the promise favouring the third party. Acceptance by the third party, which Grotius still demanded, was not needed. It was the will of the third party rejecting the promise which 'void[ed] it and ma[de] it return'.[49]

Christian Thomasius remarked, in his comment on Ulrik Huber, that '*moribus hodiernis, vel paciscendo, vel legem dicendo, vel stipulando, alterum alteri cavere posse, et ita subtilitatem jurisprudentiae Romanae esse sublatam*' – an allusion to the Roman law principle of *alteri stipulari non potest*.[50] Case law may also be found,[51] in which a seventeenth-century Wittenberg case shows the influence of Grotius.[52] This influence is also visible in scholarly work, custom and municipal law, as well as in the codes of Bavaria (1754), Prussia (ALR, 1794) and Austria (ABGB, 1811).[53] In reasoning towards a recognition of the third-party stance,

---

47 Stair, *Institutions of the Law of Scotland* (1681), 1.10.5, arguing on the basis of his stance that even unilateral promises are binding, without acceptance. Grotius does not go that far. On Stair's stance on this, see H.L. MacQueen, 'Third party rights in contract: Ius Quaesitum Tertio' in K. Reid and R. Zimmermann (eds), *A History of Private Law in Scotland*, vol. 2, OUP, Oxford 2000, pp. 220–52; H.L. MacQueen and D.H. Sellar, 'Scots law: Ius Quaesitum Tertio, Promise and Irevocability' in E.J.H. Schrage (ed), above n. 6, pp. 357–83.

48 See 1.10.5.

49 Stair, above n. 47, 1.10.10. On the distinctions between Stair and Grotius, see also T.B. Smith, 'Pollicitatio – promise and offer: Stair v. Grotius' (1958) *Acta Juridica* 141, reprinted in T.B. Smith, *Studies Critical and Comparative*, W. Green, Edinburgh 1962, pp. 168–82.

50 '[A]ccording to contemporary custom either by agreement, by prescribing a condition or by stipulating one may bind another, and thus the subtility of Roman jurisprudence is abolished.' Thomasius cites Joannes Jacob Wissenbach. Thomasius on Ulrik Huber, *Praelectionum Iuris Civilis*, Francofurti et Lipsii 1749, lib. III, tit. XX, p. 303. The text of D. 50.17.73.4 reads '*Nec paciscendo nec legem dicendo nec stipulando quisquam alteri cavere potest*': 'Not by agreement, not by prescribing a condition nor by stipulating one may bind another'.

51 Van Bijnckershoek provides a decision on the acceptance of a third-party right: *Observationes Tumultuariae*, 2792, a decision by the Hoge Raad of 27 October 1733.

52 Was a sale to be conducted on a fixed price or on the true price to a third person? The decision in the case referred to comparable *mutuum* cases, where the third party was indeed accepted, and to Mevius and Stryk, and was also explicitly based on Grotius, II.11.18, cited and translated above. See M. Pennitz, 'Ius Quaesitum Tertio: German Legal Doctrine and Practice in the 18th and 19th Century' in E.J.H. Schrage (ed), above n. 6, pp. 255–56.

53 M. Pennitz, above n. 52, p. 251 and pp. 268–69. See e.g. W.X.A. von Kreittmayer's *Codex Maximilianeus Bavaricus Civilis*, 4.1.13.1: '*Kann fuer alle jene, welche mann von vaeterliche Gewalt, Curatel, Anwartschaft oder sonst von Rechts wegen zu vertreten hat, stipuliert werden. Fuer andere Dritte hingegen gehet solches nur so weit an, als ihnen dieses nuetzlich seyn mag, und nach der Hand ratificirt oder angenommen wird*' (May be stipulated for all those, who have to be represented by fatherly power, curatorship, expectation-interest, or for any other reason. For all other third parties only until so far as it serves their interest, and is accepted or ratified afterwards).

the concept of agency starts to appear more and more. If the third party has ratified being bound, there is a contract of mandate with an *ex tunc* force. The third party is seen as a principal, and acquires an *actio utilis ex facto* – an action on the basis of the facts.[54]

Jacobus Voorda, in his lectures at Utrecht University from 1744 to 1760, in the *ius hodiernum* (contemporary law), was quite clear: 'nowadays, one man can come to an agreement in favour of another'.[55] Not Roman law, but contemporary custom, based on *ius naturale*, legitimised this order of the law as it stood: 'The reason for this is that it is not contrary to the law of nature, but accords well with it, and also that it is in my interest that another should benefit through me.'[56] However, not necessarily all scholars departed all that easily from the principle that third parties could not be bound by another's stipulations.[57]

2.4. MODERN HESITANCE

Rather than developing into a uniformity, discussion remained in the early modern *ius commune*, where scholarship was the principal source of law. Some were hesitant in leaving the *alteri stipulari non potest* principle. Huber points to the catalysing force of commerce in the acceptance of the third party: *mercaturae causae in quibusdam casibus id est receptum*. Yet in Huber's exposition, it is only accepted in certain specified cases, such as bills of exchange.[58] Huber's stance may have been influenced by the presence of Roman-Frisian law, which was the most Roman variety of all regional laws.[59] In the sources, '*une grande confusion*' – a great confusion – is concluded in the French tradition,[60] as well as in the German tradition, in scholarly works as well as in case law.[61] Natural law does not necessarily have to open up the acceptance and enforceability of the third party's claim on the ground of the contracting parties' will. The third party's individual autonomy might also lead to an underlining of the necessity of consensus by the

54 Schilter, 1698, as mentioned by M. Pennitz, above n. 52, p. 259.

55 J. Voorda, *Dictata ad Ius Hodiernum I* (ed. M. Hewett, KNAW, Amsterdam 2005), pp. 148–49, para. II, on D. 2, 14.

56 J. Voorda, above n. 55, pp. 151–53: '*quia illus non est contrarium, sed bene congruit iure naturali: et quia mea nonnihil interest, alterum per me beneficio affici.*'

57 J.G. Kees followed Justinian law: see *Commentarius ad D. Iustiniani Institutionum Imperialium IV libros*, Bousquet, Coloniae Allobrogum 1759, ad Inst. 3.20.3 and 4 and 3.19.

58 '*[U]t in cambis, cum mercator stipulator sibi*', in U. Huber, *Praelectionum Iuris Civilis*, Francofurti et Lipsii 1749, lib. III, tit. XX, p. 303.

59 According to Jacobus Voorda: '*de frisia sola, iuris civilis religiosissima custode, dubito*' (I have doubts about Friesland, that scrupulous guardian of civil law). The doubts were on Friesland's adherence to the principle of *alteri stipulari non potest*, which Voorda finds in Huber's Eunomia Romana, D. 50.17.156.1. See J. Voorda, above n. 55, pp. 152–53.

60 J. Brissaud, above n. 34, p. 494, fn. 3.

61 M. Pennitz, above n. 52, p. 252.

third party. Jean Domat was explicit: as contracts are concluded by consensus, persons may not contract for another person, unless the promisor has the power to do so.[62] In this line, Pothier furthered the argument, and caused the return of French law to the classical Roman position[63] – a Romanistic regression.[64] It is *'une tradition quelque-peu genante'*, qualified Deroussin.[65] Pothier's stance served as an inspiration for the French Civil Code, and consequently a more restrictive codified rule has dominated the French jurisdiction and those based on the French Civil Code. Nevertheless, scholars and courts did manage, in their interpretations, to find an appropriate meaning of the rule, and thus an acceptance of the third party: *'les regles posees pour interpretation sont mobilisee en faveur des promesses pour autrui'*.[66]

Within the German scholarly tradition of the Historical School, a return to Roman law in a *'usus modernus'* fashion has been observed, as with von Savigny, Vangerow and others, who argued the third party's position from the initial prohibition, over the theoretical roads of agency and sometimes cession as well.[67] These theories did not satisfy the 'standards of legislation, nor meet the practical requirements of that time'.[68] Von Jhering remarked in 1886 that *'erst unsere moderne Theorie hat in der Lehre von den Verträgen zu Gunsten Dritter denselben Schritt für das Verkehrsrecht getan'*.[69] It was Joseph Unger who exercised influence towards the outright recognition in the codifications of Germany, Austria and Switzerland.[70] Among many more things, §328 BGB (German Civil Code, *Bürgerliches Gesetzbuch*) has led to the acceptance of the *Schutzwirkung zugunsten Dritter*, which enables employees as third parties to use exemption clauses in their employers' contracts with others.

62 *'Comme les conventions se forment par le consentement, personne ne peut en faire pour une autre, si'il n'a pouvoir de lui'*, which of course amounts to some form of agency: J. Domat, *Les loix civiles dans leur ordre naturel* 1.1.3 (Paris 1745), 1.10.2.3.

63 R.J. Pothier, *Traite des obligations*, 1.1.V, van Leeuwen, Leiden 1873, pp. 23–35. In Art. 1121 of the French Civil Code (CC), *'[o]n peut pareillement stipuler au profit d'un tiers lorsque telle est la condition d'une stipulation que l'on fait pour soi-même ou d'une donation que l'on fait à un autre. Celui qui a fait cette stipulation ne peut plus la révoquer si le tiers a déclaré vouloir en profiter.'*

64 J.A. Ankum, *De Voorouders van een tweehoofdig twistziek monster*, above n. 15, p. 36.

65 D. Deroussin, 'La Stipulation pour autrui de l'ancien droit français au XIXeme siècle, ou comment se débarrasser d'une tradition gênante' in E.J.H. Schrage (ed), above n. 6, p. 222; J.A. Ankum, *De voorouders van een tweehoofdig twistziek monster*, above n. 15, pp. 30 ff.; 'not wholeheartedly accepted' is the qualification made by H.L. MacQueen, above n. 47, p. 220.

66 D. Deroussin, above n. 65, p. 233.

67 F.C. von Savigny, *Obligationenrecht II*, Bei Veit und Comp., Berlin 1853, pp. 74 ff., building on the *usus modernus* of the earlier writers; see M. Pennitz, above n. 52, pp. 276–77.

68 M. Pennitz, above n. 52, p. 277.

69 'Our modern theory has, for the first time, taken the same step in the case of third-party rights': R. von Jhering, 'Die aktive Solidarobligation' in *Jahbüchern für Dogmatik* 24 (1886), p. 138.

70 J. Unger 'Verträge zugunsten Dritter', *Jherings Jahrbuecher* 10 (1871), p. 63. BGB 328, ABGB 881, ZGB 1881, 128; ZGB 1912, 112.

English law has, in respect of third-party rights in contract, been described as 'the most Roman of all legal systems in Europe',[71] as the privity of contract doctrine came to be established in the nineteenth century.[72] The earlier history of privity of contract in common law is far from clear-cut.[73] The high number of cases, as well as the liberal results achieved therein, have been characterised as 'a creative mingling of ideas', in which the reasoning applied used concepts such as interest, benefit or trust, agency, and consideration, with an increasing involvement of the Court of Chancery in situations involving third-party beneficiaries,[74] creating a landscape of various paths towards third-party rights, before the advent of the Contracts (Rights of Third Parties) Act 1999.[75]

3. AGENCY

Agency has already appeared, in the preceding paragraphs, as a technique and explanation for the third party being bound. It appeared in the expositions of early modern *usus modernus* scholars, as well as those of nineteenth-century *Pandektist* scholars, and was also, in the common law tradition, considered a relatively late-appearing general concept. 'It must never be forgotten that agency did not become a single or significant subject until (very roughly) the turn of the nineteenth century', Stoljar states.[76] Direct agency results in binding a principal to another person through an intermediary. An obligation being seen as a personal bond, as well as the *alteri stipulari nemo potest* rule, barred acceptance of direct agency. This is stated clearly in Roman law, in the case of acquiring property by another, which was considered an impossibility – *per extraneam personam non adquiri posse*[77] – but also in the case of being bound by an obligational bond – 'acquiring' an obligation – through another.

---

71 H.L. MacQueen, above n. 47, p. 221.

72 *Dunlop Pneumatic Tyre Co Ltd v. Selfridge & Co Ltd* [1915] UKHL 1 – following *Tweddle v. Atkinson*, above n. 4.

73 On which, see V.V. Palmer, 'The History of Privity – The Formative Period (1500–1680)' (1989) 33 *American Journal of Legal History* 3; N. Jones, 'Aspects of Privity in England: Equity to 1680' in E.J.H. Schrage, above n. 6, pp. 135–74.

74 D.J. Ibbetson and W. Swain, 'Third Party Beneficiaries in English Law' in E.J.H. Schrage (ed), above n. 6, pp. 191–213, p. 201.

75 V.V. Palmer, above n. 73, pp. 3–52; see, on the developments since 1880, W. Swain, 'Third Party Beneficiaries in English Law, 1880–2004' in E.J.H. Schrage (ed), above n. 6, pp. 331–56.

76 L.J. Stoljar, *The law of agency*, Sweet & Maxwell, London 1961, p. 14.

77 I. 2.9.5: 'through an outsider, one may not acquire'. See also Julius Paulus in D. 45.1.126.2: *'per liberam personam, quae iuri nostro subjecta est neque bona fide nobis servit, obligationem nullam adquirere possumus'* (that we cannot acquire any obligation by means of any free person who is not subject to our authority, or does not serve us in good faith as a slave). See also C. 4.27.1.

Roman law did not have a general concept of agency,[78] and consequently the conceptual difference between an obligation favouring a third party and an agency construction is not clearly, if at all, visible there. But just as in the case of the *stipulatio alterii* described above, important exceptions were present, making a kind of agency possible in specific situations,[79] such as the obvious possibility of indirect representation, and thus having two contractual relations;[80] the use of an intermediate person, a *nuntius*, as a mere technicality in communication;[81] the use of *fiducia cum creditore* or *amico*;[82] the acquisition of possession by the tutor, and hence, in the case of *traditio*, the acquisition of ownership for the ward;[83] the *pater familias* being bound by *alieni iuris* in his power;[84] the use of procedural representation – *procuratio*.[85] The contract of *mandatum* allowed the procurator to represent the principal procedurally. It was said that '[t]he use of procurators is absolutely necessary, in order that those who are either unwilling, or unable to attend to their own affairs, may sue or be sued by means of others.'[86] 'If their traditionalism led the Roman lawyers to retain the principle [*alteri stipulari*], their pragmatism allowed for exceptions where necessary', Zimmermann concludes.[87]

Again, the *alteri stipulari* principle was received more strongly than it was understood in Roman law, thus barring third parties from others' obligations through agency. Procedural representation was accompanied by Irnerius' *glossa 'generale est, ex alterius stipulatione alteri accionem non queri'*,[88] which became generally accepted. Only the contracting party, and not a principal, would acquire an action,[89] yet the exceptions in the *Corpus Iuris* are also listed.[90] Again, as can be inferred from Hugolinus and Accursius, Martinus had a different opinion, based firmly on fairness: *'Nulla (sc. obligatio) acquiritur de stricto iure, sed de aequitate sic, secundum M(artinum) quod J(ohannem) non placet.'*[91]

---

78 M. Kaser, above n. 10, para. 62, p. 260; R. Zimmermann, above n. 6, pp. 47–48.
79 See R. Zimmermann, above n. 6, pp. 49–56.
80 D. 46.8.12.1; M. Kaser, above n. 10, para. 62, pp. 264–65.
81 D. 18.1.1.2; see also D. 3.3.1.1 – procurator by operating as a *nuntius*.
82 Gaius Inst. 2.60.
83 D. 41.1.13.pr. (Neratius): 'If my agent, by my direction, should purchase anything for me, and it is delivered to him in my name, the ownership of the article, that is to say, the title to it, is acquired by me, even if I am not aware of the fact'; D. 41.2.1.20 (Paulus) – possession is acquired by us by means of an agent, a guardian, or a curator.
84 Among which those like the *sui iuris*, the *pater familias*, bound by his *alieni iuris* children and slaves – see Inst. 2.9.1; on the concept of *procuratio*, see Inst. 2.9.5.
85 D. 3.3 *De procuratoribus et defensoribus*. Inst. 4.10.pr.
86 D. 3.3.1.2 (Ulpian).
87 R. Zimmermann, above n. 6, pp. 48–49.
88 Irnerius, Glossa ad D. 3.3.27.1, as in U. Müller, above n. 21, p. 30.
89 See the sources mentioned by U. Müller, above n. 21, p. 30 and fn. 16.
90 U. Müller, above n. 21, p. 32.
91 Accursius, Glossa nulla to C. 4.27.1, as cited by U. Müller, above n. 21, p. 45.

The *actio utilis* was the route which allowed the third-party principal to acquire an action, according to Martinus and commentators,[92] and local statutory law also accepted such direct representation, for reasons of commercial practice.[93]

The doctrinal separation between agency and third-party rights would, however, be made first by Grotius, in his *Inleidinge* (1619), as well as in *De Iure Belli ac Pacis* (1625). The distinction is made clearly:

> *solent et controversiae incidere de acceptatione pro altero facta; in quibus distinguendum est inter promissionem mihi factam de re danda alteri, et inter promissionem in ipsius nomen collatam, cui res danda est* – there are usual conflicts in the acceptance of deeds for others, in which there needs to be made a distinction between a promise made by me to give a thing to another, and a promise made in that very person's name, to whom the thing has to be given.[94]

Natural law provided Grotius with a line of reasoning to admit the third party, by means of agency, to the contract. Inleidinge III.1.28, and, again, II.1.36, provide the still-existing principle, 'generally speaking, no one can bind another, because an obligation comes from the power which each man has over his own acts'.[95] But agency is a necessity. In the event that a person's 'free exercise of the will' is hindered by an incapability in understanding (III.1.19), no obligations will arise. But 'in the general interest', Grotius resumes, 'the laws have enacted ... that certain persons are bound by others'.[96] Here, agency is clearly and distinctly inserted. Guardians bind their wards (whether as minors or the insane).[97] And the second exception concerns merchants and shopkeepers, as 'both are bound by the administrators of their business by sea and by land, that is to say, within the scope of their authority, and not beyond, and not if their authority is revoked'.[98] Agency is separate from, but related to, third-party rights in others' contracts. In the practice of local and customary law, the prohibition of representation was not actually adopted at all, but through a variety of informal customs forms of representation

92 See, for a detailed exposition, U. Müller, above n. 21, pp. 29–54.

93 U. Müller, above n. 21, pp. 55–60 – *'grundsaetzlich anerkannt'*, p. 60.

94 Grotius, *De Iure Belli ac Pacis* II.11.18. Translation by the author.

95 Grotius, *Inleidinge* III.1.28, translated by R.W. Lee, above n. 37; *Inleidinge* II.1.36 repeats, without giving a reason, but with the option of transfer, using the concept of cession: 'Again, no one can acquire a personal right through another without cession.'

96 Grotius, *Inleidinge* III, 1.29.

97 Ibid., 1.30.

98 Ibid., 1.31: Grotius distinguishes further between the Roman law *in solidum* liability of the individual merchant in the case of co-ownership of ships or joint trade operations (D. 14.1.1.25), which is, 'with us' (*'by ons'*, in the province of Holland), not admitted as being harmful to business. Liability follows only for the merchant's pro rata share in the business.

become visible.[99] In common law, agency came, in the late eighteenth and early nineteenth centuries, to be seen as an exception to the privity requirement of contract law.[100]

4. TRANSFER OF THE CLAIM

The personal nature of the obligation between debtor and creditor made a transfer of this personal legal relationship dogmatically just as impossible as the third party being bound by somebody else's contract, and as agency.[101] The route to a similar result to a transfer was either through novation – renewing the obligation through a stipulation[102] – or through delegation, whereby the creditor allowed their debtor to pay the 'new' creditor.[103] The debtor's cooperation was needed, and hence probably also the use of procedural representation. This mandate then enabled the 'cessionary' to claim from the debtor as *'procurator in rem suam'*, to acquire the proceeds for himself, in his own patrimony.[104] The 'cedent' dogmatically remained the creditor, which probably led to the gradual casuistic development of providing the 'cessionary' with an *actio utilis*,[105] while the cedent's *actio directa* was barred.[106] In Justinian times, it was held convincingly that the cessionary was considered to be the creditor, after a continuous and casuistic eroding of the claims' untransferability.[107] The last decision on claims transferred (D. 8.54.3) completes a general picture: 'We hereby abolish that perplexing rule.'[108] Justinian law, as with third-party

99 J. Brissaud, above n. 34, ch. 3, para. 6, no. 4 (pp. 493–500).

100 V.V. Palmer, above n. 73, 36.

101 M. Kaser, above n. 10, para. 153, p. 652. K. Luig, *Zur Geschichte der Zessionslehre*, Böhlau-Verlag, Köln/Graz, 1966, p. 2; R. Zimmermann, above n. 6, p. 58.

102 Gaius Inst. 2.38; On novation in Justinian law, see D. 46.2.

103 M. Kaser, above n. 10, para. 152, p. 650 – *delegatio solvendi.*

104 Gaius Inst. 2.39; M. Kaser, above n. 10, p. 653. Hence also the concept *cedere*, meant to signify the procedural change as the cedent 'leaves' the cessionary to proceed in the procedure.

105 D. 2.24.16.pr. (Ulpian) on the sale of a heritage; C. 4.10.2 (on the sale of an individual claim); C. 4.10.1 (on a donation); C. 6.37.18 (on a claim being legated); C. 8.53.33 (on a donation); See K. Luig, above n. 101, pp. 2–9; J.C. van Oven, *Leerboek van Romeinsch Privaatrecht*, Brill, Leiden 1948, pp. 414–15.

106 See e.g. D. 2.15.17. Unlikely by an *exceptio doli*, argues J.C. van Oven, above n. 105, pp. 415–16; more likely by a *denuntiatio* or *significatio* to the debtor, referring to C. 8.16.4 and C. 8.41.3. K. Luig, above n. 101, pp. 6–7, provides both options as possibilities; M. Kaser, above n. 10, pp. 653–54.

107 K. Luig, above n. 101, p. 6; R. Zimmermann, above n. 6, pp. 58–63.

108 '[U]nder which persons who receive the assignment of actions as donations are not permitted to transmit them to their heirs, unless they have already instituted proceedings in court with reference to the same, or obtained an Imperial Rescript releasing them from this requirement. For as it is permitted for rights of action attaching to sales to be transmitted to heirs after assignment, and before issue has been joined, so We desire that such as have been donated shall be transferred to them, even though no proceedings have been instituted, nor

contracts, functionally allowed the transfer of claims. Outside the scholarly legal domain, indeed in antique practice, the habit of mentioning the creditor, or *ad quem ea res pertinebit* – to 'whom it will concern' – made transfer an early classic reality.[109]

This is in sharp contrast to the strict application of the principle of untransferability in the times of reception,[110] which held that the action is so strongly connected to the person of the creditor that it cannot be separated from it, just as the soul cannot be separated from its body: *nomina adeo ossibus hominum inhaerent, ut nunquam separentur, non possunt separari a domino, sicut nec anima a corpore*. A claim, therefore, 'clung to the bones' of the person, so that they may never be separated, nor it can be separated from its owner, just like a soul may not be separated from its body.[111] The glossators proceed alongside the aforementioned examples in the Justinian corpus, as strict exceptions to the principled rule of untransferability, and thus proceeded on the basis of the mandate and *procuratio in rem suam* – which they called cession – to bring the cedent's *actio directa* exercised by the cessionary in the name of the cedent. Next to this there is a variety in providing the cessionary with an *actio utilis*, which has the *actio directa* remain with the cedent. Azo stated, on the first technique, '*[c]essione autem actionem facta utetur emptor directis actionibus competentibus venditori*, and, on the second, '*haec tamen cessio nihil videtur proficere emptori cum et sine cessione habeat utilem actionem*'.[112]

Glossators, as well as commentators, do show a large variety of detailed exceptions, but these did not in themselves reach the practical result of transferability achieved by Justinian law. Nevertheless, the parallel to things and their transfer was drawn: where things were transferred with a *traditio*, the claim could be seen as having been transferred with a *cessio*.[113] Bartolus remarked

---

any demand made for payment. This rule shall also be applicable to an attorney appointed to conduct cases of this kind, so that the person to whom the rights of action have been assigned will not be prevented from employing an attorney to bring suit, even though issue has not been joined, or through any legal demand has previously been made. We decree that these provisions shall only apply to persons who are known to be living at this time, and to whom rights of action by means of a donation have been assigned. For where persons of this kind are dead, We permit the ancient laws enacted with reference to such assignments to be observed. Given at Constantinople, during the month of June, under the second Consulate of the Emperor Justinian, 528.' Translation by Scott.

109 L. Goldschmidt, 'Inhaber-, Order- und executorische Urkunden im classischen Alterthum' in *Zeitschrift der Savigny-Stiftung, Romanistische Abteilung* Bd. 10 (1889), pp. 352–96.

110 In general, on the developments, see K. Luig, above n. 101; R. Zimmermann, above n. 6, pp. 58–67; R. Anderson, *Assignation*, Edinburgh Legal Education Trust, Edinburgh 2008, ch. 4.

111 Glossa In nominibus ad D. 15.1.16. The untransferability is very clearly stated in Gaius' *Institutes*; it may be concluded from various fragments in the Justinian *Codex* and *Digest*.

112 Azo, *Summa Codice* 4.39.4. (ed. Speyer, Peter Drach 1482) – the first fragment reads 'further, by this cession of the claim, the buyer will use the direct actions of the seller'; the second fragment reads 'and this [latter] cession does not seem advantageous for the buyer as without a cession he would only have an *actio utilis*'.

113 Bartolus ad C. 4.10.1, no. 8.

that the notary public sought to mobilise all concepts in order to have everything transferred to the cessionary – *actio utilis* as well as *actio directa* – '*et sic notarii in instrumento cessionum apponunt omnia ista verba, dedit, cedit, concessit et transtulit, atque mandavit ut ex hoc competant utiles et directae*'.[114] It was, in particular, commercial needs which provided justifications from outside the realm of learned law to reach at least a functional equivalent to transfer, or even an outright transfer. Part of the story contains, therefore, the continuing systematic separation between the law of obligations and the law of property.

Legal scholars in the humanist tradition stuck more to the original Roman law principle of untransferability, but sought to find a similar leniency in the law of obligations, by using mandate *(procuratio in rem suam)* and the *actio utilis*, in order, ultimately, to reach a kind of functional transfer. Indeed, Donellus reasoned closely along the Roman *limes*, denying the outright transfer of the creditor's action: '*quia ratio iuris non patitur, ullas actiones directas in alium recta transferre*' – 'as it is not allowed to justly transfer any direct action to another'[115] Thus, claims were not objects which could be transferred.[116] Mandate made the 'cessionary' the *procurator in rem suam* (for which the term '*cedere*' was used), whereby they acquired the *actio utilis*,[117] but the cedent remained the holder of the *actio directa*, even after the debtor had been informed of the transaction. In the event that the cedent made a claim, this would be against justice (*aequitas*), and the debtor would have an exception *(exceptio doli)*.[118] In the course of Donellus' reasoning, the lack of an easy transfer of a claim was emphasised: it would be so much easier if, so to speak, all actions would be transferred to the acquirer *('res esset expeditior ... ut simul omnis actio ... translata in accipientem')*.[119] Donellus had a large influence, but a modern use of Roman law came to compete with this.

This modern use happened piecemeal in the streams of thought on natural law, customary law and statutory law, in various places within the *ius commune*. While the untransferability was still mentioned, and still frontstage, transferability started shining through. Carpzov mentioned the phrase '*ossibus inhaeret*', yet elsewhere,

---

114 '[A]nd thus the notaries added to the deed of cession all these words as: he has given, ceded, allowed and transferred and mandated such that from these the *actiones directa* and *utilis* would follow' (ibid., no. 10); K. Luig, above n. 101, p. 14.

115 Donellus, *Commentarii in iure civili* 15, 44, pp. 447–69 *(De obligatione accessoria sive adventitia)*; see K. Luig, above n. 101, pp. 16–22, with Donellus, Faber and Johannes van de Sande as key authors.

116 Donellus, above n. 115, ad para. 14 *in fine* – *traditionibus et usucapionibus iure directo transferuntur*, thus reasoning in analogy to the transfer of things in C. 2.3.20 – *traditionibus et usucapionibus non nudis pactis dominia rerum transferuntur* – ownership of things is transferred by delivery and acquisitive prescription, not by bare agreements.

117 Donellus, above n. 115, §15 *in fine*, p. 462.

118 Ibid., §22, p. 469.

119 Ibid., §18, p. 465.

inspired by Tiraquellus, qualified cession as a transfer, and also referred to a case: *nam omnis actio omneque ius quod quis sibi ex speciali pacto acquisivit, in alium per cessionem transfertur.*[120] The case reveals, in its citation, the relative ease with which a claim – the claim to have preference in buying a house transferred earlier – is considered to have been transferred. Elsewhere, it appeared more fully. In France, Tiraquellus, as well as Rebuffus, spoke in terms of a change of creditors.[121] No *actio directa* remained with the cedent. In the Netherlands, analyses incorporated commercial customary practice fuelled by natural law.

In commercial custom, the claims to order as well as bearer rose to prominence. In this area, Grotius may also be seen as a pivotal author.[122] He qualified the claim as an object of property: 'we have said that the other sort of property is obligation'.[123] Assignation, which entails a creditor's request to the debtor to pay another creditor, was introduced in his *Inleidinge*. Acquiring somebody else's personal right, particularly through the techniques of order or bearer bonds, was placed in the institutional framework of his *Inleidinge*.[124] Later on, Voet left no doubt at all about a customary transferability on the basis of consensus between cedent and cessionary alone, without the debtor cessus agreeing or being notified: *plane nostris moribus circa cessas actiones magis placuit, ius omne cedentis cessione extinctus esse, nec amplius cedentem, sed solum cessionarium, compellere posse debitorem invitum ad solutionem.*[125] Mere agreement on the transfer of a claim brought about a transfer, on the basis of 'our clear custom' – *plane nostris moribus*. In the natural law tradition, claims are seen as an object of ownership and, consequently, are fit to be transferred. Wolff held that '*res etiam incorporales in dominio esse possunt*': even intangibles

120 B. Carpzov, *Jurisprudentia forensis romano-saxonica*, Pars 2, Const. 32, Def. 20 (1638, ed. 1662), p. 709 – 'as all action and right which he for himself by a special agreement has acquired, is transferred to another by cession'.

121 K. Luig, above n. 101, p. 30.

122 Zimmermann pinpoints particularly the moment, halfway through the nineteenth century, when the old untransferability principle, particularly in German scholarship (Muhlenbruch), finally gave way to the outright possibility of transfer (Windscheid). See R. Zimmermann, above n. 6, p. 64.

123 Grotius, *Inleidinge* III.1.1, in the translation by R.W. Lee, above n. 37. But Grotius did not provide a place for a personal claim in his chapter on transferring ownership. Later natural lawyers, Pufendorff and Wolff, would do so.

124 Ibid., 45. On Grotius' contribution to developing the systematic incorporation of assignation as a means of transferring bearer bonds, see D. De Ruysscher, 'Innovating Financial Law in the Early Modern Netherlands and Europe: Transfers of Commercial Paper and Recourse Liability in Legislation and *Ius Commune* (Sixteenth to Eighteenth Centuries)' (2011) 5 *European Review of Private Law* 505–18.

125 'Clearly according to our customs concerning cession it makes more sense that the cedent's right to all transferred, is extinguished, and no longer the cedent but only the cessionary may compel an unwilling debtor to pay' (J. Voet, *Commentarius ad Pandectas* (1698–1702), XVIII, 4, 15).

may be held in ownership.[126] And so, with Pufendorff, a transfer of a claim was systematically placed under the heading of transfer of ownership.[127] In Prussia's Allgemeine Landrecht für die Preußischen Staaten (1794), transferability became codified.[128] German *Pandektist* scholarship produced a Romanistic regression, with Mühlenbruch advancing an untransferability school of thought in the first half of the nineteenth century.[129] However, Windscheid came to mark a nineteenth-century turning point towards transferability, which came to be incorporated in the BGB.[130]

A similar foundation of untransferability of contractual claims was inherent to English law as well. In *Lampet's case*, the statement of Coke, often cited, gave more than dogmatic reasons for this principle:

> no ... thing in action shall be granted or assigned to strangers, for that would be the occasion of multiplying of contemptions and suits, of the great oppression of the people, and chiefly of terretenants, and the subversion of the due and equal execution of justice.[131]

Blackstone likewise described those contractual obligations, being not property in possession, but merely in action:

> wherefor it could not be transferred to another person by the strict rules of the ancient common law: for no chose in action could be assigned or granted over, because it was thought to be a great encouragement to litigiousness, if a man were allowed to make over to a stranger his right of going to law.[132]

But 'this nicety is now disregarded', Blackstone proceeded. Indeed, in the course of the seventeenth century and thereafter, due to the needs of practice, the impossibility of transferring claims started to disappear, through the channels of equity in particular.[133] The streamlining of procedure by the Judicature Act 1873

126 C. Wolff, *Institutionis iuris naturae et gentium*, para. 206; K. Luig, above n. 101, p. 41.

127 S. Pufendorff, *De Iure Naturae et Gentium* (1672), 4.9.2.

128 ALR I, 11, paras. 376–77.

129 K. Luig, above n. 101, pp. 47 ff.

130 B. Windscheid, *Die Actio des römischen Civilrechts vom Standpunkte des heutigen Rechts*, Julius Budaeus, Düsseldorf 1856.

131 *Lampet's case*, 77 Eng. Rep. 994 (K.B. 1612): 'no possibility, right, title, nor thing in action, shall be granted or assigned to strangers'; W. Blackstone, *Commentaries 2* (1768), p. 442; W.S. Holdsworth, 'The History of the Treatment of "Choses" in Action by the Common Law' (1920) 33 *Harvard Law Review* 997.

132 W. Blackstone, above n. 131, p. 442.

133 In the United States, Joseph Story summarises the practice in US courts in 1816 in *Welch v. Mandeville*, 1 Wheat. 233, 236 as follows: 'Courts of law, following in this respect the rules of equity, now take notice of assignments of choses in action, and exert themselves to afford them every support and protection', disregarding the strictness of the common law,

is seen as having been an important impetus for a more uniform doctrine of assignment.[134]

5. OBLIGATIONS *'CIRCA REM'*

Third parties have, in various ways, found themselves bound by rights and duties concerning things acquired. Property law is a clear-cut source of rights and duties – negative duties, involving abstaining from doing. Property rights burdening things may have been seen as developing on the basis of the Roman law concept of ownership, which Roman jurists never defined. Bartolus coined our modern definition of ownership as the *ius in re corporali perfecte disponendi, nisi lege prohibeatur.*[135] Property rights developed from this ownership concept, but also proceeded from a Roman catalogue of *actiones in rem* – property actions – towards a restricted catalogue of subjective property rights: ownership, and property rights to use or to dispose of.[136] The subsequent principled development towards a (kind of) *numerus clausus* of property rights proceeded along the lines of publicity and specificity, providing certainty and clarity for third parties concerning their rights and duties when acquiring objects.[137] One might, however, also argue that the normal typology in old customary law – or at least Germanic law – started from the principle that all obligations concerning land run with the land.[138] Local indigenous law – Germanic law – can be seen and heard, through the reception of Roman law, to this day.

---

protecting the rights of the assignee – indeed also referring to the parallel developments in the civilian tradition. See, in general, W.W. Cook, 'The Alienability of Choses in Action' (1916) 29 *Harvard Law Review* 816.

134 S.J. Bailey, 'Assignment of debts in England from the twelfth to the twentieth century' (1932) 48 *Law Quarterly Review* 248, 578–79; see R. Zimmermann, above n. 6, p. 67.

135 On which, see T. Rufner, 'The Roman Concept of Ownership and the Medieval Doctrine of *Dominium Utile*' in J. Cairns and P. du Plessis (eds), *The Creation of the* Ius Commune*: From Casus to Regula*, Edinburgh University Press, Edinburgh 2012, pp. 127 ff.

136 Heinrich Hahn's pentarchy *(dominium, possessio, hereditas, pignus* and *servitus)*, in his 1639 Helmstedt dissertation, has been identified as the influential source for this catalogue: E.M. Meijers, 'Artikel 584 en de zakelijke rechten', *Rechtsgeleerd Magazijn* 1907.

137 Various techniques are available when establishing such a system, e.g. having a legislative *numerus clausus*, with the judiciary perhaps assisting when needed (e.g. Germany), or having a restricted approach in case law, as e.g. in South Africa, where new property rights may be added using the 'subtraction from dominium' test. See M.J. de Waal, 'Identifying real rights in South African law: the "subtraction from the dominium" test and its application' in S.E. Bartels and J.M. Milo, *Contents of Real Rights*, WLP, Nijmegen 2004, pp. 83–98; and in the same volume (pp. 99–113), C.G. van der Merwe, '*Numerus clausus* and the development of new real rights in South Africa'; on the *numerus clausus* in general, see B. Akkermans, *The* Numerus Clausus *in European Property Law*, Intersentia, Antwerp 2008; T.H.M. Struycken, *De* numerus clausus *in het goederenrecht*, Kluwer, Deventer 2007.

138 A.S. de Blecourt and H.F.W.D. Fischer, above n. 34, pp. 286–87.

In the English common law tradition, equity brought forward, in *Tulk v. Moxhay* (1848), the restrictive covenant that runs with the land, prohibiting the performance of certain acts.[139] It is instructive to see that, in more recent cases, it has been held that a positive covenant cannot not run with the land:

> Equity cannot compel an owner to comply with a positive covenant entered into by his predecessors without flatly contradicting the common law rule that a person cannot be made liable upon a contract unless he was a party to it. Enforcement of a positive covenant lies in contract; a positive covenant compels an owner to exercise his rights. Enforcement of a negative covenant lies in property; a negative covenant deprives the owner of a right over property.[140]

These positive duties may, however, be seen in various typologies appearing over time in various jurisdictions, arising from the law of obligations as well as feudal law. Examples include the German *Reallast*,[141] and the Scottish real burden.[142] Obligations sometimes get promoted over time, such that the creditor of the obligation is suddenly also able to exercise their personal right in the land towards acquirers of the land. An example is the development of the long lease *(emphytheusis, erfpacht)* into a property right,[143] which may be seen as parallel to, or part of, the development in feudal law in which the holder of the *dominium utile* would eventually come to be considered the true owner.[144] Another illustration of this construction is the rule that the transfer of a residential immoveable does not infringe on the rights of a tenant – *emptio non tollit locatum*[145] – deviating from the opposing Roman law principle of *emptio tollit locatum*.[146] In the event that the owner of a residential immoveable

139 *Tulk v. Moxhay* (1848) 2 Ph. 774. Swadling remarks that the *numerus clausus* principle is 'probably secure' at common law, yet equity, the source of *Tulk v. Moxhay*, has a 'creative capacity' ('The Law of Property' in P. Birks, *English Private Law*, OUP, Oxford 2000, para. 4.22).

140 *Rhone v. Stephens* [1994] UKHL 3.

141 Which entitles the holder to the delivery of money or services burdening the land, varying from *'zu Martini eine Gans'* to the delivery of energy. See F. Baur and R. Sturner, *Sachenrecht*, Beck, München 2009, para. 35.

142 K.G.C. Reid, 'Real rights and real obligations' in S.E. Bartels and J.M. Milo, above n. 137, pp. 25–45, in particular para. 13, pp. 38–41.

143 It is to be found in its two-sided character as a contract, but also as a property right, in Grotius' *Inleidinge*, in II.40 and III.18.

144 See e.g. J. Brissaud, above n. 34, p. 243: *'le tenancier investi du domaine utile fut considere comme le vrai proprietaire'* (the tenant invested with *dominium utile* has to be considered true owner).

145 On the tradition of the protection of the tenant in general, see D. Magalhães, *A evolução da protecção do arrendatário*, 2018.

146 D. 19.2.25.1 (Gaius). Fockema Andreae did notice older sources in the Netherlands following the Roman strand *emptio tollit locatum*, and newer sources protecting the lessee, *non tollit locatum*: S.J. Fockema Andreae, *Oud-Nederlandsch Burgerlijk Recht*, Bohn, Haarlem 1906, pp. 344–46.

transfers the immoveable to an acquirer, the acquirer is bound as a debtor to the lease contract. In various jurisdictions the tenant acquired this protection through local statutory law.[147]

Obligations may be qualified as personal, but a category of so-called real obligations was carved out in older French jurisprudence.[148] Toullier argued real obligations to be present,[149] even though the French Civil Code, as well as Pothier, were silent on the matter. The fragment in the Digests (D. 2.14.7.8) was Toullier's formal source, *fondée sur la raison*:[150]

> There are certain agreements which relate to real property, and others which relate to personal property. Those that relate to real property are those by which I agree, in general terms, not to bring suit; those which relate to personal property are those in which I agree not to sue a certain individual, for instance: 'I will not sue Lucius Titius.' Whether an agreement is made with reference to property or to a person is to be ascertained not only from the language, but also from the intention of the contracting parties; since generally, (as Pedius says) the name of the person is inserted in the contract, not for the purpose of rendering it personal, but that it may be shown with whom the contract was made.[151]

Toullier became the verbatim source of inspiration for the Louisiana Civil Code 1825, which replaced the Louisiana Civil Code of 1808.[152] Toullier classified obligations as personal, heritable or real: those that are real may result in the land, and not the person owning the land, being bound with a benefit or burden. A contract concluded to improve the land – for example, by an architect to build on the land – is an example of such a benefit, binding the land; a contract of sale with the condition to pay the agreed price is seen as a burden which binds the land. Third parties acquire the land subject to these real obligations, as the obligations follow the land *comme l'ombre suit le corps*.[153] This is quite similar to an interpretation of the French Art. 1122 Code Civil, and its literally translated

---

147 See e.g. M. Hogg, 'Leases: Four Historical Portraits' in K. Reid and R. Zimmermann (eds), *A History of Private Law in Scotland*, vol. I, OUP, Oxford 2000, pp. 363–98.

148 On their very limited position in (more recent) French and Belgian tradition, see V. Sagaert, 'Real rights and real obligations in Belgian and French law' in S.E. Bartels and J.M. Milo, above n. 137, pp. 47–70.

149 C.B.M. Toullier, *Le droit civil Français, suivant l'ordre du code* 6, Stapleaux, Bruxelles 1821, paras. 397–462.

150 Ibid., para. 424.

151 D. 2.14.7.8: *'Pactorum quaedam in rem sunt, quaedam in personam. In rem sunt, quotiens generaliter paciscor ne petam: in personam, quotiens ne a persona petam, id est ne a Lucio Titio petam. Utrum autem in rem an in personam pactum factum est, non minus ex verbis quam ex mente convenientium aestimandum est: plerumque enim, ut Pedius ait, persona pacto inseritur, non ut personale pactum fiat, sed ut demonstretur, cum quo pactum factum est.'*

152 A.N. Yiannopoulos, 'Real Rights in Louisiana and Comparative Law: Part II' (1963) 23(3) *Louisiana Law Review* 518 ff.

153 C.B.M. Toullier, above n. 149, para. 462.

Dutch sibling Art. 1354 Dutch Civil Code (Burgelijk Wetboek (Old, 1838)), in which positive duties were read, an interpretation which took place in the Netherlands until the decision of the Dutch Supreme Court (Hoge Raad) in the *Blaauboer/Berlips* case ended this option. The court's arguments were founded (rather creatively) in legal history, as well as in principled arguments: that contracts bind parties; that property rights cannot be created by mere contracts, as these property rights need publicity; and that duties to act are against the principle *'servitus in faciendo consistere nequit'*.[154] The decision may be seen as a restatement of the Enlightenment-coined freedom of the individual person, particularly concerning their property, on a free market.

6. THE *ACTIO PAULIANA* OR REVOCATORY ACTION

The individual person's freedom has an age-old limitation, in one of Ulpian's foundational principles of law: *neminem laedere* – to harm no one.[155] This foundational norm also concerns the person's property, as a fraudulent alienation would harm the person's creditor:

> *In Fabiana quoque actione et Pauliana, per quam quae in fraudem creditorem alienata sunt revocantur, fructus quoque restituuntur* – In both the actio Fabiana and the actio Pauliana, by means of which property is recovered, which has been transferred defrauding creditors, also the fruits are returned.[156]

This is the only fragment where we find the still household name of this action: the *actio Pauliana*. It is also to be found in the *Institutes* (Inst. 4.6.6), as well as extensively in the *Digests* – *Quas in fraudem creditorum facta sunt ut restituantur* – concerning restitution where fraudulent acts have been committed against creditors (D. 42.8), and in the *Codex* – *De revocandis his quae per fraudem alienata sunt* – concerning the revocation of contracts by which property has been alienated for the purpose of defrauding creditors (C. 7.75).[157] The action based on these excerpts – the *actio revocatoria* – is expressed in Inst. 4.6.6:

> moreover, where anyone has transferred his property to another for the purpose of defrauding his creditors, and the latter have been placed in possession of said property

154 The principle is to be read in D. 8.1.15.1 (Pomponius); on *Blaauboer/Berlips* (HR 03-03-1905, Weekblad van het Recht 1905, 8191) see S.E. Bartels and J.M. Milo, 'Contents of Real Rights. Personal or Proprietary' in S.E. Bartels and J.M. Milo, above n. 137, pp. 1–23, in particular pp. 6–7.

155 D. 1.1.10.1 (Ulpian).

156 D. 22.1.38.4. Translation by the author.

157 In other fragments, actions in the case of fraud are provided: D. 12.2.9.5; D. 36.1.69.1–2; D. 42.5.25; D. 42.5.8.1; D. 46.3.96.

> by the decision of a magistrate, the creditors are authorized to set aside the transfer and bring an action for the property, that is to say, allege that it never was transferred and for this reason remained a part of the property of the debtor.

The creditor thereby had an action against the third-party acquirer. This Roman law *actio revocatoria* has been received throughout Europe,[158] and beyond, in civil as well as common law.[159] It has become a common heritage of the various European jurisdictions, as Heinrich Dernburg remarked.[160] At various stages of its reception, there were clarifications, corrections and novel additions made, in a continuous debate by scholars, legislators and judges.[161]

In this seemingly straightforward development and its analysis, unexpected and inspiring confrontations happened. The creditor's present-day possibility to have recourse to all the debtor's property may be absent in a tradition where family and feudality, as well as a property scheme whereby land was not owned by the individual, bar the execution of the debtor's immoveable property. In the French tradition, the home-grown principles '*meubles sont le siège des dettes*' and '*les fiefs ne portent aucune dette*'[162] became, in the High Middle Ages' changing culture and growing economy, too restrictive. In this context, the so-called '*clause obligatoire*', whereby the debtor binds 'all his property', became standardly used; this clause grew to become the (Roman law-received) hypothecary security. In the event that the immoveable was transferred, the creditor could 'follow' the immoveable; in the case of moveables, the old customary French (Germanic) principle '*meubles n'ont pas de suite par hypothèque*' happened to be without effect in the event of a transfer, '*pour frauder les creanciers: car la coustume est telle, que biens meubles n'ont point de suite, se ils ne sont pas transportez pour fraudez les creanciers, ou quel cas tu feras faire execution sur les dits biens et vauldra l'execution*'. This fragment from the *Grand Coutumier de France* has been qualified as a manifestation of the revocatory action,[163] visible as well in the floodlights of good faith: '*meubles n'a point de suite, c'est a ententre quand est tenu a juste titre et a bonne foy*'.[164]

---

158 J.A. Ankum, *De geschiedenis der 'Actio Pauliana'*, Tjeenk-Willink, Zwolle 1962, p. 17.

159 E.g. the Fraudulent Conveyances Act of 1581, referred to e.g. by Blackstone, above n. 131 (ed. E. Duyckinck et al., New York 1827), p. 441: 'And by statute 13 Eliz. c. 5. every grant or gift of chattels, as well as lands, with an intent to defraud creditors or others, (b) shall be void as against such persons to whom such fraud would be prejudicial'.

160 H. Dernburg, *Pandekten II*, para. 146.

161 J.A. Ankum, above n. 158 contains a detailed history.

162 J. Brissaud, above n. 34, p. 539 – '*les meubles qui font corps avec la personne (ossibus inhaerent)* [sic]' – 'the moveables that form one body with the person (they stick to the bones)'. See also J.A. Ankum, *De geschiedenis der 'Actio Pauliana'*, above n. 158, p. 271.

163 J.A. Ankum, *De geschiedenis der 'Actio Pauliana'*, above n. 158, p. 279.

164 Ibid.

7. CONCLUDING REMARKS

The third party has been dogma's litmus test over time, in various conceptual streams of thought, in meandering interplay. Third parties made their appearance early on in the legal arena, facing the *nemo potest* of another's contract; of representation; of acquiring another's claim. But they never came in from the cold, as social practice or custom always reigns in any society. In Roman law, traditional principles were accompanied by casuistic pragmatism. But this historic reality is difficult to see through the casuistic compilations, and the rise of principled dogma in the debate, therefore, does not surprise, particularly not if one keeps in mind that the prevailing theories of legal reasoning may demand that more or less weight be given to the arguments derived from the legal text itself and its authority.

Glossators, humanists, *Pandektists* and positivists had, through their strong argumentative bonds with the historic texts, contemporary codified texts, or the line of most recently decided cases, less room to offer the third party's stance. At the same time, courts, custom and local written laws were much more flexible, and remarkable lines of reasoning may be present, even if they did not prevail at the time. Martinus' *aequitas*, or natural justice, did not remain unnoticed at all, and the canonists had a consistent line of reasoning which strongly anchored the fundaments of law in justice. Promises, including those concerning third persons, were to be kept.

Commentators, *usus modernus*, *ius hodiernum*, *Interessenjurisprudenz*, sociological jurisprudence: scholars did – often as a reaction to preceding textual *auctoritas* – incorporate in their reasoning the foundations of law in justice, allowing more leniency in the historic texts, to come to an acceptable meaning, and incorporating indigenous customary and statutory law, and particularly commercial custom. The combination of these legal formants came to fruition in Grotius' *Inleidinge*, as well as in his *De Iure Belli ac Pacis*, giving third parties a place at the scholarly table of brotherhood.

Since these early modern times, subjective rights and their fundamental protection have made the person the pivotal concept we still know today – in codified, uncodified, civil, common or mixed jurisdictions – whereby the third person, like any other person, weak or strong, may find its place secure in a solemn sphere, the ίερος κυκλος of *lex, ius* and bona fides.

EXPANDING CONTRACT AND TORT FOR THE PROTECTION OF THIRD PARTIES*

Miquel Martín-Casals

1. THE CONTRACT/TORT DIVIDE

1.1. A BLURRING BORDERLINE

It is well known that classical legal thinking imposed a sharp distinction between contract and tort. It considered that contract was the essential manifestation of the power of self-determination of the parties (private autonomy), where the breach of pre-existing obligations created by contract gave rise to different remedies – damages being one of them – that could be claimed either on their own or in addition to other remedies. In tort law, damages were also an important remedy – probably the most important one – but in contrast to contract, liability arising from tort had its origin in the infringement of interests protected by law rather than by private arrangement.[1]

---

* This chapter has been elaborated within the framework of Research Project PID2022-136571NB-I00, funded by the Spanish Ministry of Science and Innovation (2022–25), in which Josep Solé Feliu and the author are principal researchers.

1 This chapter draws on some of my previous research projects and publications, including M. Martín-Casals (ed), *The Borderlines of Tort Law: Interactions with Contract Law*, Intersentia, Cambridge 2019. For a general overview on contract law from a comparative perspective, see H. Beale, B. Fauvarque-Cosson, J. Rutgers and S. Vogenauer (eds), *Cases, Materials and Text on Contract Law*, 3rd ed., Hart, Oxford/Portland 2018; J.M. Smits, *Contract Law: A Comparative Introduction*, 2nd ed., Edward Elgar, Cheltenham 2017; H Kötz, *European Contract Law*, 2nd ed., OUP, Oxford 2017; R. Cabrillac, *Droit européen comparé des contrats*, 2nd ed., LGDJ – Lextenso, Paris 2016; N. Jansen and R. Zimmermann (eds), *Commentaries on European Contract Laws*, OUP, Oxford 2018. As regards tort law, see W. van Gerven, P. Larouche and J. Lever, *Cases, Materials and Text on National, Supranational and International Tort Law*, Hart, Oxford/Portland 2000; H. Koziol, *Basic Questions of Tort Law from a Comparative Perspective*, Jan Sramek, Vienna 2015; and the corresponding volumes of the 'Principles of European Tort Law' series of the European Group on Tort Law. Other relevant books for the variety of topics dealt with in this book are A.S. Hartkamp et al. (eds), *Towards a European Civil Code*, 4th ed., Ars Aequi Libri/Kluwer Law International, Nijmegen/The Hague 2011 and J. Basedow, K. Hopt and R. Zimmermann, *The Max Planck Encyclopedia of European Private Law* (2 vols.), OUP, Oxford 2012 (quoted hereinafter as MPI/Author, Word).

However, this sharp distinction has been eroded over time and no longer reflects the current situation. Even the first European civil codes established obligations between contractual parties which were based, not on the parties' consent, but on general duties of conduct established by the law, as in the case of good faith in the creation or performance of contracts.[2] Growing state interventionism and the need to protect vulnerable parties have given rise to more obligations imposed by law, as in the case of professional liability, and in some cases even to entirely new areas of law, such as labour law or consumer law. In the tort law area, it is no longer true that all obligations arise independently of the defendant's will. In the context of comparative law, the emergence and development of liability for pure economic loss in negligence claims has led to the admission of liability on the basis of the existence of a 'special relationship', the creation of a 'reasonable trust', or the 'assumption of responsibility', as, for example, in cases of the liability of auditors towards non-contracting third parties, all of which has also brought liability in contract and tort closer together.[3]

This does not mean, however, that the two orders of responsibility have merged into a kind of common space – what some authors have called 'contorts'[4] – wherever the functions they perform and the applicable rules are the same. Contract is still a socio-economic institution which aims, through private negotiations, to increase the expected utility of the parties and, therefore, social welfare.[5] Consequently, the main objective of contract law is to enforce agreements that parties have voluntarily negotiated. Tort law, on the other hand, aims at the protection of legitimate interests from interference by third parties, and at transferring the infringement of these interests into consequences for those who have infringed them. In this context, the basic rule of the whole system of interaction between the two orders is that no legal system can allow the application of the more general rules of tort liability to destroy the balance of interests achieved by parties in their contractual agreements.

---

2 R. Zimmermann and S. Whittaker, *Good Faith in European Contract Law*, CUP, Cambridge 2000, pp. 675 ff.

3 R. Kreitner, 'Fault at the Contract-Tort Interface' in O. Ben-Shahar, *Fault in American Contract Law*, CUP, Cambridge/New York 2010, pp. 108 ff.

4 The term 'contort' has been coined by some scholars to describe situations where an actor breaches a voluntarily assumed contractual duty that is identical or closely related to one otherwise owed to the world at large, regardless of the existence of a contract: see G. Gilmore, *The Death of Contract*, Ohio State University Press, Columbus 1974, pp. 95–98. Other scholars have used the term to describe obligations consisting of a blend of elements deriving from both contract and tort. See e.g. S. Litvinoff, 'Contract, Delict, Morals, and Law' (1999) 45(1) *Loyola Law Review* 43. See also G. Brüggemeier, 'Perspectives on the Law of "Contorts", A Discussion of the Dominant Trends in West German Tort Law' (1983) 6 *Hastings International & Comparative Law Review* 355.

5 I. Gilead, 'Non-Consensual Liability of a Contracting Party: Contract, Negligence, Both, or In-Between?' (2002) 3 *Theoretical Inquires in Law* 1, 20.

When the legal effects are the same, it is immaterial to qualify an action as contractual or tortious, or to discuss concurrence or non-concurrence between contract and tort law claims. The distinction, however, becomes crucial when the effects are different and the claimant can gain something with the contractual or tortious classification or, conversely, when such differences may improve the defendant's position. Over the past decades, the rules governing liability in contract and liability in tort have come together remarkably in some areas, such as compensation for non-pecuniary loss, and the rules on prescription. As regards compensation for non-pecuniary loss, although developments regarding compensation in contract have always lagged behind those occurring in tort, and the positions of European jurisdictions still vary substantially, the differences between these two areas have been significantly reduced. Currently, almost all jurisdictions accept compensation of non-pecuniary loss in contract.[6] The reform of the prescription rules, carried out in most European jurisdictions over the last few decades, is probably even more important for the approximation of the two areas. The new regulations have followed a clear tendency towards unified, general and much shorter prescription periods in contract and in tort, thereby avoiding endless discussions on the contractual or tortious character of a claim, which are still common in countries where unification has not yet taken place.[7]

1.2. A 'GREY ZONE'

Generally speaking, it is also doubtful whether an interim or third category between contract and tort has developed in the case of pre-contractual liability, although it is true that in most jurisdictions it is a 'grey zone' which gives rise to many doubts.[8] Legislation or case law in many continental jurisdictions establish

---

6 In the area of contract, see V.V. Palmer, *The Recovery of Non-Pecuniary Loss in European Contract Law*, CUP, Cambridge 2015. In the area of tort, see U. Magnus (ed), *Unification of Tort Law: Damages*, Kluwer International, The Hague 2001; W.V. Horton Rogers (ed), *Damages for Non-Pecuniary Loss in a Comparative Perspective*, Springer, New York/Vienna 2001; and B. Winiger, H. Koziol, A. Koch and R. Zimmermann (eds), *Digest of European Tort Law, vol 2: Essential Cases on Damage*, De Gruyter, Berlin 2011, 11/1–13/29, pp. 493–705 and CR 13/30, pp. 706–18.

7 See R. Zimmermann, *Comparative Foundations of a European Law of Set-Off and Prescription*, CUP, Cambridge 2002, p. 80 and I. Gilead and B. Askeland (eds), *Prescription in Tort Law: Analytical and Comparative Perspectives*, Intersentia, Cambridge 2020. See also R. Zimmermann and J Kleinschmidt, 'Prescription: General Framework and Special Problems Concerning Damages Claims' in H. Koziol and B.C. Steininger (eds), *European Tort Law 2007*, Springer, Vienna 2008, pp. 26–78; MPI/R. Zimmermann, 'Prescription' (pp. 1306–10) and M.J. Bonell, 'Limitation Periods' in A. Hartkamp et al. (eds), above n. 1, pp. 715–32.

8 J. Cartwright and M. Hesselink, *Precontractual Liability in European Private Law*, CUP, Cambridge 2008; M. Hogg, *Promises and Contract Law: Comparative Perspectives*,

a general duty to negotiate contracts in good faith, which if breached may give rise to pre-contractual liability. Related to this general duty, other duties may arise, such as those referring to the disclosure of information, the confidentiality of the information obtained or when breaking off contract negotiations. Common to all these countries is that they consider the negotiation of a contract to place the parties in a relationship which deserves legal protection. Although negotiations are not yet a contract, and so the form and scope of their protection cannot be exactly the same, negotiations give rise to duties between the prospective parties, the enforcement of which must be made compatible with the basic principle of freedom of contract. Whereas in some jurisdictions pre-contractual liability comes close to a third category which is governed by contract law rules,[9] other jurisdictions tend to apply tort law.[10] By contrast, a general duty to bargain in good faith is unknown in common law jurisdictions. These jurisdictions do not recognise the pre-contractual stage as a legally relevant relationship which, as such, deserves the general protection of the law, and, when faced with similar problems, they solve them according to specific torts, or even according to unjust enrichment rules.[11]

Professional liability also falls into a grey zone where the distinction between contract and tort has lost importance over the years. In this context, the professions referred to are not exactly the same in all countries, but the core of the relevant professional activities relates to the provision of healthcare, legal or financial services, and includes accountants, tax advisors, bank employees and, sometimes, architects; the basic distinction probably lies between the so-called 'liberal professions' and other professions.[12] One of the main traits that distinguishes liberal professions from the others is that they require formal training; that is, the acquisition of knowledge and skills specific to the profession

---

CUP, Cambridge 2011, pp. 180 ff., 189. See also MPI/J. von Hein, 'Culpa in contrahendo' (pp. 430–33) and J. Dietrich, 'Classifying precontractual liability: a comparative analysis' (2000) 21(2) *Legal Studies* 153–91.

9 This is the case in Germany, where the 2002 reform of the law of obligations introduced into the German Civil Code all the constellations of cases previously dealt with by case law, which continue to be governed by contract law rules (see §311 (2) and (3) BGB). For these cases, it uses the term 'obligations similar to legal transactions (*rechtsgeschäftsähnliche Schuldverhältnisse*)'.

10 Pre-contractual liability is regulated in the civil codes of Italy (Arts. 1137 and 1138 CC), Greece (Art. 197), Poland (Art. 72 §2 and Art. 721 §§1 and 2), the Czech Republic (§§1728–30) and, more recently, in France (Arts. 1112, 1112-1 and 1112-2 Code civil). Without excluding the occasional application of contract rules in some of these systems, courts tend to apply tort law rules, and the area is considered a 'grey zone'. See M. Martín-Casals (ed), above n. 1, pp. 793–802 and the corresponding national reports.

11 MPI/Von Hein, above n. 8, p. 431; J. Dietrich, above n. 8, pp. 156 ff.

12 In this sense, see E. Hondius, 'Professional Liability' in M. Bussani and A.J. Sebok (eds), *Comparative Tort Law: Global Perspectives*, 2nd ed, Edward Elgar, Cheltenham 2021, pp. 214–35, p. 227.

in question, which usually involves complex activities and decisions which cannot easily be assessed by non-professionals. Often, the practising of these professions also requires a licence that empowers and legitimates those who possess it to practise the profession within the relevant community. Due to the complexity and specific characteristics of the services provided, and to the imbalance of knowledge between the professional and the other contractual party, those contracting with professionals cannot easily ascertain to what extent professionals are complying with their contractual duties. For this reason, the conduct of these professionals is not governed solely by contract or tort rules but, to a large extent, by codes of conduct, codes of ethics or similar professional rules, usually issued and enforced by the corresponding professional public or private bodies established to regulate the profession in question. These internal rules set the standards of conduct that all members of the relevant profession must observe, and from which they cannot deviate in their particular contracts. All these elements create legitimate expectations on the part of persons who contract with such professionals, and show not only that the contractual rules bargained for by the parties are not the main rules setting the standards in the relationship, but also that the general contract or tort law rules would be inadequate were they not interpreted in light of this professional setting. Thus, irrespective of the basis of the claim – whether tort or contract – professionals are responsible for typical skills of their profession, and have to abide by a standard of care which depends on their specific profession, and is higher than that required of an ordinary person outside the profession.[13]

Although most jurisdictions consider that professional liability is primarily a matter of contract law, there is a general agreement that both contract and tort law rules may apply; obviously, this does not apply in those few countries, such as France,[14] in which the *non-cumul* rule applies. In the healthcare sector, the boundary between contract and tort is very fluid, and in some countries liability has been switching between the two over the last few decades.[15]

13 See E. Karner and B.A. Koch, 'Austria' (Mn. 56); B. Askeland, 'Norway' (Mn. 74 ff.); A. Keirse, 'The Netherlands' (Mn. 85 f.); and P. Machnikowski, 'Poland' (Mn. 157 ff.) in M. Martín-Casals (ed), above n. 1.

14 J.S. Borghetti, 'France' (Mn. 84) in M. Martín-Casals (ed), above n. 1.

15 Thus, Art. 7:453 of the Dutch Civil Code provides a specific duty of care which, in spite of the wording of the code, is a contractual duty that must be understood according to the specific standards established in the model contract drawn up by the Royal Dutch Society of Medicine and the National Patients Platform. The new Czech Civil Code, effective from 1 January 2014, inspired by Dutch law and under the strong influence of the contract of treatment in the DCFR (Art IV. C. 8:101), has also introduced a new contract for healthcare services (§§2636–51, Czech CC), establishing the obligations of the provider towards the patient (see L. Tichý, 'Czech and European Law of Obligations at a Turning Point' in R. Schulze and F. Zoll (eds),

2. THE EXPANSION OF THE PROTECTIVE AREA OF CONTRACT LAW

2.1. THE PROTECTION OF THIRD PARTIES BEYOND 'CONTRACTS FOR THE BENEFIT OF THIRD PARTIES'

The principle of privity or relativity of contract does not allow a general extension of the protective scope of the contract to third parties who have not been mentioned in the contract, or at least not to those whose protection cannot result from an interpretation of the contractual will of the parties.[16] In some legal systems, the gap in protection is filled by stretching the scope of contract law, whereas in others it is filled by tort law. The interaction of contract law with tort law depends largely on the basic approach and structure of the system of tort law in the relevant legal jurisdiction. A basic idea is that where the approach to tort law is very stringent, with a more or less closed list of protected interests, an expansion of contract law becomes a way to iron out some of tort law's shortcomings. Sometimes the problems resulting from a rigid tort law system are coupled with the existence of tort law rules which courts sense do not solve these problems properly, and which, for this reason, have successfully been curbed by the courts over the years. This is the case, for instance, of the so-called 'contract with protective effects to third parties' *(Vertrag mit Schutzwirkung zugunsten Dritter)*, which, together with the so-called 'direct claim' *(action directe)* in the case of certain 'chains of contracts', constitute the two main exceptions to the principle of relativity of contract.

The Law of Obligations in Europe: A New Wave of Codifications, Sellier, Munich 2013, 40.2. A move to contract law has also taken place in Germany, where the Patient Law Act 2013 (Patientenrechtsgesetz) has codified medical liability, so far based on negligence in tort or in contract, in the part of the Civil Code devoted to the 'contract of treatment' (§§630a–630h BGB) (see Act of 26 February 2013, BGBl I, 277 and M. Stauch, 'The 2013 German Patients' Rights Act – Codifying Medical Malpractice Compensation' (2015) *Journal of European Tort Law* 85–94). By contrast, in Italy, the Gelli-Bianco Act (Act of 8 March 2017, no. 24) has scheduled a double track of liability, where liability is contractual as regards the institution providing healthcare, whether public or private, and non-contractual in relation to healthcare professionals. Nevertheless, wherever the healthcare professional and the patient have, in fact, entered into an actual contract for the provision of healthcare services, liability will be in contract (see G. Montari Vergallo, *La nuova responsabilità medica doppo la riforma Gelli-Bianco*, Dike, Rome 2017, pp. 68 ff.).

16 The principle is recognised in many civil codes (thus, expressly in Art. 1165 French CC, Art. 1372 Italian CC and Art. 1257 Spanish CC, and tacitly in §§241, 305 BGB). For England and Wales, see M. Furstom and G.J. Tolhurst, *Privity of Contract*, OUP, Oxford 2015, pp. 28 ff.; and for a comparative approach, see E. du Perron, 'Contract and Third Parties' in A. Hartkamp et al. (eds), *Towards a European Civil Code*, 2nd ed., Ars Aequi Libri/Kluwer Law International, Nijmegen/The Hague 1998, pp. 331–26; H. Kötz, *European Contract Law*, above n. 1, pp. 319 ff.; J.M. Smits, above n. 1, pp. 245 ff.; R. Cabrillac, above n. 1, pp. 123 ff.

2.2. CONTRACTS WITH PROTECTIVE EFFECTS TO THIRD PARTIES

With the so-called 'contract with protective effects to third parties' *(Vertrag mit Schutzwirkung zugunsten Dritter)*, German law developed, from the beginning of the twentieth century, a contractual approach to the protection of the interests of third parties.[17] By contrast to contracts for the benefit of third parties, these contracts do not grant third parties a right to claim performance, but only secondary duties of care and protection which, in the case of infringement, entitle them to bring a claim for damages in contract.

During the First World War, the Reichsgericht started including third parties in the protective scope of the contract, on the basis of the interpretation of the contract, by using devices such as the objective meaning and scope of the contract, *boni mores*, supplementary contract interpretation, or implied agreement of the parties. In the 1950s, following Karl Larenz, the Bundesgerichtshof coined the current name of this institution, and justified it on the grounds of the responsibility of the contractual creditor for the weal and woe *(Wohl und Wehe)* of the third party, and the courts started to loosen ties with the clear fiction of the hypothetical will of the parties, without breaking with the grounds mentioned earlier.[18]

The protected interests were regularly personal injury or property damage suffered by family members, workers or tenants, and the underpinning idea of this new institution was the protection of vulnerable third parties. These interests were already protected in tort, pursuant to §823, paragraph 1, BGB, but the contractual route was used to overcome what was perceived as a shortcoming of German tort law, which, in contrast to vicarious liability in contract (§278 BGB), requires fault of the principal to establish liability for his auxiliaries in tort (§831 BGB). The advantage offered by the contract route, however, was at the price of not being able to recover non-pecuniary loss, and having to put up with defences, such as limitation of liability or shorter contractual prescription periods. The removal of the exclusion on non-pecuniary loss recovery in contract, as a result of the 2002 reform, has made recourse to tort law no longer necessary.[19]

The application of the 'contract with protective effects to third parties' to compensate pure economic losses started in the mid-1960s, with a case imposing liability on a notary, towards disappointed beneficiaries of a testator.[20] During

---

17 S. Vogenauer, '§§328–335, "Versprechen der Leistung an einen Dritten"' in M. Schmoeckel, J. Rückert and R. Zimmermann (eds), *Historisch-kritischer Kommentar zum BGB*, II/2, Mohr Siebeck, Tübingen 2007, pp. 2031 ff.

18 Ibid.

19 G. Wagner, *Deliktsrecht*, 14th ed., Franz Vahlen, München 2021, pp. 124 ff., Mn. 43 ff.

20 A case similar to the English case *White v. Jones* [1995] 2 AC 207. See G. Kegel, 'Die lachenden Doppelerben: Erbfolge beim Versagen von Urkundspersonen' in *FS für Werner Flume zum*

those years, this institution also started being applied to pre-contractual liability, and in the 1970s the 'weal and woe' idea lost strength, and the institution was increasingly applied to non-vulnerable persons, including legal persons.[21]

Finally, the 2002 reform introduced the institution into the German Civil Code (§311 III 1 BGB), which now provides that a contractual obligation 'may also come into existence in relation to persons who are not themselves intended to be parties to the contract'. The legal provision does not mention the conditions that must be met, but according to case law: (1) the claimant must be endangered by the defendant's behaviour in the same way as the defendant's contract partner *(Leistungsnähe)*; (2) the contract partner must be interested in the extension of the contractual effects, and the contract must be able to be interpreted accordingly (*Einbeziehungsinteresse*); and (3) the defendant must have been able to know of the claimant's endangerment and interest *(Erkennbarkeit)*. However, even if all these requirements have been met, it is generally contended that a further requirement is necessary, i.e. (4) that the third party has a need for protection. No such need exists, and thus no such protection is required, if the third party has a claim – either in contract or in tort – of their own.[22]

Since pure economic loss is not recoverable under liability for fault, as it is not included in the list of interests protected by §823, paragraph 1, BGB, the main question here is whether it should be recoverable according to this contractual approach. The bitter criticism raised by some authors against this legal institution should probably be focused more on these types of cases. The echoes of the floodgates argument seem to reverberate in our ears when critical voices affirm that this institution has been possible thanks

> to the conversion of contractual obligations into a social institution underpinned with aims of social protection, so that it should generate protective effects to an incalculable number of persons who were unknown to the debtor when the contract was concluded and who had not participated in the contract.[23]

With some exaggeration, the institution is attributed to the 'advancement of socialist ideas in private law', and it is then contended that 'it does not only sacrifice the will of the contractual parties to societal goals, but also demolishes the borders between contractual and tortious liability'.[24] In fact, where pure

70. Geburtstag, O. Schmidt, Köln 1978, I, pp. 545–58. See also M. Makowsky, 'Schadensersatz für entgangene Zuwendungen im Todesfall – von "lachenden Doppelerben" und "verzückten Doppelberechtigten"' (2016) 216 *AcP* 497–557.

21 S. Vogenauer, above n. 17, pp. 2031 ff.

22 H. Kötz, *Vertragsrecht*, 2nd ed., Mohr Siebeck, Tübingen 2012, pp. 217 ff., and D. Looschelders, *Schuldrecht: Allgemeiner Teil*, 15th ed., Franz Vahlen, München 2017, Mn. 164–66.

23 H. Hattenhauer, *Grundbegriffe des Bürgerlichen Rechts*, 2nd ed., Beck, München 2000, p. 106.

24 Ibid., pp. 106 ff.

economic loss is at stake, the constellation of cases solved, in practice, with this institution comes very close to those solved in other legal systems by tort law rules, and which constitute exceptions to the non-recoverability of pure economic losses.

Besides Germany, only a few European countries, such as Austria, Greece and, at least occasionally, Italy,[25] seem to have adopted this extension of the contract to matters which, in most European jurisdictions, are dealt with according to tort law rules. The English Law Commission explicitly rejected the adoption of the institution when considering the so-called 'test of enforceability' – that is, when and in what circumstances third parties have the right to enforce a contract or contractual provision to which they are not a party – and excluded from the notion of contracts for the benefit of third parties those cases where the third party, albeit expressly designated 'as a beneficiary' in the contract, has no presumed right of enforcement.[26] Harmonisation and international texts also seem to ignore 'contracts with protective effects to third parties', and it has been contended that it seems better to leave it to national lawmakers to decide whether liability in tort is justified in some of the pertinent scenarios, rather than to 'resort to *strained and unnatural interpretations*' of contractual agreements'.[27]

2.3. DIRECT CLAIM *(ACTION DIRECTE)*

A direct claim gives a contractual party an action in contract against a party to another contract, as long as there is some sort of close relationship between their contracts that shows that events occurring in relation to one contract can have effects on the other. This direct claim, which is considered to be a claim in contract, must then abide by the terms that the party against whom the claim is addressed has agreed to in their contract.[28]

There are specific provisions in many legal systems that allow a 'direct action' *(action directe)* in particular situations; that is, which provide that a third party to the contract may bring a claim against the 'debtor of his debtor', to the extent of anything still owed by both of them. This is the case, for instance, where a landlord who is owed rent by their tenant is allowed to make a direct claim against the subtenant;[29] or where a principal is allowed to bring a claim against

25 E. Karner and B.A. Koch, 'Austria' (Mn. 31); E. Dacoronia, 'Greece' (Mn. 41); C. Amato and G. Comandé, 'Italy' (Mn. 71–73), in M. Martín-Casals (ed), above n. 1.

26 The Law Commission, *Privity of Contract: Contracts for the Benefit of Third Parties* (Law Com No. 242, 1996), Mn. 7-25 and fn. 22.

27 S. Vogenauer, 'Stipulation in Favour of a Third Party' in N. Jansen and R. Zimmerman (eds), above n. 1, pp. 883–84, Mn. 25 and 26. Emphasis in the original.

28 In relation to France, see M. Fabre-Magnan, *Droit des obligations I*, 4th ed., PUF, Paris 2016, pp. 606–12.

29 Art. 1753 French CC; Art. 1595 Italian CC; Art. 1552 Spanish CC; Art. 599.2 Greek CC.

a subagent to whom their agent has delegated the contracted task;[30] or, more generally, in the case of the so-called 'direct right of action' that, in cases of traffic accidents, injured parties may bring 'against the insurance undertaking covering the person responsible against civil liability'.[31] A direct claim limited to a specific situation can occasionally be created by case law, as in the Spanish case STS 11 March 2020 (RJ 2020,752), where, in relation to the so-called 'dieselgate' scandal, the Supreme Court unexpectedly approved a direct claim by a purchaser of a vehicle fitted with a defeat device, against the manufacturer.[32] However, leaving aside these specific cases, most countries do not allow, in general terms, the protective scope of the contract to be stretched to include third parties through a direct claim.

A clear exception to this general trend is France, where such an approach does not seem to have disappeared, despite the restrictive approach of the new Art. 1341-3 of the French CC,[33] which refers only to claims for payment.[34] The starting point for this more general *'action directe'* was the theory of contract groups *('groupes de contrats')*, developed in the 1970s, and approved in the 1980s

---

30 Art. 1992 French CC; Art. 1705 (2) Italian CC; Art. 1722 Spanish CC; Art. 716.3 Greek CC.

31 See Art. 18 of the Directive 2009/103/EC of the European Parliament and of the Council of 16 September 2009 relating to insurance against civil liability in respect of the use of motor vehicles, and the enforcement of the obligation to insure against such liability [2009] OJ L263/11.

32 In this judgment, the Spanish Supreme Court compared the automotive industry with the construction industry, where case law had extended to the buyer the action that the developer had against the contractor or the architect, based on Art. 1591 of the Civil Code and extended the principle applicable in the construction industry to the buyers of vehicles. The Court held that 'contracting in the automotive sector also has particularities that justify limiting or excepting in certain cases the principle of relativity of contracts, given the special links that are created between the manufacturer, dealers and buyers, the importance of the manufacturer's brand, the loyalty of the consumer to said brand, its influence on the decision of the purchaser of a car, and the massive affectation, to a plurality of purchasers, who usually cause manufacturing defects'.

33 Art. 1341-3: *'Dans les cas déterminés par la loi, le créancier peut agir directement en paiement de sa créance contre un débiteur de son débiteur'* ('In cases determined by legislation, a creditor may sue directly to obtain satisfaction from a debtor of his own debtor' (English translation offered by the French government, available at http://www.textes.justice.gouv.fr/art_pix/THE-LAW-OF-CONTRACT-2-5-16.pdf)).

34 The 'Rapport au Président de la République relatif à l'ordonnance no 2016-131 du 10 février 2016 portant réforme du droit des contrats, du régime général et de la preuve des obligations', *Journal Officiel de la République Française*, No. 35, du 11 février 2016, stated that: *'Le chapitre se clôt par une disposition sur les actions directes en paiement, absentes du code civil, qui vise à énoncer que ces actions existent dans les cas déterminés par la loi (article 1341-3). … Ce texte n'est toutefois relatif qu'aux actions directes en paiement et ne concerne pas les actions directes en responsabilité ou en garantie, de sorte que les solutions jurisprudentielles actuelles, notamment sur les chaînes translatives de propriété, ne sont pas affectées par ce texte'* ('The chapter ends with a provision on direct actions for payment, absent from the Civil Code, which aims to state that these actions exist in the cases established by law (article 1341-3). … This text, however, only relates to direct actions for payment and does not concern direct actions for liability or guarantee, so that the current case law solutions, in particular on transfer chains of ownership, are not affected by this text').

by the First Chamber of the Cour de cassation, while being strongly disapproved by the Third Chamber of that court. This theory gave a contractual party an action in contract against a contractual party with whom they were not in privity, as long as there was, between their contracts, a relationship that was so close that the events occurring in relation to one contract could have effects on the other. After an expansive trend,[35] the Plenary Assembly of the Cour de Cassation rejected this theory in the *arrêt Besse* (12 July 1991),[36] since it considered that it violated the principle of relativity of contract (see Art. 1199, formerly Art. 1165, French CC). Although it did not do away with a general '*action directe*', it confined it to certain 'chains of contracts'.[37]

Thus, the current position provides that there is an '*action directe*' in all chains of contracts that have the aim of transferring property, regardless of whether they are homogeneous (i.e. chains of contracts of sale) or heterogeneous (i.e. chains including at least one sale, together with other commercial contracts).[38] This theory considers that the direct claim is transferred together with the contract, as an accessory to it, a solution that the Cour de cassation has considered compatible with the principle of relativity of contract. This direct claim, which is contractual in nature, must therefore respect the terms that the party against whom the claim is addressed has agreed in their contract. In order to honour these terms, the claimant cannot oblige this party to more than what this party owes their own creditor; conversely, the claimant cannot obtain from this other party along the chain more than what they would have obtained had they brought their claim against their own debtor.[39]

A more recent and practically important exception to the principle of relativity of contract results from the 2006 *Myr'ho* decision, where the Cour de cassation ruled that 'a third party to a contract may, on the basis of tortious liability, invoke a breach of contract whenever this breach has caused him harm'. It has been contended that this rule does away with the principle of relativity of contract in many cases, in spite of the fact that the liability it creates is in tort, and not in contract.[40] The French Projet de réforme 2017, by contrast to the

35 For the details, see M. Fabre-Magnan, above n. 28, pp. 606–12.

36 No. 90-13603; D 1991, 549, note J. Ghestin; JCP 1991, II, 21743, note G. Viney. For an English version, see W. van Gerven, P. Larouche and J. Lever, above n. 1, Supplement Tort 43/2 ff.

37 See H. Kötz, *European Contract Law*, above n. 1, pp. 328–31; H. Beale, B. Fauvarque-Cosson, J. Rutgers and S. Vogenauer (eds), above n. 1, pp. 1319–22.

38 For more, in detail, see M. Fabre-Magnan, above n. 28, pp. 611 ff.; J.S. Borghetti, 'Breach of Contract and Liability to Third Parties in French Law: How to Break the Deadlock?' (2010) 2 *ZEuP* 279–303.

39 M. Fabre-Magnan, above n. 28, p. 611 and *passim*.

40 Cass. ass. Plén., 6 October 2006, *Loubeyre et autres v. SATL Myr'Ho et autre*, no. 05-13.255, P+B+R+I, Bull, Civ. ass. Plén. no. 9; D 2006, 2825, note G. Viney, JCP 2006, II, 10181, avis Garazzio et note M. Billiau; RTD civ 2007, 123, obs. Jourdain. See J.S. Borghetti, above n. 38, pp. 289 ff. See also J.S. Borghetti, 'Strict Liability in Tort and the Boundaries of Tort' in H. Koziol and U. Magnus, *Essays in Honour of Jaap Spier*, Sramek, Vienna 2016, pp. 19–54, pp. 33 ff.

Avant-Projet 2016, seems to create a major exception to this tort law route, when it provides that a third party can choose to bring a claim in contract against the party in breach, if they can prove that they had a legitimate interest in the proper performance of the contract.[41] Considering the different positions that can be found in legal writing,[42] and in case law,[43] it seems that the question will not be settled until the reform bill becomes law.

3. THE EXPANSION OF THE PROTECTIVE AREA OF TORT LAW

3.1. THE NOTION OF 'PURE ECONOMIC LOSS'

The expansion of tort law through a growing number of cases where pure economic loss is compensated in tort has also contributed to blurring the boundaries between contract and tort. In these cases, the existence of a close

---

41 Art. 1234, al 1: '*Lorsque l'inexécution du contrat cause un dommage à un tiers, celui-ci ne peut demander réparation de ses conséquences au débiteur que sur le fondement de la responsabilité extracontractuelle, à charge pour lui de rapporter la preuve de l'un des faits générateurs visés à la section II du chapitre II*' ('Where non-performance of a contract causes harm to a third-party, the latter can claim reparation of its consequences from the debtor only on the basis of extra-contractual liability, and subject to that third-party's establishing one of the actions giving rise to liability targeted by Section II of Chapter II' (English translation offered by the French government, available at http://www.textes.justice.gouv.fr/art_pix/reform_bill_on_civil_liability_march_2017.pdf)). While this rule appeared as absolute in the Avant-Projet, the Projet de réforme 2017 adds that: '*Toutefois, le tiers ayant un intérêt légitime à la bonne exécution d'un contrat et ne disposant d'aucune autre action en réparation pour le préjudice subi du fait de sa mauvaise exécution, peut également invoquer, sur le fondement de la responsabilité contractuelle, un manquement contractuel dès lors que celui-ci lui a causé un dommage. Les conditions et limites de la responsabilité qui s'appliquent dans les relations entre les contractants lui sont opposables*' (Nevertheless, a third party who has a legitimate interest in the proper performance of a contract can equally invoke, on the basis of contractual liability, a contractual failing where the latter has caused him harm. The conditions and limitations on this liability which are applicable in the relations between the contracting parties may be set up against him. Any contract term which limits the contractual liability of a party to the contract in relation to a third party is deemed not written).

42 Against the proposed rule, see J.S. Borghetti, 'La responsabilité des contractants à l'égard des tiers dans le projet de réforme de la responsabilité civile', D 2017, 1846, who considers that the 'legitimate interest' requirement will hardly limit the scope of this contractual liability. In favour, see M. Leveneur, 'Une solution convaincante pour l'engagement de la responsabilité des contractants par les tiers. À propos de l'article 1234 du projet de réforme de la responsabilité', JCPG 2017, 1182.

43 Cour de cassation, civile, Chambre commerciale, 18 janvier 2017, 14-16.442 14-18.832, and Cour de cassation, civile, Chambre civile 3, 18 mai 2017, 16-11.203, Publié au bulletin, seem to contradict the 2006 decision. In fact, the second of these 2017 decisions declares that the possibility for a third party to a contract to invoke, on the basis of tort, a breach of contract which has caused them damage, cannot result from the sole breach of a contractual *obligation de résultat* to deliver a work in conformity and defect-free.

relationship of proximity between the parties, involving the defendant's voluntary assumption of responsibility towards the claimant, either individually or as the member of an identifiable class, has become a way to fill gaps that are similar to those solved by stretching contract law rules in other legal systems.

Economic loss, and more precisely pure economic loss in negligence, has been one of the most debated issues in tort law over the last few decades.[44] Surprisingly enough, the concept of 'pure economic loss' is unknown in many legal jurisdictions, and in those that do use it, there is no generally agreed definition. A standard definition can be found in §2 of the *Restatement (Third) of Torts: Liability for Economic Harm*, which provides that, 'for purposes of this Restatement, "economic loss" is pecuniary damage not arising from injury to the plaintiff's person or from physical harm to the plaintiff's property'.[45]

It has been contended that the word 'pure' plays a central role here. Pure economic loss is a stand-alone pecuniary loss which affects the patrimony of the defendant as such; that is, without harming their person or specific items of their property – as has been graphically described, it 'strikes the victim's wallet and nothing else'.[46] If economic loss is connected with harm to the person or property of the claimant, even if this is slight, it becomes a 'consequential economic loss', which gives rise to a completely different situation.[47] Both in countries that use the notion of economic loss, and in those which do not, if all the other usual conditions for liability are met, consequential economic loss may be recovered without question.

---

44 E.K. Banakas (ed), *Tortious Liability for Pure Economic Loss: A Comparative Study*, Hellenic Institute of International and Foreign Law, Athens 1989; B. Feldthusen, *Economic Negligence: The Recovery of Pure Economic Loss*, 6th ed., Carswell, Toronto 2012; M. Bussani and V.V. Palmer (eds), *Pure Economic Loss in Europe*, CUP, Cambridge 2003; W.H. van Boom, H. Koziol and C.A. Witting (eds), *Pure Economic Loss*, Springer, New York/Vienna 2003; V.V. Palmer and M. Bussani (eds), *Pure Economic Loss: New Horizons in Comparative Law*, Routledge-Cavendish, London 2009; V.V. Palmer, 'A comparative law sketch of pure economic loss' in M. Bussani and A.J. Sebok, above n. 12, pp. 284–304. See also M. Martín-Casals and J. Ribot, '"Pure Economic Loss": la indemnización de los daños patrimoniales puros' in S. Cámara Lapuente (coord.), *Derecho privado Europeo*, Colex, Madrid 2003, pp. 883–920; M. Bussani and V.V. Palmer, 'The Frontier between Contractual and Tortious Liability in Europe: Insights from the Case of Compensation for Pure Economic Loss' in A.S. Hartkamp et al. (eds), above n. 1, pp. 945–76. From an economic analysis point of view, see J. De Mot, 'Pure economic loss' in M. Faure (ed), *Tort Law and Economics*, Edward Elgar, Cheltenham 2009, pp. 201–14.

45 The American Law Institute, *Restatement (Third) of Law of Torts: Liability for Economic Harm*, American Law Institute Publishers, St. Paul 2020, §2.

46 In this sense, see M. Bussani and V.V. Palmer, 'The Frontier', above n. 44, p. 947; V.V. Palmer, 'A comparative law sketch of pure economic loss', above n. 44, p. 286.

47 The *Restatement (Third) of Law of Torts*, above n. 45, after explaining the distinction and recognising that courts often refer to these losses as 'purely' economic, omits this qualification and points out in a comment that 'economic' loss in this Restatement normally means 'pure economic loss'. See §2, Comment a., Definitional note.

A second important distinction as regards the problems associated with recovery of pure economic loss is that the conduct that gives rise to liability is merely negligent. If pure economic loss is caused by intentional conduct that is against *boni mores* or contrary to public policy, legal systems generally agree in recognising recoverability.[48] This is also the case with the so-called 'economic torts', which are named torts developed in order to regulate excessive competitive practice, and to protect claimants' economic interests, in the sense of their existing wealth or financial expectations, and which in English law include torts such as the tort of inducing breach of contract, the unlawful means tort, intimidation, lawful means conspiracy, unlawful means conspiracy, deceit, malicious falsehood and passing off.[49] Although these torts have their own specific rules, the significant thing about them is that they generally reject liability based upon negligence, instead requiring intent. Even civil law countries that do not recognise the notion of named economic torts or the concept of pure economic loss have solved many of the problems posed by recoverability of economic losses through specific regulations dealing with the protection of pure economic losses in different areas; in many cases, these have been transpositions of European directives or the result of European regulations.[50] To summarise, the problematic notion is then 'pure' or stand-alone economic loss in negligence.

3.2. JURISDICTIONS THAT USE THE NOTION OF 'PURE ECONOMIC LOSS'

In legal systems that operate with the notion of pure economic loss, and base their tort law on a more or less closed list of absolute rights, such as Germany and Austria, since the protection of patrimony as such is not included in those lists, recovery for pure economic loss must be sought on the basis of more specific tort provisions, or

48 See, for instance, §826 BGB or §§1295, para. 2 and 1300 ABGB, and, probably, this is also the case with the use of the doctrine of 'abuse of rights' as, for instance, in Art 7.2 of the Spanish CC.

49 See H. Carty, *An Analysis of the Economic Torts*, 2nd ed., OUP, Oxford 2010; D.B. Dobbs, P.T. Hayden and E.M. Bublick, *Hornbook on Torts*, 2nd ed., West, St. Paul 2016, pp. 1059 ff.

50 For instance, Directive 2005/29/EC of the European Parliament and of the Council of 11 May 2005 concerning unfair business-to-consumer commercial practices in the internal market and amending Council Directive 84/450/EEC, Directives 97/7/EC, 98/27/EC and 2002/65/EC of the European Parliament and of the Council and Regulation (EC) No. 2006/2004 of the European Parliament and of the Council ('Unfair Commercial Practices Directive') [2005] OJ L149/22; Directive 2014/104/EU of the European Parliament and of the Council of 26 November 2014 on certain rules governing actions for damages under national law for infringements of the competition law provisions of the Member States and of the European Union (Text with EEA relevance) [2014] OJ L349/1; or Regulation (EU) No. 462/2013 of the European Parliament and of the Council of 21 May 2013 amending Regulation (EC) No. 1060/2009 on credit rating agencies (Text with EEA relevance) [2013] OJ L146/1.

through an expansive application of contract principles.[51] Other legal systems, such as England and Wales, Israel, the Netherlands, South Africa and the United States, also adopt the pure economic loss notion but develop a more pragmatic approach; that is, they operate on a case-by-case basis, not driven by a list of absolute rights, but by a careful study of the specific socio-economic implications of recovery and they use the 'duty of care' concept, which is openly based on policy grounds, as a screening device between deserving and undeserving claims.[52]

Legal writing often refers to the 'economic loss rule' when discussing whether or not a bright-line rule can be drawn between recoverable and non-recoverable stand-alone pure economic losses in negligence.[53] However, no single normative principle can be used to solve all the problems posed by pure economic loss. For this reason, it is necessary to organise all the problems that it may give rise to into different groups of cases, in what some authors call a 'legal taxonomy'.[54] This chapter will refer only to those groups of cases more closely related to protection from pure economic loss caused by negligence between contracting parties, or between parties not bound by a previous contractual relationship. This distinction is important not only because, in some legal systems, the 'economic loss rule' plays a sort of boundary-line function between contract and tort,[55] but mainly because the reasons for denying tort liability differ between the two cases. Thus, while recoverability in tort between contracting parties raises concerns as regards the need to preserve the consensual allocation of risks and interests that the parties have bargained for in the contract, recoverability between non-contracting parties may involve, among other factors, concerns about unpredictable and limitless liability.

3.2.1. *Economic Loss between Contracting Parties*

3.2.1.1. The General Approach

In a market economy, the protection of economic interests is left to the self-determination of the parties, and primarily to contract law. If the parties

---

51 U. Magnus, 'Germany' (Mn. 4 and 30), and E. Karner and Koch, 'Austria' (Mn. 2 and 25) in M. Martín-Casals (ed), above n. 1.

52 K. Oliphant and V. Wilcox, 'England and Wales' (Mn. 70 ff.); I. Gilead, 'Israel' (Mn. 35); Keirse, 'The Netherlands' (Mn. 47 f.); J. Neethling, 'South Africa' (Mn. 17–19) and J. Cardi and M.D. Green, 'United States' (Mn. 35 ff.), all in M. Martín-Casals (ed), above n. 1. In this sense, see also M. Bussani and V.V. Palmer, 'The Frontier', above n. 44, pp. 954 ff.; V.V. Palmer, 'A comparative law sketch of pure economic loss', above n. 44, p. 294.

53 See, in more detail, J. Cardi and M.D. Green, 'United States' (Mn. 37 ff.) in M. Martín-Casals (ed), above n. 1.

54 M. Bussani and V.V. Palmer, 'The Frontier', above n. 44, p. 98; V.V. Palmer, 'A comparative law sketch of pure economic loss', above n. 44, p. 286.

55 V. Johnson, 'The Boundary-Line Function of the Economic Loss Rule' (2009) 66 *Washington & Lee Law Review* 533.

involved are contracting parties, they have already established their preferences by deciding to enter into a contractual relationship and, through a bargaining process, they have defined performance and allocated the relevant economic risks involved. In so doing, they may have availed themselves of a wide variety of legal devices, such as warranties, time limitations and exclusion or limitation clauses, to contour the scope of the risk that they are willing to run. If, in one aspect or another, the parties have not made any use of the possibilities of the private ordering of their interests offered by the legal system, then the default rules – generally tailored to what parties regularly agree when they bargain on these aspects – apply. In all legal systems, economic losses resulting from the non-performance or breach of a contract are considered recoverable without debate – subject to certain rules such as foreseeability – since they refer to the frustration of the expectations of gain that can rightly be founded on the contractual agreement.

Needless to say, by entering into a contract, the parties do not waive other interests, and all legal systems afford them protection against personal injury and property damage arising from the performance or non-performance of the contract. This protection, however, may be carried out differently; that is, either by applying tort law rules or by extending contract rules or other sorts of rules. However, economic interests, the infringement of which give rise to pure economic losses, have been bargained for in the contract, and the contractual expectations cannot be overridden by tort law. For this reason, for instance, §3 of the *Restatement (Third) of Torts: Liability for Economic Harm* precludes tort liability between contracting parties by establishing a general 'exclusionary economic loss rule', subject to specific exceptions.[56]

A rule that excludes liability in tort between contracting parties, such as this one, serves several purposes. Seen from the bargaining moment, the rule allows the parties to make reliable allocations of financial risk without fear that tort law will later be used to undo them. Seen from the moment when the dispute arises, the rule protects the bargain the parties have made against disruption by a claim in tort. Viewed in the long term, the rule prevents the erosion of contract rules through the use of tort law to work around them, and also reduces the confusion that can result when a party brings a claim on the same facts under contract and under tort.[57] The rule has its origin in cases involving product liability, where the demarcation between quality defects, sounding in contract, and safety defects, sounding in tort, has also given rise to serious problems

56 The *Restatement (Third) of Law of Torts*, above n. 45, §3 Preclusion of Tort Liability Arising from Contract (Economic-Loss Rule). 'Except as provided elsewhere in this Restatement, there is no liability in tort for economic loss caused by negligence in the performance or negotiation of a contract between the parties.'

57 In more detail, see ibid., §3, Comment b).

in the legal systems of other countries, such as Germany, England and Wales, South Africa and the United States.[58]

3.2.1.2. The Professional Liability Exception

A clear exception to this exclusionary rule between contracting parties is professional negligence (also known as malpractice), since the reasons to draw as clear a line as possible between contract and tort (i.e. to prevent tort rules from interfering with the allocation of risks taken on by the contractual parties, and to promote the parties' self-determination by leaving to them what they want to regulate, and to what extent) are weak as regards the relationships some professionals establish with persons who require their services. For the reasons mentioned above, the conduct of these professionals is not governed only by contract or tort rules, but mainly by codes of conduct, codes of ethics or similar internal rules issued by the relevant professional bodies. Thus, irrespective of the basis of the claim – whether tort or contract – and regardless of whether they cause personal injury, property damage or just pure economic loss, professionals are responsible for the losses that result from the breach of their professional duties. Professional rules may allow caps and other limitations in the contract between the parties, but they normally forbid the members of the profession from disclaiming responsibility for taking due care in performing it.[59]

3.2.2. Economic Loss between Non-Contracting Parties

Where the parties in a claim for pure economic loss are not linked by a contractual relationship, the problems associated with recoverability of pure economic losses arise in all their crudity in legal systems that start from a tort law system based on the negligent infringement of a more or less closed list of protected interests which does not include a general protection of economic interests as such – as is the case, for instance, in Germany (see §823 BGB) – or which, as in the common law jurisdictions, is based on a set of specific torts, of which the most general is the tort of negligence. These legal systems have in common the fact that economic interests enjoy a lower protection in tort and, when necessary, protection is generally afforded through provisions requiring intentional harm which is immoral or against public policy (for instance, §826 BGB);[60] or through

---

58 U. Magnus, 'Germany' (Mn. 29 f.), K. Oliphant and V. Wilcox, 'England and Wales' (Mn. 71), J. Neethling, 'South Africa' (Mn. 18) and J. Cardi and M.D. Green, 'United States' (Mn. 37 ff.), all in M. Martín-Casals (ed), above n. 1.

59 As regards economic loss, §4 of *Restatement (Third) of Law of Torts*, above n. 45, provides that 'a professional is subject to liability in tort for economic loss caused by the negligent performance of an undertaking to serve a client'.

60 See G. Wagner, *Deliktsrecht*, above n. 19, pp. 100–06, Mn. 126–36.

piecemeal specific torts (economic torts),[61] which are regularly also based on intention; or through sectoral legislation developed to address particular kinds of economic harm in order to protect business relationships, fair competition and, in general, the good functioning of private law relationships in the market.

Therefore, a general principle of liability for negligently inflicted economic harm does not exist, because it could be seriously detrimental to the good functioning of the economy. This does not mean, however, that economic interests whose infringement gives rise to pure economic loss are not protected at all pursuant to the general negligence rules. The constellation of cases where such protection is afforded extends from cases where there is a widespread trend towards accepting compensation under certain conditions, to cases where the trend is to exclude compensation, with groups of cases in between, which are still in historical evolution and covered by a dark shadow of doubt.

3.2.2.1. Negligent Provision of Information

A first group of cases relates to the negligent provision of information that gives rise to economic loss, to third parties to the contract who acted on reliance of the information furnished.[62]

An example regarding negligent provision of information (negligent misrepresentation) is the well-known English case of *Hedley Byrne v. Heller & Partners Ltd*,[63] where the claimant had relied on information provided by the defendants regarding the financial position and creditworthiness of a client, and lost £17,000 when the client went bankrupt. The court held that, although there was no contractual relationship between the claimant and the defendants, if the defendants had not expressly disclaimed their liability – as in fact they had – they would have 'assumed responsibility' towards the claimant by voluntarily entering into a 'special relationship' which created a duty of care. The court considered that it was reasonable for the defendants to have known that the information they had given would likely have been relied upon for entering into a contract of some sort, and this would give rise, the court said, to a 'special relationship', in which the defendants would have to take sufficient care in giving advice, to avoid liability in negligence.[64]

---

61 H. Carty, above n. 49, pp. 301 ff. and D.B. Dobbs, P.T. Hayden and E.M. Bublick, above n. 50, pp. 1059 ff.

62 M. Bussani and V.V. Palmer, *Pure Economic Loss in Europe*, above n. 44, pp. 13 ff.; W.H. van Boom, H. Koziol and C.A. Witting (eds), above n. 44, pp. 19 ff. See also *Restatement (Third) of Law of Torts*, above n. 45, §5 Negligent Misrepresentation.

63 [1964] AC 465, noted by K. Oliphant and V. Wilcox, 'England and Wales' in B. Winiger, E. Karner and K. Oliphant (eds), *Digest of European Tort Law, vol 3: Essential Cases on Misconduct*, de Gruyter, Berlin/Boston 2018, 3e/12, pp. 507 ff.

64 See K. Oliphant and V. Wilcox, above n. 63. In more detail, see K. Barker, R. Grantham and W. Swain (eds), *The Law of Misstatements: 50 Years on from Hedley Byrne v Heller*, Hart, Oxford 2015.

In these cases, it is important, in order to confine liability to cases where information is offered in a sufficiently serious manner, that the relevant false information was supplied professionally or with a pecuniary interest, something which would exclude information given for free in a daily life situation, but would include information given for free in order to promote a business or an economic interest. The person giving the information must know that it will be used for the guidance of persons who could legitimately rely on it, and liability will usually be limited to loss suffered by the person or persons pertaining to this group, and in the transaction for which the information was intended or a similar transaction, or where the person providing the information knew that the recipient would use it. However, where there is a public duty to supply the information, liability extends to loss suffered by any of the class of persons for whose benefit the duty is created, in any of the transactions in which it is intended to protect them.[65]

All these limitations restrict the recoverability in tort of negligently inflicted pure economic losses to cases where the fear of indeterminacy is overcome by the close relationship of proximity between the parties, involving the defendant's voluntary assumption of responsibility to the claimant either individually or as the member of an identifiable class.[66]

3.2.2.2. Negligent Performance of a Service

These cases are very similar to those in the previous category, but here economic loss is caused in the course of the negligent provision of a professional service by performing an activity, which is different from providing information.[67] These cases would include, among others, cases of pure economic loss caused by legal and financial professionals, such as lawyers, public notaries, insurance brokers, accountants and auditors.

A good example regarding the negligent performance of services is the English case *White v. Jones*,[68] where a solicitor was told to draw up a new will, splitting the testator's estate between the two plaintiffs – his daughters. He negligently failed to do this by the time of the testator's death, and the estate passed in accordance with the testator's wishes expressed in a previous will. The daughters sued the solicitor in negligence. It was held that the solicitor had assumed a special relationship towards them, creating a duty of care which he had carried out negligently, and therefore had to indemnify them for their loss.

---

65 See B. Feldthusen, above n. 44, pp. 77 ff.; §5 of the *Restatement (Third) of Law of Torts*, above n. 45.

66 See K. Oliphant and V. Wilcox, 'England and Wales' (Mn. 70 and 71) in M. Martín-Casals (ed), above n. 1.

67 See *Restatement (Third) of Law of Torts*, above n. 45, §6 Negligent Performance of Services.

68 [1995] 2 AC 207.

In such cases, conditions which are similar to those applicable to the negligent provision of information apply, and thus, for the required reliance to arise, the service must be provided on a professional basis. In order to avoid indeterminate or disproportionate liability, claimants must belong to a limited group of persons for whose guidance the defendant intended the services; they must belong to the group of persons for whose benefit the defendant performed the service.[69]

3.2.2.3. Relational Economic Loss: The Exclusionary Rule and its Exceptions

3.2.2.3.1. The General Exclusionary Rule

One of the broadest categories of economic loss is so-called 'relational economic loss'; that is, where personal injury or property damage caused by the defendant, D, to a primary victim, X, causes a specific economic loss to a secondary victim, C, who suffers it because of some special relationship she has with the primary victim X. The case law of most jurisdictions supports, in these cases, a firm exclusionary rule – although subject to many exceptions – which precludes the recovery of pure economic loss in negligence when it is consequent upon personal injury or property damage affecting a third party.[70]

3.2.2.3.2. Exceptions to the General Rule

Among the exceptions, the most common and accepted refers to loss of earnings suffered by family members or close persons as a result of the death or personal injury of a relative or close person on whom they were economically dependent. The extent of the circle of relatives or close persons entitled to recovery varies between legal systems, but this form of pure economic loss is generally considered recoverable. There is, however, a widespread tendency to exclude compensation for economic loss suffered by other persons outside this circle, such as employers, except where such persons are claiming for amounts corresponding to salaries that they must keep on paying for some time, in the event of the temporary disability of the employee who has suffered personal injury.[71]

---

69 M. Bussani and V.V. Palmer, *Pure Economic Loss in Europe*, above n. 44, pp. 13 ff.; W.H. van Boom, H. Koziol and C.A. Witting (eds), above n. 44, pp. 19 ff.

70 B. Feldthusen, above n. 44, pp. 209 ff. Now, §7 of the *Restatement (Third) of Law of Torts*, above n. 45, establishes this exclusionary rule when it provides that, 'except as provided elsewhere in this Restatement, a claimant cannot recover for economic loss caused by: (a) unintentional injury to another person; or (b) unintentional injury to property in which the claimant has no proprietary interest'.

71 C. van Dam, E. Engelhard and I. Giesen, 'Third Party Losses in a Comparative Perspective – Three Short Lectures in Honour of W.H.V. Rogers' (2007) 3 *Utrecht Law Review* 70–99,

If the damage caused has been to the property of the primary victim, the exclusionary rule also tends to apply.[72]

Another exception to the exclusionary rule in the case of relational economic loss is the so-called 'transferred loss'; that is, a loss that would ordinarily fall on a primary victim, but which has been transferred to a secondary victim by the operation of the law, or by contracts, such as leases or sales or insurance agreements, that separate property rights from rights of use or specifically reallocate risk bearing. Sometimes the claimant is in a position similar to that of an insurer who needs to recover by subrogation in order to prevent unjust enrichment of the defendant, such as, for instance, when X retains title but has transferred the risks of property to C, and D destroys X's property, so that X, who is the owner, suffers no harm, but C suffers pure economic loss only, because she is not yet the owner.[73] Sometimes the claimant is under an obligation to bear the loss directly, such as, for instance, where C commits herself by a contract to maintain X's bridge in a good state of repair and D negligently damages the bridge.[74] Transferred loss cases do not increase the liability of tortfeasors, since what is compensated for is the same loss that the primary victim – that is, the victim suffering personal injury or property damage – would have suffered. Since the primary victim cannot recover what would not be recoverable by the secondary victim, the tortfeasor would benefit from the situation and end up scot-free.[75] The difference between this case and the above-mentioned economic loss suffered by relatives is that, in the case of harm suffered by relatives, the secondary victim suffers a harm that is different from any economic harm that the primary victim might have suffered.

A subgroup of relational economic losses are those cases where the loss arises through damage to resources not privately owned, as occurs where economic harm results from the destruction or closure of public infrastructure, or from impairment of natural resources that affects the economic activities of those who thereby suffer economic loss. Here, the most general trend is to award compensation, if any, to the class of victims whose livelihoods are more seriously impaired by the event causing economic loss, because their losses are somewhat 'special' or 'different in kind' compared with the losses suffered

---

complaining that the employer's losses have not been mentioned in any of the European soft-law projects on tort law. For Italy, see also R. Omodei-Sale and A. Zaccaria, 'Compensation for Pure Economic Loss Under Italian Law' in W.H. van Boom, H. Koziol and C.A. Witting (eds), above n. 44, pp. 50 ff.

72 B. Feldthusen, above n. 44, pp. 209 ff., 235 ff.

73 Ibid., pp. 261 ff.

74 Ibid., p. 263.

75 M. Bussani and V.V. Palmer, *Pure Economic Loss in Europe*, above n. 44, pp. 11 ff. and *passim*, with further examples. Also W.H. van Boom, H. Koziol and C.A. Witting (eds), above n. 44, pp. 20–31.

by the other groups of affected victims.[76] Nevertheless, it remains difficult to establish a clear yardstick to distinguish between deserving and undeserving victims.[77]

3.3. ECONOMIC LOSS IN JURISDICTIONS THAT DO NOT ACKNOWLEDGE THIS CONCEPT

3.3.1. General Overview

The notion of pure economic loss is not used by legal provisions or case law in countries where tort liability is not based on a closed list of protected interests, or on duties imposed by case law, but on a general clause which does not exclude the protection of pure economic loss as a matter of course. However, even in these systems, the notion of pure economic loss can be a useful analytical tool to deal with problems which would not otherwise be openly perceived.

For a legal system to be placed in this group, it is important that, in spite of the silence as regards protected interests and rights, case law and legal writing do not read into the system's general clause a system protecting absolute rights.[78] Since the starting point in these jurisdictions is that all interests, including pure or stand-alone economic ones, deserve legal protection in tort, the courts must try to demarcate those cases in which there is a recoverable damage from those where there is not. In the absence of a general provision with this purpose, the delimitation task is rather difficult. The civil law tradition does not, in these systems, facilitate judges openly manifesting policy choices, and they must try to solve the same concerns about unpredictable and limitless expansion of liability in tort by using other instruments. In this context, and in spite of different general approaches, the most important technical arguments used by interpreters in order to restrict (and, if necessary, widen) the circle of recoverable pure economic losses in tort have proven to be causation and scope of liability, together with the conditions for damage.[79]

---

76 B. Feldthusen, above n. 44, pp. 267 ff.; V.V. Palmer, 'A comparative law sketch of pure economic loss', above n. 44, pp. 288–89; W.H. van Boom, H. Koziol and C.A. Witting (eds), above n. 44, pp. 26 ff. Now, §8 of the *Restatement (Third) of Law of Torts*, above n. 45, terms this type of economic loss 'public nuisance resulting in economic loss', and provides that 'an actor whose wrongful conduct harms or obstructs a public resource or public property is subject to liability for resulting economic loss if the court concludes that the claimant's losses are distinct in kind from those suffered by members of the affected community in general'.

77 See, however, §8 of *Restatement (Third) of Law of Torts*, above n. 45, Comment c) Special injury.

78 As, for instance, was the case in Italy until the 1970s, and is still argued in modern Austrian law.

79 In this sense, see W.H. van Boom, H. Koziol and C.A. Witting (eds), above n. 44, pp. 9, 12, 28 and *passim*, and see there as well the French (p. 45) and Spanish reports (pp. 63 and 73).

3.3.2. *Economic Loss between Contracting Parties*

As between contracting parties, it has been contended that one of these instruments is the *non-cumul* rule; that is, the rule that forbids parties contractually bound to each other from bringing claims in tort against each other for any harm connected with the contractual performance, which, according to this opinion, would be a 'necessary corollary' of the extension of tort law to economic loss.[80] However, this would not explain the fact that, among the European jurisdictions that have a general clause of tortious liability based on fault, only a few, such as France and – following suit – Romania and Hungary,[81] have adopted this rule, while the others have opted for one or other form of concurring liabilities. Without denying that the *non-cumul* or non-concurrence of actions rule can be a useful device to protect contracts from being undermined by tort, it is true that most systems that have a general clause of tort liability can do without the rule. As French legal writing has pointed out, the *non-cumul* rule is a national French phenomenon that results from the particular doctrine of custodians' liability *(responsabilité du fait des choses)* to protect contracts against the disruption that this expansion of strict liability could have caused between contracting parties by allowing them to escape fault liability in contract, in the case of obligations to use reasonable care *(obligations de moyens)*, thereby upsetting the allocation of risk implicitly agreed by them in contract.[82]

Countries that allow concurrence of actions in contract or in tort, although they generally allow victims to choose the most favourable grounds, make exceptions and introduce some limitations that are aimed at preventing tort law rules that may undermine contract law rules.[83]

For Italy, and referring in general to civil law jurisdictions, see M. Bussani, *L'illecito civile*, Edizioni scientifiche italiane, Napoli 2020, pp. 374 ff.

80 G. Wagner, 'Grundstrukturen' in R. Zimmermann (ed), *Grundstrukturen des Europäischen Deliktsrechts*, Nomos, Baden-Baden 2003, p. 233. In the same sense, see R. Zimmermann, *The Law of Obligations: Roman Foundations of the Civilian Tradition*, Clarendon Press, Oxford 1996, p. 906, who holds that the admission of an elective concurrence of liability would lead every culpable breach of contract to become actionable in tort, too, and as a result, French doctrine has to protect the rules relating to contractual liability by means of the principle of *non-cumul*.

81 Art. 1350.3 Romanian CC(3) provides that, '[u]nless otherwise stated by law, neither party may replace the application of the rules concerning contractual liability by reference to other rules that would be more favourable.' See also §6:145 Hungarian CC.

82 J.S. Borghetti, 'Strict Liability in Tort and the Boundaries of Tort Law', above n. 40, pp. 20, 34.

83 See M. Martín-Casals (ed), above n. 1, pp. 787–93. See also R. de Graaff, 'Concurrent Claims in Contract and Tort: A Comparative Perspective' (2017) 25(4) *European Review of Private Law* 701–26.

3.3.3. *Economic Loss between Non-Contracting Parties*

As regards non-contracting parties, probably the most extended general theory distinguishes between direct or indirect damage and direct or indirect victims. Legal writing speaks of 'direct damage' where the person claiming compensation is precisely the person who has directly suffered the harm on their person or property (a 'direct victim'), and of 'indirect damage' or 'ricochet damage', where damage is indirectly suffered by other people (indirect victims) as a consequence of the damage to the physical integrity or patrimony of the direct victim. The distinction may also refer to the need for a direct causal link between the damaging event and the damage suffered.[84] As a general rule, this terminology is used to refer to cases where damage is recoverable, in spite of the fact that victims are 'indirect', as is the case of damage suffered by a certain circle of relatives and close persons of deceased or seriously injured 'direct' or primary victims; but it can also be used to refer to loss of business due to personal injury to one's employees or clients, constituting 'indirect' damage, which, in principle, should not be compensated in tort.[85] Some jurisdictions consider that the cases of relatives or close persons constitute an exception that proves the existence of the rule that excludes from compensation persons 'indirectly' harmed, and operate with the distinction between 'direct' and 'indirect' damage in order to keep economic loss within limits.[86] However, beyond these cases of economic loss by relatives and close persons, the fact that damage is direct or indirect, although it may flash a yellow warning light when damage is indirect, does not say much about the reason why pure economic loss must not be compensated when damage is indirect, or – even more importantly – in which cases, even on an exceptions basis, indirect damage must be compensated.

A second theory, of Italian origin, is the so-called '*tutela aquiliana del diritto de credito*' or tort law protection of rights *in personam*.[87] In spite of the existence of a general clause, the initial conception in Italian tort law was that the concept of 'unjust damage' *(danno ingiusto)*, required to establish liability (Art. 2043 Italian CC), referred only to the so-called 'absolute rights' – that is, personal

---

84 F. Terré, P. Simler, Y. Lequette and F. Chénedé, *Droit civil: Les obligations*, 12th ed., Dalloz, Paris 2018, Mn. 926 ff. and 1089 ff.

85 Ibid., Mn. 935; G. Viney, P. Jourdain and S. Carval, *Traité de Droit civil: Les conditions de la responsabilité*, 4th ed., LGDJ, Paris 2013, pp. 208 ff. and 216 ff.

86 See P. Machnikowski, 'Poland' (Mn. 70 ff.) and E. Dacoronia, 'Greece' (Mn. 23) in M. Martín-Casals (ed), above n. 1; and T. Pajor, 'Poland' in V.V. Palmer and M. Bussani (eds), *Pure Economic Loss: New Horizons*, above n. 44, pp. 261 ff.

87 See R. Omodei-Sale and A. Zaccaria, above n. 71, pp. 48–55; M. Bussani, *L'illecito civile*, above n. 79, pp. 367 ff. This doctrine is also mentioned in Spanish legal writing: see M.J. Pérez García, *La protección aquiliana del derecho de crédito*, Colegio de Registradores de la Propiedad y Mercantiles de España, Madrid 2005.

injury, property damage and rights of personality – and did not include rights *in personam* or of credit. Compensation for pure economic loss was recognised by extending the traditional notion of 'unjust damage' under Art. 2043 CC beyond absolute rights, so as to include the infringement of subjective interests that could be described as 'rights of credit'. The principle of the tort law protection of the right of credit was definitively affirmed in Italian case law at the beginning of the 1970s, with the sentence of Joint Sections 174/1971 (the *Meroni* case), where the court held that Art. 2043 Italian CC did not make a distinction between absolute and relative rights in determining whether or not redress could be obtained. The court did recognise, however, that, in order to establish the liability of the third party with sufficient certainty and within strict limits, the causal link between damage to the creditor and the third party's conduct had to be assessed precisely, and held that injury to credit could be redressed in tort law only where such injury was definitive and irreparable, as in the case of the killing of an irreplaceable debtor.[88] Thus, under Italian law, the issue is not whether pure economic loss can be compensated or not, but simply whether the infringement of subjective interests that could be described as 'rights of credit' can also be considered unjust damage according to Art. 2043 Italian CC. The violation of these interests is nothing but a pure economic loss, in spite of the fact that the notion of the protection of rights *in personam* in tort law does not cover all of the area covered by pure economic loss in negligence, and also extends to problems associated with intentional infliction of pure economic loss. Competing theories, such as an alleged right for the protection of the whole patrimony as such, although occasionally applied by courts, have given rise to a strong debate and have had little success. However, the doctrine of the tort law protection of rights *in personam*, which, as a matter of principle, should stand for the general recoverability of all pure economic losses caused to third parties by the infringement of such rights, also does not offer a clear basis to establish which cases should be compensated and which should not, and in practice, in most of the problematic cases, such as misleading information, prospectus liability, credit rating agency contracts, and liability of lawyers, notaries and other professionals, protection against pure economic loss suffered by third parties takes place according to specific regulations.

To sum up, in systems that have a general clause for liability in tort, compensation of pure economic loss is normally controlled either by specific legislation which has been drafted over time to clarify specific situations, or by the courts, which make use of general doctrines, such as causation and scope

88 Cf. Cass., S.U., 26 gennaio 1971, n. 174 (in Foro it., 1971, I, c. 1284 ss, con nota di F.D. Busnelli, 'Un clamoroso "revirement" della Cassazione: dalla "questione di Superga" al "Caso Meroni"').

of liability or certainty of damage, to keep compensation of pure economic loss within limits, notwithstanding the fact that these systems may also resort to specific theories.[89]

4. CONCLUSION

The distinction between contract and tort has been eroded over time, and is not located in exactly the same place in all jurisdictions. Between contract and tort there is a grey zone, as in the cases of pre-contractual liability and professional liability, where it is doubtful whether liability is in contract or in tort. Moreover, in most jurisdictions there is also an overlap area; that is, situations where the same facts can give rise to actions either in contract or in tort.

Pursuant to the principle of privity or relativity of contract, most jurisdictions do not generally allow an extension of the protective scope of the contract to third parties who have not been mentioned in it or, at least, whose protection cannot result from an interpretation of the contractual will of the parties. A clear exception to this principle is the doctrine of the protective effects of the contract with regard to third parties *(Vertrag mit Schutzwirkung zugunsten Dritter)*, which, in contrast to contracts for the benefit of third parties, does not grant third parties a right to claim performance, but only secondary duties of care and protection which, in the case of infringement, entitle them to bring a claim for damages in contract. This doctrine is used not only to iron out what are considered shortcomings of some tort law rules, but also to protect interests not included in a rigid list of those protected in tort. Another exception is the so-called *action directe*, which gives a contractual party an action in contract against a contractual party with whom he or she is not in privity, as long as there is, between their contracts, a relationship that is so close that the events occurring in one contract could have effects on the other. This doctrine, which is accepted in rather general terms in France, is also accepted as a piecemeal solution for specific cases in most countries.

As regards the expansion of tort law, a useful analytical tool, even for those jurisdictions which are not familiar with it, is the doctrine of pure economic loss. In common law jurisdictions, and in some mixed jurisdictions, the expansion is carried out through a growing number of situations where it is considered that there is a duty of care based on a special relationship between the parties which

89 See the reports on France (pp. 128–29), Belgium (pp. 131–33), Spain (pp. 136–37) and Greece (p. 138) in M. Bussani and V.V. Palmer, *Pure Economic Loss in Europe*, above n. 44. See also M. Martín-Casals and J. Ribot, 'Compensation for Pure Economic Loss Under Spanish Law' in W.H. van Boom, H. Koziol and C.A. Witting (eds), above n. 44, pp. 62–76, and the reports by P. Machnikowski, 'Poland' (Mn. 70 ff.) and E. Dacoronia, 'Greece' (Mn. 23) in M. Martín-Casals (ed), above n. 1.

justifies an exception to a more general rule that excludes compensation of pure economic loss in negligence. This expansion aims at protecting interests that are similar to those protected by stretching contract law rules in jurisdictions that have a rigid list of protected interests in tort law. By contrast, jurisdictions that base tort liability on a general clause protect, in tort, similar interests, on the grounds that, as a matter of principle, all interests, including those that would be called pure or stand-alone economic losses, deserve legal protection in tort. Such jurisdictions try to prevent an unpredictable and limitless expansion of liability by couching policy decisions under traditional legal doctrines, such as the certainty of damage or causation, or, more precisely, scope of liability. In all jurisdictions, specific legislation also plays a very important role in the growing need to protect purely economic interests in many areas of activity.

PART II

CASE STUDIES

CASE 1: CLAUSE IN FAVOUR OF A THIRD PARTY

1. CASE

Sell Co Holdings Ltd ('Holdings') is the parent company of a group of companies, The Sell Co Group. Recently, Holdings outsourced certain of the group's IT functions to Digital Age Services Ltd ('Digital Age'). The contract between Holdings and Digital Age provides, inter alia, that Digital Age will provide certain IT services to the companies set out in a schedule to the contract, from 1 February 2016 until 31 January 2021; that Holdings can add to, remove or replace any company in the schedule on giving written notice to Digital Age; and that Holdings are responsible for making all payments to Digital Age. The schedule lists a number of companies in the Sell Co Group, including Sell Co Direct Ltd ('Direct').

Due to a breach of the contract by Digital Age, Direct suffer loss, due to lost sales, in the region of €10 million.

The directors of Holdings make clear that Holdings will not raise court proceedings against Digital Age for breach of contract.

To date, Holdings have sent notices to remove two group companies from, and add another group company to, the schedule to the contract. Direct have not been removed from the schedule.

Questions

1. Can Direct take action against Digital Age for breach of contract?
2. Would Direct be able to force Holdings to raise proceedings against Digital Age to recover Direct's losses?

In answering the above questions, assume that causation is not an issue, i.e. assume that Direct would be able to prove that the losses they have suffered are as a result of Digital Age's breach of contract.

2. DISCUSSIONS

2.1. BELGIUM

Siel Demeyere and Vincent Sagaert

I. *Operative Rules*

1. Direct can take action against Digital Age.
2. Direct cannot force Holdings to raise proceedings against Digital Age to recover their losses. Direct can raise an action against Digital Age, based on its own right of action. Direct could, however, raise an action in the name of, and for the account of, Holdings, through an oblique action (cf. Case 6, question 3 below).

II. *Descriptive Formants*

In Belgian law, the rights of third parties are addressed by the general law of obligations, but some situations intersect with tort law and, occasionally, property law. The law of obligations and property law have recently been reformed, and are no longer subject to the French Code Napoléon, dating from 1804 (Belgium was then a French province). Tort law is still currently under reform, as are the rules on specific contracts. Where the legislator remained largely silent, case law and scholarship further completed the obsolete statutory rules, and many of these have been integrated into the new Civil Code (BCC).[1] Many of the aspects considered in the cases below have, moreover, been elaborately addressed in doctoral theses of Belgian scholars, to which we will refer in the appropriate places.[2] Given the recent reform, the Explanatory Memorandum is an important source to understand the new Civil Code, and to more generally grasp current Belgian law.

While Belgium is a federal state with extensive powers of the regions and communities, the current Belgian law of obligations is still federal law, and thus identical for the entire Belgian territory, which does not, however, prevent French-speaking and Dutch-speaking courts from proposing different interpretations. The Hof van Cassatie/Cour de Cassation (Court of Cassation)

---

1 The legislator envisaged creating a more accessible law by codifying case law. See Explanatory Memorandum to the Draft Statute of 24 February 2021 on introduction of Book 5 'Obligations', *Parl.St.* 2020–21, 1806/1, www.dekamer.be, 2021, 7.

2 The pioneer in Belgian law for the analysis of the position of third parties in relation to contractual rights must be Eric Dirix, who in 1984 published his doctoral thesis covering most of the areas addressed here: E. Dirix, *Obligatoire verhoudingen tussen contractanten en derden*, Kluwer, Antwerp 1984.

intervenes, or should intervene, to guarantee a lawful and uniform application of the law. The current BCC and other current Belgian legislation can be found online, in both Dutch- and French-language versions.[3] Both versions are equally official.

Before going into the cases, a brief overview of the concept of 'third parties' in Belgian law is appropriate. In Belgian law, third parties are defined in a negative manner, as anyone who is not a contracting party.[4] A contracting party is anyone who has consented to the contract, whether directly or through representation, or created a legitimate confidence in doing so.[5] The main principle governing the relations between contracting parties and third parties is the *relativiteitsbeginsel/ principe de relativité (des effets internes du contrat)* (principle of privity). This principle provides that a contract (or contracting parties) cannot grant rights to a third party, and neither can a contract impose obligations upon a third party.[6] However, when it comes to the rights, several exceptions exist, while the privity principle is strictly upheld with regard to the obligations; contracting parties can never impose an obligation upon a third party who did not consent to this.[7]

---

3 www.ejustice.just.fgov.be/wet/wet.htm.

4 H. De Page, *Traité élémentaire de droit civil belge*, I, Bruylant, Brussels 1962–64, no. 117; I. Durant, 'Tiers et biens en Belgique' in Bruylant and LB2V (eds), *Les tiers – Journées panaméennes*, Bruylant, Brussels 2016, 320, no. 4; R. Jafferali, 'Tiers et contrat en Belgique' in Bruylant and LB2V (eds), *Les tiers – Journées panaméennes*, Bruylant, Brussels 2016, 55, no. 1; F. Laurent, *Principes de droit civil*, Bruylant-Christophe, Brussels 1887, XVI, 436, no. 371; S. Stijns, 'Les contrats et les tiers' in P. Wéry (ed), *Le droit des obligations contractuelles et le bicentenaire du Code civil*, die Keure, Bruges 2004, 199, no. 17; S. Stijns, *Verbintenissenrecht. Leerboek 1*, die Keure, Bruges 2009–16, 232, no. 306; W. Van Gerven and A. Van Oevelen, *Verbintenissenrecht*, Acco, Leuven 2015, 221; P. Wéry, *Droit des obligations: Théorie générale du contrat*, I, Larcier, Brussels 2011, 800.

5 H. De Page, *Traité élémentaire de droit civil belge*, I, Bruylant, Brussels 1962–64, no. 120bis; E. Dirix, *Obligatoire verhoudingen tussen contractanten en derden*, Kluwer, Antwerp 1984, 22, no. 3; I. Durant, 'Tiers et biens en Belgique' in Bruylant and LB2V (eds), *Les tiers – Journées panaméennes*, Bruylant, Brussels 2016, 320, no. 4; F. Laurent, *Principes de droit civil*, Bruylant-Christophe, Brussels 1887, XVI, 436, no. 371; S. Stijns, 'Les contrats et les tiers' in P. Wéry (ed), *Le droit des obligations contractuelles et le bicentenaire du Code civil*, die Keure, Bruges 2004, 199, no. 18 ff.; W. Van Gerven and A. Van Oevelen, *Verbintenissenrecht*, Acco, Leuven 2015, 221; P. Van Ommeslaghe, *Traité de droit civil belge. II. Les obligations. Vol. 1*, Bruylant, Brussels 2013, 647–48.

6 Art. 5.103 of the Belgian Civil Code (BCC); Cass. 14 February 1980, *Pas.* 1980, I, 692; Cass. 22 January 1990, *Pas.* 1990, I, 598; Cass. 30 June 1995, no. C.93.0230.N, *Pas.* 1995, I, 723; H. De Page, *Traité élémentaire de droit civil belge*, I, Bruylant, Brussels 1962–64, no. 117 and 117bis; De Page, *Les incapables. Les obligations (première partie)*, II, 616, no. 614; F. Laurent, *Principes de droit civil*, Bruylant-Christophe, Brussels 1887, XVI, 436, no. 371 ff.; S. Stijns, 'Les contrats et les tiers' in P. Wéry (ed), *Le droit des obligations contractuelles et le bicentenaire du Code civil*, die Keure, Bruges 2004, 192, no. 9; W. Van Gerven and A. Van Oevelen, *Verbintenissenrecht*, Acco, Leuven 2015, 232; P. Van Ommeslaghe, *Traité de droit civil belge. II. Les obligations. Vol. 1*, Bruylant, Brussels 2013, no. 411; P. Wéry, *Droit des obligations: Théorie générale du contrat*, I, Larcier, Brussels 2011, 803.

7 H. De Page, 'Les incapables. Les obligations (première partie)', II, in *Traité élémentaire de droit civil belge*, Bruylant, Brussels 1962–64, 702, no. 729B; S. Stijns, 'Les contrats et les tiers'

The rights and obligations are the internal effects of the contract, and are governed by the relativity principle. The external effects, however – that is, the existence of the contract and its consequences – are *tegenwerpelijk/opposable* (effective) against third parties, meaning that such parties can invoke, and have to respect, the existence and the effects of a contract.[8] This is reflected in the potential tortious liability because of third-party complicity in a contractual breach (cf. Case 8 below). Simulation (cf. Case 10) and the *actio Pauliana* (cf. Case 11) are exceptions to the principle of effectiveness of the external effects of a contract.

Regarding question 1, the contract between Digital Age and Holdings contains a *derdenbeding/stipulation pour autrui* (clause in favour of a third party). On the basis of this clause, Direct can claim damages directly from Digital Age. A clause in favour of a third party is a contractual clause by which one of the contracting parties demands, from its counterparty, performance in favour of a third party who is not a party to the contract.[9] The contract need not explicitly state that the clause is a clause in favour of a third party, and need not even explicitly mention the right of the third party, as the third-party right can also be agreed upon implicitly.[10] The third party is designated as the *derde-begunstigde/tiers bénéficiaire* (third-party beneficiary).

Article 5.107 of the BCC provides the legal grounds for clauses in favour of a third party. There are four conditions for the validity of such a clause:[11]

(a) The contract between the *bedinger/stipulant* (stipulator) and *belover/promettant* (promisor) must be valid. There is nothing to indicate that this would be an issue in the present case.

---

in P. Wéry (ed), *Le droit des obligations contractuelles et le bicentenaire du Code civil*, die Keure, Bruges 2004, 196, no. 12.

8 Art. 5.103, second clause, BCC; Cass. be. 27 May 1909, *Pas.* 1909, I, 272; Cass. be. 9 March 1950, *Pas.* 1950, I, 491–92; Cass. be. 27 June 2013, no. C.11.0562.F, *Pas.* 2013, 1485; Cass. be. 20 June 2016, no. C.15.0478.F; H. De Page, *Traité élémentaire de droit civil belge*, I, Bruylant, Brussels 1962–64, no. 117bis; R. Jafferali, 'Tiers et contrat en Belgique' in Bruylant and LB2V (eds), *Les tiers – Journées panaméennes*, Bruylant, Brussels 2016, 56, no. 1 and 60, no. 8; S. Stijns, *Verbintenissenrecht. Leerboek 1*, die Keure, Bruges 2009–16, 231, no. 303; W. Van Gerven and A. Van Oevelen, *Verbintenissenrecht*, Acco, Leuven 2015, 224; P. Van Ommeslaghe, *Traité de droit civil belge. II. Les obligations. Vol. 1*, Bruylant, Brussels 2013, 659; P. Wéry, *Droit des obligations: Théorie générale du contrat*, I, Larcier, Brussels 2011, 864.

9 Based on W. Van Gerven and A. Van Oevelen, *Verbintenissenrecht*, Acco, Leuven 2015, 235. See also N. Carette, *Derdenbeding*, Intersentia, Antwerp 2011, 141, no. 140; S. Stijns, *Verbintenissenrecht. Leerboek 1*, die Keure, Bruges 2009–16, 257, no. 336; P. Wéry, *Droit des obligations: Théorie générale du contrat*, I, Larcier, Brussels 2011, 815, no. 860.

10 N. Carette, *Derdenbeding*, Intersentia, Antwerp 2011, 292, no. 367; N. Carette, 'Het derdenbeding: wanneer heeft een beding de strekking van een derdenbeding naar Belgisch recht?' in I Samoy (ed), *Derden in het contractenrecht*, Intersentia, Antwerp 2009, 87, no. 11; P. Wéry, *Droit des obligations: Théorie générale du contrat*, I, Larcier, Brussels 2011, 819, no. 866.

11 See Cass. 23 March 2006, no. C.03.0598.N, *Arr.Cass.* 2006, 684, *Pas.* 2006, 667; Ghent 8 October 2003, *TBH* 2005, 43; N. Carette, *Derdenbeding*, Intersentia, Antwerp 2011, 166, no. 168

(b) The stipulator must have a personal interest in the clause in favour of a third party, although this need not be a direct advantage for themself.[12] In this case, Holdings definitely has a personal interest in the clause in favour of the third party, as the provision gives a right to Direct, which is one of Holding's subsidiaries.

(c) The promisor and the stipulator must clearly have the intention to grant the third party a right. This cannot reasonably be doubted in this case either. Digital Age and Holdings intend to grant Direct its own right to enforce the contract for IT services, given the explicit mention of Direct in the schedule to the contract. The presence of intention on the part of the contracting parties can thus be accepted rather easily, and the case does not contain any contraindications.

(d) The third party must be identified or identifiable at the moment the provision has effect. In this regard, the list of benefiting companies which Holdings can unilaterally change does not provide a problem. The third party need not be identified (or identifiable) at the moment the contract is concluded, but only at the moment the IT services are delivered. If Direct had been added to the schedule after conclusion of the contract, Holdings would have been using its ability to unilaterally determine an element of the contract, which is designated as a *partijbeslissing/décision de partie* (party decision).[13] According to a minority view in Belgian case law and scholarship, this is only possible if the criteria for the decision have been predetermined in the contract.[14] In such a case, the court must factually assess whether this is so. In such a sovereign appreciation, the judge can take into account all relevant circumstances.

An extra aspect of a clause in favour of a third party, which does not influence its validity, is that the stipulator can withdraw their obligations at any time before the

---

(not separately distinguishing the second condition); S. Stijns, *Verbintenissenrecht. Leerboek 1*, die Keure, Bruges 2009–16, 259, no. 339; W. Van Gerven and A. Van Oevelen, *Verbintenissenrecht*, Acco, Leuven 2015, 235; P. Van Ommeslaghe, *Traité de droit civil belge. II. Les obligations. Vol. 1*, Bruylant, Brussels 2013, 686, no. 444; P. Wéry, *Droit des obligations: Théorie générale du contrat*, I, Larcier, Brussels 2011, 819, no. 865. Not all authors list the exact same conditions, but the application of the conditions nevertheless leads to the same result. There is, especially, a difference between Dutch-speaking and French-speaking authors.

12 This condition is sometimes worded differently; the provision must be an accessory to a provision for the stipulator themself, or to a donation.

13 Art. 5.71, second para. BCC; I. Samoy and Maes, 'Over het beding dat de bevoegdheid verleent om een partijbeslissing te nemen en de vraag of de opname van objectieve criteria noodzakelijk is voor de geldigheid ervan', *TBBR* (2010), 310, no. 4.

14 See I. Samoy and A. Maes, 'Over het beding dat de bevoegdheid verleent om een partijbeslissing te nemen en de vraag of de opname van objectieve criteria noodzakelijk is voor de geldigheid ervan', *TBBR* (2010), 312, no. 8. Samoy and Maes oppose this need for specific objective criteria.

third party has accepted the right.[15] From the time of acceptance, the right can no longer be revoked. In the present case, Holdings has not revoked Direct's right.

The consequence of a clause in favour of a third party is that the third party has a direct contractual right against the promisor.[16] This means that Direct can claim contractual compensation from Digital Age for its loss of €10 million.

Regarding question 2, Direct have no legal ground to force Holdings to raise proceedings against Digital Age in order to recover Direct's loss, in the absence of contractual provisions determining otherwise. This is not necessary in this case, as the clause in favour of a third party provides a sufficient basis for Direct themselves to raise proceedings in order to recover the entire loss they have suffered from the contractual breach.

2.2. BULGARIA

Petar Topurov

I. *Operative Rules*

1. Direct is the beneficiary of the contract between Holdings and Digital Age, and as such can claim against Digital Age for performance, and compensation for the damage suffered.
2. Direct cannot undertake legal action forcing Holdings to initiate court proceedings against Digital Age on account of the contract non-performance. There might be one exception, in the case that Direct owns part of the capital of Holdings and can influence the company's decisions.

II. *Descriptive Formants*

In accordance with Art. 22 of the Law on Obligations and Contracts (LOC),[17] the parties to a certain contract may also negotiate in favour of a third party.

---

15 Art. 5.107 *in fine* BCC; N. Carette, *Derdenbeding*, Intersentia, Antwerp 2011, 487, no. 592 ff.; P. Wéry, *Droit des obligations: Théorie générale du contrat*, I, Larcier, Brussels 2011, 825, no. 878.

16 Art. 5.107, second para. BCC, Cass. 16 January 2006, no. C.04.0302.F, *Arr.Cass.* 2006, 153, *Pas.* 2006, 163; N. Carette, *Derdenbeding*, Intersentia, Antwerp 2011, 662, no. 729 ff.; S. Stijns, *Verbintenissenrecht. Leerboek 1*, die Keure, Bruges 2009–16, 260, no. 341; W. Van Gerven and A. Van Oevelen, *Verbintenissenrecht*, Acco, Leuven 2015, 237; P. Van Ommeslaghe, *Traité de droit civil belge. II. Les obligations. Vol. 1*, Bruylant, Brussels 2013, 691, no. 445; P. Wéry, *Droit des obligations: Théorie générale du contrat*, I, Larcier, Brussels 2011, 823, no. 874. According to Carette and Wéry, this right has a contractual nature: N. Carette, *Derdenbeding*, Intersentia, Antwerp 2011, 666, no. 732; P. Wéry, *Droit des obligations: Théorie générale du contrat*, I, Larcier, Brussels 2011, 823, no. 875.

17 Promulgated, SG No. 275 of 22.11.1950, in force from 01.01.1951, last supplemented, SG No. 42 of 22.05.2018 (LOC).

In this particular case, Holdings (in its capacity as the promisee/*stipulans*) and Digital Age (in the capacity of promisor/*promittens*) conclude a contract in favour of a definable third party/beneficiary – the subsidiaries of Direct. Many Bulgarian court decisions assume that, by virtue of the contract in favour of a third party, there is an option for the beneficiary to claim actual performance from the promisor, including undertaking actions to find the promisor liable for compensation in the case of damage suffered because of culpable failure.[18]

III. Meta-Legal Formants

The prevailing part of the Bulgarian legal doctrine assumes that, by virtue of the contract in favour of a third party, there is an option for the beneficiary to claim actual performance from the promisor.[19] Meanwhile, some authors offer arguments for a different time of creation of the right in favour of the third party. Some of them believe that, before explicitly accepting and notifying the promisor or the promisee thereof, the right of the beneficiary is in the state of legal expectation,[20] while others assume that only the right to accept or revoke what had already been promised in their favour has arisen for the third party.[21] The same authors criticise the option for the beneficiary to acquire the right to property in real estate without participating in the conclusion of the contract by a notary.[22]

Furthermore, the Interpretative Decision No. 30 of 17 June 1981, by the General Assembly of Civil College (GACC) of the Bulgarian Supreme Court of Cassation (BSCC), rules that the third party acts in different capacities in its

---

18 Interpretative Decision No. 30 of 17.06.1981, GACC of the Supreme Court of Cassation; Order No. 122 of 14.02.2013 of the Supreme Court of Cassation on case No. 904/2012, II fiscal unit.

19 N. Mevorah, D. Lidgi and L. Farhi, *Commentary on Law of Obligations and Contracts. Art. 1–333*, Fotinov Cooperative Printing House, Sofia 1924, p. 91; L. Dikov, *Civil Law Course. Contractual Law. General part*, vol. 3, Royal Printing House, Sofia 1934; Phototype edition of 'St Kliment Ohridski' University Publishing House, Sofia 2015, p. 279; I. Apostolov, *Legal transactions affecting a foreign legal sphere*, M. Staykov's printing house, Sofia 1937, p. 181; A. Kozhuharov, *Contractual Law. General concepts of contractual relationship*, new edition and supplements by P. Petkov, 'St Kliment Ohridski' University Publishing House/Jurispress, Sofia 2002, p. 105; M. Markov, *Contractual Law*, Sibi, Sofia 2011, p. 92; A. Kalaydzhiev, *Contractual Law. General part*, 5th ed., Sibi, Sofia 2010, p. 167; P. Goleva, *Contractual Law*, New Star, Sofia 2015, p. 106; P. Topurov, 'Fulfilling a contract in favour of a third party' in H. Paunov (compilor), *Compendium 'Law – traditions and perspectives'*, Ciela, Sofia 2018, p. 297.

20 I. Ruschev, 'Acquiring rights under contract in favour of a third party' in *Research studies of the University of Russe* (2015, vol. 54, series 7), p. 199.

21 S. Bashov, 'Contract in favour of a third party. Concept and action' (2016) 10 *Property and Law* 12–20.

22 Various theories are analysed by P. Topurov, 'Legal status of the contract in favour of a third party – Critical notes on the theory of direct emergence of rights' in *Compendium of reports from the VII National Conference of PhD students in legal studies*, Institute on State and Legal Studies, Sofia 2017, pp. 190–97.

relations with the promisor and with the stipulant. As regards the promisor, the third party acts in the capacity of creditor, while as regards the stipulant, the third party acts in the capacity of beneficiary. If a case arises in which the third party states their intention to avail themselves of the contract, then the third-party rights are addressed to the promisor, who turns out to be their debtor.

The court practice, in turn, assumes that the stipulant may file a claim against the promisor, compelling the latter to pay its debt to the beneficiary.[23] There may simultaneously exist a wide range of relations between the stipulant and the beneficiary. The former could be in debt to the beneficiary, or could conclude the contract with *solvendi, acquirendi* or *donandi causa*.[24] We should, therefore, accept that where the third party is also the creditor of the stipulant, they cannot seek to exercise their rights by filing a claim according to Art. 134 LOC, thus exercising the stipulant's right to demand performance in their favour by the promisor. This ensues from the fact that, in such a case, there would be no risk of detriment, considering the option for the beneficiary themselves to file a claim for performance against the promisee.

When complying with the facts regarding the specific Case 1, what should be accounted for are the existing particular relations between the stipulant and the beneficiary. Here, the former presents as the holding company and the latter as its subsidiary. In view of this, another option to influence the holding company's decision to file a claim against the promisor would exist if Direct owned a part of Holdings' capital; that is, if there were a possibility to influence the company's decisions.

On the other hand, although Direct is an independent legal entity,[25] decision-making within the company depends on Holdings. According to Art. 277 of the Commerce Act (CA),[26] the dependence between a holding company and its subsidiary may find expression either in the former owning a big part of the latter's capital, or in the managing process of the subsidiary.[27]

In the first case, pursuant to Art. 277, paragraph 3 CA, a holding company is defined as one that owns or controls, either directly or indirectly, at least 25 per cent of the shares or units of the subsidiary. As far as the decision on filing claims regarding contractual non-performance, where the subsidiary is the beneficiary, may be within the holding company's competency, according to the founding

---

23 Decision No. 1829/13.03.2000 of the Supreme Court of Cassation under civil case No. 1241/2000.

24 A. Kalaydzhiev, *Contractual Law. General part*, 5th ed., Sibi, Sofia 2010, p. 169.

25 Decision No. 41/1993 on fiscal case 214/1992 of the Supreme Court (BSC); Order No. 399/1994 of the BSC; Decision No. 19/1995 of the BSC.

26 Promulgated SG No. 48/18.06.1991, in force from 01.07.1991, last am. SG No. 88/ 23.10.2018.

27 P. Goleva, *Commercial Law. General part. Traders*, Apis Publishing House, Sofia 2014, p. 569.

document of the company (Art. 221 CA), the holding company may decide to vote against taking such a decision.

In accordance with Art. 277, paragraph 3, the holding company's participation in the managing process of the subsidiary has to, at least, involve determining, directly or indirectly, more than half of the members of the subsidiary's board of directors, which, in turn, could also impact on the subsidiary's decision-making, and the undertaking of actions to lay a claim against the promisor of the contract in favour of the subsidiary company.

In Case 1, the directors of Holdings make clear that Holdings will not raise court proceedings against Digital Age for breach of contract. It is not clear from the facts of the case what the exact legal relationship is between Holdings and Direct, so it cannot be determined with certainty whether Holdings could impose this decision via Direct's board of directors.

2.3. CZECH REPUBLIC

Tomáš Richter

I. *Operative Rules*

1. Direct *will probably be able* to take action against Digital Age for breach of contract.
2. The answer is not clear, but Direct will *probably not be able to* force Holdings to raise proceedings against Digital Age to recover Direct's losses.

II. *Descriptive Formants*

For the purposes of answering *the first question*, the key statutory rule is section 1759 of the Civil Code (CC), which provides that:

> A contract binds the parties thereto. A contract may only be amended or cancelled with the agreement of all parties or based on other grounds prescribed by the law. *A contract has effects vis-à-vis other persons only in cases prescribed by the law.*

The third sentence (emphasis added) contains the relevant rule. The statutory rule cross-referred to is, for the present purposes, to be found in section 1767 CC, which, under the heading 'A contract for the benefit of a third person', provides that:

> (1) If, pursuant to a contract, the debtor is obligated to perform to a third person, the creditor may demand that the debtor performs to such third person.
> (2) It shall depend on the contents, the nature and the purpose of the contract whether, and if so when, such a third person also acquires the direct right to

demand performance. A third person shall presumably have acquired such right if the performance shall be effected mainly for its own benefit.

(3) The debtor may invoke objections arising out of the contract against such third person as well.

All of the above-mentioned rules appear in Part 4 of the CC (entitled 'Relative Property Rights'), Catch I (entitled 'General Provisions of Obligations'), subpart 2 (entitled 'Contract'). One may, therefore, unequivocally categorise the rules as contract law rules.

There is a further rule in section 2913(1) CC, which, under the heading 'Breach of a Contractual Obligation', provides that:

(1) If a party breaches a duty arising out of a contract, it shall remedy the damages suffered as the result by the other party *or also to a person whose interests the performance of the agreed duty should have obviously served.*

The relevant rule appears at the end of the clause (emphasis added). It appears in Part 4 of the CC (entitled 'Relative Property Rights'), Catch III (entitled 'Delictual Obligations'), Part 1 (entitled 'Remedy of proprietary and non-proprietary harm'), subpart 2 (entitled 'The duty to remedy damages'). Given its specific title, 'Breach of a Contractual Obligation', it is also possible to categorise the rule as a contract law rule.

It has been said that the third person may claim based either on section 1767(2), which would be a claim for the enforcement of contract performance, or on section 2913(1), which would be a claim for damages, but not on both.[28] Whether Direct would formulate the action as an action under section 1767(2) or section 2913(1) would depend on the actual drafting of the relevant provision of the contract between Holdings and Digital Age: the content of the actual contractual clause would determine the remedy available.

Either way, it seems that, based on the facts of Case 1, Direct would likely be able to take direct action against Digital Age as the result of the breach of contract.

The answer to the second question is negative.

Section 1767(1) expressly provides that, 'if, pursuant to a contract, the debtor is obligated to perform to a third person, *the creditor may demand* that the debtor performs to such third person' (emphasis added). It would seem quite a

28 M. Hulmák, in M. Hulmák et al., *Občanský zákoník V, Závazkové právo, Obecná část (§1721–2054), První vydání*, C.H. Beck, Praha 2014, p. 242 at 38, 40. It should be noted that, under s. 2951(1) CC, damages will primarily be remedied 'in kind', i.e. through restitution into the previous condition. However, damages will be remedied through monetary payment where restitution is not possible, or where the plaintiff so demands.

stretch to interpret these words so as to construe an obligation on the part of the creditor (in this case, Holdings), rather than its discretionary right.

In the absence of a contract with, or a specific statutory duty towards, Direct (which does not appear to be the case in this instance), Direct could only attempt to recover their loss from Holdings under section 2900 CC. Under the heading 'Prevention', section 2900 provides that:

> If the circumstances of the case or the common habits of private life so require, everyone must conduct his or her affairs such that unnecessary harm to the liberty, life, health or the property of others is avoided.

Clearly, the provision is worded in very general terms, and is thus open to interpretation, including arguments to the effect that section 2900 in essence expresses a principle more than an actionable rule.[29] The more probable outcome would seem to be that Direct could not use section 2900 to force Holdings to recover Direct's losses.[30]

III. Meta-Legal Formants

The CC came into force on 1 January 2014, superseding the previous Civil Code of 1964 (CC 1964), as well as the Commercial Code of 1991 (CommC), which contained, in addition to the law of business corporations, the law of commercial contracts. There is still very little by way of published case law of higher-instance courts on the CC.

With respect to Case 1, two notes on recent changes in the law are in order. First, section 2900 CC superseded section 415 CC 1964, and narrowed the rule down significantly.[31] Secondly, section 2913(1) CC has been adopted with the specific aim of narrowing down pre-2014 case law by the Supreme Court, which, disturbingly, conveyed on third persons a much broader ability to recover under contracts to which they were not parties than is the case under current law.[32]

---

29 F. Melzer, in F. Melzer, P. Tégl et al., *Občanský zákoník, §2894–3081. Velký komentář. Svazek IX. První vydání*, Leges, Praha 2018, pp. 75–91.

30 Ibid., who argues at pp. 90 and 91 that the section needs to be used with restraint in the context of construing claims for pure economic loss.

31 Ibid, pp. 86–88; M. Pašek, in J. Petrov, M. Výtisk, V. Beran et al., *Občanský zákoník. Komentář. 2. Vydání*, C.H. Beck, Praha 2019, p. 3014. S. 415 CC 1964 read '[e]veryone must act so that damages to health, property, the nature and the environment are avoided.'

32 F. Melzer, in F. Melzer, P. Tégl et al., *Občanský zákoník, §2894–3081. Velký komentář. Svazek IX. První vydání*, Leges, Praha 2018, pp. 323–24; M. Pašek, in J. Petrov, M. Výtisk, V. Beran et al., *Občanský zákoník. Komentář. 2. Vydání*, C.H. Beck, Praha 2019, p. 3033.

2.4. ENGLAND AND WALES

T.T. Arvind

I. Operative Rules

1. Under English law,[33] it is likely that Direct will be able to bring an action against Digital Age as a third-party beneficiary under the Contract (Rights of Third Parties) Act 1999 (CRTPA), as long as their right to do so is not excluded by the contract between Holdings and Digital Age.
2. Direct are unlikely to be able to force Holdings to raise proceedings against Digital Age.

II. Descriptive Formants

Question 1

The CRTPA permits third parties to enforce a term of the contract in their own right in two types of circumstances. Firstly, they can do so if the contract expressly provides that they may.[34] Secondly, they can do so if the contractual term 'purports to confer a benefit' on them,[35] unless it appears 'on a proper construction of the contract' that the parties did not intend the third party to be able to enforce the term.[36] In either case, the third party must be expressly identified in the contract, either by name, or as a member of a class, or as answering a particular description.[37]

In this case, Direct are likely to attempt to claim that they are covered by the CRTPA. To successfully do this, they will need to show that they were expressly identified in the contract, and that the contract purported to confer a benefit on them. Their inclusion in a schedule will satisfy the first of these requirements, as they are expressly identified by name. The requirement that the contract 'purport' to confer a benefit on the third party has been interpreted by the courts to mean that benefiting the third party must have been one of the purposes of the parties' bargain, rather than an incidental effect.[38] The fact that the purpose of the contract between Digital and Holdings is the provision of IT services

---

33 For reasons of conciseness, this report uses the phrase 'English law' rather than 'law of England and Wales', although it covers both England and Wales.
34 Contract (Rights of Third Parties) Act 1999 (CRTPA), s. 1(1)(a).
35 Ibid., s. 1(1)(b).
36 Ibid., s. 1(2).
37 Ibid., s. 1(3).
38 *Dolphin Maritime & Aviation Services Ltd v. Sveriges Angfartygs Assurans Forening* [2009] EWHC 716 (Comm), [2009] 2 Lloyd's Rep. 123 [8] (Christopher Clarke J).

to Direct (amongst other parties) is likely to be sufficient to establish that the contract does purport to confer a benefit on Direct.

The CRTPA is, however, subject to the parties' contract. Section 1(2) of CRTPA provides that the third party will be unable to enforce a contractual term if a proper construction of the contract reveals that the parties did not intend to give it the right to enforce the term. One way of achieving this is through an express provision in the contract denying the third party the right to enforce a term, and cases under CRTPA make it clear that Direct will have no right to sue Digital Age if the contract between Holdings and Digital Age has such a provision.[39] There is no authoritative judicial statement on when, in the absence of an express provision, a 'proper construction' will lead to the conclusion that the parties did not intend to give the third party the right to enforce a term. Prior cases have suggested that industry practice may be relevant,[40] as may the existence of other remedies or routes of recovery for the claimant.[41] Neither of these is likely to apply to this case. As a result, it is unlikely that Digital Age will be able to prove that Direct were not intended to have the right to enforce the IT services contract, absent an express provision to that effect.

Question 2

Neither the CRTPA nor any other statutory or common law rule gives third parties a general right to compel a party to enforce the contract. Such rights exist only in a small number of very specific circumstances, none of which apply to this case: for example, if Holdings had entered into the contract with Digital Age as Direct's agent, or if Holdings and Direct had themselves entered into a contract which gave Direct the right to compel Holdings to bring proceedings against Digital Age.

III. Meta-Legal Formants

Question 1

The traditional rule at common law was that only parties to a contract could sue or be sued under the contract. This rule, called 'privity of contract', meant that, until 1999, third-party beneficiaries had no general right to bring an action to enforce contractual provisions in their favour.[42] There were several exceptions

39 *Hurley Palmer Flatt Ltd v. Barclays Bank Ltd* [2014] EWHC 3042 (TCC), [2015] Bus LR 106 [20]–[23].

40 *Laemthong International Lines Co. Ltd v. Artis (The Laemthong Glory) (No. 2)* [2005] EWCA Civ 519, [2005] 1 Lloyd's Rep. 688 [53]–[54] (Clarke LJ).

41 *Royal Bank of Scotland Plc v. McCarthy* [2015] EWHC 3626 (QB) [141]–[143] (Picken J).

42 For the classic statement of this rule, see *Tweddle v. Atkinson* (1861) 1 B&S 393, 121 ER 762 (QB) and *Dunlop Pneumatic Tyre Co. Ltd v. Selfridge & Co. Ltd* [1915] AC 847 (HL).

to this rule. These exceptions generally operated by classifying particular types of situations as falling within some other area of law which was not subject to the doctrine of privity, such as agency (see Cases 4 and 6 below) or property (see Cases 5 and 7). As a result, they only applied to narrow subsets of cases.

The doctrine of privity was quite deeply entrenched in the conceptual basis of English contract law, and was seen as representing the principle that contractual obligations are particular to the parties to the contract. As a result, although it was well recognised that the doctrine created problems in practice, it nevertheless continued in force until 1999. In 1999 the law was reformed through the CRTPA, which created a new statutory exception to the doctrine of privity, applicable to contracts entered into after 11 May 2000. It is important to note that this new exception is based wholly on the intention of the parties (and, thus, on the principle of freedom of contract), rather than on a broader policy in favour of third-party beneficiaries. Because of the conceptual weight attached to the doctrine of privity, the CRTPA did not abolish the doctrine, which continues to subsist. As a result, if a particular situation does not satisfy the requirements of the CRTPA, and also does not fall within any of the older exceptions to privity, the doctrine of privity will apply, and the third party will have no right to enforce the contractual term.

Question 2

The position that a third party cannot compel a party to enforce a contract in its favour reflects the broader position that English law does not, in general, compel a person to act for the benefit of another, in the absence of a specific legal obligation requiring them to do so. Obligations of this type are usually created by specific contractual provisions, and can also be created by certain other types of relationships, for example the duty of loyalty which a trustee owes to the beneficiary. In the absence of a specific obligation of this type, however, a party is not under any obligation to assist another in recovering a loss.

2.5. FRANCE

Sylvain Ravenne and Flora Vern

I. Operative Rules

1. Direct can take action against Digital Age for breach of contract.
2. Direct will not be able to force Holdings to raise proceedings against Digital Age to recover Direct's losses, unless there is a specific provision in the contract between Holdings and Digital Age, or in a contract between Holdings and Direct, to this effect.

II. *Descriptive Formants*

Question 1

Under French law the provision of the contract between Holdings and Digital Age which provides that the latter will provide IT services to companies set out by the former would be regarded as a '*stipulation pour autrui*' (stipulation for another person).

A major reform of contract law was adopted on 10 February 2016, which is applicable to contracts concluded after 1 October 2016. Therefore, this case should be dealt with under the former contract law, as the contract between Holdings and Digital Age was concluded before February 2016. However, while the phrasing of the law has changed, the solutions derived from it on this particular topic are identical.

The former Article 1121 of the French Civil Code (FCC) provided:

> One may likewise stipulate for the benefit of a third party when such is the condition for a stipulation that one makes for oneself or for a donation which one makes to another. He who made that stipulation may no longer revoke it if the third party has declared that he wishes to take advantage of it.

The current Article 1205 of this Code states:

> A person may make a stipulation for another person.
>
> One of the parties to a contract (the 'stipulator' [or the 'promisee']) may require a promise from the other party (the 'promisor') to accomplish an act of performance for the benefit of a third party (the 'beneficiary'). The third party may be a future person but must be exactly identified or must be able to be determined at the time of the performance of the promise.

Thus, Holding is the promisee, Digital Age the promisor, and Direct the beneficiary.

The beneficiary is not technically a party to the agreement between the promisor and the promisee, even if they have accepted the stipulation. French law considers that acceptance of the benefit of the stipulation does not imply agreement to the contract between the promisee and promisor, which may include other provisions. Thus, the beneficiary does not have a claim to the termination of this agreement. However, early case law from the Cour de cassation (French Supreme Court) granted the beneficiary a direct right against the promisor for performance of the stipulation.[43] This solution has

[43] Cass., civ., 16 janv. 1888, *DP* 1888, 1, 77; Cass., req., 30 avr. 1888, *DP* 1888, 1, 291; Cass., com., 20. déc. 2017, n° 16-20501.

been kept in the new Article 1206 of the FCC: 'The beneficiary is vested in a direct right to the act of performance against the promisor from the time of the stipulation.'

As a result, under both the former contract law and the current law, the beneficiary is vested in this direct right, even if they have not accepted the stipulation.[44] Consequently, the promisor cannot revoke their commitment to the beneficiary, even if the latter has not yet accepted the stipulation,[45] and if the beneficiary dies before having accepted it, their heirs could still accept the stipulation.

Therefore, as the beneficiary of the stipulation provided by the contract between Holdings and Digital Age, Direct have a claim at law against Digital Age for breach of contract.[46]

Question 2

The promisee may require the promisor to perform the contract for the benefit of the beneficiary, even without any specific provision in the contract to this effect.[47] However, in principle, the promisee does not undertake engagement in their own name to the beneficiary. Therefore, the beneficiary cannot take action against the promisee to force them to sue the promisor.[48] This solution is consistent with the fact that the beneficiary has a direct claim against the promisor and does not need the help of the promisee in order to force the promisor to perform the contract or pay damages.

2.6. GERMANY

Sonja Meier

I. Operative Rules

1. Direct will probably be able to take action against Digital Age for breach of contract.
2. Direct will not be able to force Holdings to sue Digital Age.

---

44 Under the pre-2016 contract law, the question was disputed: in ancient cases, the Cour de cassation decided that the beneficiary needed to have accepted the stipulation, but most authors in recent decades have thought otherwise (*contra* J. Ghestin, C. Jamin and M. Billiau, *Traité de droit civil, les effets du contrat*, 3rd ed. (Paris: LGDJ, 2001), n° 1014 *in fine*).

45 Cass., com., 23 févr. 1993, n° 89-17670, Bull. civ. IV, n° 69.

46 Cass., com., 7 oct. 1997, n° 95-18119.

47 Cass., civ. 1, 14 déc. 1999, n° 97-20040, and current Art. 1209 of the FCC.

48 Cass., req., 6 juin 1888, *DP* 1889, 1, 55.

II. *Descriptive Formants*

Question 1

A court will likely find that a genuine *'Vertrag zugunsten Dritter'* (contract for the benefit of third parties) has been concluded between Holdings and Digital Age. According to §328 (1) Bürgerliches Gesetzbuch (German Civil Code, BGB), the contracting parties may stipulate that a third party shall have the right to claim the contractual performance and take action against the debtor independently from the party to whom the contractual promise was made. Whether the third party was intended to have that right or was only meant to profit from the contract indirectly depends on the construction of the contract. Absent an express provision, all circumstances of the case must be considered, particularly the purpose of the contract (§328 (2) BGB) and, according to the courts and commentators, the specific characteristics of the contract, the ease of its performance, and the performance interest of the third party.[49] In the present case, the contractual performance consists in IT services provided to Direct and is, therefore, primarily Direct's interest. A direct contractual claim by Direct against Digital Age facilitates the performance of the contract, since problems can be solved directly between them. Both considerations are indicative of a genuine contract for the benefit of a third party. The fact that Holdings can remove Direct from the schedule, thereby depriving them of their potential right, is irrelevant. It is generally acknowledged, and also mentioned in §328 (2) BGB, that the right of the third party may be revocable.

While it is disputed whether remedies (such as termination) that affect the obligation of the contracting party have to be exercised by the contracting party, the third party or both, there is consensus that a simple claim for damages for breach can be raised by the third party on its own.[50] The basis for such a claim can be found in §280 (1) BGB, which requires a *'Schuldverhältnis'* (obligational relationship) between the claimant and the defendant. While the core case of such a *Schuldverhältnis* is a contract between the parties, in the present case it is constituted by Direct's right against Digital Age under the contract between Holdings and Digital Age.

Question 2

In case of a *Vertrag zugunsten Dritter*, §335 BGB allows the contracting party to whom the promise was made (the promisee, in this case Holdings) to claim

49 Cf. BGH *NJW* 1991, 2209; P. Gottwald in *Münchener Kommentar zum BGB*, vol. 3 (9th ed., Beck 2022), §328, [33].

50 P. Gottwald in *Münchener Kommentar zum BGB*, vol. 3 (9th ed., Beck 2022), §335, [14]; S. Klumpp in *J. von Staudingers Kommentar zum Bürgerlichen Gesetzbuch*, vol. §§328–45 (Sellier – de Gruyter 2020), §328, [81]; §335, [22] ff.

performance from the debtor to the third party, except where the parties have provided otherwise. It is generally agreed that §335 BGB extends to damages, so that the promisee can bring a claim for damages to be paid to the third party.[51] Holdings will, therefore, have the right to recover Direct's losses from Digital Age.

However, the law does not provide for a right of the third party to force the promisee to bring such proceedings, since the third party can take action itself. Such a right can only be established by a contract between Direct and Holdings.

2.7. ITALY

Camilla Crea

I. Operative Rules

1. Direct can take direct action against Digital Age.
2. Direct are not entitled to force Holdings to raise proceedings against Digital Age to recover Direct's losses. Indeed, Direct have an independent direct claim.

II. Descriptive Formants

The solution to the case lies in the rules concerning the so-called '*contratto a favore di terzo*' (contract in favour of third parties), which are set forth in Arts. 1411 ff. of the Italian Civil Code (c.c.). This is a contract whereby the parties – the 'stipulator' and the 'promisor' – agree that the performance owed by the promisor be made in favour of a third-party beneficiary, unless the parties have agreed otherwise. In the Italian legal system, the effects the contract has vis-à-vis third parties must be in favour of them and consist in the attribution of personal rights or real rights. Real rights might burden the beneficiary, but it should be noted that the third party can always refuse the attribution.[52]

This contract scheme can apply to any contracts, be they typical or atypical.[53] The latter description applies to contracts which are not explicitly regulated in

---

51 BGH *NJW* 1974, 502; BGH *NJW* 2010, 2950, [15]; P. Gottwald in *Münchener Kommentar zum BGB*, vol. 3 (9th ed., Beck 2022), §335, [4]; S. Klumpp in *J. von Staudingers Kommentar zum Bürgerlichen Gesetzbuch*, vol. §§328–45 (Sellier – de Gruyter 2020), §335, [9].

52 Cass., 14 November 1986, no. 6688, *DeJure Giuffrè*; Cass., 1 December 2003, no. 18321, *Rivista del notariato*, II (2004), p. 1228; Cass., 27 June 2011, no. 14180, *DeJure Giuffrè*, in relation to easement entitlements.

53 See Cass., 16 October 2019, no. 26212, *Foro italiano*, I (2019), p. 3895, referring to an atypical agreement which was stipulated between a trade union association of workers and a lawyer providing legal services in favour of the workers as beneficiaries. Some well-known examples

the Civil Code or other laws, as long as they are created by party autonomy (Art. 1322 c.c.). The clause containing the stipulation in favour of a third party can be included in any contract.[54]

The key element is that the third party *directly* acquires the rights but not the duties arising from the contract, without having to accept them formally. Under Art. 1411, paragraph 2, c.c., 'the stipulation, however, can be revoked or modified by the stipulator until the third person declares to the promisor, that he intends to avail himself of the stipulation'. The '*dichiarazione di volerne profittare*' (declaration that the third party intends to avail themselves of the stipulation) can also result from *facta concludentia* (conclusive facts).[55] It does not determine the acquisition of the right against the promisor but merely corroborates that acquisition, as it prevents the stipulator from revoking or modifying the stipulation. Technically speaking, the beneficiary[56] is not a party, either formally or substantially, to the contract, because they did not contribute to the definition of the contract rules, and the stipulator acts in their own name.

The third-party beneficiary can neutralise the acquisition of the rights arising from the contract through a refusal (Art. 1411, paragraph 3, c.c.). The power to refuse is not subject to any time limitation, but as soon as it is exercised the contract will have effects only on the stipulator rather than the third party, and the stipulator will be bound to fulfil the obligations imposed on them by the contract, and will be the holder of all legal rights arising from the contract (unless it appears otherwise from the intention of the parties or the very nature of the contract).

In order for the stipulation in favour of a third party to be valid, the stipulator must have an interest therein,[57] which can be either economic or non-economic

of typical contracts in favour of third parties are insurance contracts (Cass., 30 January 2019, no. 2688, *Banca dati Il Foro Italiano*) as well as transport agreements (Cass., 15 May 2018, no. 11744, *Banca dati Il Foro Italiano*).

54 U. Majello, 'Contratto a favore del terzo', *Digesto discipline privatistiche, sez. civ.* (Turin: UTET, 1989), IV, pp. 237, 242; G. Gorla, 'Contratto a favore di terzi e nudo patto', *Rivista di diritto civile*, I (1959), p. 587; M. Tamponi, 'Il contratto a favore di terzo' in M. Bessone (ed), *Trattato di diritto privato* (Turin: Giappichelli, 2000), XIII, p. 368.

55 Cass., 24 December 1992, no. 13661, *Vita notarile* (1993), p. 769.

56 The third party must be determined (i.e. identified) or at least determinable based on the contract entered into by the stipulator and the promisor: Cass., s.u., 26 June 2001, no. 8744, *Il diritto marittimo* (2002), p. 241; Cass., 18 July 2002, no. 10403, *Società* (2003), p. 1513; Cass., 17 September 2019, no. 23125, *Banca dati Il Foro Italiano*.

57 Creditor's interest in the performance (Art. 1174 c.c.: E. Betti, *Teoria generale del negozio giuridico* (Naples: Edizioni Scientifiche Italiane, 1994), p. 549) but, above all, an interest worthy of legal protection (Art. 1322 c.c.): U. Majello, *L'interesse dello stipulante nel contratto a favore di terzi* (Naples: Jovene, 1962); F. Girino, *Studi in tema di stipulazione a favore di terzi* (Milan: Giuffrè, 1963), p. 114; M. Sesta, 'Interesse, causa e motivi nella stipulazione a favore di terzo', *Studi in memoria di G. Gorla* (Milan: Giuffrè, 1994), vol. 3, p. 2073; V.L. Moscarini, 'Il contratto a favore di terzo. Artt. 1411–1413' in P. Schlesinger and D. Busnelli (eds), *Il Codice civile commentato* (Milan: Giuffrè, 2012), p. 102.

(or even moral).[58] This interest often results from factual and objective elements (for example, a shareholder stipulating in favour of a company, a husband stipulating in favour of his wife or children, etc.). Generally speaking, the interest of the stipulator can be established by analysing the 'legal relationship' – but not the contract – between the stipulator and the third party which justifies the attribution of rights (which may, for example, be discharging a duty of the stipulator to the beneficiary (the so-called *causa solvendi*), or a gift (*causa donandi*)).

In the event of the promisor's failure to perform the contract, the third-party beneficiary can sue the promisor directly, without the stipulator's consent, or even against the stipulator's wishes, as the beneficiary can rely on their right to enforce their credit directly.[59]

It is also believed that the third party and the stipulator are both entitled to claim performance of the contract and compensation for damages against the promisor.[60] But these are independent claims which can only be raised as alternatives to one another.

Accordingly, the third party cannot force the stipulator to claim compensation for damages, because they have their own direct action; that is, an independent right to claim compensation for the damages they have suffered.

III. Meta-Legal Formants

Scholars argue over whether a contract in favour of third parties is an exception to the privity of contract principle laid down in Art. 1372, paragraph 2, c.c.[61] Historically, the ancient brocard '*res inter alios acta tertio nec nocet nec prodest*' has militated against the contract in favour of third parties.[62] However, beginning with the Civil Code of 1865, and then the Commercial Code of 1882, the legal system acknowledged the idea that a contract can have effects on third parties.

---

58 Cass., 3 July 1979, no. 3749, *DeJure Giuffré*; Cass., 4 May 2005, no. 9284, *Giustizia civile*, 12, I (2006), p. 2881; Cass., 5 June 2007, no. 13058, *Il diritto marittimo* (2008), p. 468.

59 Cass., 1 December 2003, no. 18321, *Rivista del notariato*, II (2004); Cass., 18 September 2008, no. 23844, *Giustizia civile*, 3, I (2009), p. 630.

60 M. Franzoni, 'Il contratto e i terzi' in E. Gabrielli (ed), *I contratti in generale. Trattato dei contratti diretto da Rescigno e Gabrielli* (Turin: UTET, 2006), pp. 1183, 1237; A. Fusaro, 'Il contratto a favore di terzi' in V. Roppo (ed), *Trattato del contratto* (Milan: Giuffrè, 2006), vol. III, p. 175; L.V. Moscarini, *I negozi a favore di terzo* (Milan: Giuffrè, 1970), p. 205; Cass., 9 October 1997, no. 9810, *Giurisprudenza italiana* (1998), p. 1096; Cass., 9 April 2014, no. 8272, *DeJure Giuffré*.

61 F. Galgano, 'Degli effetti del contratto. Sub Art. 1372', *Commentario del codice civile Scialoja e Branca* (Bologna/Rome: Zanichelli-Il Foro italiano, 1993), p. 1.

62 G. Amadio and F. Macario (eds), 'Il contratto a favore di terzi', *Il diritto civile, Norme, questioni, concetti* (Bologna: Il Mulino, 2014), p. 776. For the historical origins, see L.V. Moscarini, *I negozi a favore di terzo* (Milan: Giuffrè, 1970), p. 5.

On one hand, Art. 44 of the 'Italian–French Project of Obligations'[63] reads that 'contracts ... shall not prejudice third parties, but they can advantage them in the cases provided for by the law', and on the other, the official commentary on the current Italian Civil Code of 1942 (no. 643) holds that 'the rule establishing the nullity of contracts in favour of third parties was passed on from classical Roman law to the Code of 1865, with some adjustments that classical and Justinian law had gradually received. Modern codes have turned that rule into a principle of validity, and Art. 1411 c.c. has followed suit'.

This is an extremely complicated issue whose solution depends on the different ways that privity of contract has been understood over the years. This principle is grounded in connection with other implicit meta-legal formants, such as the consent theory of contract and the principle of 'inviolability of the legal positions of third parties'. Eventually, the privity of contract principle came to be downplayed in such a way that, today, it is believed to be less imperative and more flexible, allowing for a contract to affect third parties regardless of their consent. However, two requirements have to be met: (a) the effects vis-à-vis the third party should be beneficial; and (b) the third party should always be able to refuse them.[64] The beneficiary's power of refusal means that third parties can receive 'advantages without their consent, but never against their consent'.[65]

2.8. THE NETHERLANDS

Jan Biemans

I. Operative Rules

1. Direct can take action against Digital Age for breach of contract.
2. Direct cannot, in principle, force Holdings to raise proceedings against Digital Age to recover Direct's losses.

II. Descriptive Formants

From the contract between Holdings and Digital Age, combined with the schedule to the contract listing Direct (among other companies), it follows that

63 D. Deroussin, 'Le Projet de Code des obligations et des contrats franco-italien de 1927: chant du cygne de la culture juridique latine?', *Clio@Themis, Revue eléctronique d'histoire du droit*, II (2009), www.cliothemis.com/Le-Projet-de-Code-des-obligations.

64 C. Donisi, *Il problema dei negozi giuridici unilaterali* (1972) (Naples: Edizioni Scientifiche Italiane, 2010), p. 139; G. Benedetti, *Dal contratto al negozio unilaterale* (1969) (Milan: Giuffrè, 2007), p. 197.

65 V. Roppo, 'Il contratto' in G. Iudica and P. Zatti (eds), *Trattato di diritto privato* (Milan: Giuffrè, 2001).

Holdings have stipulated that Digital Age will provide IT services to Direct from 1 February 2016 until 31 January 2021, and that Holdings are responsible for making all payments to Digital Age. This stipulation in the contract between Holdings and Digital Age qualifies as a third-party clause *(derdenbeding)* as meant in Article 6:253 of the Dutch Civil Code (DCC).[66] According to Article 6:253 (1) DCC, an agreement creates the right for a third party to claim performance from one of the parties or to appeal otherwise against one of them for the observance of their agreement, if the agreement contains a stipulation to that effect (third-party clause) and the third party has accepted this stipulation. The rules on third-party clauses are non-mandatory rules in the DCC.

Since Direct have suffered loss due to a breach of the contract by Digital Age, which indicates that Digital Age were providing certain IT services to Direct, it can, therefore, be concluded that Direct have accepted the third-party clause. Such acceptance is necessary, as the third-party clause in the contract is revocable. If the stipulation (third-party clause) had been made irrevocable, and had been stipulated in favour of the third party gratuitously, it would have been regarded as having been accepted if the third party had not rejected it immediately after they had obtained knowledge of its existence (Article 6:253 (4) DCC). However, in this case, although the third-party clause has been made gratuitously in favour of Direct, Holdings can add to, remove or replace any company in the schedule, according to the contract, on giving written notice to Digital Age, which makes the third-party clause revocable, and makes it necessary for Direct to accept. The third party accepts or rejects the stipulation (third-party clause) by making a declaration to one of the parties to the agreement (Article 6:253 (3) DCC). Being a legal act *(rechtshandeling)*, the acceptance can, in principle, be expressed in any form, and may even be implied in certain legal acts (Article 3:37 DCC), such as Direct asking Digital Age to provide IT services to Direct.

The contractual possibility of Holdings removing or replacing any company in the schedule after such company (such as Direct, being the third party) has accepted the third-party clause, making the third-party clause *revocable*,[67] should be distinguished from the statutory possibility that the contracting party that has stipulated the third-party clause may revoke this stipulation (as such) up until the moment it has been accepted by the third party (Article 6:253 (2) DCC). Article 6:255 DCC provides for the situation in which a third-party clause has no effect for the third party. The party who has stipulated the clause may appoint either themselves or another third person as the person who can draw rights

66 See C.H. Sieburgh, *Mr. C. Assers Handleiding tot de beoefening van het Nederlands Burgerlijk Recht. 6. Verbintenissenrecht. Deel III. Algemeen overeenkomstenrecht*, Deventer: Wolters Kluwer 2022, pp. 564 ff.

67 In the sense that Holding can replace Direct with another party, which can be considered as a revocation of Direct's third-party right.

from it (Article 6:255 (1) DCC).[68] The party who has made the stipulation (third-party clause) is regarded as having appointed themselves as the person who can draw rights from it, when their counterparty to that stipulation, on whom the stipulation imposes an obligation, has set them a reasonable period and they have not appointed someone else within that period (Article 6:255 (2) DCC).

According to the case, Direct have suffered loss due to lost sales, due to a breach of the contract by Digital Age. Direct can take action against Digital Age for breach of contract. The reason for this is that, after the third party has accepted the stipulation as meant in Article 6:253 (1) DCC (the third-party clause), it will be a full party to the agreement (Article 6:254 (1) DCC).[69] The third party may even (as well), to the extent that this is in conformity with the underlying purpose of the stipulation (the third-party clause), derive rights from it over the period prior to the moment they accepted the stipulation (Article 6:254 (2) DCC). The answer would not have been different had Holdings removed Direct from the schedule after the breach of contract by Digital Age, as that would only have meant that Digital Age were no longer obliged to provide IT services to Direct, but not that Digital Age would not have to make up for the loss during the period that Direct were a (full) party to the contract.

Direct cannot, in principle, force Holdings to raise proceedings against Digital Age to recover Direct's losses. As follows from the above, it is not necessary for Direct to do so, as Direct themselves can take action against Digital Age for breach of contract. However, Holdings could also raise proceedings against Digital Age to recover Direct's losses. According to Article 6:256 DCC, the party that has stipulated the third-party clause (Holdings) on behalf of a third party (Direct), may demand from its counterparty to that third-party clause, on whom the third-party clause imposes an obligation (Digital Age), that it performs the obligation to the third party, unless the third party opposes this. Although both parties could raise proceedings, both claims cannot succeed, since that would be double recovery.

III. Meta-Legal Formants

The provision in Article 6:253 (2) DCC on the revocation of the third-party clause, as well as the possibility to revoke an accepted third-party clause, as implied in Article 6:253 (4) DCC, shows similarities with the provisions on the formation of agreements in general (Articles 6:217 ff. DCC), and in particular Article 6:219 DCC on revocable offers.

---

68 C.H. Sieburgh, *Mr. C. Assers Handleiding tot de beoefening van het Nederlands Burgerlijk Recht. 6. Verbintenissenrecht. Deel III. Algemeen overeenkomstenrecht*, Deventer: Wolters Kluwer 2022, p. 580.

69 Ibid., pp. 572 and 573.

The rule of Article 6:253 (4) DDC that, if the third-party clause is irrevocable and made gratuitously towards the third party, it will be regarded as having been accepted if the third party did not reject it immediately after obtaining knowledge of its existence, is comparable to the acceptance of a bequest in a last will (Article 4:201 (1) DCC) or a donation (Article 7:175 (2) DCC). The acceptance is necessary, as a person cannot be forced to have contractual rights against their will.[70]

Life insurance (or 'sum' insurance), where the policyholder appoints a third party as the beneficiary of the insurance, as meant in Articles 7:964 ff. DCC, is considered to be a particular application of the third-party clause.

2.9. POLAND

Bartosz Kucia

I. Operative Rules

1. Direct have a claim against Digital Age for breach of contract (under Art. 393 §1 in conjunction with Arts. 471 ff. of the Polish Civil Code (PCC)), which may be brought by action.
2. In the described facts, Direct may not demand that Holdings raise proceedings against Digital Age to recover Direct's losses.

II. Descriptive Formants

In relation to the first question, a contract for the benefit of a third party *(pactum in favorem tertii)*, which is the mechanism used between Holdings and Digital Age, is an exception to the principle that the effects of the agreement apply only to its parties *(inter partes)*. It is a supplementary provision (clause) added to an obligatory relationship (for example, a contractual relationship) to redirect the benefit due to the creditor to a third party.[71]

In the agreement between the creditor (Holdings) and the debtor (Digital Age), the parties may agree that the debtor will perform a service, not to the creditor, but directly to a third party (Direct),[72] who may, in turn, demand

70 Ibid., p. 562.

71 See the judgment of the Supreme Court (Sąd Najwyższy, SN) of 07.05.2003, IV CKN 101/01. See also e.g. Arts. 785, 808, 831, 908 §3 PCC.

72 That person should be indicated in the contract in a way that enables the person to be identified, e.g. by indicating the manner in which he or she will be indicated, e.g. by the creditor or another authorised person. See the judgments of the SN of 07.10.1971,

the performance directly from the debtor (Art. 393 §1 PCC).[73] *Pactum in favorem tertii* then combines three obligatory relationships between the creditor, the debtor and a third party. These include the so-called '*stosunek pokrycia*' (coverage relationship) binding the debtor and the creditor, and the so-called '*stosunek zapłaty*' (payment relationship) between the debtor and the authorised third party. In addition, the so-called '*stosunek waluty*' (currency relationship), binding the creditor with a third party, can be distinguished. Because of this relationship, the creditor usually enters into a *pactum in favorem tertii.*[74]

Therefore, the debtor is – in relation to the creditor and to a third party separately – obliged to perform the service directly to the third party.[75] The third party thus obtains their own claim against the debtor for the performance of their benefit (as an additional creditor), although they are not a party to a *pactum* in their own favour.[76] Unless agreed otherwise, the creditor may also require the debtor to perform the benefit to the third party (this action will not be dismissed, even if the third party did not participate in the process).[77]

If the debtor fails to perform the service to the third party, or performs it improperly, both the third party and the creditor may file compensation claims against them for the damage suffered (Arts. 471 ff. PCC). The third party then makes a claim for non-performance or improper performance of the obligatory relationship binding them with the debtor *(stosunek zapłaty)*. However, the legal

III CRN 255/71, OSNC 1972/3/59; 30.03.1983, I CR 344/82, OSNC 1983/11/184; 28.11.2003, IV CK 206/02 and 09.05.2014, I PK 268/13, OSNP 2015/10/134. See also A. Ohanowicz and J. Górski, *Zarys prawa zobowiązań*, Warsaw 1970, p. 104.

73 The parties may, however, arrange things differently, e.g. only authorise a third party to receive the benefit, without granting him or her a claim (an inappropriate contract for the benefit of a third party). See judgment of the Court of Appeal (Sąd Apelacyjny, SA) in Katowice of 19.02.2004, I ACa 885/03.

74 See the judgments of the SN of 05.06.2014, IV CSK 585/13 and 15.05.2015, V CSK 491/14, OSNC-ZD 2016/4/62, and also the judgment of the SA in Warsaw of 14.09.2018, V ACa 899/17.

75 Fulfilling the benefit to the creditor does not, therefore, remit the debtor's obligation to a third party (the judgment of the SN of 05.07.2000, I CKN 711/00; the judgment of the SA in Cracow of 19.02.2013, I ACa 14/13). See, however, the judgment of the SN of 30.03.1983, I CR 344/82, OSNC 1983/11/184 (the third party did not meet the requirements set out in the contract) or W. Czachórski, *Zobowiązania. Zarys wykładu*, Warsaw 2002 (edition supplemented by A. Brzozowski, M. Safjan, E. Skowrońska-Bocian), p. 177 and W. Popiołek in K. Pietrzykowski (ed), *Kodeks cywilny. Tom I. Komentarz. Art. 1–449(10)*, Warsaw 2018, p. 1355 (the third party refused to accept a benefit).

76 See e.g. the judgments of the SN of 19.02.2002, IV CKN 786/00; 17.11.2006, V CSK 268/06, OSNC 2007/9/142; 20.04.2011, I CSK 478/10; 27.07.2016, V CSK 605/15; 25.01.2018, IV CSK 215/17; and, among others, A. Kubas, *Umowa na rzecz osoby trzeciej*, Warsaw/Cracow 1976, p. 36; Z. Radwański in Z. Radwański (ed), *System prawa cywilnego. Tom III. Prawo zobowiązań – część ogólna*, Wrocław 1981, p. 448.

77 See the judgments of the SN of 21.06.2002, V CKN 1069/00, OSNC 2003/11/149 and 03.04.2014, IV CSK 309/13. See also the judgment of the SA in Poznań of 22.02.2006, I ACa 882/05 and e.g. A. Ohanowicz and J. Górski, *Zarys prawa zobowiązań*, Warsaw 1970, p. 105.

basis of the debtor's liability towards the creditor is the *stosunek pokrycia*, which covers the damage caused to the creditor due to the debtor's failure to properly perform their obligations arising from the legal relationship between the creditor and the debtor, as well as the damage suffered by the creditor due to the fact that the creditor's obligation to a third party (resulting from the *stosunek waluty*) has not been fulfilled, which would otherwise have happened if the debtor had duly performed their obligation towards the third party.[78] Although the creditor has the right to demand fulfilment of the benefit to the third party, the doctrine does not provide them with a right to claim in respect of damages suffered by the third party.[79]

In addition, there is no doubt that the creditor is not *ex definitione* a third party's representative (agent) and may not claim compensation on behalf of the third party (if there is no power of attorney authorising them to act in such a capacity). At the same time, the circumstances of the case do not allow the conclusion that the creditor was acting as the so-called *'zastępca pośredni'* (indirect substitute), who, unlike a representative, acts in their own name only (with legal consequences in their own legal sphere), but for the account of another person. In particular, it is unlikely that the third party will have contracted the creditor to claim compensation.

In relation to the second question, *pactum in favorem tertii* does not create rights or obligations for a third party (Direct) with respect to the creditor (Holdings).[80] This would prevent Direct from requiring Holdings to make a claim against Digital Age. The obligation to pursue a claim may result from a different legal relationship between the creditor and the third party[81] (*stosunek waluty* or other contractual relationship).

III. Meta-Legal Formants

The provision analysed above (Art. 393 PCC) is designed to respond to the need to simplify legal transactions by eliminating the need to satisfy benefits cascading between related persons associated through various obligatory relationships

---

78 See, further, A. Kubas, *Umowa na rzecz osoby trzeciej*, Warsaw/Cracow 1976, p. 123; M. Kaliński, *Szkoda na mieniu i jej naprawienie*, Warsaw 2014, p. 86; P. Machnikowski in E. Gniewek and P. Machnikowski (eds), *Kodeks cywilny. Komentarz*, Warsaw 2014, p. 777; A. Olejniczak in A. Kidyba (ed), *Kodeks cywilny. Komentarz. Tom III. Zobowiązania – część ogólna*, Warsaw 2014, p. 319; A. Kubas in K. Osajda (ed), *System prawa prywatnego. Tom 5. Prawo zobowiązań – część ogólna*, Warsaw 2020, p. 1188. To some extent differently, see P. Zakrzewski in M. Habdas and M. Fras (eds), *Kodeks cywilny. Komentarz. Tom III. Zobowiązania. Część ogólna (art. 353–534)*, Warsaw 2018, p. 306 (a claim for non-performance is due only to the creditor, not to a third party).

79 A. Kubas, *Umowa na rzecz osoby trzeciej*, Warsaw/Cracow 1976, p. 124.

80 See the judgments of the SN of 31.01.2003, IV CKN 1716/00 and 15.05.2015, V CSK 491/14, OSNC-ZD 2016/4/62.

81 F. Błahuta in Z. Resich (ed), *Kodeks cywilny. Komentarz. Tom 2*, Warsaw 1972, p. 937.

(that is, by a debtor to a creditor, and by a creditor to a third party). This leads to the cancellation of the two obligations arising from these relationships (between the debtor and creditor, as well as between the creditor and third party) due to one direct provision of the debtor towards a third party, while still satisfying the interests of both the creditor and third party.[82]

2.10. SCOTLAND

Lorna MacFarlane

I. *Operative Rules*

1. Direct *can* take action against Digital Age for breach of contract (on the basis that a revocable *jus quaesitum tertio* is enforceable).
   Variation: Direct *cannot* take action against Digital Age for breach of contract (on the basis that a revocable *jus quaesitum tertio* is not enforceable).
2. Direct *cannot* force Holdings to raise proceedings against Digital Age to recover Direct's losses.

II. *Descriptive Formants*

It is possible to confer an enforceable 'third-party right' in Scots law, in accordance with the Contract (Third Party Rights) (Scotland) Act 2017 ('the Act'). The Act came into force on 26 February 2018. As the contract between Holdings and Digital Age was presumably concluded on or before 1 February 2016, the contract is subject to the common law which predates the Act.

Scots law has a long tradition of upholding third-party rights. The historic third-party right, known as a *jus quaesitum tertio*,[83] was recognised from at least the sixteenth century.[84] The contracting parties were referred to as the debtor and the stipulator (the former is responsible for rendering performance to the

82 See the judgments of the SN of 29.06.2012, I CSK 606/11 and 05.06.2014, IV CSK 585/13.

83 W.W. McBryde, *The Law of Contract in Scotland*, 3rd ed. (Thomson/W. Green, Edinburgh 2007), para. 10-01. The term '*jus quaesitum tertio*' means 'the third party has acquired a right', and the Scottish Law Commission has suggested that the term was adopted by Stair due to the influence of civilian jurisprudence: Scottish Law Commission, *Memorandum on Constitution and Proof of Voluntary Obligations: Stipulations in Favour of Third Parties* (Memorandum No. 38, March 1977), p. 2.

84 See e.g. *Wood v. Moncur* (1591) Mor. 7719 at 7719; *Renton v. Ayton* (1634) Mor. 7721; *Supplicants v. Nimmo* (1627) Mor. 7740. In commentary, see T. Hope, *Major Practicks* (Neill & Co, Edinburgh 1608–33), para. 2.3.37; J. Erskine, *An Institute of the Law of Scotland*, 8th ed. (Law Society of Scotland/Butterworths, Edinburgh 1871), para. 3.1.8; and J.D. Stair, *The Institutions of the Law of Scotland*, 3rd ed. (G. Hamilton and J. Balfour, Edinburgh 1759), para. 1.10.5.

third party), and the third party was known as the *tertius*. The benefit conferred on a *tertius* can take the form of a monetary right, the transfer of property or the rendering of services.[85]

In terms of formation requirements, a *jus quaesitum tertio* requires that the benefit to the *tertius* derives from a contract between the contracting parties,[86] and that the parties (expressly or impliedly) intended to benefit the *tertius*.[87] It is clear that Holdings and Digital Age have concluded a contract expressing their intention to confer a benefit of IT services on Direct.

Further, in order to confer an enforceable right on the third party, the document containing the *jus quaesitum tertio* must be delivered to the *tertius*, or there must be an equivalent action on the part of the contracting parties.[88] In case law, intimation to the *tertius* has been found to be a functional equivalent of delivery.[89] It is assumed that Direct have been informed of the contract between Holdings and Digital Age, as they are aware of the IT services.

The historic law permitted *tertii* to be identified as a member of a class of beneficiaries.[90] In *Kelly v. Cornhill Insurance Co*,[91] for example, it was found that a motor-vehicle insurer did not need to know exactly who would receive payments under the policy: it was sufficient to define the class of *tertii* as any party who drove the car with the permission of the policyholder. In the present case, the fact that Holdings can amend the schedule to the contract does not impact on the validity of the *jus quaesitum tertio*. The class of beneficiaries can be defined as those set out in the schedule.

It was also clear in the historic law that the *tertius* need not be in existence when the contract was concluded.[92] As such, it would be inconsequential if the contract had been finalised prior to the incorporation of Direct, or if Direct had been added to the schedule after the formation of the contract between Holdings and Digital Age.

---

85 W.W. McBryde, *The Law of Contract in Scotland*, 3rd ed. (Thomson/W. Green, Edinburgh 2007), paras. 10-03 and 10-04 (Scots law).

86 *Hislop v. MacRitchie's Trs* 1881 8 R (HL) 95 at 102 per Lord Watson. Lord President Dunedin said, in *Nicholson v. Glasgow Blind Asylum* 1991 SC 391 at 400, that *Hislop* 'settled that the title of a *tertius* … depends upon an agreement between the parties to the contract'. See also D.M. Walker, *The Law of Contracts and Related Obligations in Scotland*, 3rd ed. (T & T Clark, London 1995), para. 29.11; W.W. McBryde, *The Law of Contract in Scotland*, 3rd ed. (Thomson/W. Green, Edinburgh 2007), para. 10-09.

87 *Finnie v. Glasgow and South-Western Railway Co.* (1857) 20 D (HL) 2 at 4 per Lord Cranworth.

88 *Ogilvie and Grant v. Ker* (1664) Mor. 7740 at 7741; *Allan's Trs v. Lord Advocate* 1971 SC (HL) 45 at 55 per Lord Reid.

89 *Burr v. Bo'ness Comrs* (1896) 24 R 148.

90 E.g. *Wood v. Moncur* (1591) Mor. 7719 (in which the class was constituted by tenants) and *Love v. Amalgamated Society of Lithographic Printers of Great Britain and Ireland* 1912 SC 1078 (in which the class was defined as dependents of members of a society).

91 *Kelly v. Cornhill Insurance Co.* 1964 SC (HL) 46.

92 *Auchmoutie v. Hay* (1609) Mor. 12126; *Morton's Trustees v. Aged Christian Friend Society of Scotland* (1899) 2 F 82.

Prior to the enactment of the Act, there was academic and judicial disagreement as to whether a *jus quaesitum tertio* must necessarily be irrevocable.[93] Stair, one of Scots law's institutional writers,[94] stated that:

> when parties contract, if there be any article in favour of a third party, at any time, *est jus quaesitum tertio*, which cannot be recalled by either or both of them to exhibit the contract, and thereupon the obliged may be compelled to perform.[95]

Some interpreted this to mean that irrevocability was a requirement of a valid *jus quaesitum tertio*.[96] Others, however, asserted that the contracting parties cannot revoke a *jus quaesitum tertio* once the third party has become aware of it or acted in reliance of it, but that the right can otherwise be revoked.[97]

In this case, Holdings can add, remove or replace any company in the schedule, on providing written notice to Digital Age. Any right conferred on Direct is, therefore, revocable. On the assumption that the latter category of commentators mentioned above are correct, it appears that Holdings and Digital Age have conferred an enforceable *jus quaesitum tertio* on Direct. *Tertii* are permitted to claim damages in respect of defective performance of a *jus quaesitum tertio* conferred upon them.[98] Direct can, therefore, take action against Digital Age for breach of contract in respect of the lost sales.

However, it cannot be said with certainty that a revocable third-party right would be upheld. The Scottish Law Commission acknowledged that the then current law on the revocability of third-party rights was considered inadequate, but thought it necessary to expressly provide for the abolition of any law providing that third-party rights must be made irrevocable, in their recent reforms of the *jus quaesitum tertio*.[99] Accordingly, it is possible that Direct would not be entitled to enforce the contract against Digital Age.

---

93 For an overview of the commentary, see M. Hogg, *Promises and Contract Law: Comparative Perspectives* (CUP, Cambridge 2011), p. 205.

94 The institutional writers were Scots legal commentators whose writings are considered to be a primary source of Scots law. See, further, A. Rahmatian, 'The role of institutional writers in Scots law' (2018) 1 *Juridical Review* 42.

95 J.D. Stair, *The Institutions of the Law of Scotland*, 3rd ed. (G. Hamilton and J. Balfour, Edinburgh 1759), para. 1.10.5.

96 *Carmichael v. Carmichael's Executrix* 1920 SC (HL) 195 at 200 per Lord Dunedin; J.T. Cameron, '*Jus Quaesitum Tertio*: The True Meaning of Stair I.x.5' (1961) *Juridical Review* 103, 118.

97 W.M. Gloag, *The Law of Contract: A Treatise on the Principles of Contract in the Law of Scotland*, 2nd ed. (W. Green, Edinburgh 1929), p. 242; D.M. Walker, *The Law of Contracts and Related Obligations in Scotland*, 3rd ed. (T & T Clark, London 1995), para. 29.13; D.N. MacCormick, '*Jus Quaesitum Tertio: Stair v. Dunedin*' (1970) *Juridical Review* 228.

98 *Scott Lithgow v. GEC Electrical Projects Ltd* 1989 SC 412 at 438 per Lord Clyde; *Blumer & Co v. Scott & Sons* (1874) 1 R 379. See also W.W. McBryde, *The Law of Contract in Scotland*, 3rd ed. (Thomson/W. Green, Edinburgh 2007), para. 10-24.

99 Scottish Law Commission, *Report on Third Party Rights* (Scot Law Com No. 245, 2016), para. 5.5.

There is no authority in the historic law which requires the stipulator to bring an action against the debtor on behalf of the *tertius*. In the event that Direct are the recipients of a *jus quaesitum tertio*, they cannot force Holdings to raise an action against Digital Age to recover their losses.

III. Meta-Legal Formants

As mentioned above, Scots law now recognises a statutory third-party right. The terminology has been modernised: the legislation refers to the 'contracting parties' and the 'third party'.[100]

The formation requirements of the new third-party right largely mirror the previous law. The Act provides that a third-party right arises where the contracting parties intend to confer an enforceable benefit on a third party, and a contractual term specifies that at least one of the contracting parties will do or not do something for the third party's benefit.[101] The contracting parties' intention to confer an enforceable benefit upon the third party can be express or implied.[102] The 'person who is to acquire a third-party right under a contract must be identifiable from the contract by being either named or described in it'.[103] The Act further provides that a third-party right can be acquired by a party who, at the time the contract was constituted, 'did not fall within the description of persons (if any) whom the contracting parties intended should benefit from, and be legally entitled to enforce or otherwise invoke, the undertaking'.[104] This means that, as in the previous law, the third-party right can be conferred on members of a 'class' of beneficiaries, and the scope of members of this class can fluctuate over time. Furthermore, the third party need not be in existence at the point at which the third-party right was created.[105]

However, the Act has clarified the law relating to the revocability of third-party rights. Subject to contrary provision in the contract, the right cannot be revoked or modified where the third party relies on their right and their reliance has affected their position to a material extent, where either the contracting parties acquiesced in the third party's reliance or could reasonably have foreseen that the third party would rely on the contractual undertaking.[106] It is otherwise permissible for the contracting parties to revoke or modify the third party's right.[107]

---

100 Ibid., para. 3.6.
101 Contract (Third Party Rights) (Scotland) Act 2017, s. 1(1)(a)–(b).
102 Ibid., s. 2(3).
103 Ibid., s. 1(3).
104 Ibid., s. 1(4)(b).
105 Ibid., s. 1(4)(a).
106 Ibid., s. 6(1) and (3).
107 Ibid., s. 3(1).

If the present case were to be determined in accordance with the Act, the validity of the third-party right would not be affected by the fact that Holdings can remove Direct from the schedule, nor by Holdings' ability to alter the number of companies benefited in the Schedule. Direct could raise an action for breach of their third-party right, seeking 'any remedy for breach which a contracting party would be entitled to be the undertaking one in favour of the contracting party'.[108] This means that Direct could raise an action for damages for breach of contract even if Holdings do not wish to do so themselves. This is subject to any contrary term in the contract.[109] Thus, provided that Holdings and Digital Age have not restricted third-party claims, or capped liability at a certain amount, Direct would be able to make a claim for the full €10 million.

The Act does not provide, however, that a third party can compel the party not bound to perform in its favour to raise an action on its behalf, although it does not prevent that contracting party from raising proceedings to enforce the third-party right. The Scottish Law Commission noted that the third party and the contracting parties may have concurrent rights, and did not consider that express provision was required to enable the contracting party to enforce any term of the contract (including the third-party right).[110] However, these issues have not been subject to judicial discussion.

In terms of policy considerations, the Scottish Law Commission noted that recognition of third-party rights upholds the 'fundamental' principle of recognising the intentions of contracting parties.[111] Third-party rights are of particular importance in the insurance industry,[112] and are also found in the context of partnership agreements for the benefit of a third person, contracts made by municipalities for the benefit of inhabitants, indemnification terms in construction contracts, and collective labour agreements.[113] Third-party rights thus reflect a policy objective of a commercially efficient means of contracting.

In considering reform of the *jus quaesitum tertio*, the Scottish Law Commission emphasised the practical and commercial importance of permitting

---

108 Ibid., s. 7(2).

109 Ibid., s. 7(3).

110 Scottish Law Commission, *Report on Third Party Rights* (Scot Law Com No. 245, 2016), paras. 6.52–6.54.

111 Scottish Law Commission, *Discussion Paper on Third Party Rights in Contract* (Scot Law Com DP No. 157, 2014), para. 2.15. See also P. Sutherland, 'Third-Party Contracts' in H. MacQueen and R. Zimmermann (eds), *European Contract Law: Scots and South African Perspectives* (Edinburgh University Press, Edinburgh 2006), p. 201 at p. 205.

112 H.L. MacQueen, *The Laws of Scotland: Stair Memorial Encyclopaedia: Obligations: Contract*, vol. 15 (LexisNexis/Law Society of Scotland, London/Edinburgh 1995), para. 841.

113 Scottish Law Commission, *Report on Third Party Rights* (Scot Law Com No. 245, 2016), para. 1.13. This list is not exhaustive.

third parties to be recognised as members of a class of beneficiaries, identifying that this mechanism may be used in the context of company groups, 'where the contracting company wishes to confer rights upon other companies in the group, some of which may not yet exist, or to achieve the settlement of a claim against it which may also involve other group members'.[114]

As noted above, there was a lack of consensus among judges and commentators as to whether a *jus quaesitum tertio* had to be irrevocable.[115] Practitioners were critical of the law and viewed the Scots third-party right as inflexible.[116] This was a 'central issue'[117] in the Scottish Law Commission's *Report on Third Party Rights*,[118] and the Act has clarified that revocable third-party rights are permissible.

The Scottish Law Commission noted that allowing the third party to sue in its own name without involving any contracting parties (other than that which it wishes to sue) is 'significantly more convenient and efficient than requiring that one or more of the contracting parties sue alongside the third party'.[119] There is a lack of policy discussion in Scots law on why the third party cannot force the contracting party not due to perform in its favour to raise proceedings on its behalf. However, it may be possible to draw a parallel between this aspect of the Scots third-party right and section 9 of the Act, which provides that the third party is to be treated as party to any arbitration agreement mentioned in the contract, such that they may be required to engage in arbitration to enforce the right. The benefit of the third-party right is treated as conditional on the requirement to participate in the arbitration.[120] Similarly, it could be said that the right is conditional on the third party's acceptance that it may need to raise proceedings against the party in breach if it wishes to enforce the right.

---

114 Ibid., para. 4.4.

115 See *Carmichael v. Carmichael's Executrix* 1920 SC (HL) 195 at 200 per Lord Dunedin; J.T. Cameron, '*Jus Quaesitum Tertio*: The True Meaning of Stair I.x.5' (1961) *Juridical Review* 103, 118. Opposing views, according to which a third-party right need not be irrevocable, include M. Hogg, *Promises and Contract Law: Comparative Perspectives* (CUP, Cambridge 2011), pp. 305–06; D.N. MacCormick, '*Jus Quaesitum Tertio*: *Stair v. Dunedin*' (1970) *Juridical Review* 228, 236–41; and W.M. Gloag, *The Law of Contract: A Treatise on the Principles of Contract in the Law of Scotland*, 2nd ed. (W. Green, Edinburgh 1929), p. 242.

116 Scottish Law Commission, *Discussion Paper on Third Party Rights in Contract* (Scot Law Com DP No. 157, 2014), ch. 3; Scottish Law Commission, *Report on Third Party Rights* (Scot Law Com No. 245, 2016), ch. 5.

117 Scottish Law Commission, *Report on Third Party Rights* (Scot Law Com No. 245, 2016), para. 2.16.

118 Scottish Law Commission, *Report on Third Party Rights* (Scot Law Com No. 245, 2016).

119 Ibid., para. 6.55.

120 Ibid., paras 7.5–7.6.

2.11. SLOVAKIA

Kristián Csach, Monika Jurčová, Peter Mészáros and Veronika Zoričáková

I. Operative Rules

1. Direct are the determined person to accept the performance, and the place of performance, but not a party to the contract. Direct cannot raise any proceedings against Digital Age for breach of contract. Tortious claims are not excluded in general.
2. Direct are not able to force Holdings to raise proceedings against Digital Age, but might be able to claim compensation based on breach of contract (between Direct and Holdings) or breach of the shareholder's corporate loyalty.

II. Descriptive Formants

Regarding question 1, no contract in favour of third parties has been entered into between Holdings and Digital Age, given the facts of the case. The companies within the Sell Co Group are only denominated persons to whom the performance is provided (and also the defined place of performance). From the facts provided, the intention of the parties was not to create an obligation between Digital Age and Direct. The theory of contracts for the benefit of third parties is underdeveloped in Slovak legal doctrine, and case law is scarce. The law draws a difference between a contract for the benefit of third parties (ss. 289–92 of the Slovak Commercial Code (SCommC)) and the designation of a person (s. 333 SCommC) to whom the performance is to be addressed, or a place of performance (s. 335 SCommC). The distinguishing factor is the intention of the parties to create a separate title of the third party to require performance. Unless such intention is proven, the denomination of a third party to whom the contract is to be performed is not sufficient for a contract for the benefit of a third party.[121]

This is evidenced in the present case by the fact that Holdings were only responsible for the identification of the place of performance, and for the persons to whom the performance was to be provided. In addition, Digital Age could not object to the amendment of these places of performance. This is also an indication that there was no contract in favour of a third party.

[121] See the decision of the second-instance court, Regional Court in Žilina, file no. 6 Co 587/2014 dated 25.03.2015 (reviewed by the Constitutional Court in the case file no. II. ÚS 862/2016 dated 16.11.2016).

Regarding question 2, the physical performance of Digital Age requires Direct's consent (allowing Digital Age entry to their premises or digital infrastructure for the performance of the contract). The consent enables Digital Age to perform their part of the obligation (towards Holdings), but also is directed towards Holdings, allowing them to arrange the IT services for Direct. Accordingly, the consent represents the (albeit implicit) contractual arrangement between Direct and Holdings. This contract (due to its gratuitous arrangement) could be construed as a *'príkazná zmluva'* (agency contract) governed by civil law, which obliges the agent to perform with the same level of care as in their own affairs. This might provide a basis for a contractual obligation, between Holdings and Direct, not to cause harm to Direct through the performance of the third party (Digital Age). We have assumed here that consent for the activity had been given by Direct. Otherwise, Holdings would be liable based on rules of *negotiorum gestio* for any damage caused by the intervention (s. 744 SCC), as Digital Age would have intervened in Direct's affairs without their consent. In general, Holdings would be liable for the intervention into Direct's affairs, as Digital Age were performing their contract following the commands of Holdings.[122] However, it is highly disputable whether Direct's consent would be sufficient to establish a direct relation between Direct and Digital Age. Given the facts of the case, we tend towards the conclusion that there was no will between Digital Age and Direct to enter into a legally binding relationship with each other (given the agreement on the renumeration, and the fact that it was Holdings who agreed the contract and chose Digital Age as their contractual partner).

From a corporate point of view, bearing in mind that there is a lack of regulation on groups of companies, the shareholder (Holdings) nevertheless has at least a corporate duty of loyalty, comprising the duty not to intentionally harm the company (Direct) without legitimate grounds.[123] The acceptance of faulty IT services harming the subsidiary might be considered a breach of corporate loyalty of a shareholder (Holdings) against the company (Direct). Direct may

---

122 The identification of the person responsible for the tort or *negotiorum gestio* when an agent acts under the command of another person is highly disputed. See V. Trojčáková, 'Pričítanie škody spôsobenej pomocníkom; Zodpovednosť na pomedzí porušenia zmluvnej povinnosti a deliktu [Attribution of damage caused by the assisting person, between contractual and tortious liability]' in Z. Nevolná and D. Hlobíková (eds), *Porušenie zmluvných povinností v súkromnom práve a jeho následky*, Trnava: Právnická fakulta Trnavskej univerzity v Trnave, 2018, pp. 154–78.

123 The duty of corporate loyalty of a shareholder is not elaborated either in Slovak corporate case law or in legal writing. For a particular analysis of the corporate loyalty of a shareholder in the joint-stock company, see M. Patakyová in M. Patakyová et al., *Obchodný zákonník. Komentár [Commentary on Commercial Code]*, 4th ed., Praha: C.H. Beck, 2013, pp. 698, 710. For a general corporate loyalty, see K. Csach in O. Ovečková et al., *Obchodný zákonník. Veľký komentár, vol. I [Commentary on Commercial Code I]*, Bratislava: Wolters Kluwer, 2017, pp. 380 ff.

claim not only financial compensation for the breach of loyalty (causing harm to Direct) but also restitution in kind (reparation into the previous state), and thereby only indirectly force Holdings to demand restitution from Digital Age.

III. Meta-Legal Formants

Moreover, it is far from clear whether, under circumstances such as those in this case, a contract for the benefit of a third party who is not clearly identified, and might be subject to change, is valid. According to the authors of commentaries, the third party does not need to be identified, but must be identifiable by objective criteria.[124] Fekete speaks out in favour of the validity of a contract for the benefit of a third person even if that third person is to be ascertained by the creditor.[125] We would assume that the position requiring sufficient identification of a third party through objective criteria is prevalent, as it reflects the judgment of the Czech Supreme Court[126] (given that Czech Supreme Court decisions have a high informal authority in Slovak case law).

2.12. SPAIN

Carles Vendrell Cervantes

I. Operative Rules

1. Direct *would be entitled* to take action against Digital Age for breach of contract.
2. Direct *would not be able* to force Holdings to bring proceedings against Digital Age to recover Direct's losses.

II. Descriptive Formants

Question 1

Under Spanish law, as established in Article 1257 I of the Spanish Civil Code, contracts are only binding between the parties who execute them. However, Article 1257 II of the Civil Code establishes that, 'if the contract includes an

124 See R. Dobrovodský in M. Števček, A. Dulak, J. Bajánková, M. Fečík, F. Sedlačko, M. Tomašovič et al., *Občiansky zákonník I, sect. 1–450. Komentár [Commentary on Civil Code I, ss. 1–450]*, Prague: C.H. Beck, 2015, p. 425.

125 I. Fekete, *Občiansky zákonník, Komentár [Commentary on Civil Code I], sect. 1–sect. 122*, Bratislava: Eurokódex, 2017, p. 757.

126 Judgment of the Czech Supreme Court file no. 22 Cdo 2643/99 dated 13.02.2001.

agreement to confer a right in favour of a third party, the latter may demand the enforcement of the agreement if the third party should have made known its acceptance to the obligor before it is revoked'.

In this regard, the Spanish Supreme Court, in decision no. 708/2002 of 8 July 2017, has established that 'the third party is entitled to demand the enforceability of the contractual clause established in his favour if he accepted it and made that acceptance known to the liable party'. The acceptance can be tacit, as interpreted by the Spanish Supreme Court in several decisions (for example, Judgment of 6 March 1989), and can be given through inaction or through words. On the basis of the case law, which is not conclusive or recent, the prevailing legal literature has added that, in fact, acceptance by the third party is not a requirement *(conditio iuris)* of the existence of the right in favour of that third party.[127]

Under Spanish law, the contract between Holdings and Digital Age clearly contains a 'stipulation in favour of a third party' (i.e. regarding the provision of IT services). Consequently, these third parties (inter alia, Direct) obtain the right to claim for the enforcement of the stipulation established in their favour. If a party has a right to enforce a contractual obligation, it is clear that they will also have remedies for breach of contract.

The fact that Direct have been included in the schedule, and that Holdings have the right to so include them, is enough to conclude that Direct were expressly identified when executing the contract. In any event, under Spanish law, the third party need not be identified at the time the agreement is concluded.[128]

Given the stated facts of the case, it is likely to be considered, under Spanish law, that Direct accepted the clause, and that this acceptance was communicated to Digital Age (as required by Article 1257 II of the Civil Code). Two main reasons support this conclusion: (1) Direct are a company belonging to the Sell Co Group, Holdings being the parent company of this group and the contracting party which decided to include Direct as an entitled third party in the contract. Thus, Direct were aware, or should reasonably have been aware, of the contract and/or the schedule (in truth, Direct were clearly aware of the fact that Digital Age have been providing IT services to them); furthermore, Direct did not reject the right; (2) as indicated in legal literature, acceptance is not a requirement of the acquisition of the third-party right, but only a way to avoid, under general

127 Á. Carrasco, *Derecho de contratos* (3rd ed., Thomson-Aranzadi, 2021), 682; A.M. Morillo, 'El contrato o estipulación a favor de tercero a la luz del Derecho comparado y del moderno Derecho de contratos', *Anuario de Derecho Civil*, 2020, 586–87.

128 Judgment of Supreme Court, 14 April 1986 (RJ 1986/1849). A.M. Morillo, 'El contrato o estipulación a favor de tercero a la luz del Derecho comparado y del moderno Derecho de contratos', *Anuario de Derecho Civil*, 2020, 579.

circumstances, the parties to the contract revoking the third party's right.[129] However, in the given case, it is clear that Direct's acceptance will not remove Holdings' right to remove Direct's position in the contract and, therefore, revoke Direct's right, as the contract provided that Holdings can add to, remove or replace any company in the schedule, on giving written notice to Digital Age.

Consequently, the critical question, as indicated by the Supreme Court,[130] is whether the right of the third party (in this case, Direct) was revoked before that right was claimed. As this is not the case here, Direct have the right to take action against Digital Age for breach of contract.

Question 2

As indicated above, a third party (such as Direct), in favour of whom a third-party right in contract has been established, has the right to bring proceedings against the debtor of the contract, if that debtor did not perform adequately. There is, however, no general rule under Spanish law that would grant Direct the right to force Holdings to bring proceedings. This kind of right is only established under Spanish law in specific sectors, such as under the Patent Law[131] (Article 117.3) as regards licensees of patent rights. Licensees do not have standing to sue, but are entitled to request the patent-holder to bring actions against the infringer. In the event that the patent-holder does not do so, licensees would then be entitled to bring such actions.

III. Meta-Legal Formants

As indicated above, the requirement, established by Article 1257 of the Civil Code, that the third party needs to accept (expressly or tacitly) its right under the contract, and communicate this acceptance to the obligor, has been interpreted by case law in a very broad and flexible way. According to this case law, the third party acquires the right before that requirement is fulfilled.

This is the reason why an amendment of the Spanish Civil Code was suggested in the 2009 Bill of Amendment of the Spanish Civil Code regarding the Law of Obligations and Contracts. Specifically, the suggested new provision concerning the contractual right in favour of a third party clarified, in line with the indicated case law, that the third party acquires the right immediately (unless otherwise provided in the contract), but that the right may be revoked before the third party has communicated its acceptance to the parties of the contract.

---

129 Á. Carrasco, *Derecho de contratos* (3rd ed., Thomson-Aranzadi, 2021), 682.
130 Judgment of Supreme Court, 7 July 1976 (RJ 1976/3441).
131 Law 24/2015, of 24 July, on Patents.

2.13. SWEDEN

Oskar Mossberg

I. Operative Rules

1. Direct would *not be able* to take action against Digital Age for breach of contract. Direct would *probably not be able* to claim damages on any other basis. (In principle, Holdings would be able to take action against Digital Age, but Digital Age's likely objection to such an action, that Holdings has not itself suffered any damages, would likely be successful.)
2. Direct would *not be able* to force Holdings to raise proceedings against Digital Age to recover Direct's losses.

II. Descriptive Formants

Regarding question 1, a fundamental principle of Swedish contract law is '*principen om avtals subjektiva begränsningar*' (the principle of the subjective limitations of contracts). According to this principle, which is not found in statutory law, the legal effects of contracts are limited to the spheres of the parties. This means that, as a general rule, contracts do not have third-party effects. Swedish contract law is, to a large extent, uncodified and based on general principles, analogies and case law. The current principle is an uncodified '*allmän obligationsrättslig princip*' (general principle of the law of obligations), which can be invoked directly as a source of law. It has been invoked in several Supreme Court cases – some similar to the present one. These include NJA 1997 p. 44 and NJA 2001 p. 711.[132] In the 1997 case, the Swedish Supreme Court (Högsta domstolen (HD)) held that (translated as literally as possible):

> The general rule in Swedish law is that a contractual relationship binds a party only towards his direct co-contractor, not against his co-contractor's co-contractor. In accordance herewith, liability can in principle only be invoked between the direct contractual parties in a contractual relationship.[133]

---

132 Since 1874, Swedish Supreme Court (Högsta domstolen (HD)) cases have been collected in the quasi-official (government funded, but privately owned and operated) 'Nytt juridiskt arkiv' (New Legal Archive), abbreviated 'NJA'. Cases are referenced by annual volume and the page on which they start, and are only published in Swedish. All translations are the author's own.

133 In the original Swedish: '*Den allmänna regeln i svensk rätt är att ett kontraktsförhållande binder part endast gentemot sin direkte medkontrahent, inte gentemot sin medkontrahents medkontrahent. I enlighet härmed kan i princip ansvar göras gällande endast mellan de direkta avtalsparterna i ett kontraktsrättsligt förhållande.*'

As there is no contract directly between Direct and Digital Age, Direct would be unable to raise a contractual claim against Digital Age. Therefore, Direct would not be able to take action for breach of contract, which is by definition a contractual claim, according to Swedish law.

There are exceptions to this general rule. Given the circumstances of the case, the most feasible one would be to construct[134] the contract between Holdings and Digital Age as a *'tredjemansavtal'* (third-party contract or, literally, 'third man's contract'). By entering into such a contract, the parties can give a third party a right to independently claim performance from them. This follows from uncodified general contractual principles. There are many relevant examples in case law, notably NJA 1956 p. 209, NJA 2005 p. 142 and NJA 2013 p. 491. In 2005, the HD wrote:

> ([T]he rules about third party contracts) entail that a contract between two parties can immediately entitle a third party, if this is apparent from the contract or according to standard rules of interpretation can be considered to be what the parties intended. According to practice, evidence is required that the parties intended that the third party shall be given such a right and thus, without being party to the contract, be able to invoke it against the obliged (party).[135]

The third party's rights thus hinge on contractual interpretation, to be performed on the basis of evidence supplied by the person bearing the burden of proof, which would, in cases like the present one, be the third party.[136] (In procedural terms, *'partsavsikt'* (party intent) is regarded as a question of fact, meaning that it is something that can and needs to be proven.) Pursuant to case law, and most

134 The word construction is here used in a wide sense, covering both the process of interpreting the wording and understanding the contents of a contract (*tolkning*) and the process of supplementing a contract that has been understood to be incomplete (*utfyllning*). In theory, the distinction is operative in Swedish contract law (see generally e.g. E. Runesson, 'Construction of Commercial Contracts in Nordic Law and The Role of Prudence' in *The Nordic Contracts Act: Essays in Celebration of its One Hundredth Anniversary*, Djøf Publishing, Copenhagen 2015, pp. 217–27). However, in practice, courts often express themselves ambiguously or in ways that make it difficult or impossible to discern whether the construction of a contract involved only interpretation in the narrow sense (*tolkning*) or if it also included supplementation (*utfyllning*).

135 In the original Swedish, *'reglerna om tredjemansavtal. Dessa innebär att ett avtal mellan två parter kan omedelbart berättiga en tredje man, om detta framgår av avtalet eller enligt vanliga tolkningsregler kan anses vara vad parterna åsyftat. Enligt praxis krävs bevis om att parterna avsett att tredjemannen skall erhålla en sådan rätt och således, utan att vara part i avtalet, kunna åberopa det mot den förpliktade.'*

136 This follows from NJA 2005 p. 142. See e.g. R. Nordh, 'Bevisbörda och beviskrav i tvistemål', *Svensk juristtidning* 2012, pp. 781–99, pp. 794 ff. or O. Mossberg, *Avtalets räckvidd I: Om avtals tredjemansverkningar, särskilt vid tredjemansavtal och direktkrav*, Iustus, Uppsala 2020, pp. 459 ff.

notably the cases NJA 2013 p. 491 and NJA 2005 p. 142, the criteria for a third-party contract are twofold: (1) the parties should intend to give the third party a right; and (2) the parties should intend this right to be exercised independently.

Given the circumstances, it seems unlikely that Direct would be able to supply adequate evidence that Holdings and Digital Age had a relevant '*tredjemansberättigande avsikt*' (intention to entitle a third party) at contract formation. Provided that all the facts of the case are known (=proven), the question depends on how these facts are judged. Swedish case law differs on how much proof of intention is required. In some cases, the demands have been quite low;[137] in others, considerably higher.[138] Other than the fact that Digital Age is supposed to in fact supply IT support to Direct, there is nothing that seems to suggest that Direct was ever intended to be able to demand such support independently of Holdings (the second part (2) of the aforementioned criteria). In particular, the fact that the IT services were intended to be supplied in accordance with a schedule exclusively controlled by Holdings seems to contradict the existence of a relevant intention of the parties to the contract (i.e. Holdings and Digital Age) that Direct should be able to exercise any rights under the contract independently.

The circumstances thus suggest that any contractual breach would only be considered to have occurred in relation to Holdings – not against Direct, which would, thus, not be able to take action for breach of contract on the basis of a '*tredjemansavtal*'. As Holdings is party to the contract, Holdings would (in principle, had the company wanted to) be able to take action against Digital Age for the breach of contract. However, Digital Age could then object that Holdings has not itself suffered any loss. Swedish law does not have a developed doctrine of transferred loss, and for Holdings' action to be successful, Holdings would need to prove it had suffered losses ('*skada*' (harm)) of their own. Direct would not have any action against Holdings, should Holdings fail to enforce the contract with Digital Age (see Case 2 below). Holdings would, therefore, likely be considered not to have suffered any relevant losses (of their own), and thus Digital Age's objection about not having harmed the contracting party would likely hold, thereby barring '*skadestånd*' (damages) as a contractual remedy. This legal position indirectly enforces the aforementioned general rule of the Swedish law of obligation – the principle of the subjective limitations of contracts.

---

137 E.g. NJA 1995 p. 197, NJA 1996 p. 400 and NJA 2000 p. 48, where the HD, on the basis of meagre evidence, found that '*tredjemansavtal*' existed. These holdings have been regarded as entailing '*fiktiva tredjemansavtal*' (fictious third-party contracts), due to a perceived lack of evidence of party intent. See also NJA 2010 p. 559 (where the court constructed a presumptive rule of interpretation, the application of which meant that a contract concerning the licensing of copyright was given effect in favour of a third party, meaning that the third party could make copies without copyright infringement) and Case 3 below on NJA 2007 p. 758 and NJA 2010 p. 629.

138 E.g. NJA 2005 p. 142.

There are other exceptions to the general rule. An important group of exceptions is found under the heading *'direktkrav'* (direct claims/actions). These concern statutory or case law-based actions of a *sui generis* kind, according to which a person can demand performance from their co-contractor's co-contractor (see the passage from NJA 1997 p. 44, quoted above). However, there is no established exception directly applicable in the present case. The future development of further exceptions, including one applicable to the present case, is not unthinkable, but there is no real *de lege lata* support for a direct claim in the present situation.

Without a contractually based claim of some kind, Direct will not be able to take action for breach of contract or claim damages from Digital Age, as the non-contractual rules concerning pure economic loss normally require the damages to be the result of a criminal act (see Case 9 below).

Regarding question 2, there is no rule or principle according to which companies can force their parent companies to raise proceedings against the parent companies' contractual counterparties.

III. *Meta-Legal Formants*

The notion that contracts have effects only for the parties has been called a historically transmitted dogma.[139] In Swedish legal consciousness, it is tied up with ideas of individual autonomy (this is, to some extent, illustrated by the fact that the parties-only principle has a kindred principle called *'självbindningens princip'* (the principle of binding oneself), the effect of which is to explain why an 'agent' not authorised by the principal cannot effectively act on behalf of the principal).

The main current rationale for the privity principle, quoted by the HD in NJA 1997 p. 44, is that it 'furthers clarity in the legal relations if one and all stick to their co-contractor'.[140] Another prevalent argument is that the principle supports the main rule in insolvency proceedings, according to which creditors are treated equally in the sense that they all receive dividends in proportion to their respective claims, following Articles 1 and 18 of Förmånsrättslagen (1970:979)[141] (the Act on Advantageous Rights). If contracts were more

---

[139] See e.g. K. Grönfors, *Avtalsgrundande rättsfakta*, Nerénius och Santerus förlag, Stockholm 2013, pp. 129 ff.

[140] In Swedish: *'Argumentet för huvudregeln är att det befordrar klarheten i rättsförhållandena att var och en håller sig till sin medkontrahent.'*

[141] This is the official way of referencing Swedish legislation. First, the year (1970) the law was enacted is given, followed by its number (979) in the Swedish Code of Statutes (*Svensk författningssamling*, SFS), the official and authentic version of Acts, Ordinances, and certain government regulations.

regularly given third-party effects, creditors entitled by these contracts (A) could bypass their insolvent debtors (B) and demand performance directly from the debtor's debtor (C), circumventing the insolvency proceedings (regarding B).[142] Restrictiveness in allowing third-party contracts is, thus, a way of upholding the *'princip om borgenärernas lika rätt i konkurs'* (principle of equal treatment of the creditors in bankruptcy proceedings). This restrictiveness can manifest itself in the interpretation of potential third-party contracts, and imply an ungenerous application of the third party-criteria, meaning that more proof of relevant party intention is required. There are other rationales for the parties-only principle, but these are the main ones. The current legal situation is assumed to have desirable economic effects, as the clarity is assumed to make risk calculation easier, furthering economic turnover.

The principle and the effects it produces have been controversial in Swedish literature, case law and legislation, and the issue has been debated for some time.[143] This has led to the evolution of further exceptions to what has thus become increasingly important to describe as 'the general rule'. These exceptions are stated in different legal rules, which are in turn based on different rationales.[144] Generally speaking, these rules are often based on the interests of: (1) respecting the intentions of the contracting parties; (2) allowing for adequate measures to protect third-party interests (for example, in cases where the party is a consumer (see Cases 2 and 10 below)); (3) legal and procedural economy, as allowing a third party A to make their claim directly against C eliminates the need for double procedures, or indeed a series of procedures (whereby A sues B, who then sues C, and so on); and (4) achieving a level of coordination in contractual chains, where there is a functional connection between the performance of the different contracts (for example, B buys something from C, to sell to A). There are also a few other, more controversial, rationales which have been proposed as arguments for bestowing third-party rights. These include: (5) the interest of avoiding unjustified enrichment (this argument is controversial, in part due to the fact that, traditionally, unjustified enrichment has been a highly controversial

---

142 See e.g. NJA 2012 p. 697; L. Zackariasson, 'Privity of Contract and Direct Claims' in T. Håstad (ed), *The Nordic Contracts Act: Essays in Celebration of its One Hundredth Anniversary*, Djøf Publishing, Copenhagen 2015, p. 229; O. Mossberg, *Avtalets räckvidd I: Om avtals tredjemansverkningar, särskilt vid tredjemansavtal och direktkrav*, Iustus, Uppsala 2020, pp. 571 ff. and 592 ff.

143 For an overview, see e.g. S. Lindskog, *Betalning: Om kongruent infriande av penningskulder och andra betalningsrättsliga frågor*, 2nd ed., Norstedts juridik, Stockholm 2018, pp. 223 ff. In English, see e.g. L. Zackariasson, 'Privity of Contract and Direct Claims' in T. Håstad (ed), *The Nordic Contracts Act: Essays in Celebration of its One Hundredth Anniversary*, Djøf Publishing, Copenhagen 2015, pp. 229 ff.

144 For the following, see O. Mossberg, *Avtalets räckvidd I: Om avtals tredjemansverkningar, särskilt vid tredjemansavtal och direktkrav*, Iustus, Uppsala 2020, pp. 679–840, providing an extensive critical overview of the more or less recurring arguments for bestowing rights on a third party, and providing ample further references.

doctrine in Swedish and Nordic law); and (6) an interest in legal harmonisation between the Nordic countries, in which Norwegian and Danish law can be said to be more accommodating, when it comes to third party rights, than Swedish law (and possibly Finnish law).

As mentioned above, the third-party contract would be the most appropriate *'rättsfigur'* (legal figure) for the circumstances of the case. The third-party contract is among the oldest of the exceptions to the general principle of privity. It should be noted, that, in Swedish law, the *'tredjemansavtal'* (third-party contract) or, more specifically,[145] the *'avtal till förmån för tredjeman'* (contract for the benefit of a third party) is viewed as a separate *'rättsfigur'* (legal figure). This means that the third-party contract is viewed as something separate, *sui generis*, with its own specific legal rules which are applicable to third-party contracts and not to anything else.

Obviously, allowing the contracting parties to confer rights on a third party is a way of respecting the intentions of the parties (see rationale (1) above), in cases where there is freedom of contract. As regards the question of whether or not the parties should, in fact, have the freedom to contract in favour of a third party – that is, as regards the rationales for the legal validity of a third-party contract – one of the leading contract law textbooks simply states that this 'fills certain practical needs': it achieves a legal-technical simplification, since it removes the need for assignment, and fills an important practical function, not least in cases where it is necessary to give persons rights which can only be designated indirectly, and might not be individualised until later, such as many insurance contracts for the benefit of third parties (see Case 5 below).[146] The general stance of Swedish contract law is likely that there is often simply no valid reason not to recognise third-party effects of a contract, if the parties want to create such effects.

3. COMPARATIVE REMARKS

Jan Biemans and Lorna Richardson

This case sketches a contract between a parent company (A) and its counterparty (B), which contract stipulates that B will provide services to the companies as set out in the schedule to the contract, including C. Whereas A pays for the services, C has suffered loss after default by B. The question is whether C can sue B directly

145 Even though it may seem improper, under Swedish law, onerous third-party contracts, that is, agreements intended to be disadvantageous to the third party, are also considered third-party contracts in the broad sense of the term. However, this is merely a matter of terminology. According to Swedish law, as a clear general rule, agreements that are disadvantageous to a third party have no effect on the third party.

146 A. Adlercreutz and L. Gorton, *Avtalsrätt I*, 13th ed., Juristförlaget i Lund, Lund 2011, p. 154.

and/or force A to sue B for this loss. In this case, the party suffering loss due to the default is not a party to the contract. The question, therefore, is what action a party can take where it is not a party to a contract, but where it benefits from the contract (is a beneficiary), in the event of default by one of the contract parties, and against which of the two contract parties this action should be taken. Broadly speaking, the answer depends on whether a legal system recognises the concept of the third-party stipulation in a contract, in which case the beneficiary can sue the non-performing contract party for breach of contract, and if not, alternatively, whether the beneficiary can force the stipulating contract party to do so for the beneficiary's benefit.

Question 1

In all jurisdictions (in this volume), the concept of a third-party stipulation is recognised as such. It serves as an exception to the principle that a contract only has legal consequences between its parties. Although all jurisdictions are familiar with this concept, there are differences with regard to what is required in the contract to create such a third-party right, which often involves construction and/or interpretation of the contract in order to determine the intention of the contracting parties.

In most jurisdictions (Belgium, Bulgaria, Czech Republic, England, France, Germany, Italy, the Netherlands, Poland, Scotland and Spain) the intention of the contracting parties to grant the third party such a right (to enforce the contract) is easily accepted and/or does not seem to be an issue, if it is clear that the third party benefits from the stipulation and/or the clause is made for their benefit. The third party needs to be identified or identifiable[147] by the time performance is due under the contract.[148] In some jurisdictions (such as England), it is sufficient that such a right is not (explicitly) excluded in the contract. As a consequence, in these jurisdictions, the facts of the case are sufficient to create a third-party right for Direct.

In the Netherlands, Direct have to accept the right before it will be created. In none of the jurisdictions except Scotland is the fact that Holdings could alter the schedule to the contract by giving notice to Digital Age problematic for the creation of a third-party right in Direct's favour. In Scots law there has, historically, been some debate about the need for the right to be irrevocable before a third-party right can be created, but legislative change, which came into

[147] The third party need not be named, but may instead fall within a particular class of persons or answer to a description given in the contract.

[148] The third party need not be identified or identifiable at the time of contract formation. For instance, A and B could enter into a contract for the benefit of C, who did not exist at the date of contract formation, but will exist by the time B is to render performance under the contract.

force in 2018, has clarified that revocable third-party rights can be created. In Belgium, Spain and the Netherlands, Holdings would have been able to revoke the third-party right in Direct's favour until such time as Direct had accepted it. Similarly, in Italy the right can be revoked until the third party declares their intention to avail themselves of it.

In other jurisdictions, however, a third-party right is not easily created. The stipulation in the contract is, for example, understood merely to be a clause in the contractual relationship between Holdings and Digital Age, designating to which person and in what place Digital Age should provide their performance (towards Holdings), but not a third-party clause constituting a direct enforceable obligation from Digital Age to Direct to provide the performance (Slovakia). In Sweden, the question whether a third-party right has been conferred is also a matter of interpretation, and depends on whether the parties intended to give the third party a right which can be exercised independently of the stipulator. In this case, this would most likely be answered in the negative. The Swedish reporter notes that it follows from the facts of the case that, although Digital Age have to 'in fact' supply to Direct, nothing in the case suggests that the contacting parties intended that Direct should also be able to *demand* such support independently of Holdings. The approaches of Slovakia and Sweden, as applied to this case, are very similar.

Question 2

In all jurisdictions, although Holdings can sue Digital Age,[149] Direct cannot, in principle, force Holdings to do so. For those jurisdictions in which Direct can sue Digital Age directly on the basis of the third-party stipulation (the majority), action by Holdings on Direct's behalf is not necessary, as Direct have their own right to sue for damages.

In addition, some reports mention situations in which Direct would be able to force Holdings to take action against Digital Age, but which are inapplicable to the facts of the case. These are rooted in corporate law (Bulgaria), agency (England) or would arise where there was a contract or contractual provisions between Holdings and Direct to that effect (Belgium, England, Germany).

In Slovakia, Direct may have a claim against Holdings on two bases: (1) an agency arrangement between Direct and Holdings, which Holdings breached by virtue of the breach of contract by Digital Age; or (2) breach of the shareholder's corporate loyalty. In Sweden, Direct would have no legal remedy if Holdings decided not to sue Digital Age.

---

149 Although such a claim may be unsuccessful, given that Holdings themselves have not suffered any loss. Holdings' claim would be successful where Holdings are able to sue Digital Age to recover Direct's losses and pass the damages on to Direct, as is the position in German and Bulgarian law.

CASE 2: ASSET DAMAGED WITH LOSS TO A SUBSEQUENT OWNER

1. CASE

Alpha Inc. enter into a contract with Beta plc for significant works to be carried out to their head office premises. When the works are complete, Alpha resume full operations from the refurbished premises. Two years later, Alpha decide to sell the premises, and enter into a contract of sale with Delta GmbH.

In terms of the contract between Alpha and Delta, Delta must satisfy themselves on the quality of the premises. Alpha will not provide any warranties to Delta in relation to the premises or their condition. Delta buy the premises from Alpha for their full market value of €5 million. This price is based on the premises being in good condition, with no major works being required.

A year after Delta move into the premises, cracks start to appear in some of the walls. Investigations show that the cracks are due to work having been carried out defectively by Beta, in breach of their contractual obligations to Alpha. Further investigations determine that it will cost €1.5 million for the problem to be repaired. The nature of the problem means that Delta could not have found out about it before the sale.

There is no breach of contract by Alpha that would allow Delta to raise proceedings against Alpha. Alpha refuse to transfer their rights under the works contract with Beta to Delta. Having received full market value for the premises, Alpha have suffered no loss as a result of Beta's breach of contract.

Questions

1. Who can take action against Beta to recover Delta's €1.5 million loss, and on what basis?
2. Can Delta force Alpha to take any action or require Alpha to do anything that would assist Delta in recovering their loss from Beta?

2. DISCUSSIONS

2.1. BELGIUM

Siel Demeyere and Vincent Sagaert

I. Operative Rules

1. Delta can take action against Beta, based on Article 1792 of the old Belgian Civil Code (old BCC).[1] This provision forms part of the rules for contracting, and is still in force, but must be referred to as part of the 'old' BCC, in contrast to the 'Civil Code', as gradually introduced.
2. Delta cannot force Alpha to submit a claim against Beta, and given the answer to the first question, this would not be necessary. Moreover, a claim by Alpha against Beta would most likely be unsuccessful, as Alpha has not suffered damage under the contract, and thus has nothing to claim for.

II. Descriptive Formants

Regarding question 1, in this case, a third party suffers damage from a contractual breach, while the contracting party suffers no loss. No specific legal device has been designed for such a situation (cf. Case 9 below), but in these circumstances Delta can invoke a right *propter rem* against Beta.[2]

Delta can argue on the basis of a *kwalitatief recht/droit propter rem* (right *propter rem*), grounded in Article 1792, old BCC,[3] to overcome the principle of privity of contract and rely on the contract between Alpha and Beta. The right *propter rem* is a right that is so closely connected with a good that it transfers automatically with it.[4] The automatic transfer was already widely accepted under the old BCC, and has received a legal basis in Article 5.105 BCC. This provision defines such rights as the transferable rights which are so closely connected with a good that the interest in those rights depends on the ownership of that good.[5]

---

1 This code is still in force for the parts of law that have not yet been reformed and introduced in the (new) Belgian Civil Code, but must be referred to as 'old' Belgian Civil Code, in contrast to the 'Civil Code' as gradually introduced.

2 Should these circumstances not be fulfilled, Belgian tort law is so permissive that it can, nevertheless, provide a remedy for the third party suffering loss, i.e. Delta: Art. 1382, old BCC.

3 Cass. 18 May 2006, no. C.05.0097.N, *Arr.Cass.* 2006, 1118, concl. Adv. Gen. Dubrulle.

4 S. Stijns, *Verbintenissenrecht. Leerboek 1*, die Keure, Bruges 2009–16, 235, no. 310; P. Van Ommeslaghe, *Traité de droit civil belge. II. Les obligations. Vol. 1*, Bruylant, Brussels 2013, 754, no. 496; P. Wéry, *Droit des obligations: Théorie générale du contrat*, I, Larcier, Brussels 2011, 848, no. 905. A *goed/bien* (good) can, in Belgian law, be moveable or immoveable; corporeal or incorporeal.

5 Explanatory Memorandum to the Draft Statute of 24 February 2021 on introduction of Book 5 'Obligations', *Parl.St.* 2020–21, 1806/1, www.dekamer.be, 173 ff.

Such rights automatically transfer with the good, unless otherwise provided by law. A right *propter rem*, developed originally in Dutch scholarship, should, however, more precisely be described as a right held by its holder in a certain capacity, for example the owner of a building, but which is of no use separate from that capacity.[6] Because of the connection of the right to that capacity, the right transfers automatically with the capacity, for example in the event of sale of the building. The category of rights *propter rem* is not delineated in a general sense in Belgian law, but Article 1792, old BCC, definitely provides a claim to the owner of a building against the architect and contractor of the construction work, for a deficiency in that work. It is widely accepted that the right pursuant to Article 1792, old BCC, is a right *propter rem*. A deficiency in the construction work is a factual condition for the right *propter rem* to apply, and since Delta has been confronted with cracks in some of the walls, Delta will be entitled to claim on the basis of the right *propter rem*, based on Article 1792, old BCC.

Alpha would have a cause of action against Beta based on contractual breach, but has suffered no damage, and will not, therefore, raise proceedings.

Regarding question 2, as stated above, Delta cannot force Alpha to submit a claim against Beta, and given the answer to the first question, this would not be necessary. The *aanvullende werking van de goede trouw/la function complétive de la bonne foi* (complementary function of good faith),[7] however, could result in an obligation for Alpha to assist Delta in exercising its right, by, for instance, transferring to Delta all relevant information, such as the construction contract between Alpha and Beta. The complementary function of good faith includes that contracting parties are not only bound by what is explicitly mentioned in their contracts, *in casu* the contract between Alpha and Delta, but are also required to take any action required by good faith, for a loyal cooperation and fruitful performance of the contract.

2.2. BULGARIA

Petar Topurov

I. Operative Rules

1. Alpha could file a claim against Beta, based on their contract and the warranty liability of Beta, but only for damages suffered by Alpha. According

---

6 W. Van Gerven and A. Van Oevelen, *Verbintenissenrecht*, Acco, Leuven 2015, 222.

7 Art. 5.71 BCC; W. Van Gerven and A. Van Oevelen, *Verbintenissenrecht*, Acco, Leuven 2015, 98; P. Van Ommeslaghe, *Traité de droit civil belge. II. Les obligations. Vol. 1*, Bruylant, Brussels 2013, 193, no. 99.

to the prevailing opinions from the jurisprudence,[8] Delta could file only a special delict claim against Beta.

2. Within the course of the trial against Beta, Delta could require that Alpha present evidence concerning the contract for construction work with Beta.

II. Descriptive Formants

According to Art. 193 LOC, the seller is responsible if an item sold has a defect that that substantially reduces its value or suitability for use, even if they did not know about the defect. At the same time, Art. 194 LOC holds that, after accepting the item, the buyer must review it with such a time period as is usually necessary in such cases, and immediately notify the seller of any deficiencies noted. If they fail to do so, the property is deemed approved unless a defect is later discovered that could not have been noticed in a simple review. In the latter case, the buyer's rights are retained if they immediately notify the seller of the defect found. Where the seller was aware of the item's defect, no notification is required. At the same time, Art. 197 LOC stipulates that the purchaser's claims against the seller are declared terminated after one year, in a sale of real estate; if, however, the seller deliberately ignored the defect, the term is three years. Guilt is not a prerequisite for making the seller liable for deficiencies.[9] These provisions are applicable in all contracts for the sale of real estate in Bulgaria, even where there is no breach of a term of the contract. Judicial practice is controversial on the issue of the moment when the term specified by Art. 197 LOC starts: the issue is whether this is the moment when the item is handed over, or the moment when the deficiency is detected.[10]

---

8 Interpretative Decision No. 37/13.11.1984 of the BSC; Decision No. 611 from 20.09.2012 r. of the BSCC, commercial case No. 859/2011 r.; Decision from 04.08.2014 of the RDC, civil case No. 32132/2013; Decision No. 217 from 30.12.2015 of the RCPo, civil case No. 687/2014; Decision from 03.02.2014 of the RCR, civil case No. 5076/2013; Decision No. 554 from 28.03.2018 of the RCPlo, case No. 553/2018; Decision No. 66 from 26.02.2016 of the DCP, civil case No. 989/2015; Decision No. 1473 from 23.10.2015 of the RCP, civil case No. 2264/2015; Decision No. 5 from 04.01.2013 r. DCR, commercial case No. 18/2012; Decision No. 463573 from 02.08.2018 r. of the SRC, civil case No. 51110/2015. The exceptions to the opinion of the prevailing jurisprudence are Decision from 20.01.2016 of the SRC, civil case No. 46679/2013 and Decision No. 104 from 14.04.2016 of the RCB, civil case No. 825/2015 r. At the same time, the legal doctrine supports the position that all third parties may file a claim against the builders, based on the warranty liability, whether or not this right has been expressly transferred to them by the seller of the property: S. Popova, *Contractual relations in the construction*, Southwestern University Publishing House, Blagoevgrad 2012, p. 233.

9 M. Markov, *Contractual Law*, Sibi, Sofia 2011, p. 276; P. Goleva, *Contractual Law*, New Star, Sofia 2015, p. 281; A. Kozhuharov, *Contractual Law. General concepts of contractual relationship*, new edition and supplements by P. Petkov, 'St Kliment Ohridski' University Publishing House/Jurispress, Sofia 2002, p. 102.

10 Order No. 57/2009 r. BSCC civil case No. 3460/2008 r.; Decision No. 82/2010 r. BSCC civil case 34060/2008 r.

Furthermore, construction and repair contractors are responsible for the warranty liability. According to the case law, (implied) warranty liability does not follow the property. If the property purchaser wants to base their claim on it, they should have the rights of the party contracting with the contractor expressly transferred.[11]

The purchaser (Delta) can claim redress from Beta with a claim for unlawful damage.[12] The claim is based on the legal norm from Art. 163, paragraph 3 of the Spatial Development Act.[13] Within the course of the trial, the purchaser may require that the court oblige the seller to present documentation by means of which it is easier to prove that Beta's repair works caused the damage. This special delict claim is granted to all third parties who have suffered damage due to culpable actions of the builder.

2.3. CZECH REPUBLIC

Tomáš Richter

I. *Operative Rules*

1. *Alpha can, in principle, take action against Beta* for such remedies as are available to Alpha under the construction contract with Beta.

   Delta might be able to enforce against Beta such rights as Alpha had against Beta at the time of the sale of the premises to Delta. However, the facts as stipulated are not clear enough to allow for a detailed analysis, and the law on the point is rather uncertain too.
2. *Delta will probably not be able to effectively force* Alpha to assist it in recovering Delta's loss from Beta.

II. *Descriptive Formants*

Czech law differentiates between liability for defects in performance as at the time of performance (even if such defects only become apparent later), on the one hand, and a warranty that the thing sold will maintain certain parameters for a certain period of time after the sale, on the other.

---

11 Interpretative Decision No. 37/13.11.1984 in civil case No. 16/84, BSC.

12 Interpretative Decision No. 54/23.06.1986 г. BSC.

13 Promulgated, SG No. 1 of 02.01.2001, last supplemented, SG No. 17 of 25.02.2020. The Spatial Development Act contains rules about the development of the territories, and the investment in, design and construction of buildings, and determines the restrictions of ownership for development purposes.

The former concept is referred to as *'práva z vadného plnění'* (rights arising from defective performance), and is governed by sections 1916 to 1925 CC, in general, and sections 2099 to 2012 CC, with respect to the sale of moveables in particular, with an additional special rule in section 2129 CC, applicable to the sale of immoveables. These rules apply by default, but are not mandatory: the parties (and certainly commercial parties) are free to fully contract out of them (section 1916(2) CC).[14]

The latter concept is referred to as *'záruka za jakost'* (a warranty of quality), and is governed by section 1919 CC, in general, and sections 2113 to 2117 and section 2131 CC, with respect to sales of moveables and immoveables in particular. In contracts between commercial parties, the warranty of quality must be contractually agreed; that is, it does not apply by default.

Against this legal background, the facts of the hypothetical case require certain further assumptions to be made.

The factual stipulation that, '[i]n terms of the contract between Alpha and Delta, Delta must satisfy themselves on the quality of the premises. *Alpha will not provide any warranties to Delta in relation to the premises or their condition*' (emphasis added) will be taken to mean that Alpha has not agreed to extend a 'warranty of quality' pursuant to sections 2113 ff. CC to Delta.

There is a further stipulation that '[t]here is *no breach of contract* by Alpha that would allow Delta to raise proceedings against Alpha' (emphasis added). This sentence could be taken to mean that Delta has no rights against Alpha in relation to the defects of the premises at all, since the parties have contracted out of the default statutory rules on 'rights arising from defective performance', including section 2129(2) CC, whereunder a buyer of a building has up to five years after the purchase of the building to notify the seller of hidden defects therein. Alternatively, it could be read more narrowly, in the sense that Alpha has breached no explicit provisions of the contract, but Delta may still be able to invoke rights under the statutory rules on 'rights arising from defective performance', because these have not been disapplied by the contract. On the latter, narrower reading, it is notable that Delta would be well within the five-year statutory time limit under section 2129(2) CC, and may actually have direct recourse against Alpha.

As regards Delta's potential recourse against Beta, the case stipulates that 'Alpha refuse to transfer their rights under the works contract with Beta to Delta.' Under section 1106 CC, an acquirer of ownership also acquires rights and obligations pertaining to the thing acquired. Accordingly, if the contract between Alpha and Delta was silent about the issue, and the stipulation refers to the situation *ex post*, it might not matter much that Alpha is refusing to transfer its rights under

14 J. Šilhán, in M. Hulmák et al., *Občanský zákoník V, Závazkové právo, Obecná část (§1721–2054), První vydání*, C.H. Beck, Praha 2014, p. 877 at 29.

the construction contract with Beta to Delta – those rights might already have passed to Delta by operation of section 1106 CC. But apart from the uncertainty about the stipulated facts, the law on the point is also very uncertain. Section 1106 CC has no direct predecessor, either in the CC 1964 or in the CommC, and it is presently unclear whether it would really operate so as to achieve a transfer of Alpha's rights against Beta (be they 'rights arising from defective performance' or rights arising out of a 'warranty of quality') to Delta, together with the transfer of ownership of the premises. None of the commentaries so far published on the new CC have dealt with the question of whether or not section 1106 would achieve such a transfer. The question will have to be answered by the courts when the opportunity arises. Given the size of the loss suffered by Delta as a result of the defects, it is quite likely that Delta would test section 1106 CC in the courts, potentially leading to an important judicial clarification of the law on the point.

As regards the relationship between Alpha and Beta, the case stipulates nothing at all about the construction contract between these two parties. However, the basic position would be that the mere fact of Alpha selling the premises would not, per se, prevent Alpha from enforcing any 'rights arising from defective performance' or any rights arising out of any 'warranty of quality' which may have arisen out of Alpha's construction contract with Beta. Under section 2615(2) CC, employers' rights against contractors arising out of defects in the work contracted for would essentially be governed by the same rules as stated above in the context of the sale contract. Alpha, as an employer, would therefore be able to claim against Beta, as the contractor, on any grounds available to it under its construction contract with Beta or in connection with it, such as the statutory rules on 'rights arising from defective performance', to the extent these had not been contracted out of. Alpha could, in particular, claim a reduction in the price of the construction works (section 2106(1)(c) CC, section 2107 CC), or the repair of the defect in kind (section 2106(1)(b) CC, section 2107 CC).[15] Unlike a damages claim, a claim for defects does not require the claimant to prove loss (indeed, a claim for the repair of a defect in kind, by definition, does not involve any quantification on the plaintiff's side at all).

Having said the above, and assuming that Beta is able to ascertain the terms of the sale contract between Alpha and Delta,[16] one can assume that Beta would resist any claim made by Alpha to the extent that Alpha itself resists compensating

---

15 Trying to enforce the right to avoid the construction contract might be difficult and lead to unpredictable results, due to the rather poorly formulated s. 2110 CC, which seems to try to set out rules similar in their effect to Arts. 82 and 84 CISG (United Nations Convention on Contracts for the International Sale of Goods); however, it is not very clear what the end effect of that attempt is.

16 Beta could inspect the contract of sale at the land register, assuming that what the case describes as 'premises' were, as a matter of law, real estate registered in the land register (s. 52 of Act No. 256/2013 Coll., on the real estate cadastre).

Delta for the defect in the premises. One can assume that Beta would invoke the CC's rules on unjust enrichment, whereby a person who enriches him- or herself to the detriment of another without a just cause must return such enrichment (section 2991 CC), or the rules enforcing fair and equitable dealing (in particular, section 6(1) CC, whereby everyone must act fairly in legal relationships, section 6(2) CC, whereby no one must benefit from his or her unfair or illegal acts, and section 8 CC, whereby a manifest abuse of rights shall not enjoy the protection of the law). It would seem quite obvious that an attempt by Alpha to claim from Beta on the grounds of a hidden defect in the premises, while at the same time refusing to compensate Delta for the same defect, would be a natural candidate for a bar to recovery under the broad principles of fair and equitable dealing set out in sections 6, 8 and 2991 CC. If, on the other hand, Alpha was intending to pass on to Delta the compensation recovered from Beta (notwithstanding the fact that it is not obligated to do so under the stipulations of the case), there would seem to be no reason to apply any such bar.

That being said, and once again making the assumptions about the contract between Alpha and Delta made above, it seems quite unlikely that Delta would be able to force Alpha into cooperation vis-à-vis Beta if Alpha were not willing to do this voluntarily.

2.4. ENGLAND AND WALES

T.T. Arvind

I. Operative Rules

1. The answer to this case will depend on the terms of the contract between Alpha and Beta. If the contract is structured to confer rights on subsequent purchasers of the premises which are enforceable under the CRTPA, then only Delta (and not Alpha) can take action to recover the loss. If the contract is not so structured, then Alpha may be able to take action on Delta's behalf to recover the loss suffered by Delta, but Delta will not be able to take action. In the specific scenario presented by the facts of this case, it is likely that Delta will be able to sue Beta.
2. Delta are unlikely to be able to force Alpha to assist them against Beta.

II. Descriptive Formants

Question 1

Under the CRTPA, third parties do not acquire a right to sue simply because the contract benefits them. As discussed under Case 1 above, they must also be identified in the contract by name, class or description,[17] and the contract must either expressly provide that they have the right to enforce its terms[18] or, alternatively, purport to confer a benefit on them.[19] Most of the standard contracts used in the construction industry in England and Wales now include provisions giving subsequent purchasers (and, in some cases, tenants) a defined and delineated set of rights against the contractor, structured to satisfy the requirements of the CRTPA.[20] If the works contract between Beta and Alpha includes equivalent provisions, Delta will have the right to recover its loss from Beta.

If, however, the works contract departs from standard English contracting practice, and does not contain provisions either expressly giving enforcement rights to subsequent purchasers or purporting to confer benefits on them, the CRTPA's requirements will not be satisfied. In such a case, the doctrine of privity will apply, and Delta will have no right of action against Beta for breach of contract. Delta will also have no action in tort against Beta for negligence, as damage of this kind is considered pure economic loss in English law, for which compensation is not recoverable in the absence of a voluntary assumption of responsibility by Beta to Delta in respect of that type of loss.[21]

Ordinarily, Alpha will not be able to recover 'substantial' damages (that is, damages awarded in compensation for actual economic or other recoverable loss suffered in consequence of breach) against Beta, because Alpha have not themselves suffered any loss. Alpha will only be able to recover 'nominal' damages (that is, damages of a token sum, usually £1, awarded to the claimant in cases where the claimant suffered no recoverable loss, in recognition of the fact that the contract was breached). However, case law has recognised an exception to this general principle, usually called the *Albazero* principle or the *Linden Gardens* principle, after the key cases in which it was developed.[22] Under this exception, Alpha can recover against Beta for Delta's loss if three conditions are satisfied. Firstly, the loss must relate to property; although the courts have spoken in favour of recognising a broader 'transferred loss' principle that goes beyond property, they have not yet actually done so.[23] Secondly, Alpha and Beta must have known, or been able to foresee, that damage caused by breach would cause loss to a later owner, and not just Alpha. Thirdly, the ultimate purchaser

17 CRTPA, s. 1(3).

18 Ibid., s. 1(1)(a).

19 Ibid., s. 1(1)(b).

20 See e.g. clauses 7A, 7C and 7E of the Joint Contracts Tribunal Standard Building Contract (2016 edition), and the discussion in D. Chappell, *Understanding JCT Standard Building Contracts*, 10th ed. (Abingdon: Routledge, 2017), ch. 3.

21 See *Murphy v. Brentwood District Council* [1992] AC 398 (HL).

22 *Albacruz (Cargo Owners) v. Albazero (Owners)* [1977] AC 774 (HL) and *Linden Gardens Trust v. Lenesta Sludge Disposals Ltd* [1994] 1 AC 85 (HL).

23 See e.g. *Swynson Ltd v. Lowick Rose LLP* [2017] UKSC 32, [2018] 1 AC 313 [17].

must lack a direct cause of action against Beta. If all three conditions are satisfied, then the law treats the parties as having entered into the contract on the basis that Alpha would be able to enforce the contract against Beta for the benefit of anyone who suffered from defective performance, but could not themselves enforce the contract.[24] On the facts, all three conditions do appear to be satisfied. As a result, if Delta do not have any direct right of action against Beta under the CRTPA, Alpha will be able to recover the loss from Beta on the basis of the *Linden Gardens* rule, and will be accountable to Delta for any amount so recovered.[25]

Question 2

In English law, this situation is identical to Case 1, question 2. For the reasons discussed there, Delta will not be able to force Alpha to take action or assist Delta in recovering from Beta, in the absence of a contractual provision requiring Alpha to do so. This is the case notwithstanding the fact that Alpha's claim against Beta on the basis of the *Linden Gardens* rule may be the only way in which Delta could seek to recover Delta's loss.

III. Meta-Legal Formants

Question 1

The *Albazero/Linden Gardens* principle reflects a balance between two different basic principles of English law. The first is that damages in contract only compensate a party for losses which they themselves have suffered (the 'own loss' principle). The second is the principle that, 'where a real loss has been caused by a real breach of contract, then there should if at all possible be a real remedy which directs recovery from the defendant towards the party which has suffered the loss'.[26] The precise manner in which the balance between the two is drawn, however, has been coloured by the doctrine of privity of contract. As a result, the exceptions that have been developed to the 'own loss' principle have tended to be very specific, as the three conditions set out in *Linden Gardens* demonstrate, and have been construed strictly: in cases where one of the conditions has not been satisfied, or where the contracting party has been unwilling to be joined in the litigation, the third party has had no remedy for the loss it has suffered as a result of breach of contract.[27] The cases have also tended to require that the claim be

---

24 *Linden Gardens Trust v. Lenesta Sludge Disposals Ltd* [1994] 1 AC 85 (HL), 114–15.
25 *Albacruz (Cargo Owners) v. Albazero (Owners)* [1977] AC 774 (HL), 844.
26 *Offer-Hoar v. Larkstore Ltd* [2006] EWCA Civ 1079, [2006] 1 WLR 2926 [85] (Rix LJ).
27 See e.g. *Alfred McAlpine Construction Ltd v. Panatown Ltd (No. 1)* [2001] 1 AC 518 (HL).

brought by, or on behalf of, the contracting party, rather than giving the third party a direct right of action. The provisions of the CRTPA remain the clearest and most certain way to give the third party a direct right of action.

2.5. FRANCE

Sylvain Ravenne and Flora Vern

I. Operative Rules

1. Delta can take action against Beta to recover their loss.
2. Delta cannot force Alpha to take action or require Alpha to do anything to assist Delta. This is unnecessary given Delta's direct claim against Beta, noted above.

II. Descriptive Formants

Question 1

The situation described in this case would be dealt with, under French law, as a '*contrat d'entreprise*' (contract for the supply of services), whereby a person agrees to perform a predetermined work for another, in exchange for a price. Beta are the contractors who renovate Alpha's building. After the work is done, Alpha sell the building to Delta, who then discover cracks in the walls, establishing that the work has been carried out defectively by Beta. This situation will, therefore, be dealt with from the perspective of contracts for services.

Under French law, a person may take action against another only if they have an interest in the success or dismissal of a claim.[28] As a result, Delta could take action against Beta to recover their loss, as opposed to Alpha, who do not have any interest in the success or dismissal of the claim, having sold the building to Delta.[29] Delta's claim would be based on the rules relating to contracts for services, namely Article 1792 of the FCC, which states:

> Any builder of a work is liable as a matter of law to the owner or to the buyer of the work for the damages … that compromise the stability of the building or that, by affecting it in one of its essential component parts or one of its complementary elements, render it unsuitable for its purposes.

28 Art. 31 Code of Civil Procedure.
29 As explained in Question 2, para. (a).

This Article applies not only to constructors of new buildings, but also to any workers who perform significant work, such as restoration, renovation or rehabilitation, on existing buildings.[30] It would, therefore, be applicable to the present case. Even though Delta were not a party to the original contract for services, as buyer of the building, they have an *'action directe'* (direct claim) against Beta.

This answer is based on the theory according to which claims relative to a thing will follow that thing into the hands of subsequent owners,[31] because they are so-called accessories of the thing itself.[32] No specific contractual clause is needed in this case, because Alpha's claim is automatically transferred to the buyer.

Question 2

Delta, who are a third party to the improperly performed enterprise contract, already have a valid claim against Beta. As a result, Delta do not need Alpha's assistance in order to recover their losses, and therefore cannot require Alpha to take any action against Beta, because, as noted above, Alpha no longer have such a claim, which was transferred to Delta along with the building. However, Delta could sue Alpha to obtain any information regarding the renovation, which may be necessary to argue the claim in court.

However, in the event of Beta's insolvency (for example, if they are not insured), or if Delta prefer to sue Alpha alone, or Alpha as well as Beta, French law would allow Delta to sue Alpha on two different grounds:

(a) Alpha would be liable to Delta on the basis of the existence of hidden defects at the time of the sale. This type of liability is not based on actual breach of contract, but on a legal warranty under Article 1641 FCC in the law of sales.[33] In the present case, this warranty would, however, effectively be waived by the contractual clause excluding Alpha's liability as a seller, based on Article 1643 FCC, to the extent that Alpha are not real estate professionals, and are therefore presumed to have ignored the defects. This is because the Cour de cassation considers that warranty waivers are inoperative when the vendor acted in bad faith (i.e. with knowledge of the hidden defects).[34] In order to protect the buyer, the Court also ruled that professional vendors are presumed to know of any hidden defects of the

30 Cass., civ. 3e, 3 mai 1990, no 88-19642; Cass., civ. 3e, 30 mars 1994, no 92-11996.
31 Cass., civ. 1re, 28 nov. 1967, Bull. civ. I, no 348.
32 Cass., civ. 3e, 23 sept. 2009, no 08-13470.
33 Cass., com., 19 mars 2013, no 11-26566.
34 Cass., civ. 3e, 12 nov. 1975, no 74-13775.

thing, as long as it is within their area of expertise.[35] Similarly, the person who constructed or repaired the building would be presumed to know of any subsequent defects.[36] Thus, in this case, if Alpha were real estate professionals, or had done the repairs themselves, the warranty waiver would not be effective against Delta.

(b) Alpha would also be directly liable to Delta for the defects in the building because Article 1792-1 FCC extends the status – and liability – of the builder to the owner who subsequently sells the new or renovated building.[37] It should be noted that, by contrast with the clauses in a sales contract which can exclude a non-professional's liability, clauses that limit or waive the builder's liability are null and void, according to Article 1792-5 FCC. The fact that Alpha provided no warranties in the sales contract regarding the building or its condition would not waive Alpha's liability under Article 1792-1 FCC. After paying for the damage sustained by Delta, Alpha would, however, have a claim against Beta to recover the sum paid to Delta, although this action would only allow Alpha to recover part of the costs sustained, if Beta were indeed insolvent.

2.6. GERMANY

Sonja Meier

I. Operative Rules

1. Alpha will be able to bring a contractual claim. Depending on the circumstances, they may also be able to bring a delictual claim. Delta will not be able to take action against Beta.
2. Delta will probably not be able to require Alpha to commence proceedings or take any other action.

II. Descriptive Formants

Question 1

Alpha will be able to claim damages for breach of contract under §280 (1) BGB if they have suffered a loss.[38] Assuming that the property suffered damage at the

35 Cass., com., 27 nov. 1991, n° 89-19546.

36 Cass., civ. 3e, 26 févr. 1980, n° 78-15566; Cass., civ. 3e, 28 mars 2007, n° 06-12299.

37 Cass., civ. 3e, 9 déc. 1992, n° 91-12097; Cass., civ. 3e, 28 mai 2002, n° 01-01881.

38 If Beta were contractually obliged to maintain the walls themselves, the cracks could be regarded as a *'Sachmangel'* (defective work) under §633 (2) BGB. In this case, Alpha would

time of Beta's performance (as opposed to at a later time), Alpha have suffered a loss, because the objective value of their property dropped significantly. It is irrelevant that this was not detectable at that moment.

However, the sale to Delta at the full market price may have had the effect of reducing Alpha's loss to zero. According to the doctrine of *'Vorteilsausgleichung'* (offset of an advantage), a benefit to the injured party caused by the same event that caused the loss can sometimes be set off against the loss.[39] In order to determine whether this is possible, the judge has to take all the circumstances of the case into account, particularly the nature of the benefit and the purpose of the liability. Contracts with third parties on favourable terms will not generally reduce the loss suffered. According to the courts and commentators, where contracted work on a building is defective, the owner's claim for damages is not extinguished by the fact that they afterwards sold the property to a third party for a price that did not reflect the defects.[40] The reason for this is to avoid the contract with the third-party buyer benefiting the contractor, and to enable the former owner to assign their claims against the contractor to the third party (irrespective of whether they have actually done so).

Since Alpha were the owners of the premises and the walls were intact before Beta began their works, Alpha may also be able to bring a delictual claim for damage to their property under §823 (1) BGB, if they can show that Beta were negligent by infringing the duty of care expected from building contractors.

In principle, delictual claims are not excluded by the existence of contractual claims. However, where the loss suffered by the claimant is exactly the same loss as that which was caused by the disappointment of the claimant's contractual performance interest, the Federal Court does not grant the claimant delictual claims.[41] According to the Court, the mere fact that contracted work had to be done on property belonging to the claimant cannot justify the existence of delictual claims, which might circumvent the limitations and restrictions of the contractual claims already available. However, where the loss caused by the contractor exceeds the performance interest of the claimant, for example

be able to demand *'Nacherfüllung'* (cure of performance) under §635 BGB. After expiry of a reasonable time Alpha will also be able to repair the walls themselves and demand reimbursement for their expenses under §637 BGB. Since both rights are regarded as a modified form of specific performance, they are not affected by the transfer of property as long as cure is possible, i.e. Delta is willing to allow the repairs.

39 H. Oetker in *Münchener Kommentar zum BGB*, vol. 2 (9th ed., Beck 2022), §249, [228] ff.; C. Höpfner in *J. von Staudingers Kommentar zum Bürgerlichen Gesetzbuch*, vol. §§249–54 (Sellier – de Gruyter 2021), §249, [133] ff.

40 *BGHZ* 99, 81; BGH *NJW-RR* 2004, 1462; F. Peters in *J. von Staudingers Kommentar zum Bürgerlichen Gesetzbuch*, vol. §§631–50v (Sellier – de Gruyter 2019), §634, [150]; see also BGH *NJW* 1981, 45 at 47; OLG Hamm, *NJW* 1974, 2091; H. Oetker in *Münchener Kommentar zum BGB*, vol. 2 (9th ed., Beck 2022), §249, [274]; C. Höpfner in *J. von Staudingers Kommentar zum Bürgerlichen Gesetzbuch*, vol. §§249–54 (Sellier – de Gruyter 2021), §249, [150].

41 *BGHZ* 162, 86.

where the contractor damages property that was not the object of the particular contract, delictual claims are generally possible.[42] On this basis, Alpha would have no delictual claim if Beta damaged the very part of the property they were working on. The distinction between losses corresponding to the contractual performance interest and losses exceeding the contractual performance interest has been criticised by many commentators, who argue that the owner should never lose their delictual protection by commissioning work from the contractor.[43]

Delta have no contractual claims, since they are not a party to the contract between Alpha and Beta, and this contract is not a *'Vertrag mit Schutzwirkung für Dritte'* (contract with protective effects towards third parties).[44] There is no indication that the contracting parties intended to give protection to unknown prospective transferees.

A delictual claim under §823 (1) BGB requires that Beta damaged Delta's property. However, the property was damaged at a time when it was Alpha's and not Delta's. Accordingly, it is only Alpha, and not Delta, who can avail themselves of a delictual claim.

Question 2

The usual way of protecting the injured party in cases where another party has claims against the wrongdoer is to require the claim-holder to assign their claims to the injured party. Rights to force another party to sue, while not unknown in general, are therefore not discussed in this situation.

§285 BGB provides that where performance of a contract is, or becomes, impossible, and the event causing the impossibility gives rise to a claim of the debtor against a third party (for example, an insurance company or a tortfeasor), the debtor is obliged to assign this 'surrogate claim' to the creditor. In the present case, performance of the contract of sale between Alpha and Delta will not be impossible, since even if Alpha were obliged to transfer the property without any defects, the walls can still be repaired. However, §285 (1) could be applied by analogy, requiring Alpha to assign their rights against Beta to Delta.

A right to have claims assigned can also be derived from an *'ergänzende Vertragsauslegung'* (supplementary interpretation of the contract). This concept is used where a particular state of affairs exists which had not been in the contemplation of the parties, and allows the court to apply the rule which

---

42 OLG Koblenz, *NJW* 2014, 1246; F. Peters in *J. von Staudingers Kommentar zum Bürgerlichen Gesetzbuch*, vol. §§631–50v (Sellier – de Gruyter 2019), §634, [165]–[167].

43 J. Hager in *J. von Staudingers Kommentar zum Bürgerlichen Gesetzbuch*, vol. §§823 A–D (Sellier – de Gruyter 2017), §823, [B 107]; G. Wagner in *Münchener Kommentar zum BGB*, vol. 7 (9th ed., Beck 2024), §823, [340]–[341].

44 As to this concept, see Case 4, question 1, and Case 9.

reasonable parties would have agreed on had they considered the problem.[45] It is sometimes used by the Federal Court in order to establish a right to have claims against third parties assigned.[46]

When considering whether such a right should be implied into the contract at hand, it has to be taken into account that Alpha is not contractually liable for the defects since their contract with Delta provides that they do not provide any warranties and Delta must satisfy themselves on the quality of the premises. Under German law, this means that Alpha's liability for defects was excluded in the contract. In legal doctrine, it is a matter of debate whether a right to have claims assigned can be derived from *ergänzende Vertragsauslegung* in cases of exemption of liability.[47] It has been argued that exemption clauses of this type support the implication of a right to assignment, since the buyer would otherwise be left without any remedy. Conversely, it has been argued that the exemption shows that the parties, when concluding the contract, considered the possibility of the performance being defective, so that there is no room for an *ergänzende Vertragsauslegung*. This is the opinion of the Federal Court: where there is an exemption clause, a right to have claims against third parties assigned can only be derived from *ergänzende Vertragsauslegung* if it concerns extraordinary facts which the parties would not have contemplated at the moment of contracting.[48] This is not the case here, since hidden defects in the building are nothing extraordinary.

2.7. ITALY

Pasquale Femia

I. Operative Rules

1. Delta can take a direct action as 'successor in interest' of Alpha under Art. 1669 c.c. (extracontractual or contractual liability).
2. Delta could theoretically act through a subrogation action, exercising the creditor rights that Alpha holds against Beta in place of Alpha; however, this is extremely unlikely in practice, as the primary remedy is the direct action.

---

45 J. Busche in *Münchener Kommentar zum BGB*, vol. 1 (9th ed., Beck 2021), §157, [26]–[59].
46 BGH *NJW* 1997, 652.
47 Cf. G. Caspers in *J. von Staudingers Kommentar zum Bürgerlichen Gesetzbuch*, vol. §§255–304 (Sellier – de Gruyter 2019), §285, [17] with further references.
48 BGH *NJW* 1997, 652; BGH *NJW* 2004, 1873.

II. *Descriptive Formants*

Regarding question 1, Art. 1669, paragraph 1, c.c. reads as follows:

> In the case of buildings or other immovables intended by their nature to last for a long period of time, if within ten years from completion the work is totally or partially destroyed by reason of defects in the soil or in construction, or if such work appears to be in evident danger of destruction or reveals serious deficiencies, the contractor is liable with respect to the customer *and his successors in interest*, provided notice of said destruction or defects has been given within one year of their discovery. This rule applies to contracts for works to buildings as well as to contracts for the construction of buildings. The right of the customer is prescribed in one year from the notice.[49]

This rule explicitly extends the contractor's liability to successors in interest, who are not parties to the contract.[50]

It is controversial whether Beta's liability to Delta is contractual[51] or extracontractual.[52] A strict interpretation would point to an extracontractual liability because Delta are a third party to the contract between Alpha and Beta. However, Art. 1669 c.c., which lays down the rules on liability for failure to perform the construction contract, mentions the contractor's liability to the customer (who is a party to the contract) and their 'successors in interest'. This provision may support an explicit extension of contractual liability for the benefit of the successor in interest; that is, the party who acquired the property built by the contractor and then sold by their customer.[53]

Regarding question 2, since Delta have a direct course of action against Beta, Delta's interest in Alpha taking action against Beta is marginal. The issue

---

49 S. Beltramo (ed), *Italian Civil Code and Complementary Legislation*, tr. in 1969 by M. Beltramo, G.E. Longo and J.H. Merryman (Dobbs Ferry, NY: Oceana, 1991–c2010), p. 353.

50 Courts endorse the buyer's action by postponing the start of the one-year limitation period to exercise the action. The *dies a quo* is set at the moment the buyer had knowledge of the 'severe defects'; thus, the limitation period starts when the buyer, mostly based on an expert opinion, becomes aware that the property they have bought is marred by defects: Cass., 1 February 2008, no. 2460, *Massimario Giustizia civile* (2008), p. 146.

51 D. Rubino and G. Iudica, 'Dell'appalto, *sub* Art. 1669', *Commentario del codice civile Scialoja e Branca* (Bologna/Rome: Zanichelli-Foro italiano, 4th ed., 2007), p. 452; M. Mattioni, 'Una pronuncia esemplare sull'ambito di applicazione (e sulla natura) della responsabilità ex Art. 1669 cod. civ.', *Nuova giurisprudenza civile commentata* (2017), p. 1193.

52 In case law: Cass., 27 November 2017, no. 28233, *Massimario Giustizia civile* (2018); Cass., 9 November 2017, no. 26552, *Guida al diritto* (2018), p. 39. In scholarship: F. Galgano (ed), *Trattato di diritto civile* (Padua: Cedam, 2015), II, p. 749. On the contractor's liability to the successor in interest see also S. Polidori, 'Appalto', *Trattato di diritto civile del Consiglio nazionale del notariato* (Naples: Edizioni Scientifiche Italiane, 2015), p. 358.

53 Apparently arguing this way, though it is an *obiter dictum*, see Cass., s.u., 27 March 2017, no. 7756, *Responsabilità Civile e Previdenza*, 4 (2017), p. 1210.

would have practical significance if: (a) Delta lost their right to take direct action against Beta under Art. 1669 (for example, if they expressly waived their right to compensation, retaining the power to take action against Alpha); or (b) Delta took action against Alpha claiming compensation for damages based on the rules on sale (Art. 1495 c.c.), provided that this action is still possible.[54] If (a) and (b) occur, then, (c), by means of an action on the contract between Alpha and Beta, Alpha, who have been sued by Delta for compensation for damages based on the rules on sale, would sue Beta in order to make Beta liable to Alpha for the damages that Alpha, as seller, may have to pay to Delta, as purchaser. If Alpha failed to exercise their rights against Beta and, due to this failure, Delta would not be compensated by Alpha for its credit (because Alpha's money and estate would be too scarce to compensate Delta), Delta could take an action in subrogation (Art. 2900 c.c.), thereby replacing Alpha in the action on a guarantee.

This solution, however, cannot be considered unanimous under Italian law, and can be upheld only by overcoming an obstacle. Delta can take an action in subrogation, replacing Alpha in the exercise of Alpha's right to be compensated by Beta for the failure to perform the construction contract, only if such a right already exists in Alpha's patrimony at the time Delta's action in subrogation is taken (that is, Delta replaces Alpha in the action against Beta). In the case at issue, however, the right does not pre-exist in Alpha's patrimony, because Alpha have not suffered an actual loss: the damage revealed itself only after Alpha had sold the property to Delta. Yet, it may be argued that Delta's action against Alpha, as described in the previous paragraph, would result in damage being suffered by Alpha themselves,[55] and Beta would no doubt be liable for this damage due to their failure to perform the contract. Accordingly, such failure would be in a 'lag phase' until Delta took legal action against Alpha. At the moment when Alpha is sued with the direct action (*sub* 1) by Delta, Alpha then has a right to compensation against Beta, and it is this right that Delta can exercise by subrogating Alpha.

A recent decision of the Court of Cassation[56] seems to pave the way for a new solution which would benefit Delta. In this case, Delta may take direct action against the seller, Alpha, under Art. 1669 c.c. The abstract of the judgment reads as follows: 'The seller that, under his direction and control, had renovation or long-term maintenance works performed on the property

---

54 Art. 1495, paras. 1 and 2, c.c. stipulate that the buyer forfeits the right of warranty if they fail to notify the seller of the defects within eight days from their discovery (unless the seller concealed them in bad faith). Courts take the view that the eight-day limitation period starts when the buyer had knowledge of the defects (Cass., s.u., 11 July 2019, no. 18672, *Massimario Giustizia civile* (2019)). The action prescribes one year from discovery (Art. 1495, para. 3, c.c.).

55 Being called to court to respond to a claim for damages could be considered, for Alpha, a harm in itself, as the risk of having to pay the compensation is already considered a harm; this fulfills the conditions for exercising the subrogation action.

56 Cass., 28 July 2017, no. 18891, *Foro italiano*, I (2018), p. 2169.

that he later transferred, is liable to the buyer under art. 1669 c.c. where those works are destroyed or present serious defects.' Alpha (seller) would, therefore, have to compensate Delta directly, without Delta having to sue Beta (i.e. the contractor that performed negligent works). However, this solution results from a misunderstanding, originated by legislative policy (see below).

III. Meta-Legal Formants

Beta's contractual liability towards the third party is supported by strong arguments of *policy* (based on a standard of reasonableness)[57] in all cases in which, as in the case at hand, the contract concerns the construction or maintenance of a building. Since the construction contract is the ordinary instrument for performing works on buildings, it is reasonable that the contractor's obligations exist against anyone who is damaged by their failure to perform the contract.

An additional direct consequence of the standard of reasonableness[58] is the avoidance of unequal treatment in the regime of liability for the parties to the contract and third parties. Unequal treatment would be unreasonable because the customer and their successors in interest are entitled to equal treatment in their ownership of the property. Accordingly, it would be unreasonable to allow the customer ten years (the limitation period for contractual liability actions) but the successor in interest only five years (the limitation period for extracontractual liability actions) to raise an action.

The courts' policy encourages the transfer of losses resulting from defects in construction or renovation to contractors, even where they affect only the successors in interest. In this way, the wall of privity of contract is breached, to the benefit of the third party. This principle has understandable explanations, but it would be better to pursue it overtly (the policy of urban regulation imposes

---

57 Reliance on public policy reflects a non-regulated urban planning and marks a hybridisation of public and private law. Reliance on reasons of '*sûreté publique*' can be found in the preparatory works of the French Code Civil too: P.-A. Fenet (ed), *Recueil complet des travaux préparatoires du Code civil* (Paris: Videcoq, 1836), t. 14, p. 263; Art. 1792 of the Code was then construed as a provision of *ordre public*: R.T. Troplong, *Le droit civil expliqué suivant l'ordre du Code. De l'échange et du louage, ou commentaire des titres VII et VIII du livre III du Code civil* (Bruxelles: Meline, Cans et co., 1841), §995, p. 272. Reference to public policy is made by the scholarship on the previous civil code of 1865 (Art. 1639 c.c. of 1865): M. Vita Levi, *Della locazione di opere e più specialmente degli appalti* (Turin: Unione Tipografico-Editrice, 1876), vol. II, §152, p. 106; the invocation of public policy was rejected by modern scholarship: D. Rubino and G. Iudica, 'Dell'appalto, *sub* Art. 1669', *Commentario del codice civile Scialoja e Branca* (Bologna/Rome: Zanichelli-Foro italiano, 4th ed., 2007), pp. 452 ff. Today, the public aspect of construction is urban planning law; the private aspect is the construction contract, which extends the protection against failure of performance to successors in interest.

58 On the value of this formula, see G. Perlingieri, *Profili applicativi della ragionevolezza nel diritto civile* (Naples: Edizioni Scientifiche Italiane, 2015), pp. 125 ff.; N. Lipari, *Diritto civile e ragione* (Milan: Giuffrè, 2019), pp. 48 ff. and 105 ff.

that Delta have a direct contractual action against Alpha),[59] and not through the artifices of an extension of extracontractual liability under Art. 1669 c.c.[60] Under the extracontractual regime, the damage would be attributed jointly to the seller (Alpha) and the contractor (Beta): they would be jointly and severally liable for causing extracontractual damage.[61] Under a contractual liability regime, the burden of proof would instead favour Delta.[62] The Court of Cassation's opinion about the extracontractual nature of liability builds on a precedent[63] in which the extracontractual nature of liability under Art. 1669 was questioned to a considerable extent. It would be better to classify, at first hand, the liability under Art. 1669 for the loss suffered by the third party as contractual. Actually, current case law on extracontractual liability represents the right solution achieved in the wrong way.

2.8. THE NETHERLANDS

Jan Biemans

I. *Operative Rules*

1. Delta can take action against Beta to recover their loss, on the basis that Delta acquired the rights of Alpha against Beta when acquiring the property. Delta might possibly also do so on the basis of an unlawful act by Beta.
2. Delta can demand that Alpha assist Delta in preparing their claim and proceedings against Beta, but cannot force Alpha to take action to recover the loss from Beta directly.

II. *Descriptive Formants*

Delta can take action against Beta to recover their loss, on the basis that Delta acquired the rights of Alpha against Beta when acquiring the property.

---

59 This is a direct consequence of the application of constitutional principles mediated by the public order clause, interpreted according to the directives of urban regulation. The urban regulation is public law, but affects the construction of private law actions of the third-party purchaser against defects that can be ascribed to the contractor.

60 Cass., 28 July 2017, no. 18891, *Foro italiano*, I (2018), §III.2 of reasoning.

61 If the rules of non-contractual liability were applied, the conclusion would be that the damage to Delta has been jointly caused by Beta (who carried out defective building work) and Alpha (who sold a defective good), in which case they would both be jointly and severally liable to pay damages (Art. 2055 c.c.).

62 In contractual liability, the burden of proof is on the party that caused the damage (debtor); in non-contractual liability, it is on the injured party (creditor of the compensation debt). Arts. 1218 and 2043 c.c.

63 Cass., s.u., 27 March 2017, no. 7756, *Responsabilità Civile e Previdenza*, 4 (2017), §VII of reasoning.

Alpha entered into a contract with Beta for works to be carried out to the property, and later sold (and transferred) the property to Delta. The damage – the cracks in the walls – is due to work carried out defectively by Beta. It is a given that this constitutes a breach of the contractual obligations of Beta towards Alpha (Article 6:74 DCC).

First, Delta has acquired the right of Alpha against Beta to have the works to the property carried out correctly, and thus without defects. When Alpha transferred the property to Delta, Delta also acquired this right by operation of law. According to Article 6:251 (1) DCC, where a transferable right arising from an agreement is connected in such a way to a specific property of the creditor (Alpha) that the creditor only has any interest in that right for as long as they retain this property, this right will pass by operation of law to the person that acquires the property (Delta) under particular title (for example, sale). The rights in Article 6:251 (1) DCC are called 'qualitative rights' *(kwalitatieve rechten)*, as they follow the person of the owner of the good to which they are connected.[64] Another example of such qualitative rights may be a guarantee of the seller of a good, with regard to a product sold, in which the owner of the good only has an interest for as long as they retain this good. Upon the sale of the good to another person, the qualitative right transfers to the new owner of the good by operation of law.

It is crucial that the cracks appeared a year after the sale and transfer of the property to Delta. If the cracks had appeared before the sale and transfer, Alpha would have held the right to claim damages. Article 6:251 DCC does not apply to already-existing compensatory claims for damages.[65] Alpha would have had to transfer (assign) such a claim separately to Delta, in order to have it pass to Delta. Such transfers often happen in practice.

Second, in more exceptional circumstances, the defective work by Beta to the property could constitute an unlawful act against the acquirer of the property. The Dutch Supreme Court has decided that bringing polluted premises into trade by a municipality without warning about the pollution may constitute an unlawful act, not only against the buyer, but also against third parties that later acquire the property, if there are exceptional additional circumstances (such as a building obligation implicitly guaranteeing that the property is not polluted).[66] In different case law,[67] the Dutch Supreme Court has also ruled that a producer

---

64 Ibid., pp. 541 ff.

65 M.v.A. II, Parl. Gesch. Boek 6, p. 933; J.W.A. Biemans, *Rechtsgevolgen van stille cessie*, Deventer: Kluwer 2011, no. 334 and 417.

66 Dutch Supreme Court, 24 March 2006, ECLI:NL:HR:2006:AU7492, NJ 2007/377 *(Geldermalsen/Plameco)*.

67 Dutch Supreme Court, 22 October 1999, ECLI:NL:HR:1999:ZC2994, NJ 2000/159 *(Koolhaas/Rockwool)*; Dutch Supreme Court, 22 September 2000, ECLI:NL:HR:2000:AA7239, NJ 2000/644 *(Haagman/Vaessen-Schoemaker)*; Dutch Supreme Court, 13 January 2017, ECLI:NL:HR:2017:32, NJ 2017/48 *(DAF/Achmea)*.

who puts into circulation a product that causes damage during normal usage for which the product is intended may be liable not only towards consumers, on the basis of product liability, but also towards third parties in general, on the basis of an unlawful act. It could be argued that, if the works constitute a 'product' causing danger of collapse (and/or other safety risks), Beta would be directly liable towards Delta. In other circumstances, it is very uncertain whether a direct action by Delta against Beta would be possible.[68]

Delta cannot force Alpha to take action to recover the loss from Beta directly. The most important reason for this is that Alpha have no claim against Beta, as the right has passed to Delta, as explained above. Moreover, Alpha have no loss: they have sold the property to Delta for its full market value, based on the premises being in good condition with no major works being required, and Delta had to satisfy themselves on the quality of the premises, meaning that Delta cannot claim damages from Alpha. If Delta could have claimed damages from Alpha, this could at least have qualified as a loss for Alpha, but this is not the case. However, it could be argued that Alpha, being a party to the contract, with considerable knowledge about the works carried out by Beta, are obliged to assist Delta in their proceedings against Beta, based on the standards of reasonableness and fairness (Article 6:248 DCC), combined with the rights and obligations of the old and new creditors of claims (Articles 6:142 ff. DCC).[69] According to Article 6:248 (1) DCC, an agreement not only has the legal effects which parties have agreed upon, but also those which, due to the nature of the agreement, arise from law, usage (common practice) or the standards of reasonableness and fairness.

III. Meta-Legal Formants

Article 6:251 (2) to (4) DCC contain more provisions, which do not apply in this case. Article 6:251 (2) DCC provides what should happen with remaining (counter-)obligations of the (previous) owner: where, in the exchange of a qualitative right, a counter-performance has been agreed upon between the transferor and the third party, this counter-performance obligation also passes to the new owner, as far as it relates to the period after the passage of the right connected with the transferred property. Although this counter-performance

---

68 Another point of view, with a different criterion from Dutch Supreme Court, 24 September 2004, ECLI:NL:HR:2004:AO9069, NJ 2008/587 *(Vleesmeesters/Alog)*, can be found in Dutch Supreme Court, 20 January 2012, ECLI:NL:HR:2012:BT7496, NJ 2012/59, where the client could (successfully) sue a subcontractor for defective work on the basis on an unlawful act. Among other things, the liability was constituted on the fact that the subcontractor knew that, ultimately, through a chain of contracts, a third party (the client) had an interest in the work being executed, which makes it different from the present case.

69 See, generally, J.W.A. Biemans, *Rechtsgevolgen van stille cessie*, Deventer: Kluwer 2011.

obligation passes to the acquiring party, the former owner (the alienating or transferring party) remains liable for the counter-performance. The former owner is not liable for this counter-performance insofar as the counterparty to the agreement is able to release themselves, after the passing of the property (and the passing of the right), from their obligation towards the acquiring party, by a rescission or termination of that agreement (from which the qualitative right and the counter-performance arise) on the basis of non-performance by the acquiring party of the counter-performance.

According to Article 6:251 (3) DCC, Article 6:251 (1) and (2) DCC do not apply if the acquiring party (Delta) has notified the counterparty to the agreement (Beta) that they do not accept the passing of the right, which is not the case here. The juridical act under which the property has been transferred may result in no rights from the agreement passing to another party (Article 6:251 (4) DCC), meaning that the qualitative rights may be excluded in the transfer between the current and new owners of the property.

2.9. POLAND

Dariusz Szostek

I. Operative Rules

1. The provisions of Polish law do not provide any possibility for Delta to take direct action against Beta in order to recover the loss of €1.5 million. Furthermore, Alpha cannot take action against Beta to recover Delta's loss of €1.5 million; Alpha can only transfer to Delta the right to demand a reduction in the price of the real estate.
2. Delta do not have any real means of forcing Alpha to take action against Beta in order to recover the loss. A subsidiary solution may be that Delta claims their rights against Alpha (on the basis of contractual breach or implied warranty) and then Alpha exercise the right of recourse against Beta, or the transfer to Delta of rights under the provisions of the PCC regarding the implied warranty.

II. Descriptive Formants

According to the facts presented, Alpha did not violate the provisions of the agreement between Alpha and Delta. Delta are entitled to take action resulting from the provisions of the PCC regarding the implied warranty (in Polish, '*rękojmia*'): that is, (1) to submit a statement on the price reduction; (2) to withdraw from the contract, on the basis of Article 560 §1 PCC; (3) to request a replacement of the item (thing) by one free from defects; or (4) to request the removal of the defect, on the basis of Article 561 §1 PCC.[70] Pursuant to Article 568 §§2 and 3 PCC, Delta are entitled, within one year of finding a defect, to file a claim against Alpha,[71] demanding that Alpha remove the defect or replace the item (thing) sold with one free from defects, or to submit a declaration of withdrawal from the agreement, or to demand a price reduction due to the item's defects.[72] Under Article 568 §1 PCC, 'the seller is liable under implied warranty if a physical defect is found within two years, and in the case of defects in real estate, within five years of the thing being handed over to the buyer'.

Further to the above-mentioned provisions, Alpha, as the sellers, are responsible to Delta for the real estate's physical defects, provided that these are identified within five years from the date of transfer of the real estate to Delta.[73] If Alpha refuse to rectify the defects, the buyer may direct other requests to the seller. In the event that Alpha continue to refuse, Delta have the right to bring appropriate legal actions against Alpha before the civil or commercial court, in order to reduce the price of the real estate by the amount of €1.5 million lost as a result of the cost of the works to rectify the defective renovation works.[74] Delta have no claim against Beta; under Polish law, they only have a claim against the seller of the property (Alpha).

At the same time, the sale of the item (thing) does not result in the transfer to the purchaser of rights under the warranty for its physical defects.[75] The seller (Alpha) may, however, transfer to the buyer (Delta) the right to request a price reduction, the removal of the defect, or the provision of a thing free from defects.[76] If Beta gave a guarantee for the performance of the renovation, or if these rights result from non-compliance with the contract, Alpha may transfer these rights to Delta. If, however, no warranty or non-conformity with the contract has been given, or its term has expired, there is no basis for Alpha to transfer the rights.

The provisions of Polish law do not allow Delta to take direct action against Beta in order to recover the loss of €1.5 million. In the event that a loss has

70 A. Kubiak-Cyrul, 'Komentarz do art. 560' in M. Załucki (ed), *Kodeks cywilny. Komentarz*, Warsaw 2019; A. Brzozowski, 'Komentarz do art. 561' in K. Pietrzykowski (ed), *Kodeks cywilny. T II. Komentarz. Art. 450–1088. Przepisy wprowadzające*, Warsaw 2018.

71 J.P. Naworski, 'Terminy rękojmi za wady fizyczne – glosa – III CZP 39/02', *Monitor Prawniczy* 2004, no. 1, p. 146.

72 F. Zoll, *Rękojmia. Odpowiedzialność sprzedawcy*, Warsaw 2018.

73 K. Haładyj and M. Tulibacka, 'Komentarz do art. 560' in K. Osajda (ed), *Kodeks cywilny. Komentarz*, Warsaw 2019.

74 K. Żok, 'Obniżenie ceny w świetle znowelizowanych przepisów o rękojmi', *Ius Novum* 2016, no. 4, p. 170.

75 K. Koch, 'Przejście uprawnień z tytułu rękojmi na kolejnego nabywcę rzeczy – glosa – III CZP 96/03', *Monitor Prawniczy* 2007, no. 3, p. 156.

76 Resolution of the Supreme Court (Sąd Najwyższy, SN) of 5 May 2004, ref. file no. III CZP 96/03.

occurred, the only options for Delta to seek compensation for the loss are to obtain a reduction in the sale price, require the seller to remedy the defect, or – where it is either not a physical defect, or is a defect impossible to repair – withdraw from the contract. It is worth noting that, according to Polish regulations, a seller has a return claim against Beta. Significantly, such claim would be available if non-compliance with the contract has been shown, or if a guarantee has been invoked (if such a guarantee has been established).[77]

2.10. SCOTLAND

Lorna MacFarlane

I. *Operative Rules*

1. *Alpha* can take action against Beta to recover Delta's loss.
2. Delta *cannot* force Alpha to make a claim against Beta.

II. *Descriptive Formants*

This case would be resolved in accordance with the 'transferred loss doctrine', which has been developed in Scotland through case law. Where loss results from a breach of a contract between two parties, but the loss has somehow (wholly or partly) 'transferred' to another, there is a legal 'black hole'.[78] This is because the party on which the loss falls has no title to sue under the contract between the two contracting parties, and the party which did not cause the loss has no interest to sue, because it has transferred its interest in the relevant property to the third party. The transferred loss doctrine allows the contracting party which did not cause the loss (i.e. the party that transferred the property) to claim against the other contracting party in respect of the loss suffered by the party on which the loss falls.[79]

---

77 E. Habryn-Chojnacka, 'Komentarz do art. 568' in M. Gutowski (ed), *Kodeks cywilny. Tom II. Komentarz, Art. 353–626*, Warsaw 2019.

78 *J Dykes Ltd. v. Littlewoods Mail Order Stores Ltd* 1982 SLT 50 at 54 per Lord Stewart.

79 *McLaren Murdoch & Hamilton Ltd v. The Abercromby Motor Group* 2003 SCLR 323 at para. 33 per Lord Drummond Young; *Axon Well Intervention Products Holdings v. Michael Craig* [2015] CSOH 4 at para. 29 per Lord Doherty; *The Most Honourable Alexander George Gordon, Marquess of Aberdeen and Temair v. Messrs Turcan Connell* [2008] CSOH 183 at para. 45 per Lady Smith. For discussion in commentary, see G. Jackson, *The Laws of Scotland: Stair Memorial Encyclopaedia: Building Contracts*, reissue (LexisNexis/Law Society of Scotland, London/Edinburgh 2012), para. 158; M. Hogg, *Obligations*, 2nd ed. (Avizandum, Edinburgh 2006), para. 3.174; J. Thomson, 'Restitutionary and performance damages' (2001) 8 *Scots Law Times (News)* 71, 73–74.

The party on which the loss falls cannot, however, recover damages at its own suit: it must rely on the contracting party to sue on its behalf, and it cannot force the party to bring a claim.[80] There are two possible reasons for this. Firstly, it is recognised in case law that the party on whom the loss falls is not the recipient of a third-party right,[81] and so the basis of any claim by that party is unclear. Secondly, there are two possible explanations for the recovery of the third party's loss: the 'broad' and 'narrow' grounds. The narrow ground, which is dominant in Scots law,[82] provides that the loss falls on the party to which the property is transferred, and the contracting party which transferred the property is entitled to recover on its behalf.[83] According to the broad ground, however, the loss falls on the contracting party which transferred the property, because that contracting party did not obtain the performance it bargained for in its contract with the party who caused the loss.[84] In terms of the narrow ground, the contracting party which transferred the property recovers on behalf of the third party, whereas the broad ground provides that the contracting party recovers its own loss. In English law, judicial and academic opinion on the two grounds are mixed,[85] and the adoption of transferred loss in Scots law was based on an English case decided in the House of Lords.[86] It is possible that judicial reluctance to consider whether the party on whom the loss falls should be able to make a direct claim stems from the ongoing uncertainty as to whether the loss should, in fact, be treated as that of the contracting party which transferred the property.

---

80 *McLaren Murdoch & Hamilton Ltd v. The Abercromby Motor Group* 2003 SCLR 323 at para. 42 per Lord Drummond Young; *The Most Honourable Alexander George Gordon, Marquess of Aberdeen and Temair v. Messrs Turcan Connell* [2008] CSOH 183 at para. 46 per Lady Smith; M. Hogg, *Obligations*, 2nd ed. (Avizandum, Edinburgh 2006), para. 3.188.

81 *McLaren Murdoch & Hamilton Ltd v. The Abercromby Motor Group* 2003 SCLR 323 at para. 39 per Lord Drummond Young. See also Scottish Law Commission, *Report on Third Party Rights* (Scot Law Com No. 245, 2016), para. 6.16.

82 *McLaren Murdoch & Hamilton Ltd v. The Abercromby Motor Group* 2003 SCLR 323 at paras. 40–41 per Lord Drummond Young.

83 See the English case of *Panatown Ltd v. Alfred McAlpine Construction Ltd* [2001] 1 AC 518 at 529 and 535 per Lord Clyde.

84 *Panatown Ltd v. Alfred McAlpine Construction Ltd* [2001] 1 AC 518 at 543–46 per Lord Goff of Chieveley, and at 586–92 per Lord Millett.

85 Compare e.g. I.N.D. Wallace, 'Third party damages: no legal black hole?' (1999) 115(Jul) *Law Quarterly Review* 394; B. Coote, 'The Performance Interest, Panatown, and the Problem of Loss' (2001) 117(Jan) *Law Quarterly Review* 81; G.H. Treitel, *The Law of Contract*, 9th ed. (Sweet & Maxwell, London 1995), p. 546 (broad ground); and H. Unberath, 'Third party losses and black holes: another view' (1999) 115(Jul) *Law Quarterly* Review 535, 540; and A. Mason, 'Privity – A Rule in Search of Decent Burial?' in P. Kincaid (ed), *Privity: Private Justice of Public Regulation* (Ashgate, Dartmouth 2001), p. 88 at p. 95 (narrow ground).

86 *McLaren Murdoch & Hamilton Ltd v. The Abercromby Motor Group* 2003 SCLR 323, in which Lord Drummond Young described *Panatown Ltd v. Alfred McAlpine Construction Ltd* [2001] 1 AC 518 as compatible with Scots law.

In this case, the parties to the works contract are Alpha and Beta. Beta's breach of contract has resulted in a €1.5 million loss, which has transferred to Delta because of the sale contract between Alpha and Delta. If Alpha wishes, it can take action against Beta to recover the loss, but it is not obliged to do so.

III. Meta-Legal Formants

There is some confusion in Scots law as to whether transferred loss operates in accordance with the intentions of the contracting parties. In the most recent case on the matter, Lord Doherty indicated that the transferred loss doctrine can apply where it is the 'imputed intention of the contracting parties' that the contract should benefit the third party.[87] However, this contradicts previous judicial comment: according to Lord Drummond Young[88] and Lady Smith,[89] transferred loss operates as a matter of general legal policy regardless of the intentions of the contracting parties.[90] While the role of intention in transferred loss cases is, thus, currently a point of uncertainty, transferred loss is underpinned by clear policy considerations, as case law[91] and commentary[92] recognise the importance of preventing damages 'black holes'.

The Scottish Law Commission recently contemplated reform of the transferred loss doctrine so as to allow the party which suffers the loss to have a direct claim against the party who caused the loss, without requiring the involvement of, or permission from, the other contracting party.[93] This difficulty has also been recognised in commentary: Hawkes observes that a contracting party in a company group 'might have no hesitation in doing the decent thing' in terms of handing over damages recovered in respect of loss suffered by another

---

87 *Axon Well Intervention Products Holdings v. Michael Craig* [2015] CSOH 4 at para. 45 per Lord Doherty.

88 *McLaren Murdoch & Hamilton Ltd v. The Abercromby Motor Group* 2003 SCLR 323 at para. 42 per Lord Drummond Young.

89 *The Most Honourable Alexander George Gordon, Marquess of Aberdeen and Temair v. Messrs Turcan Connell* [2008] CSOH 183 at para. 45 per Lady Smith.

90 See also M. Hogg, *Obligations*, 2nd ed. (Avizandum, Edinburgh 2006), para. 3.188; L. MacFarlane, 'Black Holes and Revelations on the Transferred Loss Doctrine' (2015) 19(3) *Edinburgh Law Review* 388.

91 *McLaren Murdoch & Hamilton Ltd v. The Abercromby Motor Group* 2003 SCLR 323 at para. 33 per Lord Drummond Young; *Axon Well Intervention Products Holdings v. Michael Craig* [2015] CSOH 4 at para. 29 per Lord Doherty. See also *The Most Honourable Alexander George Gordon, Marquess of Aberdeen and Temair v. Messrs Turcan Connell* [2008] CSOH 183 at para. 45 per Lady Smith.

92 G. Jackson, *The Laws of Scotland: Stair Memorial Encyclopaedia: Building Contracts*, reissue (LexisNexis/Law Society of Scotland, London/Edinburgh 2012), para. 158; G. Hawkes, 'Emerging from a Black Hole' (2003) 38 *Scots Law Times* 285, 288. See also Scottish Law Commission, *Report on Review of Contract Law: Formation, Interpretation, Remedies for Breach, and Penalty Clauses* (Scot Law Com No. 252, 2018), para. 18.28.

93 Scottish Law Commission, *Report on Review of Contract Law: Formation, Interpretation, Remedies for Breach, and Penalty Clauses* (Scot Law Com No. 252, 2018), paras. 18.36–18.41.

company in the group, but questions the practical implications of permitting only the contracting party to recover where its relationship with the third party is at arm's length.[94] However, the Scottish Law Commission concluded that it could not provide 'a satisfactory solution to the difficulties raised by [the third party's] present inability to recover transferred loss directly without much further investigation of the various commercial and other contexts in which the issue may arise'.[95] Accordingly, further research on the point is required, in Scots law, to explore whether there are sound policy considerations to support a direct third-party claim.[96]

In the leading English case on transferred loss, *Panatown Ltd v. Alfred McAlpine Construction Ltd*,[97] the doctrine was treated as a remedy of last resort. The transferred loss claim was unsuccessful because the party that suffered the loss had a right of action against the party in breach under a duty of care deed to which it was party. A recent Scottish case, *Axon Well Intervention Products Holdings v. Michael Craig*,[98] recognised that, where the contracting parties provide a third-party right or an alternative direct right of claim for the party which suffered the loss, a transferred loss claim will not be possible. However, Lord Docherty also stated that, where the contracting parties have not provided a means for the third party to make a direct claim, but a non-contractual remedy is available, this must provide 'equivalent means of redress and equivalent prospects of success to an action for damages for breach of contract', in order to exclude a transferred loss claim.[99] In Scots law, the transferred loss doctrine does not operate where the third party can make a contractual claim, but allows for recovery of the loss where the third party is unable to make a claim equivalent to a claim for damages for breach of contract.

2.11. SLOVAKIA

Kristián Csach, Monika Jurčová, Peter Mészáros and Veronika Zoričáková

I. Operative Rules

1. Delta can take action against Beta, provided the contract on transfer of premises is classified as a contract on sale of an enterprise under Slovak law, requiring all assets, or a part of the enterprise forming a cluster of assets, to

94 G. Hawkes, 'Emerging from a Black Hole' (2003) 38 *Scots Law Times* 285, 286.
95 Scottish Law Commission, *Report on Review of Contract Law: Formation, Interpretation, Remedies for Breach, and Penalty Clauses* (Scot Law Com No. 252, 2018), para. 18.56.
96 Ibid., para. 18.58.
97 *Panatown Ltd v. Alfred McAlpine Construction Ltd* [2001] 1 AC 518.
98 *Axon Well Intervention Products Holdings v. Michael Craig* [2015] CSOH 4.
99 Ibid., para. 42.

be transferred. Otherwise, the contract is an ordinary sales contract under which no claims are transferred to the buyer and Delta cannot directly sue Beta.

2. No, Delta can neither force Alpha to take any action against Beta nor require them to assist Delta in taking such action.

II. Descriptive Formants

Regarding question 1, the answer depends upon the qualification of the contractual relation between Alpha and Delta.

If the contract is a *contract on sale of a 'podnik'* (enterprise), all liabilities and rights of the seller (Alpha) regarding the undertaking against third parties are *ex lege* transferred to the buyer (Delta). According to section 476 (1) SCommC:

> Under a contract of sale of an enterprise, the seller undertakes to transfer to the buyer title to the things, other rights and other tangible values which are utilized in the operation of the respective enterprise, and the buyer undertakes to assume the obligations of the seller related to the enterprise and to pay the purchase price.

No contractual arrangement regarding non-liability of the parties (Alpha and Delta) in their mutual agreement will have an effect on third parties (such as Beta). A contract is considered a transfer of an enterprise if the entire enterprise is transferred. According to section 5 of the SCommC, the term 'enterprise' shall mean the whole of the tangible, intangible and personnel assets which are used in business. The enterprise comprises assets, rights and other valuables which belong to the entrepreneur and are – or, due to their characteristics, are supposed to be – used for the operation of the enterprise.

The same rules apply to contracts under which a certain part of an enterprise, being an independent organisational unit, is transferred (s. 487 SCommC). The term 'organisational unit' is not defined in, but only described by, the law (s. 7(1) SCommC), and its definition is disputed. According to legal writings, the organisational unit must represent a specific accounting subunit in order to constitute a part of the enterprise.[100]

If the premises in question form the enterprise of the seller (i.e. represent their entire operating assets) or a sufficiently stand-alone part of the enterprise forming an independent organisational unit, the contract will be characterised as a transfer of enterprise, with the effect of transferring the entire bundle of rights and obligations of the seller (relating to the enterprise) to the buyer. The buyer will step into the position of the seller and become their legal successor.

---

100 See M. Rušín, 'Schvaľovanie zmluvy o predaji (časti) podniku valným zhromaždením' [The approval of the contract on the transfer of enterprise by the shareholder assembly]', *Súkromné právo*, 6–7 (2015), p. 32.

The question whether some obligations or rights (such as a claim against Beta arising from the contract of work) forming part of the transferred enterprise might be excluded from the transfer of enterprise is disputed, but generally denied.[101] The aforementioned contractual arrangement between Alpha and Delta, stating that Alpha does not provide any warranty to Delta in relation to the premises, does not modify the object of the transfer – the extent of the rights and obligations against third parties that form part of the enterprise to be transferred. Such a contractual arrangement defines only the mutual relation between the seller and the purchaser arising from the transfer contract, and not the object of the transfer.

Therefore, under the contract on sale of an enterprise (or a part thereof), Alpha's claim against Beta would be transferred to Delta. It is assumed that the cracks in the walls are a defect caused by the work carried out by Beta. Delta (as Alpha's successor in the contractual arrangement) will have all the rights arising from the contract of work, and would have been obliged to notify Beta of the defect (s. 562 SCommC) as soon as it became noticeable, otherwise Beta might raise an objection of late notification, effectively barring the claim (ss. 564 ff. SCommC). If the defect was notified as soon as it appeared, Delta will have the possibility to demand, at its discretion, either partial return of the price paid, termination of the contract, repair, or compensation for damage incurred. Provided that no different contractual arrangements have been made, Delta may choose only one of the listed rights and cannot alter their choice afterwards without the consent of Beta. Given the facts of the case, the partial return of the price might be demanded. The calculated costs of the repair cannot be required directly,[102] but only if Beta fails to repair the defects as requested by Delta, and Delta arranges the repair at the expense of Beta.

If the transfer is instead considered a *pure contract of sale of premises* (or multiple contracts of sale of individual tangible and non-tangible assets), then no claim against Beta will have been transferred. As the object of the transfer comprises immoveable property, the rules on sales contracts in the Slovak Civil Code (SCC) would apply.[103] The liability for defects (Alpha against Beta) is a contractual liability, and would not automatically be transferred to Delta, as the

---

[101] See E. Valko and B. Jablonka, 'Zmluva o predaji podniku nepripúšťa dohodu o vylúčení niektorých práv a povinností (reakcia na článok) [Transfer of enterprise does not allow any arrangement on exclusion of certain rights or liabilites (a reaction)]', *Obchodné právo*, 8–9 (2004), pp. 22–23. In favour of a potential modification, see K. Csach in O. Ovečková et al., *Obchodný zákonník. Veľký komentár, vol. II [Commentary on Commercial Code II]*, Bratislava: Wolters Kluwer, 2017, s. 476.

[102] See P. Lukáčka, L. Dufalová and K. Lenhartová, *Zodpovednosť za vady diela [Liability for defects of the work]*, Bratislava: Wolters Kluwer, 2016, p. 141, approving the position of the Czech Supreme Court file no. 29 Odo 556/2003 dated 15.04.2004.

[103] According to s. 409 SCommC, the object of a commercial sales contract can only be goods (moveable things).

buyer of the asset. It is generally accepted that the liability for defects is not a liability *in rem* that would stick to the object transferred, and that it retains its *inter partes* contractual nature even after the object has been transferred,[104] unless special legislation provides otherwise.[105]

The contract of work between Alpha and Beta is not considered a contract in favour of potential third parties who might buy the object in the future, and the duties and liabilities of Beta are owed only to Alpha. Alpha and Beta have not entered into the contract with the will to create a separate title for Delta, who were not even known to Beta.

Regarding question 2, there is no acknowledged rule on loyalty between contractual parties, nor is there a duty to assist one's contractual partner in taking action against third parties, and the rules on liability for defects applicable in the relationship between Alpha and Delta do not give rise to any such right. The rules on liability for defects between Alpha and Delta (as in general) are non-mandatory for both situations (transfer of an enterprise according to the SCommC, or the sales contract according to the SCC). Parties may, therefore, effectively waive all claims for liability for defects. The illustrated arrangement between Alpha and Delta will be interpreted as the amendment of default liability rules and the exclusion of any claims by Delta against Alpha. Moreover, in the given scenario, the parties (Alpha and Delta) have made a clear arrangement regarding the quality of the premises, which might be interpreted as a way of dividing risk between the parties.

To conclude, neither an express nor an implicit duty of Alpha to assign its claims against Beta, nor a duty for Alpha to assist Delta, are provided for under Slovak law.

2.12. SPAIN

Carles Vendrell Cervantes

I. *Operative Rules*

1. *Delta* would be able to take action against Beta to recover their €1.5 million loss, on the basis of the non-contractual liability established in the Spanish

[104] The singular opposite view relating to the *ex lege* liability for defects (legal warranty), which will be interpreted as a liability sticking to the thing *(in rem)* in the event of its transfer, has been promoted by P. Vojčík, *Občianske právo hmotné II [Substantive Civil Law II]*, Košice: UPJŠ, 2006, p. 61.

[105] According to s. 9 of the Act on Ownership of Flats, claims against the party who built an apartment block, arising from liability for defects, are transferred from the original owner of the building to the owners of the flats.

Law 38/1999 of 5 November, on building regulation ('Ley de ordenación de la edificación'), if applicable.

2. Delta *would not be able* to require Alpha to do anything in connection with the potential recovery from Beta. Delta may only request Alpha to provide the necessary documentation in order to prepare their case against Beta (on the basis of the general rule of civil procedure regulation, namely Law 1/2000 of 7 January, on civil procedure).

On a different note, Alpha would theoretically be entitled to make a claim against Beta on the basis of the contract concluded with Beta for the works carried out to Alpha's premises, and request specific performance (i.e. performance in kind) under Article 1124(2) of the Spanish Civil Code, in order to have Beta repair the walls (as their performance would amount to a defective performance). The specific performance claim, which, under Spanish law,[106] clearly includes the 'remedying of a defective performance', does not require the claimant to evidence a loss (which is only a requirement for damages claim).

II. Descriptive Formants

Question 1

As far as the works carried out by Beta are 'significant', the Spanish Law 38/1999 of 5 November, on building regulation ('Ley de ordenación de la edificación') may apply. This law applies, amongst other things, to any works carried out on a building (a concept in which Alpha's head office premises should be included) that imply an alteration of the building's architectural configuration (which also seems likely, given the stated facts of the case).

Law 38/1999 recognises the right of the owner or the third-party purchaser (in this case, Delta) to take action against the natural or legal persons involved in the construction process (i.e. Beta).

If Law 38/1999 were inapplicable (which would depend, as mentioned, on the type of works carried out by Beta), Delta's potential claim against Beta would not necessarily be excluded, as it might be construed as a general non-contractual liability (i.e. a general tort law claim or an unjustified enrichment claim), based on the Spanish Civil Code. It is clear that the contractual liability and consequent remedies that result from the contract between Alpha and Beta were not transferred to Delta on the basis of the contract of sale of the premises. Therefore, if Law 38/1999 were inapplicable, the only possible claim between Delta and Alpha should be sought on non-contractual bases; that is, (1) the general clause of Article 1902 of the Civil Code that states that 'the person who,

[106] Á. Carrasco, *Derecho de contratos* (3rd ed., Thomson-Aranzadi, 2021), 1170.

as a result of an action or omission, causes damage to another by his fault or negligence shall be obliged to repair the damage caused'; or (2) an unjustified enrichment claim (which is, in Spain, an institution created by case law, as the Spanish Civil Code does not establish it). Albeit that they are not excluded, both claims are difficult to envisage in this case, as it is very uncertain: (1) whether the damage suffered by Delta is directly attributable to Beta (for instance, it may be argued that it is, in part, attributable to the decision of Delta to not establish a contractual provision with Alpha to cover this potential liability); and (2) whether the enrichment experienced by Beta is justified because of the contract between Alpha and Beta.

Question 2

Spanish law does not provide for any specific claim that would entitle Delta to force Alpha to assist Delta in enforcing Delta's claim against Beta. As indicated above, the only provision that would be relevant is the law on civil procedure, in connection with the production of evidence necessary to enforce that claim against Delta.

2.13. SWEDEN

Oskar Mossberg

I. *Operative Rules*

1. *Neither Alpha nor Delta* can take action against Beta to recover Delta's loss.
2. *Delta cannot force Alpha* to take any action or require Alpha to do anything that would assist Delta in recovering their loss from Beta.

II. *Descriptive Formants*

Regarding question 1, Delta do not have any contractual recourse against Alpha, as according to the express wording of the case there is no breach of contract. There is simply no legal support for such a claim.

However, parenthetically (and this is going to be a rather long parenthesis, spanning the whole current paragraph), it should be noted that, according to Swedish law, the factual situation would most likely include a breach of contract in the form of a *'faktiskt fel'* (factual error), leading to the availability of contractual remedies for Delta against Alpha, including *'ersättning för avhjälpandekostnader'* (recompense for correction costs). This form of compensation does not require any warranties. Provided that the premises are considered *'lös egendom'* (loose/non-real property), the right to remedies follows from the supplementary derogatory rules in the Sale of Goods Act (Köplagen (1990:931) (the Purchase Act)), which would be applicable as long as the parties have not contracted out of them. If the premises are, instead, considered *'fast egendom'* (land/real property), the applicable rules would be found in Jordabalken (the Earth Balk (1970:994)), which is the central Swedish statutory Act on real property. The relevant rule on *'fel'* (error) is found in its Chapter 4, section 19, which would be applicable (provided the parties have not opted out from it). There are thus two alternatives concerning the rules applicable. Which of these alternatives is 'right' depends on how the case is interpreted, and in particular how the word 'premises' is read. (The national reporter who authored the text you are currently reading initially, albeit without much reflection, found the 'non-real property' interpretation to be more plausible.[107] This volume's editors then proposed that the 'real property' reading was to be preferred as the intended meaning.)[108] The Swedish rules concerning *'fel'* (error) are generally similar for non-real and real property. One difference, however, is that Jordabalken (concerning real property) does not include recompense for correction costs *('ersättning för avhjälpandekostnader')* as a contractual remedy which does not require negligence or a warranty. For real property, the remedies available are *'skadestånd'* (damages) and *'prisavdrag'* (price reduction). In practice, the purchaser could try to claim compensation by demanding a price reduction. In litigation, this can be done by stating something like, 'due to the state of the property, at the time of the passing of risk, i.e. at the time the purchaser got access to the property, it was worth less than what the purchaser paid'. However, in principle, it is more formally correct to consider the costs incurred (recompense for correction costs) as a form of injury to be remedied by compensation for damages. The purchaser would, therefore, need to claim damages, which (unlike price reduction, or, in the non-real property system, compensation for correction costs) according to Chapter 4, section 19, would require either: (1) negligence on the part of the seller; or (2) an (implied) warranty granted by the seller. As already mentioned, however, according to the wording of the case there is no breach of contract, and thus this is merely a comment on a hypothetical case.

---

107 From a Swedish perspective, the 'non-real' interpretation seemed closer to hand. Directly translated, the word 'premises' does not mean *'hus'* (house) or *'byggnad'* (building), in which case the 'real' interpretation would have seemed closer to hand: rather, it means *'lokal'* (premises), a concept which, in Swedish legal nomenclature, is closely tied to *'hyresgästens nyttjanderätt'* (the tenants right of use), as the *'lokal'* is the thing to which the tenant's right entitles them. In practice, a tenant's right of use (the contractual right of a tenant pursuant to the contract with the landlord) is often sold (by the tenant, to a new tenant) as an object of non-real property (see also Case 6 below).

108 The national reporter found this to be an illustrative example of how translatability issues can affect comparative studies.

As exemplified by the quote from NJA 1997 p. 44, cited in the answers to Case 1 above, Delta does not derive any rights from the contract between Alpha and Beta. In the present case, there are no applicable exceptions to this general rule, and any potential claim Alpha might have against Beta would not benefit Delta. This has been viewed as a shortcoming of Swedish law, and there are statutory exceptions for some consumer cases.[109]

As Alpha has not suffered any losses, Alpha would not have any action against Beta; no harm has befallen Alpha, and therefore Alpha has no recourse against Beta. Had Alpha incurred costs for correcting an error (for example, due to having to pay Delta), Alpha would, in principle, have a right to claim *'påföljder på grund av avtalsbrott'* (recourses due to a breach of contract) from Beta. As any costs Alpha has had in relation to Delta would be viewed as *'ekonomisk skada'* (economic loss), the applicable recourse would be *'skadestånd'* (damages). However, a breach of contract, as such, does not suffice as a basis for liability in damages, which, according to general rules, requires either negligence or breach of warranty. As there is no indication that Alpha has given any guarantees, or been negligent in relation to Delta, Delta would not be able to claim damages. If Alpha were to pay Delta, despite not needing to pursuant to their contractual relationship, this would most likely be regarded as a kind of *'gåva'* (gift), and Alpha would not be able to recover the cost from Beta (this follows from the principle of NJA 2010 p. 629).

There is a non-contractual rule regarding property damage in Skadeståndslagen (1972:207) (the Act on Damages), Chapter 2, Article 2. Skadeståndslagen is a generally applicable statutory law concerning tortious damages (see Case 3 below). The provision in Chapter 2, Article 2 can be described as a general tort of negligence. It is applicable even in contractual relations (unless the parties have agreed to limit their liability for negligence by including a non-liability clause of some kind), which means that negligently caused property damage can give rise to a claim for non-contractual damages. This rule is applicable to *'entreprenadavtal'* (development contracts); that is, contracts regarding work on buildings. However, as there is no indication that Beta has been negligent in relation to Delta, Delta would be unable to claim such damages.

The fact that the nature of the damage to the building meant that Delta could not have found out about it before the sale could, in principle, affect Delta's right to take action against Alpha. However, as Delta do not have any such right, this is of no consequence here.

109 Interestingly, the otherwise quite similar Norwegian Law of Sales (Lov om Kjøp, Art. 84(1)) has been amended to allow a purchaser to make *'krav som følge av mangel'* (claims that follow from error), the equivalent of the Swedish *'fel'*, directly against the seller's seller, provided that the seller could make an equivalent claim. The doctrinal explanation is that the sales contract entails a transfer of some of the seller's rights from the previous sales contract (an implicit assignment of claim).

Regarding question 2, there are no legal grounds which would allow Delta to force Alpha to take any action, or require Alpha to do anything that would assist Delta in recovering their loss from Beta. There are no rules conferring such rights on Delta. The right to *'väcka talan'* (file suit) – to take action in court, including the (negative) right to abstain from taking action – is viewed as an important part of the autonomy of individuals, and there are no rules conferring a right to demand specific performance in the form of demanding another person to bring an action in court. Given the basic freedom of contract *('avtalsfrihet')*, the parties can, of course, assume different duties, including the duty to take action. In practice, the parties to a contract might also agree upon various *'viten'* (penalty fees) which can be used by the creditor as a way of exerting pressure on the debtor to perform or abstain from doing something, including taking action. In the absence of such provisions (and in the absence of other remedies of contractual breach providing economic incentives to aid Delta), there is, however, not much a party in Delta's position can do to force another person to do their bidding.

III. Meta-Legal Formants

The basic idea and traditional stance of Swedish contract law is that claims should be channelled *('kanaliserade')* through a series of claims throughout the chain of contracts. The rationales for this stance have been touched upon in Case 1 above. The stance has been criticised and, even though one can never be certain, future developments toward a more liberal stance on third-party effects do not seem unlikely.

As has already been mentioned, there are several exceptions to, and ways of circumventing, this main principle (for example, voluntary assignment of claims, which can make the channelling process less cumbersome).

Many of the existing exceptions are justified on the grounds of third-party protection, especially where the third party is a consumer or has suffered damages. For example, the Act on Consumer Purchases (Konsumentköplagen (2022:260)), Chapter 8, Article 5, allows a consumer (A) a direct claim against the seller's (B's) seller (C), if the goods are defective and the seller (B) is in default, provided that the seller (B) would have had an equivalent claim against the previous seller (C). This rule is based on pragmatic rationales regarding the need for consumer protection. Another example can be found in the Act on Insurance Contracts (Försäkringsavtalslagen (2005:104)), Chapter 9, Article 7, which allows a party who has suffered loss to make claims directly against the injuring party's liability insurer. This rule is based, inter alia, on the interest of protecting injured parties. If it were not for the rule, the insurance monies could, for example, be paid out to the injuring party's insolvency estate, and then divided equally between all the creditors (pursuant to the principle of equal treatment of the creditors (see section III of Case 1 above)). This would mean that the injured party would typically only get a small portion of the compensation. This result is avoided by the rule in the Act on Insurance Contracts.[110]

3. COMPARATIVE REMARKS

Jan Biemans and Lorna Richardson

This case considers the situation in which a loss is caused to one party (X) by the actions or omissions of another (Y), with whom X is not in a contractual relationship. The loss has resulted due to a breach of contract where the contract is between Y and another party (Z). There is another contract or transaction between X and Z, but no breach by Z thereunder entitling X to claim damages or any other remedy. As a result, the party who has title to sue (Z) has suffered no loss as a result of Y's actions or omissions, and the party who has suffered loss (X) has no title to sue.[111] The case asks what happens in this scenario – can X or Z take action against Y to recover X's loss? Can X force Z to take action against Y, or take any steps that would assist X to recover its loss?

Question 1

The responses to this question were far from unanimous; there were varying conclusions across the jurisdictions. There were also different legal bases used by the different legal systems, even where they came to the same result.

In the majority of jurisdictions surveyed in this volume, Delta would have a right to take action against Beta to recover their loss. In Belgium, France and the Netherlands, the right to sue Beta passed to Delta, as the claim followed ownership of the building. It was thought that a claim on this basis might also be possible in Czech law. In a similar vein, in Italy, Delta could sue as a successor to the owner. Delta's right to sue Beta on the basis of non-contractual liability is regulated by specific building regulations in Spain, but might also, theoretically,

[110] See O. Mossberg, *Avtalets räckvidd I: Om avtals tredjemansverkningar, särskilt vid tredjemansavtal och direktkrav*, Iustus, Uppsala 2020, pp. 694 ff. In English, see L. Zackariasson, 'Privity of Contract and Direct Claims' in T. Håstad (ed), *The Nordic Contracts Act: Essays in Celebration of its One Hundredth Anniversary*, Djøf Publishing, Copenhagen 2015, pp. 229 ff.

[111] Although the outcome may look similar to the scenario where Y, acting under a contract with Z, causes a loss to X, in which case some jurisdictions, such as Dutch and German law, would consider whether the doctrine of transferred loss *(Drittschadensliquidation)* should apply, this is not the case here, as Z entered into the contract on their own behalf, not on behalf of X. *Drittschadensliquidation* is considered in Case 4 below.

be based, albeit with some difficulties, on a general tort law or unjustified enrichment claim.

In other jurisdictions, such as Bulgaria and England, the claim against Beta would not follow the ownership of the building, but Delta could, nevertheless, sue Beta. In English law, Delta would have a third-party right from the contract between Alpha and Beta if the contract for the works followed current industry practice. In Bulgaria, Delta would have a special delict claim against Beta.

In some jurisdictions, Alpha would be able to sue Beta in order to recover Delta's loss. In Scotland, and in England (if a third-party right could not be established), Alpha could seek to recover the loss suffered by Delta, on Delta's behalf. In Czech law, Alpha could take action against Beta, and any claim by Alpha against Beta would likely be successfully defended if Alpha did not intend to pass any damages recovered from Beta on to Delta. In German law, Alpha could seek damages for the loss they suffered, which amounted to the drop in the value of the property as a result of Beta's breach of contract. The fact that Delta subsequently paid Alpha market value for the property would not cause difficulties with this claim. The legal ground for Alpha's claim could be both contractual and delictual.

In a minority of jurisdictions (Poland, Slovakia and Sweden), neither Alpha nor Delta would be able to take action against Beta. In Slovakia, the only exception that would allow Delta to take action against Beta would be where the contract for transfer of the premises was classified as a contract for the sale of an enterprise, which includes the transfer of all related assets.

Some reporters noted warranty provisions in their legal systems that would protect purchasers where there were defects in a property. As such, it was thought that Delta might have a claim against Alpha, as the contract exclusions might not affect a claim based on such a warranty (Bulgaria, Poland, Czech Republic). In Italy, recent case law would allow Delta to sue Alpha for their loss, although this is believed by the Italian reporters to be based on a misunderstanding and, as such, is controversial.

A number of reporters noted that the way matters would be dealt with in their jurisdiction would involve Alpha assigning their claim against Beta to Delta (although the facts of this case rule out that possibility).

Question 2

In none of the jurisdictions surveyed would Delta be able to force Alpha to sue Beta, either because Delta have no such right against Alpha (for example, because Delta have no interest in such a claim, in those jurisdictions where Delta can sue Beta directly) or because Alpha have no claim against Beta, since there is no loss on Alpha's part. As a general rule, it is clear that it is not possible for one party to force another party to sue to recover the first party's loss. Some reporters noted that some action could be taken by Delta against Alpha to ensure that Alpha provided assistance in Delta's claim against Beta. This included making a claim, in terms of civil procedure rules, for necessary documentation which would assist Delta in making their case against Beta (Bulgaria, Spain), or being required to assist Delta in preparing their claim, based on standards of reasonableness and fairness and the provision on the legal effects of the assignment of claims (the Netherlands), or on the basis of good faith (Belgium).

CASE 3: LIMITATION OF LIABILITY OF A SUBCONTRACTOR

1. CASE

Duff Inc. are appointed main contractors under a construction contract by Cairn Products plc, to build an apartment block. The contract between Cairn and Duff provides, inter alia, that 'Duff Inc.'s liability for loss will be limited to $10 million'. Assume this is a valid limitation of liability, not open to challenge.

Duff enter into a subcontract with Spark Ltd, to carry out the electrical work on the apartment block. Due to Spark's negligence in carrying out the electrical works, certain floors in the apartment block are damaged. This will cost $15 milion to rectify.

Given the limit on Duff's liability, Cairn raise proceedings in tort against Spark. Assume that this is a valid claim, the requirements of a relevant claim in tort having been satisfied by Cairn. In defending the action, Spark seek to rely upon the limitation of liability clause in the contract between Cairn and Duff.

Questions

1. Can Spark rely on the limitation of liability clause?
2. Would your answer to 1 be different if the contract between Cairn and Duff provided that 'Duff Inc. and its agents' (including independent contractors') liability for loss will be limited to $10 million'?

2. DISCUSSIONS

2.1. BELGIUM

Siel Demeyere and Vincent Sagaert

I. Operative Rules

1. Spark cannot rely on the limitation of liability clause.
2. In this scenario, Spark could rely on the limitation of liability clause.

II. Descriptive Formants

Regarding question 1, Spark cannot rely on the clause in the contract between Cairn and Duff, since Spark is a third party to that contract, and cannot normally derive rights from that contract. This is an application of the principle of privity of contract (see section II of Case 1 above).[1]

However, a preliminary question in Belgian law is whether Spark can be held liable by Duff at all. Duff has a contractual claim against Spark, since there is a breach of contract, but Cairn has to base its claim against Spark on tort law[2] – more specifically, on Article 1382, old BCC. However, since Spark assisted Duff in the performance of the contract with Cairn, Belgian law does not allow Cairn to claim in tort against Spark, save where specific conditions are satisfied. Spark is only liable in tort: (1) when the tort amounts to a crime,[3] which is not the case here; or (2) when the contractual breach also constitutes an extracontractual fault, and the damage differs from the damage which would arise from non-compliance with contractual obligations.[4] The latter condition is hard to satisfy, and is not satisfied here. This means that Spark could escape liability, as only Duff may hold Spark liable, based on their contract. This is called the quasi-immunity of the execution agent.

Regarding question 2, If the contractual clause provides that the liability of 'Duff Inc. and its agents' is limited, this could be interpreted as a clause in favour of a third party (cf. Case 1 above), and would indeed benefit Spark. However, as just demonstrated, this is not necessary, to the extent that Spark benefits from the rule on the quasi-immunity of the execution agent (being Spark).

III. Meta-Legal Formants

This rule of *quasi-immuniteit van de uitvoeringsagent/quasi-immunité de l'agent d'exécution* (quasi-immunity of the execution agent) has been developed in case law, based on the reasoning that tort law should not be used to overcome

---

1 Art. 5.103 BCC.

2 Not on a contractual basis: Cass. 15 September 1977, *RCJB* 1978, 426, comment R.-O. Dalcq and F. Glansdorff; Cass. 13 April 1984, *Pas.* 1984, I, 1022; P. Wéry, *Droit des obligations: Théorie générale du contrat*, I, Larcier, Brussels 2011, 606, no. 644.

3 Cass. 26 October 1990, *Pas.* 1991, I, 216, *RCJB* 1992, 497, comment R.O. Dalcq.

4 Cass. 7 December 1973, *Arr.Cass.* 1974, 395, concl. Adv. Gen. Mahaux, *Pas.* 1974, 376, *RGAR* 1974, no. 9.317, comment J.L. Fagnart, *RJCB* 1976, 15, comment R.O. Dalcq and F. Glansdorff, *RW* 1973–74, 1597, comment J.H. Herbots (with a stricter fault requirement); Cass. 24 March 2016, no. C.14.0329.N, *TBH* 2017, 200, comment R. Steennot; S. Stijns, *Verbintenissenrecht leerboek 1bis*, die Keure, Bruges 2009–16, 146, no. 180; W. Van Gerven and A. Van Oevelen, *Verbintenissenrecht*, Acco, Leuven 2015, 317 ff.; P. Van Ommeslaghe, *Traité de droit civil belge. II. Les obligations. Vol. 2*, Bruylant, Brussels 2013, 1201, no. 819; P. Wéry, *Droit des obligations: Théorie générale du contrat*, I, Larcier, Brussels 2011, 608, no. 645 ff.

limitations of contract law. In other words, an agent, such as Spark, cannot be liable in tort more easily than the contracting party (Duff), because the agent is conceived as the 'economical substitute or representative' of the contracting party.[5] Based on the *samenloopverbod/la prohibition du concours des responsabilités* (prohibition of concurrence), a contracting party can only be liable in tort where the conditions mentioned above are fulfilled.[6] Extracontractual liability of a contracting party is considered undesirable, because it would potentially disrupt the contractual allocation of risks, as agreed upon between the contracting parties.[7] The quasi-immunity of the execution agent is also referred to as a situation of *actieve co-existentie/coexistence active*[8] (active coexistence) of contractual and extracontractual liability, since one person, *in casu* Cairn, has (or may have) a contractual claim against one person, *in casu* Duff, and an extracontractual claim against another person, *in casu* Spark, based on the same (set of) fact(s).[9]

In this case, the Draft Statute Tort Law provides for a different solution, since the principled prohibition of concurrence between contracting parties is reversed and the quasi-immunity of the execution agent is not upheld. An extracontractual claim does not, under the Draft Statute, prohibit a claim with another legal basis, such as contractual liability, unless the contrary follows from statute or contract.[10] The claimant can choose between invoking contractual or extracontractual liability.[11] Even in the case of an extracontractual claim, however, the contractual limitations of liability apply.[12] Because of the widening scope of contractual liability, based on obligations read into the

5 S. Stijns, *Verbintenissenrecht leerboek 1bis*, die Keure, Bruges 2009–16, 147, no. 181. Cf. T. Vansweevelt and B. Weyts, *Handboek buitencontractueel aansprakelijkheidsrecht*, Intersentia, Antwerp 2009, 112, no. 149. *Contra*: I. Claeys, *Samenhangende overeenkomsten en aansprakelijkheid*, Intersentia, Antwerp 2003, 217, no. 188.

6 Cass. 4 June 1971, *Arr.Cass.* 1971, 989, *RW* 1971–72, 371 (with a stricter fault requirement); Cass. 29 September 2006, *Arr.Cass.* 2006, 1863, *NJW* 2006, 946, comment I. Boone, *RW* 2006–07, 1717, comment A. Van Oevelen; S. Stijns, *Verbintenissenrecht leerboek 1bis*, die Keure, Bruges 2009–16, 135, no. 171; W. Van Gerven and A. Van Oevelen, *Verbintenissenrecht*, Acco, Leuven 2015, 309 ff.; P. Van Ommeslaghe, *Traité de droit civil belge. II. Les obligations. Vol. 2*, Bruylant, Brussels 2013, 1200, no. 818; P. Wéry, *Droit des obligations: Théorie générale du contrat*, I, Larcier, Brussels 2011, 602, no. 638 ff.

7 E. Dirix, 'Samenloop van aansprakelijkheid en allocatie van risico's' in I. Boone, I. Claeys and L. Lavrysen (eds), *Liber amicorum Hubert Bocken. Dare la Luce*, die Keure, Bruges 2009, 59.

8 This term is mainly used in Dutch-language scholarship, not in French-language scholarship.

9 S. Stijns, *Verbintenissenrecht leerboek 1bis*, die Keure, Bruges 2009–16, 143, no. 178. The opposite situation, in which one person is confronted with claims from several other persons, is less problematic under Belgian law.

10 Art. 6.3 Draft Statute Tort Law.

11 Ibid., Art. 6.4; Explanatory Memorandum to the Draft Statute of 8 March 2023 on introduction of Book 6 'Tort Law', *Parl.St.* 2022–23, 3213/1, www.dekamer.be, 20 ff.

12 Art. 6.4, §1, second clause, Draft Statute Tort Law.

contract by the complementary function of good faith, the defendant cannot benefit from any advantages extracontractual liability may give rise to, such as insurance coverage for civil liability.[13] Also, an execution agent can now be liable on an extracontractual basis. The execution agent can, nevertheless, rely on the limitations of liability in the main contract, on the basis of the proposed Article 6.4, §2 Draft Statute Tort Law. Essentially, Cairn can engage the extracontractual liability of Spark, but the latter will be able to invoke the limitation of liability to $10 million, contained in the contract between Cairn and Duff. The new rule on concurrence and liability of the agent, in the Draft Statute Tort Law, must help restore the balance between the parties, and also protect the party whose liability is invoked.

2.2. BULGARIA

Petar Topurov

I. Operative Rules

1. Spark Ltd cannot refer to the limitation of liability clause.
2. The response would not differ even if the contract between Cairn and Duff contained such an explicit provision.

II. Descriptive Formants

The current Bulgarian legal regulations establish that provisions which preclude or restrict the debtor's liability for intentional or gross negligence are void (Art. 94 LOC). Such provisions can only be made after the damage has been sustained. When interpreting the given provision, court practice assumes that Art. 94 LOC presupposes an option for limiting civil liability only because of non-performance of contractual obligations, while the same does not apply to delictual liability. Thus, Decision No. 47 of 16 January 1970 on criminal case No. 780/1969, II c.u. of the BSC expresses the opinion that delictual liability may not be excluded by exemption clauses leading to the detriment of the other party, even where there is no intentional or gross negligence. Conclusions of this type are supported by the latest legal cases, which take it for granted that the Art. 94 LOC provision is inapplicable to delictual liability, its field of application being restricted only to the hypotheses of civil liability arising from non-performance of an obligation

[13] Explanatory Memorandum to the Draft Statute of 8 March 2023 on introduction of Book 6 'Tort Law', *Parl.St.* 2022–23, 3213/1, www.dekamer.be, 27; Cass. 27 November 2003, no. C.99.0410.N, *Cigna Insurance Company of Europe/Vermeulen.*

specified in a contract.[14] The decisions cited here need not be followed by other courts, given they are not interpretive decisions of the Supreme Court.

III. Meta-Legal Formants

There is an argument in legal doctrine on whether the Art. 94 LOC rule is applicable with regard to delictual liability. Some authors believe that it is inapplicable, because delictual liability is regulated by imperative legal arrangements, which are not subject to derogation by contractual means.[15] Other authors are of the opinion that it is possible, by means of a contract in favour of a third party, to negotiate exemption clauses or limited liability for the third party, whereby the benefit for the third party is the reduction of its liabilities. Based on the exemption clauses in favour of the third party, a civil procedural objection will arise, whereby the third party could oppose the creditor's claim for benefits that have been excluded by a clause in the contract. This proposition is supported by the text of Art. 22 LOC, which stipulates that the parties to a contract may negotiate 'benefit', where the legislator has used a wider concept than 'right'. Meanwhile, the law provides for the third party to make objections based on contractual relations to which they are not a party (Art. 142 LOC and Art. 151 LOC).[16] Authors who accept the admissibility of exemption clauses concerning delictual liability, however, accept that such clauses would be void in the following cases:

- actions performed with an intention to cause detriment or gross negligence;
- clauses which oppose imperative legal norms or good manners;[17] and
- cases where parties agree to do harm to someone's life, health and bodily inviolability.[18]

In the absence of such an exemption clause in favour of a third party, liability would be realised under the rules of tort.[19]

---

14 Decision No. 8820 of Sofia Civil Court from 22.12.2015 on civil appeals No. 12437/2014.

15 A. Kalaydzhiev, *Contractual Law. General part*, 5th ed., Sibi, Sofia 2010, p. 438; A. Kozhuharov, *Contractual Law. General concepts of contractual relationship*, new edition and supplements by P. Petkov, 'St Kliment Ohridski' University Publishing House/Jurispress, Sofia 2002, p. 323; P. Goleva, *Contractual Law*, New Star, Sofia 2015, p. 465.

16 K. Mitev, 'Exemption Clauses in Contracts and Third Parties' (2005) 4 *Legal Studies* 18–35.

17 Ibid., p. 110. Good manners are moral norms that exist in modern society, and to which the law gives legal significance. The consequences of their violation are equated to a contradiction of the contract with the law. Whether there is a contradiction of good manners depends on whether a contractual clause corresponds to the moral ideas embedded by the legislator in the content of the legal system, especially in accordance with legal principles.

18 Ibid., p. 119.

19 Ibid., p. 100.

2.3. CZECH REPUBLIC

Tomáš Richter

I. Operative Rules

1. Spark *might be able to rely on the limitation clause*, although this is not free of doubt.
2. A provision along the lines posited in this question would greatly improve the likelihood that the view expressed above in relation to question 1 would prevail.

II. Descriptive Formants

This case is really interesting because Czech law has a new, explicit and rather unusual statutory rule on subcontractor liability. That rule is section 2630 CC, which appears in the code's provisions on the contract for works, subpart 3, dealing with construction contracts, under subheading 'Vady stavby' (Construction defects), and provides as follows:

> (1) If there are defects in the performance, *the following persons shall be bound jointly and severally with the contractor in respect of what they had themselves performed*:
> (a) *the contractor's sub-contractor*, unless it can prove that the defect had been caused solely by a decision by the contractor or by the construction oversight,
> (b) the author of the construction design documentation, unless it can prove that the defect had not been caused by a mistake in the construction design documentation,
> (c) the person having oversight over the construction, unless he or she can prove that the defect had not been caused by a failure of construction oversight.
> (2) The contractor shall be absolved of liability for the defect of the construction if it can prove that the defect had only been caused by a mistake in the construction design documentation supplied by an author selected by the employer or a failure of construction oversight provided by a person selected by the employer. (emphasis added)

Although the rule is not mandatory, nothing in the facts of the case suggest that it has been contractually disapplied or modified. Accordingly, Duff and Spark would be jointly and severally liable to Cairn for the defects of the electrical work, pursuant to section 2630(1)(a) CC.

Under section 1872 CC, entitled 'Debtors obligated jointly and severally', the following rules apply:

(1) Where more debtors are obligated to perform jointly and severally, they must perform one for all and all for one. The creditor may demand the entire performance or any part thereof from all of the co-debtors, some of them only, or from any one of them.
(2) A particular understanding between the creditor and a co-debtor shall have no effect vis-à-vis other co-debtors.

It is clear from the above that, on the facts of the case, Cairn will have direct recourse against Spark as a joint and several co-debtor with Duff.

It is less clear whether Spark will be able to rely on the limitation clause in Duff's contract with Cairn. On the one hand, one can argue that if there is a valid limitation on the main contractor's liability to the employer, the subcontractor's liability towards the employer (qua the contractor's co-debtor by operation of section 2630(1) CC) should not exceed that limit simply because their liability is joint and several. On the other hand, and complicatedly, section 1872(2) CC specifically provides that 'particular [i.e. separate, or bilateral] understanding[s] between the creditor and a co-debtor shall have no effect vis-à-vis other co-debtors'. This rule was inspired by section 894 of the Austrian ABGB (Civil Code) (which was part of Czech law before 1950), whereunder a co-debtor may not inflict a burden on other co-debtors by agreeing tougher conditions with the creditor, nor convey benefits to other co-debtors through releases or waivers granted to one co-debtor.[20] That rule seems to have been thought to apply to *ex post* agreements and arrangements,[21] whereas on the facts of the case, the limitation clause between Cairn and Duff has been agreed upfront. It was also thought that, even in the *ex post* situation, the rule prevented a co-debtor from inflicting a burden on their co-debtors, but not from agreeing benefits on their behalf by way of entering into a contract for the benefit of a third party.[22] One could, therefore, cautiously argue that the correct outcome would be that Spark should be able to invoke the limitation agreed between Cairn and Duff. However, this argument is open to challenge, and one cannot exclude the possibility that a case would be decided against Spark.

It also follows from the above that an augmented contractual wording such as that posited in question 2 should greatly improve the chances that Spark, as Duff's subcontractor and co-debtor pursuant to section 2630 CC, could rely on the limitation clause.

---

20 P. Lavický in M. Hulmák et al., *Občanský zákoník V, Závazkové právo, Obecná část (§1721–2054), První vydání*, C.H. Beck, Praha 2014, p. 696 at 69.

21 J. Sedláček in F. Rouček and J. Sedláček, *Komentář k Československému obecnému zákoníku občanskému a občanské právo platné na Slovensku a v Podkarpatské Rusi. Díl čtvrtý (§859 až 1089)*, Nakladatelství V. Linhart, Praha 1936 (reprint ASPI Publishing, Praha 1998), p. 227 at 1.

22 i.e. for the benefit of Spark (ibid. at 2).

III. Meta-Legal Formants

Section 2630 CC is a very new rule: it first came into force, with the rest of the CC, on 1 January 2014, there having been no similar rule in the preceding codes. The case thus highlights some of the new questions that Czech courts will have to answer when applying it.

Also, there is very little case law in the Czech Republic on limitation clauses in general, since they were widely thought to be unenforceable before 2012, when section 386(1) of the CommC expressly allowed them in relationships governed by that code.

The case, therefore, combines two very untested issues.

2.4. ENGLAND AND WALES

T.T. Arvind

I. Operative Rules

1. Spark are unlikely to be able to rely on the limitation of liability clause.
2. Spark will be able to rely on the limitation of liability clause to limit its liability.

II. Descriptive Formants

Question 1

Under the doctrine of privity, only the parties to a contract can benefit from clauses in the contract which exclude or limit liability.[23] For Spark to be able to rely on the limitation of liability clause, they must show that that the case falls either within the CRTPA or one of the other exceptions to privity. On the facts, they are unlikely to be able to do either, with the result that they are unlikely to be able to rely on the limitation of liability clause.

Under the CRTPA, a third party can rely on a term excluding or limiting liability in the same way, and subject to the same requirements, as any other term.[24] This means that, for Spark to be able to rely on the clause, it must purport to confer a benefit on Spark,[25] and Spark must be expressly identified in the

23 *Scruttons Ltd v. Midland Silicones Ltd* [1962] AC 446 (HL).
24 CRTPA, s. 1(6).
25 Ibid., s. 1(1)(b).

contract.[26] For a term to 'purport' to confer a benefit on Spark, as required by section 1(1)(b) CRTPA, Spark must show that conferring a benefit on them was one of the contracting parties' purposes, and not just an incidental effect.[27] This is a matter of contractual interpretation,[28] and the fact that the clause refers only to 'Duff Inc.'s liability for loss' makes it very unlikely that the clause will be read as purporting to confer a benefit on Spark.

Spark are also unlikely to meet the requirement of identification in CRTPA, section 1(3), under which the third party must be expressly identified in the contract by name, class or description. In *The Alexandros T*, the High Court held that it could, on the basis of contextual evidence, interpret the phrase 'underwriters' to mean 'underwriters, servants and agents', and that that would meet the requirement of identification.[29] This approach has been criticised by some commentators, who have argued that it ignores the fact that the requirements of sections 1(1)(b) and 1(3) CRTPA are intended to be cumulative,[30] but it has, nevertheless, been reiterated in subsequent cases.[31] Even so, it is unlikely that the very specific reference to 'Duff Inc.' can be interpreted to mean 'Duff Inc. and its subcontractors'. Nor will the courts imply a term identifying third parties into the contract in the absence of an express term: section 1(3) CRTPA has consistently been interpreted to mean that there must be an express term in the contract from which the identification of the third-party beneficiary proceeds.[32]

A third party can also rely on an exclusion clause if one of the parties contracted as its agent. This technique was successfully used, before the advent of the CRTPA, to enable subcontractors to benefit from clauses limiting liability.[33] For Spark to be able to use this exception, however, they will need to show that Cairn in fact signed the contract as their agent. If (as the case details suggest) Spark were not appointed as subcontractor until after the main contract was signed, they are unlikely to be able to do this.

---

26 Ibid., s. 1(3).

27 *Dolphin Maritime & Aviation Services Ltd v. Sveriges Angfartygs Assurans Forening* [2009] EWHC 716 (Comm), [2009] 2 Lloyd's Rep 123 [8] (Christopher Clarke J).

28 *Prudential Assurance Co Ltd v. Ayres* [2008] EWCA Civ 52.

29 *Starlight Shipping Co v. Allianz Versicherungs AG (The Alexandros T)* [2014] EWHC 3068 (Comm), [2014] 2 Lloyd's Rep. 579 [88].

30 H. Beale (ed), *Chitty on Contracts*, 33rd ed., 2 vols. (London: Sweet and Maxwell, 2019), para. 18-097.

31 *Chudley v. Clydesdale Bank plc* [2019] EWCA Civ 344, [2020] 1 QB 284 [77].

32 *Themis Avraamides v. Mark Colwill* [2006] EWCA Civ 1533, [2007] BLR 76.

33 See e.g. *New Zealand Shipping Co. Ltd v. AM Satterthwaite & Co. Ltd (The Eurymedon)* [1975] AC 154 (PC).

Question 2

Until recently, opinion was divided on whether the requirements of CRTPA, sections 1(1)(b) and 1(3), needed to be satisfied separately, through a separate term identifying the third-party beneficiary. In the recent case of *Chudley v. Clydesdale Bank plc*,[34] however, the Court of Appeal resolved the issue, and held that a term which purports to confer a benefit on the third party can also satisfy the requirement that the third party must be identified. Applying that reasoning, it is likely that a reference to 'Duff Inc. and its agents (including independent contractors)' in the limitation clause will be sufficient to meet both requirements, enabling Spark to rely on the limitation of liability clause.

2.5. FRANCE

Sylvain Ravenne and Flora Vern

I. Operative Rules

1. Spark cannot rely on the limitation of liability clause.
2. Likewise, Spark cannot rely on the limitation of liability clause.

II. Descriptive Formants

Question 1

This case would be described under French law as one of *'sous-traitance'* (subcontract for the supply of services). Damage has been suffered by the client, who is the owner of the premises, due to the negligence of the subcontractor.

Subcontracting for services is governed by a specific statute which provides that the main contractor is fully liable for the wrongful performance of the contract by the subcontractor.[35] This implies that the client has no direct claim against the subcontractor who does not perform the contract, or commits a fault in doing so. In reverse, the law creates a direct claim in that case, for the subcontractor to sue the client, where the main contractor fails to pay for the subcontractor's services.[36] Hence, in the present case, the main contractor is liable towards the client, and will then have a contractual claim against the subcontractor.[37]

---

34 [2019] EWCA Civ 344, [2020] 1 QB 284.
35 Art. 1er of the Loi nº 75-1334 du 31 décembre 1975 relative à la sous-traitance.
36 Ibid., Art. 12.
37 Cass., civ. 3e, 11 mai 2006, nº 05-13254.

Two alternative solutions are, however, possible:

(a) Cairn may rely on Spark's tort liability, as is proposed in the case, if the conditions for such a claim are met. In that event, the contractual clause between Cairn and Duff cannot be invoked by Spark, who are not a party to the contract containing the limitation of liability provision. The FCC provides that contracts do not, in principle, affect third parties. As a result, the contract cannot create an obligation for Cairn to limit their claim to damages.[38] Correlatively, Spark cannot require Cairn to abide by a particular clause of a contract with a third party.[39]

    It is interesting to note that the Cour de cassation has repeatedly ruled that a third party may invoke the improper performance of a contract as a ground for tort liability.[40] As a result, Cairn will have a claim in tort against Spark if they can prove that Spark committed a fault in the performance of the contract with Duff, and that Cairn suffered damage as a result. In that case, the wrongful element of tort liability is automatically established, to the benefit of the third party.
(b) If the damage were incurred due to a defect in the materials used by Spark, the solution would be different. In that situation, case law recognises that a claim runs with the thing itself because of the chain of contracts transferring ownership, which is independent from the subcontract.[41] As a result, Cairn could sue Spark because of a defect in the thing, as Spark bought and eventually delivered a defective product to Cairn. The clause limiting Duff's liability will have no effect on Spark, who cannot use it to defend the claim by Cairn.

Question 2

The answer would be identical if the main contract provided that the clause limited the liability of the main contractor and their agents, understood as encompassing subcontractors. Such a clause is inapplicable to tort liability. The Cour de cassation has, for a long time, ruled that all clauses which limit a person's tort liability are null and void, on the ground that the victim of a tort may not renounce their right to damages before said damages are incurred.[42] As a result, even if the contract contained a clause limiting the liability of the main contractor's agents, Cairn could still rely on tort liability to circumvent the clause.

---

38 Art. 1199, §1, FCC.
39 Ibid., Art. 1199, §2.
40 Cass., ass. plén., 6 oct. 2006, *Bootshop*, n° 05-13255; Cass., ass. plén., 13 janv. 2020, n° 17-19963.
41 Cass., com., 22 mai 2002, n° 99-11113.
42 Cass., civ., 3 janv. 1933, *DH* 1933.113; Cass., civ. 2ᵉ, 17 févr. 1977, *GAJC*, 11ᵉ éd., n° 178.

2.6. GERMANY

Sonja Meier

I. Operative Rules

1. Spark will probably not be able to rely on the limitation of liability clause.
2. In this alternative scenario, Spark will be able to rely on the clause.

II. Descriptive Formants

Question 1

German law does not have a general rule providing that a subcontractor can rely on a limitation of liability clause contained in the contract between the main contractor and the creditor. Statutory rules of this kind exist for particular kinds of contract,[43] such as commercial contracts of carriage,[44] but not for building contracts. Accordingly, the question whether the limitation of liability clause can be relied on by Spark depends on the construction of the contract between Cairn and Duff. The wording seems to imply that only Duff's liability is limited. However, another result can be reached through a purposive interpretation, or by way of an *'ergänzende Vertragsauslegung'* (supplementary interpretation of the contract).[45]

If the third party is an employee of the party protected by the limitation of liability clause, they will, according to the courts and commentators, generally enjoy the benefit of the clause.[46] It is argued that an employer has a contractual duty to protect their employees from delictual liability arising from their work, and that it can be assumed that the employer is willing to comply with this duty. Further, an employee who is liable towards a third party because of an act done in the course of the work has, in principle, a contractual right against their employer to relieve them from liability. If, therefore, the limitation of liability clause in the contract between the employer and their contractual partner was restricted to the employer themselves, it would be of only limited use to the employer, since the employer would remain subject to a claim by their employee

43 For an overview, see P. Gottwald in *Münchener Kommentar zum BGB*, vol. 3 (9th ed., Beck 2022), §328, [258].

44 §436 HGB.

45 See Case 2, question 2.

46 BGH *NJW* 1962, 388; BGH *VersR* 1985, 595; P. Gottwald in *Münchener Kommentar zum BGB*, vol. 3 (9th ed., Beck 2022), §328, [258], [260]; S. Klumpp in *J. von Staudingers Kommentar zum Bürgerlichen Gesetzbuch*, vol. §§328–45 (Sellier – de Gruyter 2020), §328, [154].

to relieve them from their delictual liability towards the employer's contractual partner. According to the Federal Court, the same considerations apply to subcontractors where their position towards the main contractor is economically similar to that of an employee.[47] This ruling was made in a case where the contract provided detailed instructions to the subcontractor, barred him from delegating his contractual duties, subjected him to a restraint of competition, and fixed an hourly wage. There is no indication that such a relationship exists between Duff and Cairn.

Some commentators submit that subcontractors should generally profit from a limitation of liability clause agreed between the creditor and the main contractor, at least where it is foreseeable for the creditor that the debtor will engage third parties to perform the contract.[48] It is argued that the limitation of liability clause is 'paid for' through a reduction of the contract price, and that it would be unfair if the creditor benefited from the low price and could also recover their damage in full only because the contractual debtor used subcontractors instead of employees. Although this argument can also be found in judgments of the Federal Court,[49] the Court does not yet seem to have extended a limitation of liability clause to an independent subcontractor by way of supplementary interpretation.

Question 2

The principle of freedom of contract and the *ratio* of §328 BGB, which allows contracts for the benefit of a third party, enable the parties to a contract to limit the liability of a third party towards them. The effects of such a clause are subject to debate. According to some writers, the liability of the third party towards the contractual party will automatically *(ipso iure)* be limited to the agreed amount.[50] The courts, however, maintain that such an agreement can only have the effect of a usual contract for the benefit of a third party, which is to create an obligation. The clause will, then, only give rise to an obligation of the injured party towards the third party not to enforce their damages claim insofar as it exceeds the agreed limit *(pactum de non petendo)*.[51]

---

47 *BGHZ* 130, 223.

48 See S. Klumpp in *J. von Staudingers Kommentar zum Bürgerlichen Gesetzbuch*, vol. §§328–45 (Sellier – de Gruyter 2020), §328, [154]; P. Gottwald in *Münchener Kommentar zum BGB*, vol. 3 (9th ed., Beck 2022), §328, [258].

49 BGH *VersR* 1960, 727; *BGHZ* 130, 223.

50 P. Gottwald in *Münchener Kommentar zum BGB*, vol. 3 (9th ed., Beck 2022), §328, [261]; S. Klumpp in *J. von Staudingers Kommentar zum Bürgerlichen Gesetzbuch*, vol. §§328–45 (Sellier – de Gruyter 2020), §328, [154].

51 BGH *NJW* 1994, 2483 at 2484; BGH *NJW* 2010, 64 at [16]; OLG Karlsruhe, *NJW-RR* 2014, 692 at 693.

2.7. ITALY

Pasquale Femia

I. Operative Rules

1. Spark cannot rely on the limitation of liability clause.
2. The solution could be different in the case of a limitation of liability clause, but it is unclear whether this clause in the contract between Cairn and Duff would automatically extend the limitation of liability for the benefit of Spark.

II. Descriptive Formants

Regarding question 1, scholars and courts insist on the autonomy of the construction contract and the construction subcontract.[52] Courts explicitly add[53] that the terms and conditions of the construction contract do not transfer to the subcontract. It follows that the customer (parties to the construction contract are the contractor and the customer) does not have an action against the subcontractor (parties to the construction subcontract are the contractor in the first contract and the subcontractor), and vice versa. The only possible action of the customer against the subcontractor is an extracontractual one under Art. 2043 c.c., due to the breach of the customer's right against the contractor for full performance. In fact, Cairn have a credit against Duff, as Duff have a duty to perform the contract exactly; since the construction was defective, Duff are in breach of contract and Cairn have a right to recover the loss.[54] Under Italian case law, the breach of this contract counts as extracontractual damage caused by Spark to Cairn.

Given that Duff appear here to have discharged the burden of proof (which is actually quite simple under the contractual liability regime, on the basis of *res ipsa loquitur*), only one doubt remains as to whether the limitation of liability provision is relevant vis-à-vis third parties, so that Spark may benefit therefrom. Duff have a limitation of contractual damages in their relations with Cairn (Art. 1229 c.c.) and Spark's conduct amounts to an extracontractual breach of credit (as Spark have violated Cairn's credit against Duff). Accordingly, Spark's duty to compensate Cairn would be based on Art. 2043 c.c.: Spark would then be debtor to Cairn as a result of an obligation independent from that between Cairn and Duff, and Spark's obligation would not be subject to the limitation

---

52 M.C. Cervale, 'Subappalto, *sub* Art. 1656' in P. Cendon (ed), *Commentario al codice civile* (Milan: Giuffrè, 2008), p. 55.

53 Cass., 19 July 2018, no. 19296, *Foro Amministrativo* (2019), p. 628, §3 of reasoning.

54 Cass., s.u., 26 January 1971, no. 174, *Foro italiano*, I (1971), p. 342; and, in literature, F.D. Busnelli, *La lesione del credito da parte di terzi* (Milan: Giuffrè, 1964).

which applies to the different obligation between Cairn and Duff. Spark cannot, therefore, rely on the limitation clause.

Regarding question 2, Cairn and Duff's statement that the limitation of liability agreed upon in the construction contract extends to the parties to the construction subcontract does not amount to representation: neither Cairn nor Duff can be considered *falsi procurators*, because the construction subcontract has been concluded by Spark in their own name. There are two possibilities for how the contract clause containing a benefit for the third-party subcontractor might be viewed. Firstly, it might be viewed as a contract in favour of third parties (Art. 1411 c.c.), whereby Cairn promise to Duff not to recover damages from Spark of more than $10 million. In this event, Spark will have a right against Cairn in relation to the latter's promise not to recover amounts beyond the limitation clause (the contract in favour of a third party gives Spark a direct right against Cairn). More likely, perhaps, is that it is instead an obligation *inter partes* undertaken by Cairn against Duff not to claim against Spark a sum higher than the one Cairn themselves can claim against Duff as a result of the construction contract. In this second case, however, Spark have no direct right against Cairn (who are under an obligation in relation to Duff only). In this case, Spark would have no direct action for full recovery (only Duff could have an action against Cairn), but Cairn's action against Spark to recover the entire loss would be paralysed by a case law remedy – the *exceptio doli* – a judicial exception to prevent an abuse of a right.[55] There is no regulation for this unique *pactum de non petendo* against the third party, but the solution results from the general principles of obligations.

III. Meta-Legal Formants

An alternative option lies in considering the construction subcontract as a phenomenon of economic integration among enterprises through contractual networks.[56]

As for Spark's breach of Cairn's credit against Duff, Spark are not a third party to the contract, but are a party to a contract which is functionally connected. The autonomy of both contracts (construction and subconstruction) would theoretically imply that the liability regimes and related contractual balances might differ when the contracts are considered individually as opposed to when they are viewed collectively as an interconnected network.[57] Autonomy of subcontract is a useful instrument to differentiate the liability regimes according

55 In Italian law: L. Tullio, *Eccezione di dolo e funzione negoziale* (Naples: Edizioni Scientifiche Italiane, 2005).

56 G. Teubner, *Netzwerk als Vertragsverbund: Virtuelle Unternehmen, Franchising, just-in-time in sozialwissenschaftlicher und juristischer Sicht* (Baden Baden: Nomos, 2004); C. Crea, *Reti contrattuali e organizzazione dell'attività di impresa* (Naples: Edizioni Scientifiche Italiane, 2008).

57 D. Rubino and G. Iudica, 'Dell'appalto, *sub* Art. 1669', *Commentario del codice civile Scialoja e Branca* (Bologna/Rome: Zanichelli-Foro italiano, 4th ed., 2007), p. 219.

to the very contractual influence beneath the network. Consider a case in which a contractor is only a shell company, serving as a vehicle for a deal, behind which contractor several non-shell company subcontractors act: in this case, the limitation would be reasonable for the contractor and unreasonable for the subcontractor, and the case law solution (in which the non-shell subcontractor may not benefit from the limitation of liability obtained by the main contractor) fits the socio-economic rationality.

Participants in a contractual network (in which subcontracting is one of the forms of participation, on the basis of division of contractual work) do not have an imperative right to equal treatment, but to equality; that is, to equal treatment within homogeneous situations.[58] The autonomous differentiation of each contract involved in the network is a characteristic that contributes to the network's efficiency.

2.8. THE NETHERLANDS

Jan Biemans

I. Operative Rules

1. Spark can rely on the limitation of liability clause.
2. The outcome would not be different if the contract between Cairn and Duff provided that 'Duff Inc. and its agents' (including independent contractors') liability for loss will be limited to $10 million'.

II. Descriptive Formants

Spark can rely on the limitation of liability clause, as the DCC contains a specific provision on this subject. According to Article 6:257 DCC, if a party to an agreement, in order to ward off their liability for damages caused by one of their subordinates, may raise a defence against their counterparty in any action that directly or indirectly results from their agreement with that counterparty, then their subordinate, if they are held liable for these damages to the counterparty, may also raise that defence as if they themselves were a party to that agreement.[59] A subordinate can be an employee of the party to the agreement, or a subcontractor. Thus, as the contract between Cairn and Duff

58 On equality in contractual networks, see G. Teubner, *Netzwerk als Vertragsverbund: Virtuelle Unternehmen, Franchising, just-in-time in sozialwissenschaftlicher und juristischer Sicht* (Baden Baden: Nomos, 2004), p. 153.

59 C.H. Sieburgh, *Mr. C. Assers Handleiding tot de beoefening van het Nederlands Burgerlijk Recht. 6. Verbintenissenrecht. Deel III. Algemeen overeenkomstenrecht*, Deventer: Wolters Kluwer 2022, pp. 581 ff.

limits the liability for loss to $10 million, and Duff may raise this clause against Cairn to fend off liability, the subcontractor Spark, if held liable for these damages to Cairn, may also raise this clause against Cairn. The provision is known as the 'blocking the horse movement' *(blokkering paardensprong)*. The term is derived from the game of chess, where the horse (or knight) can jump over pieces to reach its destination (moving two squares vertically and one square horizontally, or two squares horizontally and one square vertically, both forming the shape of an L).

It should be noted, generally, that Cairn's claim against Duff would be based on a breach of contract by Duff, as Duff are, in principle, liable for the work of their subordinates (Article 6:74 in conjunction with Article 6:75 DCC), whereas Cairn's claim against Spark would be based on an unlawful act by Spark (Article 6:162 DCC).[60] Spark can use the clause limiting the liability as if they had concluded the contract themselves.

The use of the clause by Spark is not unlimited. It is not possible for a contracting party to conclude a clause limiting liability to the extent it would lead to a situation in which that party could act with gross negligence or wilful misconduct.[61] To that extent, the clause would be void, as such exclusion or limitation of liability is contrary to public order and good morals *(goede zeden)* (Article 3:40 DCC). As a consequence, if there has been gross negligence or wilful misconduct on the part of Spark, Duff could rely on the clause (as it is valid to exclude or limit liability for the gross negligence or wilful misconduct of others), but Spark could not.

In relation to the second question, the outcome would not be different if the contract between Cairn and Duff provided that 'Duff Inc. and its agents' (including independent contractors) liability for loss will be limited to $10 million'. Such provision in the contract could be interpreted as a third-party clause, and would have the same effect as Article 6:257 DCC.

2.9. POLAND

Bartosz Kucia

I. Operative Rules

1. It is doubtful whether Spark could rely on the clause limiting Duff's liability for damages.
2. Spark would usually be able to invoke a limitation of liability clause that extends to Duff's agents (including independent contractors).

---

60 Ibid., p. 584.

61 Ibid., p. 585; C.H. Sieburgh, *Mr. C. Assers Handleiding tot de beoefening van het Nederlands Burgerlijk Recht. 6. Verbintenissenrecht. Deel I. De verbintenis in het algemeen, eerste gedeelte*, Deventer: Wolters Kluwer 2020, p. 365; Parl. Gesch. BW Boek 6 1981, p. 964, Parl. Gesch. BW Boek 8 1992, pp. 332 and 361.

II. Descriptive Formants

In relation to the first question, the principle of freedom of contract (Art. 353^1 PCC) allows the parties to modify the statutory liability model of *ex contractu* liability,[62] through extending (for example, by making liability independent from fault) or limiting (for example, as to the specific degree of fault, type of damage or maximum amount of liability) its scope. However, a reservation that excludes liability for damage that the debtor may cause to the creditor intentionally is invalid (Art. 473 §2 PCC),[63] including where it concerns the liability of the debtor for the subcontractor (Art. 474 PCC).[64]

There is no doubt that such clauses are effective between the parties to a given contract, to the extent permitted by the principle of freedom of contract. The main contractor (Duff) may, therefore, invoke the limitation of their liability resulting from the contractual clause concluded with the investor (Cairn).[65]

However, it is doubtful whether the same clause (arising from the construction contract between Cairn and Duff) may be invoked by Duff's subcontractor (Spark), who in this situation would need to rely on the limitation of their tort

62 This view plays a dominant role in literature (see e.g. W. Warkałło, 'Klauzule wyłączające odpowiedzialność za szkodę a ubezpieczenie odpowiedzialności cywilnej', *Ruch Prawniczy Ekonomiczny i Socjologiczny (Ruch PES)* 1974, no. 3, p. 331) and in case law (see, in particular, judgments of the SN of 08.07.2004, IV CK 583/03; 29.11.2002, IV CKN 1553/00; and 16.01.2013, II CSK 331/12). Art. 443 PCC allows, on this occasion (though not in all cases), the limitation of the *ex delicto* liability of the debtor. See e.g. W. Czachórski, 'Odpowiedzialność kontraktowa i jej stosunek do odpowiedzialności deliktowej wg k.c.', *Nowe Prawo (NP)* 1964, no. 10, p. 959; A. Ohanowicz, 'Zbieg norm w kodeksie cywilnym', *NP* 1966, no. 12, p. 1505; A. Śmieja in A. Olejniczak, *System prawa prywatnego. Tom 6. Prawo zobowiązań – część ogólna*, Warsaw 2023, pp. 741–42; Ł. Błaszczak and J. Kuźmicka-Sulikowska, 'Zbieg roszczeń ex contractu i ex delicto na tle art. 443 k.c. w ujęciu materialnoprawnym i procesowym', *Transformacje Prawa Prywatnego (TPP)* 2013, no. 3, p. 32; in the opposite direction, see A. Szpunar, 'Zbieg roszczeń odszkodowawczych', *Ruch PES* 1974, no. 1, p. 47.

63 The contractual reservation that the debtor bore liability for the damage resulting from the creditor's circumstances has also been considered inadmissible. See judgments of the Supreme Court (Sąd Najwyższy, SN) of 06.05.1970, II CR 145/70 and 27.09.2013, I CSK 748/12, OSNC 2014/6/67. W. Popiołek in K. Pietrzykowski, *Kodeks cywilny. Tom II. Komentarz. Art. 450–1088*, Warsaw 2021, art. 473, no. 2; P. Machnikowski in P. Machnikowski (ed), *Zobowiązania. Część ogólna. Tom II. Komentarz*, Warsaw 2024, art. 473, no. 18. See also general provisions affecting the permissible contractual modification of liability: Arts. 58 and 353^1 PCC. In contracts with consumers, these restrictions are further-reaching. See, inter alia, A. Śmieja, 'Umowna modyfikacja zasad odpowiedzialności kontraktowej', *Iustitia* 2011, no. 3, pp. 117 ff.; M. Kaliński, *Szkoda na mieniu i jej naprawienie*, Warsaw 2014, pp. 582 ff.; J. Jastrzębski, 'O umownych modyfikacjach podstawy odpoowiedzialności odszkodowawczej dłużnika', *Kwartalnik Prawa Prywatnego (KPP)* 2007, no. 3, pp. 823 ff.

64 See judgment of the SA in Gdańsk of 25.10.1996, I ACr 822/96, OSA 1997/10/58, and A. Rembieliński, 'Kontraktowa odpowiedzialność dłużnika za osoby trzecie w prawie cywilnym i w prawie obrotu uspołecznionego', *Studia Prawno-Ekonomiczne (SPE)* 1974, t. XII, p. 61.

65 The case whereby such a clause is reserved in the subcontract lies outside the scope of this study.

liability (since the subcontractor is not a party to the construction contract,[66] and as a result may be held liable only in tort).[67] There are not many answers to this question in Polish literature and case law. Two positions have been presented in this respect: liberal (allowing the aforementioned possibility)[68] and restrictive (limiting the effectiveness of the clause only to the parties to a given contract), of which the second is more deserving of approval.[69] The second view is supported by the legal nature of a contract *(inter partes)*, as well as a need to protect the creditor (investor), who usually has no influence on the selection of subcontractors (Art. 356 §1 PCC). The contractual exclusion or limitation of liability requires the creditor's consent (see, for example, Articles 55^1 *in fine*, 483 §2 and 508 PCC), which in relation to the subcontractor was not expressed in the given contract.

No specific statutory provision of the PCC is devoted to the issue. Article 474 PCC concerns only the liability of the debtor (the main contractor) to their creditor (investor).[70]

In relation to the second question, the result will be different in the case of a contractual clause including, in addition to the main contractor, their subcontractors (assuming that the parties to the given contract were also considering limiting tort liability, since this is the only basis on which the subcontractor is liable to the investor in relation to their works). Such a clause

---

66 Similarly, the investor is not a party to the subcontract agreement, even if they have agreed to its conclusion between the investor and the subcontractor (judgment of the SN of 21.10.2016, IV CSK 834/15); the investor's consent remains, however, relevant to the investor's liability for paying the subcontractor's remuneration (Art. 647^1 PCC).

67 However, only if the subcontractor's act or omission can be attributed to the tort. The breach of a subcontract agreement may be considered a tort only if it simultaneously violates the general obligation incumbent upon any entity. See judgment of the SN of 19.09.2013, I CSK 687/12, OSNC-ZD 2015/1/1 (improper car repair was not considered a tort under the circumstances of the case). See also W. Robaczyński and P. Księżak, 'Niewykonanie lub nienależyte wykonanie zobowiązania jako czyn niedozwolony' in M. Nesterowicz (ed), *Czyny niedozwolone w prawie polskim i prawie porównawczym*, Warsaw 2012, pp. 339 ff. P. Machnikowski in P. Machnikowski (ed), *Zobowiązania. Część ogólna. Tom II. Komentarz*, Warsaw 2024, art. 474, no. 44; W. Borysiak in K. Osajda and W. Borysiak (eds), *Kodeks cywilny. Komentarz*, Warsaw 2024, art. 474, no. 57.

68 See A. Kubas, *Umowa na rzecz osoby trzeciej*, Warsaw/Cracow 1976, p. 69 (noting the need to balance economic risk).

69 See Z. Gordon, 'Umowne klauzule egzoneracyjne w stosunkach obrotu uspołecznionego', *Acta Universitatis Lodziensis, Folia Iuridica* 1988, no. 34, p. 46 (clauses of this type distribute the risk as defined by the parties themselves, and are not intended to eliminate such risk, as such); A. Śmieja, 'O dopuszczalnych granicach umownej modyfikacji zasad i przesłanek odpowiedzialności odszkodowawczej' in W. Robaczyński (ed), *Czynić postęp w prawie. Księga jubileuszowa dedykowana Profesor Birucie Lewaszkiewicz Petrykowskiej*, Łódź 2017, p. 383.

70 As well as their own actions (including omissions), the main contractor is also liable for actions (including omissions) of subcontractors to whom they have entrusted the performance of the contract (Art. 474 PCC), and may not free themselves from this liability by demonstrating their lack of fault in choosing a subcontractor or supervising them (in this sense, the main contractor bears the risk of their subcontractor's actions). See the resolution of the SN of 25.02.1986, III CZP 2/86, OSNCP 1987/1/10; judgment of the SA in Warsaw of 14.11.2012, VI ACa 802/12; judgment of the SA in Łódź of 13.12.2016,

will not itself exempt the subcontractor from future liability, since the subcontractor's consent is required for this purpose (Art. 508 PCC). However, the intention of the parties is best reflected (Art. 65 §2 PCC) by the assumption that, to the extent covered by the relevant clause, the investor undertook to release subcontractors from the debt that would result from their torts in future *(pactum in favorem tertii)*. The subcontractor may then request the investor to conclude a debt relief agreement within the meaning of Art. 508 PCC, which may also apply to future debts (Art. 64 PCC).[71] However, the present clause might also, depending on the circumstances of a particular case, be classified as *pactum de non petendo*, also based on the *pactum in favorem tertii* mechanism (that is, as a result of the agreement with Duff, Cairn undertake not to pursue a claim against Spark; this usually allows the subcontractor to raise a plea against such a claim, although it does not release them from liability for damage).[72]

III. Meta-Legal Formants

The legal status of the subcontractor, as presented here, favours them incurring high economic risks associated with the investment process (with the subcontractor having *ex delicto* liability to the full extent, in comparison with the limited liability of the main contractor). In the literature, therefore, attempts have been made to reinterpret the law with reference to teleological arguments, which is not always possible without prejudice to the dogmatic assumptions of civil law. Those risks are not always eliminated by an appropriate subcontracting agreement. On the other hand, it is necessary to protect the investor, who often has no input into the selection of subcontractors.

Finally, it is worth noting that contractual clauses extending the scope of the contractor's responsibility for construction works have become increasingly popular, in practice, in recent years.[73] This phenomenon is also encountered in the case of subcontracts.

I ACa 717/16. See also A. Rembieliński, 'Kontraktowa odpowiedzialność dłużnika za osoby trzecie w prawie cywilnym i w prawie obrotu uspołecznionego', *SPE* 1974, t. XII, pp. 42, 50; T. Pajor, *Odpowiedzialność dłużnika za niewykonanie zobowiązania*, Warsaw 1982, pp. 223, 259; R. Strugała, 'Odpowiedzialność dłużnika w razie wykonywania zobowiązania przez osoby trzecie (art. 474 k.c.)', *Przegląd Sądowy (PS)* 2017, no. 11–12, p. 106. With regard to liability *ex delicto*, see, in particular, Arts. 415, 416, 428 and 429 PCC, as well as Art. 120 Labour Code (damage caused by an employee).

71 There is also a liberal view, under which the limitation of the subcontractor's liability is a consequence of the consent of the injured party, which excludes the unlawfulness of a perpetrator's behaviour (one of the required conditions for tort liability). See A. Kubas, *Umowa na rzecz osoby trzeciej*, Warsaw/Cracow 1976, p. 72.

72 See ibid., p. 71.

73 Recently, courts have been cautious about such clauses. This is reflected in the restrictive approach to the statutory (derived from Art. 473 §1 PCC) requirement to specify

2.10. SCOTLAND

Lorna MacFarlane

I. Operative Rules

1. Spark *cannot* rely on the limitation of liability clause.
2. If the clause provided that 'Duff Inc. and its agents' (including independent contractors') liability for loss will be limited to $10 million', Spark *could* rely on this clause in limiting their liability.

II. Descriptive Formants

The benefit conferred by a 'third-party right' can consist of the limitation of liability on the part of the third party. Section 2(6) of the Contract (Third Party Rights) (Scotland) Act 2017 provides that a third-party right can include an enforceable undertaking 'not to enforce, or to enforce in full, a person's liability in a matter'. The formulation in the first question does not appear to confer any benefit on Spark. A statement of the limitation of Duff's loss does not, however, provide for a third-party right in favour of Spark, nor give rise to any other protection for Spark. As noted in the discussion on Case 1 above, the Act requires that the 'person who is to acquire a third-party right under a contract must be identifiable from the contract by being either named or described in it'. Spark are not identifiable in the first version of the limitation of liability clause, and cannot, therefore, rely on the limitation of liability clause, because they are not the recipient of a third-party right.

---

circumstances covered by extended liability. See e.g. judgment of the SN of 16.11.2017, V CSK 28/17; judgment of the SA in Katowice of 28.11.2018, V AGa 235/18; judgment of the SA in Szczecin of 14.09.2017, I ACa 309/17; see also: A. Śmieja, 'Umowna modyfikacja zasad odpowiedzialności kontraktowej', *Iustitia* 2011, no. 3, p. 119; M. Gutowski in M. Gutowski (ed), *Kodeks cywilny. Tom II. Komentarz. Art. 353–626*; K. Zagrobelny in E. Gniewek and P. Machnikowski (eds), *Kodeks cywilny. Komentarz*, Warsaw 2021, art. 473, no. 7 (finding it sufficient to indicate the borderline circumstances); F. Zoll in A. Olejniczak (ed), *System Prawa Prywatnego. Tom 6. Prawo zobowiązań – część ogólna*, Warsaw 2018, pp. 1173–74 and F. Zoll and M. Bujalski in A. Olejniczak (ed), *System Prawa Prywatnego. Tom 6. Prawo zobowiązań – część ogólna*, Warsaw 2023, p. 1242 (with the observation that the statute does not regulate the manner in which the said circumstances must be specified). In search of a liberal interpretation, however, see e.g. judgment of the SN of 16.01.2013, II CSK 331/12, as well as W. Popiołek in K. Pietrzykowski (ed), *Kodeks cywilny. Tom II. Komentarz. Art. 450–1088*, Warsaw 2021, art. 473, no. 1; W. Borysiak in K. Osajda and W. Borysiak (eds), *Kodeks cywilny. Komentarz*, Warsaw 2024, art. 473, no. 27 (both accepting to specify only the scope of extended liability). The statutory requirement to specify circumstances covered by the extended liability, as well as its restrictive interpretation, have recently been subject to a critical examination in P. Machnikowski in P. Machnikowski (ed), *Zobowiązania. Część ogólna. Tom II. Komentarz*, Warsaw 2024, art. 473, no. 12–17.

However, in the second question, the contract between Cairn and Duff provides for a third-party right in the form of a limitation of liability clause in favour of Spark. The reference to Duff's agents 'including independent contractors' clearly encompasses Spark (as discussed in Case 1, it is possible for the recipient of a third-party right to be identified as a member of a class of beneficiaries).

It is unlikely that Spark would be considered, in Scots law, to be acting as an agent for Duff. In the Scots conception of agency, the agent acts to produce legally binding effects for the principal, rather than carrying out the work on the principal's behalf. Spark is operating under a subcontract with Duff rather than working directly with Cairn to enter into transactions on Duff's behalf. Duff and Spark are not, therefore, operating as principal and agent.

III. Meta-Legal Formants

Prior to the Act, there was some uncertainty as to the extent to which limitation of liability clauses would be recognised in respect of a third party.[74] Cases which upheld such clauses did so as a result of applying the law on third-party rights, but did not discuss any specific policy reasoning justifying third-party rights in the form of limitation of liability clauses.[75] Section 2(6) of the Act has not yet been the subject of judicial comment. However, the relevant provisions in the Act resulted from the Scottish Law Commission's finding that such clauses are 'particularly useful in business contexts involving multiple actors, such as construction projects',[76] and that 'an opportunity to provide … convenience and efficiency to Scottish parties should not be missed',[77] reflecting policy objectives of commercial convenience and upholding contractual intention.

2.11. SLOVAKIA

Kristián Csach, Monika Jurčová, Peter Mészáros and Veronika Zoričáková

I. Operative Rules

1. Although third parties may not, in general, rely on contractual arrangements between the parties to a contract, the contractual definition of 'protected

74 Scottish Law Commission, *Discussion Paper on Third Party Rights in Contract* (Scot Law Com DP No. 157, 2014), para. 2.24.

75 Such clauses were upheld in e.g. *Renton v. Ayton* (1634) Mor. 7721; *Magistrates of Dunbar v. Mackersy* 1931 SC 180; and *Melrose v. Davidson* 1993 SC 288.

76 Scottish Law Commission, *Report on Third Party Rights* (Scot Law Com No. 245, 2016), para. 4.26.

77 Scottish Law Commission, *Discussion Paper on Third Party Rights in Contract* (Scot Law Com DP No. 157, 2014), para. 5.25.

interest' might also be significant for third parties. Therefore, under the circumstances of the case, Spark can rely on the limitation of liability clause.

2. No, but the third party might, in such a case, have a much stronger argument for the limitation.

II. Descriptive Formants

Regarding question 1, the effect of contractual limitations of liability on third parties is neither debated in Slovak literature nor is it the subject of case law. In the present authors' view, contractual limitations of liability can have effect only between the parties to the contract.[78] However, this view has been articulated in relation to situations where the party in breach wants to rely on the limitation clause against tortious claims of third parties. A different point of view should be taken in a situation where a third party (X) is in breach of a duty that leads to the breach of contract of Y vis-à-vis Z, with a limitation of liability clause in the contract between Y and Z. Under such circumstances, the limitation of liability clause will also have the effect of defining the scope of potential loss to be compensated (whether by the party in breach or by any other third party). Any loss exceeding the limitation based on the breach of a contractual duty (a breach that is substantively the breach of a contractual duty, disregarding whether it also gives grounds for a tortious claim against a third party) will not be compensated. The contracting party, Z, having agreed to a limitation clause, will not have the advantage of an unlimited claim against a third party, X, who was introduced into the performance of the contract by the other contracting party, Y. The limitations of liability are possibly part of a price-setting mechanism, not only in the relationship between the contracting parties adhering to the limitation of liability clause (Duff and Cairn), but also in the chain of subcontractors of a contractual party.

Regarding question 2, the position would be clearer under such circumstances; there is much stronger reasoning for allowing subcontractors to rely on the limitation clause. The clause would favour any third party that was an agent of Duff, as it might be construed as a public offer for a contractual arrangement (s. 276 SCommC) on the limitation of damages between Duff and Spark. Such a public offer is a proposal made to the public to conclude a contract. The limitation of damages could be considered an innominate contract between Duff and Spark.

78 See K. Csach in K. Csach, T. Doležal, J. Husár, J. Suchoža and Ľ. Siricová, *Profesijná zodpovednosť [Professional negligence]*, Košice: UPJŠ, 2011, pp. 223–28, in relation to the liability of solicitors.

III. Meta-Legal Formants

A tortious claim against Spark would most likely be barred under Slovak law. In general, no claims by a third party may arise from a breach of a contract between other parties. Although the Slovak Supreme Court (SSC) has not excluded such a possibility,[79] and recently decided on a limited scope of third-party protection derived from a contract between a bank and their client,[80] there is, to our knowledge, no judgment of the SSC that would allow a tortious claim brought by a third party against a party in breach of contract. The lower courts sometimes allow a tortious claim against a subcontractor,[81] while identifying a breach of a general statutory duty to prevent damage. The legal writing does not address this issue besides two conflicting points of view.[82] However, the present writers assume that two situations are to be distinguished: firstly, the breach of a statutory duty relating to the performance of a contract and, secondly, the breach of a separate statutory duty, leading to a special tortious claim (application of different liability clause) – that is, the intentional infliction of damage by acting contrary to good morals. In both cases, a stand-alone title, separate and parallel to the contractual claim, arises, and might also be brought against third persons. The contractual arrangements between contractual parties should not protrude into the tortious claim. However, as stated above in response to question 1, if the contractual arrangement also defines the scope of a potential protected interest, it might be argued that it also limits the scope of potential loss (and damages), although there is no legal or doctrinal source to support this position.

The present writers assume that the lack of doctrine on the interaction between contractual and tortious liability is derived from a unified liability that has a single general liability clause comprising both contractual and tortious liability. Slovak civil law is built on a rather unusual concept of the so-called unitary concept of civil liability or unitary concept of civil wrong. This means that Slovak civil law regulation does not distinguish between tortious liability and contractual liability for damages, but operates only with concept of a general clause on liability for damages and additional special clauses on liability, some of which are considered to be of a contractual nature, and others to be of a tortious nature. Accordingly, there is no set of rules applicable only to tortious

79 As an *obiter dictum* in the rather procedural decision of SSC file no. 4 Cdo 319/2008 dated 28.04.2010.

80 Decision of the SSC file no. 7 Cdo 163/2020 dated 28.02.2020 (R 18/2022).

81 Regional Court in Žilina file no. 7 Co 3/2012 dated 15.02.2012.

82 Rather unclear on the applicability of the concept in Slovak law, and referring to the Czech case law, see A. Dulak in M. Števček, A. Dulak, J. Bajánková, M. Fečík, F. Sedlačko, M. Tomašovič et al., *Občiansky zákonník I, sect. 1–450. Komentár [Commentary on Civil Code I, ss. 1–450]*, Prague: C.H. Beck, 2015, p. 1337; opposing such a possibility, while formulating exceptions, see K. Csach in K. Csach, T. Doležal, J. Husár, J. Suchoža and Ľ. Siricová, *Profesijná zodpovednosť [Professional negligence]*, Košice: UPJŠ, 2011, p. 147.

or to contractual liability. Therefore, the issue in question is not one of grounds of liability but, rather, whether an existing obligation has been breached. The unified system of liability, therefore, brings a shift in perspective which leaves some issues on the interaction between the two systems of liability unconsidered.

2.12. SPAIN

Carles Vendrell Cervantes

I. Operative Rules

1. It is *unlikely* that *Spark* would be able to benefit from Duff's limitation of liability.
2. *Yes*, in that case, the contract between Cairn and Duff would expressly confer a right upon third parties such as Spark.

II. Descriptive Formants

Question 1

The fact that the contract between Cairn and Duff expressly provides that the party with limited liability is Duff makes the possibility of extending this limitation to Spark difficult. In Spain, it is very common, in practice, to agree between the principal and the main contractor that limitation of liability will extend to any subcontractor;[83] the lack of such specific agreement here may imply that parties did not want to provide for that extension, so there is little room to interpret that an implied agreement exists. The legal question involved would be determined by interpreting the contract and, ultimately, determining the shared intentions of Cairn and Duff, which will depend on the circumstances of their contractual relationship.

Question 2

The extension of the limitation to Duff's 'agents (including independent contractors)' clearly expresses the intention of both parties to the contract to include third parties by granting rights to those parties. Thus, this term of the contract qualifies as a 'stipulation in favour of a third party'; under Spanish law, it is clear that such a stipulation may consist of a limitation or exoneration of liability.[84]

---

83 Á. Carrasco, *Derecho de contratos* (3rd ed., Thomson-Aranzadi, 2021), 681.
84 Ibid.

III. Meta-Legal Formants

Albeit not expressly mentioned in Article 1257 of the Civil Code, a contract clause that may benefit a third party need not be a claim aimed at giving, doing or refraining from doing something, but can also include an exclusion or limitation of liability.[85]

2.13. SWEDEN

Oskar Mossberg

I. Operative Rules

1. Spark *can most likely* rely on the limitation of liability clause.
2. Yes, then Spark *can* rely on the limitation of liability clause.

II. Descriptive Formants

At the outset, Cairn would have a tortious claim against Spark, according to the general rule on damages due to negligence, contained in Skadeståndslagen (1972:207) (the Act of Damages), Chapter 2, Article 1. According to Chapter 1, Article 1 of the Act, this rule is applicable unless there is derogatory legislation or derogation otherwise follows from contracts or rules on contracts.

As the current contracts would be regarded as *'kommersiella tjänsteavtal'* (commercial services contracts), there are no directly applicable statutory rules regarding the issue at hand, as indeed there are no such rules for this *'avtalstyp'* (type of contract). Instead, applicable rules are constructed from statutory law *ex analogia* or found in general principles of contract law. This traditional stance has been confirmed in NJA 2013 p. 1190.

However, as there are no *'tvingande kontraktsrättsliga regler'* (non-derogatory contract rules) applicable here, the parties have freedom of contract. In practice, virtually all construction contracts are regulated by some version of the system of standard terms 'Allmänna bestämmelser för entreprenader' (General Provisions for Construction Contracts) (AB), supplemented with any individual terms the parties deem suitable, for example limitation of liability clauses. There are several versions of the AB standard contracts, differing as to the parties' obligations and how the project is to be organised. The most commonly used is AB04, according to which the builder is responsible

---

[85] Á. Carrasco, *Derecho de contratos* (2nd ed., Thomson-Aranzadi, 2017), 599.

for organising and performing the works, but not for their planning. AB04 would most likely be used in a situation such as the present case. The rules are complicated, but here it suffices to say that there are provisions regarding liability for negligence. As these provisions are part of the contract, the principle of privity applies. This means that the contract's rules regarding liability can only be invoked by the contracting parties, which in turn means that Spark can only be held contractually liable by Duff (unless the contract is to be interpreted as a kind of third-party contract (see Case 1 above)). However, Cairn can hold Spark liable for negligence pursuant to the general rule on tortious liability in Chapter 2, Article 1 of the Act on Damages (see Case 2 above).

As regards the limitation of liability clause, there are two relevant cases from the HD. The first is NJA 2007 p. 758, where the parties had used the standard contract AB92 (the predecessor to the AB04 terms). A subcontractor had negligently caused damage to a house, and the owner sued the subcontractor directly, invoking tortious rules on liability due to negligence. The HD found that the claim was barred by the agreement between the owner of the house and the contractor, which contained a limitation of liability clause. The stated rationale for this is not entirely illuminating, but the HD seemed to view the owner's claim as a way of circumventing the contract with the main contractor. The result is equivalent to a '*friskrivning till förmån för tredjeman*' (limitation of liability in favour of a third party), to the benefit of the subcontractor. This is a particular type of third-party contract which awards an independent right to a third party, which takes the form of a limitation of the third party's liability against one or both of the parties to the contract.

A similar HD case is NJA 2010 p. 629. In this case, a limitation of liability clause between a subcontractor and the customer was given effect in favour of the subcontractor. The rationale for this was mainly that the loss which had occurred could easily have resulted through the actions of either the contractor or the subcontractor, and this was taken to suggest that the clause could be invoked by the subcontractor, even though the subcontractor was not a party to the contract. This ruling was given by the HD without further elaboration.[86]

---

86 Note that this is not necessarily an atypical example of an HD ruling. It is not typical either, but there is no formal requirement to invoke any particular doctrine, in the sense of a 'legal label' (such as 'third-party contract') when deciding a case. The formal requirement is to give reasons, and the described reasoning fulfils that requirement (despite potentially being perceived as unsatisfactory by legal scholarship). One could say that, traditionally, much (although nowhere near all) of the doctrinal development in Swedish law has been left to legal scholarship, which is thus charged with compiling case law into different doctrines, and the present case could be construed as representing such a division of labour. This implies that legal scholars are co-creators of the legal order and, indeed, legal scholarship is often invoked as an independent source of law, considered subordinate to the hierarchically superior sources of law (i.e. (traditionally) legislation, preparatory works and superior court case law).

It is possible to view the ruling as based on a third-party contract (in the form of a limitation of liability in favour of a third party). However, as the ruling is not explicitly based on any established doctrine, it must be considered ambiguous.

The rationales in both cases are ambiguous, but seem to suggest a tendency towards generous assessments concerning third-party effects in cases concerning commercial construction contracts. Accordingly, it seems to be in line with the reasoning of these cases to give the limitation of liability clause in the contract between Cairn and Duff effect in favour of Spark, pursuant to the general doctrine of third-party contracts *('den allmänna tredjemansavtalsläran')*.

In relation to question 2, the contract in this situation would indeed be interpreted as containing a *'friskrivning till förmån för tredjeman'* (limitation of liability in favour of a third party), a particular kind of third-party contract entailing a derogation from the general tortious rules and barring Cairn's claim to the extent that it exceeds the limitation of liability.

III. Meta-Legal Formants

Limitations of liability in favour of third parties are not regulated in statutory law. They are regarded as a form of third-party contract, and thus are subject to uncodified general principles of contract law and the rationales concerning these (see Case 1 above).

3. COMPARATIVE REMARKS

Jan Biemans and Lorna Richardson

This case considers whether a third party can utilise a limitation of liability provision in a contract between two other parties. Here, in contrast to earlier scenarios, the third-party right is not to receive something from one of the contracting parties, but to use a term of the contract as a defence to a claim by one of the contracting parties. The case is situated within a construction contract in which work has been subcontracted to a third party who tries to rely on the limitation of liability clause in the contract between the two main parties. The scenario posed seeks to identify to what extent the jurisdictions surveyed permit a third-party right to be created in relation to a contractual limitation of liability, and, if they do, what might be needed for the valid creation of that third-party right.

Question 1

In relation to this issue, the majority of legal systems surveyed would not allow Spark to rely on the limitation of liability clause in the contract between Cairn and Duff. In some systems, this was because no third-party right in Spark's favour had been created (Belgium, England, France, Scotland).

A similar stance was taken in Spanish law, in which the decision would be based on interpretation of the contract between Cairn and Duff to determine the intentions of those parties. German law also determined the outcome using interpretation. In Germany, Spark would probably not be able to rely on the limitation clause. However, the position would have been different had Spark been an employee, or a subcontractor in a similar position to an employee, due to employers' duties to protect employees from delictual liability arising as a consequence of their employment. In Italian law, Spark's obligation to Cairn arises extra-contractually and, as such, Spark could not seek to rely on the limitation clause in Cairn and Duff's contract. In Bulgaria, current case law means that delictual liability cannot competently be excluded, as opposed to contractual liability, which can be excluded unless there is intentional or gross negligence. As such, in that system the limitation clause is void.

The outcome is more doubtful in Poland, as the matter has not been the subject of any Code provisions and no cases have come before the courts for a resolution on the point. The Polish reporters came to the view that a restrictive approach, with the limitation clause benefiting Duff only, would more likely be taken by the courts.

In relation to the jurisdictions where Spark would be able to rely on the clause, there were varying reasons for this. In the Netherlands, there is a specific provision in the Civil Code dealing with the issue: Spark could only rely on Duff's limitation of liability clause for their own delictual liability insofar as Duff could have relied on the clause for their contractual liability against Cairn (meaning that Spark could not rely on it in the case of intentional or gross negligence). In Sweden, the limitation clause can be invoked by Spark as, without this being permitted, Cairn would be circumventing the contract with Duff. In Czech law, there is a specific statutory provision making Duff and Spark jointly and severally liable to Cairn. On that basis, the Czech reporter was of the view – although there were arguments going the other way – that Spark should not have greater liability than the main contractor. In Slovakia, the matter was not beyond doubt, given that there has been no case law on the point and no legal literature considering the matter. The reporters took the view that the limitation clause had the effect of defining the scope of potential loss to be compensated, whether by Cairn or by someone else. Thus, in both Czech and Slovakian law, the answers were reached by considering the scope of liability agreed to by Cairn and Duff.

Question 2

In contrast to the position in question 1, most of the jurisdictions would permit Spark to rely on the limitation clause with the additional wording included.

In most jurisdictions (Belgium, England, Germany, the Netherlands, Poland, Scotland, Spain and Sweden), a third-party right in favour of Spark would be created.

The position is unclear in Italian law, but the reporters took the view that Spark would be able to use the *exceptio doli* to prevent Cairn from abusing their rights, should they seek sums in excess of the $10 million limit.

In neither Bulgaria nor France can Spark rely on the clause. In both jurisdictions, delictual liability could not be excluded.

CASE 4: INDIRECT AGENCY AND RENTAL CONTRACTS

1. CASE

Mr Kane, a real estate investor, acquires real property in order to rent it out to companies. Mr Kane has hired a real estate agent, Waltmann & Co., to rent out his properties. Waltmann sign the rental contracts for the account of Kane, but in their own name; the rental contracts are concluded between Waltmann and the tenants. Waltmann carry out a number of administrative obligations, including giving the keys to the tenant at the start of the rental period and inspecting the properties after the end of the rental period. Waltmann also send invoices, collect the rent, deduct a fee, and then pay the remainder to Kane. Kane never comes into contact with the tenants, and most tenants have no particular knowledge of Kane being the owner of the property, although they could find out through the land registry, or by inquiring with Waltmann. One of the tenants, MyPad Inc., have damaged the property it has rented.

Questions

1. Can Waltmann sue MyPad for compensation for the damage caused to the property?
2. If Waltmann become insolvent after concluding a new rental contract with Nickel & Dime Ltd, what remedies do Nickel & Dime and Kane have against each other to safeguard their respective interests under this contract (access to and use of the building, and payment of the rent, respectively)?

2. DISCUSSIONS

2.1. BELGIUM

Siel Demeyere and Vincent Sagaert

I. Operative Rules

1. Waltmann can sue MyPad.
2. Nickel & Dime would be able to use the building. Kane would be able to seek payment of the rent.

II. Descriptive Formants

Question 1

This is a case of *middellijke vertegenwoordiging/représentation imparfaite* (indirect agency),[1] since the agent has entered into the agreement for the account of another, but in their own name. The contract between Waltmann and Kane is probably a *commissieovereenkomst/contrat de commission*[2] (commission contract), as Waltmann is aware of the existence of the agency (even if they are not aware of the identity of the principal). Agency for real estate transactions is a professional activity of Waltmann and contracting parties know this.[3] In cases where the agency is intentionally hidden, there is a situation of *naamlening/prête-nom* (name lending).[4]

The contractual effects of the contract arise, in the case of indirect agency, between the agent (Waltmann) and the counterparty (MyPad Inc.). There is no contractual bond between the principal (Kane) and the contracting party (in this case, MyPad Inc.).[5] However, the legal effects on the proprietary level,[6] if any, arise immediately between these two parties.[7] This entails that Waltmann will be allowed to sue MyPad, in order to seek damages for the damage caused to the property. Kane can subsequently claim the damages from Waltmann.

Waltmann could also claim the damages as a representative of Kane, by way of an oblique action (cf. Case 6, question 3).

Indirect agency must be distinguished from direct agency, in which the agent acts in the name of, and for the account of, the principal. If this were the case here, all consequences would arise in the relation between the contracting

1 Art. 1.8 BCC.

2 See I. Samoy, *Middellijke vertegenwoordiging: vertegenwoordiging herbekeken vanuit het optreden in eigen naam voor andermans rekening*, Intersentia, Antwerp 2005, 194, no. 286.

3 P. Van Ommeslaghe, *Traité de droit civil belge. II. Les obligations. Vol. 1*, Bruylant, Brussels 2013, 650, no. 417.

4 See I. Samoy, *Middellijke vertegenwoordiging: vertegenwoordiging herbekeken vanuit het optreden in eigen naam voor andermans rekening*, Intersentia, Antwerp 2005, 125, no. 169.

5 Art. 1.8, §3, second para., BCC; E. Dirix, 'De rechtsverhouding tussen principaal, commissionair en derde' in E. Dirix, P. Senaeve, W. Pintens and S. Stijns (eds), *Liber Amicorum Jacques Herbots*, Kluwer, Deurne 2002, 106, no. 10; I. Samoy, *Middellijke vertegenwoordiging: vertegenwoordiging herbekeken vanuit het optreden in eigen naam voor andermans rekening*, Intersentia, Antwerp 2005, 271, no. 406; M.E. Storme, 'Van Trust gespeend? Trusts en fiduciaire figuren in het Belgisch privaatrecht', *TPR* 1998, 766, no. 99.

6 For instance, a transfer of ownership.

7 Explanatory Memorandum Book 1, *Parl.St.* 2020–21, 1806/1, p. 20; E. Dirix, 'De rechtsverhouding tussen principaal, commissionair en derde' in E. Dirix, P. Senaeve, W. Pintens and S. Stijns (eds), *Liber Amicorum Jacques Herbots*, Kluwer, Deurne 2002, 100, no. 4 and 106, no. 10; I. Samoy, *Middellijke vertegenwoordiging: vertegenwoordiging herbekeken vanuit het optreden in eigen naam voor andermans rekening*, Intersentia, Antwerp 2005, 322, no. 493; M.E. Storme, 'Van Trust gespeend? Trusts en fiduciaire figuren in het Belgisch privaatrecht', *TPR*, 1998, 766, no. 99.

party (MyPad) and the principal (Kane), without any legal effects (rights or obligations) arising on the part of the agent.[8]

Question 2

In principle, the consequences of the contract arise between the agent, Waltmann, and Nickel & Dime, and not immediately between Nickel & Dime and Kane. The insolvency of the principal or agent is one of the grounds for termination of the agency agreement (Art. 2003, old BCC). However, Nickel & Dime cannot avoid the need to go to the bankruptcy trustee dealing with Waltmann's affairs.[9] The bankruptcy trustee can, theoretically, decide not to respect the lease.[10] However, the Court of Cassation has ruled that the option not to continue compliance with an agreement only exists if this is necessary for the compulsory sale of the real estate.[11]

In any case, Kane can claim property rights in the claim for payment of the rent against Nickel & Dime, despite the insolvency of Waltmann. Article XX.196, paragraph 2 WER protects the claim for payment of the price arising from a sales contract concluded by an indirect agent. However, this protection can analogously be applied to all claims arising from the juridical act which the agent has agreed with the contracting party, for the account of the principal.[12] On the proprietary level, the principal owns these claims in the relationship between Kane and Nickel & Dime.

2.2. BULGARIA

Petar Topurov

I. Operative Rules

1. Waltmann can file a claim against MyPad for compensation for the damage caused to the property.

---

8 S. Stijns, *Verbintenissenrecht. Leerboek 1*, die Keure, Bruges 2009–16, 133, no. 169; P. Wéry, *Droit des obligations: Théorie générale du contrat*, I, Larcier, Brussels 2011, 181, no. 165.

9 See I. Samoy, *Middellijke vertegenwoordiging: vertegenwoordiging herbekeken vanuit het optreden in eigen naam voor andermans rekening*, Intersentia, Antwerp 2005, 342, no. 520.

10 Art. XX.139 Code of Economic Law of 28 February 2013 (*Wetboek Economisch recht/Code de droit économique*) (WER); V. Sagaert and S. Baeyens, 'De beëindiging van overeenkomsten in geval van insolventie van de partijen: loopt het insolventierecht uit de pas van het verbintenissenrecht?' in N. Carette and B. Weyts (eds.), *Verantwoord aansprakelijkheidsrecht. Liber amicorum Aloïs Van Oevelen*, Intersentia, Antwerp 2017, 487 ff.

11 Cass. 10 April 2008, *Arr. Cass.* 2008, 878, *JT* 2008, 349, comment T. Hürner.

12 I. Samoy, *Middellijke vertegenwoordiging: vertegenwoordiging herbekeken vanuit het optreden in eigen naam voor andermans rekening*, Intersentia, Antwerp 2005, 337, no. 512.

2. In the event of Waltmann's insolvency, Mr Kane could claim transfer of rights under the lease, and Nickel & Dime could express their consent to have Waltmann, in the capacity of a lessor, replaced by Mr Kane.

II. Descriptive Formants

Regarding question 1 above, Art. 228 LOC stipulates that, under the lease, the lessor undertakes to provide the tenant with a temporary use of a certain property. The law does not require that the lessor should be this property's owner, which makes it completely possible to rent out someone else's property.[13] Simultaneously, according to Art. 233, paragraph 1, sentence 2 LOC, the tenant owes compensation for damage caused by them during their use of the property. Furthermore, the regulation of the public property register does not include the presumption that third parties should be aware of who owns a certain property.[14] Based on the above, it should be assumed that Waltmann can file a claim against MyPad for compensation for damage inflicted on the property. Although the damage is to Mr Kane's property, Waltmann can file a claim against MyPad, based on the contract between them, according to which MyPad should use the property without damaging it. Such damages would also affect Waltmann's property (*patrimonium*), since it would be obliged to repair the damage under the contract with Mr Kane. According to Art. 233, paragraph 1, sentence 3 LOC, the tenant owes compensation for damage caused by their subtenants.

Regarding question 2 above, and considering the facts of this case, Mr Kane has authorised Waltmann to conclude leases on his property, whereby leases have been concluded at the expense of the owner, but on behalf of the commissioner.[15] The facts of the case lead to the conclusion that there exists a commission contract, as far as Waltmann presents in the capacity of a commission merchant.[16] Along these lines, Art. 352, paragraph 2 CA provides that it is only after the transfer of rights, acquired at the expense of the principal, that the counterparty to the execution transaction may enter into a legal transaction with the principal, and be entitled to request that the commission merchant perform their legal obligations.[17] Meanwhile, Art. 349,

13 M. Markov, *Contractual Law*, Sibi, Sofia 2011, p. 335; P. Goleva, *Contractual Law*, New Star, Sofia 2015, p. 332; Decision No. 725 of the BSCC from 04.11.2008 in case No. 163/2008.

14 I. Vassilev, 'Publicity of the entry under Bulgarian property law' in H. Paunov (compilor), *Compendium 'Law – Traditions and Perspectives'*, Ciela, Sofia 2018, pp. 251–62.

15 According to Art. 348 Commerce Act, '[u]nder a commission contract the commission merchant shall undertake, for a commission and upon the mandate of the principal, to perform on his own behalf and for the account of the principal one or more transactions. In this sentence "on his own behalf" is used with the meaning "on his own name"'.

16 T. Yossifova, *The commission contract*, Sibi, Sofia 2006, p. 18.

17 M. Pavlova, *Civil Law. General Part*, Sophie-P, Sofia 2002, p. 598.

paragraph 2 CA poses the fiction that the rights acquired by the commission merchant, or granted thereto by the principal, shall be deemed, with respect to the commission merchant's creditors, rights of the principal, even before they have been transferred to the principal. The commission merchant's creditors cannot be satisfied by the rights acquired by the former, because this occurred at the expense of the principal.[18]

What follows is that, notwithstanding Waltmann's insolvency, receivables under the lease are deemed rights outwith the commission agent's insolvent estate, provided the principal has performed their obligations.[19] It is necessary, however, after initiating the insolvency proceedings, for the syndic[20] of the insolvent company to transfer in Mr Kane's favour the rights acquired by Waltmann ensuing from the execution transaction, while Nickel & Dime give their consent to replace the commission merchant, as a debtor, with the principal, on the grounds of Art. 102, paragraph 1 LOC.[21] Mr Kane could also demand the separation of rights acquired at his expense, based on the fiction according to Art. 349, paragraph 2 CA.[22] The commissioner's creditors cannot seek payment from the assets and rights held by the commissioner for the principal, notwithstanding the fact that those assets and rights have not yet been transferred to the principal. Where the syndic refuses to cooperate, legal doctrine accepts the option that the principal has the right to file a claim under Art. 349, paragraph 2 CA,[23] for a court decision that the principal is the holder of certain rights.

Such an opinion, however, conflicts with the prohibition on opening new judicial proceedings against the company, following the institution of bankruptcy proceedings against it (Art. 637, paragraph 6 CA). Until the company is declared bankrupt, the commission contract may continue to operate, provided that supervision is guaranteed on the part of the syndic.[24] It is only when the commission merchant has been declared bankrupt that the commission contract will be terminated.[25] Following the contract's termination, Mr Kane and Nickel & Dime may have a new opportunity for rearranging their relationship through

18 O. Gerdzhikov, *Commercial Transactions*, Publisher Work-and-law, Sofia 2006, p. 135.

19 G. Grigorov, *Insolvency*, Sibi, Sofia 2017, p. 166; T. Yossifova, *The commission contract*, Sibi, Sofia 2006, p. 97.

20 Person who manages a company after bankruptcy. The court of insolvency appoints this person.

21 Decision No. 220/29.02.1996 of the BSC; Decision No 392/12.10.1994 of the BSC; T. Yossifova, *The commission contract*, Sibi, Sofia 2006, p. 95.

22 T. Yossifova, *The commission contract*, Sibi, Sofia 2006, p. 97.

23 Ibid., p. 61.

24 As a consequence of this, Nickel & Dime can continue to occupy the premises and pay the rent to the syndic, who must hold the rent for the benefit of Mr Kane.

25 T. Yossifova, *The commission contract*, Sibi, Sofia 2006, p. 185.

a new lease, or may decide to avail themselves of the contract concluded under the rights transfer in Mr Kane's favour by the commissioner, as well as of the expressed consent from the lessee about the replacement of the commissioner with Mr Kane in the contractual relationship between the lessee and the commissioner.[26]

2.3. CZECH REPUBLIC

Tomáš Richter

I. Operative Rules

1. *Waltmann can sue MyPad* for damages.
2. *Very few effective remedies would be available to Nickel & Dime*, while *Kane would be able to rely on a rule* which would prevent Waltmann's other creditors from having recourse to as-yet-uncollected rental receivables owed by Nickel & Dime.

II. Descriptive Formants

In sections 2455 to 2470, the CC has specific rules on what one could call undisclosed agency, and what the CC calls *'komise'* (commission). The basic provisions describe the contract between *'komisionář'* (the agent) and *'komitent'* (the principal) as a contract whereby the agent undertakes to procure a certain matter for the principal's account but in the agent's own name, and the principal undertakes to pay the agent a fee therefor (section 2455 CC). Transactions conducted by the agent vis-à-vis third parties do not give rise to rights and obligations on the part of the principal, but rather on the part of the agent themselves (section 2456).

As regards the enforcement of the tenants' obligations under the rental agreements entered into by Waltmann for the account of Kane, one would rely on section 2466 CC, which provides (in its first sentence) that where a third party defaults on an obligation under a contract concluded with the agent, the agent shall enforce such obligations for the principal's account. The second sentence of section 2466 CC provides that, where the principal so agrees, the agent may assign such enforcement rights to the principal.

Assuming that MyPad is indeed liable for the damage under the terms of the relevant rental agreement (or the statutory provisions buttressing it), and

26 According to Art. 102, para. 1 LOC, a third party may substitute for the debtor only with the creditor's explicit consent.

that no assignment pursuant to section 2466, second sentence, has taken place, Waltmann can indeed sue MyPad under the provision of section 2466 CC, first sentence.

The analysis would be much more complicated with respect to the second question, concerning the legal situation upon Waltmann's insolvency. The Civil Code has only very rudimentary provisions in the subpart on '*komise*' (undisclosed agency) which can facilitate such an analysis. These rules appear in sections 2464 and 2465 CC, which, however, quite clearly assume that the agent has been retained in order to procure the sale of a tangible asset for the principal, rather than entering into a more complex and long-term transaction such as a lease of real estate. Section 2464 CC provides that:

> (1) A thing entrusted to the agent for the purposes of a sale remains the property of the principal until ownership is transferred to a third party.
> (2) A receivable arising under a contract entered into by the agent for the principal's account shall be deemed, for the purposes of the relationship between the principal and the agent or the agent's creditors, to belong to the principal.

In relation to the facts of the case, this provision provides only a very limited basis for reliable conclusions. It seems to follow clearly from section 2464(2) CC that receivables such as the payment of rent (as well as other payments to be made) under the rental agreement entered into by Waltmann with Nickel & Dime would be deemed to belong directly to Kane, and this effect would obtain not only internally between Kane and Waltmann, but vis-à-vis Waltmann's other creditors as well.

However, neither this provision nor any of the CC's other rules help much further. It is, for example, unclear whether the same 'ring-fencing' effect would apply to payments on account of those receivables already collected by Waltmann prior to the onset of insolvency but not yet paid out to Kane. It has been suggested that the provision should indeed be construed broadly in order to achieve that effect.[27] While the provision speaks about receivables arising out of a transaction entered into by the agent for the principal's account, it is silent about the corresponding obligations. It has, accordingly, also been suggested that the provision ought to be interpreted broadly, so as to apply not only to receivables involved in transactions entered into by the agent, but also to the matching obligations 'going the other way', in effect leading to the constitution of a 'ring-fenced patrimony' in the hands of the agent, which would effectively belong to the principal and not the agent.[28] While such suggestions might be

[27] V. Pihera in M. Hulmák et al., *Občanský zákoník V, Závazkové právo, Obecná část (§1721–2054), První vydání*, C.H. Beck, Praha 2014, p. 854 at 15.

[28] Ibid. at 14.

intuitively appealing, there is very little basis for such outcomes in the language of the law. In fact, the CC, in its sections 1488 ff., regulating *'svěřenský fond'* (the trust fund), allows a similar outcome to obtain, only subject to rather strict formal requirements, including the adoption of a founding charter of the trust fund by way of a public deed entered into before a notary (section 1452(3) CC), and subject to the registration of the trust fund in a register of trust funds (section 1451(2) CC). The broad interpretation also conflicts with the basic rule in section 2456 CC, in terms of which transactions conducted by the agent vis-à-vis third parties do not give rise to rights and obligations on the part of the principal, but rather the agent themselves.

In addition to section 2464 CC, which provides only limited protection to Kane, and none to Nickel & Dime, there is section 2467 CC, which provides that the principal (Kane) may demand performance procured by the agents from the third party (Nickel & Dime), in the event that the agents (Waltmann) are not capable of doing so for reasons arising on the agents' part. It is not at all clear whether or not the agents' insolvency would qualify as a ground to invoke section 2467 CC, but even if it did, it would clearly protect only Kane, and not Nickel & Dime, and only for so long as the lease itself was not prejudiced by Waltmann's insolvency. One would be well advised to assume that the lease, being a contract entered into by Waltmann, might indeed be impacted on by the insolvency proceedings to the same extent as any other executory contracts of the same kind would be liable to be so impacted under the relevant insolvency law.

The answer to question 2 could, therefore, be summarised by stating that the legal situation is rather unclear, and would expose both Kane and Nickel & Dime to significant legal uncertainty. The one reasonably clear protection provided by the CC would be the 'ring-fencing' against recourse by Waltmann's other creditors, conferred by section 2464(2) CC on as-yet-uncollected receivables, in relation to the rental payments owed by Nickel & Dime.

2.4. ENGLAND AND WALES

T.T. Arvind

I. Operative Rules

1. Waltmann may be able to sue MyPad for compensation for damage caused to the property if MyPad were unaware that Waltmann were acting on behalf of someone else, but not otherwise.
2. In the event of Waltmann's insolvency, Kane and Nickel & Dime will have full rights against each other under the tenancy.

II. Descriptive Formants

Question 1

The relationship between Waltmann and Kane will be one of principal and agent, because Waltmann have the authority to enter into binding transactions on Kane's behalf. Principal–agent relations are governed by special rules derived from case law, which differ from the ordinary rules of contract. In general, only the principal can sue or be sued under the contract. Agents are not party to contracts entered into on behalf of their principals, even if it is the agent who signs the contract.[29] As a result, under the doctrine of privity, the agent cannot sue[30] or be sued[31] under the contract, unless the parties have provided for them to be liable concurrently with, or to the exclusion of, the principal.[32] Although older cases suggest that the agent has a right to sue, instead of the principal, the consensus among commentators is that subsequent developments mean those cases no longer apply.[33]

This general rule, however, only applies if the other party is aware that the agent is acting on behalf of someone else (a 'disclosed principal'). It does not apply if the other party is unaware, at the time of contracting, that the agent is contracting on behalf of someone else (an 'undisclosed principal'). Where the principal is undisclosed at the time of contracting, the agent is treated as a party to the contract; the agent can bring an action to enforce the contract, and the other party can choose to sue the agent under the contract.[34] This does not exclude the rights and liabilities of the undisclosed principal, who can also sue or be sued under the contract, if the agent acted within the scope of their actual authority (see, further, question 2 below).

A principal is not undisclosed merely because the third party is unaware of the principal's identity. If the other party knows that the agent is contracting on someone else's behalf but does not know who that someone else is, then in law the principal is not undisclosed but merely unidentified. Thus, if MyPad were aware that Waltmann were acting on behalf of someone else, but did not know who the principal was, Kane will be an unidentified (but not undisclosed) principal. In such a case, any action to enforce the contract must be brought by or against Kane. If, however, MyPad did not know that Waltmann were

29 *Montgomerie v. UK Mutual SS Association Ltd* [1891] 1 QB 370.
30 *Fairlie v. Fenton* (1870) LR 5 Exch 169.
31 *Paquin v. Beauclerk* [1906] AC 148.
32 *Montgomerie v. UK Mutual SS Association Ltd* [1891] 1 QB 370, 372.
33 P.G. Watts and F.M.B. Reynolds (eds), *Bowstead & Reynolds on Agency*, 21st ed. (London: Sweet & Maxwell, 2017), para. 9-010.
34 *Siu Yin Kwan v. Eastern Insurance Co. Ltd* [1994] 2 AC 199 (HL), 207.

acting on behalf of someone else, and believed them to be acting on their own behalf, then Kane will be an undisclosed principal. In such a case, either Kane or Waltmann may sue or be sued under the contract. In practice, the distinction between undisclosed and unidentified principals is not always easy to draw, and commentators have argued that agents should prima facie be liable together with the principal even where the principal is unidentified rather than undisclosed.[35] However, this position has not yet been accepted in case law.

Whether a particular situation is one of an undisclosed or an unidentified principal tends to depend on the context and background. Prior cases have shown, for example, that a broker will usually be assumed to be trading on behalf of someone else, thus making cases involving brokers cases of unidentified, but not undisclosed, principals.[36] In contrast, a purchaser at an auction could be trading either on their own account or on behalf of someone else, thus making cases involving such purchasers cases of undisclosed principals.[37] Applying this distinction to the present case, then if Waltmann are established as estate agents, it is likely that Kane will be an unidentified but not undisclosed principal, as estate agents typically contract on behalf of others. If, however, Waltmann are established as a property company, then it is possible that Kane might be treated as an undisclosed principal, as property companies can also contract on their own behalf. Waltmann will be able to sue MyPad in the latter case, but not in the former.

Question 2

The general rule is that a disclosed principal, whether identified or unidentified, may sue or be sued on any contract made on their behalf by an agent, as long as the contract was within the scope of the agent's authority, or was subsequently ratified by the principal. This is very well established in the case law, and is generally taken to reflect a broader underlying principle that the contract is the principal's contract rather than the agent's.[38]

Case law has held that this principle also applies where the principal is undisclosed, but only if the agent was acting within their actual authority.[39] Unlike a disclosed principal, an undisclosed principal cannot ratify acts outside the scope of the agent's actual authority.[40] Either way, on the facts it is apparent

---

35 P.G. Watts and F.M.B. Reynolds (eds), *Bowstead & Reynolds on Agency*, 21st ed. (London: Sweet & Maxwell, 2017), para. 9-016.

36 *Baring v. Corrie* (1818) 2 B&A 137.

37 *Williamson v. Barton* (1862) 7 H&N 899; *Chadwick v. Maden* (1851) 9 Hare 188.

38 P.G. Watts and F.M.B. Reynolds (eds), *Bowstead & Reynolds on Agency*, 21st ed. (London: Sweet & Maxwell, 2017), paras. 8-001 to 8-002.

39 *Siu Yin Kwan v. Eastern Insurance Co Ltd* [1994] 2 AC 199 (HL), 207.

40 *Keighley, Maxsted & Co v. Durant* [1901] AC 240.

that the contract was within Waltmann's actual authority, and it will therefore create rights as between Kane and Nickel & Dime, even if they were not aware of each other's identity, and regardless of whether Kane is a disclosed or undisclosed principal.

III. Meta-Legal Formants

Question 2

Commentators have questioned whether the application, to undisclosed principals, of the rule that principals may sue or be sued under contracts made by an agent is compatible with orthodox theories of contract. It has been pointed out, for example, that the cases doing so sit uneasily with the standard understanding of consent and the doctrine of privity. Taken together, consent and privity would seem to militate against permitting a third party who was unaware that the agent was contracting on behalf of an undisclosed principal to be sued by that undisclosed principal. Nevertheless, it is generally accepted that the rule serves an important commercial function, and is, therefore, a commercially expedient exception to privity.[41]

2.5. FRANCE

Sylvain Ravenne and Flora Vern

I. Operative Rules

1. Waltmann can sue MyPad for compensation for the damage caused to the property.
2. Kane would have an oblique action against Nickel & Dime for the rent. It is more doubtful, however, whether Nickel & Dime would have a remedy against Kane for access to and use of the building.

II. Descriptive Formants

Question 1

In this case the real estate agent concludes rental contracts in their own name, but on behalf of the landowner. According to Article L.132-1 of the French

41 P.G. Watts and F.M.B. Reynolds (eds), *Bowstead & Reynolds on Agency*, 21st ed. (London: Sweet & Maxwell, 2017), para. 8-069.

Commercial Code, a person who acts in their own name (or under a company name) on behalf of a *'commettant'* (principal) is a *'commissionnaire'* (agent on commission).

Unlike a mandatary, who acts in the name of a principal (Art. 1984 FCC), an agent on commission acts in their own name and is personally bound by the contracts they undertake. Correlatively, the principal is a third party to the contracts undertaken by the agent on commission. As a result, there is no direct relation between a principal and the co-contracting party of their agent,[42] even if the co-contracting party has knowledge of the commission contract, and of the identity of the principal.[43]

The reform of contract law has set this principle out in legislation, and the current Article 1154 of the FCC, which is applicable to contracts concluded after 1 October 2016, states accordingly:

> Where a representative acts within their authority, in the name and on behalf of the person whom they represent, only the latter is bound to the undertaking so contracted.
>
> Where a representative states that they are acting on behalf of another person but contracts in their own name, they alone are bound towards the other contracting party.

The first paragraph of the Article refers, for instance, to a mandatary, whereas the second paragraph describes the obligations of an agent on commission. Since Waltmann are an agent on commission of the owner, they can sue the tenant, MyPad, who have damaged the property in violation of the lease, which creates an obligation to return the thing in its original condition.[44] An agent on commission is liable to their principal for faults, such as a lack of diligence, in their management (Arts. 1991 and 1992 FCC). Thus, if Waltmann did not sue MyPad, they would be liable to Kane for the damage caused by MyPad.

Waltmann will have to either use the compensation to repair the property or account for it to Kane as their principal (Art. 1993 FCC).

Question 2

Case law from the Cour de cassation provides that a principal and the co-contracting party of their agent on commission have no direct claim against each other.[45] However, both the principal and the third party have a claim against the agent on commission.

---

42 Cass., com., 15 juill. 1963, Bull. civ. IV, n° 378.

43 Cass., com., 7 juill. 1962, Bull. civ. IV, n° 240.

44 Art. 1728 ff. FCC.

45 Cass., civ., 20 juill. 1871, *DP* 1871, 1, 232; Cass., com., 15 juill. 1963; Cass., com., 30 oct. 2000, n° 98-12236.

Nevertheless, the former Article 1166 and the current Article 1341-1 of the FCC provide that a creditor may exercise, on behalf of their debtor, the patrimonial rights of the latter through an *'action oblique'* (indirect or oblique action). This action is open whenever the debtor (Waltmann, in this case) fails to exercise their own rights. Thus, Kane could sue Nickel & Dime and request the payment of the rent. However, this claim would be exercised on behalf of Waltmann. Nickel & Dime could invoke the *'exception d'inexécution'* (defence of non-performance) and refuse to pay the rent (Art. 1219 FCC) because the lessors are under a duty to provide the tenant with access to and use of the building *('obligation de faire jouir')*. On the other hand, Kane has no contractual obligation to grant Waltmann, as an agent on commission, personal access to, and use of, the building. Only Waltmann, who are the lessors, have such an obligation, which is owed to Nickel & Dime. Kane only has an obligation to give Waltmann the means to give access and use to the tenants (for example, by providing keys). Therefore, Nickel & Dime could only demand that Kane give Waltmann access to the building.

Furthermore, some authors consider that the principal and the co-contracting party of the agent should be able to sue each other after the principal has declared their intention to benefit from the contract, which could be done any time, since the commission contract is concluded in the exclusive interest of the principal. According to these authors, the principal would, by making this declaration, accept being bound by the contract between the agent and the co-contracting party and be substituted for the agent on commission.[46] Thus, by declaring their intention to benefit from the rental contracts, Kane would become the lessor of Nickel & Dime. As a result, Kane would be bound to guarantee the lessee access to, and use of, the building in exchange for a direct claim to the payment of the rent.

2.6. GERMANY

Sonja Meier

I. Operative Rules

1. Waltmann will most likely be able to sue MyPad in contract.
2. Kane will not have any claims against Nickel & Dime. However, he can claim an assignment of Waltmann's claims for unpaid rent against Nickel & Dime from Waltmann's insolvency administrator. Nickel & Dime do not have any remedies against Kane.

[46] P. Delebecque and F. Collart-Dutilleul, *Contrats Civils & Commerciaux*, 12th ed. (Paris: Dalloz, 2023), n° 663; J.L. Aubert, É. Savaux and J. Flour, *Droit Civil. Les Obligations. L'Acte Juridique*, 17th ed. (Paris: Sirey, 2022), n° 389.

II. Descriptive Formants

Question 1

When contracting with MyPad, Waltmann did not act as Kane's direct agent under §164 BGB because they did not act in the name of Kane. The parties to the rental contract, therefore, are Waltmann and MyPad. Damaging the rented property constitutes a breach of contract by MyPad under §280 (1) BGB, entitling Waltmann to contractual damages for any loss they have suffered. Waltmann would have suffered a loss had they been liable to pay damages under their contract with Kane. However, there is no indication that Waltmann can be held responsible for the acts of MyPad vis-à-vis Kane. Therefore, it is not Waltmann who have suffered a loss, but Kane.

In exceptional cases, the claimant can liquidate the loss of a third person by way of '*Drittschadensliquidation*' (liquidation of a damage of a third party).[47] This doctrine is not expressly mentioned in the BGB, but has been developed by courts and commentators. It requires a '*Schadensverlagerung*' (shift of loss); that is, that a loss which under normal circumstances would be borne by the claimant has shifted to a third party, due to a special relationship between the claimant and the third party.[48] Courts and writers have developed certain groups of cases where *Drittschadensliquidation* is allowed. One of the most important of these is '*mittelbare Stellvertretung*' (indirect agency).[49] This applies where the claimant concludes a contract in their own name but for the account of a third party, and this indirect agency causes the loss to be shifted from the claimant to the third party. The present case falls into this category, since a third party had to bear the loss only because Waltmann acted as Kane's indirect agent.

An alternative to using the concept of *Drittschadensliquidation* is to regard the contract between Waltmann and MyPad as a '*Vertrag mit Schutzwirkung für Dritte*' (contract with protective effects towards third parties). This doctrine has been developed by the courts and commentators, and implies that a contract between two parties can create contractual duties of care and protection towards

---

47 See, generally, *BGHZ* 40, 91; BGH *NJW-RR* 2008, 786 at [18]; H. Oetker in *Münchener Kommentar zum BGB*, vol. 2 (9th ed., Beck 2022), §249, [289] ff.; C. Höpfner in *J. von Staudingers Kommentar zum Bürgerlichen Gesetzbuch*, vol. §§249–54 (Sellier – de Gruyter 2021), before §249, [62] ff.

48 *BGHZ* 51, 91; *BGHZ* 133, 36.

49 C. Höpfner in *J. von Staudingers Kommentar zum Bürgerlichen Gesetzbuch*, vol. §§249–54 (Sellier – de Gruyter 2021), before §249, [69]–[70]; H. Oetker in *Münchener Kommentar zum BGB*, vol. 2 (9th ed., Beck 2022), §249, [296]; BGH *NJW* 1967, 930; BGH *WM* 1987, 581; BGH *NJW* 1988, 1864; *BGHZ* 176, 281 at [35].

certain third parties.[50] Under this doctrine, the third party will not be entitled to the contractual performance, but will have the right to claim contractual damages if its pre-existing rights and interests are infringed by the contractual debtor. While some authors regard the doctrine as a case of established judicial lawmaking, the courts base it on a supplementary interpretation of the contract. In the present case, it could be argued that Kane was included within the protective ambit of the contract, since he was subject to the risk of MyPad damaging the property, and Waltmann had a legitimate interest in extending the contractual protection to Kane, which could have been anticipated by MyPad, since they must have been aware of the possibility that Waltmann were not the owners but contracting on account of someone else.

Both doctrines are functionally similar, allowing the recovery of a third party's loss by way of contractual remedies. In general, *Drittschadensliquidation* will be applied where there is a unique loss which has shifted from the creditor to the third party. A *Vertrag mit Schutzwirkung*, by contrast, will be assumed where the third party's loss is a separate loss which can exist alongside a loss of the creditor, for example a breach of contract by the landlord in not maintaining the premises that results in an accident in which the tenant (creditor) and their family (third parties) are injured.[51] In the present case, a court will probably apply the *Drittschadensliquidation* rather than the *Vertrag mit Schutzwirkung*, because the loss arising from the damage to the property is a loss which shifted from Waltmann to Kane rather than an additional loss on the part of Kane.

Kane has a claim in delict against MyPad for violation of his right of ownership of the premises under §823 (1) BGB if the damage was either negligently inflicted by a legal representative of MyPad (§31 BGB) or by one of MyPad's employees in relation to whom MyPad cannot show that they acted with necessary care in selecting and supervising them (§831 BGB). According to some authors, the existence of a delictual claim excludes the application of *Drittschadensliquidation*, because the third party is sufficiently protected.[52] The courts, by contrast, regularly allow a *Drittschadensliquidation* even where the

50 See, generally, *BGHZ* 176, 281 at [27]; *BGH NJW-RR* 2017, 888 at [15]–[19]; P. Gottwald in *Münchener Kommentar zum BGB*, vol. 3 (9th ed., Beck 2022), §328, [167] ff., [181] ff.; S. Klumpp in *J. von Staudingers Kommentar zum Bürgerlichen Gesetzbuch*, vol. §§328–45 (Sellier – de Gruyter 2020), §328, [92] ff.

51 H. Oetker in *Münchener Kommentar zum BGB*, vol. 2 (9th ed., Beck 2022), §249, [292]; P. Gottwald in *Münchener Kommentar zum BGB*, vol. 3 (9th ed., Beck 2022), §328, [195]; C. Höpfner in *J. von Staudingers Kommentar zum Bürgerlichen Gesetzbuch*, vol. §§249–54 (Sellier – de Gruyter 2021), before §249, [64].

52 Cf. H. Oetker in *Münchener Kommentar zum BGB*, vol. 2 (9th ed., Beck 2022), §249, [305]; C. Höpfner in *J. von Staudingers Kommentar zum Bürgerlichen Gesetzbuch*, vol. §§249–54 (Sellier – de Gruyter 2021), before §249, [72].

injured party has delictual claims, since a contractual claim generally offers more protection (for example, regarding the onus of proof) than a delictual one.[53]

The effect of *Drittschadensliquidation* is that the creditor (Waltmann) has a claim for damages against the debtor for the third party's (Kane's) loss. The creditor can either assign this claim to the third party or enforce the claim themselves and pass the proceeds on to the third party. Therefore, a *Drittschadensliquidation* will not be allowed where it is certain that the claimant is neither obliged nor willing to do either.[54] However, this is not the case here. According to §§675 and 667 BGB and §384 (2) HGB, a mandatee (a person tasked with concluding contracts for another person, either as a direct agent or as an intermediary) has to surrender to the principal everything received in the course of their mandate. Waltmann will, therefore, be obliged to assign their claim against MyPad to Kane.

Waltmann will not have any delictual claim against MyPad, since they are not the owners of the damaged property.

Question 2

Since the rental contract was concluded by Waltmann in their own name, Kane does not have any contractual remedies against Nickel & Dime.

He may, however, try to get hold of any claims Waltmann may have against Nickel & Dime for unpaid rent. According to §§675 and 667 BGB and §384 (2) HGB, a mandatee is obliged to account to the principal for everything they have received in the course of their mandate. This means that Kane has a contractual right against Waltmann to have any claims against Nickel & Dime assigned to him. However, for as long as Waltmann have not done so, Kane does not have any rights against Nickel & Dime.

For contracts with commission agents, there is a special rule in §392 HGB. A commission agent is a person who, as part of their business, buys or sells goods or bonds in their own name, but for the account of another person (§383 (1) HGB). §406 (1) HGB, which extends the rules on commission agents to other contracts made for the account of others, is construed in such a way that the rules on commission contracts apply in every case where a business person undertakes, in the course of their business, to act as an indirect agent of their client.[55] Since Waltmann are a business, the rules on commission contracts will apply in the present case.

---

53 *RGZ* 93, 39; *RGZ* 170, 246, 250; BGH *NJW* 1985, 2411.

54 H. Oetker in *Münchener Kommentar zum BGB*, vol. 2 (9th ed., Beck 2022), §249, [295], [297].

55 C. Kumpan in K. Hopt, *Handelsgesetzbuch* (43rd ed., Beck 2024), §406, [2]; F. Häuser in *Münchener Kommentar zum Handelsgesetzbuch*, vol. 5 (5th ed., Beck 2021), §406, [8].

According to §392 HGB, rights under the contract concluded by the commission agent can be asserted by the principal against the third party only after they have been assigned to the principal by the commission agent. However, such claims against the third party are deemed claims of the principal in the relationship between the principal, on the one hand, and the commission agent and their creditors, on the other. This means that, in the insolvency of the commission agent, the *'Insolvenzverwalter'* (insolvency administrator) cannot use the claim to satisfy the general creditors of the insolvent commission agent. The principal is entitled to an *'Aussonderung'* (separation) of the claim, according to §47 InsO. This means that they can claim the assignment from the *Insolvenzverwalter* outside the insolvency proceedings.[56] Thus, Kane will have the right to have the claims against Nickel & Dime assigned to him irrespective of the insolvency of Waltmann. After the assignment, he can sue Nickel & Dime.

Regarding the rights of Nickel & Dime, their rental contract with Waltmann continues in existence despite Waltmann's insolvency (§108 (1) InsO). Kane cannot object to Nickel & Dime using the building, as long as the management contract between Kane and Waltmann is still valid. This contract survives Waltmann's insolvency (§103 InsO).[57] However, Kane can bring the contract to an end either by way of extraordinary termination under §626 BGB, on the ground of Waltmann's insolvency, or by way of an ordinary termination on 14 days' notice, under §621 no. 5 BGB.[58] After terminating his agency contract with Waltmann, Kane can eject Nickel & Dime independently of their rental contract with Waltmann, and Nickel & Dime will not have any remedies against Kane.

If Nickel & Dime had rented the rooms out for residential purposes, they might have been able to profit from §565 (1) BGB. According to this provision, if a landlord rents out rooms to a tenant with the agreement that the tenant will commercially rent out the rooms to third parties for residential purposes, the landlord will, in the event that their contract with the tenant comes to an end, become the third party's landlord. The purpose of this provision is to protect tenants of residential premises who conclude their rental contracts with an intermediary rather than an owner. Some commentators argue in favour of applying §565 BGB by analogy to the case where the owner uses a manager who rents out the residential premises in their own name.[59] In the present case,

---

56 C. Kumpan in K. Hopt, *Handelsgesetzbuch* (43rd ed., Beck 2024), §392, [9]; F. Häuser in *Münchener Kommentar zum Handelsgesetzbuch*, vol. 5 (5th ed., Beck 2021), §392, [36].

57 BGH *NJW* 2002, 2783; M. Huber in *Münchener Kommentar zur Insolvenzordnung*, vol. 2 (4th ed., Beck 2019), §103, [4a].

58 For the general applicability of the norms on the termination of service contracts, see BGH *NJW* 1983, 42; P. Heermann in *Münchener Kommentar zum BGB*, vol. 6 (9th ed., Beck 2023), §675, [25].

59 P. Derleder and K. Bartels, *JZ* 1997, 981 at 989; U. Herrmann in W. Hau and R. Poseck, *BeckOK BGB* (70th ed., 2024), §565, [4].

this would mean that, if Nickel & Dime had rented out the rooms for residential purposes, Kane would be their new landlord. However, the protection afforded by §565 BGB is restricted to tenants of residential premises, and is not applied by analogy to tenants renting commercial premises.[60]

2.7. ITALY

Luca Ettore Perriello

I. Operative Rules

1. Waltman can claim compensation against MyPad for the damage caused to the property.
2. Kane can bring an action against Nickel & Dime for payment of the rent. It is unlikely that Nickel & Dime can claim access to, and use of, the building against Kane.

II. Descriptive Formants

Regarding question 1, the case at issue involves the '*mandato*' (mandate), which is defined by Art. 1703 of the Italian c.c. as a contract whereby a party undertakes to perform one or more legal acts for the account of the other party.

The '*mandatario*' (mandatary) must act for the account of the '*mandante*' (mandator); that is, they must serve an interest belonging to the latter. However, a clear dividing line exists between mandate with or without '*rappresentanza*' (representation). Under the former (Art. 1704 c.c.), the mandatary acts in the name of the mandator, who consequently acquires the rights and undertakes the duties arising from the contract entered into by the mandatary. As the rules on representation apply (Arts. 1387 ff. c.c.), the two legal relations (mandate and representation) overlap but pursue different scopes: mandate concerns the relationship between the parties, and representation concerns the effects vis-à-vis third parties.

It is precisely when it comes to the effects vis-à-vis third parties that the mandate without representation differs from its counterpart. Indeed, the mandatary acting in their own name (i.e. without representation) is vested with the rights and obligations resulting from the contracts they sign with third parties, even where these third parties have knowledge of the mandate (Art. 1705, paragraph 1, c.c.). Thus, Waltmann can sue MyPad for compensation

60 V. Emmerich in *J. von Staudingers Kommentar zum Bürgerlichen Gesetzbuch*, vol. §§557–80 a (Sellier – de Gruyter 2021), §565, [4].

for the damage caused to the property, because Waltmann benefit from the rights, including the legal actions for damage to the rented property, arising from the rental contract they have signed for the account of Kane but in their own name. The rules on rental contracts (Arts. 1588 ff. c.c.) provide that the tenant must compensate the landlord for the damage to the property. Waltmann qualify as a landlord and acquire all the rights arising from the rental contract, including the right to claim such compensation.

Regarding question 2, third parties have no relationship whatsoever with the mandator without representation (Art. 1705, paragraph 2, c.c.). However, the same rule lays down an exception. The mandator, in lieu of the mandatary, can claim the credits arising from the contracts entered into by the mandatary, unless this is detrimental to the rights that Arts. 1706 ff. c.c. afford the mandatary (that is, their right to obtain remuneration, refunds of expenses, and compensation for damages suffered by reason of their undertaking).

Hence, Kane can claim payment of the rent against Nickel & Dime should Waltmann become insolvent after concluding the rental contract. Rent qualifies as a credit under Art. 1705, paragraph 2, c.c.

III. Meta-Legal Formants

In the mandate without representation, while the mandator can enforce their credits against the third party, it is unclear whether the third party can claim any rights against the mandator, given that Art. 1705, paragraph 2, c.c. makes it quite clear that third parties have no relationship with the mandator. The courts consider that there is no right for third parties to claim against the mandator, on the ground of the exceptionality of the mandator's power, meaning that their power to claim the credits arising from the performance of the mandate without representation derogates from the general rule and, hence, this exception cannot apply by way of analogy to the credits vested with third parties.[61] However, a minority view argues that, once the mandator has claimed their credits in lieu of the mandatary, a legal relation between the mandator and the third party ensues, meaning that the latter is entitled to enforce all the rights arising from the contract against the mandator. Put differently, the third party becomes a fully fledged party to the agreement with the mandator. Indeed, it would be unreasonable to apply Art. 1705, paragraph 2, c.c. in such a way that it would be beneficial to the mandator only.[62]

Accordingly, as the case law currently stands, it is unlikely that Nickel & Dime could obtain access to, and use of, the building against Kane, in the event

[61] Cass., 7 January 1993, no. 78, *Massimario Giustizia civile* (1993), p. 15.

[62] D. Minussi, 'Azione del terzo nei confronti del mandante', *WikiJus*, 6 July 2010, www.e-glossa.it/wiki/azione_del_terzo_nei_confronti_del_mandante.aspx.

of Waltmann's insolvency. For these purposes, Nickel & Dime have a right of action only against Waltmann. The opposite solution would apply should the scholarly view prevail.

2.8. THE NETHERLANDS

Jan Biemans

I. *Operative Rules*

1. Waltmann can sue MyPad for compensation for the damage caused to the property.
2. If Waltmann become insolvent after concluding a new rental contract with Nickel & Dime Ltd, Nickel & Dime and Kane can circumvent Waltmann and claim directly from each other: Kane can claim payment from (only) Nickel & Dime, and Nickel & Dime can claim access to and use of the building from Kane (in addition to Waltmann).

II. *Descriptive Formants*

Waltmann can sue MyPad for compensation for the damage caused to the property. The relationship between Nickel & Dime and Waltmann is a contract of mandate (or commission *(lastgeving)*). A mandate agreement is a service provision agreement under which one of the parties ('the mandatary' or 'agent') has engaged themselves towards the other party ('the mandator' or 'principal'), to perform one or more juridical acts for the account of the mandator (Article 7:414 (1) DCC).[63] The agreement may engage the mandatary to perform juridical acts in their own name, but may also engage them to perform juridical acts in the name of the mandator (Article 7:414 (2) DCC). Thus, the mandatary may act as an indirect agent, in their own name, or as a direct agent, in the name of the principal.

In the case of *Stolte/Schiphoff* (or *'Kribbebijter'*),[64] the Dutch Supreme Court ruled that whether the mandatary has acted in their own name – meaning as

---

[63] See, generally, S.C.J.J. Kortman, L.J.M. de Leede and H.O. Thunissen, *Mr. C. Assers Handleiding tot de beoefening van het Nederlands Burgerlijk Recht. 5. Deel III. Overeenkomst van opdracht, arbeidsovereenkomst, aaneming van werk*, Zwolle: W.E.J. Tjeenk Willink 1994; T.F.E. Tjong Tjin Tai, *Mr. C. Assers Handleiding tot de beoefening van het Nederlands Burgerlijk Recht. 7. Bijzondere overeenkomsten. Deel IV. Opdracht, incl. de geneeskundige behandelingsovereenkomst en de reisovereenkomst*, Deventer: Wolters Kluwer 2022.

[64] Dutch Supreme Court, 11 March 1977, ECLI:NL:HR:1977:AC1877, NJ 1977/521 (*Stolte/ Schiphoff* or *'Kribbebijter'*).

the contracting party – depends on what the mandatary and their counterparty have declared to each other, and have derived from, and could reasonably derive from, each other's statements and behaviour. A positive answer to this question is possible even where the counterparty knew that the mandatary was not acting for its own account, but on behalf of another person – the mandator. The Dutch Supreme Court has confirmed this case law in later cases.[65]

As stated above, if the mandatary performs juridical acts in the name of the mandator, the mandatary will also act as a direct agent for the mandator. In such a case, the direct agent will act upon a power of attorney (Articles 3:60 ff. DCC). If the mandatary acts as a direct agent when concluding a contract for the account of the mandator, the mandator will become the contracting party.

In this case, the mandatary (Waltmann) has acted in their own name. The contract between Kane and Waltmann provides for the power to act on account of the principal, which power may be limited, just as a power of attorney can be provided under certain conditions.[66] If the mandatary (Waltmann) acts as an indirect agent when concluding a contract for the account of the mandator (Kane), the indirect agent themselves will become the contracting party. Consequently, although Waltmann are not the owners of the building, they are, under the rental contract, both obliged to give the tenant access to Kane's building (in addition to other obligations, such as giving the keys to the tenant at the start of the rental period and inspecting the properties after its end) and entitled to the rent (and, thus, to send invoices and collect the rent), of which, however, they will have to pay Kane the remainder after deduction of their fee, probably consisting of their costs and remuneration (Article 7:405 DCC).

The person owning the building and the person renting out the building are different persons, which leads to complications. As the building belongs to Kane, Waltmann will not suffer any loss if MyPad have damaged the property they have rented. And since Waltmann, and not Kane, are party to the rental contract, Kane cannot sue MyPad for damages for breach of contract. In order to solve this problem, the DCC contains a special provision. According to Article 7:419 DCC, if a mandatary has entered, in their own name, into an agreement with a third person who subsequently fails to comply with their obligations under that agreement, then this third person is also liable towards the mandatary for the damage which the mandator has indirectly suffered from their non-performance, although not beyond the limits to which they, apart from this provision, are bound by law with regard to their obligations to repair damages. This kind of

65 Dutch Supreme Court, 28 November 2014, ECLI:NL:HR:2014:3460, JOR 2015/26 *(Snippers q.q./Rabobank)*; Dutch Supreme Court, 30 November 2018, ECLI:NL:HR:2018:2217, JOR 2019/96.

66 Dutch Supreme Court, 10 December 2010, ECLI:NL:HR:2010:BN6386, NJ 2010/669 *(Mesdag)*.

damage is called third-party damage (using the German term '*Drittschade*').[67] Thus, Waltmann can sue MyPad for damaging Kane's building. After collecting damages, Waltmann will, in principle, have to pay these to Kane.[68]

In addition, one could argue that Kane could also sue MyPad directly, on the basis of an unlawful act that MyPad committed against Kane by damaging his property. Kane's loss would need to have been foreseeable to MyPad (Article 6:98 DCC),[69] but this requirement would easily be met in the case of damaging property.

In the event of default by, or insolvency of, the indirect agent (the mandatary acting in their own name, in this case Waltmann), Articles 7:420 and 7:421 DCC provide a solution.[70] Article 7:420 DCC allows the mandator (Kane) to transfer all rights from the contract Waltmann have entered into on his behalf to himself, and Article 7:421 DCC allows Nickel & Dime to have Kane as an alternative contracting party to the bankrupt Waltmann.

According to Article 7:420 (1) DCC, if an indirect agent (a mandatary acting in their own name, in this case Waltmann) who has entered into an agreement with a third person (Nickel & Dime) does not comply with their obligations towards the mandator (Kane), is declared bankrupt, or becomes subject to the Debt Repayment Scheme for Natural Persons, then the mandator (the principal) may, by means of a written declaration addressed to both the mandatary and the third person, take over the transferable rights which the mandatary has towards the third party, except as far as these rights, within the mutual relationship between the mandator and mandatary, belong to the mandatary. The mandator has the same powers if the third person does not comply with their obligations

---

67 S.C.J.J. Kortmann (in cooperation with J.S. Kortmann), *Mr. C. Assers Handleiding tot de beoefening van het Nederlands Burgerlijk Recht. 3. Deel III. Vermogensrecht algemeen. Volmacht en vertegenwoordiging*, Deventer: Wolters Kluwer 2017, p. 108; T.F.E. Tjong Tjin Tai, *Mr. C. Assers Handleiding tot de beoefening van het Nederlands Burgerlijk Recht. 7. Bijzondere overeenkomsten. Deel IV. Opdracht, incl. de geneeskundige behandelingsovereenkomst en de reisovereenkomst*, Deventer: Wolters Kluwer 2022, p. 252.

68 S.C.J.J. Kortmann (in cooperation with J.S. Kortmann), *Mr. C. Assers Handleiding tot de beoefening van het Nederlands Burgerlijk Recht. 3. Deel III. Vermogensrecht algemeen. Volmacht en vertegenwoordiging*, Deventer: Wolters Kluwer 2017, p. 108; T.F.E. Tjong Tjin Tai, *Mr. C. Assers Handleiding tot de beoefening van het Nederlands Burgerlijk Recht. 7. Bijzondere overeenkomsten. Deel IV. Opdracht, incl. de geneeskundige behandelingsovereenkomst en de reisovereenkomst*, Deventer: Wolters Kluwer 2022, p. 254.

69 S.C.J.J. Kortman, L.J.M. de Leede and H.O. Thunissen, *Mr. C. Assers Handleiding tot de beoefening van het Nederlands Burgerlijk Recht. 5. Deel III. Overeenkomst van opdracht, arbeidsovereenkomst, aaneming van werk*, Zwolle: W.E.J. Tjeenk Willink 1994, p. 155; T.F.E. Tjong Tjin Tai, *Mr. C. Assers Handleiding tot de beoefening van het Nederlands Burgerlijk Recht. 7. Bijzondere overeenkomsten. Deel IV. Opdracht, incl. de geneeskundige behandelingsovereenkomst en de reisovereenkomst*, Deventer: Wolters Kluwer 2022, p. 253.

70 T.F.E. Tjong Tjin Tai, *Mr. C. Assers Handleiding tot de beoefening van het Nederlands Burgerlijk Recht. 7. Bijzondere overeenkomsten. Deel IV. Opdracht, incl. de geneeskundige behandelingsovereenkomst en de reisovereenkomst*, Deventer: Wolters Kluwer 2022, pp. 255 ff.

towards the mandatary, unless the mandatary satisfies the mandator as though the third person had performed their obligations (Article 7:420 (2) DCC). The justification for Article 7:420 (2) DCC can be found in the need to cut out the middleman if there are complications with the third party. In such a case, there will be more communication between the opposing parties, which would have become (too) complicated with a mandatary in between.[71] There is obviously no need for the transfer of rights if the mandatary performs towards the mandator as if the third party had complied with their obligations towards the mandatary (and thus, indirectly, towards the mandator).

According to Article 7:421 DCC, if an indirect agent (a mandatary acting in their own name, in this case Waltmann) who has entered into an agreement with a third person (Nickel & Dime) does not comply with their obligations towards that third person, is declared bankrupt, or becomes subject to the Debt Repayment Scheme for Natural Persons, then this third person may, by means of a written declaration addressed to both the mandatary and the mandator, exercise their rights under this agreement against the mandator, but only to the extent that the mandator, at the moment when the declaration was made, was correspondingly obliged to perform towards the mandatary. If the mandator has, for example, already paid a custody fee to the mandatary, but the mandatary has not paid this to the third party, the mandator is not obliged to pay twice.[72]

The mandatary has the obligation to inform the mandator, upon their request, of the name of the third person (Article 7:420 (3) DCC), and vice versa (Article 7:421 (2) DCC).

The result of these two provisions is that, if Waltmann become insolvent after concluding a new rental contract with Nickel & Dime, both other parties can circumvent Waltmann and claim directly from each other: Kane can claim payment from Nickel & Dime, and Nickel & Dime can claim access to and use of the building from Kane, in addition to Waltmann.

III. Meta-Legal Formants

Before the Dutch Civil Code entered into force in 1992, the Dutch Supreme Court already allowed for the possibility of claiming *Drittschade*, in the aforementioned *Stolte/Schiphoff* case. Article 7:419 is a codification of this case law.[73]

---

71 Ibid., p. 260.

72 Dutch Supreme Court, 28 June 1996, NJ 1997, 494 *(KVV/Moksel)*; ibid., p. 277.

73 Dutch Supreme Court, 11 March 1977, NJ 1977/521 (*Stolte/Schiphoff* or *'Kribbebijter'*). See Parl. Gesch. BW Boek 7 (Inv. 3, 5 en 6), p. 351; T.F.E. Tjong Tjin Tai, *Mr. C. Assers Handleiding tot de beoefening van het Nederlands Burgerlijk Recht. 7. Bijzondere overeenkomsten. Deel IV. Opdracht, incl. de geneeskundige behandelingsovereenkomst en de reisovereenkomst*, Deventer: Wolters Kluwer 2022, p. 252.

2.9. POLAND

Bartosz Kucia

I. Operative Rules

1. Waltmann may sue MyPad for compensation for the damage caused to the property.
2. Waltmann's insolvency does not itself create mutual remedies for Kane and Nickel & Dime under the concluded lease agreement. The lease agreement remains in force despite Waltmann's insolvency. Waltmann's rights and obligations resulting from the lease agreement will not automatically pass to Kane by virtue of law.

II. Descriptive Formants

In relation to the first question, if the tenant (MyPad) intentionally or negligently damage the subject of the lease, they violate the obligations under the lease agreement with the lessors (Waltmann),[74] as well as Kane's right as owner (Art. 415 PCC).

As Waltmann (the lessors) are not the owners of the real estate,[75] they may, on their own, require the tenant (MyPad) to compensate them for the damage they have suffered as a result of the breach of the lease contract. This would include Waltmann's loss resulting from the fact that they were obliged to compensate the property owner for the damage caused to the property under the obligatory relationship between the lessors and the owner (a third party to the lease contract).[76] Where the lessor has no such obligation towards the owner,[77] the owner would be able to assert their claim for damages only against the tenant (as perpetrator), under the *ex delicto* liability regime. Therefore, it was proposed in literature to grant the lessors (Waltmann) the right to pursue, on account of the suffering owner of the property (Kane), a contractual claim

---

74 See judgments of the Supreme Court (Sąd Najwyższy, SN) of 12.08.1975, II CR 387/75, OSNC 1976/7-8/166 and 13.11.1987, IV CR 313/87, OSNC 1990/1/16.

75 The lessor does not have to be the owner of the rented property (see judgments of the SN of 14.04.1961, III CR 806/60, OSNC 1962/3/101, and 08.06.1999, II CKN 701/98).

76 See, in particular, K. Zagrobelny, 'W sprawie szkody występującej pod postacią zwiększenia się pasywów poszkodowanego', *Acta Universitatis Wratislaviensis, Prawo 2009*, t. CCCVIII, p. 577, and the resolution of the SN of 10.07.2008, III CZP 62/08, OSP 2010/12/126 (however, with questionably far-reaching restriction). See also M. Kaliński, *Szkoda na mieniu i jej naprawienie*, Warsaw 2014, pp. 270–71 (accepting damage on the part of the injured creditor only after compensation for damage to a third party).

77 In the case of '*zastępstwo pośrednie*' (indirect substitution), to which this case seems to refer, such obligation usually does not exist.

for damages against the tenant (MyPad), regardless of whether the lessors bear liability towards the owner for damages.[78]

In relation to the second question, Waltmann's rights and obligations resulting from the lease agreement will not automatically pass to Kane by virtue of law, in the event of Waltmann's insolvency. A lease agreement has an effect between its parties (but would not, as a rule, create any mutual remedies between the owner and the tenant, in a case such as the one at hand). Polish law allows a change of lessor (for example, Kane instead of Waltmann), though this requires the use of the institutions of '*przelew*' (assignment) (Arts. 509 ff. PCC) and '*przejęcie długu*' (debt takeover) (Arts. 519 ff. PCC).[79] As a result, a person who had previously remained outside the contractual relationship would replace an existing party to the contract. The lessors' insolvency does not, in principle, exclude the use of this mechanism. In such a case, however, these legal actions may be declared ineffective where they are taken knowingly by the lessors, to the detriment of their creditors (Arts. 527 ff. PCC), or, if the lessors have been declared bankrupt, where they are carried out within the specified time preceding the submission of the bankruptcy petition (Arts. 127 ff. Bankruptcy Act 2003).[80]

Polish law distinguishes insolvency from bankruptcy, with the former being a prerequisite for declaring the latter (Art. 10 Bankruptcy Act 2003). A lease agreement for real estate remains in force despite the lessor's insolvency or bankruptcy (Art. 107 Bankruptcy Act 2003),[81] even if the lessors (in this case, Waltmann) were not the owners of the real estate.[82] The tenant (Nickel & Dime)

---

78 See A. Ohanowicz and J. Górski, *Zarys prawa zobowiązań*, Warsaw 1970, p. 183; M. Piekarski in Z. Resich (ed), *Kodeks cywilny. Komentarz. Tom 2*, Warsaw 1972, p. 1157; T. Pajor, *Odpowiedzialność dłużnika za niewykonanie zobowiązania*, Warsaw 1982, pp. 138–40; W. Popiołek in K. Pietrzykowski (ed), *Kodeks cywilny. Tom II. Komentarz. Art. 450–1088. Przepisy wprowadzające*, Warsaw 2018, pp. 47–48; W. Borysiak in K. Osajda (ed), *Kodeks cywilny. Komentarz. Zobowiązania – część ogólna*, Warsaw 2017, p. 994; G. Stojek in M. Habdas and M. Fras (eds), *Kodeks cywilny. Komentarz. Tom III. Zobowiązania, Część ogólna (art. 353–534)*, p. 834; K. Zagrobelny in E. Gniewek and P. Machnikowski (eds), *Kodeks cywilny. Komentarz*, Warsaw 2017, p. 996 (with an accurate reservation as to the creditor who did not themselves suffer the damage). See also judgment of the SN of 07.05.2009, III CZP 7/09 (the administrator, as an indirect substitute, may file a claim for the issue of the object rented to its owner). But see also the opposite position: M. Kaliński, *Szkoda na mieniu i jej naprawienie*, Warsaw 2014, pp. 89–90 (an indirect substitute may only demand compensation for their own damage, while a third party only has an *ex delicto* claim).

79 See order of the SN of 21.03.2013, II CSK 396/12 and judgment of the District Court (Sąd Okręgowy, SO) in Gliwice of 11.02.2016, X GC 336/15.

80 Ustawa z dnia 28 lutego 2003 r. – Prawo upadłościowe (Polish Act of 28 February 2003 – Law of Bankruptcy). See judgment of the SA in Poznań of 28.01.2015, I ACa 894/14. See also judgment of the SN of 13.10.2005, IV CSK 170/05.

81 A bankruptcy trustee may, however, withdraw from the agreement with effect as of the date of declaration of a lessor's bankruptcy, if the real estate was not delivered to tenant before that date (Art. 98, s. 1, and Art. 107, s. 1, Bankruptcy Act 2003).

82 See, inter alia, S. Gurgul, *Prawo upadłościowe. Prawo restrukturyzacyjne. Komentarz*, Warsaw 2018, p. 288.

may still occupy the real estate upon payment of the rent. In the event of the lessors' bankruptcy, however, the rent would be paid to the bankruptcy trustee, and consequently the owner (Kane) would be able to submit his claim for rent clearance to the lessor's bankruptcy estate (Art. 102 Bankruptcy Act 2003 *a contrario*). The bankruptcy trustee, however, on the basis of a decision of the judge-commissioner, can terminate the agreement with three months' notice, even if termination of the agreement by the bankrupt would not be allowed according to the general principles set out in the agreement or in statutory law (Art. 109, s. 1, Bankruptcy Act 2003).

It should be noted that, in the facts described, Kane remains the owner of the real estate (regardless of Waltmann's position), and has rights under property law. Should Nickel & Dime continue to use the real estate despite the termination of the lease agreement, Kane could claim the return of the real property (Art. 222 PCC), as well as compensation from the holder (Nickel & Dime) for the use of the real estate (Art. 224, para. 2, and Art. 225 PCC).

III. Meta-Legal Formants

The above interpretation of the provisions regulating the possibility of claiming damages due to the damage to the subject of the lease takes into account the requirements set by equity considerations. The restrictive view, denying the '*zastępca pośredni*' (indirect substitute) the right to claim compensation on the account of the owner of the damaged item, would limit the protection of the owner only to the *ex delicto* liability regime, which, because of the grounds for this liability, would make it more difficult for the aggrieved owner to be compensated for the damage suffered.

The mechanisms adopted in Polish law, as they relate to the lessors' insolvency or bankruptcy, correspond to the *pacta sunt servanda* principle. Kane derives his title to the real estate from his right of ownership. His interest may, therefore, be safeguarded on general principles. In the event of Waltmann's bankruptcy, the lease agreement may be terminated by a bankruptcy trustee or the tenant, on general principles (i.e. upon expiration of the lease, or under contractual or statutory provisions regarding a right to terminate the lease). Kane, as the real estate owner, may then rent out his real estate, under another lease agreement, to the same or another tenant. Nickel & Dime do not, however, in principle, have a claim against the owner for the conclusion of a new lease agreement.

2.10. SCOTLAND

Lorna MacFarlane

I. Operative Rules

1. Waltmann *can* sue MyPad for the damage caused to the property.
2. If Waltmann became insolvent after concluding a rental contract with Nickel & Dime, Nickel & Dime would have *any remedies against Kane which they would have had against Waltmann.* Kane would have *any remedies against Nickel & Dime that Waltmann would have had against Nickel & Dime.*

II. Descriptive Formants

In this case, Waltmann are acting as Kane's 'undisclosed agent'. In Scots law, the undisclosed agency doctrine has been recognised in case law from at least the late seventeenth century,[83] and Macgregor suggests that its development was influenced by English law.[84] In an 'undisclosed agency' transaction, the principal instructs the agent not to disclose to third parties that it is acting on behalf of the principal,[85] and so the existence and identity of the principal is not revealed to the third party.[86] The principles of 'undisclosed agency' apply where the agent does not reveal its representative capacity, even where (as in this case) the third party could determine that the land or property in which the agent deals belongs to another party.[87]

The agent can sue the third party before and after the disclosure of the principal.[88] Waltmann can, therefore, recover damages from MyPad regardless

83 See *Street v. Hume and Bruntfield* (1699) Mor. 15122 and *Sterly v. Spence* (1687) Mor. 15127. These cases do not expressly use the term 'undisclosed principal', but the factual matrixes match the present-day undisclosed agency doctrine. See also C.G.H. Paton (ed), *Baron David Hume's Lectures, 1786–1822*, vol. II (The Stair Society, Edinburgh 1939–58), p. 160; G.J. Bell, *Principles of the Law of Scotland*, 10th ed., vol. 1 (1889, reprinted by Law Society of Scotland, Butterworths, Edinburgh 1989), para. 224A; G.J. Bell, *Commentaries on the Law of Scotland and on the Principles of Mercantile Jurisprudence*, 7th ed., vol. 1 (1870, reprinted by T&T Clark, Edinburgh 1990), p. 537.

84 L.J. Macgregor, *The Law of Agency in Scotland* (W. Green, Edinburgh 2013), para. 12.28.

85 Ibid., para. 12.25; W.M. Gloag, *The Law of Contract: A Treatise on the Principles of Contract in the Law of Scotland*, 2nd ed. (W. Green, Edinburgh 1929), p. 127; J.J.H. Pearson, 'Agency' in A.D.M. Forte (ed), *Scots Commercial Law* (Butterworths, Edinburgh 1997), p. 272, at p. 289.

86 L.J. Macgregor, *The Law of Agency in Scotland* (W. Green, Edinburgh 2013), para. 12.25.

87 This is not excluded by the Scots definitions of undisclosed agency. See L.J. Macgregor, *The Laws of Scotland: Stair Memorial Encyclopaedia: Agency and Mandate*, reissue (LexisNexis/Law Society of Scotland, London/Edinburgh 2001), para. 147.

88 *A.F. Craig & Co v. Blackater* 1923 SC 472; L.J. Macgregor, *The Laws of Scotland: Stair Memorial Encyclopaedia: Agency and Mandate*, reissue (LexisNexis/Law Society of Scotland, London/Edinburgh 2001), para. 157; T.B. Smith, *Short Commentary on the Law of Scotland* (W. Green, Edinburgh 1962), p. 777.

of whether they have disclosed that they are acting for Kane. This answer assumes that the terms of the contract concluded by Waltmann and MyPad do not exclude the operation of undisclosed agency: the doctrine of undisclosed agency cannot operate where the contract expressly or impliedly provides that the agent is not acting for an undisclosed principal.[89] If the contract expressly or impliedly excludes the possibility of an undisclosed principal, the principal will not (on disclosure or otherwise) be able to enforce the contract against the third party.[90]

Provided that the agent has acted within the limits of their authority, the undisclosed principal can 'sue or be sued by the third party as if the principal had been bound in a contract with the third party from the outset',[91] after the third party has been made aware of the principal's existence. The third party's ability to sue the principal is not dependent on the agent's insolvency or default – rather, the third party can elect to sue either party. Accordingly, Nickel & Dime can enforce their rights to access and use the building against Kane, using any remedies available under the contract they concluded with Waltmann (and would have the same remedies for breach of contract if Kane impeded their rights to use or access). The liability of Waltmann and Kane is alternative, not joint and several,[92] and Nickel & Dime can choose which to sue, by informing both parties,[93] or by its conduct.[94] In light of Waltmann's insolvency, their choice to sue Kane could be inferred simply by raising an action against him if necessary.

Equally, Kane can enforce his right to payment of the rent against Nickel & Dime, under the terms of the contract which Waltmann entered into on his behalf. The principal's right to claim against the third party is subject to any defences which the third party could have used against the agent.[95] If, for example, Nickel & Dime had already paid rent in respect of a certain period to Waltmann,

---

89 L.J. Macgregor, *The Laws of Scotland: Stair Memorial Encyclopaedia: Agency and Mandate*, reissue (LexisNexis/Law Society of Scotland, London/Edinburgh 2001), para. 153. Undisclosed agency is further prohibited in contracts to which *delectus personae* applies: L.J. Macgregor, *The Law of Agency in Scotland* (W. Green, Edinburgh 2013), para. 12.37.

90 See e.g. the English case of *Said v. Butt* [1920] 3 KB 497 and, further, L.J. Macgregor, *The Law of Agency in Scotland* (W. Green, Edinburgh 2013), para. 12.28.

91 L.J. Macgregor, *The Laws of Scotland: Stair Memorial Encyclopaedia: Agency and Mandate*, reissue (LexisNexis/Law Society of Scotland, London/Edinburgh 2001), para. 147. See also L.J. Macgregor, *The Law of Agency in Scotland* (W. Green, Edinburgh 2013), para. 12.34; G.J. Bell, *Principles of the Law of Scotland*, 10th ed., vol. 1 (1889, reprinted by Law Society of Scotland, Butterworths, Edinburgh 1989), para. 224A; *Thomson v. Davenport* 1829 9 B & C 78; *Bennet v. Inveresk Paper Co* 1891 18 R 975.

92 L.J. Macgregor, *The Law of Agency in Scotland* (W. Green, Edinburgh 2013), para. 12.34.

93 Ibid.; *Meier & Co v. Küchenmeister* (1881) 8 R 642.

94 L.J. Macgregor, *The Law of Agency in Scotland* (W. Green, Edinburgh 2013), paras. 12.40–12.42.

95 Ibid., para. 12.46, citing *Bennet v. Inveresk Paper Co* (1891) 18 R 975. See also G.J. Bell, *Principles of the Law of Scotland*, 10th ed., vol. 1 (1889, reprinted by Law Society of Scotland, Butterworths, Edinburgh 1989), para. 224A.

Kane could not claim for the same sum.[96] Nickel & Dime could also claim compensation on any debt owed to them by Waltmann, if the debt was incurred prior to them being informed of Kane's existence as an undisclosed principal.[97]

III. Meta-Legal Formants

Scots case law has recognised undisclosed agency since at least the late seventeenth century.[98] Macgregor notes the tension between the recognition of this doctrine and contractual consent, commenting that it is 'contrary to the central role of consent in contract that the third party may find that he has contractual rights and duties in a contract with a stranger'.[99] Nonetheless, undisclosed agency is thought to uphold the general policy objective of commercial convenience.[100] The concept also allows for the protection of personal information.[101] In this respect, Macgregor cites *MacPhail & Son v. Maclean's Trustee*,[102] in which a creditor appointed his debtor as the manager of his farm, through an agent, without disclosing that he was the owner. It was recognised that this was due to 'considerations of delicacy towards his client and debtor'.[103] The doctrine also arguably protects the principal from adverse trading conditions and higher prices it may experience if third parties know their identity.[104]

Bell rationalises that the third party must be able to use defences it has against the agent in respect of claims made by the principal, on the basis that the third party 'cannot be deprived of the benefit of the securities which he could fairly contemplate as resulting from the contract'.[105] Macgregor has justified the

---

96 L.J. Macgregor, *The Laws of Scotland: Stair Memorial Encyclopaedia: Agency and Mandate*, reissue (LexisNexis/Law Society of Scotland, London/Edinburgh 2001), para. 162; *International Sponge Importers Ltd v. Andrew Watt & Sons* 1911 SC (HL) 57.

97 L.J. Macgregor, *The Law of Agency in Scotland* (W. Green, Edinburgh 2013), para. 12.46; G.J. Bell, *Principles of the Law of Scotland*, 10th ed., vol. 1 (1889, reprinted by Law Society of Scotland, Butterworths, Edinburgh 1989), para. 224A; *Gall v. Murdoch* (1821) 1 S 77; *Bennet v. Inveresk Paper Co* (1891) 18 R 975 at 985 per Lord McLaren; *Wester Moffat Colliery Co. Ltd v. A Jeffrey & Co.* 1911 SC 346.

98 C.G.H. Paton (ed), *Baron David Hume's Lectures, 1786–1822*, vol. II (The Stair Society, Edinburgh 1939–58), p. 160.

99 L.J. Macgregor, *The Laws of Scotland: Stair Memorial Encyclopaedia: Agency and Mandate*, reissue (LexisNexis/Law Society of Scotland, London/Edinburgh 2001), para. 148.

100 Ibid.

101 L.J. Macgregor, *The Law of Agency in Scotland* (W. Green, Edinburgh 2013), para. 12.31.

102 *MacPhail & Son v. Maclean's Trustee* (1887) 15 R 4.

103 Ibid. at 54 per Lord Young.

104 R. Barnett, 'Squaring undisclosed agency law with contract theory' (1987) 75 *California Law Review* 1969, 1976–77; G. Fridman, 'Undisclosed Principals and the Sale of Goods' in D. Busch, L. Macgregor and P. Watts (eds), *Agency Law in Commercial Practice* (Oxford University Press, Oxford 2016), pp. 70, 79.

105 G.J. Bell, *Commentaries on the Law of Scotland and on the Principles of Mercantile Jurisprudence*, 7th ed., vol. 1 (1870, reprinted by T&T Clark, Edinburgh 1990), vol. 1, pp. 527–29. See also p. 537.

third party's ability to use compensation against the principal on the grounds that the third party understood the contract to be with the agent.[106] These rules thus protect the third party from prejudice resulting from the principal's disclosure,[107] demonstrating a general policy objective of protecting the third party.

2.11. SLOVAKIA

Kristián Csach, Monika Jurčová, Peter Mészáros and Veronika Zoričáková

I. Operative Rules

1. Waltmann can sue MyPad for compensation for the damage caused to the property.
2. If Nickel & Dime have not yet paid the rent, Kane may require payment of the rent directly from them, as the tenant. If Nickel & Dime have already paid the rent to Waltmann (prior to their insolvency), Kane could submit his claim in the bankruptcy proceeding.

   The tenants' access to, and use of, the building would probably not be influenced by Waltmann's insolvency.

II. Descriptive Formants

The contract concluded between Kane and Waltmann will be qualified as a commission agent's agreement contract, under section 577 SCommC. Under this contract, the commission agents (Waltmann) undertake to arrange a certain business matter for the principal in the agents' own name, but on the principal's account, and the principal (Kane) undertakes to pay the agents commission. If the subject of a commission agent's obligation is a permanent activity, the provisions of the SCommC regulating a contract on commercial representation will, accordingly, apply to the relation between the principal and the commission agent. The commission agent's agreement contract is considered a specific contract in the Slovak legal order, applicable for the arrangement of another's affairs, and one of the most appropriate types of contract for management of another's property.[108]

---

106 L.J. Macgregor, *The Law of Agency in Scotland* (W. Green, Edinburgh 2013), para. 12.46.

107 Ibid.

108 V. Janáč, 'Komisionárska zmluva a správa cudzieho majetku' in O. Ovečková et al., *Obchodný zákonník. Veľký komentár, vol. II*, Bratislava: Wolters Kluwer, 2017, pp. 985, 1003, 1013, 1396; J. Husár, 'Správa cudzieho majetku [Administration of assets belonging to others]' in J. Suchoža and J. Husár (eds), *Obchodné právo a jeho širšie kontexty*, Košice: UPJŠ, 2010, p. 170.

Regarding question 1, the tenants are entitled to use the property in the manner stipulated in the agreement, and, unless agreed otherwise, this corresponds to the nature and purpose of the property. The tenants are obliged to ensure that no damage occurs to the property. If one of the tenants has damaged the property, they would probably be liable for breach of the contractual duty based on the rental relationship and, therefore, liable for damage inflicted on the property due to this breach. If a party with whom the commission agent has concluded a contract (MyPad) breaches their obligations, the commission agent is obliged, under section 586 SCommC, to claim fulfilment of these obligations on the principal's account or, if the principal agrees, to assign the receivables corresponding to these obligations to the principal.[109] Therefore, Waltmann might be entitled, under this provision, to claim damages from MyPad. The obligation to claim fulfilment of the third party's obligations after they have been breached will cover all possible claims arising from the breach. As the principal is excluded from any direct action against MyPad (s. 581 SCommC), the agent will have the possibility to claim damages for loss actually suffered by the principal.

Regarding question 2, the validity and effectiveness of the rental contract between MyPad and Waltmann will not be influenced by the insolvency of Waltmann. As stated above, Kane may require payment of the rent directly from the tenants (Nickel & Dime), if they have not yet paid it. The principle that neither rights nor obligations arise for the principal in relation to third parties as a result of the commission agent's conduct is overridden by the specific rule in section 581 SCommC, under which the principal may directly request a third party to hand over an item or fulfil an obligation which the commission agent has arranged for the principal, if the commission agent may not do so themselves due to circumstances relating to their person. The literature explicitly enumerates the death or insolvency of the agent as examples of such circumstances. These special circumstances transform the indirect representation to a direct link between the principal and the third party.[110]

The situation would be substantially different if Nickel & Dime have already paid the rent (or part of it) to Waltmann, and Waltmann have not yet transferred the payment (minus deduction) to Kane.[111] Kane would submit his claim in the bankruptcy proceeding declared against Waltmann under the provisions of the Act on Bankruptcy and Restructuring.[112] The Slovak legal order is reluctant to

---

109 Supreme Court decision file no. 1 M Obdo V 6/2009 dated 22.07.2010.

110 V. Janáč, 'Komisionárska zmluva a správa cudzieho majetku' in O. Ovečková et al., *Obchodný zákonník. Veľký komentár, vol. II [Commentary on Commercial Code II]*, Bratislava: Wolters Kluwer, 2017, pp. 985, 1003, 1013, 1396.

111 S. 585 of SCommC: 'The commission agent is obliged to transfer rights acquired when arranging a matter to the principal without undue delay and hand over to the principal everything they have acquired when doing so, and the principal is obliged to take such rights and items over.'

112 Act no. 7/ 2005 Coll. on Bankruptcy and Restructuring as amended.

provide special protective safeguards for parties in the indirect representation relationship influenced by insolvency (the above-mentioned section 581 SCommC serves as an exception).[113] According to section 581, in the event of non-performance by the third party (in this case, Nickel & Dime), the principal (Kane) might have a direct claim against the third party, but the third party does not have a direct claim for performance against the principal. Therefore, the right to use and access the property is derived solely from the rental contract concluded with Waltmann.

The tenants' access to, and use of, the building would not be influenced by Waltmann's insolvency, notwithstanding the factual circumstances or inconveniences mentioned in the previous paragraph; that is, that the third party (Nickel & Dime) would not have a direct claim for performance against Kane. Provided that Waltmann had the right to conclude the tenancy contract, this contract will be valid, and the right of tenants to access and use the property will not be affected by the insolvency of the property manager.

Termination of the commission agents' contract with the principal would not have any direct effect on the tenancy. According to the particular circumstances of the case, various kinds of practical problems may arise in such an event, but it is up to Kane, as the owner of the property, to tackle these problems, and the most logical step will be termination of the commission agents' contract.

The initiation of bankruptcy proceedings may prohibit Waltmann from fulfilling their obligations, because they will be obliged to limit the performance of their activities to usual acts, and to refrain from extraordinary acts. Managing the property based on the existing rental contract would generally be considered as a 'usual course of business' act; on the contrary, concluding new contracts, or termination of the contract, would probably be considered extraordinary acts. If Waltmann breach this obligation, the validity of the legal act will not thereby be affected, but the act may be contested in the bankruptcy (s. 14(5) of the Act on Bankruptcy and Restructuring). But at the moment the bankruptcy is declared, the right to act on behalf of the bankrupt debtor will be transferred to the administrator of the bankrupt's assets and, therefore, it will be up to the administrator whether the bankrupt will continue as a party to the commission agent contract. If the answer is positive, the insolvency administrator may also seek to end the rental contract. The declaration of insolvency does not lead to an automatic termination of the commission agent's contract. Moreover, there is no rule regarding an *ex lege* transfer of the contract between the agent and the third party, or regarding the assignment of claims, in the event of the agent's insolvency.[114]

---

[113] M. Jurčová and J. Zámožík, 'Ochrana majetkových záujmov komitenta v komisionárskej zmluve [Protection of property interests according to the contract on commission]', *Justičná revue*, vol. 62, 5 (2010), pp. 620–30.

[114] Ibid.

2.12. SPAIN

Carles Vendrell Cervantes

I. Operative Rules

1. Waltmann *would be entitled* to sue MyPad for compensation for the damage caused to the property.
2. *Both* Nickel & Dime and Kane would have *direct claims against each other* as an exception to the general rule of Article 1717 of the Spanish Civil Code.

II. Descriptive Formants

Question 1

In this case, Waltmann (the intermediary) are an indirect representative of Mr Kane (the principal), since Waltmann conclude the contracts in their own name. This rule is established in Article 1717 of the Spanish Civil Code:

> Where the representative should act in his own name, the principal shall have no action against the persons with whom the representative has entered into any contract, nor the latter against the principal. In this case, the representative shall be directly bound vis-à-vis the person with whom he has contracted, as if the affair were a personal affair of his own.

However, due to the fact that the contract concerns Mr Kane's own things, he could also sue MyPad for compensation for the damage.[115] This is because of the final clause of the second paragraph of the Article cited above: 'Except in case of things owned by the principal'.[116] This does not prevent Waltmann suing MyPad for compensation, since Waltmann are, as indicated, an indirect representative of Mr Kane, and are the party who has entered into the contract with MyPad.[117] As a consequence, the beneficiary of the potential compensation would be Mr Kane, since Waltmann contracted on the account of Mr Kane. MyPad may

115 See, among others, Spanish Supreme Court (Civil Chamber) judgment 251/2005 of 22 April (RJ 2005\3751).

116 This exception and its interpretation have been the subject of some debate, not only between legal scholars, but also in the case law. The literature states that the most sensible interpretation is that the principal is entitled to sue the third party directly, but not basing the claim on any reason that the representative could not use (Á. Carrasco Perera, *Derecho Civil: Introducción. Fuentes. Derecho de la Persona. Derecho Subjetivo. Derecho de Propiedad* (5th ed., Tecnos, 2016), 364).

117 See, for instance, Spanish Supreme Court (Civil Chamber) judgment of 14 October 1989 (RJ 1989\6920).

allege that the claimant (i.e. Waltmann) did not suffer an actual loss. However, Waltmann may still argue that they are a representative of Mr Kane, and are acting on his behalf, so that the damages that Waltmann may claim from MyPad should be conceived as relating to the damages caused to the principal's property.

Question 2

There are no specific rules under Spanish law regarding indirect intermediaries' insolvency, or their fundamental non-performance and its legal consequences for both the principal and the third party (such as the rules established in the DCFR III.-5:401 or DCFR III.-5:402).

However, as stated above, the general rule according to which the intermediary will be 'directly bound vis-à-vis the person with whom he has contracted, as if the affair were a personal affair of his own' has an exception under Article 1717.II of the Spanish Civil Code. This exception establishes that the third party can sue the principal 'when the affair should relate to the things owned by the principal'.

According to the general consensus,[118] this exception will apply in order to grant direct enforceability of the contract between the principal and the third party (above all in the case of insolvency of the indirect intermediary). The rationale for this exception is to avoid abuse by the principal against the third party who has legitimately contracted with his or her intermediary. Since, because of the default of the representative, the enforcement of the contract depends solely on the principal's choice (because it concerns their property), the third party is entitled to act directly against the principal.

In this regard, assuming that Waltmann can no longer comply with the contract because they are insolvent, Nickel & Dime could use the exception established in the Spanish Civil Code, together with the rule regarding the 'separation of assets' in the Spanish Insolvency Law (Article 80, which provides that 'the assets belonging to others that are in possession of the insolvent and in respect whereof he does not have right to use, secure or retain, shall be delivered to their legitimate owners'). This means, in this case, that possession should be given to Mr Kane, who is the legitimate owner. Since Waltmann would fail to comply with the lease contract because of their insolvency, and thus the enforcement of the contract would now depend entirely on the choice of Mr Kane (who is the owner of the property), Nickel & Dime can demand the enforcement directly from Mr Kane, and thus demand access to, and use of, the property from Mr Kane.

---

118 B. Fernández Gregoraci, *La representación indirecta* (Thomson Civitas, 2006), 298–306 and 320–25. This legal scholar reaches this conclusion based on decisions of the Spanish Supreme Court of 10 July 1946, 17 December 1959 and 8 June 1966.

On a different but related note, since Nickel & Dime can demand enforcement of the contract from Mr Kane, and the contract establishes mutual obligations, it has also been suggested in the literature[119] that a party in Mr Kane's position would also have the right to demand enforcement even though the exception, in principle, only concerns the right for the third party to take action against the principal. In conclusion, Mr Kane would have the right to receive the payment of the rent and, in turn, Nickel & Dime would have the right to continue to have access to, and use of, the property, as long as they continue to pay their rent.

2.13. SWEDEN

Oskar Mossberg

I. Operative Rules

1. Waltmann *can sue* MyPad for the damage caused to the property.
2. Kane could assume Waltmann's claim against Nickel & Dime. Nickel & Dime would have no remedies against Kane. However, Nickel & Dime would not (unless otherwise stated in the contract with Waltmann) need to pay until having received performance; that is, access to, and use of, the building.

II. Descriptive Formants

Regarding question 1, the case concerns Swedish rules on '*kommission*' (commission). There are statutory rules in Kommissionlagen (2009:865) (the Act on Commission) (unless otherwise stated, subsequent references under the present case refer to this Act). According to Article 1 of the Act, the Act applies to '*uppdrag att för en annan persons räkning men i eget namn sälja eller köpa lös egendom*' (agreements concerning the purchase or sale of non-real property in one's own name but for another's account). The rules of the Act are extensively applied *ex analogia*, and would be applied to the present case, which is a kind of '*tjänstekommission*' (service commission).

The contract between the principal and the agent, on the one hand, and the contract between the agent and the third party, on the other, are regarded as separate. This follows from Article 24 of the Act, which states that the third party derives no rights against the principal through the contract with the agent. According to Article 23, the principal does, however, acquire ownership of the goods bought by the commissionary agent pursuant to the contract with the

119 Ibid.

principal. The same provision also states that the third party acquires ownership of goods sold. The rationale of these rules is that the 'commission goods' are never intended to be owned by the commissionary agent, and so the goods should not be drawn into the commissionary agent's potential insolvency proceedings. Also, pursuant to Article 27, the principal has a right to a non-voluntary assignment of the agent's claim against the third party (a rule on *cessio necessaria* (see Case 2 above, and section III below)).

Waltmann can, as a commissionary agent, sue MyPad on behalf of the principal Kane, if this is deemed to be within the agent's *'uppdrag'* (agreement/mission). The question is not explicitly regulated in the Act, but such a right to sue can be deemed to exist according to the commission contract, the contents of which will be established through interpretation. Alternatively, Waltmann could be seen to have an independent claim of its own, due to having to pay Kane (channelling the damages through the chain of contracts). There are no authoritative sources regarding how the issue is to be dogmatically constructed, but the damage to the property could be viewed as a breach of the commission contract, specifically regarding the agent's duty of care in relation to the principal's property (following Articles 6 and 43 of the Act *ex analogia*). This latter possibility could, however, be seen as a way for the principal to pass on a large part of the risk concerning the property to the agent, in such a way as to entail that the agent's contracts with third parties are not really entered into on the principal's account (a large portion of the risk being on the agent himself can be taken to mean that the contracts are, in reality, on his own account).[120] It therefore seems more feasible to focus on the first possibility, under which the question would revolve around whether or not suing MyPad is included in Waltmann's *'uppdrag'*. The lawsuit would then be for the account (and benefit) of the principal. It would, however, typically be in the name of the commissionary agent.

Kane is not barred from suing MyPad, and does have an action pursuant to the general rule of tortious liability in Chapter 2, Article 1 of the Act on Damages (see Case 3 above). However, MyPad has a contractual duty of care pursuant to the rules on leasing real property contained in Jordabalken (the Earth Balk, which is the central Swedish statutory Act on real property), Chapter 12, Article 24. This contractual *'vårdplikt'* (duty of care), owed by MyPad to Waltmann pursuant to the contract, is potentially stricter than any duties based on the direct non-contractual relation between Kane and MyPad (where there is no real *'vårdplikt'* (duty of care), other than not being tortiously negligent,

120 Commission contracts are favourable in cases where the agent goes bankrupt. There are many HD cases concerning whether or not an alleged commission contract is to be considered as such, e.g. NJA 2010 p. 154, NJA 2012 p. 419. See, on these issues, e.g. S.O. Johansson, *Kommissionslagen: En kommentar*, Norstedts, Stockholm 2017, pp. 47 ff.

although, in general, Swedish lawyers do not talk about *'vårdplikter'* (duties of care) outside of contractual relations). Therefore, at the outset, Waltmann, being a party to the contract establishing the contractual duty of care, would be in a better position to raise proceedings than Kane, as Waltmann can simply sue on the basis of the rental contract. As stated above, Kane could, in principle, sue on the basis of tortious liability, but such a claim is less likely than Waltmann's to be successful, as the non-contractual 'duty of care' (i.e. not being negligent) is 'lower' than the contractual duty of care according to Chapter 12, Article 24 of Jordabalken. However, according to Article 27 of the Act on Commission, Kane can effect a non-voluntary assignment of Waltmann's claim against MyPad, after which Kane will be able to litigate 'using' this claim, thereby benefiting from the contractual duty of care.

Regarding question 2, Nickel & Dime do not, pursuant to Article 24 of the Act on Commission, derive any rights against Kane from the contract with Waltmann. Pursuant to Article 27, the principal will, in some circumstances, including *'konkurs'* (bankruptcy) of the agent, have a right to assume the agent's rights against the third party. This essentially means that the principal can effect a non-voluntary assignment to themselves of the agent's claim against the third party. (It should be noted that this does not work the other way round; the asymmetry in commissionary relations has been a source of controversy in Swedish legal debate, but the legal situation *de lege lata* is quite clear, in that the third party does not gain a right against the principal (see section II below).) In the circumstances of the case, Kane could, therefore, assume Waltmann's claim against Nickel & Dime (see section I above). According to general principles of obligations, as expressed in Article 27 of Skuldebrevslagen (the Act on Letters of Debt), an assignee does not get a *'bättre rätt'* (better right) than the assignor had, entailing that any *'invändning'* (objection) the debtor could have made in relation to the assignor can also be made against the assignee. If Nickel & Dime has not received any performance, it could (if the contract does not state otherwise) invoke a *'detentionsrätt'* (right of detention) – the right to withhold one's own performance pending performance from the other party. This right of detention could be invoked against Waltmann, and would hold against Kane as assignee.

III. Meta-Legal Formants

According to Swedish law, including the Act on Commission and uncodified general principles of commission, commission is a form of indirect agency.[121]

[121] An accessible English-language account of Nordic and Swedish rules on representation is provided in O. Lando et al., *Restatement of Nordic Contract Law*, Jurist- og Økonomforbundets forlag, Copenhagen 2016, pp. 117 ff.

It differs from direct agency *'fullmakt'* (full power) in the sense that in commission, but not in *'fullmakt'*, the agent acts in their own name. The idea of the commissionary as an agent is essential in explaining the rules. The right of the principal to effect a non-voluntary assignment of the agent's claim against the third party is based on the idea that this claim is in some sense 'owned' by, or intended to enrich, the principal.[122] The agent's rights are protected by the principal having to inform him of the assumption of the claim, and, if the agent calls for it, either paying the agent or furnishing security (for example, depositing money with or obtaining a guarantee from a bank, or pledging a lien). This is stated in Article 27, paragraph 2 of the Act on Commission. The commissionary agent's right to demand security has its basis in an interest of symmetry. According to Article 15 of the Act on Commission, the agent has a *'legal panträtt'* (statutory lien) in the claim against the third party (for example, in cases where the principal does not pay the agent, the agent can demand payment from the third party instead, invoking the lien). The agent's right pursuant to Article 27 is intended to secure the agent's interest in the claim against the third party (otherwise the principal could circumvent the agent's lien pursuant to Article 15 simply by assuming the claim pursuant to Article 27).

The current rules on commission are the result of legislative changes that took effect in 2009. The older law of commission from 1914 was, however, in many respects similar to the current one. During the legislative work on the new Act, issues regarding the relations between the principal and the third party were discussed in detail, especially as regards the asymmetry of relations: the principal does not have any direct obligations to the third party, not even in cases where the agent becomes insolvent, but the principal can assume the agent's claim against the third party, and thus take action directly against the third party. This asymmetry was criticised at an early stage in the preparatory works, and changes were cautiously suggested, with the caveat that further investigations were needed.[123] The proposed changes would have given the third

122 The Act on Commission, Article 27, first paragraph states (translated as literally as possible): 'A principal may acquire the claim against the third party based on contracts the commissionary agent has entered into with the third party for the account of the principal. If the commission contract [between the principal and agent] is commercial, the principal may however only acquire the claim if the third party is late in payment or delivery or if the commissionary agent has lapsed in his duty to account [for goods or money, to the principal], acted in bad faith against the principal or is in bankruptcy.' In other words, in commercial relations the principal's right to acquire the commissary agent's claim against the third party is not universal.

123 See SOU 1984:85 – Handelsagentur och kommission: Betänkande av Kommissionslags-kommittén, pp. 170 ff., where the proposed changes were discussed as an UNIDROIT Convention-inspired approach towards 'Anglosaxon law', and a distancing from 'German and continental law'.

party more access to sue the principal directly. At a later stage, and after the necessary further investigations, the proposed changes were, however, rejected. This was, in part, due to the fact that the proposed changes had been based on the UNIDROIT Convention on Agency in the International Sale of Goods of 1983,[124] which had not gained the adherence envisaged in the earlier preparatory works of the Act on Commission, and in part due to the fact that consultations on the proposal had been negative.[125] A supplementary reason for the current rules is that the third party, who might very well have no idea that there even is a principal, has agreed to have the agent as his contractual partner, and therefore has taken a calculated risk as regards the person of his co-contractor.[126] (Note that disclosure of the agency is irrelevant; regardless of disclosure, a third party who has contracted with an indirect agent may not rely on the principal, as the aforementioned Article 24 of the Act on Commission still applies.) As they stand, the rules on commission are regarded as a fundamental support for the principles on privity of contract in Swedish law.[127]

3. COMPARATIVE REMARKS

Jan Biemans and Lorna Richardson

This case discusses the positions of three different parties: the 'indirect' agent (Waltmann) concluding a lease contract in their own name for the benefit of the principal; the principal – the person benefiting most from the contract – who, in this case, also happens to be the owner of the building (Kane); and the counterparty, who is renting the building (MyPad, and later Nickel & Dime). The case does so by addressing these positions, first, in the case of damage caused by the counterparty to the principal's property and, second, in the case of the insolvency of the agent.

The first question relates to the ability of the agent to claim damages for the benefit of the principal. There is a discrepancy here: the agent sues in their own

---

124 UNIDROIT Convention on Agency in the International Sale of Goods of 1983 (Geneva 17 February 1983).

125 SOU 1988:63 – Kommission och dylikt: Sakrättsliga frågor vid kommission, återtagandeförbehåll, konsignation, legotillverkning, kommissionärsbolag, pp. 139 ff., conclusion at pp. 161 ff. The legislative background is described in S.O. Johansson, *Kommissionslagen: En kommentar*, Norstedts, Stockholm 2017, pp. 291 ff.

126 See e.g. O. Lando et al., *Restatement of Nordic Contract Law*, Jurist- og Økonomforbundets forlag, Copenhagen 2016, p. 128.

127 See e.g. J. Hellner, R. Hager and A.H. Persson, *Speciell avtalsrätt II: Kontraktsrätt: 2 häftet. Allmänna ämnen*, 6th ed., Wolters Kluwer, Stockholm 2016, pp. 131 ff.; L. Zackariasson, 'Privity of Contract and Direct Claims' in T. Håstad (ed), *The Nordic Contracts Act: Essays in Celebration of its One Hundredth Anniversary*, Djøf Publishing, Copenhagen 2015, pp. 229 ff.

name for breach of the lease contract in their capacity as a contracting party, whereas the principal has suffered the actual damage, being the owner of the building.

The second question relates to the power of the principal and the counterparty to sue each other directly in the event of the agent's insolvency. The question is whether the indirect agent remains an obstacle between the two interested parties (Kane and Nickel & Dime), or whether the law allows the parties to address (and sue) each other directly.

Question 1

In all jurisdictions except England, Waltmann would be able to sue MyPad for the benefit of Kane; and, except in Belgium, Waltmann could do so on the basis of the contract concluded between Waltmann and MyPad.

In most jurisdictions (Belgium, Czech Republic, France, Germany, Italy, the Netherlands, Slovakia, Spain, Sweden, and probably also Bulgaria and Poland), the agency in this case is considered to be 'indirect agency', and the contract between the principal and the agent to be an agreement of commission. (The counterparty will generally be aware that the indirect agent is not acting on their own behalf, even though the counterparty will not know the identity of the principal.) In these jurisdictions, if the indirect agent concludes the contract, the contractual effects of the contract will be between the indirect agent and the counterparty. There is no contractual bond between Kane and MyPad. If it had been direct agency, where the agent acts in the name of the principal, the contract would have been concluded between the principal and the counterparty, without legal effects for the direct agent.

In Belgium, the 'proprietary' aspect of the damage would allow the indirect agent to sue the counterparty for compensation for the damage caused to the principal's property, thereafter (following payment by the counterparty) allowing the principal to claim the compensation from the indirect agent.

In other jurisdictions, there is an explicit legal ground for the possibility of the indirect agent suing, on the basis of the contract concluded between the indirect agent and the counterparty, for damages for the benefit of the principal (Czech Republic, Germany, the Netherlands). In Germany and the Netherlands, this is called 'third-person damage' *(Drittschaden)* or the liquidation of this damage *(Drittschadensliquidation)*, which in the Netherlands has a statutory basis. In Germany, the legal construction of 'the contract with protective effects towards third parties' *(Vertrag mit Schutzwirkung für Dritte)* leads to a similar (contractual-based) outcome, but is unlikely to be used in this scenario, in which the *Drittschadensliquidation* would operate to compensate Kane. Legal rules in other jurisdictions (Bulgaria, France, Italy, Poland, Scotland, Slovakia, Spain and Sweden) lead to the same outcome as the third-person damage, but without such an explicit legal ground. Such jurisdictions reason, for example, that the law allows the renting out of someone's property, and that the tenant has to compensate for damage caused by them to the property, irrespective of who owns it. In these jurisdictions, the indirect agent is liable to the principal (on the basis of the agreement of commission) either to repair the property or pay over to the principal the damages paid by the counterparty to the agent, which adds to the agent's authority to sue the counterparty. In several jurisdictions, such as the Czech Republic, Germany, the Netherlands and Slovakia, the indirect agent can also assign their claim for damages to the principal. Indeed, in some jurisdictions, such as Germany, the Netherlands and Sweden, the principal even has the right to have the agent's claim against the third party assigned to them.

With respect to some jurisdictions (for instance, Belgium, France, Germany, the Netherlands, Poland, Slovakia, Spain and Sweden), it has been noted that the principal would have a claim for damages of their own relating to their property, irrespective of the contract concluded between the indirect agent and the counterparty, based on an unlawful act by the counterparty.[128] The principal, or the agent on behalf of the principal, could sue on this basis. In Belgium, this seems to be the only way for the agent to claim damages for the benefit of the principal, as a contractual claim by the indirect agent against the counterparty is not permitted.

England and Scotland take a different position. In England, whether or not the (disclosed) agent has acted as an indirect or direct agent (including in cases where the counterparty is unaware of the identity of the principal), the contractual effects of the contract are only between the principal and the counterparty – thus, very much like the effect of direct agency in other jurisdictions. Only if the counterparty did not know that the (indirect) agent was acting on behalf of a principal – 'the undisclosed principal' – would the agent be bound by the contract, and the agent and the counterparty be able to sue each other. The outcome would then be similar to that in the aforementioned jurisdictions, meaning that the agent of the undisclosed principal could sue the counterparty on the basis of the contract. In this case, however, the agent cannot sue the counterparty, and only the principal can, unless the counterparty was unaware that the agent was acting on behalf of the principal as property owner, which, according to English law, is unlikely.

Scotland makes a similar distinction between disclosed and undisclosed agency, but the outcome in this case seems to differ from England, as the reporter considers Waltmann to be an undisclosed agent. According to Scots law, if the agency is disclosed at some point, not only the principal, but also the agent, can sue and be sued by the counterparty.

---

128 Some reporters mentioned this right of action in their national reports. Others did not, considering it a purely tortious claim and, as such, outwith the scope of considering third-party rights.

Question 2

The answers to this question lead to very different outcomes. In both England and Scotland, Kane and Nickel & Dime can always sue each other directly, irrespective of the default or insolvency of Waltmann, and, in the case of Scotland, assuming that Waltmann's agency has now been disclosed to Nickel & Dime. This outcome follows from the principles of agency described above.

In Bulgaria, the Netherlands and Spain (and possibly also France (see below)), Kane and Nickel & Dime could sue each other directly in the event of Waltmann's insolvency, which would include the transfer of Waltmann's rights against Nickel & Dime to Kane. Kane and Nickel & Dime can, thus, address each other directly, establishing mutual obligations and leaving Waltmann out. In France, it may be necessary for Kane to take action first. Although based on different grounds, these outcomes are similar to those in England and Scotland.

In most other jurisdictions, the rules in the event of default by, or insolvency of, Waltmann are not always clear, but point in the direction that only Kane, who would 'own' or be entitled (in a proprietary sense) to the claims for rent, would be able to sue Nickel & Dime, but that Nickel & Dime would not be able to directly sue Kane to have access to the building or continue the lease (Belgium, Czech Republic, France, Germany, Italy, Poland, Slovakia and Sweden). Nickel & Dime would have to file their claim with Waltmann's bankruptcy administrator. This approach seems to lead to an unbalanced protection of Kane. In France Kane's action could possibly lead to the replacement, in the rental contract, of Waltmann by Kane, thus allowing Nickel & Dime to sue Kane as the new lessor, instead of Waltmann, after Kane has chosen to sue Nickel & Dime directly; for practical purposes, the outcome would be similar to that under Spanish law. Under Bulgarian law, Nickel & Dime would have to consent to the substitution of Waltmann, as debtor, with Kane. In other jurisdictions (Poland, Slovakia), Waltmann's insolvency could lead to the termination, by the bankruptcy administrator, of the rental agreement with Nickel & Dime. In Sweden, Nickel & Dime could invoke the right to withhold the rental payment, as the payment obligation is reciprocal to the right of access to, and use of, the premises.

CASE 5: TRANSFER OF ASSET AND ASSOCIATED CONTRACTUAL RIGHTS

1. CASE

Mr Joyce, a real estate investor, decides to sell one of his buildings. Prior to the sale, Joyce had concluded a rental contract for a period of two years with Adams Corp. In addition, Joyce had entered into an insurance contract with an insurance company, in relation to the property. Furthermore, the building has recently been undergoing renovation, for which Joyce entered into a contract for works with Schwarzmann. Although the contract price has been paid, the renovation is not yet finished. Schwarzmann has promised to finish the renovation in a couple of months. In the meantime, Joyce sells and transfers ownership of the building to Mr Watts.

Question

Do any of the rights and obligations under the contracts between Joyce and third parties transfer to Watts? If so, on what basis do they transfer?

2. DISCUSSIONS

2.1. BELGIUM

Siel Demeyere and Vincent Sagaert

I. Operative Rules

The rights and obligations under the lease may transfer to Watts. The rights and obligations under the insurance contract do transfer (for a three-month period). The rights under the construction contract may transfer. No obligations under that contract (if there are any) will transfer.

II. Descriptive Formants

Tenants are protected against a sale of the let premises, under condition that the lease contract has a *vaste datum/date certaine* (fixed date),[1] obtained, for instance, through registration at the tax office.[2] This entails that the new owner must respect and further perform the lease contract. In the case of a commercial lease, the tenant is also protected against termination of the lease by the new owner where the lease does not have a fixed date, if the tenant has used the premises for at least six months before the sale.[3] In the case at hand, we cannot assess whether the lease contract has a fixed date, or whether Adams Corp. have been able to use the premises for a six-month period prior to the sale, and whether they would, therefore, be protected against the sale of the premises to Watts.

The insurance contract survives the change of ownership of the premises. According to Article 111 of the Belgian Insurance Act, non-life insurance automatically transfers upon the sale of insured property and ends three months after the signing of the official (title) deed. The insurance coverage is available until then, except where the buyer has their own coverage under another insurance contract.

Although this term is not really common in Belgian law, both the lease and the insurance contract can be designated as *kwalitatieve overeenkomsten/ contrats propter rem* (qualitative contracts), by analogy with rights *propter rem* (cf. Case 2 above), since these contracts are connected with the property, and not in the first place with a person, and remain in force despite the sale of the property. This is generally characterised as a statutory transfer of contract.[4]

The contract for works is not addressed by the legislator as constituting a qualitative contract, and is, therefore, not transferred by statute to the new owner, Watts. However, the claim to execute the renovations could be characterised as a right *propter rem*, since the execution of the contract is in the interests of the owner of the building, whoever that may be, and not necessarily

---

1 Art. 1743 old BCC. Residential lease law has recently been regulated on regional level. Provisions with similar content can be found in Art. 38 Flemish Woninghuurdecreet of 9 November 2018; Art. 40 (Walloon) Decree of 15 March 2018 relatif au bail d'habitation; Art. 229 Brussels Huisvestingscode/Code du logement.

2 According to Art. 1328 old BCC, private deeds have a fixed date on either the day the deed is registered, the day one of the signing parties dies (because they cannot have signed it after that date) or the date the content of the deed has been ascertained in an official deed, such as an estate description or registration at the tax office.

3 Art. 12 Handelshuurwet/Loi des baux commerciaux 1951 (Act on Commercial Lease).

4 R. Jansen, 'Overdracht van het verhuurde goed' in G.-L. Ballon, H. De Decker, V. Sagaert, E. Terryn, B. Tilleman and A.L. Verbeke (eds), *Contractuele clausules – Huur*, Intersentia, Antwerp 2016, 425; W. Van Gerven and A. Van Oevelen, *Verbintenissenrecht*, Acco, Leuven 2015, 593; V. Withofs, *Contractsoverdracht*, die Keure, Bruges 2015, 229, no. 170.

in the interests of Mr Joyce, who concluded the contract (cf. Case 2 above). The characterisation as a right *propter rem* leads to the automatic transfer of the right to Watts. However, the transfer to Watts of obligations under the contract of works is not possible, because of the privity principle (cf. Case 3 above). No statutory provision deviates from the principle in this specific situation. If there are any obligations (beyond payment), these will not transfer.

III. Meta-Legal Formants

The reforms for specific contracts, such as lease contracts, insurance contracts and contracts for works, are still ongoing, and no draft statutes have yet been published. Thus, the influence of such reforms on the solutions to this case cannot yet be assessed. However, rights *propter rem* have been recognised more generally (cf. Case 2 above), such that it will be easier for Watts to demand the renovation from Schwarzmann. Moreover, the transfer of contracts has been regulated by the legislator,[5] although the statutory transfers of lease contracts and insurance contracts are not affected by this general regulation.

2.2. BULGARIA

Petar Topurov

I. Operative Rules

1. The rights and obligations under the rental agreement will be transferred to Watts in accordance with the law, depending on whether (alternatively):
   (a) the rental agreement is duly registered with the correct date of registration;
   (b) the rental agreement has an authentic date[6] of the conclusion of the agreement;
   (c) the tenant is in possession of the property;
   (d) the acquirer is informed about the rental agreement prior to the transfer of ownership.

---

5 Art. 5.193 BCC.

6 According to Art. 181 of the Code of Civil Procedure (Promulgated, SG, No. 59 of 20.07.2007, in force since 01.03.2018, last am. No. 100 of 20.12.2019), a private document shall have an authentic date for third persons (alternatively): (a) from the day on which it was certified; (b) from the day of the death or occurred physical disability to sign of the person who has signed the document; (c) from the day on which the content of the document was reproduced in an official document; or (d) from the day on which another fact appeared, certifying in an unquestionable way the preceding drafting of the document.

2. The rights and obligations under the insurance contract will be transferred in favour of Watts, in accordance with the law.
3. The rights under the renovation contract can be transferred on the grounds of an additional clause or contract between Joyce and Watts.

II. Descriptive Formants

1. The legal consequences for the property owner, ensuing from the property transfer with respect to the rented property, have an explicit legal framework.

(a) According to Art. 237 LOC, transfer of immoveable property is accompanied by the rental agreement remaining in force vis-à-vis the acquirer, provided it was duly entered into the property register.
(b) Where such an entry is absent, and the rental agreement was concluded prior to the property transfer and has an authentic date of the conclusion of the agreement, the rental agreement remains compulsory for the acquirer for the term specified in the agreement, which cannot exceed the transfer date by more than a year.
(c) Where the rental agreement does not contain an authentic date of the conclusion of the agreement, and the tenant is in possession of the property, the contract is compulsory for the acquirer, as a rental agreement without a fixed term, and the new owner of the property is entitled to terminate it on one month's written prior notification.
(d) The last case presents an example of replacement of the landlord by the acquirer in the rental relationship, which occurs under the law. There is controversy in legal doctrine on the contract's opposability to the acquirer, inasmuch as it is not registered and lacks an authentic date of conclusion, but the buyer is informed of the existing rental relationship.[7] The case law accepts that the contract is protected from acquirers[8] who act in bad faith.[9]

2. Regarding the concluded insurance contract, there are explicit legal provisions as well. Art. 413(1) of the Insurance Code (IC)[10] stipulates that if,

---

7 T. Yossifova, *Effect of the contract concerning persons* Sibi, Sofia 2019, p. 111.

8 The normative status of a contract, expressed in the possibility for the parties to the contract to protect or save their rights under the contract against third parties. The possibility of protection is usually based on legal requirements for certain publicity of the contract, but it is also possible for it to be based on the possession of the property by a party to the contract.

9 Decision No. 1608 of 11.06.1966 on civil case No. 1081/66. If the purchaser of the property knows that the previous owner has entered into a lease agreement, but nevertheless wishes to terminate the contract immediately, they would be acting in bad faith.

10 Code of Insurance, Promulgated, SG, No. 102 of 29.12.2015, in force since 01.01.2016, last am. No. 17 of 06.02.2019.

during the term of the insurance contract, the insured property is transferred, the acquirer shall assume the rights and obligations of the insured person under the insurance contract. This succession of rights occurs *ex lege*, without the need for any additional actions on the part of the acquirer.[11]

In cases under Article 413(1) IC:

(a) The insurer has the right to terminate the insurance legal relation with the acquirer of the insured property, by one month's prior written notification. This right of termination by the insurer expires where it is not exercised by them within one month from gaining knowledge of the change in the ownership title to the insured property.
(b) In terms of Art. 414(1) and (2) IC, the acquirer of the insured property has the right to terminate the insurance legal relation immediately, by notifying the insurer in writing of this. The right of termination by the acquirer expires if it is not exercised by them either within one month after the acquisition or, if the acquirer was not aware of the existence of the insurance contract, within one month after them becoming aware of the insurance contract.

3. As regards the renovation contract, in order to transfer the rights to the seller it is necessary either to incorporate a cession agreement in the sales contract itself, or to conclude such a contract between the seller and the buyer at a later stage, as these rights do not transfer automatically by operation of law.

2.3. CZECH REPUBLIC

Tomáš Richter

I. *Operative Rules*

Joyce's rights and obligations under *the rental contract with Adams* transfer to Watts. The situation is unclear with respect to the insurance and building contracts, but the more likely answer is that these will not transfer to Watts.

II. *Descriptive Formants*

The one instance in which one can answer the question unequivocally is with respect to the rental contract with Adams. This is due to the rule in section 2221 CC

[11] O. Gerdzhikov, *Commercial Transactions*, Publisher Work-and-law, Sofia 2006, p. 210.

(appearing in the subpart governing leases, and entitled 'Change of ownership'), which provides that:

> (1) If the owner of the [rented] thing changes, the rights and obligations under the lease shall pass on to the new owner.
> (2) Where the lessor transfers ownership to the [rented] thing, the new owner is not bound by contractual provisions setting out lessor's obligations which do not follow from the law. The rule [in the previous sentence] does not apply to contractual provisions which were known to the new owner.

As already mentioned in relation to Case 2 above, the CC contains section 1106, pursuant to which an acquirer of ownership also acquires rights and obligations pertaining to the thing acquired. While it is not yet clear what the provision actually means, there seem to be no suggestions that the rule could imply the automatic transfer of as-yet-unperformed contracts relating to the thing sold. On the contrary, the existence of section 2221 CC is thought to be an exception to the principle of the relative nature of contractual obligations.[12]

2.4. ENGLAND AND WALES

T.T. Arvind

I. Operative Rules

The tenancy will automatically transfer to Watts with the sale, but Joyce will continue to be bound by some obligations unless he is released from them by Adams. The rights and obligations under the works contract with Schwarzmann and the insurance contract will not automatically pass to Watts without further action, which is likely to require the consent of the other party.

II. Descriptive Formants

The position in relation to tenancies involves three sets of formants which are mutually complementary: the general legal principles derived from case law in relation to the nature of leases, the rules in the Law of Property Act 1925 (LPA) concerning the transfer of tenanted property, and the provisions of the Landlord and Tenant (Covenants) Act 1995 (LTCA) on the obligations of the former landlord.

---

12 M. Hulmák in M. Hulmák et al., *Občanský zákoník V, Závazkové právo, Obecná část (§1721–2054), První vydání*, C.H. Beck, Praha 2014, p. 295 at 1, 2.

In English law, tenancies are not merely contracts. They also create a legal estate (that is, a set of conveyable rights over the land), called a leasehold or 'a term of years absolute',[13] in the property to which they relate. As a result, there is a separate relationship, called 'privity of estate', between the landlord and the tenant, over and above the contractual relationship.[14] A landlord who sells tenanted land is, in law, treated as having assigned the 'reversionary interest' (that is, the right to recover possession of the property after the tenancy ends) to the purchaser. The assignment of the reversion creates privity of estate between the tenant and the new landlord, and the existence of such privity of estate means that the new landlord takes the land subject to the tenancy, even though they were not a party to the original tenancy agreement.

Until fairly recently, privity of estate and privity of contract were treated as two different things.[15] As a result, a distinction was drawn between rights and obligations in the tenancy agreement that are merely personal, and those that 'touch and concern' the land.[16] The latter were governed by privity of estate and passed automatically to the new owner of the land,[17] but the former were governed by privity of contract and were not passed. Leases granted before 1 January 1996 are still governed by these rules, but leases granted on or after that date are governed by a simpler regime contained in the LTCA, under which the benefit and burden of all landlord and tenant covenants pass on assignment of the reversion,[18] unless the covenant is expressly stated to be personal to one of the parties.[19]

The passing of the tenancy and covenants to Watts under the LTCA does not, however, release Joyce. The tenant's consent is required for release, and Joyce must seek release by sending a notice to Adams within four weeks of the assignment. If notice is not sent, Joyce will remain liable for any breach of the landlord's covenants, despite the transfer.[20] If Adams object, Joyce will only be released if the court finds release reasonable.[21]

---

13 Law of Property Act 1925 (LPA), s. 1(1)(b).

14 See the discussion in K.M. Lewison et al. (eds), *Woodfall on Landlord and Tenant*, Release 120, 4 vols. (London: Sweet and Maxwell, 2020), vol. 1, para. 11.032.

15 For an overview of the development of this distinction and its consequences, see S. Goulding, 'Privity of estate and the enforcement of real covenants' (2007) 63 *Common Law World Review* 193.

16 For a discussion of the meaning of this phrase and its application in the courts, see K.M. Lewison et al. (eds), *Woodfall on Landlord and Tenant*, Release 120, 4 vols. (London: Sweet and Maxwell, 2020), vol. 1, para. 11.048 ff. (esp. 11.051).

17 LPA, ss. 78(1), 79(1), 141, 142.

18 Landlord and Tenant (Covenants) Act 1995 (LTCA), s. 3.

19 Ibid., s. 3(6)(a).

20 See *Reeves v. Sandhu* [2015] EWHC 985 (Ch) [32]–[35].

21 LTCA, ss. 6, 8.

Contractual rights other than tenancy are not automatically transferred by the sale of property, as they do not run with the land.[22] They must be transferred separately. A contractual right (but not a contractual duty) is, in English law, considered a 'chose in action' or 'thing in action', and can be transferred by assignment under LPA, section 136, which specifies that the assignment must be in writing, that it must be absolute (and not conditional), and that written notice must be given to the other party to the contract being assigned. However, while the benefit of the contract can be assigned, the burden cannot, and Joyce will remain responsible for all obligations under any assigned contract.

Not all contractual rights are capable of assignment.[23] It is well established that insurance policies cannot be assigned without the insurer's consent (other than marine and life insurance, which are subject to special statutory rules). Further, if the subject matter of the policy is transferred by the assured then the policy will lapse, as the assured will cease to have an insurable interest.[24] Joyce will, therefore, be unable to transfer the benefit of the insurance policy to Watts.

Rights under a contract also cannot be assigned if the contract's terms prohibit assignment.[25] It is common for works contracts and construction contracts to explicitly prohibit assignment without the contractor's consent.[26] If the works contract with Schwarzmann follows standard contracting practice, Joyce will, therefore, not be entitled to assign the rights arising out of the contract to Watts without Schwarzmann's consent.

The only effective way of fully transferring both the benefit and burden under the contracts with Schwarzmann and the insurers would be through novation. Novation would require the parties to each of the original contracts to agree that Watts will take Joyce's place under each contract. The effect of novation is to extinguish the original contract and create a new contract with the new party on the same terms.[27] Absent a novation, it is unlikely that the contracts will be transferred.

---

22 *Rayner v. Preston* (1881) 18 Ch D 1.

23 See G.J. Tolhurst, *The Assignment of Contractual Rights*, 2nd ed. (Oxford: Hart Publishing, 2016), ch. 8.

24 J. Birds, B. Lynch and S. Paul (eds), *MacGillivray on Insurance Law*, 14th ed. (London: Sweet & Maxwell, 2014), paras. 22-06 to 22-08.

25 *Linden Gardens Trust v. Lenesta Sludge Disposals Ltd* [1994] 1 AC 85 (HL).

26 See e.g. clause 7.1 of the Joint Contracts Tribunal Standard Building Contract (2016 edition), and D. Chappell, *Understanding JCT Standard Building Contracts*, 10th ed. (Abingdon: Routledge, 2017), s. 3.1.

27 H. Beale (ed), *Chitty on Contracts*, 33rd ed., 2 vols. (London: Sweet and Maxwell, 2019), para. 19-087.

2.5. FRANCE

Sylvain Ravenne and Flora Vern

I. Operative Rules

The right and obligations under the rental contract may transfer to Watts, depending on the terms of the sales contract and the rental contract.

The rights and obligations under the insurance contract will transfer to Watts.

The claims for damages in relation to the property that arise from (or will arise from) the contract with Schwarzmann are transferred to Watts. No other rights under the contract with Schwarzmann are transferred to Watts.

II. Descriptive Formants

In this case, a real estate investor has entered into three different contracts, the performance of each of which is still ongoing, before selling the property. The question is whether the rights and obligations created by those contracts are transferred to the buyer.

Under French law, a contract that is an *'accessoire'* (accessory) to a thing, or to the performance of another agreement, is generally transferred with the thing or the agreement, even though there is no general rule providing this.[28] As a result, the extent of the rights, obligations or claims transferred may vary depending on the type of contract. This means that contracts that are accessories to real property will run with the land. While this is true in theory, however, the practical implementation of this rule is quite difficult for two reasons: firstly, it is sometimes difficult to determine whether the contract is accessory to the property; secondly, the buyer may not know about the existence of the contract, and may therefore be unable to comply with it. Conversely, the third party to the sales contract may also have legitimate reasons to refuse to be bound to the buyer against their will. In order to simplify contractual relations, the law usually states expressly that the buyer and the third party will be bound by certain contracts concluded before the sale. It is, therefore, necessary to look for legal provisions or case law in each specific situation.

(a) Joyce has entered into a fixed-term rental contract with Adams Corp. According to Article 1743 of the FCC, a buyer will be bound to respect a

---

[28] F. Terré, P. Simler, Y. Lequette and F. Chénedé, *Droit civil, les obligations*, 13th ed. (Paris: Dalloz, 2022), n° 1666 and 1670 ; J.L. Aubert, É. Savaux and J. Flour, *Droit Civil. Les Obligations. L'Acte Juridique*, 17th ed. (Paris: Sirey, 2022), n°s 671 ff.

rental contract which has been concluded prior to a sale, if the lease has acquired a legal date. This happens when one of the parties to the original rental contract dies, when the contract is registered as a deed, or when it is merely mentioned in a deed. If the sales contract, in the form of a deed, mentions the existence of the rental contract and the price of the rent, Watts will be bound by it, and Adams Corp. will have to pay the rent directly to Watts as soon as they have been notified of the sale. Claims that arose from the rental contract prior to the sale will not be transferred, and should be settled between Adams Corp. and Joyce.

(b) Joyce has also subscribed an insurance contract relative to the property. The general rule is that insurance contracts that cover damage caused to the thing, or by the thing, are automatically transferred to the buyer.[29] This rule applies, for instance, to an insurance contract covering damage to a property caused by a natural disaster. In such a case, the buyer may claim the insurance money even if the damage occurred before the transfer of ownership, but was revealed or consolidated afterwards.[30] The outcome would be identical if the insurance were meant to cover payment for any renovation works subsequent to the damage.[31] Either way, the insurance contract would be transferred by law to Watts, who should fulfil the obligations laid out in the contract, such as paying the premium, since the contract would otherwise be terminated.[32] Upon informing the insurance company of the sale, the seller will no longer be liable for payment of future premiums, and upon failure of the buyer to make such payments, the insurance company will have a claim against Watts for the unpaid premiums.

(c) Finally, Joyce has entered a '*contrat d'entreprise*' (a contract for the supply of services) with Schwarzmann. The price has been paid, but the works are still ongoing at the time of the sale. In that specific case, while the price was paid by the original owner of the property, the contractor will be liable to any subsequent buyer for any damages that fall within their responsibility under the contract for services. In this case, it is not so much the contract for services which is transferred to the buyer (who has not directly paid the contractor), as the claims arising from it, insofar as these relate to damage to the property which has been transferred. This solution is provided for by Article 1792 of the FCC. Case law explicitly considers that this solution rests on the idea that the accessory follows the fate of

29 Art. L.121-10 §3, Code des assurances.
30 Cass., civ. 3e, 7 mai 2014, no 13-16400.
31 Art. L.242-1 §1, Code des assurances.
32 Cass., civ. 3e, 20 oct. 2004, no 03-13599.

the principal; that is, the warranty relative to the works runs with the thing, and is attached to the owner thereof.[33] The buyer's claim is then deemed to be contractual in nature, due to the transmission of the original claim along with the thing.[34]

However, since this transfer of the legal claim is organised by the law, it will be excluded in certain circumstances. The original owner will still have a claim against the contractor if the damage was discovered before the sale and impacted on the price,[35] or if the seller has agreed to repair the damage for the buyer,[36] or been judicially required to do so.[37] The logic behind these rules is that the buyer should not enrich themselves unjustly where the seller is the one paying for the actual damage. Correlatively, another limitation is that the contractor may not be required to compensate for more than the actual price of the repairs. This means that, if one of the successive owners sues the contractor because they have incurred the full economic burden of the damage in lieu of the previous owner, others will be barred from doing the same, in order to prevent double recovery from the breach of contract. If the damage consolidated over time, however, it is possible that successive buyers could each claim compensation for the economic loss they personally incurred, up to the actual price of the repairs.

2.6. GERMANY

Sonja Meier

I. *Operative Rules*

The rights and obligations under the rental contract between Joyce and Adams Corp. will transfer to Watts by operation of law. The same goes for the rights and obligations under the insurance contract, although the insurance company will only be bound from the moment they receive notice of the change in ownership. The rights and obligations under the renovation contract, by contrast, will only transfer to Watts if all three parties have expressly or impliedly agreed to that transfer.

---

33 Cass., civ. 1re, 28 nov. 1967, Bull. civ. I, n° 348; Cass, civ. 3e, 23 sept. 2009, n° 08-13470.

34 Cass., civ. 3e, 8 oct. 1997, n° 96-11155.

35 Cass., civ. 3e, 26 avr. 1983, n° 81-11865.

36 Cass., civ. 3e, 11 déc. 1991, n° 90-17489.

37 Cass., civ. 3e, 20 avr. 1982, n° 81-10026.

II. Descriptive Formants

1. §566 (1) BGB states that all rights and obligations under a contract for the lease of residential premises will transfer to the acquirer by operation of law if ownership of the premises is transferred after the tenant has acquired possession of the premises. §578 BGB extends the scope of this provision to all contracts for the lease of land (which, according to §94 (1) BGB, includes buildings erected on the land), as well as other premises not constituting residential premises. Assuming that Adams Corp. acquired possession of the premises before the property was transferred to Watts, the rights and obligations under the rental contract will transfer to Watts under §§566 (1), 578 BGB, irrespective of whether or not the lessee (Adams Corp.) has been informed of the change of ownership or acquired knowledge of it in a different way.[38] However, it is generally accepted that the parties can agree that the rights and obligations should remain with the original lessor. For such an agreement to be valid, however, the consent of the lessee is necessary.[39]

2. According to §95 (1) Versicherungsvertragsgesetz (Law on Insurance Contracts, VVG), all rights and obligations under a contract insuring damage to property will transfer to the acquirer by operation of law if ownership of the property is transferred. In contrast to the lessee, however, the insurer will only be bound vis-à-vis the acquirer once it has knowledge of the transfer of ownership (§95 (3) VVG). Although there is no similar provision in relation to policies insuring risks flowing from property (for example, the risk of water escaping), the prevailing (but not unanimous) view among commentators is that §95 VVG should apply by analogy to such contracts.[40]

3. Regarding the renovation contract, there is no statutory provision similar to those mentioned above. However, it is possible for the parties involved to expressly or impliedly stipulate that the rights and obligations under the renovation contract should be transferred to the new owner of the building. This agreement, called *Vertragsübernahme*, results in the transfer to the third party of the whole contractual position of one of the contracting parties.[41] *Vertragsübernahme* can only be effected if all of the parties involved agree to the transfer.

---

38 In the event that Adams Corp., in ignorance of the transfer, pay the rent to their former contract partner Joyce or agree a reduction with him, they will be protected vis-à-vis Watts under §407 BGB (a provision primarily applicable to assignments but, according to §412 BGB, also to other cases of transfers of claims).

39 M. Häublein in *Münchener Kommentar zum BGB*, vol. 5 (9th ed., Beck 2023), §566, [62].

40 P. Reusch in *Münchener Kommentar zum Versicherungsvertragsgesetz*, vol. 1 (3rd ed., Beck 2022), §95, [32]; C. Armbrüster in *Prölss/Martin Versicherungsvertragsgesetz* (31st ed., Beck 2021), §95, [3].

41 BGH *NJW* 2013, 1083 at [19]; S. Heinemeyer in *Münchener Kommentar zum BGB*, vol. 3 (9th ed., Beck 2022), before §414, [7]–[8].

2.7. ITALY

Claudia Amodio

I. Operative Rules

1. The rights and obligations under the rental contract will most likely transfer to Watts, regardless of Adams Corp.'s consent (Arts. 1599 c.c. ff.).
2. The rights and obligations under the insurance contract might transfer to Watts on the basis of the 'silent consent' of both Watts and the insurance company (Art. 1918 c.c.).
3. The right to claim performance of the renovation works Schwarzmann has promised to finish will transfer to Watts, as long as '*cessione del credito*' (assignment of credit) is concluded between Joyce and Watts, with or without the consent of Schwarzmann (Arts. 1260 c.c. ff.).

II. Descriptive Formants

The fact that the rental contract has a certified date preceding the date of the contract of sale should suffice to render it '*opponibile*' (invocable) against a subsequent third-party purchaser. Art. 1599 of the Italian c.c. lays down this principle of the '*opponibilità*' (invocability), as an exception to the privity of contract and the non-transferability of the contractual relationship.[42]

The general rule in such a case is that a statutory substitution will take effect, so that the rental contract remains in force upon the property being alienated *(emptio non tollit locatum)*, regardless of whether or not the tenant has given consent (Art. 1602 c.c.).[43]

Although party autonomy plays an important role in Italian law, this is not an 'opt-out' system. According to a specific legal provision dealing with landlord and tenant relationships, any contractual provision providing for the termination of the rental contract in the event of a transfer of the rented property is deemed to be void on grounds of public policy.[44]

---

42 R. Calvo, 'La locazione' in M. Bessone (ed), *Trattato di diritto privato* (Turin: Giappichelli, 2016), vol. XIV, p. 139. If the rental contract has been registered, the invocability regime applies for a period that might exceed nine years (Art. 1599, c. 3). If it has not been registered, the rental contract with a certified date preceding the date of the contract of sale is invocable (thus enforceable against the third party) for a period that cannot exceed nine years from the date of the rental contract.

43 Cass., 13 July 2018, no. 18536, *Massimario Giustizia civile* (2018).

44 Art. 7 L. 27 luglio 1978, no. 392, Disciplina delle locazioni di immobili urbani. Moreover, according to other specific legal provisions to be found in L. 27 luglio 1978, no. 392, Disciplina delle locazioni di immobili urbani (namely Arts. 27 and 28), a subsequent purchaser who wants to get out of the rental agreement will be rather restricted, as they would be entitled to do so only if they respect the minimum lease duration and provide the tenant with an appropriate notice period.

The issue of the transfer of an insured property is also specifically addressed by the Italian Civil Code (Art. 1918 c.c.).[45] While this provision states that there is no automatic termination of the insurance contract due to the transfer of the property, it adopts what might be called a flexible 'substitution approach',[46] granting the insurer and the transferee the right to terminate the contract and thus avoid the statutory substitution.

In the present case, the rights and obligations under the insurance contract will likely transfer to Mr Watts unless he or the insurance company decide the contract is not to be continued. To this end, they must both be informed in due course by the policyholder of, respectively, the existence of the insurance contract and the transfer of the insured property. Whereas the insurance company is granted the right to terminate the contract within ten days from the policyholder's notice, Mr Watts would have to terminate the contract within a mandatory transitional ten-day period starting from the date on which the first premium subsequent to the transfer is due. Should Joyce not comply with the aforementioned duty to inform the insurance company and the transferee, he will remain fully bound to the insurance contract even after the transfer.

As for Joyce's right to claim performance of the renovation works, it might transfer to Watts on the basis of a '*cessione del credito*' (assignment of credit).[47] Unlike the assignment of a contract, which transfers the whole contractual position, including any rights and duties, from the assignor to the assignee, the assignment of credit has more limited effects, as it concerns only the right to credit which the assignor acquired in the contract (Arts. 1260 c.c. ff.).

More specifically, Joyce may agree to assign the credit to Watts either '*pro soluto*' (that is, without recourse, so that in the event of the debtor's non-performance, the assignee will have no right to take legal steps against the assignor) or '*pro solvendo*' (that is, with recourse, so that, in the event of the debtor's non-performance, the assignee will retain the right to take legal steps against the assignor).[48] Only in the former case would Watts agree to bear the risk of Schwarzmann's non-performance.

The assignment of credit must be notified to the debtor, but their consent is not necessary. If the contract contains a non-assignment clause, this cannot be invoked against the third party unless it can be proved that they knew about it.

III. Meta-Legal Formants

Underlying the statutory substitution mechanism in rental contracts is the *tenant's stake* in the property. Accordingly, when balancing the interests of a

[45] G. De Zuliani, *Successione di diritto nel rapporto assicurativo* (Milan: Giuffrè, 1960).
[46] J. Basedow (ed), *Principles of European Insurance Contract Law* (Munich: Sellier European Law Publishers, 2009), p. 277.
[47] P. Perlingieri, *Cessione dei crediti* (Naples: Edizioni Scientifiche Italiane, 2010), p. 1.
[48] Ibid., p. 282.

third-party purchaser and those of the tenant, courts generally give greater weight to the latter.

However, it is assumed that the change of landlord does not make any relevant difference to the tenant. Of course, the former landlord must still inform the tenant in due course of the transfer of the property, so that the substitution is effective, but the tenant's consent to the transfer is not necessary (Art. 1599 c.c.).[49]

The dogmatic differences between substitution in rental contracts and assignment of credit have been put in perspective by the Italian courts.[50] In both cases, the position of the debtor should not worsen as a result of the change of creditor, and there is no need for the debtor's approval – rather, the debtor must simply be notified about it. In both cases, until the debtor has been notified, the debtor may still effectively perform towards the old creditor, unless the new creditor proves that the debtor knew about the transfer anyway.

In the case of the insurance contract, the main reason why substitution appears to be the default rule only in the absence of a different intention expressed either by the third party or the insurance company is the *intuitu personae* character of the contract. What is relevant here is a sort of statutory 'silent consent' mechanism. By the end of the aforementioned termination periods, the insurance company and the transferee can indeed be deemed to have accepted the substitution effect.

2.8. THE NETHERLANDS

Jan Biemans

I. *Operative Rules*

1. The rights and obligations under the rental contract between Joyce and Adams Corp. transfer to Watts by operation of law, on the basis of Article 7:226 DCC.
2. The rights and obligations under the insurance contract between Joyce and the insurance company transfer to Watts by operation of law, ceasing after one month, on the basis of Article 7:948 DCC.
3. The rights (and obligations) under the contract for works between Joyce and Schwarzmann transfer to Watts by operation of law, on the basis of Article 6:251 DCC.

---

[49] Cass., 13 July 2018, no. 18536, *Massimario Giustizia civile* (2018).
[50] Cass., 14 January 2005, no. 674, *Massimario Giustizia civile* (2005).

II. Descriptive Formants

The general rule in Dutch private law is that the rights and obligations of a contract which a property owner has concluded with a counterparty with regard to their property do not transfer by operation of law to the new owner of that property. This principle is generally considered to be based on the 1905 Dutch Supreme Court *Blaauboer/Berlips* case.[51] Despite the *Blaauboer/Berlips* case, the DCC contains several exceptions which almost obliterate this general rule, especially when it comes to contracts and real property.[52]

In the *Blaauboer/Berlips*[53] case, the former owner (Berlips) had promised Blaauboer that he would pave a strip of land in between two building plots which Berlips had sold to Blaauboer. Berlips later sold the strip to the widow Maks. When Blaauboer and their legal successor Kloots later sued Berlips to pave the strip of land, as he had promised, Berlips defended himself by arguing that Maks was now the owner of the strip of land, and therefore obliged to pave it. The Dutch Supreme Court ruled that the obligation was still with Berlips, as it is, in principle, not possible for a party (debtor) to bind a third party without their consent. There is, thus, no such thing as a 'third-party obligation' in a contract. Although the *Blaauboer/Berlips* case seems to have been transformed by legal doctrine into a general rule that contractual rights and obligations relating to a property do not transfer to the new owner of the property, but remain with the former owner and the contracting party, there are many exceptions to this rule.

First, the rights and obligations under the rental contract between Joyce and Adams Corp. transfer to Watts by operation of law, on the basis of Article 7:226 DCC. According to Article 7:226 (1) DCC, a transfer by the lessor of property to which a lease agreement relates, or the establishment or transfer by the lessor of an independent usufruct, long leasehold or building rights on the property to which the lease agreement relates, makes the rights and obligations of the lessor, derived from the lease agreement, due and demandable as of that moment, pass to the acquiring party. In fact, the rental contract is transferred by operation of law from the former owner to the new owner, who becomes the new lessor. The acquiring party is bound only by those contractual provisions of the lease agreement that directly relate to the use of the leased property as granted by the lessor in exchange for the counter-performance of the lessee (Article 7:226 (3) DCC).

Second, the rights and obligations under the (non-life) insurance contract between Joyce and the insurance company transfer to Watts by operation of law,

---

51 Dutch Supreme Court, 3 March 1905, W 1905/8191 *(Blaauboer/Berlips)*.

52 J.W.A. Biemans, *Rechtsgevolgen van stille cessie*, Deventer: Kluwer 2011, no. 414, note 14.

53 Dutch Supreme Court, 3 March 1905, W 1905/8191 *(Blaauboer/Berlips)*.

on the basis of Article 7:948 DCC.[54] According to Article 7:948 (1) DCC, upon a transfer of a thing or a limited property right with which a thing is encumbered, the rights and obligations derived from the insurance agreement, covering the interests of the alienator that this thing is preserved, pass, together with the risk, to the acquiring party, even where the risk had already passed to the acquiring party before the thing or limited property right was legally transferred.[55] The insurance agreement ceases to exist one month after it passes over to the new insured person (the new owner), unless, within this period, the new insured person notifies the insurer that they want to continue the insurance agreement. In that event, the insurer may, within two months after receiving such notification, terminate the insurance agreement under observance of a term of notice of one month (Article 7:948 (2) DCC). Insurance premiums due and demandable before the new insured person has notified the insurer that he wants to continue the insurance agreement are debts of the original owner only as the policyholder (Article 7:948 (3) DCC).[56]

The rights under the contract for works between Joyce and Schwarzmann transfer to Watts by operation of law, on the basis of Article 6:251 DCC. This provision has been explained under Case 2 above. According to the case details, the contract price has been paid; if this were not the case, Joyce and Watts would have been jointly and severally liable for this.

III. Meta-Legal Formants

A transfer of leased property by a creditor of the lessor, including a mortgagee (bank), is equated with a transfer by the lessor themselves (Article 7:226 (2) DCC). Because of this, banks (as mortgagees) often stipulate that the homeowner is not allowed to rent out the property without the consent of the bank – a so-called 'lease clause'. If the mortgage deed contains such a lease clause, the mortgagee may invoke this clause against parties who have acquired the mortgaged property, and against the lessee (tenant). Article 3:264 DCC contains several procedural requirements the mortgagee has to take into account.

---

54 C.H. Sieburgh, *Mr. C. Assers Handleiding tot de beoefening van het Nederlands Burgerlijk Recht. 6. Verbintenissenrecht. Deel III. Algemeen overeenkomstenrecht*, Deventer: Wolters Kluwer 2022, p. 542.

55 The same applies to secondary insurances which came to existence at the conclusion of this same insurance agreement. No passage will take place if this is indicated by the juridical act under which the thing is transferred or through a declaration of the new interested party to the insurer.

56 The provisions in Art. 7:948 (2) do not lead to a lengthening of the duration of the insurance agreement, nor to a restriction of the right to terminate this agreement on another ground (Art. 7:948 (4) DCC). Paras. 1–4 of this Article do not apply if the insurance agreement itself points out the acquiring party as a third party who is appointed as a beneficiary in the sense of Art. 7:947 DCC (Art. 7:948 (5) DCC).

Article 7:226 DCC shows that a rental contract may transfer by operation of law. Article 3:217 DCC contains a similar provision for a rental contract entered into by a usufructuary *(vruchtgebruiker)*, and Article 7:228 DCC does so for the succession of rental contracts in the event of the lessor's death.

Although Article 7:948 DCC and Article 6:251 DCC especially see to the transfer, by operation of law, of rights under a contract, these provisions also lead to the joint and several liability of the former and the new owners with regard to any counter-obligation(s) to the right(s) acquired, which almost resembles a transfer of contract (Article 6:159 DCC), in which case contractual rights and liabilities both also transfer. Articles 7:226 (in conjunction with Article 7:201 (2) DCC) and Article 6:251 DCC relate to goods (*goederen*; both tangibles and intangibles) in general; Article 7:948 DCC relates, in particular, to insured 'things' (*zaken*; tangibles only).

According to Article 3:168 (1) and (4) DCC, regarding community assets (both tangibles and intangibles), co-proprietors may make a contractual arrangement for the enjoyment, use and administration of the community assets which is binding for their legal successors. The legal successor could, for example, be a buyer (and as a result thereof, an acquirer) of a share in the particular community asset. This could also be regarded as an exception to the *Blaauboer/Berlips* rule.

In addition to these provisions, the DCC also contains the possibility of a so-called *qualitative obligation* with regard to real property, which differs in several respects from a qualitative right (as described in Case 2 above), as will be shown in the following sentences. According to Article 6:252 (1) DCC, it is possible to stipulate by agreement that the obligation of one of the parties to tolerate something or refrain from doing something, with regard to their own registered property, shall pass to all persons who acquire that registered property under particular title, and that this obligation also has to be observed by persons who obtain a right of use of the registered property from a person who has acquired the registered property under the effect of such stipulation.[57] Such stipulation (as meant in Article 6:252 (1) DCC) shall only be effective if the agreement in which it is written down is drawn up by notarial deed, followed by the registration of this deed in the public registers for registered property (Article 6:252 (2), first sentence, DCC). Such qualitative obligations cannot be used to impose an active obligation on one of the parties, such as paving a strip of land. Even after the stipulation has been registered in the public registers, it shall have no effect: (a) against persons who already, before its registration, had acquired under particular title a right in the registered

57 C.H. Sieburgh, *Mr. C. Assers Handleiding tot de beoefening van het Nederlands Burgerlijk Recht. 6. Verbintenissenrecht. Deel III. Algemeen overeenkomstenrecht*, Deventer: Wolters Kluwer 2022, pp. 550 ff.

property or a right of use of that property; (b) against a person who has seized the registered property or a limited property right with which it has been encumbered, if the stipulated obligation was not yet registered at the moment on which the warrant of seizure was registered in the public registers; and (c) against persons who have acquired their right from someone who, pursuant to the provisions under point (a) or (b), was not bound by the stipulated obligation (Article 6:252 (3) DCC). Where, in exchange for the stipulated obligation, a counter-performance has been agreed upon, the right to claim this counter-performance also passes, together with the stipulated obligation, to the party who has acquired the registered property, as far as this right is related to the period after the passage of the stipulated obligation, and provided that the stipulation under which the counter-performance is due is also registered in the public registers (Article 6:252 (4) DCC). Article 6:252 DCC does not apply to (and cannot be used for) obligations that limit a proprietor's powers to alienate or encumber the registered property (Article 6:252 (5) DCC).

2.9. POLAND

Dariusz Szostek

I. Operative Rules

1. Joyce's rights and obligations resulting from the lease agreement concluded with Adams Corp. will automatically pass, by virtue of law, to Watts.
2. As a general rule, Joyce's rights and obligations resulting from the insurance agreement will not automatically pass, by virtue of law, to Watts. Joyce's rights and obligations resulting from this agreement may be transferred to Watts, but this would require the conclusion of a special agreement on the transfer of rights, with the consent of the insurer.
3. In general, the provisions of Polish law do not provide the possibility of an automatic transfer, to the buyer, of rights resulting from a contract for construction works that was previously concluded by the seller. Joyce's rights and obligations resulting from the contract for construction works can be transferred to Watts, but will not automatically pass to Watts by virtue of law.

II. Descriptive Formants

According to Article 678 §1 PCC, 'if a rented thing is disposed of during the tenancy period, the acquirer becomes a party to the tenancy in place of the transferor; it may, however, terminate the tenancy observing statutory notice periods'.[58] Moreover, pursuant to Article 680 PCC, 'the provisions of the preceding chapter apply to the tenancy of premises, subject to the following provisions', including the aforementioned Article 678 PCC. In view of the above, Joyce's rights and obligations resulting from the lease agreement concluded with Adams Corp. will automatically pass, by virtue of law, to Watts.[59] Adams Corp. have to take possession of the item in order to lease it. This results from Article 662 of the Civil Code, in conjunction with Article 680 PCC.

Based on Article 823 §1 PCC:

> if the object of the insurance is transferred, the rights under the insurance contract may be transferred to the acquirer of the insurance object. The transfer of those rights requires the insurer's consent, unless the insurance contract or the general terms and conditions of insurance provide otherwise.[60]

As a general rule, Joyce's rights and obligations resulting from the insurance agreement would not automatically pass, by virtue of law, to Watts.[61] However, based on the above-mentioned provision, Joyce's rights and obligations resulting from the insurance agreement could be transferred to Watts, though this would require the conclusion of an assignation of the rights, with the consent of the insurer.

The provisions of the PCC regarding contracts for construction works do not contain regulations forming the basis for subjective changes in such contracts, whether on the part of the contractor or the investor (Joyce, in the present case).[62] Thus, in general, the provisions of Polish law do not provide for the possibility of an automatic transfer to the buyer (Watts) of rights resulting from the contract for construction works concluded previously by the seller (Joyce). However, at the same time, the provisions of Article 509 §1 PCC provide for the possibility of transferring rights (assignment) to a third party,[63] who in the present case would be Watts. Therefore, Joyce's rights and obligations resulting from the contract for construction works can be transferred to Watts pursuant to Article 509 §1 PCC on the transfer of rights (the consent of the contractor is not required here), but will not automatically pass to Watts by virtue of law.

---

58 J. Jezioro, 'Komentarz do art. 678' in E. Gniewek and P. Machnikowski (eds), *Kodeks cywilny. Komentarz*, Warsaw 2017.

59 W. Koczara and A. Brzoza, 'Przejście praw z umowy najmu nieruchomości w razie zbycia rzeczy najętej', *Nieruchomości* 2009, no. 2, p. 10; K. Siwiec, 'Zmiana stron umowy najmu i dzierżawy w czasie obowiązywania umowy, cz. I', *Nieruchomości* 2013, no. 8, p. 7.

60 J.M. Kondek, 'Komentarz do art. 823' in K. Osajda (ed), *Kodeks cywilny. Komentarz*, Warsaw 2019.

61 R. Golat, 'Skutki zbycia ubezpieczonej nieruchomości', *Nieruchomości* 2009, no. 2, p. 15.

62 J. Pokrzywniak, 'Klauzula zezwalająca na przeniesienie praw i obowiązków z umowy', *Monitor Prawniczy* 2004, no. 24, p. 1154.

63 J. Mojak, 'Komentarz do art. 509' in K. Pietrzykowski (ed), *Kodeks cywilny. T II. Komentarz. Art. 450–1088. Przepisy wprowadzające*, Warsaw 2018.

2.10. SCOTLAND

Lorna MacFarlane

I. Operative Rules

None of the rights and obligations under these contracts automatically transfer to Mr Watts. The rental agreement will transfer, provided certain conditions are fulfilled.

II. Descriptive Formants

The 'privity doctrine' is recognised in Scots law, in both legal commentary and case law, although it has no statutory footing. This doctrine prevents the transfer of both burdens and contractual benefits to non-contractual parties. For example, Walker states that it is

> clear and well settled, that under a contract between two parties no third party either acquires rights or comes under duties by virtue of the contract. Consequently no third party can, in general, sue for performance of a contract or for damages for breach thereof, nor be sued for performance or for damages.[64]

Privity is judicially described as a 'well established rule'.[65]

Taking both aspects of privity together, this means that Mr Watts cannot sue or be sued on any of the contracts concluded by Mr Joyce and his counterparties (namely, the insurance company, Schwarzmann, and Adams Corp.). There is no legal basis on which Mr Joyce's duties towards the three parties, or his rights under his contracts with them, would transfer to Mr Watts. Equally, the three parties would not become bound to perform their contractual duties in favour of Mr Watts by virtue of the transfer of the building, nor could they enforce their contractual rights against him.

It should, however, be noted that the building may be 'conveyed' (transferred) to Mr Watts subject to the rental agreement with Adams Corp.

The first question in ascertaining whether the rental agreement remains enforceable after the transfer of the property is whether the agreement is a

---

64 D.M. Walker, *The Law of Contracts and Related Obligations in Scotland*, 3rd ed. (T & T Clark, London 1995), para. 29.1. See also H. MacQueen and Lord Eassie (eds), *Gloag and Henderson: The Law of Scotland*, 14th ed. (W. Green, Edinburgh 2017), para. 8.01.

65 *Duke of Queensberry's Executors v. Maxwell* (1831) 5 W & S 771 at 766 per Lord Eassie. See also *Laurence McIntosh Limited v. Balfour Beatty Group Limited and The Trustees of the National Library of Scotland* [2006] CSOH 197 at para. 33 per Lord Drummond Young; *MacLaren and Others v. Mayberry and Others* (1904) 11 SLT 636 at 637 per Lord Low.

'lease' or merely a 'licence'. The agreement is a lease if it meets the following requirements of the Leases Act 1449: there must be a landlord and tenant; the parties must have reached *consensus in idem* (agreement on the essential terms of the lease); the lease must be over heritable subjects (i.e. land or buildings); there must be rental payments due under the lease; and the subjects must be let for a period of time.[66] If these requirements are met, the agreement is a lease. If the agreement between Mr Joyce and Adams Corp. does not meet these requirements, it is a licence. A licence grants a contractual right to use land or buildings (for example, to set up a kiosk in a shopping centre or use a particular parking space in an office building). If Adams Corp. is a licensee, it will be able to enforce the agreement against only the original licensor (Mr Joyce).[67] Assuming that Adams Corp. owes rent under the contract, the contract is a lease: Mr Joyce (landlord) and Adams Corp. (tenant) have reached an agreement as expressed in their rental contract over the heritable subjects (the building), for a period of time (two years).

If the agreement meets the requirements under the 1449 Act and certain other conditions, it is a real right: a right in the building itself, which is enforceable against anyone (as opposed to a personal right, which would be enforceable against Mr Joyce only).[68] The other conditions are that the lease is in writing (unless it is for less than one year); the tenant has taken possession of the land/building (unless the lease is for more than twenty years); the lease is registered in the Land Register of Scotland, if the tenant's interest in the lease will or may last for more than twenty years; and the landlord was the registered owner when the lease was granted.[69] If the lease meets these conditions and Adams Corp. has a real right in the lease, Adams Corp. will be able to enforce the lease against Mr Watts as the new owner of the building.[70] Consequently, Mr Watts would not be able, in any way, to alter Adams Corp.'s rights under the lease or prevent it from occupying the building. Mr Watts and Adams Corp. would be subject to the terms of the lease unless they contracted otherwise – the lease would essentially transfer to Mr Watts on point of sale.[71]

66 G.C.H. Paton and J.G.S. Cameron, *The Law of Landlord and Tenant in Scotland* (W. Green, Edinburgh 1967), p. 5; K. Gerber, *Commercial Leases in Scotland*, 3rd ed. (W. Green, Edinburgh 2016), para. 2.05.

67 K. Gerber, *Commercial Leases in Scotland*, 3rd ed. (W. Green, Edinburgh 2016), paras. 2.02–2.03.

68 R. Rennie, *Leases* (W. Green, Edinburgh 2015), paras. 1.01–1.08 and 5.01; K.G.C. Reid, *The Laws of Scotland: Stair Memorial Encyclopaedia: Property: Part 1 – General Law*, vol. 18 (LexisNexis/Law Society of Scotland, London/Edinburgh 1993), paras. 4 and 5. See G.C.H. Paton and J.G.S. Cameron, *The Law of Landlord and Tenant in Scotland* (W. Green, Edinburgh 1967), p. 5.

69 K. Gerber, *Commercial Leases in Scotland*, 3rd ed. (W. Green, Edinburgh 2016), para. 2.06.

70 Ibid., para. 2.02.

71 K. Gerber, *Commercial Leases in Scotland*, 3rd ed. (W. Green, Edinburgh 2016), para. 22.01, citing *Hall v. M'Gill* (1847) 9 D. 1557 at 1566 and *M'Gillivray's Executors v. Masson* (1857) 19 D. 1334.

In Scotland, this is a matter of common law.[72] If, however, there are any personal obligations in the lease (such as an option to take a lease over another property), these will not transfer to the new landlord.[73]

If Mr Watts wished to have the benefit of the insurance contract or the contract for works, Mr Joyce could potentially arrange for one or both of these to be assigned to him (see discussion of the rules of assignation in Cases 7 and 10 below).

Mr Joyce could also negotiate for a 'collateral warranty' to be granted by Schwarzmann in favour of Mr Watts. A collateral warranty acts as a guarantee on the part of the grantor, in favour of the grantee,[74] allowing for a right of action by a party otherwise unconnected by contract. These are used frequently in construction contexts, as where building works, including renovation, are defective or not completed timeously, this might result in loss on the part of a party other than the party to the contract, because the interest in the building has passed to another party.[75]

III. Meta-Legal Formants

Scots law does not have the benefit of extensive judicial or academic reflection on the policy considerations underpinning privity. However, recognition of the doctrine appears to reflect the importance of upholding contractual intentions. For example, Gloag emphasises that one cannot assume from a party's decision to enter into a contractual obligation that the party intends to be bound to 'anyone who may think that the fulfilment of that obligation would be advantageous to him, and hence it is a general rule that only the parties to a contract have a title to sue upon it'.[76] Privity is thus recognised in Scots law as ensuring that contracting parties' intentions in respect of their contractual partners are upheld.

Collateral warranties are considered to be 'an important feature of modern practice in the construction industry',[77] and have arisen due to policy considerations of contractual and commercial efficiency.

---

72 K. Gerber, *Commercial Leases in Scotland*, 3rd ed. (W. Green, Edinburgh 2016), para. 22.03.

73 Ibid., para. 22.05.

74 *Scottish Widows Services Ltd v. Harmon/CRM Facades Ltd (in liquidation)* 2010 SLT 1102 at paras. 1 and 17 per Lord Drummond Young.

75 Ibid., para. 1 per Lord Drummond Young. In *Macdonald Estates Plc v. Regenesis (2005) Dunfermline Ltd* 2007 SLT 791, for example, collateral warranties had been used to give tenants in a shopping centre the right to claim against the developer of the site for any defects in their units (they had a direct contractual claim only with the owner of the centre).

76 W.M. Gloag, *The Law of Contract: A Treatise on the Principles of Contract in the Law of Scotland*, 2nd ed. (W. Green, Edinburgh 1929), p. 218.

77 *Scottish Widows Services Ltd v. Harmon/CRM Facades Ltd (in liquidation)* 2010 SLT 1102 at para. 1 per Lord Drummond Young.

2.11. SLOVAKIA

Kristián Csach, Monika Jurčová, Peter Mészáros and Veronika Zoričáková

I. Operative Rules

According to the legislature (s. 680(2) SCC), only rights and obligations arising from the rental contract will be (automatically) transferred to Watts, unless the transfer of the building is considered a sale of an enterprise (s. 476 SCommC), in which case all rights and obligations will be transferred automatically. The assignment of individual rights is also possible, but would require action on the part of the parties.

II. Descriptive Formants

This answer is based on the assumption that the transfer of the building was not a transfer of an enterprise (see Case 2 above).

The contract on work (renovation) between Joyce and Schwarzmann is a personal contract which would not automatically be transferred to the new owner of the asset that underwent renovation.

According to section 680(2) SCC, the new owner is the legal successor of the previous owner with regard to the rental contract.

According to section 812 SCC, the insurance ceases to exist if the insured property is transferred to another person, unless otherwise provided for by the general terms of the insurance contract. According to the stated provisions, general insurance terms may provide that the previous owner retains the obligations from the insurance contract even after the insured thing has been transferred. It is also possible for the general insurance terms to allow the transfer of the contractual arrangement, but the new owner of the insured object will not be bound by the insurance contract unless the buyer agrees to this.[78]

2.12. SPAIN

Carles Vendrell Cervantes

I. Operative Rules

Only the rights and obligations under *the rental and insurance contracts* would be transferred to Mr Watts after the sale.

---

[78] M. Šulíková in M. Števček, A. Dulak, J. Bajánková, M. Fečík, F. Sedlačko, M. Tomašovič et al., *Občiansky zákonník II, sect. 451–880 [Commentary on Civil Code II, ss. 451–880]*, Prague: C.H. Beck, 2015, p. 2971.

II. *Descriptive Formants*

This case involves three contractual relationships: a rental contract, an insurance contract and a construction or works contract.

Lease Contract

Article 1571 of the Spanish Civil Code provides that the acquirer of a leased property is entitled to terminate the lease agreement, unless otherwise agreed, and except as otherwise provided in the Spanish Mortgage Law (*Ley Hipotecaria*).

However, as an exception to this general rule, Article 29 of the Spanish Law on Urban Leases,[79] which is applicable to leases for non-residential uses, states that 'the acquirer of the leased property will be subrogated in the lessor's rights and obligations deriving from the rental contract, unless the conditions for the application of art. 34 of the Spanish Mortgage Law (Ley Hipotecaria) can be satisfied'. Article 34 has a broad scope because it states, generally speaking, that a third party who in good faith purchases a right from a person who, according to the property register, is entitled to transfer that right, will maintain their acquisition once their right has been inscribed, even if the grantor's right is later resolved or annulled due to circumstances which are not reflected in the register. In contrast, an acquisition by a third party who acted in bad faith will not be maintained, because they will not be able to benefit from the assumption of the correctness of the property register.

Accordingly, if the rental contract with Adams Corp. has been recorded in the property register, the rights and obligations under this contract will be transferred to Mr Watts after the sale. If the rental contract has not been recorded, Mr Watts will be entitled to terminate the lease agreement, unless it can be proven that he did not act in good faith. In this regard, Article 34 of the Spanish Mortgage Law also provides that the third party's good faith is presumed unless it is proven that he or she knew about the inaccuracy of the information recorded in the property register.

Insurance Contract

According to Article 34 of Law 50/1980 of 8 October on Insurance Contracts (the 'Spanish Law on Insurance Contracts'), transfer of the ownership of an insured object implies the subrogation of the acquirer in the rights and obligations of the former owner under the insurance contract (for the same period of time, and under the same conditions, as originally concluded). There

[79] Law 29/1994, of 24 November.

is an exception to this rule, which requires that the insurance contract is not mandatory, that it has adopted the form of a nominative insurance policy (i.e. a policy that covers the person designated in it, and which was issued in favour of a certain person), and that the automatic subrogation is expressly excluded by the general conditions. If the insurance contract in relation to the acquired property meets these requirements, the rights and obligations under the agreement will not be transferred to Mr Watts after the sale.

Regarding the insurance contract, it is important to bear in mind that Article 34 of the Spanish Law on Insurance Contracts obliges the seller of the insured object to inform the acquirer, in writing, of the existence of the insurance contract. The seller is also obliged to inform the insurer or their representatives about the transfer of ownership, in writing, and within 15 days from the date it took place. The Spanish Law on Insurance Contracts states that the acquirer and the former owner will be jointly liable for payment of the premiums which are due after the transfer takes place.

Works Contract

There are no provisions under Spanish law that establish the subrogation of the acquirer in the rights and obligations of the seller regarding contracts for works to be performed on the acquired object. It is unlikely that a court would establish the subrogation of the acquirer of the rights and obligations of the seller under the works contracts either, since there is no legal basis for this. However, since the contract price has already been paid by Mr Joyce, the only right that is yet to be satisfied is the right of the client that the works be completed. This right could be transferred to Mr Watts without requiring the contractor's agreement, and even if it is not stipulated in the purchase contract, as a consequence of the transfer of ownership of the building and the acquirer's interest in the good condition of the property, as a legal consequence of the contractual good faith obligation under Article 1258 of the Spanish Civil Code.

2.13. SWEDEN

Oskar Mossberg

I. *Operative Rules*

The insurance would benefit Mr Watts, on the basis of statutory law.

The position regarding the rental contract would depend on the circumstances. If the renter has a written contract and has occupied the property, their rights of use will hold against the purchaser, who will then be considered the new landlord. The basis for this is statutory law.

In relation to the construction contract, Mr Watts will not receive any rights on the basis of the contract for sale of the property. Mr Joyce's rights against Schwarzmann can be assigned to Mr Watts, but this requires a separate contract.

II. Descriptive Formants

Insurance contracts have some effects in favour of third parties, according to Försäkringsavtalslagen (the Act on Insurance Contracts). Chapter 9, Article 1 states that an insurance policy concerning the value of a *'fastighet'* (piece of real estate) has effects in favour not only of the policyholder, but also other persons who have a right of ownership protected against the creditors of the policyholder. This rule is supplemented, in Article 2, by a non-derogatory rule according to which the insurance applies in favour of purchasers for seven days after the passing of risk (the time of transfer of possession), provided the purchaser is a consumer. However, the fact that Watts purchased the entire building indicates that he is likely acting for business purposes; hence, Article 2 would not be applicable. The insurance would last for the insured period stated in the policy. Provided that this period stretches past the time of the transfer of ownership, and neither of the parties terminate the insurance contract, Watts would be protected by the insurance. In essence, the application of the rules in the Insurance Contracts Act makes the situation equivalent to one where a third-party contract in favour of the purchaser exists. In consumer cases, if the insurance contract states that the insurance discontinues if ownership of the insured property is transferred, the insurance would still apply for seven days after the passing of risk. After the seven-day period, the purchaser of the property would need to get new insurance.

Regarding the rental contract, the ownership of real estate can be transferred irrespective of any existing rental contracts relating to the property. The general rule of Swedish law is captured in a centuries-old legal maxim known as *'köp bryter legostämma'* (purchase severs claim of lease), which entails that non-ownership rights against the seller regarding the property are not effective in relation to the purchaser. This rule has many exceptions, including ones relevant to the present case. According to Jordabalken (the Earth Balk, which is the central statutory Act on real property), Chapter 7, Article 11, a seller of a piece of real estate *'belastad av nyttjanderätt'* (burdened by right(s) of use) must make reservations to the purchaser about the burden, unless it has been documented in the land registry. If reservation or registration is made, the burden holds against the purchaser. Without reservation or registration, the general rule applies, which means the right of use (i.e. rental rights) cannot be invoked against the purchaser – unless there is a written rental agreement and the renter has occupied the property, according to Chapter 7, Article 13 of Jordabalken. In cases where the burden is not registered, the seller's obligation to make a reservation is compulsory. However, failure to comply will only result in an obligation to pay damages to the *'nyttjanderättshavare'* (lessee), who will lose their right to the property. After the date of sale, the new owner, Watts, will be the new creditor as regards payment of rent, according to Chapter 7, Article 17 of Jordabalken. If the rent relates to a period before the date of transfer of possession to the purchaser under the contract of sale (in the sense that the date on which payment is due is before this time), the rent is to be accounted for (paid) to the seller; if it relates to the period after the sale, it has to be paid to the purchaser. This follows from Chapter 4, Article 10, paragraph 2 of Jordabalken.

In relation to the construction contract, the sale of the property does not, in itself, change any rights or obligations. As a general rule, the purchaser derives no rights from the contracts of the seller. As elaborated in Cases 1 and 3 above, the construction contract can be interpreted as a contract in favour of a third party. However, given the circumstances, such an interpretation seems to be without merit here. The parties to the sales contract can assign the seller's rights under the construction contract to the purchaser, but this would require a separate contract between the seller as assignor (Joyce) and purchaser as assignee (Watts). The debtor need not be involved. As there are no formal requirements for such a contract, it can, however, be considered to have been entered into through the (non-verbal) actions of the parties, or even silently. However, for the assignment to be valid against the seller's creditors, the assignor or assignee must give formal notice (preferably, but not necessarily, written) to the debtor, pursuant to Article 31 of Skuldebrevslagen (the Act on Letters of Debt) *ex analogia*.[80]

III. Meta-Legal Formants

This case revolves around two relatively well-regulated areas of Swedish contract law: insurance contracts and real estate contracts. These are some of the most comprehensively legislated contracts under Swedish law.

The rules on insurance contracts for the benefit of third parties have a long history. For present purposes, a suitable cut-off point might be the previous law on insurance contracts, from 1927. The present law on insurance contracts is from 2005, but its preparatory works do not shed much light on the issue of third-party contracts. However, in the preparatory works for the 1927 Act, the older equivalents of the currently applicable rules touched upon above are viewed as third-party contracts.[81] As no relevant changes were intended

80 See the HD case NJA 2005 p. 87.

81 SOU 1925:21 – Förslag till lag om försäkringsavtal m.m., p. 144; NJA II 1927 – proposition 1927:33, Kungl. Maj:ts proposition till riksdagen med förslag till lag om försäkringsavtal m.m., p. 449. See also SOU 1989:88 – Skadeförsäkringslag: slutbetänkande av Försäkringsrättskommittén, p. 206.

by the promulgation of the 2005 Act, the statements in the older preparatory works still have relevance. The rules in the older Act were meant as aids for the interpretation of insurance contracts, and were intended to protect third parties and ensure that the value of the insurance accrued to the person entitled to the value of the insured object. The rules in the current Act on Insurance Contracts acknowledge these rationales, even though they do not touch upon the issue of whether or not insurance contracts should be seen as contracts in favour of a third party, or whether the doctrinal explanation is to be found elsewhere. It is likely that the doctrinal explanation of the third-party effects was deemed to be of little practical importance.

The touched-upon rules on real property are based on the idea that the landlord is seen primarily as a creditor in relation to the tenant. Any *'borgenärsförpliktelser'* (obligations of the creditor) are considered to be tied to the building rather than the contracting landlord's person. Therefore, a building can be sold quite freely, affecting a change of creditor (whereas a change of debtor (tenant) requires the consent of the creditor (landlord)). To mitigate unwanted consequences for the tenant due to the liberal rules on transferability of the property, exceptions have been introduced to the general rule that purchase breaks actions of lease. These exceptions are intended to protect the tenant's legitimate interest of tenancy, as well as investments made by commercial tenants. The rules attempt to strike a balance between the parties' often incompatible interests, and in effect prevent landlords from getting rid of all their tenants by selling properties.[82]

As regards the construction contract, see Cases 1 and 3 above.

3. COMPARATIVE REMARKS

Jan Biemans and Lorna Richardson

This case study sought to explore the extent to which contracts relating to an asset pass with the asset when it transfers from one owner to another. Would the related contract pass by operation of law, or would some act be required on the part of the existing or the new owner, or both? Other issues that arise are whether some types of contract transfer but others do not, and, if so, why this is the case. Would obligations under the contract transfer, or only rights? The given scenario considers a lease of real estate, an insurance contract for the property, and a contract for works to the property.

---

[82] See e.g. E. Björkdahl, *Hyra av bostad och lokal*, 2nd ed., Iustus, Uppsala 2018, pp. 263 ff.

The Rental Contract

In all of the jurisdictions surveyed, the rental contract passes from Mr Joyce to Mr Watts (but no novation). All jurisdictions have specific provisions in their Civil Codes or other legislation dealing with the situation.

Some reporters noted that certain conditions would, however, have to be satisfied before the transfer would take place. In many jurisdictions (Belgium, Bulgaria, France, Scotland, Spain and Sweden), registration of the rental contract – for example, in the property register or with the tax authority – would be necessary. The rationale of the registration requirement seems to be the prevention of ante-dating the rental contract. As an alternative to registration, there could, in some jurisdictions (Belgium, Bulgaria, Germany, Scotland and Sweden), have been occupation of the property by Adams Corp. prior to the sale of the building to Watts, which also relates to publicity. In Scotland and Sweden, occupation of the property would have to be accompanied by a written rental contract. Another condition was that Watts had been made aware of the lease (Bulgaria and Sweden), or that the contract for the sale of the building mentioned the rental agreement and the amount of rent (France). In the Czech Republic, the new owner is bound only by contractual provisions setting out the lessor's obligations which follow from the law, or other provisions which are known to the new owner. This is similar to the position in Scotland, where only the rights and obligations that are *inter naturalia* of the lease pass to the new owner; that is, those rights that are not considered as personal rights between the contracting parties (for instance, an option to purchase the leased premises would be considered a personal right). Some jurisdictions, such as the Netherlands and Poland, do not impose any additional requirements: the rental contract always passes by operation of law, giving the most protection to the lessee.

Interestingly, in English law, while the rental contract would automatically transfer to Watts, certain obligations under it would remain with Joyce until he is released from them by Adams Corp. Joyce would be required, by legislation, to seek such release within four weeks of the transfer of the building to Watts.

The Insurance Contract

On this issue, there was a division in the legal systems surveyed, with the rights and obligations under the contract passing to Watts in the majority of jurisdictions (Belgium, Bulgaria, France, Germany, the Netherlands, Spain and Sweden). In all of these jurisdictions, there were specific legal provisions regulating the matter. Some reporters (Belgium, the Netherlands) mentioned that the rights and obligations passed for an initial period of time to Watts following the sale of the building, allowing the new owner to conclude a new insurance contract in the meantime. In Belgian, Bulgarian, French, German and Spanish law, the transfer was based on the fact that the insurance contract passed with the building.

The Italian reporters considered it possible that the rights and obligations under the contract would pass, but the Czech reporters considered this unlikely in their jurisdiction. In the remaining jurisdictions (England, Poland, Scotland and Slovakia), the rights and obligations would not automatically pass, but could be transferred by further actions – assignment or novation – by Joyce and Watts. In Slovakia, the claim would be transferred were the sale to be classified as a sale of an enterprise, which would include the transfer of all related assets.

The Contract for Works

In relation to this contract, there is a clear split between those jurisdictions which recognise that certain contracts might be an accessory to an asset and, as such, pass automatically with it, and those which do not. This part of the case shows similarities with Case 2 above. In Belgian and Dutch law, rights under the contract pass to Watts, as qualitative rights related to the 'quality' of the new owner. Only in the Netherlands might the new owner become liable for the obligations arising out of the contract. In French law, any claim to damages arising under the contract passes, but not any other rights or obligations arising from it.

The Bulgarian reporter noted that the rights and obligations under the contract would pass to Watts if a provision to that effect was made in the sales contract or by separate agreement. The German reporter commented that the rights and obligations would transfer to Watts if all parties had expressly or impliedly agreed to this. The fact that the contract can be assigned impliedly brings German law closer to the automatic transfer of the claims similar to the jurisdictions mentioned in the preceding paragraph.

In the other jurisdictions surveyed, the rights and obligations would not automatically pass to Watts, but the reporters mentioned that they could be assigned or novated.

CASE 6: INDIRECT AGENCY AND SALES CONTRACTS

1. CASE

Xervix Inc. sells and acquires paintings and real estate for wealthy private clients who wish to remain anonymous. Xervix enters into contracts with the sellers and buyers of the valuable items, and receives the money in the event of a sale, and the paintings or real estate in the event of a purchase, each time in its own name for the benefit of its private clients.

In particular, the money is wired to one of Xervix's bank accounts, paintings are handed over to Xervix and stored on Xervix's premises, and deeds of transfer for disposal of real property are signed by Xervix, with the keys of real property acquired being handed over to Xervix. The parties dealing with Xervix know that Xervix acts as an intermediary.

On Wednesday 22 February 2017, Xervix sells two Mesdag paintings to Mr Ross for €180,000, for the benefit of Mrs Brown. Mr Ross has not yet paid. Xervix acquires a Van Dyck painting worth €3 million, for the benefit of Mr Landwell. The painting is handed over to an employee of Xervix. Xervix also acquires an apartment for Mr and Mrs Astor.

Assume that Xervix have not yet taken any action by Thursday 23 February 2017.

Questions

1. On that date, who are the owners of the Van Dyck painting and the apartment?
2. Assuming Xervix are the owners of the Van Dyck painting and the apartment, if Xervix become insolvent do Mr Landwell and Mr and Mrs Astor have any rights in relation to those assets in preference to Xervix's general creditors?
3. As at 23 February 2017, can Mrs Brown sue Mr Ross for the purchase price of the Mesdag paintings?
4. Does your answer to question 3 change if Xervix are insolvent?
5. What happens if Mr Ross pays the purchase price for the Mesdag paintings into Xervix's bank account and Xervix become insolvent before they have paid the money over to Mrs Brown?

2. DISCUSSIONS

2.1. BELGIUM

Siel Demeyere and Vincent Sagaert

I. Operative Rules

1. The principals own the Van Dyck painting and the apartment.
2. Ownership is transferred immediately to the principals, so that Xervix's general creditors have no right to it.
3. Mrs Brown can claim payment on Xervix's behalf.
4. Mrs Brown can claim payment from Mr Ross directly.
5. Mrs Brown would have to seek payment of the money as an ordinary creditor of Xervix.

II. Descriptive Formants

This is a case of indirect agency (cf. Case 4 above), more precisely a *commissieovereenkomst/contrat de commission* (commission contract), where the fact of the agency is known to the contracting parties. As previously explained, the contractual rights and obligations arise between the agent and the contracting party, while the proprietary legal effects of the contract arise immediately between the contracting party and the principal. Moreover, ownership passes, in Belgian law, from the moment of consent between the contracting parties, without any need for formalisation, both with regard to moveables and immoveables.[1] This is the principle of 'consensual transfer'.

Regarding question 1, the above-mentioned principles result in the conclusion that the principals – Mr Landwell and Mr and Mrs Astor, respectively – own the Van Dyck painting and the apartment.[2]

Regarding question 2, as mentioned above, the principal immediately becomes the owner of the goods acquired by the agent on their behalf, which entails that they have a right of ownership. The principal's right of ownership is protected against the insolvency of the agent, and the true owner can lodge

1 Art. 3.14, §2 BCC.

2 A transfer of ownership (even of immoveable property) does not require registration in order to be valid between the contracting parties. The registration, which is, however, necessary to ensure third-party effectiveness of the transfer, will be done in the name of the principals, since they own the apartment.

a proprietary claim for delivery from the agent's bankruptcy trustee, through a revindication, while the property is still in the possession of Xervix.[3]

Third parties in good faith, however, can treat Xervix as the owners. A third party in good faith with a concurring right on the apartment would, therefore, have preference over Mr and Mrs Astor if the ownership title had not yet been transferred into the public register in their names.[4]

Regarding question 3, the payment of the purchase price is a contractual obligation, and is thus not situated on a proprietary level.[5] Thus, it is not possible to avoid Xervix; Mrs Brown has to claim the price from Xervix. Nevertheless, Mrs Brown can claim the payment from Mr Ross through a *zijdelingse vordering/action oblique* (oblique action), except if Xervix have gone bankrupt.[6] An oblique action would entails that she act as a representative of Xervix, and Mr Ross would have to pay the money to Xervix rather than directly to Mrs Brown.

Regarding question 4, in the event of insolvency of the agent, the principal is better protected. Mrs Brown can claim the payment of the price pursuant to a sales agreement entered into by an agent, directly from the counterparty, Mr Ross. Article XX.196, paragraph 2 WER protects the claim for payment of the price arising from a sales contract concluded by an indirect agent, against the insolvency of that agent (cf. Case 4 above).[7]

Regarding question 5, as money is a *genus* good, the money paid intermixes with the rest of the money in Xervix's bank account, such that the money obtained for Mrs Brown cannot be separated from the other money therein. Therefore, Mrs Brown cannot exercise any proprietary claim against Xervix.[8] The result would be different if the money was wired to a protected *derdenrekening/compte tiers* (third-party account) of persons with a profession within which such accounts are imposed by professional rules (attorneys, public notaries, bailiffs and real estate brokers) are protected against the insolvency of such persons.[9] Mrs Brown has a claim against Xervix for the money.

---

3 I. Samoy, *Middellijke vertegenwoordiging: vertegenwoordiging herbekeken vanuit het optreden in eigen naam voor andermans rekening*, Intersentia, Antwerp 2005, 341, no. 519.

4 Art. 3.30 BCC.

5 Even if a claim for money could be considered property, this is not how this is dealt with in view of indirect agency in current Belgian law.

6 Art. 5.242 BCC; I. Samoy, *Middellijke vertegenwoordiging: vertegenwoordiging herbekeken vanuit het optreden in eigen naam voor andermans rekening*, Intersentia, Antwerp 2005, 276, no. 414.

7 Art. XX.196, second clause, WER; I. Samoy, *Middellijke vertegenwoordiging: vertegenwoordiging herbekeken vanuit het optreden in eigen naam voor andermans rekening*, Intersentia, Antwerp 2005, 332, no. 508.

8 Cass. 30 October 1947, *Arr.Cass.* 1947, 341.

9 Art. 3.37 BCC.

2.2. BULGARIA

Petar Topurov

I. *Operative Rules*

1. On 23 February 2017, Xervix is the owner of both the Van Dyck painting and the apartment, with regard to all third parties. Considering the relationship with Mr Landwell and Mr and Mrs Astor, the property is deemed to be the rights of the principals (i.e. Mr and Mrs Astor).
2. If Xervix falls into insolvency, the rights over the painting and the apartment should be considered Mr Landwell's and Mr and Mrs Astor's rights with respect to the company's creditors.
3. On 23 February 2017, Mrs Brown cannot file a claim against Mr Ross over the purchase price of the Mesdag painting.
4. The answer will not differ should Xervix fall into insolvency.
5. The sum paid by Mr Ross shall be paid to Mrs Brown by the syndic of Xervix.

II. *Descriptive Formants*

Relations between Xervix and its customers lead to the conclusion of a commission contract under which the company concludes certain transactions in its own name, but for the benefit of its clients, who wish to remain anonymous.

The specificity of the legal framework of that contract is that the law contains a legal fiction on holding over the rights acquired by the commissioner at the expense of the principal. This fiction consists in the fact that the rights acquired by the commissioner are considered to be the rights of the principal vis-à-vis the creditors of the commission agent and the agent himself, even though these rights have not been transferred (Art. 349, paragraph 2 CA). At the same time, under the transaction concluded with the third party in fulfilment of the principal's order, the rights and obligations arise for the commissioner (Art. 349, paragraph 1 CA).

The deliberations given in Case 4 above hold true here to substantiate the findings in the answer to question 2. The option for the principal of a commission contract to file a claim against the third party with whom the commissioner is in a contractual relationship is regulated in Art. 349, paragraph 4 CA. The principal may exercise the rights with respect to a third person only after the transfer thereof by the commission merchant, and on condition that the third party has not yet performed their obligations towards the commission merchant.[10]

[10] T. Yossifova, *The commission contract*, Sibi, Sofia 2006, p. 43.

With regard to the conclusions on questions 4 and 5, the applicable argumentation is that detailed in Case 4 above. Notwithstanding Xervix's insolvency, receivables under the contract of sale are deemed rights outwith the commissioner's insolvent estate, provided the principal has performed his/her obligations.[11] It is necessary, however, after initiating the insolvency proceedings, for the syndic[12] of the insolvent company to transfer in Mrs Brown's favour the rights acquired from Mr Ross, ensuing from the execution transaction (the contract of sale). Mrs Brown could also demand the separation of rights acquired at her expense, based on the fiction according to Art. 349, paragraph 2 CA.[13] The rights acquired by the commissioner shall be considered against his creditors for principal's rights, even before their transfer to the latter. Where the syndic refuses to cooperate, legal doctrine accepts the option that the principal has the right to file a claim under Art. 349, paragraph 2 CA,[14] seeking a court decision that the principal is the holder of certain rights.

Mrs Brown would be entitled to receive the purchase price from Xervix's bank account. However, if there are no sums left in the bank account, Mrs Brown could file a revocation claim, resulting in the sums representing the sale price having to be returned to Xervix, and then transferred to her by the syndic of the company.

III. Meta-Legal Formants

The moment and manner of transferring ownership of the right acquired by the commissioner is an issue of debate in legal doctrine. According to some authors, the ownership of individual moveables passes automatically, while others believe that, for this purpose, an additional transfer needs to take place between the commissioner and the principal.[15] A number of examples in the existing case law show that the principal may file a claim for the establishment of their property against the commission agent without concluding a transfer deal between the commissioner and the principal.[16]

---

11 G. Grigorov, *Insolvency*, Sibi, Sofia 2017, p. 166; T. Yossifova, *The commission contract*, Sibi, Sofia 2006, p. 97.

12 Person who manages a company after bankruptcy.

13 T. Yossifova, *The commission contract*, Sibi, Sofia 2006, p. 97.

14 Ibid., p. 61.

15 See different views described in T. Yossifova, *The commission contract*, Sibi, Sofia 2006, pp. 37–46.

16 Decision No. 375 of 03.01.2012 of the BSCC on civil case No. 288/2011; Order No. 726 of 02.07.2009 of the BSCC on civil case No. 842/2009.

2.3. CZECH REPUBLIC

Tomáš Richter

I. Operative Rules

As regards question 1, *Xervix would be the owner of the Van Dyck painting and the apartment* on 23 February 2017.

As regards question 2, *it is presently unclear* whether Mr Landwell and Mr and Mrs Astor would have any rights in relation to the assets in question. This would depend on whether the courts took a narrow or an expansive view of a particular provision of the CC.

As regards questions 3 and 4, *Mrs Brown will likely not be able to sue Mr Ross unless Xervix or its insolvency administrator cooperate* with Mrs Brown to that end.

As regards question 5, the *money paid to Xervix by Mr Ross will probably belong to Xervix's insolvent estate*, unless the courts take an expansive view of a particular provision of the CC.

II. Descriptive Formants

Most of the relevant rules on *'komise'* (undisclosed agency) have been described and discussed in relation to Case 4 above. In this Case 6, these rules fit the facts better than in Case 4, since the CC's rules actually clearly assume that the transaction to be procured by the agent is a sale and purchase transaction. Having said that, this does not mean that clear answers always follow from those rules.

In relation to question 1, it seems clear from section 2456 CC that Xervix, not Mr Landwell or Mr and Mrs Astor, acquired ownership of the Van Dyck painting and apartment on 22 February 2017.

In relation to question 2, the outcome would depend on whether one construed the rule in section 2464(2) CC (discussed in relation to Case 4) narrowly or broadly. To recap, the rule in section 2464(2) CC provides that a receivable arising under a contract entered into by the agent for the principal's account shall be deemed, for the purposes of the relationship between the principal and the agent *or the agent's creditors* (emphasis added), to belong to the principal. On the facts of Case 6, there seem to be no more outstanding receivables with respect to the transaction involving the Van Dyck painting (the facts posit that the painting was handed over to an employee of Xervix) or the apartment (the apartment is said to have been 'acquired', i.e. ownership title to the apartment has, presumably, already passed from the seller). Therefore, if one reads the rule narrowly, there would have been no receivables on 23 February 2017 which could enjoy the protection against Xervix's other creditors afforded by section 2464(2) CC. If, on the other hand, one read the rule broadly in order to also include the proceeds of those receivables collected by the agent,[17] Mr Landwell and Mr and Mrs Astor could argue that the Van Dyck painting and the apartment do not belong to Xervix's insolvent estate. Presumably, given the obvious value of those assets, the question would need to be litigated in Xervix's insolvency proceedings, which might lead to judicial clarification of the meaning of section 2464(2) CC.

In relation to questions 3 and 4, it is clear that Mrs Brown enjoys the protection afforded by section 2464(2) CC, even on its narrow construction, since, as the facts posit, Mr Ross has not yet paid the purchase price of the two Mesdag paintings. Therefore, there is an outstanding receivable to which section 2464(2) CC applies. Whether Mrs Brown can sue Mr Ross in order to enforce that receivable depends on the construction of sections 2466 and 2467 CC. To recap, section 2466 CC provides, in its first sentence, that where a third party defaults on an obligation under a contract concluded with an agent, the agent shall enforce such obligations for the principal's account. The second sentence of section 2466 CC provides that, where the principal so agrees, the agent may delegate (or 'assign', in a verbatim translation of the provision's words) such enforcement rights to the principal. Section 2467 CC provides that the principal may demand performance procured by the agent from the third party in the event that the agent is not capable of doing so for reasons arising on the agent's part. It is clear from these rules that it is primarily the agent (Xervix) who has the standing to sue Mr Ross for the payment of the purchase price of the two Mesdag paintings. However, it is also clear that neither Xervix nor any of its other creditors will obtain any real benefit from such enforcement action, because section 2464(2) CC means that those receivables are deemed to belong to Mrs Brown, not Xervix or its estate. Xervix would, therefore, have to incur the costs of the enforcement action but obtain no real benefits from it, since these benefits would pertain to the principals.[18] One may, therefore, assume that Xervix (or their insolvency administrator, depending on who holds the relevant power at which point in the insolvency proceedings) might be willing to delegate the enforcement rights to Mrs Brown pursuant to the second sentence of section 2466 CC. Whether the insolvency of Xervix would, of itself, amount to a circumstance qualifying as an event rendering the agent incapable of enforcing the receivables for the purposes of section 2467 CC is an open question; however, such an interpretation seems rather unlikely.

In relation to question 5, the answer is essentially the same as those to questions 1 and 2; that is, Xervix would probably be considered the owner of the

17 See V. Pihera in M. Hulmák et al., *Občanský zákoník V, Závazkové právo, Obecná část (§1721–2054), První vydání*, C.H. Beck, Praha 2014.

18 The details of this analysis would, of course, depend on the actual terms of the contract between Mrs Brown and Xervix as regards Xervix's fees and expenses, as to which the facts of the case posit nothing, as well as on the impacts of Xervix's insolvency on that contract.

money paid to it by Mr Ross, and the money would be treated as belonging to Xervix's insolvent estate. A different outcome would only obtain if Mrs Brown managed to persuade the courts that the rule in section 2464(2) CC (discussed above) should be construed broadly and 'ring-fence' not only claims arising under a contract entered into by the agent for the principal's account but also collections made on such claims. As explained above, this is an open question.

III. Meta-Legal Formants

Notably, the lot of Mr Landwell is much worse under the CC than it would have been prior to 31 December 2013 under the CommC. That code provided, in section 583, second sentence, that the principal acquired ownership of moveables purchased for his or her account directly at the moment the purchased thing was handed over to the agent. The CC did not carry this rule over, resulting in a legal outcome whereby, in purchase transactions conducted via *'komise'* (undisclosed agency), the ownership is now acquired by the agent, who must then transfer the thing acquired on to the principal.[19]

2.4. ENGLAND AND WALES

T.T. Arvind

I. Operative Rules

1. The ownership of the Van Dyck painting will remain with the original seller until property passes, at which stage it will pass directly to Mr Landwell. The ownership of the apartment will depend on who has been registered as the owner. If Xervix are the registered owner, they will be deemed to hold the apartment in trust for the Astors.
2. Landwell is unlikely to have any preferential rights to the painting if Xervix are the owners. The Astors, as owners of the beneficial interest in the apartment, will be able to have it excluded from Xervix's estate in the insolvency.
3. Mrs Brown can sue Mr Ross for the purchase price of the painting if it has fallen due.
4. The agent's insolvency does not affect the answer to question 3.
5. Mrs Brown will be in the position of an unsecured creditor in relation to money paid into Xervix's account.

---

[19] V. Pihera in M. Hulmák et al., *Občanský zákoník V, Závazkové právo, Obecná část (§1721–2054), První vydání*, C.H. Beck, Praha 2014, p. 852 at 6.

II. *Descriptive Formants*

Question 1

Given that the parties dealing with Xervix know that Xervix is acting on behalf of another person, Xervix will, in law, be the agent of a disclosed but unidentified principal (see Case 4 above). The general rule established by case law is that, in a contract for sale of goods entered into by an agent, property in the goods passes directly from the principal to the purchaser. If an agent is in possession of the property in their capacity as agent, the agent's possession is, in law, deemed to be the principal's possession.[20] As a result, the seller of the Van Dyck painting will remain the owner of the property until such time as property passes to Mr Landwell. The time when property passes depends on the parties' intention,[21] but in the absence of any indication of a contrary intention, the property in the painting will pass as soon as the contract to sell it has been made.[22] In such a case, Mr Landwell will be the owner on 23 February 2017.

Legal ownership of the apartment will vest in whoever has been registered as the owner in the Land Registry.[23] If this was the Astors, then they will be the owners, even if the transaction was wholly carried out by Xervix. If, however, the apartment was registered in Xervix's name, then Xervix will be deemed by law to be the legal owners by virtue of registration. If so, it is settled law that Xervix will hold the property as trustee for their principals – in this case, the Astors.[24] Where a trust exists, English law recognises two different types of ownership in the property. The first is 'legal ownership', which vests with the trustee. At the same time, however, the beneficiaries of the trust also have a proprietary interest in the property, which is called 'beneficial ownership' or 'equitable title'. The Astors will, therefore, have beneficial ownership of the apartment, even if Xervix are the registered owners.

Question 2

In English law, property acquired by an agent in their capacity as agent is treated as the principal's property (see question 1 above). As a result, Xervix would only be the owners of the Van Dyck painting if they had acquired the painting on their own behalf rather than as Landwell's agent, and subsequently resold it to Landwell, as the general principle is that a person who purchases goods

---

20 *John Cooper v. Fermin De Tastet* [1829] Tamlyn 178, (1829) 48 ER 71, 72.
21 Sale of Goods Act 1979 (SOGA), s. 17(1).
22 Ibid., s. 18, Rule 1.
23 Land Registration Act 2002 (LRA), s. 58.
24 P.G. Watts and F.M.B. Reynolds (eds), *Bowstead & Reynolds on Agency*, 21st ed. (London: Sweet & Maxwell, 2017), para. 2-037.

as an agent does not become the owner of the goods. In such a case, Xervix's relationship with Landwell is that of buyer and seller. Case law has established that, where property in goods has not passed to the buyer, the buyer has only a personal claim for breach of contract against the seller, even if they have paid the full price.[25] Landwell will, therefore, not have any preferential claim against Xervix.

The position is different as regards the Astors' claim to the apartment. As discussed in the response to question 1, the Astors will have beneficial ownership of the apartment and Xervix will hold the apartment on trust for them. Property held as trustee is not considered part of the bankrupt's estate under the Insolvency Act 1986.[26] As a result, the apartment will not form part of Xervix's assets in insolvency and the Astors will be able to maintain their beneficial ownership.

Question 3

As discussed in Case 4 above, a disclosed principal can sue on a contract entered into by their agent, as long as the transaction is either within the agent's authority or subsequently ratified by the principal. This case is likely to fall into the former category, giving Mrs Brown the right to sue Mr Ross for payment of the purchase price once it falls due.

Question 4

The right of a principal to sue on a contract within the agent's authority is not affected by the agent's insolvency. This is because, as discussed under Case 4, English law treats contracts made by an agent as being the principal's contract and not the agent's.

Question 5

English law treats money held by the agent for the principal differently from goods or other property. Older authority suggested that the agent would, in some situations, be in a position akin to that of a trustee in relation to money which it held for its principal,[27] especially if the money was received after the agent's insolvency.[28] However, these cases are no longer followed, and in a recent case the

---

25 *Carlos Federspiel & Co. SA v. Charles Twigg & Co. Ltd* [1957] 1 Lloyd's Rep. 240.
26 Insolvency Act 1986, s. 283(3).
27 *Scott v. Surman* (1743) Willes 400, (1743) 125 ER 1235.
28 *Neste Oy v. Lloyds Bank plc* [1983] 2 Lloyd's Rep. 658.

Supreme Court expressed the view that the older decisions cannot be justified.[29] The current approach is better represented by cases like *Triffit Nurseries v. Salads Etcetera Ltd*,[30] in which it was held that a grower of salad vegetables who transacted with supermarkets through an agent did not have a preferential claim to the proceeds of sale held by the agent, and was merely an unsecured creditor in the agent's insolvency. In essence, the court is, in these cases, asking whether it is appropriate to import a trust into an ordinary commercial relationship. It is, therefore, possible for parties to structure their transactions in a manner that makes the agent a trustee of money it receives on behalf of the principal, for example by requiring the money to be held in a segregated account and only used for specified purposes rather than being mingled with the agent's general funds.[31] Absent such specific arrangements, however, Mrs Brown will stand in the position of an unsecured creditor in relation to proceeds of sale held by Xervix.

III. Meta-Legal Formants

Question 1

English law regards the key aspect of an agency as being the legal power of the agent to bind the principal, and thus to alter the principal's legal relations with third parties. This has led to a number of duties being imposed on agents in relation to the manner in which they exercise that legal power. The duties that bind agents are, in consequence, far stricter than those that apply in other types of commercial contracts.[32] One manifestation of this is that agents owe very strict duties to their principals when it comes to title to property. Property acquired by agents in their capacity as agents is treated as being not their own property, but the principal's property, and agents are legally precluded from asserting that they have a title superior to their principal's, to such property.[33] An agent such as Xervix will, in consequence, only acquire title to property if they can clearly demonstrate that their acquisition of that property was not done in respect of the agency.[34]

---

29 *Angove's Pty Ltd v. Bailey* [2016] UKSC 47, [2016] 1 WLR 3179 [31].

30 [2000] 2 Lloyd's Rep. 74 (CA).

31 *Barclays Bank Ltd v. Quistclose Investments Ltd* [1970] AC 567 (HL); *Cooper v. PRG Powerhouse Ltd* [2008] EWHC 498 (Ch), [2008] 2 All ER (Comm) 964.

32 For an overview, see F.E. Dowrick, 'The Relationship of Principal and Agent' (1954) 17 *Modern Law Review* 24.

33 P.G. Watts and F.M.B. Reynolds (eds), *Bowstead & Reynolds on Agency*, 21st ed. (London: Sweet & Maxwell, 2017), para. 6-111.

34 *Attorney-General v. Corporation of London* (1850) 2 Mac & G 247, 259 (Lord Cottenham LC).

Question 5

The decision of the Supreme Court in *Angove's Pty Ltd v. Bailey*[35] sheds light on the reasons underpinning the differential treatment of goods and money in English law. In general, English law avoids reassigning property rights after the fact. If a trust is to be recognised, it is crucial that the property over which the trust is recognised be *both* identifiable *and* not available to the person holding it as part of their general assets.[36] This will almost never be the case in relation to money held by an agent as part of their general funds: even if the money is identifiable, it will still be available to the agent as part of their general assets, unless it is held in a segregated bank account subject to special requirements. As a result, the money will be treated as the agent's money, and the principal will only be in the position of an unsecured creditor in relation to that money.

2.5. FRANCE

Sylvain Ravenne and Flora Vern

I. *Operative Rules*

1. Mr Landwell owns the Van Dyck painting. The Astors own the apartment.
2. There is no need for a preference, given the answer to question 1.
3. Mrs Brown would be able to sue Mr Ross if Xervix failed to seek payment from him.
4. Mrs Brown would be able to sue Mr Ross.
5. Mrs Brown cannot take action against Mr Ross. She would have to claim the purchase price in Xervix's insolvency.

II. *Descriptive Formants*

Question 1

In this case the fact that Xervix are acting as an intermediary is known by all of the parties. Therefore, Xervix are not acting as a *'prête-nom'* (undisclosed mandatary) in a simulated contract, but as a *'commissionaire'* (agent on commission), according to Article L.132-1 of the Commercial Code.

While an agent on commission is personally bound by the contracts they undertake, ownership of the thing which is sold or bought is transferred directly

[35] [2016] UKSC 47, [2016] 1 WLR 3179.
[36] Ibid., [27]–[29].

from the principal to the buyer, or from the seller to the principal.[37] Thus, Xervix never owned the Van Dyck painting or the apartment: they are owned by Mr Landwell and the Astors respectively. Under French law, the transfer of ownership of both moveable and immoveable things happens whenever their sale is concluded, unless the parties agree to delay the transfer.[38] Land registration is not a condition for the effectiveness of the transfer of ownership of the apartment. To be recorded in the land register, Mr and Mrs Astor would need to have the sales contract between the seller and Xervix, as well as their own agreement with Xervix, authenticated by a notary. Otherwise, only Xervix could be registered, as the sales contract bears their name.

Question 2

Question 2 is irrelevant in French law, considering the answer to question 1. Nevertheless, if Xervix had been a '*prête-nom*' (undisclosed mandatary) and, as such, had become the owner of the painting and the apartment, the transfer of ownership would be subject to the rules relative to '*simulation*' (simulated contracts). On this hypothesis, the sales contracts would be the 'apparent contract', concealing the fact that Xervix are merely a '*prête-nom*' and not the intended owners of the property. As a result, the intended sales contracts would be simulated, because the contract between the original owners and the mandatary would be hidden from the buyers. In that specific case, Article 1201 of the FCC provides that the '*contre-lettre*' – the hidden contract between the prospective buyers and Xervix – would take effect between the parties to it, but produce no binding effect with respect to third parties (who, on the other hand, could still rely on it whenever it was in their interests to do so). Accordingly, the agreements between Xervix and the prospective buyers – Mr Landwell and the Astors, respectively – would not be enforceable against Xervix's general creditors, who are third parties to these agreements. Mr Landwell and the Astors would have no right in preference to the creditors.[39]

However, by means of an action in declaration of simulation, the prospective buyers can prevent the apparent contract from being invoked against them. Thus, they can reveal the existence of the '*contre-lettre*' and claim that Xervix were merely an undisclosed mandatary who never acquired the apartment or the painting. Because the hidden contract would thereby become apparent, third parties – among them, Xervix's creditors – would no longer be able to invoke the apparent contract.

---

37 Cass., crim., 18 nov. 1882, D. 1883, 1, 230; Cass., com., 7 mars 2000, Bull. civ. IV, n° 46.

38 Arts. 1196 and 1583 FCC.

39 F. Terré, P. Simler, Y. Lequette and F. Chénedé, *Droit civil, les obligations*, 13th ed. (Paris: Dalloz, 2022), n° 739; J.L. Aubert, É. Savaux and J. Flour, *Droit Civil. Les Obligations. L'Acte Juridique*, 17th ed. (Paris: Sirey, 2022), n° 613.

Question 3

As explained above,[40] case law from the Cour de cassation provides that, where an agent on commission acts as an intermediary between the principal and a third party, each of them has a claim against the agent, but they have no direct claim against each other.[41]

However, should Xervix fail to claim payment of the purchase price of the painting from Mr Ross, Mrs Brown might sue the latter on the behalf of the former through an '*action oblique*' (indirect or oblique action).[42] This action is only meant to protect a creditor against their debtor's inaction. In the present situation, the purchase price would, at least in theory, be paid to Xervix before reaching Mrs Brown, implying that it may be seized by other creditors should Xervix already be insolvent.

Moreover, according to some authors,[43] Mrs Brown could declare her intention to benefit from the contract, regardless of whether or not Xervix failed to claim payment. Thus, she would be substituted for the agent on commission, Xervix, and become the seller. As a consequence, she would be able to sue Mr Ross for the outstanding price of the painting.

Question 4

If Xervix were insolvent, it would be against Mrs Brown's interests to sue Mr Ross through an oblique action, because the price would be paid to Xervix. In this situation, she should declare her intention to benefit from the sale and sue Mr Ross.

Question 5

If Mr Ross pays the purchase price to Xervix before Mrs Brown has declared her intention to benefit from the sale, she, as the principal, has no choice but to sue Xervix, her agent on commission, in restitution of this sum of money. The Cour de cassation does not recognise property claims on money.[44] Therefore, Mrs Brown only has a contractual claim against Xervix. This implies that her claim will be subject to the rules of Xervix's insolvency procedure. If, however,

---

40 See Case 4.

41 Cass., civ., 20 juill. 1871, DP 1871, 1, 232; Cass., com., 15 juill. 1963, Bull. civ., 1963 IV, n° 378; Cass., com., 30 oct. 2000, n° 98-12236.

42 Art. 1341-1 FCC.

43 P. Delebecque and F. Collart-Dutilleul, *Contrats Civils & Commerciaux*, 12th ed. (Paris: Dalloz, 2023), n° 663; J.L. Aubert, É. Savaux and J. Flour, *Droit Civil. Les Obligations. L'Acte Juridique*, 17th ed. (Paris: Sirey, 2022), n° 389.

44 Cass., com., 22 mai 2013, Bull. civ. IV, n° 87.

both requirements have been fulfilled – namely that Mrs Brown has declared her intention to benefit from the sale, and this is known to Mr Ross – payment by Mr Ross to Xervix would not be valid and Mrs Brown would be able to sue Mr Ross for the price.

2.6. GERMANY

Sonja Meier

I. *Operative Rules*

1. Xervix are the owners of the painting and, assuming that they have been registered as proprietor in the land register, the apartment.
2. According to the courts, Mr Landwell and the Astors will not have any rights in preference to the general creditors.
3. Mrs Brown cannot sue Mr Ross.
4. Presently, Mrs Brown cannot sue Mr Ross, but she will be able to sue him after an assignment of the claim.
5. According to the courts, the purchase price becomes part of the insolvency estate of Xervix. Most commentators, in contrast, would allow Mrs Brown to claim the money in preference to the general creditors, as long as it can be traced and identified.

II. *Descriptive Formants*

Question 1

1. According to §929 BGB, a transfer of property in moveable goods like a painting requires an agreement between the transferor and the transferee. This agreement is a contract to which the general rules on agency apply. Agency requires the agent to act in the name of the principal (§164 BGB). An exception, called *'Vertrag für den, den es angeht'* (transaction for whom it concerns), is sometimes made where the identity of their contractual partner is not relevant to a party. This is assumed in the case of cash transactions in daily life, but not where, as in the present case, valuable goods are involved.[45] Since Xervix contracted in their own name, the parties to the agreement are the seller and

[45] C. Schubert in *Münchener Kommentar zum BGB*, vol. 1 (9th ed., Beck 2021), §164, [140]–[148]; E. Schilken in *J. von Staudingers Kommentar zum Bürgerlichen Gesetzbuch*, vol. §§164–240 (Sellier – de Gruyter 2019), before §164, [53]–[54].

Xervix. §929 BGB further requires the delivery of possession to the transferee. This took place when the painting was handed over to Xervix's employee, for, according to §855 BGB, physical control of an object by the employee constitutes possession on the part of the employer (in this case, Xervix).

If the parties to the commission contract want Mr Landwell to acquire ownership of the painting at the earliest possible moment, they can provide for a second transfer of ownership immediately after Xervix acquire ownership from the seller. The necessary agreement between Xervix and Mr Landwell can be made beforehand (a so-called anticipated transfer of ownership). Such a transfer will not usually be made under §929 BGB, which requires the delivery of possession to the transferee (Mr Landwell), since Xervix will not usually be able to deliver the painting immediately to the transferee; instead, it will be made under §930 BGB. According to this provision, physical delivery of the object from the transferor (Xervix) to the transferee (Mr Landwell) can be substituted by an agreement between the parties that the transferor (Xervix) remains in physical possession but possesses the object henceforth on behalf of the transferee (the so-called *constitutum possessorium*). The effect of such an agreement would be that ownership is firstly transferred from the seller to Xervix and then immediately from Xervix to Mr Landwell.[46] Since Xervix will at least briefly acquire ownership of the painting, this solution could be risky for Mr Landwell in the event of Xervix's insolvency.

The only way the parties can avoid an intermediary acquisition by Xervix and provide for a direct transfer from the seller to Mr Landwell is for Xervix to conclude the contract with the seller openly as an agent; that is, by way of direct representation under §164 BGB. However, this requires that the agent acts in the name of another person, and thus makes clear to the third party that the effects of the contract will only affect the principal and not the agent. The identity of the principal does not necessarily have to be revealed to the third party by the agent. If the agent makes clear that they are acting, not in their own name, but for a principal who does not want to reveal their identity, and the third party agrees with this course of action, the contract will take effect between the third party and the principal.[47] Thus, the seller has the possibility to transfer ownership directly to an unknown person. A further possibility is that the agent concludes the contract in the name of a person to be identified by the agent in the future, if the other party agrees to this course of action. In this case, the contract will only

46 C. Schubert in *Münchener Kommentar zum BGB*, vol. 1 (9th ed., Beck 2021), §164, [53]; J. Oechsler in *Münchener Kommentar zum BGB*, vol. 8 (9th ed., Beck 2023), §930, [27]; F. Häuser in *Münchener Kommentar zum Handelsgesetzbuch*, vol. 5 (5th ed., Beck 2021), §392, [45].

47 C. Schubert in *Münchener Kommentar zum BGB*, vol. 1 (9th ed., Beck 2021), §164, [138]; E. Schilken in *J. von Staudingers Kommentar zum Bürgerlichen Gesetzbuch*, vol. §§164–240 (Sellier - de Gruyter 2019), before §164, [35a].

become effective (prospectively) if a third person willing to become a principal is identified. If the agent cannot name a principal in due course, they will be liable to the third party in a similar way to an agent acting without authority.[48]

2. Ownership of the apartment is a form of ownership of land. According to §§873, 925 BGB, the transfer of ownership of land requires a formal agreement between transferor and transferee, made before a notary, and a recording of the change in the Grundbuch (Land Register). Since Xervix have concluded the contract of transfer in their own name, they will become the owners as soon as they have been registered as the new proprietors. In order to transfer the apartment to Mr and Mrs Astor, Xervix will have to conclude a contract of transfer with them, and they will have to be registered as the new owners.

Since a transfer of land causes notary fees, registration fees and tax to be incurred, parties will, in practice, avoid making two successive transfers. The contract of transfer will be concluded between the seller and the principal or the commission agent acting in the principal's name, and the principal will be registered directly in the land register.

Question 2

According to the general rules, Mr Landwell and Mr and Mrs Astor would be insolvency creditors, since their claims to the items of property are only personal in nature. However, they would have a right to claim the items in priority to other creditors, under §47 InsO, called '*Aussonderung*', if §392 HGB could be applied in their favour. Xervix are commercial commission agents within the meaning of §§383, 406 HGB. According to §392 HGB, claims of a commission agent arising from their contracts with third parties are deemed to be claims of the principals in the relationship between the principals, on the one hand, and the commission agent and their creditors, on the other.[49] If the painting and the apartment had not yet been transferred to Xervix, Xervix would have had claims against the sellers for the transfer of the property, and §392 HGB would have enabled the clients to claim the assignment of these claims from the insolvency administrator in priority to other creditors. However, the wording of §392 HGB is confined to '*Forderungen*' (claims). According to the courts, the provision cannot be applied to surrogates of a claim.[50] Where the third party renders performance to the commission agent by transferring money or property to them, §392 HGB will not give the principal a right to these assets in preference to the general creditors.

---

48 C. Schubert in *Münchener Kommentar zum BGB*, vol. 1 (9th ed., Beck 2021), §164, [125], [138]–[139].

49 See Case 4, question 2 above.

50 BGH *NJW* 1974, 456; *BGHZ* 79, 89; OLG Hamm, *ZIP* 2003, 2262; BGH *NJW* 2010, 3578 at [15].

In contrast, the majority of writers want to apply §392 (2) HGB, by way of analogy, to surrogates of the claim.[51] It is argued that there is no reason why the protection of the principal should cease the moment the third party fulfils their obligation towards the commission agent. Such writers also point to recent statutory provisions which extend the protection of an indirect principal to surrogates of the claim, for example §457 HGB, in the law of transport. If §392 (2) HGB is applied, the clients will have the right, under §47 InsO, to prevent the sale of the painting and the apartment, and to have these items of property transferred to them in preference to the other creditors.

Question 3

Since Xervix acted in their own name, the parties to the contract of sale are Mr Ross and Xervix. Xervix can claim the purchase price, and Mrs Brown has a contractual right to an assignment of that claim. However, unless Xervix have assigned the claim to her, Mrs Brown cannot sue Mr Ross (§392 HGB).[52]

Question 4

According to §392 HGB, the claim for the purchase price is deemed to be a claim of the principal (Mrs Brown), in the relationship between her and the creditors of Xervix. In Xervix's insolvency, Mrs Brown has a right to *Aussonderung* according to §47 InsO, allowing her to prevent a realisation of the claim in favour of the general creditors, and to claim the assignment of the claim in a regular lawsuit outside the insolvency proceedings.[53] After the assignment, she will be able to sue Mr Ross.

Question 5

According to the courts, §392 (2) HGB does not apply to the surrogate of a claim, such as money paid in fulfilment of the obligation. The money in Xervix's bank account will, therefore, be part of the insolvency estate, to be realised for the benefit of the general creditors. Mrs Brown will have to claim the purchase price obtained by Xervix as a general creditor in the insolvency procedure.

---

51 C. Kumpan in K. Hopt, *Handelsgesetzbuch* (43rd ed., Beck 2024), §392, [7]; J.T. Füller in C.T. Ebenroth, K. Boujong, D. Joost and L. Strohn, *Handelsgesetzbuch*, vol. 2 (5th ed., Vahlen 2024), §392, [7]; H.G. Ganter in *Münchener Kommentar zur Insolvenzordnung*, vol. 1 (4th ed., Beck 2019), §47, [289]; E. Bäuerle in E. Braun and E. Bäuerle, *Insolvenzordnung* (9th ed., Beck 2022), §47, [87].

52 See Case 4, question 2.

53 Ibid.

According to the prevailing view among commentators, §392 (2) HGB has to be applied, by way of analogy, to the surrogate of a claim of the commission agent against the third party. Following this, Mrs Brown may have a right to *Aussonderung* of the purchase money, according to §47 InsO; that is, a right to have the money transferred to her outside the insolvency proceedings, and in preference to the general creditors. However, such a right requires that the money can still be identified as a separate asset in the patrimony of the commission agent.[54] If money has been paid into a bank account of the insolvency debtor that is also used for other transactions, courts will generally deny that the money is still identifiable, as long as the account is not used exclusively as a trust account.[55]

2.7. ITALY

Luca Ettore Perriello

I. *Operative Rules*

1. Mr Landwell is the owner of the Van Dyck painting. Xervix are the owners of the apartment.
2. Mr Landwell and Mr and Mrs Astor will take precedence over Xervix's general creditors.
3. Mrs Brown can sue Mr Ross for the purchase price of the Mesdag painting.
4. Mrs Brown can claim the purchase price even where Xervix are insolvent.
5. Mrs Brown will prevail over Xervix's creditors.

II. *Descriptive Formants*

A '*mandato senza rappresentanza*' (mandate without representation) is a contract whereby a party, known as '*mandatario*' (mandatary), undertakes to perform one or more legal acts for the account of the other party, the '*mandante*' (mandator), but in their own name. The mandatary acquires the rights and undertakes the duties arising from the contracts they conclude with third parties, even where

54 C. Kumpan in K. Hopt, *Handelsgesetzbuch* (43rd ed., Beck 2024), §392, [7]; F. Häuser in *Münchener Kommentar zum Handelsgesetzbuch*, vol. 5 (5th ed., Beck 2021), §392, [43]; J.T. Füller in C.T. Ebenroth, K. Boujong, D. Joost and L. Strohn, *Handelsgesetzbuch*, vol. 2 (5th ed., Vahlen 2024), §392, [7], [15]; H.G. Ganter in *Münchener Kommentar zur Insolvenzordnung*, vol. 1 (4th ed., Beck 2019), §47, [289]; E. Bäuerle in E. Braun and E. Bäuerle, *Insolvenzordnung* (9th ed., Beck 2022), §47, [87].

55 BGH *NJW-RR* 2003, 1375; BGH *NJW* 2010, 3578, [14]–[15]; *BGHZ* 188, 317, [15], [23]; OLG Hamm, *ZIP* 2003, 2262.

these third parties had knowledge of the mandate (Art. 1705, paragraph 1, c.c.). Third parties have no relationship whatsoever with the mandator (Art. 1705, paragraph 2, c.c.).

When the mandatary without representation acquires immoveable property or registered moveable property, they must transfer it to the mandator immediately (Art. 1706, paragraph 2, c.c.). Where the mandatary fails to transfer the property, the mandator can apply for a judgment having the same effects as the transfer agreement the mandatary refused to sign.[56] Thus, Xervix are the owners of the apartment acquired in their own name but for the benefit of Mr and Mrs Astor, and Xervix are under an obligation to transfer the property to Mr and Mrs Astor.

On the other hand, the mandator can claim the credits arising from the contracts entered into by the mandatary (Art. 1705 c.c.; see Case 4 above for further details). Also, they can claim the moveable property that the mandatary has acquired in their own name, without prejudice to the rights of third parties as a result of good-faith possession (Art. 1706, paragraph 1, c.c.). Some scholars and courts consider this an exception to the rule that the mandate does not transfer property but merely creates rights and obligations.[57] Thus, when the mandatary acquires the moveable property, this immediately transfers to the mandator, who is then entitled to bring a *rei vindicatio*. Others contend that the mandate to acquire moveable property transfers the property directly to the mandator, without first transferring it to the mandatary.[58] Either way, the rights that third parties in good faith have acquired from the mandatary will not be affected. Accordingly, Mr Landwell is the owner of the painting acquired by Xervix in their own name but for the benefit of Mr Landwell. The *rei vindicatio* requires that Mr Landwell be the owner of the property claimed.

As at 23 February 2017, Mrs Brown can claim the purchase price of the Mesdag painting from Mr Ross. Although the mandate is without representation, and Mrs Brown has no relationship with Mr Ross, Mrs Brown, in lieu of Xervix, can claim the credits arising from the contract entered into by Xervix (Art. 1705, paragraph 2, c.c.). While the mandator (Mrs Brown) has a direct action against the third party (Mr Ross) for the purchase price, the third party has no direct action against the mandator, but only against the mandatary. This results from the wording of the Civil Code, and is the rule upheld by the courts, on the ground that the mandator's power to claim the credits arising from the mandate without representation is deemed to be 'exceptional' and, as such, is not to be applied by way of analogy to the rights vested with third parties.

---

56 Cass., 9 March 1994, no. 2301, *Giustizia civile*, I (1994), p. 1887.

57 A. Luminoso, 'Mandato, commissione, spedizione' in A. Cicu, F. Messineo and L. Mengoni (eds), *Trattato di diritto civile e commerciale* (Milan: Giuffrè, 1984), vol. XXXII, p. 209. In case law, see Cass., 26 January 1994, no. 728, *Giustizia civile*, I (1994), p. 1528.

58 R. Sacco, 'Principio consensualistico ed effetti del mandato', *Foro padano*, I (1966), p. 1390.

Mrs Brown has the power to claim the purchase price irrespective of Xervix being insolvent. As will be seen below, Mrs Brown's credit will take precedence over Xervix's creditors, with the proviso that the mandate be evidenced by writing bearing a certain date prior to foreclosure.

The mandatary's creditors cannot have recourse against the assets the mandatary has acquired in their own name for the account of the mandator, provided that, in the case of unregistered moveable property or rights, the mandate be evidenced by writing bearing a certain date prior to foreclosure, and, in the case of immoveable or registered moveable property, the transfer agreement or the legal action seeking transfer be registered prior to foreclosure (Art. 1707 c.c.). Accordingly, Mr Landwell and Mr and Mrs Astor have all the rights in relation to the property acquired by Xervix in preference to Xervix's general creditors, assuming that all the other requirements laid down in Art. 1707 c.c. have been met. Moreover, Mrs Brown will take precedence over Xervix's creditors if Mr Ross pays the purchase price for the Mesdag painting into Xervix's bank account and Xervix become insolvent, provided that the mandate can be evidenced by writing bearing a certain date prior to foreclosure.

III. Meta-Legal Formants

It is believed that the mandator cannot claim immoveable property the mandatary has acquired in their own name, as is the case with moveable property.[59] The mandatary must transfer the property through a contract with the mandator or a unilateral act. Claiming otherwise would turn the mandate itself into a transfer agreement, subject to registration, while the contract or unilateral act that subsequently transfers the property to the mandator would amount to a mere recognition of the transfer. On the other hand, money is moveable property that the mandator can claim against the mandatary directly.

2.8. THE NETHERLANDS

Jan Biemans

I. Operative Rules

1. On 23 February 2017, Mr Landwell is the owner of the Van Dyck painting and Xervix are the owners of the apartment.
2. Assuming Xervix are the owners of the Van Dyck painting and the apartment, if Xervix become insolvent then Mr Landwell and Mr and Mrs Astor do not

---

59 S. Pugliatti, 'La rappresentanza indiretta e la morte del rappresentante', *Foro padano*, III (1953), p. 88.

have any rights in relation to those assets in preference to Xervix's general creditors.

3. On 23 February 2017, Mrs Brown cannot sue Mr Ross for the purchase price of the Mesdag painting.
4. If Xervix are insolvent, Mrs Brown can sue Mr Ross for the purchase price of the Mesdag painting, if Mrs Brown makes a declaration that she asserts her contractual right to the purchase price to Mr Ross, and to the insolvency administrator of Xervix.
5. If Mr Ross pays the purchase price for the Mesdag painting into Xervix's bank account and Xervix become insolvent before they have paid over the money to Mrs Brown, the purchase price is part of the insolvency estate.

II. Descriptive Formants

Question 1 deals with acquisition through an intermediary acting in their own name. According to Article 3:110 DCC, if the legal relationship between two persons implies that, when one of them acquires something in a specific way, they will hold it for the other, then they will, in compliance with that relationship, immediately hold what they have acquired for that other person. This is called 'direct' acquisition through an intermediary. From this provision it follows that, if a mandatary acquires moveable tangible property for the account of the mandator, the mandatary does not become the owner of that property. Instead, as soon as the moveable tangible property is delivered to the mandatary, the mandator directly acquires ownership. The moveable tangible property thus directly becomes part of the patrimony of the mandator, and the mandatary is only the holder, as a third party, of the moveable tangible property on behalf of the mandator. The mandatary is obliged to provide the moveable tangible property to the mandator. However, it is not necessary for the mandatary to legally transfer that property to the mandator, as it is already in the mandator's patrimony; it is only a personal obligation of the mandatary to deliver the property to the mandatary, rather than any question of ownership.

Although Article 3:110 DCC is drafted broadly, and may seem to imply that the provision concerns goods of all kinds, it applies only to moveable tangibles, such as paintings. From Dutch Supreme Court case law it follows that the provision does not apply to those goods where the ascription of the good is decisive for the question of who becomes its owner, as is the case, for example, with real estate, and with bank accounts with book-entry money and book-entry securities, as these types of goods are all 'registered' or 'administered' in someone's name.[60] In the *Modehuis Nolly* (fashion house Nolly) case,[61] a man

[60] J.W.A. Biemans, *Rechtsgevolgen van stille cessie*, Deventer: Kluwer 2011, no. 84–87.

[61] Dutch Supreme Court, 2 April 1976, ECLI:NL:HR:1976:AB6874, NJ 1976/450 *(Modehuis Nolly I)*.

acquired real estate on the account of his wife. Although his wife paid for the real estate, the name of the man was mentioned in all deeds of transfer, and his name was registered as the owner in the public land registry. This was done for tax purposes. After their divorce, the woman claimed that she was the owner of the real estate, as the man had only acted as an intermediary. The Dutch Supreme Court dismissed her claims, ruling that the name of the acquirer was decisive for the question of ownership. Less famous, but nonetheless relevant, is the sequel of this case, eight years later. In this second *Modehuis Nolly* case,[62] the Dutch Supreme Court ruled that the man was obliged to transfer all of the real estate to the woman, as he had acted as a mandatary for her account. This obligation is based on the law of the contract of mandate.[63]

In response to question 2, Dutch insolvency law, contained in the Dutch Bankruptcy Act (Faillissementswet), does not protect those creditors with a beneficial interest in goods of which the insolvent person is the legal owner. Mr Landwell and Mr and Mrs Astor, as the mandators, would have to file their claims for the transfer of the goods with the insolvency administrator of Xervix, which claims will be converted into monetary damages claims (Article 6:87 DCC) with a small chance of payment by the bankruptcy administrator.

There are some exceptions to the rule that the person contractually entitled to property is not protected against the insolvency of the owner, but these do not apply in this case. One of these exceptions is contained in Article 7:3 DCC, which provides for the possibility to register the sales contract of real property (a residence) in the public land registry, in addition to the registration of the real property transaction (Article 3:89 in conjunction with 3:84 (1) DCC) that succeeds it. For a period of six months, the buyer of the real estate is protected against various possible misfortunes in relation to the seller and/or the property, including the insolvency of the seller.

In response to question 3, Mrs Brown cannot, on 23 February 2017, sue Mr Ross for the purchase price of the Mesdag painting. As explained above, if a mandatary, such as Xervix, acts in their own name, they become the party to the agreement. Even though Xervix, as a mandatary, concluded the contract for the account and the benefit of Mrs Brown as a mandator, and Xervix are bound, eventually, to pay the purchase price to Mrs Brown, Mrs Brown is not herself a contracting party. As a consequence, she cannot sue Mr Ross for the purchase price of the Mesdag painting. Only Xervix, as the contracting party, are legally entitled to claim the purchase price from Mr Ross, as the claim to payment of the purchase price is part of the patrimony of Xervix.

---

62 Dutch Supreme Court, 16 March 1984, ECLI:NL:HR:1984:AB7952, NJ 1984/556 *(Modehuis Nolly II)*.

63 L.v.Antw. II Inv., Parl. Gesch. Boek 3 (Inv. 3, 5 en 6), p. 1204; and inter alia Dutch Supreme Court, 31 May 1974, NJ 1976/309; Dutch Supreme Court, 24 March 1995, NJ 1996/447 *(Jahn/Nask)*.

In response to question 4, if Xervix are insolvent, then Mrs Brown can sue Mr Ross for the purchase prices of the Mesdag painting, if Mrs Brown declares such to Mr Ross and to the insolvency administrator of Xervix. As explained in Case 4 above, Article 7:420 DCC provides for a solution in the event of default or insolvency of the indirect agent (the mandatary acting in its own name, in this case Xervix) by allowing the mandator (principal, in this case Mrs Brown) to take over all rights arising out of the contract by means of a written declaration addressed to both the mandatary and the contracting party.

In response to question 5, if Mr Ross pays the purchase price for the Mesdag painting into Xervix's bank account and Xervix become insolvent before they have paid over the money to Mrs Brown, the purchase price is part of Xervix's insolvency estate.

As for bank accounts with book-entry money or book-entry securities, if the bank account is opened and administered in the name of the principal (direct agency), the bank balance (meaning the claim arising out of the bank account) belongs to the principal. However, if the bank account is opened and administered in the name of the indirect agent, the bank balance belongs to the indirect agent, even though the indirect agent acted on behalf of, and for the account of, the principal when opening the bank account in their own name. For bank accounts with book-entry money, the Dutch Supreme Court decided this point in the *ProCall* case, where a collection company contracted by a hospital went bankrupt, and the book-entry moneys in the bank account of the collection company – belonging to the hospital – were deemed to form part of the bankruptcy estate of the collection company.[64] For bank accounts with book-entry securities, the Dutch Supreme Court has decided this point in the *Kas-Associatie/Drying* case.[65]

Only bailiffs, lawyers (solicitors) and civil law notaries can achieve a different result. If they open a bank account in their own name, and in their professional capacity, they are considered only to be the administrators of the account, whereas claims arising out of the account are assets of the beneficiaries (their clients). There is no beneficial ownership by the bailiffs, lawyers and civil law notaries. For bailiffs and civil law notaries, statutory bases for this can be found in Article 19 of the Bailiffs Acts (Gerechtsdeurwaarderswet) and Article 25 of the Notaries Act (Wet op het Notarisambt), respectively. For lawyers, this was decided in the aforementioned *ProCall* case.[66]

As a consequence, all payments to the bank account held and administered by Xervix will fall into the bankruptcy estate. Mrs Brown will have only an ordinary claim to payment of these book-entry moneys, with only a small chance of payment by the bankruptcy administrator.

---

64 Dutch Supreme Court, 13 June 2003, NJ 2004/196, JOR 2003/209 *(ProCall/Beatrix Ziekenhuis).*

65 Dutch Supreme Court, 23 September 1994, NJ 1996/461 *(Kas-Associatie/Drying).*

66 Dutch Supreme Court, 13 June 2003, NJ 2004/196, JOR 2003/209 *(ProCall/Beatrix Ziekenhuis).*

2.9. POLAND

Monika Jagielska

I. *Operative Rules*

1. Mr Landwell is the owner of the Van Dyck painting. The ownership of the apartment depends on the content and the form of the contract concluded.
2. If Xervix become insolvent, Mr Landwell has rights in relation to those assets in preference to Xervix's general creditors. This does not apply to the apartment, as the specific rule applies to contract of consignment only.
3. Mrs Brown *cannot* sue Mr Ross for the purchase price of the Mesdag painting.
4. Mrs Brown *cannot* sue Mr Ross for the purchase price of the Mesdag painting if Xervix are insolvent.
5. If Mr Ross pays the purchase price for the Mesdag painting into Xervix's bank account and Xervix become insolvent before they have paid the money over to Mrs Brown, the money will be held and governed by the insolvency administrator, but Mrs Brown will have her own claim for the money to be excluded from the bankruptcy estate.

II. *Descriptive Formants*

The Ownership

The Polish Civil Code recognises the contract of consignment (Art. 765 PCC), in which 'the party accepting the mandate (the consigning agent) undertakes to buy or sell moveable things within the scope of his enterprise's activity on the account of the principal (the consigning party), yet in his own name'. The contract of consignment belongs to a group of contracts for the provision of services, through which a person directly interested in the transaction (principal) may remain undisclosed to the contractor purchasing or disposing of a given item (indirect replacement). The agent acts here as an intermediary in their own name, but on behalf of the principal.

In the case of the consignment of sales, the principal authorises the agent to sell the subject of the contract of consignment, but the agent becomes a person who, although permitted to dispose of the thing, has no title to it.[67]

[67] J. Frąckowiak, 'Umowa komisu' in J. Rajski (ed), *System Prawa Prywatnego, T. 7*, Warsaw 2018.

The ownership still belongs to the principal. Thus, the property right to the thing sold by the agent passes directly from the principal to a third party.[68]

In the case of the consignment to buy, it is generally adopted in Polish law[69] that the first owner of a moveable thing purchased will be the agent, and it is only by performing the consignment contract that the agent will transfer ownership of the property, and possibly other rights they have acquired, to the principal.

At the same time, Polish law adopts the concept of the disposing effect of an obligation. According to Article 155 PCC:

> a sale, exchange, donation, disposal of real estate or other contract creating an obligation to transfer the ownership of goods in specie transfers the ownership to the acquirer unless a specific regulation provides otherwise or the parties decide otherwise. If fungibles are the subject of a contract creating an obligation to transfer ownership, then to transfer the ownership of the fungibles, the transfer of possession is required. The same applies if the subject of the contract creating an obligation to transfer ownership is future things.

Therefore, in the case of a consignment contract, the acquisition of property will take place, depending on the type of item, either at the time the contract is concluded (for moveable goods *in specie*) or when the item is handed over (in the case of *genus* moveable goods that are replaceable). In the case of goods *in specie* sold by the agent, the ownership will be transferred directly from the principal to the third party when the sales contract is concluded; in the case of goods in *specie* bought by the agent, the ownership will be transferred via the agent, but the transfer will be performed 'automatically' when the agent buys the goods. As such, as at 22 February, Mr Landwell is the owner of the Van Dyck painting.

As the agent is a party to the sales contract, and acts on their own behalf, they should be considered the creditor of the buyer, in terms of the sale price. Consequently, they will also become the owner of the money transferred.

The scope of the contract of consignment is limited to moveables only, but in the case of immoveables the concept of indirect representation may apply[70] Nevertheless, according to Article 158 PCC, a contract obliging the transfer of ownership of immoveable property must be executed in the form of a notarial

---

68 J. Frąckowiak, *Komis w eksporcie według prawa polskiego*, Wrocław 1985; A. Kędzierska-Cieślak, *Komis, zagadnienia cywilnoprawne*, Warsaw 1973; A. Szpunar, 'Stosunki własnościowe przy komisie', *Rejent* 1994, no. 1.

69 For more, see J. Frąckowiak, 'Umowa komisu' in J. Rajski (ed), *System Prawa Prywatnego, T. 7*, Warsaw 2018.

70 L. Ogiegło in K. Pietrzykowski (ed), *Kodeks cywilny. Komentarz. Tom II. Art. 450–1088*, Warsaw 2015, s. 704.

deed. The ownership of the apartment thus depends on who was revealed as its buyer (Xervix or Mrs and Mr Astor), and whether the contract was concluded in an appropriate form.

Insolvency

In accordance with Article 766 PCC, the agent shall release to the principal everything that they have obtained during the performance of the mandate: in particular, they shall transfer the receivables which they have acquired on the principal's account. These entitlements of the principal will also be effective towards the agent's creditors. The principal may, therefore, object to the seizure of property, money or claims, or demand release from execution.[71] According to Article 841 of the Polish Code of Procedure, a third party may bring an action to exempt a thing attached from execution, if the execution against that thing would violate their rights. This would provide Mr Landwell with rights to the Van Dyck painting upon Xervix's insolvency (if Xervix were presumed to be the owner). It would also provide Mrs Brown with a claim against the bankruptcy estate for the price of the Mesdag painting, although this would not be a preferential claim.

According to Article 102 §2 of the Polish Bankruptcy Act, consignment contracts concluded by the bankrupt person, in which the bankrupt person was the agent, may be terminated on the day of declaration of bankruptcy, without compensation. In the event of the insolvency of the agent, the principal may request the exclusion from the bankruptcy estate of items constituting the principal's property, if they have benefited from the possibility of terminating the commission contract. A principal to whom the agent had not released the property acquired on their behalf before the declaration of bankruptcy will not normally be interested in withdrawing from the contract.[72] Nevertheless, since such a principal would have a vindication claim against the agent, they should also be entitled to a claim against the bankruptcy estate, in order to exclude the goods owned by the principal from the bankruptcy estate.

2.10. SCOTLAND

Lorna MacFarlane

I. Operative Rules

1. *Mr Landwell* is the owner of the Van Dyck painting and *the Astors* are the owners of the apartment.

---

[71] Ibid., s. 706.
[72] J. Frąckowiak, 'Umowa komisu' in J. Rajski (ed), *System Prawa Prywatnego, T. 7*, Warsaw 2018.

2. If Xervix were the owners of the Van Dyck painting and the apartment, Mr Landwell and the Astors *would not* have any preferential rights to Xervix's general creditors.
3. On 23 February 2017, Mrs Brown *can* sue Mr Ross for the Mesdag purchase price.
4. Xervix's insolvency *does not* affect the answer to question 3.
5. Mrs Brown *can sue Mr Ross* for the purchase price.

II. Descriptive Formants

Regarding the first question, a disclosed agent is employed by a principal to carry out business on their behalf and, as such, property which the agent acquires on behalf of its principal belongs to the principal.[73] The contract brokered by the agent is between the principal and the third party, and on conclusion of the contract the property passes directly to the principal. Thus, the Astors and Mr Landwell are the owners of the paintings and the apartment, respectively. Regarding the second question, if, however, Xervix owned the assets on 23 February 2017, the Astors and Mr Landwell would not have any rights in preference to the general creditors. The relationship between agent and principal is contractual,[74] and they would, accordingly, rank with the general creditors.

Macgregor notes the lack of authority in Scots law concerning situations in which an agent acts for a disclosed but unnamed principal (i.e. the agent informs the third party that it is acting as an agent, but does not disclose the identity of the principal).[75] In particular, the question of whether the agent is bound to perform in favour of the third party in such a scenario is the subject of ongoing debate.[76] There is, however, clear judicial authority relating to the third, fourth and fifth questions. Regarding the third question, it is accepted that the principal can sue the third party.[77] Case law indicates that the third party

73 L.J. Macgregor, *The Laws of Scotland: Stair Memorial Encyclopaedia: Agency and Mandate*, reissue (LexisNexis/Law Society of Scotland, London/Edinburgh 2001), para. 55. Regarding undisclosed agency (see Case 4 above), there is some authority that the third party initially contracts with the undisclosed agent rather than the principal, in which case the property might (prior to disclosure of the principal) be regarded as the agent's. See, further, Macgregor, ibid., paras. 149–50.

74 Ibid., para. 43.

75 Ibid., para. 137.

76 See, generally, L.J. Macgregor, *The Law of Agency in Scotland* (W. Green, Edinburgh 2013), para. 12.17–12.18.

77 L.J. Macgregor, *The Laws of Scotland: Stair Memorial Encyclopaedia: Agency and Mandate*, reissue (LexisNexis/Law Society of Scotland, London/Edinburgh 2001), para. 143.

cannot claim compensation on a debt owed to them by the agent,[78] which, as noted by Macgregor, aligns with the view that the third party relies on the credit of the principal where the principal is disclosed but unnamed.[79] Accordingly, Mrs Brown can sue Mr Ross for the Mesdag purchase price, regardless of whether Xervix are insolvent. Although there is a lack of case law on the point, Macgregor surmises that the third party cannot defend a claim on the part of the principal on the basis that they have already paid the agent.[80] Mrs Brown can, therefore, claim against Mr Ross even if he has paid Xervix prior to their insolvency. The position appears to be the same had Mr Ross paid Xervix's estate following their insolvency. One of the reasons suggested for not protecting the third party from having to perform twice is that he/she knows that a principal exists and takes a risk if he/she renders performance to the agent rather than the principal. This rationale would apply more forcefully where the third party is aware of the agent's insolvency.

III. Meta-Legal Formants

Regarding the third party's remaining obligation to pay the principal, if they paid the agent prior to the agent's insolvency, Macgregor writes that:

> there seems no good reason to protect the third party from performing twice. The third party was aware from the outset that a principal existed. It is not unfair to allow the third party to bear the loss should the agent become insolvent without paying the principal. The third party could have taken steps to find out the identity of the principal.[81]

This perhaps does not account for the view that the principal ought also to bear the risk of the agent's insolvency. The principal chose to form an agency relationship with the particular agent, and was arguably in a better position than the third party to consider the agent's solvency and commercial reputation. However, it appears that, while the law and policy on this aspect of agency law are underdeveloped, the policy objective of ensuring that the third party is not prejudiced by the disclosure of the principal (discussed above in Case 4) does not extend to cases in which the identity of the principal might later be disclosed, because, in this case, the third party ought to have considered the risk of contracting with a disclosed but unnamed principal.

---

78 Ibid., para. 143, citing *Matthews v. Auld and Guild* (1873) 1 R 1224; *Lavaggi v. Pirrie & Sons* (1872) 10 M 312; *National Bank of Scotland v. Dickie's Trustees* (1895) 22 R 740.

79 L.J. Macgregor, *The Laws of Scotland: Stair Memorial Encyclopaedia: Agency and Mandate*, reissue (LexisNexis/Law Society of Scotland, London/Edinburgh 2001), para. 143.

80 Ibid., para. 146.

81 Ibid.

2.11. SLOVAKIA

Kristián Csach, Monika Jurčová, Peter Mészáros and Veronika Zoričáková

I. Operative Rules

1. The owners are either Xervix or their client, depending on the applicable regulation (commercial or civil). Given the facts of the case, it is assumed that the civil law regulation will apply, and that Xervix will be the owners.
2. Neither the Astors nor Mr Landwell would have priority rights in Xervix's bankruptcy. Nevertheless, if the parties had agreed on the application of the SCommC, the principals would have acquired ownership directly, at least regarding moveables.
3. Mrs Brown cannot sue Mr Ross unless Xervix have assigned their claim to Mrs Brown.
4. The insolvency of Xervix would give rise to a direct claim against Mr Ross only if the commercial law regulation applied.
5. Mrs Brown can only bring a claim in bankruptcy proceedings, as with other ordinary creditors of Xervix.

II. Descriptive Formants

The results in this case are dependent upon the varying applicable rules. There are two basic sets of rules regulating a commission contract, each with different and unclear regimes on the regulation of property law.

Firstly, the commercial commission contract pursuant to sections 577 ff. SCommC would apply (s. 261 SCommC), as this covers both situations – sales commission and purchase commission. It follows a simple model regarding the transfer of property: the commission agent does not become the owner of the property transferred (whether through a sale or a purchase commission). The ownership of moveables is transferred directly from the (ultimate) seller to the (ultimate) purchaser (s. 583(1) SCommC). However, this *ex lege* immediate transfer of ownership does not cover the transfer of receivables, rights or obligations, which have to be transferred by the commission agent to the principal. The commission agent is obliged and entitled personally from the contract entered into with the third party, and the principal *(komitent)* is neither obliged nor entitled from that contract, with one exception. According to section 581 SCommC, the principal is entitled to claim performance from the third party directly if the agent is not able to do so due to circumstances concerning their person. According to the doctrine, the main such circumstances are the death of the commissioner, the winding up of the company without a legal successor, or the insolvency of the agent.[82] It has been argued that the commission agency contract under the SCommC covers only commercial contracts, and is not applicable to contracts on transfers of immoveables.[83]

The commercial commission regulation applies in two basic situations: either both entities are entrepreneurs and it is obvious that they are acting in relation to their business activities (s. 261 SCommC) or the parties agree in writing to the application of the SCommC (s. 262 SCommC).

Otherwise, one of two special civil law agency contracts would be applicable: either a *'zmluva o obstaraní veci'* (the agreement on arrangement for a matter) under sections 733 ff. SCC or a *'zmluva o obstaraní predaja veci'* (an agreement on arranging for sale of a thing) under sections 737 ff. SCC. Contrary to the SCommC, the SCC does not expressly regulate the transfer of ownership. The prevailing view distinguishes between sales and purchase commissions. With a sales commission, the ownership is transferred directly to the purchaser, but under a purchase commission the agent becomes the owner of the goods, which are to be transferred to the principal afterwards.[84]

The rationale behind all of these distinctions is unclear and not very convincing. However, we shall answer the questions on this case on this legal basis.

Regarding question 1, Xervix will become the owners of the Van Dyck painting and the apartment, pursuant to the civil law purchase commission (the agreement on arrangement for a matter, according to the SCC), and must then transfer all the acquired items to the principals.

If the rules on commercial commission agency contracts had been applicable, Mr Landwell would have become the owner of the painting directly. However, due to the scope of commercial agency contracts being restricted to moveables, and the resulting application of civil law purchase commission, Xervix will, in fact, become the owners of the apartment.

Regarding question 2, and assuming that Xervix become the owners of both moveable and immoveable property, the Slovak Act on Bankruptcy and

---

82 M. Jurčová and J. Zámožík, 'Ochrana majetkových záujmov komitenta v komisionárskej zmluve [Protection of property interests according to the contract on commission]', *Justičná revue*, vol. 62, 5 (2010), pp. 620–30.

83 V. Janáč in O. Ovečková et al., *Obchodný zákonník. Veľký komentár, vol. II [Commentary on Commercial Code II]*, Bratislava: Wolters Kluwer, 2017, pp. 982 and 996. Other commentaries are silent on the issue.

84 Pursuant to Slovak civil law, when acquiring a painting for the client the ownership of the painting does not pass directly to the client. However, when selling a client's painting, the ownership passes straight from the client to the third party (the buyer). See M. Jurčová in M. Števček, A. Dulak, J. Bajánková, M. Fečík, F. Sedlačko, M. Tomašovič et al., *Občiansky zákonník II, sect. 451–880 [Commentary on Civil Code II, ss. 451–880]*, Prague: C.H. Beck, 2015, pp. 2670 and 2674.

Restructuring will not prioritise the clients of Xervix over other bankruptcy creditors. The clients mentioned in the present case will thus bear the risk of Xervix's insolvency to the same extent as other creditors. However, this applies only if an agency contract pursuant to the SCC has been concluded. Should the special commercial regulation on *ex lege* acquisition of moveable property apply, Mr Landwell would be the owner of the paintings (moveables), and therefore would not face the risk of Xervix's insolvency.

Regarding question 3, Mrs Brown cannot, under the civil law regulation, demand contractual performance from Mr Ross. The sales contract was concluded between Mr Ross and Xervix, and thus only Xervix may demand performance of the contractual obligations, including payment of the purchase price. The claim for payment of the purchase price could, however, be assigned by Xervix to Mrs Brown by a separate assignation, prior to their insolvency.

The basic rule of the commission contract regulation in the SCommC also assumes that Xervix would be the party entitled to enforce contractual obligations against third parties.

Regarding question 4, the insolvency of Xervix would not give rise to a direct claim against Mr Ross if the SCC were applicable. However, based on the exception in section 581 SCommC, Mrs Brown would be entitled to claim performance from Mr Ross if Xervix were not able to do so due to circumstances concerning their person. According to the doctrine, the main such circumstances are the death of the commissioner, the winding up of the company without a legal successor, or the insolvency of the commissioner (in this case, Xervix).[85]

Regarding question 5, Xervix's insolvency would mean that all their assets would become part of the bankruptcy estate. Pursuant to the Slovak Act on Bankruptcy and Restructuring, Mrs Brown would only be able to bring a claim in bankruptcy proceedings in the same way as other ordinary Xervix creditors. Mrs Brown will have no priority over other creditors. As the money paid to Xervix is not moveable property, the commercial law exception on direct transfer of property under section 583(1) SCommC would not apply.

2.12. SPAIN

Carles Vendrell Cervantes

I. *Operative Rules*

1. *Mr Landwell* would be considered the owner of the *Van Dyck painting*; *Mr and Mrs Astor* would be considered the owners of the *apartment*.

---

85 Ibid.

2. As stated above, *Xervix will not be considered the owners* of the Van Dyck painting and the apartment. If Xervix become insolvent, these assets will be separated from their own assets, as established in Article 80 of the Spanish Insolvency Law.

   However, assuming that Xervix are, in fact, the owners (as indicated in the question), the general rules on insolvency will apply and, therefore, Mr Landwell and the Astors will be subject to the same conditions as all the other creditors of Xervix (without any priority or higher ranking), when the insolvency proceedings are being carried out.
3. No, Mrs Brown does not have a right to take action against Mr Ross. On the contrary, Xervix could take action.
4. Yes, the answer might be different on the basis of an interpretation of Article 1717.II of the Spanish Civil Code suggested in the prevailing literature.
5. The money belongs to Mrs Brown, because Xervix have entered into the contract on behalf of Mrs Brown.

II. Descriptive Formants

Question 1

Under Spanish Law, this case qualifies as an indirect representation, as established in Article 1717 of the Spanish Civil Code together with Articles 244 ff. of the Spanish Commercial Code. Xervix are acting on their own, but on behalf of the principals: Mr Landwell and the Astors.

In principle, as indicated earlier (see Case 4 above), the rule established in Article 1717 states that the representative (i.e. intermediary) will be bound as if the business was their own; the fact that the third party knows that they are contracting with a representative does not challenge this general rule. In this regard, the principal will not be considered a party to the contract. Nevertheless, the general consensus[86] among legal scholars and judges is that this will only affect the right to take action between the principal and the third party, but not the transfer of the assets (i.e. the painting or the apartment). Once the property has been acquired, the Astors could register the property in their own names, in the property register. If Xervix validly registered the property in the property register (albeit that they are not the owners), Xervix would be presumed to be the owner (Art. 38 Spanish Mortgage Law), although this presumption may be rebutted.

---

[86] Á. Carrasco, *Derecho Civil* (6th ed., Tecnos, 2018), 362–65. This legal scholar reaches this conclusion based on the decisions of the Spanish Supreme Court of 13 April 1994 and 22 April 2005.

In this regard, Xervix have acquired the painting and apartment for, and under the instruction of, Mr Landwell and the Astors, respectively. As a consequence, they, and not Xervix, will be considered the owners.

Question 2

Assuming that Xervix are the owners of the assets, the right of separation established in Article 80 of the Spanish Insolvency Law (which provides that 'the assets belonging to others that are in possession of the insolvent and in respect whereof he does not have right to use, secure or retain, shall be delivered to their legitimate owners') will not apply. Consequently, the painting and apartment will form part of the aggregate assets of the insolvent party. As indicated above, Mr Landwell and the Astors will be subject to the same conditions as all the other creditors of Xervix, when the insolvency proceedings are being carried out.

Question 3

Article 1717 of the Spanish Civil Code provides that:

> where the representative should act in his own name, the principal shall have no action against the persons with whom the representative has entered into any contract, nor the latter against the principal. In this case, the representative shall be directly bound vis-à-vis the person with whom he has contracted, as if the affair were a personal affair of his own.

This general rule, together with Article 246 of the Spanish Commercial Code, excludes direct action between the principal (i.e. Mrs Brown) and the third party (i.e. Mr Ross). The exception to the general rule, in Article 1717 of the Spanish Civil Code (see Case 4 above), will not apply in this case, as the intermediary has not failed to comply with the contract.

Question 4

There are no specific rules as regards the insolvency of the indirect representative. However, as established above, there is an exception to the general rule that the contract between the indirect representative and the third party binds only them. This exception, established in Article 1717.II of the Spanish Civil Code, will apply only if the enforceability of the contract is subject to the principal's will, and its rationale is to protect the third party's rights (see Case 4 above).

This exception would allow the third party to take action directly against the principal. This would be applicable if Mr Ross wanted to take direct action against Mrs Brown in order to obtain the paintings. The law does not include other situations.

However, it has been suggested by the prevailing legal literature[87] that the exception would also include a potential claim by the principal against the third party (i.e. Mrs Brown could sue Mr Ross for the purchase price), in order to provide for a legal balance between the parties regarding their mutual performance obligations under the contract.

Question 5

As established above, the Spanish Insolvency Law includes a rule, under Article 80, according to which 'the assets belonging to others that are in possession of the insolvent and in respect whereof he does not have right to use, secure or retain, shall be delivered to their legitimate owners'. Therefore, Mrs Brown's money will be separated from the assets of the insolvent party, Xervix.

2.13. SWEDEN

Oskar Mossberg

I. *Operative Rules*

1. Mr Landwell is the owner of the Van Dyck painting. Mr and Mr Astor are the owners of the apartment.
2. According to Swedish law, Xervix can never be the owners of the painting or the apartment in these circumstances. Mr Landwell owns the painting, and Mr and Mrs Astor are the owners of the apartment. Their rights are preferential to those of Xervix's general creditors.
3. Given the circumstances, Mrs Brown is to be considered the principal of an indirect (commissionary) agent (Xervix), and as she has not assumed the agent's claim against Mr Ross, Mrs Brown cannot sue Mr Ross directly.
4. If Xervix is insolvent, Mrs Brown can sue Mr Ross directly.
5. The funds are to be forwarded to Mrs Brown. She has a right to separate them from the insolvency proceedings, and this right is preferential to those of Xervix's general creditors.

II. *Descriptive Formants*

The rules on commission (see Case 4 above) in Kommissionslagen (2009:865) (the Act on Commission) are directly applicable here, as Xervix has agreed to

[87] See, for instance, B. Fernández Gregoraci, *La representación indirecta* (Thomson Civitas, 2006), 310–25; or Á. Carrasco Perera, *Derecho Civil: Introducción. Fuentes. Derecho de la Persona. Derecho Subjetivo. Derecho de Propiedad* (5th ed., Tecnos, 2016), 364.

purchase and sell non-real property in its own name for the benefit of its private clients (see Article 1 of the Act on Commission). In general, 'apartments' are considered non-real property in Swedish law; or, rather, the *'rättsobjekt'* (legal object) normally sold is not the apartments as such – that is, the physical parts of a building – but, rather, (various forms of) *'nyttjanderätter'* (rights of use) associated with the apartments. The object of transfer is thus a non-physical (or immaterial) legal right which is not considered real property, as real property is basically land and things permanently fixed to the land, such as trees and houses, provided that these affixed things are owned by the owner of the land, as detailed in the first and second chapters of Jordabalken (the Earth Balk, which is the central Swedish statutory Act on real property).

The rules in the Act on Commission are based on the idea that the commissionary agent acts as an agent, and that any goods procured or sold by him are only intended to 'pass through' him, and never be owned by him. As long as the agent stays within the limits of his authority, ownership is transferred directly between the third party and principal, the instant the contract between the agent and third party is concluded (it does not matter whether or not the agency is disclosed to the third party, as disclosure is not an issue, according to the Swedish law of commission). This follows from an express statutory provision in Article 23 of the Act on Commission. The one exception to this rule is not applicable to the present case and, as such, Xervix never assumes ownership of any goods; ownership is always either retained by the seller or transferred directly to the principal.

As indicated above, the apartment would most likely be considered non-real property under Swedish law, as this is the common practice, and what has been discussed so far therefore concerns commissionary purchases of non-real property. It is, however, not impossible for an apartment to be real property, given the 2009 introduction of *'ägarlägenheter'* (owner apartments), as a result of *'tredimensionell fastighetsbildning'* (three-dimensional real property registration). Traditionally, and normally, *'fastigheter'* (pieces of real estate) are defined two-dimensionally, as plots of land, but defining them as three-dimensionally demarcated spaces entails the possibility of an apartment being a piece of real estate. The Act on Commission is only directly applicable to commission contracts regarding the sale or purchase of non-real property (as expressly stated in Article 1 of the Act) and, as such, would not be directly applicable to such a case. One could discuss *ex analogia* application of Article 23 in such a way that the principal would assume ownership immediately, through the commissionary's contract with the seller. In many cases, such an analogy would likely be deemed reasonable. However, Swedish law has formal requirements for *'fastighetsöverlåtelser'* (sales of real property) and, in general, these requirements are strictly upheld. These requirements are found in Chapter 4 of Jordabalken, where Article 1 states, inter alia, that there must be a written contract of sale, signed by the purchaser. In commission cases, the contract would, by definition, need to be signed by the agent (otherwise, the contract will not be made 'in the name of the agent' in the sense required). With reference to this, the HD has deemed that the principal does not gain ownership directly through the agent's contract with the seller in the sense that the principal's claim to the real property purchased by their commissionary agent will have priority over the agent's creditors.[88] In the HD cases NJA 2020 p. 384 and NJA 1984 p. 772, the court held that not giving the principal's claim priority over the agent's other creditors' claims was 'most in line with general principles of property law and with the formal requirement for purchases of real property'; that is, the requirement that the written sales agreement be signed by the buyer. The principal can, however, have a claim against the agent to have ownership transferred. This would be valid *inter partes*, but would not entail any property law protection against the agent's creditors, in the sense of having priority over their claims (this, too, follows from the aforementioned HD cases).

Swedish law differentiates between the law of obligations and the law of property. Within the latter subject, it further differentiates between different questions which in other jurisdictions might be collected under the heading of 'transfer of ownership'.[89] The property law issues regarding commissionary purchases of real property can be complicated, and are not entirely clear (see NJA 1984 p. 722, where the HD says the same thing). Also, despite the possibility of 'owner apartments', these are anything but common. Neither is it common practice to purchase real property through a commissionary agent. In practice, the most important cases involving such issues are family law cases concerning giving adequate protection to spouses upon divorce, where one spouse has purchased and is the registered owner of the *'fastighet'* (piece of real property) where the spouses have lived, but the other spouse has contributed economically. In such cases, there are special family law rules on *'dold samäganderätt'* (non-disclosed co-ownership). These rules are, however, irrelevant to the case at hand. On the property law requirements in general, see Case 7 below.

The following analysis concerns cases where the apartment is considered non-real property, as this is by far the most common practice in Sweden.

Given the circumstances, possession of the goods is of no consequence. (If either the third party, or the principal, or both, had also been insolvent, the issues would be more complicated, and possession would be a factor.)

The rule in Article 27 of the Act on Commission, mentioned in Case 4 above, allows for Mrs Brown to assume the claim against Mr Ross. However, as Xervix

---

88 On Swedish property law, and the differentiation of the concept of ownership into a set of different questions of priority of claims, see C. Martinson, 'How Swedish Lawyers Think about "Ownership" and "Transfer of Ownership" – Are We Just Peculiar or Actually Ahead?' in W. Faber and B. Lurger (eds), *Rules for the Transfer of Movables: A Candidate for European Harmonisation or National Reforms?*, Sellier European Law Publishers GmbH, Munich 2008.

89 See ibid.

is a business and the contracts fall within its business activities, the principal's right of assumption is limited.[90] Mrs Brown can assume the claim only if Xervix is insolvent, has acted deceitfully or has failed to render accounts (see below), or if Mr Ross is late with payment. As there is no indication that any of these is the case here, Mrs Brown would not be able to assume Xervix's claim, in the first variation of the question.

According to Article 6 of the Act on Commission, a commissionary agent is *'redovisningsskyldig'* (required to render accounts), which means that the principal has a preferential right to claim money owed, and the agent a corresponding obligation to pay such money. This right is protected against the agent's general creditors, and as long as the funds are identifiable as having been intended for Mrs Brown (for example, by being kept in a bank account labelled 'client funds'), she would be able to separate them from the insolvency proceedings. In other words, the funds can be separated from the agent's insolvency proceedings pursuant to Article 6 of the Act on Commission and *'lagen om redovisningsmedel'* (the Act on Funds Accountable), which concerns, among other things, funds that an agent is in possession of on the account of their principal.

III. Meta-Legal Formants

The commissionary agent is seen as an indirect representative, and the rules are premised on them being an agent of the principal. As such, they are never intended to own the goods sold or purchased, and therefore their general creditors, in general, have no claim on these goods. The right to separate the funds in the bank account is a consequence of this general construction of the governing principles of commission.[91]

---

90 See the Act on Commission, Article 27, first paragraph (translated as literally as possible): 'A principal may acquire the claim against the third party based on contracts the commissionary agent has entered into with the third party for the account of the principal. If the commission contract [between the principal and agent] is commercial, the principal may however only acquire the claim if the third party is late in payment or delivery or if the commissionary agent has lapsed in his duty to account [for goods or money, to the principal], acted in bad faith against the principal or is in bankruptcy.' See also S.O. Johansson, *Kommissionslagen: En kommentar*, Norstedts, Stockholm 2017, pp. 325 ff.

91 In Swedish law, these issues are considered part of the law of property rather than the law of obligations. They quickly get complicated, and it is not possible to provide a full treatment of them within the space available here. In practice, the important requirement is that the funds are identifiable. They can be held in a bank account where they are 'mixed' with other money (though some types of agents, such as lawyers, are required by public law to keep the principal's/client's funds in separate accounts). The principal can still separate the funds 'up to the least kept/held amount' *('intill lägsta behållna saldo')*. This follows from the Lag om redovisningsmedel (1944:181) (Act on Accountable Funds), and the HD cases NJA 1956 p. 485, NJA 1994 p. 506 and NJA 2009 p. 500. For a monographical treatment of this topic, see L. Zackariasson, *Borgenärsskydd och specialitet*, Iustus, Uppsala 2011.

On the principal's right to assume the agent's claim against the third party, see the comments in Case 4 above.

The rules have been hotly debated in the literature, and there are many HD cases concerning third-party issues in relation to commission. Significantly, there is a rather large group of cases concerning the area of application of the rules (not the least problematic of which relates to the requisite *'för annans räkning'* (for the benefit of/on account of another)[92] in Article 1 of the Act on Commission). That there a large number cases is, in part, due to the fact that commission lessens the principal's risk associated with the insolvency of the agent, as the principal can separate the goods associated with the contract on commission (the goods intended to be sold or purchased on the account of the principal) from the commissionary's insolvency estate.[93]

---

92 The deciding criteria, as stated in the Commission Act, Article 1, is *'för annans räkning'* (for the benefit of another). The body of cases concerning the application and development of the criteria include, among others, NJA 2012 p. 419 ('The assessment must be made after considering all relevant circumstances'); NJA 2010 p. 154; NJA 2000 p. 685; NJA 1940 p. 312; NJA 1940 p. 164 and NJA 1937 p. 591. The issue has been discussed in the preparatory works to the Act on Commission (see prop. 2008/09 – Ny kommissionslag, pp. 29 ff. and 86 ff.; SOU 1988:63 – Kommission och dylikt, pp. 49 ff.) as well as extensively in legal scholarship, see e.g. L. Zackariasson, *Borgenärsskydd och specialitet*, Iustus, Uppsala 2011, pp. 495 ff. (with further case law references); S.O. Johansson, *Kommissionslagen: En kommentar*, Norstedts, Stockholm 2017, pp. 59 ff.; and O. Mossberg, 'Spekulationer om implikationer: Om kommission och om vad NJA 2014 s. 760 egentligen innebär' in J. Samuelsson and L.M. Elvevold (eds), *Över gränsen*, Iustus, Uppsala 2024 (forthcoming), with extensive further references. One way of framing the assessment could be to ask whether the agent, given the mission and circumstances, can be considered to have only had an *intermediary role* (cf. NJA 2014 p. 760, and NJA 2000 p. 685). However, the decisive factor remains whether the legal act was conducted 'on behalf of another', and nothing else, which means that any thematic reformulations should not be taken too seriously; the requirement is the requirement! However, potentially important factors may include: (a) how the parties have designated their agreement (this may have evidentiary value, but is hardly decisive); (b) the specific content of the agreement between the principal and agent; (c) how the agent and third party perceived the matter when entering into their contract; (d) what the intermediary intended at the same time, if this can be considered proven; (e) if there are similarities with an (extensive) agency relationship (see NJA 2000 p. 685), which, however, should perhaps be regarded more as an alternative thematization rather than an independent assessment factor; and (f) the intermediary's degree of independence, especially in long-term agent relationships. However, the primary factor is perhaps (g) in *whose economic interest* the agreement between the agent and third party is entered into – which can be assessed, among other things, by considering who bears the *business risk* (the risk of loss if the deal falls through, where, in sales commission, the intermediary's potential right to return unsold goods is generally considered a significant factor) and *business interest*, that is, who benefits (most) from the deal being made. In connection with the business interest, it can be noted that an at least quasi-etymological explanation for the term *'kommission'* has been that the commissionary agent should receive a commission in the sense of a percentage of revenue generated. Hence, if the agent is deemed to profit more than just the equivalent to such a commission fee, this speaks against a commission classification.

93 See Case 4 above.

3. COMPARATIVE REMARKS

Jan Biemans and Lorna Richardson

This case deals with the acquisition of goods in the case where an indirect (disclosed) agent acting in their own name on behalf of their principal is involved in the transfer of the goods. The questions distinguish between various types of goods: tangible moveables (such as paintings), real estate property, receivables, and book-entry monies in bank accounts. Also, the questions differentiate between the acquisition of these goods by the indirect agent in their own name on behalf of their principal, on the one hand, and the transfer of these goods by the indirect agent in their own name on behalf of their principal, on the other. Lastly, the case explores the rights of the parties involved in the event of the insolvency of the indirect agent. Just as in Case 4, the indirect agent in this case concludes the sales contracts in their own name, on behalf of their principals.

Question 1: Acquisition of Van Dyck Painting and Apartment

In the first question, Xervix have bought a painting for the benefit of Mr Landwell, and an apartment for Mr and Mrs Astor. The painting has been physically handed to an employee of Xervix and stored on Xervix's premises. In the deed of transfer of the apartment, Xervix are mentioned as the recipients of the property, and the keys of the apartment have been handed over to Xervix. The question is, who are the owners of these assets?

Just as in Case 4 above, the agreement between the principal and the indirect agent is, in most jurisdictions, an agreement of commission.

In some jurisdictions (Belgium, Bulgaria, France, Spain and Sweden[94]), although the contractual rights and obligations arise between the indirect agent and the counterparty, the proprietary legal effects of the contract occur directly between the principal and the counterparty. Consequently, the principals become the owners of the painting and the apartment. In Belgium and France, ownership passes from the moment of the *consent* between the contracting parties, without any need for formalisation.

In other jurisdictions (Czech Republic, Germany and Slovakia), Xervix would become the owners of both the painting and the apartment, and would have to transfer both to the principals. In Germany, the conveyance of the painting can be done in advance, before the transfer of the painting to Xervix, resulting in the transfer of the painting from the patrimony of the agent to the principal at the moment the agent becomes the owner of it for the benefit of the principal.

---

94 It may be noted that, in Sweden, apartments are not generally considered real estate, but legal rights to access and use the property.

However, in Slovakia, if the rules on commercial commission agency contracts apply, Mr Landwell will acquire the painting directly, but Xervix will become owners of the apartment.

In other jurisdictions, the results differ between moveable and immoveable property. For the immoveable property, it will, in several jurisdictions (England, Italy, the Netherlands, Poland and Scotland), be decisive in whose name the apartment will be registered in the land registry. In other jurisdictions (for example, France), registration in the land registry is only necessary to uphold the right against a third party, such as a creditor. If the apartment is registered in the name of the indirect agent, Xervix will become the owners and will have to transfer the apartment to the principals, Mr and Mrs Astor. In England, the agent will hold the property in trust. As for the moveable property, the painting will, in England, Italy, the Netherlands and Poland, pass to the principal, meaning that the principal could revindicate it from the indirect agent. In England, the ownership of the painting will remain with the original seller until property passes, at which stage it will pass directly to the principal. In Poland, ownership of the painting will pass, through the agent, to the principal, but this will happen automatically when the agent acquires it. In Dutch law, ownership of the painting will transfer directly from the third-party seller to the principal; at no time will it form part of Xervix's patrimony. Whether ownership transfers directly from the third party to the principal, or via Xervix, is a matter of some debate in Italian law.

To conclude, in almost all jurisdictions (except Czech Republic, Germany and Slovakia) the painting will pass directly to the principal. In most jurisdictions, but not in Belgium, Bulgaria, France, Spain or Sweden, the indirect agent will become the owner of the apartment.

Question 2: Painting, Apartment and Insolvency of Xervix

In those jurisdictions where the principal directly becomes the owner of both the painting and the apartment (Belgium, Bulgaria, France,[95] Spain[96] and Sweden),

95 Although the reporters note that, had Xervix been the owners, the principals would have had no preference. In that case, Xervix would be an undisclosed mandatary, and the rules on simulated contracts would apply such that the sales contracts were 'apparent contracts' concealing the fact that Xervix are merely a *'prête-nom'* and not the intended owner of the property. As such, the sales contracts are simulated, because the contracts between the real owners and the mandatary are hidden to the buyers. In that specific case, Art. 1201 of the Civil Code provides that the *'contre-lettre'* – i.e. the hidden contract between the prospective buyers and Xervix – would take effect between parties, but produce no binding effect with respect to third parties (who, on the other hand, may still rely on it whenever it is in their interests to do so).

96 The reporters note that, if Xervix were the owners of the property, the principals would have no preferential rights.

the insolvency of Xervix would not make any difference: neither the painting nor the apartment would be part of the insolvency estate. The same holds true, as regards the painting, for those jurisdictions in which the principal directly becomes the owner of the painting (England, Italy, the Netherlands and Poland).[97]

Where the agent becomes the owner of both the painting and the apartment (Czech Republic, Germany and Slovakia), the principals will have only a non-preferential claim against the bankruptcy administrator unless an exception applies. English law dictates that the agent would hold the apartment in trust for the principals, saving the apartment from the insolvency estate, for the benefit of the Astors. In Italy and Poland, the principals would have a preference, with regard to the painting and the apartment, in the insolvency of Xervix. In Germany, despite the majority of commentators arguing for a preference, the principals would not have one where the property had already been transferred to the agent (which contrasts with the position where the third party has yet to transfer the property). In the Netherlands, Scotland and Slovakia, the principals would have no such preferential rights. In the Netherlands and Germany, if the painting and the apartment had not been transferred to the principals by the time Xervix became insolvent, the principals could sue the sellers directly, on the insolvency of the indirect agent; however, these are not the facts of the present case. In German law, the principals could sue the insolvency administrator for an assignment of the claims against the sellers; only after such an assignment would the principals be able to sue the sellers directly.

In the Czech Republic, it is unclear whether the principals would have any rights, in the insolvency of Xervix, with regard to the painting and the apartment. On a broad view, not only outstanding receivables but those already obtained by the agent would fall outside the insolvency estate, protecting the principals.

Questions 3 and 4: Purchase Price, Insolvency, and Sale of the Mesdag Paintings

In the third question, which has parallels with Case 4 above, Xervix sell and deliver to Mr Ross two Mesdag paintings, on behalf of their principal Mrs Brown, on 22 February 2017. The question is whether, on 23 February 2017, Mrs Brown can sue Mr Ross for the purchase price of the Mesdag paintings.

In those jurisdictions (England, Scotland) where disclosed agency constitutes an agreement between the principal and the counterparty, Mrs Brown can sue Mr Ross for the purchase price of the paintings. This is also the case in Italy. In all of these jurisdictions (England, Italy, Scotland), this would not change in the event of Xervix's insolvency.

In most jurisdictions (Belgium, Bulgaria, Czech Republic, France, Germany, the Netherlands, Slovakia, Spain and Sweden), the effects of the agreement only

97 For a discussion of undisclosed agency, see Case 4 above.

arise between Xervix (the indirect agent) and their counterparty (Mr Ross). In Belgian law, Mrs Brown could sue Mr Ross in an oblique action, but this would be as Xervix's representative rather than a claim for payment in her own right. As such, Mr Ross would have to pay Xervix rather than Mrs Brown, should this action be successful. An oblique action would also be possible in French law if the agent had failed to claim payment, although some authors would argue that Mrs Brown should be able to declare her intention to benefit from the contract and sue Mr Ross for the purchase price, in place of Xervix.

In these jurisdictions, the contractual relationship between Xervix and Mr Ross means that only Xervix can sue Mr Ross for the purchase price, unless, for example, Xervix become insolvent (Belgium, Germany, Slovakia (in commercial cases only) and Sweden) or, more generally, fail to seek payment from Mr Ross (the Netherlands, and possibly Spain, where the prevailing view in the literature is that such a claim should be possible), in which case Mrs Brown could also sue Mr Ross directly. In Germany, Mrs Brown would have to seek an assignment of Xervix's claim against Mr Ross before suing him. In the Netherlands, Mrs Brown would have to make a written declaration, to both Xervix's insolvency administrator and Mr Ross, that she intended to sue Mr Ross directly.

In Bulgaria and Poland, the principal would not be able to sue Mr Ross directly, unless with the cooperation of Xervix's bankruptcy administrator. In Czech law, it is unlikely that Xervix's insolvency alone would allow Mrs Brown to sue Mr Ross directly, and she would require an assignment of the claim against him from Xervix to do so. It is likely that Xervix's insolvency administrator would agree to assign the claim, given the costs of seeking payment from Mr Ross and the fact that recovering the purchase price would be for Mrs Brown's benefit rather than Xervix's body of creditors.

Question 5: Bank Account and Insolvency

The last question deals with the book-entry monies in bank accounts: can the principal, Mrs Brown, claim these monies in the situation where the purchaser, Mr Ross, has already paid the purchase price to the indirect agent, Xervix, in the event of Xervix's insolvency?

In most jurisdictions (Belgium, Czech Republic, England, France, Germany and Slovakia), the money paid into Xervix's bank account will intermix with the rest of the money in the account, meaning that it cannot be separated from the other money, and that Mrs Brown cannot exercise any proprietary claim against (the bankruptcy administrator of) Xervix. She would have to file her claim as a general, non-preferential creditor in the bankruptcy of Xervix. The outcome may be different in some jurisdictions (Belgium, the Netherlands), where exceptions apply for special bank accounts held, for example, by lawyers, bailiffs and civil law notaries, giving rise to proprietary claims to the money. In England, the money will not be held in trust, absent matters being structured in such a way as to make the agent trustee of the funds received on behalf of the principal, such as funds being placed in a segregated bank account. In Bulgaria, Mrs Brown would have a claim for payment of the monies, but it is not clear whether this claim would have proprietary effect in the event of Xervix's insolvency.

In Italy, Mrs Brown would have a preferential claim against the insolvent estate, provided the mandate in terms of which Xervix has agreed to act on Mrs Brown's behalf can be evidenced in writing, bearing a date prior to Xervix's insolvency. In Poland, it is possible that Mrs Brown will have a preferential claim. In Scotland, Mrs Brown could sue Mr Ross, even if Mr Ross has already paid Xervix. In Spain and Sweden, the principal enjoys great protection: Mrs Brown could reclaim her money from the bankruptcy estate with proprietary effect. In Swedish law, the funds would have to have been identifiable as being intended for Mrs Brown, such as having been in a client account. There is an argument in Czech law that the relevant provision of the Civil Code should receive a broad interpretation such that not only receivables due but also property and money already received by the agent under the contract entered into on behalf of the principal should be ring-fenced for the principal. The matter has not, however, been determined before the courts.

CASE 7: ASSIGNMENT OF A RECEIVABLE AND SET-OFF

1. CASE

Cloud Investments Ltd delivers IT services. On 1 January 2016, Cloud Investments enter into a loan agreement with Santa Bank for the amount of €10 million. The loan is due to be repaid to Santa Bank by 1 January 2020, with an interest rate of 2 per cent per annum.

The contract contains a clause which allows Santa Bank to raise the interest rate to 5 per cent. In security of repayment of the loan, Cloud Investments has granted a mortgage on its real property in favour of Santa Bank. The contract also allows Santa Bank to terminate the loan agreement and immediately demand payment of all outstanding amounts of principal and interest, if Cloud Investments default on the loan.

By 1 January 2017, Cloud Investments have provided several IT services to Santa Bank, worth €2 million, which have not yet been paid for.

On 31 January 2017, Santa Bank, as assignor, assigns the right to be repaid under the loan agreement to Rangifer Tarandus Bank ('RT Bank'), as assignee. The assignment is intimated to Cloud Investments.

Questions

1. Which rights remain with Santa Bank as assignor, and which rights pass to RT Bank as assignee?
2. Can Cloud Investments set off their claim of €2 million against the claim of €10 million assigned to RT Bank?

2. DISCUSSIONS

2.1. BELGIUM

Siel Demeyere and Vincent Sagaert

I. Operative Rules

1. The rights to payment and to the security over Cloud's property pass to RT Bank.
2. Cloud cannot set off their claim for €2 million against the claim for €10 million.

II. Descriptive Formants

Question 1

A creditor can assign a claim without the cooperation of the debtor, as the assignment does not affect the legal position of the debtor.[1] Where the debtor has been notified of the assignment (or has obtained knowledge of it in another way), the debtor can only discharge themselves by making payment to the assignee.[2] It is also possible to assign future claims or existing claims which are not due, as long as they have been determined or are determinable.

The BCC previously regulated the assignment of a claim as the transfer of incorporeal property,[3] but the regulation of the assignment of a claim has now been incorporated in the new Book on obligations (part of the BCC). The BCC still provides for detailed rules on the effectiveness of the assignment against certain persons, such as the debtor.[4] The right to raise the interest rate, the right to demand immediate payment on default, and the mortgage of Cloud Investment's property are conceived as *accessorium* of the claim, and automatically transfer to RT Bank with the assignment of the claim, unless specified otherwise in the transfer contract.[5] RT Bank should, nevertheless, enter its right to the

1 M. Fontaine, 'La transmission des obligations *de lege feranda*', in obligations, U. C. d. d. d. (ed), *La transmission des obligations*, Bruylant, Brussels 1980, 620; S. Stijns, *Verbintenissenrecht. 2: de algemene leer van de verbintenis*, die Keure, Bruges 2019–16, 58, no. 82; W. Van Gerven and A. Van Oevelen, *Verbintenissenrecht*, Acco, Leuven 2015, 573; P. Van Ommeslaghe, *Traité de droit civil belge. II. Les obligations. Vol. 1*, Bruylant, Brussels 2013, 385, no. 405. For a thorough analysis of the assignment of receivables, see R. Feltkamp, *De overdracht van schuldvorderingen*, 2005, Intersentia, Antwerp 2005.

2 Art. 5.181 BCC.

3 Art. 1689 old BCC.

4 Art. 5.179 BCC.

5 Ibid., Art. 5.177.

mortgage in the land register, in order to ensure the third-party effectiveness of this transfer.[6] This means that third parties cannot ignore the mortgage, and cannot acquire a property right neglecting the mortgage. The assignor is not liable towards the assignee for the insolvency of the debtor, save where they have contractually guaranteed the solvency of the latter.[7]

Question 2

In the case of *schuldvergelijking/compensation* (compensation or set-off), two persons are each other's debtor, and thus each has a claim against the other, with the effect that the smallest debt disappears.[8] There are three kinds of set-off, namely statutory, judicial and contractual set-off. In this case, set-off on a statutory basis is applicable.

Statutory set-off takes place by operation of law, without any initiative or even knowledge of the debtors,[9] as soon as four conditions have been fulfilled:[10]

(a) The claims must exist between the same persons.
(b) Both claims must consist of a sum of money (or fungible goods of the same kind).
(c) Both claims must be certain and not subject to dispute.
(d) Both claims must be due and payable.

In the present case, the first condition is no longer met after the assignment: the first claim is held by RT Bank against Cloud Investments, while Cloud Investments holds the counterclaim against Santa Bank.[11] Statutory compensation is thus not possible, although it would have been had the sums already been due before the moment of assignment. In the latter case, the set-off, which takes place automatically, would have taken place prior to the assignment (or its notification). The claim would then no longer exist.

Set-off will, nevertheless, be possible once the assignment has been notified, if the claims are *samenhangend/connexe* (connected).[12] Claims can, for instance,

6 Ibid., Art. 3.30.
7 Ibid., Art. 5.186.
8 W. Van Gerven and A. Van Oevelen, *Verbintenissenrecht*, Acco, Leuven 2015, 639; P. Wéry, *Droit des obligations: Les sources des obligations extracontractuelles. Le régime général des obligations*, II, Larcier, Brussels 2016, 677, no. 750.
9 Art. 5.255 BCC; R. Houben, *Schuldvergelijking*, Intersentia, Antwerp 2010, 404, no. 651 ff.
10 S. Stijns, *Verbintenissenrecht. 2: de algemene leer van de verbintenis*, die Keure, Bruges 2009–16, 132, no. 181; W. Van Gerven and A. Van Oevelen, *Verbintenissenrecht*, Acco, Leuven 2015, 640–41; P. Wéry, *Droit des obligations: Les sources des obligations extracontractuelles. Le régime général des obligations*, II, Larcier, Brussels 2016, 683, no. 758 ff. See, elaborately, R. Houben, *Schuldvergelijking*, Intersentia, Antwerp 2010, 137 ff.
11 Cass. 26 June 2003, *JLMB* 2005, 204, *Pas.* 2003, 1276, concl. X. De Riemaecker.
12 Art. 5.182 BCC.

be connected where they arise from the same contract. In the present case, the claims are not connected, since they arise from the IT contract, on the one hand, and the loan agreement, on the other, such that compensation is no longer possible after intimation of the assignment.

2.2. BULGARIA

Petar Topurov

I. Operative Rules

1. The right to annul the contract on the basis that the contract is voidable,[13] the right to cancel (terminate) the contract,[14] and the right to request an interest rate change will remain within Santa Bank's patrimony.[15] The right of cancellation and the right to request an interest rate change can be transferred only through an explicit agreement between the cedent and the cessionary. The loan's principal receivable, accrued interest, future interest, mortgage, and right to demand payment of all outstanding amounts of principal and interest if Cloud Investments defaults on the loan will all be transferred to RT Bank.
2. Cloud Investments could set off its claim of €2 million against the claim of €10 million assigned to RT Bank.

II. Descriptive Formants

Regarding question 1 above, the case involves a concluded contract for the transfer of claims (cession) between Santa Bank, in the capacity of the cedent, and RT Bank, in the capacity of the cessionary. According to Art. 99, paragraph 2 LOC, the transferred claim shall pass over to the new creditor with the privileges, securities and other attributes thereof, including interest accrued, unless the opposite has been agreed. The term 'interest' here includes both the interest with a remunerative nature, due for the use of the loan provided, and the interest

---

13 According to Art. 27 LOC, '[c]ontracts concluded by persons of legal incapacity, or by their agents without observing the requirements established for such agents, as well as contracts concluded under mistake, fraud, threat or extreme necessity shall be subject to invalidation.'

14 According to Art. 87, paragraph 1 LOC, '[w]here a debtor under a bilateral contract fails to perform his obligation due to a reason that he is liable for, the creditor may cancel the contract by providing the debtor with an appropriate time period for performance with a warning that he shall deem the contract cancelled upon expiration of that time period.' The cancellation of the contract in the sense of Art. 87 LOC has, as a consequence, the termination of the obligation relationship between the debtor and the creditor.

15 The legal practice states the need for an explicit agreement for the transfer of that kind of right.

established by law, which has a compensatory character, and is due in the event of non-fulfilment of a monetary obligation.[16] In turn, Art. 171 LOC stipulates that the transfer of a claim secured by mortgage must be made in writing with notarised signatures, and entered in the property register, in order for it to have effect. It is accepted that, as a rule, everything commercially belonging to the claim shall be transferred for the benefit of the cessionary, including claims of interest (whether already accrued or due in the future).[17] Concerning the right to demand payment of all outstanding amounts of principal and interest if the debtor defaults on the loan, the existing case law of the Bulgarian Supreme Court of Cassation establishes that this right is transferred to the patrimony of the new creditor.[18] We shall assume, therefore, that the right to change the interest rate on the loan could be transferred for the benefit of the cessionary, as long as this has been agreed upon in the cession contract.[19] The cession's existence does not lead to the automatic transfer of the cedent's right to request nullity, voidance or cancellation of the contract.[20] The latter could, however, be transferred to the cessionary.[21]

Regarding question 2 above, if the debtor has agreed to the transfer of the claim then, according to Art. 103 LOC, they are not entitled to set off their obligation against their claim towards the former creditor. Under an *a contrario* argument, a lack of consent would enable the debtor to object to the offsetting to the new creditor.[22] Inasmuch as the debtor's objection results from another legal relationship with a cedent, the counterclaim of the debtor should have arisen and become chargeable before the notification of the cession.[23]

---

16 A. Ivanov, *Transfer of Receivables in Commercial Turnover*, Sibi, Sofia 2010, p. 114; Decision No. 369/2005 BSC; Decision No. 208/1997 BSC.

17 Insofar as the contract is validly concluded and the debtor is informed about it: A. Kozhuharov, *Contractual Law. General concepts of contractual relationship*, new edition and supplements by P. Petkov, 'St Kliment Ohridski' University Publishing House/Jurispress, Sofia 2002, p. 481. According to Art. 99, paragraph 4 LOC, the transfer of a claim shall be binding upon third parties and the debtor from the day the latter is notified thereof by the former creditor.

18 Decision No. 204 of 25.01.2018 in case No. 2230/2016 BSCC.

19 Decision No. 62 of 15.01.2019 of Varna District Court in case No. 1656/2018.

20 A. Kozhuharov, *Contractual Law. General concepts of contractual relationship*, new edition and supplements by P. Petkov, 'St Kliment Ohridski' University Publishing House/Jurispress, Sofia 2002, p. 483. Such an opinion is justified by the fact that the contract of assignment transfers a principal right, but not the secondary rights of the creditor arising from that principal right.

21 A. Kalaydzhiev, *Contractual Law. General part*, 5th ed., Sibi, Sofia 2010, p. 500. This position is explained by the fact that the right to file a claim for annulment of a contract depends on the personal judgement of the assignor. The assignee acquires a claim, but does not become a party to the legal relationship with the debtor; therefore, they cannot request cancellation of the contract.

22 M. Markov, *Contractual Law*, Sibi, Sofia 2011, p. 202; A. Kozhuharov, *Contractual Law. General concepts of contractual relationship*, new edition and supplements by P. Petkov, 'St Kliment Ohridski' University Publishing House/Jurispress, Sofia 2002, pp. 483–84; Decision No. 2175/1955 BSC.

23 A. Kalaydzhiev, *Contractual Law. General part*, 5th ed., Sibi, Sofia 2010, p. 500.

2.3. CZECH REPUBLIC

Tomáš Richter

I. Operative Rules

1. *All rights pass to RT Bank as assignee.*
2. *Cloud can set off its €2 million claim against the €10 million* claim assigned to RT Bank.

II. Descriptive Formants

The CC legislates for assignments of claims in sections 1879 ff. Section 1879 provides that the creditor may assign a claim or a part thereof to a third party (an assignee), even without the debtor's consent. Certain doubts have been voiced, in general, as to the assignment of remedies that are conditional upon the existence of the obligation but are not exclusively related to the assigned claim.[24] There can, however, be no doubt that both the right to declare a default and the right to increase the interest rate are remedies inextricably linked to the loan receivable, and that the assignee will benefit from them. Indeed, upon assignment of loan receivables, there are not really any residual rights that would remain with the assignor.

Section 1880(1) CC provides that, upon assignment of a claim, the assignee acquires all appurtenances and rights related to the claim, including security rights. The case stipulates that 'Santa Bank, as assignor, assigns the right to be repaid under the loan agreement', which presumably means not only the right to repayment of the principal sum but also to payment of the agreed interest, and the rights to raise the interest rate and to terminate the loan. If this reading of the facts is correct, then all of Santa Bank's rights under the loan agreement would have passed to RT Bank on 31 January 2017, including the rights under the mortgage granted by Cloud over its real estate, in security of repayment of the loan. The date of the notification of the assignment is significant for certain purposes, but not as regards the effective date of the assignment for the purposes of the relationship between the assignor and the assignee.

Section 1884(1) CC provides that the debtor retains all objections against the assigned claim which the debtor had at the time of the assignment. The debtor may invoke its counterclaims against the assignee even if they were not due and payable at the time of the assignment, provided the claims existed at that time; however, the debtor must notify its counterclaims to the assignee without

24 B. Dvořák in M. Hulmák et al., *Občanský zákoník V, Závazkové právo, Obecná část (§1721–2054), První vydání*, C.H. Beck, Praha 2014, p. 730 at 33.

undue delay after becoming aware of the assignment. On the facts as stipulated in the case, one can conclude that Cloud will be able to set off its €2 million counterclaim against the €10 million claim assigned to RT Bank, provided that Cloud notifies the counterclaim to RT Bank 'without undue delay' after the assignment has been intimated to Cloud.[25]

2.4. ENGLAND AND WALES

T.T. Arvind

I. Operative Rules

1. The rights that pass to RT Bank will depend on the terms of the assignment. If only the right to be repaid is assigned, then the only rights that pass will be the right to the loan and interest.
2. Cloud Investments can set off its claim of €2 million against the claim assigned to RT Bank.

II. Descriptive Formants

Question 1

The rights under a loan agreement are (like any other contractual right) considered a 'chose in action', and are capable of assignment in accordance with LPA, section 136, which permits choses in action to be assigned unilaterally by giving written notice to the debtor (see Case 5 above).

The question of which rights pass to RT Bank will depend on the terms of the assignment. If all that is assigned is the right to be repaid, then the only rights that pass to RT Bank will be the right to payment of the loan and interest; all other rights will remain with Santa Bank, including the mortgage, the right to terminate on default, and the right to raise the interest rate. If, however, the assignment is framed to include all rights under the loan agreement and the mortgage, then all rights will pass to RT Bank.

If only the right to be repaid is transferred, then RT Bank's right to receive a higher amount if Santa Bank were to increase the rate of interest will raise specific issues. English law distinguishes between 'existing' choses in action and 'future' choses in action. Only existing choses of action are capable of assignment under LPA, section 136. Future choses in action cannot be assigned, but can be the subject of an agreement to assign, which will be effective at equity if it is made

---

25 Ibid., p. 750 at 9.

for valuable consideration.[26] There are a large number of cases on the distinction between existing and future choses in action, and making the distinction is often difficult. However, commentaries on the subject typically draw a distinction between a sum which is certain to become payable in the future (which will be an existing chose in action) and a sum which is a 'mere expectancy' (which will be a future chose in action).[27]

Applying this distinction, it is likely that the right to receive an increased rate of interest will be a future chose in action, as a 'mere expectancy', and can therefore only be the subject of an agreement to assign rather than an actual assignment under LPA, section 136. An important consequence is that neither RT Bank nor Santa Bank will be able to sue Cloud Investments for the higher rate of interest by themselves: each would need to join the other to the action as a party.[28] In contrast, an assignment of an existing chose in action makes the assignee its owner, and gives them the right to sue the debtor in their own name without joining the assignor as a party to the action.[29]

Question 2

At English law, the assignee of a chose in action – whether through a legal[30] or equitable[31] assignment – takes the assignment subject to any equities which have priority over the assignee's rights. It is well established in the case law that a right of set-off is an equity which has priority, and may be asserted against an assignee.[32] Any claim against the assignor which accrued before Cloud Investments were given notice of the assignment can be set off, regardless of whether or not it was payable on that date. In addition, if the claim arose out of the same contract or transaction as the one that was assigned, or out of a closely connected contract or transaction, it can be asserted against the assignee by way of set-off regardless of whether it accrued before or after the notice of assignment.[33]

Cloud Investment's claim in relation to the IT services does not arise in relation to the same or a closely connected transaction. Nevertheless, because it accrued before the assignment, Cloud Investments can set it off against the claim assigned to RT Bank.

---

26 *Edward Tailby v. The Official Receiver* (1888) 13 App. Cas. 523 (HL).

27 H. Beale (ed), *Chitty on Contracts*, 33rd ed., 2 vols. (London: Sweet and Maxwell, 2019), para. 19-029; J. McGhee et al. (eds), *Snell's Equity*, 34th ed. (London: Sweet & Maxwell, 2019), para. 3-030.

28 See the cases discussed in J. McGhee et al. (eds), *Snell's Equity*, 34th ed. (London: Sweet & Maxwell, 2019), para. 3-023.

29 LPA, s. 136(1)(b); *In re Westerton* [1919] 2 Ch 104.

30 LPA, s. 136(1).

31 *Phipps v. Lovegrove* (1873) LR 16 Eq 80, 88.

32 J. McGhee et al. (eds), *Snell's Equity*, 34th ed. (London: Sweet & Maxwell, 2019), para. 3-026.

33 *Business Computers Ltd v. Anglo-African Leasing Ltd* [1977] 1 WLR 578 (Ch), 585 (Templeman J).

2.5. FRANCE

Sylvain Ravenne and Flora Vern

I. Operative Rules

1. All rights in the loan, including the right to raise the interest rate and to terminate the loan, are transferred to RT Bank. The mortgage securing the loan is also transferred to RT Bank.
2. Cloud Investments cannot set off their claim for €2 million due from Santa Bank against their obligation to pay €10 million to RT Bank.

II. Descriptive Formants

Question 1

Santa Bank may transfer the right to be repaid under the loan agreement to RT Bank in one of two ways: it can either assign the entire agreement *(cession du contrat)* or merely some of the obligations arising from the agreement *(cession de la créance)*.

Concerning the assignment of the entire contract, Article 1216 of the FCC provides:

> A contracting party, the assignor, may assign their status as party to the contract to a third party, the assignee, with the agreement of their own contractual partner, the person subject to assignment.
>
> This agreement may be given in advance, notably in a contract concluded between the future assignor and person subject to assignment, in which case assignment takes effect as regards the person subject to assignment when the contract concluded between the assignor and the assignee is notified to them or when they acknowledge it.
>
> An assignment must be established in writing, on pain of nullity.

Thus, either the loan agreement provided that Santa Bank may assign the agreement, in which case the assignment would have taken effect as regards Cloud Investments when it was notified to the latter, or Santa Bank should have secured Cloud's consent to the assignment of the loan agreement. We will assume that the agreement was validly assigned either way.

As a result of the assignment of the loan, the assignee is substituted for the assignor. Therefore, the rights which the agreement confers on the assignor are transferred to the assignee. The obligations imposed on the assignor by the agreement are also transferred to the assignee. However, according to Article 1216-1 of the FCC, the assignor will be discharged only if the person subject to assignment has expressly consented to this.

In this case, the right to raise the interest rate to 5 per cent and the right to terminate the loan agreement if Cloud Investments default on the loan pass to RT Bank. The same goes for the mortgage, since, according to Article 2424 of the FCC, it 'is transferred by operation of law with the secured claim'.

If Santa Bank prefer to assign the obligation alone (cession de la créance), Article 1321, §4 of the FCC provides that 'the consent of the debtor is not required unless the obligation was stipulated to be non-assignable', but the assignment still has to be notified to Cloud Investments, unless they have already agreed to it (Art. 1324 FCC). This procedure is merely intended for the information of the debtor.

The assignment only transfers the obligation itself and its ancillary rights (Art. 1321 FCC). Therefore, the mortgage passes to RT Bank, since it is, by definition, an ancillary to the obligation to repay the loan.

The same should go for the provision which allows the bank to terminate the loan agreement *(clause résolutoire)*. Case law provides that the assignment transfers, to the assignee, the rights and claims belonging to the assignor and attached to the assigned obligation, unless otherwise stipulated.[34] However, there is no precedent concerning the transfer of either an claim in termination or a *clause résolutoire*. Most authors consider that the claim in termination should be transferred, since it is a guarantee for the assignee.[35] More accurately, however, one author proposes that the claim in termination of the contract would only be transferred if the assignor has fulfilled their own obligations towards the person subject to assignment, or has no obligation towards them; otherwise, only the assignor could, with the agreement of the assignee, pursue the termination of the contract.[36] Here, Santa Bank has fulfilled their obligations towards Cloud Investments. It can, therefore, be assumed that the action in termination would be transferred to RT Bank, and so should the *clause résolutoire* which allows the creditor to terminate the agreement on their own. Therefore, the right to terminate the contract should pass to RT Bank.

On the other hand, the clause which allows Santa Bank to raise the interest rate to 5 per cent cannot be considered a way to secure the repayment of the loan and, therefore, cannot be considered an ancillary right. As a result, it should not pass to RT Bank in the event of an assignment of the obligation to repay the loan.

---

34 Cass., civ. 1re, 24 oct. 2006, no 04-10.231 ('the assignment of a right transfers to the assignee ... the claim in liability ... resulting from the previous fault of a third party which resulted in the loss or reduction of the assigned right'); Cass., civ. 2e, 20 déc. 2001, no 00-10.806; Cass., civ. 1re, 5 jan. 1999, no 96-20.202, deciding that an arbitration clause is transferred to the assignee.

35 F. Terré, P. Simler, Y. Lequette and F. Chénedé, *Droit civil, les obligations*, 13th ed. (Paris: Dalloz, 2022), no 1641; M. Planiol and G. Ripert, *Traité pratique de droit civil français*, 2nd ed. by P. Esmein, J. Radouant and G. Gabolde (Paris: LGDJ), t. VII, 1954, no 1126; C. Aubry and C. Rau, *Droit civil français*, 6th ed. by P. Esmein (Paris: Librairies techniques, 1952), t. V, §359*bis*.

36 J. François, *Traité de droit civil, Les obligations. Régime général*, 4th ed. (Paris: Economica 2017), t. IV, no 485.

Question 2

According to Article 1347-1 of the FCC, 'set-off takes place only in the case of two fungible obligations which are certain, liquidated and enforceable'. In this case, the loan repayment has been enforceable since 1 January 2020. Therefore, there was no opportunity for Cloud Investments to set off their claim against their debt of repayment before the assignment took place. Thus, the question is whether Cloud Investments can set a claim against the assignor, Santa Bank, off against their contractual debt to the assignee, RT Bank.

Concerning the assignment of the contract, Article 1216-2, §2 of the FCC provides:

> The person subject to assignment may set up against the assignee all the defences which they could have been able to set up against the assignor.

This provision is ambiguous, and should be interpreted in light of the provision on '*cession de créance*' (assignment of rights arising from obligations), which states:

> The debtor (subject to assignment) may set up against the assignee defences inherent in the debt itself, such as nullity, the defence of non-performance, termination or *the right to set off related debts*. They may also set up defences which arose from the relations with the assignor *before the assignment became enforceable against them*, such as the grant of a deferral, the release of a debt, or *the set-off of debts which are not related*.[37]

Hence, whether Santa Bank have assigned the entire contract or only a specific obligation arising from it, if the claim of the person subject to assignment against the assignor is related to their debt to the assignee, the person subject to assignment will be able to set off their claim against their debt, *even if the conditions of set-off have been fulfilled after the assignment has taken effect as regards the person subject to assignment*.

On the other hand, if their claim against the assignor is not related to the debt, the person subject to assignment will be able to set off their claim against their debt *only if the conditions of set-off have been fulfilled before the assignment has taken effect as regards the person subject to assignment*.

In this case, it is clear that Cloud Investments' claim against Santa Bank *is not related* to the loan agreement. Therefore, Cloud Investments cannot set off their claim against their contractual debt to RT Bank, because the conditions of set-off were not yet fulfilled at the time when the assignment was notified to Cloud Investments.

37 Art. 1324, §2, FCC (emphasis added).

2.6. GERMANY

Sonja Meier

I. Operative Rules

1. The right to repayment of the loan, the right to receive the future interest, and the right to raise the interest rate will pass to RT Bank. The right to terminate the loan agreement will remain with Santa Bank. Whether the rights that arise from the mortgage agreement will pass to RT Bank depends on the circumstances.
2. Cloud Investments can set off its claim against RT Bank's claim.

II. Descriptive Formants

Question 1

According to §398 BGB, an assignment requires a contract between an assignor and an assignee, in which they agree that a right shall pass. The right to repayment has been validly assigned to RT Bank.

Whether the right to claim interest will also pass to the assignee depends on the assignment agreement in question. Where there is no express provision in the agreement, the courts will assume that the parties intended the right to receive future interest on the loan to also pass to the assignee, and this approach is supported by commentators.[38]

The right to raise the interest rate is a *'Gestaltungsrecht'* (right to influence a legal relationship by unilateral declaration). The assignability of a *Gestaltungsrecht* depends on whether it is independent (such as an option to buy) or relates to an obligation or a contract. The right to raise the interest rate is regarded as a case of unilateral determination of performance, within the meaning of §315 BGB.[39] Such a right modifies the content of an obligation and is, therefore, classified as a *forderungsbezogenes Gestaltungsrecht*; that is, as relating to an obligation. It is generally agreed that such rights automatically pass to the assignee together with the obligation, under §401 BGB.[40]

---

38 *BGHZ* 35, 172 at 173; KG *ZIP* 2009, 2256 at 2257; J. Busche in *J. von Staudingers Kommentar zum Bürgerlichen Gesetzbuch*, vol. §§397–432 (Sellier – de Gruyter 2022), §401, [45]–[46]; E.-M. Kieninger in *Münchener Kommentar zum BGB*, vol. 3 (9th ed., Beck 2022), §401, [11].

39 *BGHZ* 97, 212 at 214; K.P. Berger in *Münchener Kommentar zum BGB*, vol. 4 (8th ed., Beck 2019), §488, [173].

40 E.-M. Kieninger in *Münchener Kommentar zum BGB*, vol. 3 (9th ed., Beck 2022), §398, [97], §401, [10]; J. Busche in *J. von Staudingers Kommentar zum Bürgerlichen Gesetzbuch*, vol. §§397–432 (Sellier – de Gruyter 2022), §401, [35], §413, [13].

The right to terminate the loan agreement is also a *Gestaltungsrecht*. Since it allows the creditor to terminate the whole contract before its usual end, it is regarded as *vertragsbezogen*; that is, relating to the contract as such.[41] It is widely agreed that such rights to unilaterally change the conditions of a contract do not automatically pass to the assignee.[42] On the contrary, it is a matter of debate whether they can be separated from the underlying contract (in the present case, the contract of loan) by way of assignment at all. According to the courts and the prevailing view among commentators, freedom of contract allows parties to assign such rights, at least where they are transferred together with a connected claim.[43] It is a matter of debate whether the assignee can then exercise the right alone or only together with the assignor. The assignment need not be expressly agreed, but can be implied from the agreement between the parties.[44] In the present case, however, the right to terminate was neither expressly assigned nor are there any indications of an implied assignment.

Whether the rights that arise from the mortgage agreement will pass to RT Bank depends on whether the mortgage is a *'Hypothek'* or a *'Grundschuld'*.

The *Hypothek* (§1113 BGB) is a mortgage the existence of which depends on the claim it secures. When the claim (for example, the right to be repaid) is transferred, the *Hypothek* automatically follows and passes to the assignee (§§398, 401, 1153 BGB). It is important to note that the claim that is secured by a *Hypothek* can only be assigned if the formal requirements of §1154 BGB are met. Under this provision, the assignment of the secured claim requires a written agreement and a handing over of the mortgage certificate issued by the Grundbuchamt (Land Registry). In the event that the mortgage was exceptionally established without the issue of a certificate, the assignment of the secured claim requires an entry in the Grundbuch (Land Register). If Santa Bank complies with these formal requirements, the claim and the *Hypothek* will pass to RT Bank.

The *Grundschuld* (§1191 BGB), in contrast, is a mortgage which does not depend on the right it secures. It does not automatically follow the right it secures, but has to be transferred separately. Thus, if Santa Bank merely assigns the claim to RT Bank, which may be done informally (§398 BGB), the *Grundschuld* will not pass to RT Bank. However, Santa Bank can also assign the *Grundschuld*.

---

41 R. Freitag and P. Mülbert in *J. von Staudingers Kommentar zum Bürgerlichen Gesetzbuch*, vol. §§488–90, 607–10 (Sellier – de Gruyter 2015), §488, [260], [292].

42 J. Busche in *J. von Staudingers Kommentar zum Bürgerlichen Gesetzbuch*, vol. §§397–432 (Sellier – de Gruyter 2022), §413, [13]; E.-M. Kieninger in *Münchener Kommentar zum BGB*, vol. 3 (9th ed., Beck 2022), §398, [97].

43 BGH *NJW* 1973, 1793 at 1794; BGH *NJW* 1985, 2640; BGH *NJW* 2012, 1510 at [13]; BGH *WM* 2018, 2128 at [24]; E.-M. Kieninger in *Münchener Kommentar zum BGB*, vol. 3 (9th ed., Beck 2022), §398, [97], §413, [12]; J. Busche in *J. von Staudingers Kommentar zum Bürgerlichen Gesetzbuch*, vol. §§397–432 (Sellier – de Gruyter 2022), §413, [13].

44 W. Ernst in *Münchener Kommentar zum BGB*, vol. 3 (9th ed., Beck 2022), §323, [168].

This requires a written agreement, and either a handing over of the certificate or an entry in the Grundbuch (Land Register) (§§1192 (1), 1154 BGB).

Question 2

According to §406 BGB, a right of set-off is not lost through an assignment: the debtor can set their claim against the previous creditor off against the claim assigned to the new creditor. This right to set-off is only excluded in two situations: firstly, the debtor cannot set off their claim if they knew of the assignment when they acquired the claim against the previous creditor; secondly, even if the debtor acquired the right against the previous creditor before they learned of the assignment, they cannot set off this claim if it becomes due only after the debtor learns of the assignment *and* after the new creditor's claim has become due. These exceptions do not apply in the present case.

2.7. ITALY

Camilla Crea and Claudia Amodio

I. Operative Rules

1. Santa Bank are the contracting party and retain the right to terminate the contract. RT Bank, as assignee of the credit only, acquire a right to credit vis-à-vis Cloud Investments, including accessories (mortgage, interest and *ius variandi*).
2. Cloud Investments are entitled to set off their claim of €2 million against RT Bank.

II. Descriptive Formants

Regarding question 1, this case concerns an assignment of credit, which is governed by Arts. 1260 ff. c.c.

The contract relating to the assignment of credit does not require a specific form, and is concluded through the mere agreement of the assignor and the assignee. In order for the assignment to be effective vis-à-vis the debtor, Art. 1264 c.c.[45] provides that the assignment takes effect on the debtor when they accept it or when it is notified to them.[46]

45 S. Beltramo (ed), *Italian Civil Code and Complementary Legislation*, tr. in 1969 by M. Beltramo, G.E. Longo and J.H. Merryman (West, 2012), pp. 273–74.

46 Courts claim that the notification of the assignment does not require a specific form, and is not subject to special regimes (Cass., 12 May 1998, no. 4774, *Foro italiano*, I (1998), p. 2114).

It should be noted, however, that the notification of the assignment to the debtor and their acceptance or knowledge thereof have no bearing on the change in the active entitlement to the obligation: the assignment of credit takes effect due to the mere consent lawfully given by the assignor and the assignee, pursuant to the principle of the transferring effect of consent.[47] Accordingly, through the assignment of credit, the assignee becomes the exclusive creditor, and thus the only party entitled to claim performance, even where the debtor has not been notified under Art. 1264 c.c.

The assignment of credit transfers only the credit as such, even where this originates from a contract, and the substitution concerns the credit only. Consequently, as the assignee of the credit is not a party to the contract which originated the credit itself, they cannot exercise the powers afforded to the assignor, and so are not entitled to bring an action to terminate the contract.[48]

As a result of the assignment, the credit transfers to the assignee, including all its accessories, possible privileges and real and personal guarantees,[49] unless the parties agree that the security should not transfer (which is not the position in the present case). The assignment must be noted on the margin of the inscription of the mortgage in the land register.[50] The notation does not affect the duties of the parties (assignor and assignee of the credit), but it is required to enforce the mortgage against third parties.[51] The transfer of the credit along with its accessories (including personal and real guarantees) is an application of the Roman principle '*accessorium sequitur principale*'. Accordingly, the assignee also acquires the mortgage connected with the assigned credit, as well as the right to the interest on the credit and the *ius variandi* (the right to change the interest rate).

Regarding question 2, and pursuant to Art. 1263 c.c., the position of the debtor should not worsen as a result of the change of creditor. By virtue of the assignment, the claim is transferred to the assignee with privileges, real or personal guarantees and other accessories. Theoretically, the debtor is entitled to invoke every defence against the assignee as if they were the original creditor.

---

47 Art. 1376 c.c. (S. Beltramo (ed), *Italian Civil Code and Complementary Legislation*, tr. in 1969 by M. Beltramo, G.E. Longo and J.H. Merryman (West, 2012), p. 295).

48 Cass., 6 July 2018, no. 17727, *Guida al diritto*, 42 (2018), p. 73; Cass., 28 April 1967, no. 776, *Foro italiano*, I (1967), p. 1822. On the contrary, in legal literature, see T. Auletta, *La risoluzione per inadempimento* (Milan: Giuffrè, 1942), p. 137; D. Valentino, 'Il cessionario e l'azione di risoluzione del rapporto-fonte del credito ceduto' in R. Favale and B. Marucci (eds), *Studi in memoria di Vincenzo Ernesto Cantelmo* (Naples: Edizioni Scientifiche Italiane, 2003), pp. 893–99.

49 S. Beltramo (ed), *Italian Civil Code and Complementary Legislation*, tr. in 1969 by M. Beltramo, G.E. Longo and J.H. Merryman (West, 2012), p. 273.

50 Cass., 12 September 1997, no. 9023, *Vita notarile* (1998), p. 929; Cass., 10 August 2007, no. 17644, *Giustizia civile*, I (2008), p. 2885.

51 Cass., 23 March 1995, no. 3387, *Giustizia civile*, I (1996), p. 181; Cass., 27 December 1963, no. 3221 and no. 3222, *Foro Padano*, I (1964), p. 822.

As far as the right to set-off is concerned, it should be noted, however, that a derogation to this rule is provided for in the case of acceptance of the assignment by the debtor.[52] Art. 1248 c.c., paragraph 1, states that no set-off may be exercised by the debtor vis-à-vis the assignee if the former has accepted, purely and simply, the assignment. Hence, once the debtor has accepted the assignment, they should not be able to erode the assignee's rights. There is authority establishing that the acceptance of the assignment by the debtor 'results in the irrebuttable presumption of a tacit renunciation to rely on the set-off'.[53]

The question of whether a notice of assignment can prevent the debtor from exercising their contractual right of set-off has also been specifically addressed by the legislator. According to Art. 1248 c.c., paragraph 2, if the assignment has merely been notified (but not accepted), the debtor should be able to exercise their right of set-off, as long as the related claim existed before the assignment.

Given the facts of the case, RT Bank will most likely be bound by Cloud Investments' contractual right of set-off, as this is grounded on claims having arisen towards the assignor (Santa Bank) before the notice of the assignment.

III. Meta-Legal Formants

The Italian legal system accepts the principle that credits are, as a rule, freely transferable, even without the debtor's consent. The reason behind this principle is economic, namely safeguarding the mobility and circulation of future wealth.

2.8. THE NETHERLANDS

Jan Biemans

I. Operative Rules

1. With the assignment of the claim to be repaid under the loan agreement, all of the aforementioned rights transfer to RT Bank: the right to be paid interest of 2 per cent annually, the right to raise the interest rate to 5 per cent, the mortgage right on the real property of Cloud Investments, and the right to terminate the loan agreement and immediately demand payment of all outstanding amounts of principal and interest if Cloud Investments default on the loan.
2. Cloud Investments can set off their claim of €2 million against the claim of €10 million assigned to RT Bank, as both claims existed, and/or originated from legal relationships which existed, prior to the assignment of the claim.

52 E. Moscati, *La disciplina generale delle obbligazioni* (Turin: Giappichelli, 2015), p. 391.
53 Cass., 22 May 1980, no. 3377, *Giurisprudenza italiana*, I, 1 (1981), p. 1528.

II. Descriptive Formants

In response to question 1, Santa Bank, as assignor, assigns the right to be repaid under the loan agreement to RT Bank as assignee, and the assignment is intimated to Cloud Investments. In Dutch law, the right to be repaid under the loan agreement would be considered a claim arising out of the loan agreement for the repayment of the principal sum. If a claim *(vordering)* transfers from the former creditor *(cedent)* to the new creditor *(cessionaris)*, any accessory rights transfer automatically to the new creditor (Articles 6:142 and 3:82 DCC).[54] As a result, after the assignment, RT Bank, as the new creditor, have the right to be paid interest of 2 per cent annually, the right to raise the interest rate to 5 per cent, the mortgage right on the real property of Cloud Investments, and the right to terminate the loan agreement and immediately demand payment of all outstanding amounts of principal and interest if Cloud Investments default on the loan.

According to Article 6:142 (1) DCC, when a claim passes to a new creditor, this creditor will acquire not only the primary right to the performance but also all accessory rights attached to it, such as rights of mortgage or pledge, and rights derived from a surety *(borgtocht)*, privileges *(voorrechten)*, and the power to enforce an existing executorial title with regard to the claim or its accessory rights. Based on this provision, the right of mortgage will automatically transfer by operation of law from Santa Bank, as assignor, to RF Bank. This is especially clear in the simple case in which the right of mortgage has only been vested in favour of Santa Bank to secure the repayment of this loan. In the more complicated case in which the right of mortgage has been vested in favour of Santa Bank for all present and future claims of Santa Bank (Article 3:231 DCC), most authors assume that, if only one of these secured claims has been assigned to another party, there will be a mutual right of mortgage, held by both the former and the new creditors (Articles 3:166 ff. DCC).[55] In such a situation, RF Bank would not have to register their interest in the mortgage in the property registers, as the right of mortgage transfers by operation of law. However, for purposes of third-party protection, and in order to legitimise themselves towards third parties as a rightful (co-)mortgagor, RF Bank would be advised to do so.

According to Article 6:142 (1) DCC, the accessory rights also include the rights (entitlements) of the former creditor to contractual interest and a contractual penalty or periodic penalty payment imposed by the court, except insofar as the interest was already due and payable or the contractual penalty or periodical penalty payment had already been forfeited at the moment the claim passed to the new creditor. Based on this provision, it is clear that RF Bank,

---

54 See, in detail, on the legal consequences of the transfer of claims, including the transfer of accessory rights, J.W.A. Biemans, *Rechtsgevolgen van stille cessie*, Deventer: Kluwer 2011.

55 Ibid., paras. 5.2.2 and 5.7.2.

as the new creditor, are entitled to the right to be paid interest of 2 per cent annually, insofar as this interest was not already due and payable at the moment the claim was assigned.

A recent Dutch Supreme Court case[56] on the transferability of credit claims from banks to non-banks seems also to confirm that the contractual right to alter the interest rate – in this case, the right to raise the interest rate to 5 per cent – is an accessory right which, by operation of law, transfers as an accessory right to the new creditor, as was argued in Dutch legal doctrine.[57]

Although the underlying loan agreement itself does not transfer with the assignment of the claim arising out of it, the leading view in Dutch legal doctrine[58] is that the right to terminate the loan agreement and demand immediate payment of all outstanding amounts of principal and interest if the debtor defaults on the loan also qualifies as an accessory right, and thus transfers by operation of law to the new creditor. A pledgee or creditor seeking executory attachment of the claim have similar rights (Article 3:246 (2) DCC and Article 477 (4) Dutch Code of Civil Proceedings, respectively). According to Article 6:149 DCC, the right to rescind the contract as a result of breach (other than, in this case, defaulting under the loan) and the right to nullify the entire contract generally remain with the contracting party (the former creditor), but these rights do not see to the termination of the contract, as discussed here.

In response to question 2, Cloud Investments can set off its claim of €2 million against the claim of €10 million assigned to RT Bank, as both claims existed, and/or originated from legal relationships which existed, prior to the assignment of the claim.

The rules on set-off can be found in Articles 6:127 ff. DCC,[59] and are written from the perspective of the debtor. Among the requirements for set-off (Articles 6:127 (2), (3) and 6:136 DCC) are the requirement that the debtor exercising the right to set-off is both the debtor and creditor of the opposing party, and the requirement that the debtor can pay its debt to that party. In the case of an assignment or a pledge and attachment of the claim against the debtor, these requirements are no longer met. Article 6:130 DCC protects the reasonable expectation of the debtor to set-off, and provides for a right to set-off

---

56 Dutch Supreme Court, 10 July 2020, ECLI:NL:HR:2020:1274 *(Immobile/Promontoria)*; and Dutch Supreme Court, 10 July 2020, ECLI:NL:HR:2020:1276, JOR 2020/267.

57 See M.H.E. Rongen, *Cessie*, Deventer: Kluwer 2012, no. 1022; and T.E. Booms, *Aanvullen van subjectieve rechten*, Deventer: Wolters Kluwer 2019, no. 495 and 832. See also J.W.A. Biemans, *Rechtsgevolgen van stille cessie*, Deventer: Kluwer 2011, para. 6.8.2.

58 H.L.E. Verhagen and M.H.E. Rongen, *Cessie*, Deventer: Kluwer 2000, p. 131; J.W.A. Biemans, *Rechtsgevolgen van stille cessie*, Deventer: Kluwer 2011, no. 195–97 and Parl. Gesch. Boek 6, pp. 528 and 531.

59 See, on set-off, N.E.D. Faber, *Verrekening*, Deventer: Deventer 2005; and on Art. 6:130 DCC, J.W.A. Biemans, *Rechtsgevolgen van stille cessie*, Deventer: Kluwer 2011, para. 10.5.2.2.

within certain limits.[60] According to Article 6:130 (1) DCC, where the claim of a former creditor (Santa Bank) has passed under particular title to a new creditor (RF Bank), the debtor (Cloud Investments) is nevertheless entitled to offset a counterclaim which they had against their former creditor against the obligation they now have to perform to the new creditor, provided that this counterclaim results from the same legal relationship as the claim that has passed, or that it already belonged to the debtor and had already become due and payable before the claim passed to the new creditor.

Because the €2 million counterclaim of Cloud Investments against Santa Bank already existed before the assignment of the claim by Santa Bank to RF Bank on 31 January 2017, Cloud Investments can offset this counterclaim against the loan (the assigned claim). Cloud Investments can do so by making a statement to their new creditor, RF Bank (Article 6:127 (1) DCC).[61]

2.9. POLAND

Agata Kozioł

I. *Operative Rules*

1. *All the rights* connected with assigned claim pass to RT Bank unless otherwise stated.
2. Cloud Investments *may set off its claim against the assigned claim.*

II. *Descriptive Formants*

In relation to question 1, the assignment of a claim gives rise, according to Article 509 §2 PCC, to the transfer to the assignee of all rights and claims connected with the transferred claim. The same applies, as a rule, to mortgages; on the basis of Article 79 of the LMR Act,[62] the assignment of a claim secured by mortgage results in the transfer of the mortgage to the assignee.[63] However, if the parties to the assignment decide to exclude the mortgage from the transfer of the claim, the mortgage expires.[64]

---

60 See T.M., Parl. Gesch. Boek 6, p. 500; N.E.D. Faber, *Verrekening*, Deventer: Deventer 2005, no. 251 and 255.

61 See J.W.A. Biemans, *Rechtsgevolgen van stille cessie*, Deventer: Kluwer 2011, para. 10.5.2.2.

62 Ustawa z dnia 6 lipca 1982 r. o księgach wieczystych i hipotece (Polish Act of 6 July 1982 on Land and Mortgage Register and on Mortgage).

63 W. Kurowski, 'Komentarz do art. 509' in M. Habdas and M. Fras (eds), *Kodeks cywilny. Komentarz. Tom III. Zobowiązania. Część ogólna (art. 353–534)*, Warsaw 2018, p. 1036.

64 G. Kozieł, 'Komentarz do art. 509' in A. Kidyba (ed), *Kodeks cywilny. Komentarz. Zobowiązania. Część ogólna. Tom III*, Warsaw 2014, pp. 856, 860–61.

It must be stressed that the transfer of a claim secured with a mortgage does not result in the automatic transfer of the mortgage.[65] Pursuant to Article 245^1 PCC, for the transfer of a mortgage to be effective, it must be entered in the relevant land and mortgage register. The registration has a constitutive character, which means that the mortgage passes to the assignee at the moment the entry becomes effective (at the moment of submitting the application for an entry). In addition, as the grounds for making an entry in the land and mortgage register, the statement of intent of the assignor of the secured claim must be made in writing, with the signature authenticated by a public notary (Art. 31 of the LMR Act).

The right to terminate the contract by declaration of will of the creditor, as a right that may influence the legal position of the creditor, passes to the assignee through the contract of transfer of claim (Art. 509 §2 PCC), unless otherwise stated. The Polish Supreme Court has confirmed this rule in its judgment of 6 November 2003.[66] The right to raise the interest should be qualified in the same way (Art. 509 §2 PCC).[67]

The consent of the debtor is not required in order for the assignment of the claim to be valid.[68] However, it should be noted that the assignment becomes effective for the debtor at the moment of the notification to the debtor by the assignor (Art. 512 PCC).[69] This means that, prior to receiving the notification, the debtor may perform their obligations to the assignor in an effective manner, unless they have found out about the assignment from other source (for example, from a notification made by the assignee). The same applies to other legal acts between the debtor and the assignor (Art. 512, second sentence, PCC).[70]

In relation to question 2, the debtor may, pursuant to Article 513 §2 PCC, set off their claim against the assignor, even if it became enforceable after the notification of the assignment to the debtor. The right of set-off is, however, excluded where the mutual claim of the debtor becomes enforceable after the

65 R. Mojak, 'Komentarz do art. 509 k.c.' in K. Pietrzykowski (ed), *Kodeks cywilny. Komentarz. Tom II. Art. 450–1088. Przepisy wprowadzające*, Warsaw 2017, p. 162.

66 Act signature: II CK 16/02.

67 R. Mojak, 'Komentarz do art. 509' in K. Pietrzykowski (ed), *Kodeks cywilny. Tom II. Komentarz. Art. 450–1088. Przepisy wprowadzające*, Warsaw 2017, p. 155.

68 W. Kurowski, 'Komentarz do art. 512' in M. Habdas and M. Fras (eds), *Kodeks cywilny. Komentarz. Tom III. Zobowiązania. Część ogólna (art. 353–534)*, Warsaw 2018, p. 1059; K. Zagrobelny, 'Komentarz do art. 512' in E. Gniewek and P. Machnikowski (eds), *Kodeks cywilny. Komentarz*, Warsaw 2016, p. 1049.

69 W. Kurowski, 'Komentarz do art. 512' in M. Habdas and M. Fras (eds), *Kodeks cywilny. Komentarz. Tom III. Zobowiązania. Część ogólna (art. 353–534)*, Warsaw 2018, p. 1059; R. Mojak, 'Komentarz do art. 512 k.c.' in K. Pietrzykowski (ed), *Kodeks cywilny. Komentarz. Tom II. Art. 450–1088. Przepisy wprowadzające*, Warsaw 2017, p. 174.

70 K. Zagrobelny, 'Komentarz do art. 512' in E. Gniewek and P. Machnikowski (eds), *Kodeks cywilny. Komentarz*, Warsaw 2016, p. 1049.

enforceability of the assigned claim.[71] In the present case, the assigned claim resulted from a loan agreement that is payable by instalments, and each instalment is due on a different date. This would lead to the conclusion that Cloud Investments could set off its claim only in relation to that part of the assigned claim that was due after 1 January 2017 (date of the enforceability of Cloud Investments' claim). However, the case states that the assignment was intimated to the debtor (Cloud Investments) and, therefore, by virtue of Article 512, second sentence, of the PCC, this exclusion cannot apply.[72] Thus, Cloud Investments, as a debtor of the assigned claim, would be allowed to set off their claim against the assignor without restrictions (apart from those that result from general rules on set-off).

2.10. SCOTLAND

Lorna MacFarlane

I. *Operative Rules*

1. The *right to be repaid under the loan* passes to RT Bank as assignee, and *all other rights* remain with Santa Bank.
2. Cloud Investments *can* set off their claim of €2 million against the claim assigned to RT Bank (on the basis that the loan agreement and the IT services contract are inextricably linked).

   Variation: Cloud Investments *cannot* set off their claim of €2 million against the claim assigned to RT Bank (on the basis that the loan agreement and the IT services contract were concluded separately and are not inextricably linked).

II. *Descriptive Formants*

Assignment involves the transfer of a right from the creditor to the assignee, in order that the assignee can sue the debtor for performance of the right,[73] upon intimation of the assignation to the debtor.[74] In the present case, the assignment

---

71 W. Kurowski, 'Komentarz do art. 512' in M. Habdas and M. Fras (eds), *Kodeks cywilny. Komentarz. Tom III. Zobowiązania. Część ogólna (art. 353–534)*, Warsaw 2018, p. 1075.

72 G. Kozieł, 'Komentarz do art. 512' in A. Kidyba (ed), *Kodeks cywilny. Komentarz. Zobowiązania. Część ogólna. Tom III*, Warsaw 2014, p. 886.

73 H.L. MacQueen, *The Laws of Scotland: Stair Memorial Encyclopaedia: Obligations: Contract*, vol. 15 (LexisNexis/Law Society of Scotland, London/Edinburgh 1995), para. 855.

74 H.L. MacQueen and J. Thomson, *Contract Law in Scotland*, 4th ed. (Bloomsbury Professional Limited, West Sussex 2016), para. 2.87.

has been intimated to Cloud Investments, and so the right to repayment has been assigned from Santa Bank to RT Bank. The assignment of one of Santa Bank's contractual rights against Cloud Investments does not mean that *all* of Santa Bank's rights are transferred – the transaction is limited to the rights assigned. Accordingly, the rights to terminate the loan and alter the interest rates have likely not been assigned.

However, the security will be assigned as an accessory right. Erskine states that assignation carries to the assignee, 'all rights which corroborate or strengthen the right conveyed'.[75] In terms of a mortgage, this would mean that the assignee would have the right to have the assigned security.[76] RT Bank could, therefore, demand that the mortgage be assigned to it. The assignation in favour of RT Bank must be registered in the Land Register to effectively transfer the security to them.[77]

In terms of Cloud Investments' ability to set off the claim in respect of the IT services against the outstanding loan sums, it is noted that set-off is 'not a term of art' in Scots law, and that the 'sources in Scots law on set-off are desperately confused'.[78] However, as a general rule, the 'cedent's right is the measure of the right of the assignee'.[79] As such, it is recognised, in case law[80] and commentary,[81] that the debtor (in this case, Cloud Investments) can plead against the assignee (RT Bank) any debt due to the debtor by the cedent (Santa Bank).

According to Anderson, this is subject to the requirement that the 'defence is intrinsic to the claim assigned'.[82] This results in the variation in the answer: the answer depends on whether, on the facts of the case, the loan agreement and the IT services contract are inextricably linked. If the IT services were delivered under the same contract providing for the loan agreement, then Cloud Investments will likely have a defence of set-off. If the loan and IT agreements were concluded separately, however, the variation will apply.

---

75 J. Erskine, *An Institute of the Law of Scotland*, 8th ed. (Law Society of Scotland/Butterworths, Edinburgh 1871), para. 3.5.8; Scottish Law Commission, *Report on Moveable Transactions Volume 1: Assignation of Claims* (Scot Law Com No. 249, 2017), paras. 12.26–12.27; R.G. Anderson, *Assignation* (Edinburgh Legal Education Trust, Edinburgh 2008), paras. 2.07–2.14; R.G. Anderson and J.W.A. Biemans, 'Reform of Assignation in Security: Lessons from the Netherlands' (2012) 16(1) *Edinburgh Law Review* 24–57.

76 Scottish Law Commission, *Report on Moveable Transactions Volume 1: Assignation of Claims* (Scot Law Com No. 249, 2017), paras. 12.26–12.27.

77 Conveyancing and Feudal Reform (Scotland) Act 1970, s. 14(1).

78 R.G. Anderson, *Assignation* (Edinburgh Legal Education Trust, Edinburgh 2008), para. 8.38.

79 W.W. McBryde, *The Law of Contract in Scotland*, 3rd ed. (Thomson/W. Green, Edinburgh 2007), para. 12-69.

80 *Livingston v. Reid* (1833) 11 S 878; *Shiells v. Ferguson, Davidson & Co.* (1876) 4 R 250.

81 W.W. McBryde, *The Law of Contract in Scotland*, 3rd ed. (Thomson/W. Green, Edinburgh 2007), para. 12-70.

82 R.G. Anderson, *Assignation* (Edinburgh Legal Education Trust, Edinburgh 2008), para. 8.47.

III. *Meta-Legal Formants*

McBryde notes that assignation 'exists for a strong commercial reason. A creditor has a right which may be commercially valuable and can be sold or transferred in security. The market inexorably tries to make any asset marketable and with as few legal impediments as possible.'[83] The permissibility of assignation, accordingly, reflects policy considerations of commercial convenience and market efficiency.[84]

Regarding the assignability of the mortgage, the Scottish Law Commission considered reforming the law so as to provide the assignee a completed title to the security immediately upon assignation. However, it was thought that this would adversely impact the clarity of the law on standard securities, in particular the fact that the registered holder of a standard security would not necessarily be the assignee.[85]

2.11. SLOVAKIA

Kristián Csach, Monika Jurčová, Peter Mészáros and Veronika Zoričáková

I. *Operative Rules*

1. No rights regarding the security remain with Santa Bank. The rights transfer to RT Bank, as the assignee of the secured claim. The other contractual rights should remain with Santa Bank.
2. Cloud Investments are entitled to set off their claim of €2 million against the claim of €10 million assigned to RT Bank.

II. *Descriptive Formants*

Regarding question 1, the result will depend upon the interpretation of the words used by the parties: assignation of 'the right to be repaid under the loan agreement'. The right to be repaid is not acknowledged as a particular right detachable from the receivable (from the position of a creditor) as such. Slovak law regulates an assignment of claims (receivables), not the assignment of particular rights arising out of, or connected with, the receivables. Another

---

83 W.W. McBryde, *The Law of Contract in Scotland*, 3rd ed. (Thomson/W. Green, Edinburgh 2007), para. 12-03.

84 See also Scottish Law Commission, *Report on Moveable Transactions Volume 1: Assignation of Claims* (Scot Law Com No. 249, 2017), para. 1.55.

85 Ibid., para. 12.28.

option for the collection of claims by a third party is the so-called *inkaso* assignment, which is not expressly regulated by law, but in practice is based on the concept that the nominal assignee is entitled to bring the claim against the debtor in their own name, but for the ultimate benefit of the nominal assignor. The contractual arrangement between such parties is the contract on commission under section 577 SCommC. The right of the nominal assignee is limited to the possibility of bringing a claim before the court in their own name, despite the fact that, substantively, the nominal assignor will still be entitled to the receivable as such. However, the case law places limits on this practice. According to the Supreme Court, the usage of contract on commission in order to entitle a third person to request payment from the debtor is always dependent upon the actual assignation of the claim.[86] Accordingly, the *inkaso* assignment will always be connected with the substantive change in the creditor's position.

Given the facts of the case, the parties have entered into an arrangement which entitles RT to be repaid, and not only to demand payment which is then to be transferred back to Santa Bank. Therefore, it is assumed that this contractual arrangement is to be construed as an ordinary assignment of a secured claim, rather than an *inkaso* assignment.

After the assignation of a secured receivable, the assignee will step into the position of the secured creditor (s. 151c(3) SCC). All rights and duties of the secured creditor regarding the security are thereby transferred to the assignee. The extent of the contractual rights which are assigned to the new creditor is disputed, however. According to a recent decision of the Supreme Court, the assignee becomes the creditor of the particular obligation, and other rights connected with the receivable which are dependent on the transferred receivable, but does not enter into the basic obligatory relationship with the debtor from which the assigned receivable arose, which may comprise a significant number of rights and obligations not affected by the assignment. The assignor remains a party to the original agreement.[87] According to this position, it might be argued that the original contractual position and the contractual rights (the rights to

86 See the SSC decision file no. 1 M Obdo V 6/2009 dated 22.07.2010, published in the journal *Zo súdnej praxe*, 6 (2011), no. 59. According to the SSC, even if the parties conclude a commission contract for the collection of claims, a substantive assignment of the claim is needed. The SSC draws a sharp distinction between the internal and external effects of a commission on collection of claims. Therefore, the commission agent not only has to appear as being the creditor towards debtors, but must also be a creditor from the substantive point of view. For a remarkable critique of this decision, see M. Novotný, 'Vymáhanie cudzej pohľadávky vo vlastnom mene (Niekoľko úvah nad rozhodnutím Najvyššieho súdu SR) [Collection of claims belonging to other creditors (Some thoughts on a Supreme Court Judgment)]', *Právní rozhledy*, 23–24 (2016), pp. 818–25. The case law of lower courts is much more fragmented still. See e.g. M. Valachovič, 'Zastupovanie vlastníkov pri správe bytového domu [Representation of owners and the administration of the residential building]', *Zlepšovák*, 4–5 (2018), pp. 35–37.

87 Decision of the SSC file no. 2 Cdo 125/2018 dated 27.06.2019 (R 72/2019).

terminate the contract or to amend or adjust the contractual arrangement) remain with the assignor. However, the rights regarding the security are transferred with no limitations.

Regarding question 2, according to section 529(2) SCC the debtor may set off against the assignee the receivables that he had against the assignor at the time he was notified about the assignment, or when the assignment was proved to him, if he notified the assignee about them without undue delay. Therefore, if Cloud Investments notified RT Bank that it had claims against Santa Bank, Cloud may set off its claims for €2 million in fees unpaid by Santa Bank against the claim of €10 million that has been assigned to RT Bank.

2.12. SPAIN

Carles Vendrell Cervantes

I. Operative Rules

1. Both *the right to be repaid* (the personal claim) and the *mortgage* (the right to foreclose it) pass to RT Bank as assignee. However, other rights under the loan agreement remain with Santa Bank.
2. Cloud Investments *would not be entitled* to set off their claim of €2 million against the claim of €10 million assigned to RT Bank.

   Variation: Cloud Investments would be able to set off their claim of €2 million against the claim of €10 million assigned to RT Bank if Cloud Investments did not consent to the assignment.

II. Descriptive Formants

Question 1

Under Article 1528 of the Spanish Civil Code, the assignment of a credit involves the assignment of the associated or ancillary rights, such as securities, mortgages or pledges. Accordingly, both the credit claim and the right to foreclose the mortgage would pass to RT Bank as assignee.

The assignment of a credit, which does not require the debtor's agreement (the debtor's agreement is not a necessary requirement, but they will be given the possibility to issue their consent or not, with different consequences, as will be seen later), is not an assignment of a contract, which would require the consent of the debtor. According to the Spanish Supreme Court judgments of 23 October 1984, 26 November 1982 and 25 April 1975, only the assignment of a contract involves transfer of all the rights and obligations under that contract as a whole to a third party. As a result, since the loan agreement as a whole has not been assigned to RT Bank, neither Santa Bank's right to raise the interest rate to 5 per cent, nor its right to terminate the loan agreement and immediately demand payment of all the outstanding amounts of principal and interest if the debtor defaults on the loan, would pass to RT Bank as assignee.

Question 2

According to Article 1195 of the Spanish Civil Code, offsetting credits and debts between two parties can only happen where those parties are each other's creditor and debtor in relation to the same debt. In the present case, there is no such reciprocity between the parties after the assignment, because the assignee is only related to the debtor through the assignment of the loan claim, and the assignee has nothing to do with the other debt. As a consequence, the debtor cannot set off their claim relating to the IT services against the assignee. In this regard, paragraph 1 of Article 1198 of the Spanish Civil Code states that a debtor who consents to the assignment of rights will not be able to oppose a claim by the assignee on the grounds of their (i.e. the debtor's) own claim against the assignor (as stated above, the debtor is entitled to either issue or withhold their consent).

However, paragraph 2 of Article 1198 of the Spanish Civil Code provides a particularity: if the creditor intimates the assignment of the claim to the debtor, and the debtor does not consent to it, the debtor may exercise rights of set-off arising from claims against the assignor that arose prior to the credit assignment. Accordingly, if, following the intimation of the assignment of the credit, Cloud Investments refused consent for the assignment, they would be able to set off their claim of €2 million against the right assigned to RT Bank.

2.13. SWEDEN

Oskar Mossberg

I. *Operative Rules*

1. The *right to be repaid* and to *adjust the interest*, as well as *the mortgage*, *would all be transferred* to RT Bank.
2. It depends on the circumstances of the case, but Cloud *would most likely be able to use its counterclaim* against Santa Bank *for set-off* in relation to RT Bank.

II. *Descriptive Formants*

Regarding question 1, only rights and not obligations can be transferred through assignment, and without the consent of the debtor. Transfers of obligations (*'gäldenärsbyten'* (debtor shifts)) require the creditor's acceptance. This follows from general principles of the law of obligations. Here, a brief note on legal sources might be helpful: a general principle is considered an independent source of law, and can be invoked as such.[88] This reflects an important part of Swedish (and Nordic) legal culture, and is a reflection of the fact that we do not have more generally applicable statutory laws regarding the law of obligations, including contract law (such as, for example, the Bürgerliches Gesetzbuch or the Code Civil). Instead, the Nordic countries generally have statutory Acts regulating (only) a few specific important types of contracts (such as sale of goods contracts). Outside the scope of these statutory laws, Swedish lawyers use techniques of analogy and/or invoke uncodified general principles. Basic principles are often implied in other rules, as it is not atypical, in the Swedish legislative tradition, to give explicit rules for exceptional cases while letting the main rules remain implicit. In practice, the principles are found by looking in the books, as usual, but the books need not necessarily be cited, as the principles are considered sources of law in and of themselves (see Case 1 above, at section II).

According to the Swedish case NJA 2005 p. 142, a creditor's right to adjust the interest rate can correspond to an obligation to lower it, if the adjustment clause is, for example, intended to allow for adjustment in relation to the creditor's own costs of borrowing. As there are no circumstances in the present case to suggest such a corresponding obligation on the creditor's part (other than a general obligation not to apply the adjustment clause disloyally),[89] this right can be transferred, as the *'fordran'* (the claim, or right to be repaid) will be viewed as an integral part of the *'överlåtelseobjekt'* (object of transfer). The general obligation of loyalty would hold against the assignee, in accordance with the general principle expressed in Article 27 of Skuldebrevslagen (the Act on Debt Letters) (see Case 4 above).[90]

Mortgages can be transferred, both as regards the right to be repaid (through a *'fordringsöverlåtelse'* (assignment of claim)) and as regards any lien securing the credit. A *'fastighetspant'* (lien in real property) needs to be perfected, through transactions separate from the loan agreement, to be effective against

---

[88] A general principle is considered an independent source of law, and can be invoked as such. See Case 1, section II above, on general principles of the law of obligations. On debtor shifts, see e.g. S. Lindskog, *Betalning: Om kongruent infriande av penningskulder och andra betalningsrättsliga frågor*, 2nd ed., Norstedts juridik, Stockholm 2018, pp. 363 ff. with further references.

[89] The demand for loyal application of the adjustment clause can be viewed as a particular instance of an overarching principle of good faith and fair dealing. In Swedish legal literature, the principle has been called *'lojalitetsprincipen'* (the principle of loyalty): see e.g. the monographical treatment by J. Munukka, *Kontraktuell lojalitetsplikt*, Jure, Stockholm 2007.

[90] See, on this issue, e.g. S. Lindskog, *Betalning: Om kongruent infriande av penningskulder och andra betalningsrättsliga frågor*, 2nd ed., Norstedts juridik, Stockholm 2018, pp. 266 ff., or in English, O. Lando et al., *Restatement of Nordic Contract Law*, Jurist- og Økonomforbundets forlag, Copenhagen 2016, pp. 313 ff.

the lien's owner's general creditors. Perfection is attained either through transfer of possession *(traditio)*, if it is a physical *'pantbrev'* (lien letter), or by registration in the lien registry administered by a government authority. This follows from statutory rules in Jordabalken (the Earth Balk, the central statutory Act on real property).[91] However, these requirements do not apply where the claim is transferred through an assignment by a creditor. In such a case, the security would follow the claim, as an accessory, unless the parties to the assignment contracted differently. This follows from the statutory provision in Article 3 of Förmånsrättslagen (the Act on Advantageous Rights), which regulates the regime of preferential claims in bankruptcy; it is also the clearly held position of scholars.[92]

Regarding question 2, this issue is regulated by Articles 27 and 28 of the Act on Debt Letters. Article 28 is intended to create a measure of symmetry between payment and set-off as modes of performance, by extending the debtor's *'invändningsrätt'* (right of objection) against demands from a new creditor for payment to some set-off situations. Pursuant to Article 27, objections which would be valid against the assignor can also be made by the debtor against claims from the assignee, who in this sense does not get a *'bättre rätt'* (better right) than the assignor. Pursuant to Article 28, the debtor can use counterclaims against the assignor for set-off in relation to the assignee, unless: (a) the debtor acquired a counterclaim against the assignor when they knew or should have known that the claim had been assigned; or (b) the counterclaim was due to be paid after the debtor was made aware of the assignment, and later than the debt.

Accordingly, the general Swedish rule on set-off of claims (under Article 28) is that a debtor may set their counterclaim against the assignor off against claims made by the assignee after the assignment has taken place. There are two exceptions to this general rule. The first concerns cases where the debtor has acquired the counterclaim in bad faith; that is, where they were aware, or ought to have been aware, of the assignment. This exception is not applicable to the present case. The other exception concerns cases where the counterclaim was due to be paid after the debtor has been made aware of the assignment, and later than the assigned claim. Where these exceptions apply, set-off is not allowed.

This means that whether or not Cloud has a right to set its counterclaim off against RT Bank's claim depends on the circumstances. Given the stated facts, Cloud would likely be able to use its counterclaim for set-off against RT Bank's

---

91 See also e.g. T. Håstad, *Sakrätt avseende lös egendom*, 6th ed., Norstedts, Stockholm 1996, p. 320.

92 See e.g. G. Walin, *Förmånsrättslagen, lönegarantilagen m.m.: En kommentar*, 5th ed., Norstedts, Stockholm 2004, p. 31; G. Walin, G. Millqvist and A.H. Persson, *Panträtt*, 3rd ed., Norstedts juridik, Stockholm, 2012, pp. 107 ff., 183 ff., 230 ff.; T. Håstad (ed), *The Nordic Contracts Act: Essays in Celebration of its One Hundredth Anniversary*, Djøf Publishing, Copenhagen 2015, pp. 297 ff; O. Lando et al., *Restatement of Nordic Contract Law*, Jurist- og Økonomforbundets forlag, Copenhagen 2016, p. 317.

claim, despite the assignment and the fact that RT Bank is not the actual debtor as regards Cloud's counterclaim. This answer hinges on the assumption that payment for the services rendered was due and payable before the point that Cloud is made aware of the assignment from Santa Bank to RT Bank (given the stated facts, this is not entirely clear, but it seems like the most plausible practical case).

III. *Meta-Legal Formants*

Unless the parties contract differently (and there are no special rules applicable), a security follows the claim to which it is related, through assignment. The theoretical explanation for this is that the security is seen as an accessory to the claim, and will also become worthless to the assignor, since they have no post-assignment right to it, as a security is necessarily tied to a claim.

The rule in Article 27 of the Act on Debt Letters (see also Case 4 above) is intended to facilitate the transferability of claims without endangering the debtor's legal position too much. The rule on set-off is intended to create a measure of symmetry between payment and set-off as modes of performance, and to strike a fair balance between the interests of the debtor, the assignor and the assignee. The Swedish rules are the result of legislative cooperation among the Nordic countries, whereby large areas of private law, including the basic rules of *'fordringsrätten'* (the Swedish law of claims) – the part of the law of obligations that specifically concerns claims – are largely harmonised.

3. COMPARATIVE REMARKS

Jan Biemans and Lorna Richardson

This case deals with the effects of the assignment of receivables. In particular, it relates to the effects of the assignment between the old creditor (the assignor, A) and the new creditor (the assignee, C), with regard to the so-called 'accessory' or 'ancillary' rights – the rights that transfer with the assigned claim, by operation of law (or, in some cases, together with the claim itself). The rights in this case that may qualify as such are: (a) the right to payment of the claim itself; (b) the (contractual) right to payment of the contractual interest; (c) the contractual right to raise the interest rate; (d) the proprietary right of mortgage (established for the repayment of the loan); and (e) the contractual right to terminate the loan agreement (and demand immediate payment of all amounts outstanding) in the event of default.

In addition, the case addresses the position of the debtor of the assigned claim (B), in terms of their power to set off a claim against A after (the notification or intimation of) the assignment has taken place. As, generally, one of the requirements for statutory set-off is that the claims to be set off must exist between the same persons, the question is whether B is protected against the change of person because of the transfer of the claim.

Question 1: Accessory Rights

In all jurisdictions, it is possible to assign and transfer the receivable, as such. In the various jurisdictions, the following positions are taken with regard to whether rights are considered to be accessory rights:

(a) In most jurisdictions (Belgium, France, Germany, the Netherlands, Scotland, Slovakia, and probably Bulgaria, Czech Republic, England, Italy, Poland, Spain and Sweden), the right to payment will transfer, but as (a part of) the receivable itself, and not an accessory right to the receivable.
(b) In Belgium, the contractual right to payment of the interest is considered part of the receivable itself rather than an accessory right (the right to be paid interest, therefore, transfers with the right to payment). In Bulgaria, Czech Republic, England, France, Italy, the Netherlands, Poland, Slovakia, and probably also Scotland and Sweden, it is considered an accessory right. In German law, it is a matter of interpretation of the assignment agreement whether this right will be transferred to the assignee. As such, it is not regarded as an accessory right in a strict sense.
(c) The contractual right to raise the interest rate is considered an accessory right in Belgium, Czech Republic, Germany, Italy, the Netherlands, Poland and Sweden.
(d) The proprietary right of mortgage is considered an accessory right in Belgium, Bulgaria, Czech Republic, France, Germany, Italy, the Netherlands, Poland, Scotland, Slovakia, Spain and Sweden. In Germany, this depends on whether the mortgage is a '*Hypothek*' (the existence of which depends on the claim it secures) or a '*Grundschuld*' (which does not depend on the right it secures). A *Hypothek* would automatically pass to the assignee, whereas a *Grundschuld* would have to be transferred to the assignee separately.
(e) The contractual right to terminate the loan agreement in the event of default is considered an accessory right in Belgium, Bulgaria, Czech Republic, the Netherlands, Poland, and possibly France. In Germany, this right, if it can be assigned (which is debated), would have to be expressly assigned or for there to be an assignation implied from the parties' agreement, neither of which features in the facts of this case study.

To conclude, the right to payment of the principal sum and the interest, as well as the right of mortgage, will generally transfer, but not the right to raise the interest rate or to terminate the loan agreement.

In most jurisdictions (Belgium, Bulgaria, Czech Republic, France, Germany, Italy, the Netherlands, Scotland, Slovakia and Sweden), if a right is an accessory right, it transfers automatically with the receivable, by operation of law. In Belgium, Bulgaria, France, Germany, Italy, Poland and Sweden, parties can also (to some extent) exclude the transfer of accessory rights. In Germany, a separate transfer of the mortgage may be required: this will be the case if it is a *Grundschuld*, but not if it is a *Hypothek*.

In Bulgaria, the right to raise the interest rate could be expressly assigned to the new creditor. In England, the rights to raise the interest rate and to terminate the contract and demand immediate repayment could be expressly assigned, as could the mortgage.

In several jurisdictions (Bulgaria, Germany and Poland), the transfer of the right of mortgage would need to be filed with the public registry in order to complete the transfer, and in Germany the transfer of the assigned claim would also be filed; in others (Belgium, Italy, the Netherlands and Sweden), it would be wise to file the transfer of the mortgage for purposes of third-party protection and/or enforcement against third parties.

Question 2: Set-off

In most jurisdictions analysed in this volume (all except Belgium, France, Scotland and Spain), Cloud Investments would be able to set off its claim for €2 million against RT Bank's claim for payment of the loan. While the outcome would be the same in most jurisdictions, the applicable legal rules vary between the jurisdictions.

In most jurisdictions (Belgium, Czech Republic, Italy, Poland, Scotland and Spain), the debtor (Cloud Investments) would only be protected against the assignment of the claim if their counterclaim against the old creditor (Santa Bank) already existed prior to (the notification of) the assignment (generally whether due and payable or not). In some jurisdictions, additional requirements apply: for example, the debtor should not have consented to the assignment (Bulgaria, Italy, Spain); the debtor should have notified the assignee of their counterclaim without undue delay after notification of the assignment (Czech Republic, Slovakia); the counterclaim of the debtor should be enforceable before notification of the assignment (Bulgaria) or before the assigned claim has become enforceable (Poland); the counterclaim should be inextricably linked to the claim (Scotland). If the set-off happens by operation of law (Belgium), the two claims will have been set off before the assignment took place. If the set-off takes place after a declaration (for example, in the Netherlands), the declaration will have retroactive force.

In other jurisdictions, the debtor enjoys a broader protection. In Dutch law, as well as the debtor being able to set off their counterclaim where it existed prior to (the notification of) the assignment, they also have a right of set-off against the assignee where their claim originated from a legal relationship (or relationships) which existed prior to notification of the assignment to them. As with most other jurisdictions, in English law the debtor may also set off their claim where it existed prior to notification of the assignment. The debtor may also set off their claim where it arose out of the same, or a closely connected, contract or transaction, regardless of whether the claim accrued before or after notification of the assignment. Similarly, in France, the debtor can set off a counterclaim they have against the old creditor, against the assigned claim, if the conditions for set-off were met before (the notification of) the assignment, or if the claims are related to each other.

In Germany and Sweden, the debtor retains their full right to set-off, unless they knew of the assignment when acquiring their counterclaim against the assignor, or they acquired their counterclaim before they knew about the assignment, but the counterclaim became due after the debtor had learnt of the assignment, and after the assigned claim had become due (in Sweden, this rule serves to prevent the acquisition of a counterclaim in bad faith).

CASE 8: IMPOSING OBLIGATIONS ON A THIRD-PARTY BENEFICIARY

1. CASE

Anita decides to rent her husband, Ben, a boat from Anchors Ltd, as a gift. The contract is between Anita and Anchors, and specifies that the crew of the boat will be Ben and four friends.

Ben and his friends take the boat out. They have a great time – so great, in fact, that they are a day late in returning the boat to Anchors. Anchors tell Ben that he will have to pay a late return penalty of €750. Ben refutes this. Anchors draw Ben's attention to clause 14(a) of the contract between Anchors and Anita, which provides for a late-return fee.

Question

From whom can Anchors seek payment of the penalty?

2. DISCUSSIONS

2.1. BELGIUM

Siel Demeyere and Vincent Sagaert

I. Operative Rules

Anchors can seek payment from Anita under the contract. They may, alternatively, be able to seek damages from Ben on a non-contractual basis, as a result of Ben's complicity in contractual breach.

II. Descriptive Formants

This case can be solved in two ways, depending on whether the timely return of the boat, under penalty of the fee, is in the first place conceived as a contractual obligation, or as a burden connected with the clause in favour of a third party. Looking at it from the former point of view, Anchors can seek payment of the penalty from Anita: she is the contracting party and the breach of contract is *toerekenbaar/imputable* (accountable) to her.[1] Returning the boat in time is a *resultaatsverbintenis/obligation de résultat* (obligation to achieve a result), such that Anita is liable for not complying with the obligation, unless she is able to prove *overmacht/force majeure (vis maior)*. There is only *vis maior* when a reasonable person could not anticipate and prevent the breach of contract.[2] This is definitely not the case here, resulting in the liability of Anita for the penalty. It should be observed that penalty clauses can be mitigated in Belgian law, to the extent that they manifestly exceed the potential damage at the moment of the agreement (Art. 5.88, §2 BCC).

Ben could only be held liable on an extracontractual basis (meaning on the basis of an unlawful act),[3] more specifically based on the judge-made legal device of *derde-medeplichtigheid aan contractbreuk/tierce complicité de la violation d'une obligation contractuelle* (third-party complicity in contractual breach). The four conditions for fault in the case of third-party complicity are satisfied *in casu*:[4]

(a) There is a valid contract between Anchors and Anita.
(b) There is a breach of contract imputable to one of the contracting parties, namely Anita.
(c) The third party was aware of the contractual situation, or should reasonably have been aware of it. Even though Ben was not aware of the penalty itself, he knew he should have returned the boat one day earlier. This is enough to satisfy this condition, as the knowledge requirement is applied flexibly.
(d) The third party has actively cooperated or participated in the contractual breach. There is no doubt that this condition is satisfied as well, since it was Ben himself who returned the boat one day late.

The damage, and a causal link between the fault and the damage, must also be proven, as the situation at hand concerns general extracontractual liability. The contractually imposed late-return fee cannot be invoked against Ben, so

[1] Art. 5.225 BCC.
[2] Ibid., Art. 5.226, §1; S. Stijns, *Verbintenissenrecht. Leerboek 1*, die Keure, Bruges 2009–16, 162, no. 211; W. Van Gerven and A. Van Oevelen, *Verbintenissenrecht*, Acco, Leuven 2015, 171; P. Wéry, *Droit des obligations: Théorie générale du contrat*, I, Larcier, Brussels 2011, 540, no. 564.
[3] Art. 1382 old BCC.
[4] Art. 5.111 BCC; Cass. 22 April 1983, *Arr.Cass.* 1982–83, 1022, concl. E. Krings, *RCJB* 1984, comment Y. Merchiers, *RW* 1983–84, 427, comment E. Dirix; Cass. 28 November 2002, no. C.01.0532.F, *Pas.* 2002, 2293; S. Stijns, *Verbintenissenrecht. Leerboek 1*, die Keure, Bruges 2009–16, 246, no. 322; W. Van Gerven and A. Van Oevelen, *Verbintenissenrecht*, Acco, Leuven 2015, 245; P. Van Ommeslaghe, *Traité de droit civil belge. II. Les obligations. Vol. 1*, Bruylant, Brussels 2013, 674, no. 433; P. Wéry, *Droit des obligations: Théorie générale du contrat*, I, Larcier, Brussels 2011, 619, no. 655.

Anchors will have to prove the actual loss they have suffered. Proving the causal link will not pose a problem in this case. Ben is liable for the damage to Anchors because of the breach of contract.

Alternatively, the return of the boat, under penalty of the fee, can be conceived of as a burden connected with the clause in favour of a third party,[5] Ben, concerning the use of the boat. Traditionally, the binding nature of such a burden is denied, because it would conflict with privity of contract. A third party can only receive a right, and is not liable for the performance of any obligations. This situation should, therefore, be designated as a *stipulation de contrat pour autrui*,[6] where Ben has agreed on a separate contract with Anchors, which contract may be implied. On this hypothesis, he has failed to comply with a contractual obligation, a situation we have already analysed above for Anita.

2.2. BULGARIA

Petar Topurov

I. Operative Rules

Anchors may request payment of the punitive fee from Anita, but not from Ben.[7]

II. Descriptive Formants

Anita concludes a contract with Anchors for the rental of a boat, in favour of her husband Ben. The contract is made with an intention to donate, and is not associated with family needs; otherwise, there may arise a joint liability between Anita and Ben, by virtue of the law, and in accordance with the property regime applicable between them. The characteristic features of the relations lead to the inference that a contract has been concluded in favour of a third party, within the meaning of Art. 22 LOC. Only entitlements, not duties, may arise for the beneficiary, based on its text. The third party can fulfil the obligations of the contracting party only on a voluntary basis.[8] The contractor and the promisor[9] represent the two parties to the contract, according to Art. 22 LOC. It is, therefore, only possible to claim payment of a punitive fee from Anita.

---

5 See, elaborately, N. Carette, *Derdenbeding*, Intersentia, Antwerp 2011, 723, no. 783 ff.

6 Ibid., 737, no. 806.

7 Anchors can also seek damages from Ben on the basis of tort law, but must provide proof of the exact amount of damages suffered due to the overdue use of the boat.

8 A. Kalaydzhiev, *Contractual Law. General part*, 5th ed., Sibi, Sofia 2010, p. 168.

9 Ibid., p. 165.

2.3. CZECH REPUBLIC

Tomáš Richter

I. Operative Rules

Anchors can *most likely seek the payment of the penalty from Anita only.*

II. Descriptive Formants

The CC regulates contracts for the benefit of third parties in sections 1767 and 1768, which were already cited in response to Case 1. To recap, section 1767(1) provides that where, pursuant to a contract, the debtor must perform to a third party, the creditor may demand that the debtor performs to such third party. Section 1767(2) provides that it shall depend on the content, nature and the purpose of the contract whether such a third party is also entitled to demand performance of the contract, and, if so, when. It will be presumed that the third party has become so entitled if the performance is to be provided mainly for the third party's benefit. Section 1767(3) provides that the debtor may also invoke objections arising from the contract against the third party. Section 1768 provides that, if the third party rejects the right acquired under the contract, they shall be deemed not to have acquired such right at all. The creditor may demand the performance for itself, unless this would be contrary to the content or purpose of the contract.

It follows from the above that the actual provisions of the contract, including clause 14(a), but not only that clause, would be determinative of the liability issue. It would seem very likely that Anita would be liable to Anchors for the late fee, as Anchors' undoubted counterparty who had agreed to rent the boat. Whether Ben and/or any of his four friends would be liable alongside Anita is highly uncertain. The likely answer is no, however, since there is nothing in the facts which would suggest that either Ben or any of his four friends have themselves agreed to be bound by the terms of the contract, including in particular clause 14(a). In fact, it is not clear from the facts that they were even aware of the exact terms of the contract.

2.4. ENGLAND AND WALES

T.T. Arvind

I. Operative Rules

Anchors can seek payment from Anita, as the contracting party, but not from Ben.

II. Descriptive Formants

Although third parties can enforce and rely on contractual clauses, subject to the requirements of CRTPA, neither CRTPA nor any other common law or statutory rule permit the enforcement of contractual terms against third parties. The general rule is that a contract can only impose duties or liabilities on persons who are parties to it, and not on third parties. Although there are few recent cases directly establishing this principle, it is nevertheless implicit in many cases,[10] and the leading commentary on contract law treats the point as being 'so obvious that it scarcely needs to be stated'.[11]

The main exceptions to this rule relate to covenants concerning land, which can bind subsequent purchasers of the land (as discussed in Case 5 above), and to agency, where an undisclosed principal can be sued on a contract within the agent's actual authority (as discussed in Case 4). Neither exception applies on the facts, as the subject matter of the contract is not land, and Anita rents the boat as a gift for Ben rather than as Ben's agent.

Ben is also unlikely to have any liability in tort to Anchors. Even if Ben was negligent in returning the boat late, the loss suffered by Anchors as a result of the late return of the boat will be considered pure economic loss in English law, and liability in negligence for pure economic loss only arises where the defendant has voluntarily assumed liability to the claimant in respect of that loss (see, further, Case 9 below). More specific economic torts, such as the tort of inducing breach of contract, require the existence of a specific intention to procure a breach. It is not sufficient for breach to be a foreseeable consequence of the defendant's conduct; it must, rather, be the goal or end of their conduct.[12] On the facts, it is unlikely that this requirement will be met.

Anita, as the contracting party, is, however, bound by the obligation to return the boat on time, even if she does not herself crew it, and will be liable for the late payment fee (assuming it to be enforceable, and neither a penalty under the rule against penalties[13] nor unfair for the purposes of the Consumer Rights Act 2015).[14]

---

10 See e.g. *MacDonald Dickens & Macklin v. Costello* [2011] EWCA Civ 930, [2012] QB 244.

11 H. Beale (ed), *Chitty on Contracts*, 33rd ed., 2 vols. (London: Sweet and Maxwell, 2019), para. 18-139.

12 *OBG Ltd v. Allan* [2007] UKHL 21, [2008] 1 AC 1 [42]–[43] (Lord Hoffmann).

13 See *Cavendish Square Holding BV v. Talal El Makdessi* [2015] UKSC 67, [2016] AC 1172.

14 Consumer Rights Act 2015, s. 62.

2.5. FRANCE

Sylvain Ravenne and Flora Vern

I. Operative Rules

Anchors can seek payment of the penalty from Anita. Anchors may also be able to seek it from Ben and his friends if they were made aware of the clause before making use of the boat.

II. Descriptive Formants

The rental contract between Anita and Anchors is intended to be for the benefit of Ben and his friends, who will have effective use of the boat while Anita pays the rent, as a gift for her husband. This contract contains a '*stipulation pour autrui*' (stipulation for another person).

As discussed previously,[15] a '*stipulation pour autrui*', according to Article 1206 of the FCC, grants the beneficiary a direct claim against the promisor, which means that Ben could sue Anchors for performance of the rental contract. However, the reverse is not true. The law does not provide for any direct claim of the promisor against the beneficiary, because while a *stipulation pour autrui* is beneficial for a third party, it does not create obligations on behalf of this person. Anchors should, therefore, sue Anita for any claims relating to the performance of the rental contract.

Case law does, however, provide that, where the beneficiary accepts the *stipulation pour autrui*, they may be required to perform certain obligations[16] and, correlatively, they will be liable if they do not perform them as required. This happens, for instance, where the parties who stipulate for another person agree that this person will be bound by certain terms and conditions if they want to benefit from the clause. Such a clause is valid as long as the beneficiary has knowledge of it and can refuse the benefit of the contract accordingly. This, in turn, presupposes that the parties agreed on the terms under which the beneficiary would be bound. If these conditions were met, Ben and his friends could be required to pay the late-return penalty, if they were informed of the relevant clause by Anchors.

It seems unlikely that Ben and his friends could be liable under tort for returning the boat too late, as Anchors have suffered no specific damage from this negligence – not even business loss. In France, tort liability requires, as per Article 1240 of the FCC, not only fault, negligence or an unlawful act, but also damage or a loss that will be compensated for.[17]

---

15 See Case 1 above.

16 Cass., civ. 1re, 8 déc. 1987, n° 85-11769.

17 Cass., civ. 1re, 9 nov. 2004, n° 86-02-12506.

2.6. GERMANY

Sonja Meier

I. Operative Rules

Anchors can seek payment of the penalty only from Anita. Anchors can also claim rent for the period of delay from Anita. It is not clear whether a contractual liability to pay damages falls on Anita, Ben or both. Ben may also be liable in delict.

II. Descriptive Formants

Anchors and Anita are the only parties to the rental contract, since Anita did not act as Ben's direct agent. §1357 BGB, according to which a contract concluded by a married person covering necessaries for the members of the family generates rights and obligations for both spouses, does not apply here, since the concept of 'necessaries' does not cover a boat trip made by the husband and four friends.[18] The contract between Anita and Anchors will probably be regarded as a contract for the benefit of a third party under §328 BGB, which entitles Ben to claim the performance from Anchors but does not make him a party to the contract.[19]

Where a rental contract has been made for the benefit of a third party, it is not clear whether the contractual obligation to return the rental object to the lessor is on the contracting party (Anita), the third party (Ben) or both. The matter is disputed among commentators,[20] and there seems to be no relevant case law.

In any case, the obligation to pay the late-return fee can only fall on Anita and not Ben. Since Ben is not a party to the contract, he cannot be bound by the agreement therein of a contractual penalty. If Anita is regarded as debtor of the obligation to return the boat, the penalty will be owed under §339 BGB if she can be held responsible for the breach of contract constituted by the late return. §278 BGB makes a party responsible for the acts of persons it engages in the performance of a contract. According to the courts and commentators, a party renting property is responsible for the acts of persons who use the property with

18 See A. Roth, *Münchener Kommentar zum BGB*, vol. 9 (9th ed., Beck 2022), §1357, [17]–[24].

19 Cf. Case 1, question 1.

20 A contractual obligation of the third party to return the rented object is assumed by W. Hadding in *Soergel, Bürgerliches Gesetzbuch*, vol 5,3 (13th ed., Kohlhammer 2010), §334, [22]; H. Dörner, *Dynamische Relativität* (Beck 1985), 173, and A. Lehmann-Richter, *ZMR* 2010, 813, 820–21. It is doubted by W. Bayer, *Der Vertrag zugunsten Dritter* (Mohr Siebeck 1995), 349–50. According to Lehmann-Richter, only the third party is liable, while according to Blank, the obligation falls on both the contracting party and the third party.

that party's consent.[21] Anita will, therefore, be responsible for the late return, and will consequently be liable to pay the penalty. If, by contrast, only Ben is regarded as being obliged to return the boat, the late-return fee can be construed as a kind of guarantee in the form of a promise to pay a penalty in the event of a breach of contract by a certain third party.[22] Anita will then be liable to pay under this guarantee.

Anchors can also avail itself of other remedies for the late return of the boat, but only to the extent that the amount owed under these remedies exceeds the amount of the penalty (§§340 (2), 341 (2) BGB). Thus, double compensation is avoided.

Under §546 a of the BGB, Anchors can claim rent for the period of the delay, according to either the agreed or the market rate (whichever is higher).[23] This rent has to be paid by the person who was originally obliged to pay the rent.[24] Thus, Anchors can claim the 'delay rent' only from Anita, not from Ben.

In the event that they have suffered a loss, Anchors also have a contractual claim for damages under §§280 (1), (2), 286 BGB. In principle, damages for delayed performance (in this case, for the delay in returning the boat) require a warning notice to be issued by the creditor against the debtor. This notice, however, is not required where the parties have fixed a specific date for the required act (§286 (2) no. 1 BGB), as Anita and Anchors have done here by fixing a return date in their contract. Whether it is Anita or Ben who is liable to pay these damages depends on the disputed question, mentioned above, of who is contractually obliged to return the boat. If Anita is the obligor of the obligation to return the boat, §278 BGB makes her responsible for Ben's failure to return the boat in time,[25] and thus she will be liable to pay damages to Anchors. If the contractual duty to return the boat falls on Ben, by contrast, he will be liable to pay the contractual damages. If both are bound to return the boat, they will be jointly and severally liable to pay the damages.

In the event that Ben is not regarded as being under a contractual duty to return the boat, he may nevertheless be liable in damages for breaching a protective duty under §241 (2) BGB. The relationship between the debtor and the third party having rights under the contract is not a genuine contractual relationship. However, it is generally regarded as a special obligational relationship *(Schuldverhältnis)*, which, according to §241 (2) BGB, can generate duties to

---

21 BGH *NJW* 1991, 1750, 1752; S. Grundmann in *Münchener Kommentar zum BGB*, vol. 2 (9th ed., Beck 2022), §278, [32].

22 See P. Gottwald in *Münchener Kommentar zum BGB*, vol. 3 (9th ed., Beck 2022), §343, [37].

23 BGH *NJW* 1999, 2808.

24 A. Lehmann-Richter, *ZMR* 2010, 813, 820.

25 As mentioned above, a party renting property is responsible for the acts of persons who use the property with that party's consent.

take care of the rights and interests of the other party.[26] It is, therefore, widely acknowledged that the third party has duties to take care of the interest of the debtor.[27] Thus, they must not inflict harm on the debtor's person or property, or misuse data or confidential information obtained in the course of performance of the contract. It is, however, not clear whether these duties include a duty to timeously return a rented boat.

If Anchors are the owners of the boat, Ben can also be held liable in delict under §823 (1) BGB for wrongful detention of another's chattel. However, where the wrongdoer initially acquired possession with the permission of the owner, as is the case here, the delictual rules are modified by the rules governing the vindication claim *(Eigentümer-Besitzer-Verhältnis)*. According to §§989, 990 BGB, damages arising from a detention alone, such as the owner's loss of rent (in contrast to damage done to the substance of the chattel) can only be recovered if the possessor is obliged to give up the chattel to the owner under §985 (the vindication claim), and is, regarding this duty, in a state of formal default *(mora)* under §286 BGB.[28] As mentioned earlier, §286 requires a warning notice unless the date for the required act is fixed. It is not clear whether the fixing of a return date in the contract between Anita and Anchors fulfils this requirement and can, thus, generate delictual liability on the part of Ben.[29]

Anita is not liable in delict since she has not been at fault and is not delictually responsible for the acts of her husband.

2.7. ITALY

Camilla Crea

I. Operative Rules

Anchors can only seek payment of the penalty from Anita, and not from Ben and his friends.

---

[26] See Case 9 below.

[27] P. Gottwald in *Münchener Kommentar zum BGB*, vol. 3 (9th ed., Beck 2022), §328, [31], §334, [11]; S. Klumpp in *J. von Staudingers Kommentar zum Bürgerlichen Gesetzbuch*, vol. §§328–45 (Sellier - de Gruyter 2020), before §328, [62], §328, [25]; W. Hadding in *Soergel, Bürgerliches Gesetzbuch*, vol 5,3 (13th ed., Kohlhammer 2010), §334, [22]; BGH *NJW* 2005, 3778; H. Dörner, *Dynamische Relativität* (Beck 1985), 129, 172–73; W. Bayer, *Der Vertrag zugunsten Dritter* (Mohr Siebeck 1995), 348–51.

[28] T. Raff in *Münchener Kommentar zum BGB*, vol. 8 (9th ed., Beck 2023), §990, [38], §992, [15]; C. Thole in *J. von Staudingers Kommentar zum Bürgerlichen Gesetzbuch*, vol. §§985–1011 (Sellier - de Gruyter 2023), §989, [50].

[29] Cf. T. Raff in *Münchener Kommentar zum BGB*, vol. 8 (9th ed., Beck 2023), §990, [39]; C. Thole in *J. von Staudingers Kommentar zum Bürgerlichen Gesetzbuch*, vol. §§985–1011 (Sellier - de Gruyter 2023), §990, [109].

II. Descriptive Formants

The case at issue involves a contract in favour of a third party, a type of contract which is analysed in Case 1 above.

In the event of a stipulation in their favour, the third party, as a beneficiary, acquires the rights as they are created by the contract.[30] Furthermore, Art. 1413 c.c. states that the promisor can raise, against the third party, defences based on the contract from which the third party derives their right, but not those based on other relationships between the promisor and the stipulator.

The 'declaration that the third party intends to avail himself' (Art. 1411 c.c.) of the contract between stipulator and promisor amounts to the third party's consent to the stipulation in their favour. This declaration is not a fully fledged acceptance, although it prevents the stipulator from revoking the contract and the third party from refusing the stipulation. It entails adherence to the whole contract; that is, to all the terms therein.[31]

However, the beneficiary of a contract in their favour acquires only the rights or benefits arising therefrom. A penalty clause implies a conventional assessment of damages without a judicial review, and serves a deterrent and punitive function; that is, it prevents and punishes the failure to perform the contract and/or delay in performance, regardless of proof of damage (Art. 1382 c.c.).

In any case, paying the penalty is a duty. The promisor can bring an action, *ex contractu*, only against the stipulator. Accordingly, the courts have ruled that the stipulator is the party that must return leased property and pay the fee.[32]

III. Meta-Legal Formants

See Case 1 above.

2.8. THE NETHERLANDS

Jan Biemans

I. Operative Rules

Anchors can only seek payment of the penalty from Anita.

---

30 V. Roppo, 'Il contratto' in G. Iudica and P. Zatti (eds), *Trattato di diritto privato* (Milan: Giuffrè, 2001), p. 545.

31 Cass., 1 April 1994, no. 3207, *Rivista dell'arbitrato*, (1995), p. 69; Cass., 18 March 1997, no. 2384, *Contratti* (1997), p. 360; Cass., 10 October 2000, no. 13474, *Giustizia civile Massimario*, (2001), p. 20.

32 Cass., 22 October 2008, no. 25584, *Giustizia civile*, 7-8, I (2009), p. 1683; Cass., 20 January 2005, no. 1150, *Giustizia civile* (2006), p. 2165.

II. *Descriptive Formants*

The specification in the contract between Anita and Anchors qualifies as a third-party clause as meant in Article 6:253 DCC, as further described in Case 1 above. Although such a provision creates the right for a third party (Ben) to claim performance from one of the parties to the contract (Anchors), the effect of such a third-party clause is not that it creates obligations on the third party, or that the contracting parties may also enforce the obligations in the contract against this third party. Consequently, if Ben and his friends are a day late in returning the boat to Anchors, Anchors can only demand payment of the late-return penalty of €750 from Anita, but not from Ben and/or his friends.

Anita may, in turn, demand payment from Ben. Also, Anchors may claim damages from Ben and his friends, based on the unlawful act (Article 6:162 DCC, and Article 5:2 DCC) of infringing the property right of Anchors by returning the boat late, or on unjustified enrichment (Article 6:212 DCC). However, these actions would not be based on clause 14(a) of the contract between Anchors and Anita, which provides for a late-return fee.

In theory, it is possible for an obligation to be attached to a third-party right.[33] However, a stipulation that the person entitled to the third-party right also has an obligation towards one of the parties to the contract should be included in the contract which contains the third-party clause. The case details do not indicate that this has been done.

2.9. POLAND

Agata Kozioł

I. *Operative Rules*

Anchors can seek *payment of the penalty fee from Anita only.*

II. *Descriptive Formants*

The penalty fee, as described in this case, has its source in the contractual relation of the parties; as such, it can be sued for only on the basis of the terms of the contract.

The contract between Anita and Anchors should be classified as an *'umowa o świadczenie na rzecz osoby trzeciej'* (contract on performance to the benefit of

---

33 C.H. Sieburgh, *Mr. C. Assers Handleiding tot de beoefening van het Nederlands Burgerlijk Recht. 6. Verbintenissenrecht. Deel III. Algemeen overeenkomstenrecht*, Deventer: Wolters Kluwer 2022, pp. 564 and 575; Parl. Gesch. BW Boek 6 1981, pp. 959 and 1045.

a third party). According to Article 393 PCC, such an agreement entitles the third party to receive a benefit directly from the debtor of the contract. However, a contract on performance to the benefit of a third party does not implicitly impose any obligations on a person who is not a party to that contract.[34]

Pursuant to Article 391 PCC, a contract may provide that a third person is obliged to fulfil a described obligation. Such a contract is called an '*umowa o świadczenie przez osobę trzecią*' (contract on performance by a third party). It should be stressed that, if the third person fails to perform their obligation, the creditor cannot effectively demand performance from that person; they must direct their claim towards the debtor under the contract.[35] However, the debtor may direct their claim towards that third party if the prerequisites of the liability of the third party (usually resulting from a contract between the debtor and the third party) have been fulfilled.

It is not clear whether the obligation to pay a penalty fee was imposed by the contract on Ben, as the user of the boat, by using the institution of the contract on performance by a third party (Art. 391 PCC). Independently of the fact whether the penalty fee was imposed, taking into account Articles 391 and 393 PCC, the only person against whom Anchors can effectively enforce their claim concerning a delay in the performance of a contractual obligation is Anita, as a party to the contract.

2.10. SCOTLAND

Lorna MacFarlane

I. Operative Rules

Anchors can seek payment of the penalty from *Anita*.

II. Descriptive Formants

Anchors can recover the late-return fee from Anita by way of an action for payment, assuming that the €750 late-return fee is not a 'penalty clause'.[36]

Ben is not a party to the contract between Anita and Anchors, and so he cannot be sued under this contract. Third parties cannot be burdened under contracts to which they are not party. This is recognised as a second limb of the 'privity

34 P. Zakrzewski, 'Komentarz do art. 391' in M. Habdas and M. Fras (eds), *Kodeks cywilny. Komentarz. Tom III. Zobowiązania. Część ogólna (art. 353–534)*, Warsaw 2018, p. 299.

35 Ibid., p. 287.

36 A penalty clause is an unenforceable contractual term which provides for a remedy for one party which is extravagant, exorbitant or unconscionable. See *Cavendish Square Holding BV v. Talal El Makdessi* [2015] UKSC 67.

doctrine' in Scots law (the first, discussed in Case 5 above, being the prevention of third parties' enforcement of contractual benefits under contracts to which they are not party). In *Ashley v. Muir*,[37] for example, Lord Fullerton mentioned that a third party had 'no direct responsibility [for contractual performance], or what is called "privity of contract"'.[38] Case law on this point is otherwise thin. However, commentators firmly uphold this view. For example, Gloag notes that 'it is not within the province of contract to impose any liability upon a third party',[39] and Smith comments that a contract cannot 'bind a stranger to it'.[40] The Scottish Law Commission stresses that the contracting parties can confer rights on third parties, but not duties.[41]

It is unlikely that Anchors can make a delictual claim against Ben. If, however, Anchors successfully argued that Ben had breached a duty of care to return the property on time, such a claim would be for loss arising from the breach of that duty, rather than the specific €750 late-return fee. The finding of a delictual duty on the part of Ben does not mean that he is subject to the terms of the contract.

Anita will likely not be able to seek payment from Ben. Gifts[42] are enforceable unilateral contracts in Scots law, provided that the giver intended to make a gift to the recipient,[43] and has delivered the gift to them.[44] These requirements appear to have been met in this case: Anita intended to give Ben a present of the boat trip, and she delivered this gift by informing him of the contract with Anchors. Those who choose to give gifts cannot generally 'compel any counter-performance in return for the ... act of donation'.[45] Anita could possibly argue that Ben is subject to an implied term that he will not put Anita in breach of the contract with Anchors. Commentators refer to implied terms only in respect of the donor (for example, an implied term that the donor will not adversely affect the donee's right to gifted property in the future).[46] However, it is possible to

37 *Ashley v. Muir* (1845) 7 D 524.

38 Ibid. at 530 per Lord Fullerton. See also *Howgate Shopping Centre Ltd v. GLS 164 Ltd* 2002 SLT 820.

39 W.M. Gloag, *The Law of Contract: A Treatise on the Principles of Contract in the Law of Scotland*, 2nd ed. (W. Green, Edinburgh 1929), p. 257.

40 T.B. Smith, *Short Commentary on the Law of Scotland* (W. Green, Edinburgh 1962), p. 773. See H. MacQueen and Lord Eassie (eds), *Gloag and Henderson: The Law of Scotland*, 14th ed. (W Green, Edinburgh 2017), para. 8.01; D.M. Walker, *The Law of Contracts and Related Obligations in Scotland*, 3rd ed. (T & T Clark, London 1995), para. 29.1.

41 Scottish Law Commission, *Discussion Paper on Third Party Rights in Contract* (Scot Law Com DP No. 157, 2014), para. 2.23.

42 Also known as donation: H. MacQueen and M. Hogg, 'Donation in Scots law' (2012) *Juridical Review* 1, 1.

43 Ibid., 10.

44 Ibid., 13.

45 Ibid., 3–4.

46 W.M. Gordon, *The Laws of Scotland: Stair Memorial Encyclopaedia: Donation*, reissue (LexisNexis/Law Society of Scotland, London/Edinburgh 2011), para. 39; H. MacQueen and M. Hogg, 'Donation in Scots law' (2012) *Juridical Review* 1, 15.

give a gift subject to a condition,[47] and in this case the implied condition could be that Ben must comply with the terms of the contract. MacQueen and Hogg write that, in the context of gifts, there is 'nothing to prevent the implication of a term in the particular circumstances of an individual case, applying the usual tests of necessity and, where appropriate, business efficacy'.[48] Anita could argue that it is necessary to imply this term because she cannot control the actions of Ben and his friends. If this is successful, the donation can be reclaimed.[49] This would not specifically include payment of the late-return fee, but would allow Anita to recover the full value of the contract with Anchors.

III. Meta-Legal Formants

The policy consideration justifying the protection of third parties such as Ben from the imposition of liability is that, according to Gloag, 'parties to a contract cannot fetter the free will of a third party'.[50] The importance of protecting the third party's intentions is also recognised by McBryde, who states that it is 'axiomatic that a duty could not be imposed on the third party against its will'.[51]

Scots law's enforcement of donations is based on Roman law,[52] rather than any modern discussion on policy considerations.

2.11. SLOVAKIA

Kristián Csach, Monika Jurčová, Peter Mészáros and Veronika Zoričáková

I. Operative Rules

Anchors may seek payment of the penalty only from Anita, because she was the person with whom they entered into the contract. Even the family law rules do not give rise to a claim against Ben directly.

---

47 W.M. Gordon, *The Laws of Scotland: Stair Memorial Encyclopaedia: Donation*, reissue (LexisNexis/Law Society of Scotland, London/Edinburgh 2011), para. 40.

48 H. MacQueen and M. Hogg, 'Donation in Scots law' (2012) *Juridical Review* 1, 15.

49 W.M. Gordon, *The Laws of Scotland: Stair Memorial Encyclopaedia: Donation*, reissue (LexisNexis/Law Society of Scotland, London/Edinburgh 2011), para. 42, citing *Connell's Judicial Factor v. MacWatt* 1961 SLT 203.

50 W.M. Gloag, *The Law of Contract: A Treatise on the Principles of Contract in the Law of Scotland*, 2nd ed. (W. Green, Edinburgh 1929), p. 257.

51 W.W. McBryde, *The Law of Contract in Scotland*, 3rd ed. (Thomson/W. Green, Edinburgh 2007), para. 10-10.

52 W.M. Gordon, *The Laws of Scotland: Stair Memorial Encyclopaedia: Donation*, reissue (LexisNexis/Law Society of Scotland, London/Edinburgh 2011), para. 2.

II. *Descriptive Formants*

This contract would be considered a contract in favour of third parties. According to section 50 SCC:

(1) The participants may also conclude an agreement in favour of a third person.
(2) Unless this Act or agreement between the participants stipulate otherwise, the third person shall be entitled from the agreement from the moment when he expresses his consent to the agreement. The debtor shall be entitled to raise the same objections against this person that he can raise against the person with whom he entered into the agreement. If the third person waives his right, the debt shall be discharged unless the agreement stipulates that in such case, the debt is to be performed to the person with whom the debtor concluded the agreement.
(3) Until the third person expresses its consent, the agreement shall be valid only between those who concluded it; the right to the performance shall belong to the participant who reserved the performance in favour of the third person unless anything else was agreed. The same rule shall apply if the third person denied the consent.

Even though the sole fact that a third party is a beneficiary of the performance is not sufficient for a contract to be classified as a contract in favour of a third party (see answers to Cases 1 and 3 above),[53] Ben has, in the given contract, been specifically named as the beneficiary of the contract, and it is assumed that Ben was intended to have the possibility to demand performance from Anchors directly – he was the person who could ask that the boat be given to him. Moreover, Anita would not be on board the boat and, therefore, the parties did not intend performance to be made to Anita. Therefore, the contract might be construed as a contract in favour of a third party (Ben). After Ben expressed his consent to the contract, including through the act of making use of the boat, he became entitled to the performance of the contract (s. 50(2) SCC), but not liable for any breach of contract nor obliged to make any other counter-performance.[54] From the point of view of a contract in favour of third parties, Anita is, therefore, bound by the contract and liable for the late return of the boat. As contractual agreements are not protected by tort law, there would not be a direct tortious claim against Ben, except that a special clause of tortious liability would apply (i.e. intentionally acting contrary to good morals).[55] The circumstances of the case do not indicate that Ben is liable according to the special clauses of tortious liability.

---

53 Decision of the Regional Court in Žilina, file no. 6 Co 587/2014 dated 25.03.2015.

54 S. 50(2) SCC states that the third person shall become entitled from the agreement (but will neither become obliged nor become a party to the contract).

55 For further explanation, see Case 1 above.

The application of family law rules leads to same results. According to section 20 of the Family Act, '[e]ach of the spouses is entitled to represent the other in regular affairs, foremostly to accept regular performance rendered. Any act of a spouse while arranging regular affairs obliges both spouses jointly and severally.' However, the rental of a boat by a wife would not generally be considered an arrangement of regular affairs, unless it would be considered as such by this particular family (based on a regularity of such arrangements). Therefore, Anita's entering into a contract with Anchors neither makes Ben the contract party based on representation (s. 20, first sentence, Family Act) nor establishes joint and several liability of both spouses under the contract (s. 20, second sentence, Family Act).

However, even though the contract was entered into by Anita only, and she is, as the contracting party, liable for the late return of the boat, Anchors may satisfy the claim not only from Anita's individual property but also from the property which belongs to the *'bezpodielové spoluvlastníctvo manželov'* (non-proportional matrimonial joint ownership).

Moreover, there is no *'zmluva o združení'* (contract on partnership/association) between Ben and his four friends which could lead to their joint liability, as they have not associated themselves in order to jointly achieve an agreed goal (s. 829 SCC), and they have neither agreed to perform labour activities nor provide money or other things for the purpose of the association (s. 831 SCC).

2.12. SPAIN

Carles Vendrell Cervantes

I. Operative Rules

Anchors are only entitled to claim the agreed penalty fee from Anita.

II. Descriptive Formants

Even if the contract contains a stipulation in favour of a third party (a provision by virtue of which Ben and his four friends could use the boat), Article 1257 of the Spanish Civil Code provides that the penalty contained in the contract cannot be applied to them, as they were not parties to the contract and have not agreed to its content. Therefore, Anchors can only seek payment of the penalty fee from Anita, who is the only counterparty to the contract.

On the basis of Article 1257 of the Spanish Civil Code, which clearly states that contracts shall only be effective between the parties who execute them, case law has consistently held that, in general, what has been agreed in a contract cannot affect those who were not involved in its performance (see the decisions of the Supreme Court no. 669/1999 of 23 July and no. 269/2011 of 11 April). In particular, case law has held that Article 1257 prevents the effects of contracts from harming or adversely affecting third parties (see the decision of the Supreme Court no. 517/2015 of 6 October).

In this case, although Ben and his friends are the beneficiaries of the contract, they cannot be considered as parties to it, as they did not sign or agree to the contract, and did not act in any way that could lead Anchors to think, in good faith, that they were parties to the contract. The contract itself identifies Anita as the counterparty, and specifies that the crew (beneficiaries) would be Ben and his friends. Therefore, Anchors may only seek payment of the penalty from Anita, who is the counterparty to the contract in which the penalty was agreed.

Alternatively, Anchors might seek compensation for the damages caused by the late return from Ben and his friends by virtue of the non-contractual liability contained in Article 1902 of the Spanish Civil Code. Apart from the fact that the existence of this non-contractual claim is disputable, the potential damages would amount to the effective damage caused by the delay, and not to the penalty agreed in the contract.

2.13. SWEDEN

Oskar Mossberg

I. *Operative Rules*

Anchors can only seek payment *from Anita.*

II. *Descriptive Formants*

Whereas the contract with Anita can be invoked to demand payment from her, there is no contractual basis for a claim against Ben.

Anchors could possibly argue a claim against Ben in one of two different ways: either as a tortious claim of negligence[56] or a claim of unjustified enrichment.[57]

56 Pursuant to Ch. 2, Art. 1 of the Act on Damages: see e.g. J. Hellner and M. Radetzki, *Skadeståndsrätt*, 10th ed., Norstedts, Stockholm 2018, pp. 87 ff., 103 ff.

57 The possibility to base a claim in uncodified principles of unjustified enrichment is an old question of controversy in Nordic, and especially Swedish, law. The traditional Scandinavian Realist approach is that unjustified enrichment is not a part of Swedish law, and thus cannot be invoked as the basis for a claim. This traditional opinion has been the source of much controversy, and there are several newer cases where the HD has more or less explicitly alluded to principles of unjustified enrichment, including NJA 1993 p. 13; NJA 2007 p. 519; NJA 2009 N 40; and NJA 2019 p. 23. For scholarly discussion, see e.g. M. Schultz, 'Nya argumentationslinjer i förmögenhetsrätten: Obehörig vinst rediviva', *SvJT* 2009, pp. 946 ff.

As Anchors can demand payment for their losses from Anita, it is, however, doubtful whether there are any losses to be compensated beyond that claim. Furthermore, for negligence to suffice as a basis for tortious liability according to the general statutory law on damages, Skadeståndslagen (the Act on Damages), the losses would need to be considered as property damage, and not just pure economic loss, which as a general rule is only compensated if the damages are caused through a criminal act (Chapter 2, Articles 1 and 2 of the Act on Damages). The present case could possibly be argued as a case of *'funktionell sakskada i form av undandragen nyttjanderätt'* (functional property damages in the form of deprived rights of use), for which negligence would suffice as a basis for liability, and which has some scholarly support.[58] It is, however, highly unlikely that Anchors would be successful in claiming any payment from Ben.

This would hold even on the dubious hypothesis under which Anita should be viewed as a representative of Ben because she was acting in her own name, and therefore as a commissionary agent (on Article 24 of the Commissionary Act, see Case 4 above).[59]

III. Meta-Legal Formants

As stated in Case 1 above, Swedish contract law is based on the notion that, generally, people can bind only themselves – a notion sometimes captured in *'självbindningens princip'* (the principle of binding oneself) and *'förbudet mot betungande tredjemansavtal'* (the ban on onerous third-party contracts). (This notion also applies to representatives, as they generally derive their authority from the actions of the principal.)

On commission, see Case 4 above.

3. COMPARATIVE REMARKS

Jan Biemans and Lorna Richardson

This case considers the extent to which a contract between two parties (A and B) can impose a contractual obligation on another, who is not party to the contract (C). While it is clear from answers to earlier cases (for instance, Case 1) that A and B

(positive); J. Kleineman, 'Obehörig vinst och frågan om vårt behov av rättsliga tvångströjor', *Tidsskrift for Rettsvitenskap* 2013 (vol. 126) pp. 531–549 (more critical); or O. Mossberg, *Avtalets räckvidd I: Om avtals tredjemansverkningar, särskilt vid tredjemansavtal och direktkrav*, Iustus, Uppsala 2020, section 6.3, all with further references.

58 H. Andersson, *Ersättningsproblem i skadeståndsrätten*, Iustus, Uppsala 2017, pp. 171 ff.

59 On Art. 24 of the Act on Commission, see e.g. S.O. Johansson, *Kommissionslagen: En kommentar*, Norstedts, Stockholm 2017, pp. 291 ff.

could grant rights to C, this case considers the position vis-à-vis contractual obligations. The case examines the position where the third party (C) has enjoyed the right in their favour, and asks whether certain obligations pass to them as a result of their having utilised that right. A further issue is whether C would be under any non-contractual liability to either or both contracting parties.

In all of the jurisdictions represented in this volume, Anchors can seek payment of the contractual penalty from Anita only. All reporters note that burdens or obligations cannot be imposed on a third party who is not a party to the contract. In both France and the Netherlands, there is, however, a possibility of Ben and his friends being liable to Anchors for the penalty. This would occur if they had been aware of the penalty clause before making use of the boat. In these jurisdictions, it is permissible for the third-party right to come with conditions for its use, which conditions become obligations when the third party decides to exercise the third-party right in their favour.

In German law, Ben and his friends could potentially be liable for damages arising from breach of contract, rather than being obliged to pay the penalty set out in the contract between Anchors and Anita. In German law, it is unclear, where an item is rented on behalf of a third party, whether the obligation to return the item timeously falls on the contracting party (Anita) or the third party having use of the item (Ben).[60]

The Swedish and Dutch reporters note that Anchors may have non-contractual claims against Ben. In Sweden, such a claim could possibly be based on tort or unjust enrichment. In the Netherlands, a claim could be based on an unlawful act of infringing Anchors' property rights, or on unjust enrichment. In German law, Ben and his friends might be liable in delict for the wrongful detention of another's chattel. In Belgian law, Ben might, by returning the boat a day late, be liable on a non-contractual basis, due to his complicity in Anita's contractual breach.

[60] This is contrary to the position in Italian law, where the courts have held that the stipulator (in this case, Anita) is the party obliged to return the rented thing at the end of the hire period.

CASE 9: RELIANCE ON PROFESSIONAL STATEMENTS BY THIRD PARTIES

1. CASE

Mrs Fidel wants to buy Mr Goodman's house. Mr Goodman appoints Mr Delmonte, a surveyor, to assess the value of the house. Mr Delmonte estimates the value of the house at €700,000. In making his valuation he fails to take into account both the sharp decline in house prices in the neighbourhood in the last month and a remark in an inspection report mentioning heavy soil contamination. Based on Mr Delmonte's valuation report, Mrs Fidel purchases the house for €695,000. The bank, having seen the valuation report, provides a loan to Mrs Fidel for the same amount and takes a security over the house. Three months later, Mrs Fidel is fired from her job, and is forced to sell the house. She decides to do this, as she knows the bank will foreclose when she cannot make her loan repayments, and that this will result in additional costs. She sells the house for only €575,000, and is unable to repay the bank the residual debt.

Question

Assuming there is professional negligence on the part of Mr Delmonte, who can sue him for damages?

2. DISCUSSIONS

2.1. BELGIUM

Siel Demeyere and Vincent Sagaert

I. Operative Rules

Both Mrs Fidel and the bank can sue Mr Delmonte.

II. *Descriptive Formants*

Firstly, the professional negligence by Mr Delmonte constitutes a breach of the contract with Mr Goodman. However, Mr Goodman suffered no damage, and was even able to realise extra profit from the sale, thanks to the overvaluation of his house.

Secondly, Mrs Fidel has made a €120,000 loss in the comparison between both transactions. She will argue that Mr Delmonte has been professionally negligent, in order to have him compensate her loss. However, as she is not a party to the contract between Mr Delmonte and Mr Goodman, she cannot - according to the case law of the Belgian Court of Cassation - merely invoke the contractual breach, but must prove the existence of an extracontractual fault,[1] separate from the breach of contract.[2] The case law from the lower courts, on the contrary, takes a permissive stance in such cases, and readily acknowledges the existence of a wrongful act when a third party suffers damage from a contractual breach.[3] According to this case law, Mrs Fidel can claim damages from Mr Delmonte to the extent that his contractual breach amounts to an extracontractual fault; that is, the breach of a statutory duty or a duty of care. That does not mean, however, that she can claim damages for the full amount of €120,000. The damages for extracontractual fault will be assessed by comparing the patrimonial situation which Mrs Fidel is in now with the situation in which she would have been had there been no fault.[4] For instance, market circumstances may have affected the house price, so that not all of the loss of value may be due to professional negligence on the part of Mr Delmonte. Establishing causation will not be a problem, since there is already a causal link between the fault and the damage, as the damage would not have occurred, or at least not to such an extent, had the fault not been committed. This is referred to as the *conditio sine qua non* test.

---

1 Art. 1382 old BCC.

2 Cass. 22 June 2009, no. C.08.0546.N, *NJW* 2009, 724, comment I. Boone, *RW* 2011–12, afl. 22, 1003; Cass. 21 October 2010, no. C.08.0558.F, *Arr.Cass.* 2010, 2565; Cass. 25 October 2012, *RGDC* 2015, 563, comment P. Wéry. Recent Belgian scholarship confirms this requirement. See e.g. I. Claeys, *Samenhangende overeenkomsten en aansprakelijkheid*, Intersentia, Antwerp 2003, 44, no. 36; S. Stijns and E. Verjans, 'Variaties op het begrip "derde" in het contractenrecht' in A. De Boeck, S. Stijns, R. Van Ransbeeck, F. Brandsma, N. Carette, D. Leroy, I. Samoy and E. Verjans (eds), *Positie van de derde in het privaat vermogensrecht*, die Keure, Bruges 2012, 50; P. Van Ommeslaghe, *Traité de droit civil belge. II. Les obligations. Vol. 2*, Bruylant, Brussels 2013, 1207–08.

3 See e.g. Com. Liège 23 March 1934 (confirmed by Liège 5 January 1935), *RGAR* 1934, no. 1463; Trib. Leuven (10e k.) 9 March 2006, no. 04/2163/A, *T.App.* 2006, issue 3, 54–56. More elaborately on this issue, see S. Demeyere, *Aansprakelijkheid van een contractant jegens derden*, die Keure, Bruges 2015, 42 ff. A contractual breach is not necessary for liability on the part of Delmonte, as it suffices to prove that the independent criteria for an extracontractual fault are satisfied. However, it will generally be easier to establish the contractual breach, which is often accepted as an extracontractual fault.

4 W. Van Gerven and A. Van Oevelen, *Verbintenissenrecht*, Acco, Leuven 2015, 453.

Thirdly, the bank suffered damage when Mrs Fidel was not able to repay her loan. The bank may also sue Mr Delmonte for damages, based on the same reasoning and legal bases on which Mrs Fidel could sue Mr Delmonte.

III. Meta-Legal Formants

One could question whether the view in the case law from the lower courts is too permissive and overprotective of third parties. Scholars argue that only third parties who could rightly rely on the proper performance of the contract should be allowed to rely on the contractual breach.[5]

The Draft Statute Tort Law does not specifically target the situation of a third party suffering damage from a contractual breach. The general provision for extracontractual liability can be applied in such cases. Article 6.6 of the Draft Statute Tort Law mainly rephrases the current Article 1382 of the old BCC, and codifies the most important case law.[6]

2.2. BULGARIA

Petar Topurov

I. Operative Rules

Mrs Fidel has the right to file a delict claim against Mr Delmonte, on account of detriment she has suffered due to his professional negligence during the assessing process.

II. Descriptive Formants

Mrs Fidel and Mr Delmonte are not in a contractual relationship, since the surveyor was appointed by Mr Goodman. We should assume, therefore, that Mrs Fidel's claim for damages may be presented on a delictual basis, because of the circumstance that Mrs Fidel concluded the contract with Mr Goodman on the basis of an error in the actual market value of the house. Art. 28 LOC stipulates that an error in the subject is a ground for annulment of the deal, because it is voidable.

Legal doctrine, in turn, accepts that an error in the price does not have legal significance, as far as it does not relate to an error in the essential qualities

---

5 S. Demeyere, *Aansprakelijkheid van een contractant jegens derden*, die Keure, Bruges 2015, 135 ff.

6 Explanatory Memorandum to the Draft Statute of 8 March 2023 on introduction of Book 6 'Tort Law', *Parl.St.* 2022–23, 3213/1, www.dekamer.be, 39 ff.

of the subject.[7] Other authors share an opinion that the fact of the party's assessment of whether the deal is a profitable one does not result in invalidity (or a voidable contract).[8] Legal studies offer examples of debates on the extent to which a person who has entered into a bargain against their will is entitled to claim compensation for the detriment they suffered before the annulment of the voidable contract.[9]

We should accept that the person entering the bargain against their will could claim damages based on Art. 45 LOC, irrespective of the contract's annulment, since in these cases the invalidity of the contract is not the only possible detriment. Meanwhile, establishing a causal link between Mr Delmonte's behaviour and the damage suffered is a necessary condition for the upholding of the claim filed by Mrs Fidel. The burden of proving the existence of a causal link falls on the injured person.[10] Hence, Mrs Fidel could file a delict claim against the surveyor, but the admission of this claim would depend on proving direct and immediate damage suffered as a result of the deal made, and due to the neglectfully prepared assessment,[11] irrespective of whether or not the deal is annulled under Art. 28 LOC.

It is questionable, however, whether Mrs Fidel will succeed in proving the causal link to the damage suffered, given the existing contractual practices. The parties are not bound by the market prices when the transaction is executed, and the transaction may be executed at a price considerably higher than the market value. Some legal decisions take it for granted that privately made assessments given by surveyors tend to be deliberately higher, to enable the obtaining of a bank loan that corresponds to the collateral scheme applied by the bank.[12] To defend their interests, the buyer could have appointed their own expert. Banks also obtain their own evaluations of collaterals offered, irrespective of existing private assessments, and because of this, there is no need to discuss the possibility for the bank to claim damages. Should such a claim be initiated, the court will accept that the bank has not acted as a good merchant. Should Mrs Fidel not bring an action for the annulment of the transaction due to an error, under Art. 28 LOC, Mr Goodman would have no legal interest in filing a claim against the surveyor, since he did not suffer any damage: just the opposite – he received a higher price than the property's market value as a result of the deal.

---

7 A. Shopov, *Mistake as a ground for nullification of contracts*, Sibi, Sofia 2013, p. 199.
8 M. Pavlova, *Civil Law. General Part*, Sophie-P, Sofia 2002, p. 554.
9 M. Malchev, *Destruction of Civil Law Transactions*, Ciela, Sofia 2013, p. 266.
10 P. Goleva, *Contractual Law*, New Star, Sofia 2015, p. 474.
11 According to Art. 51, paragraph 1 LOC, compensation will be due for all damages that are a direct and immediate consequence of the tort.
12 Decision No. 233 of 24.07.2018 by Plovdiv Court of Appeal in case No. 665/2017.

2.3. CZECH REPUBLIC

Tomáš Richter

I. Operative Rules

It is *not clear that anyone may sue Mr Delmonte* for damages.

II. Descriptive Formants

Mr Delmonte had a contract with Mr Goodman. Presumably, in that contract, Mr Goodman agreed to pay Mr Delmonte a fee for his valuation report, although the facts are silent on this. There is no suggestion in the facts of the case that Mr Goodman suffered any loss at all. Nor is there any stipulation suggesting that the contract between Mr Goodman and Mr Delmonte was entered into for the benefit of third parties, such as potential bidders for Mr Goodman's house, or that Mr Delmonte was even made aware by Mr Goodman that the valuation report was intended for the purposes of being disclosed to potential bidders or the bank. The case states that Mrs Fidel purchased the house 'based on Mr Delmonte's valuation report', however there is no stipulation suggesting that Mr Delmonte accepted any reliance by Mrs Fidel at all. There is also no suggestion that Mr Goodman made any assurances to Mrs Fidel as regards the valuation report. Neither is there any suggestion that Mr Delmonte accepted that Mrs Fidel's bank, which is stated to have 'seen the valuation report', would be able to rely on the report.

On these facts, it seems most unlikely that Mr Delmonte would be liable for damages to any party for breach of contract. Whether Mr Delmonte could be liable to Mrs Fidel or her bank *ex delictu* is highly questionable, and the outcome of any suit would be highly uncertain. The rules most likely to be invoked are sections 5(1), 2900, 2910, 2912 and 2950 of the CC. Section 5(1) provides that anyone who, when dealing with others, claims professional skills as a member of a particular profession or estate, shall be considered to signal that they are able to act with such knowledge or care as pertains to such profession or estate. If they fail to use such professional care, they shall bear the burden thereof. Section 2900 provides that, where the circumstances of the case or the customs of private life so demand, everyone must act so as to avoid unreasonable harm to the liberty, life, health or property of others. Section 2910 provides, under the title 'Violation of the law', that a person who culpably breaches a duty set by the law, and thereby intrudes into an absolute right of the person damaged, shall remedy the harm caused. The same duty shall arise where the intrusion concerns other types of rights, and is caused by a culpable breach of a statutory duty set to protect such rights. Section 2912(1) provides that, where a person fails to act in a manner which may reasonably be expected of an average person in private matters, they shall be presumed to act negligently. Section 2912(2) provides that, where a person signals a special knowledge, skill or care, or where he or she agrees to provide performance which demands special knowledge, skill or care, and does not use such special faculties, they shall be presumed to act negligently. Finally, section 2950 provides, under the title 'Damages caused by information or advice', that anyone who purports to act expertly as a member of a particular profession or estate, or who otherwise purports to act as an expert, shall be liable for damages caused by incomplete or incorrect information or incorrect advice provided for consideration within the ambit of their knowledge or skill. Otherwise, a person is only liable for damages caused by defective information given or defective advice dispensed on purpose.

Although these provisions perhaps contain seeds of potential liability in delict, it is not presently clear at all whether such liability could be claimed from Mr Delmonte by either Mrs Fidel or her bank, simply because Czech law currently has no reliable rules which would help define such persons, who have neither contracted with the expert or professional in question nor been identified as the beneficiaries of such a contract, but would still have standing to sue such an expert on what could be thought of as legitimate reliance on the information provided by the expert. In particular, the CC has no rule substantially similar to Draft Common Frame of Reference (DCFR) Art. VI.-2:207.[13]

III. Meta-Legal Formants

The entire body of the CC's liability rules, which came into effect on 1 January 2014, differ significantly from the previous law, and section 2950 in particular has no precedent in Czech law after 1950. Therefore, there is very little by way of contemporary case law to refer to.

2.4. ENGLAND AND WALES

T.T. Arvind

I. Operative Rules

Neither Mrs Fidel nor the lender is likely to be able to sue Mr Delmonte. Mr Goodman can sue Mr Delmonte for breach of contract, but is unlikely to be able to recover substantial damages.

---

13 Filip Melzer refers to DCFR Art. VI.-2:207 in his commentary on s. 2950, describing the two provisions as 'very similar'. However, it should be clear from the translation provided above that such similarity is lacking, simply because the Czech rule has nothing to say on

II. *Descriptive Formants*

Whether Mrs Fidel or the lender can sue Mr Delmonte in their capacity as a third-party beneficiary under CRTPA will depend on the wording of the contract between Mr Delmonte and Mr Goodman. As discussed in Case 1 above, the CRTPA's requirement that the contract 'purport' to confer a benefit on the third party has been interpreted to mean that providing the benefit must be one of the purposes of the contract, rather than an incidental effect.[14] It is unlikely that this will be true of a contract whereby a seller commissions a valuation, unless it explicitly states that the valuation is being obtained for the benefit of potential lenders and/or purchasers.

A second potential ground for Mrs Fidel and the lender would be to bring an action in tort against the surveyor for pure economic loss caused by professional negligence. Compensation for pure economic loss requires a special relationship where the defendant has voluntarily assumed responsibility to the claimant for the correctness of the statement in question.[15] For this, the defendant must know that the advice will be communicated to the claimant and be used by them without further independent inquiry for a specific purpose.[16] Since the leading case of *Smith v. Eric S Bush*,[17] it has been well settled that these requirements are satisfied as between purchasers and lender-appointed valuers,[18] if the purchaser is a domestic householder. Most of the reported cases relate to pure economic loss caused by a failure to notice structural problems with a house, but the same principle applies to any pure economic loss that lies within the scope of the surveyor's duty of care[19] (that is, if the loss arose from risks which it was part of the surveyor's duty to protect against).[20]

However, on the facts of the case, it is unlikely that Mrs Fidel or the bank will succeed in an action for professional negligence. The duty in *Smith v. Eric S Bush* was imposed because surveyors are aware of the 'overwhelming probability' that

---

legitimate reliance in cases where the person purporting to rely on the information or advice has no grounds for such reliance in contract: F. Melzer, P. Tégl et al., *Občanský zákoník, §2894–3081. Velký komentář. Svazek IX. První vydání*, Leges, Praha 2018, p. 873 at 6. Accordingly, Melzer's commentary on s. 2950 regarding potential liability for damages caused indirectly does not allow for any reliable conclusions as to Mrs Fidel's or her bank's legal position in the context of the case at hand (ibid., pp. 886–88).

14 *Dolphin Maritime & Aviation Services Ltd v. Sveriges Angfartygs Assurans Forening* [2009] EWHC 716 (Comm), [2009] 2 Lloyd's Rep. 123 [8] (Christopher Clarke J).

15 The most recent judicial statement of the law is in *NRAM Ltd v. Steel* [2018] UKSC 13, [2018] 1 WLR 1190.

16 *Caparo Industries plc v. Dickman* [1990] 2 AC 605, 638 (Lord Oliver); *Playboy Club London Ltd v. Banca Nazionale del Lavoro SpA* [2018] UKSC 43, [2018] 1 WLR 4041 [10] (Lord Sumption).

17 [1990] 1 AC 831 (HL).

18 See e.g. *Merrett v. Babb* [2001] EWCA Civ 214, [2001] QB 1174.

19 *South Australia Asset Management Corp v. York Montague Ltd* [1997] AC 191.

20 *BPE Solicitors v. Hughes-Holland* [2017] UKSC 21, [2018] AC 599.

domestic purchasers will rely on the surveyor's valuation.[21] Subsequent cases suggest that the duty does not apply outside the 'special facts'[22] created by the specific context of a lender-commissioned survey for a domestic purchaser. An important example of this limitation, which directly affects the bank, is that surveyors are not held to have assumed responsibility towards commercial parties, such as landlords or investors, as they would reasonably expect such parties to commission their own surveys.[23] Applying this to the present case, it is very unlikely that Mr Delmonte will be held to have assumed responsibility towards the bank. Equally, the court in *Smith v. Eric S Bush* was influenced by a range of factors, including not just the fact that domestic purchasers commonly relied on lender-commissioned surveys, but also that it was typically the purchaser who paid for these surveys.[24] These cumulatively created a relationship of proximity. Neither of these factors applies to a survey commissioned by the seller, and it is therefore unlikely that Mr Delmonte will be held to have assumed responsibility to Mrs Fidel.

As a party to the contract, Mr Goodman will be able to sue Mr Delmonte for breach. Ordinarily, however, Mr Goodman will only be able to recover nominal damages, because he has not himself suffered any loss. The primary exception to this rule is the principle developed in the *Albazero*[25] and *Linden Gardens*[26] cases, discussed in more detail under Case 2 above. However, it is unlikely that that principle will apply here. Both the standard 'narrow' reading of the rule and the suggested 'broad' reading of the rule depend on the premise that the third party was intended to have the benefit of the work done under the contract.[27] Save in exceptional circumstances, it is hard to see how this could be true of a valuation commissioned by a seller. It is, therefore, unlikely that Mr Goodman will be able to recover substantial damages against Mr Delmonte on behalf of the bank or Mrs Fidel.

2.5. FRANCE

Sylvain Ravenne and Flora Vern

I. *Operative Rules*

Mr Goodman could sue Mr Delmonte, but he has suffered no loss. Mrs Fidel and the bank can sue Mr Delmonte in tort for the losses they have sustained.

---

21 *Smith v. Eric S Bush* [1990] 1 AC 831 (HL), 865 (Lord Griffiths).
22 *Williams v. Natural Life Health Foods Ltd* [1998] 1 WLR 830, 837 (HL).
23 *Scullion v. Bank of Scotland Plc* [2011] EWCA Civ 693, [2011] 1 WLR 3212.
24 *Smith v. Eric S Bush* [1990] 1 AC 831 (HL), 865 (Lord Griffiths).
25 *Albacruz (Cargo Owners) v. Albazero (Owners)* [1977] AC 774 (HL).
26 *Linden Gardens Trust v. Lenesta Sludge Disposals Ltd* [1994] 1 AC 85 (HL).
27 *Swynson Ltd v. Lowick Rose LLP* [2017] UKSC 32, [2018] 1 AC 313 [14]–[16].

II. *Descriptive Formants*

The seller of a house contracts with a surveyor for an assessment of the value of the property. Due to negligence, the surveyor overvalues the house. The buyer of the house is compelled to sell it at a loss a few months later, in order to repay a bank loan. The question is who can sue the surveyor for damages. Possible claimants are the seller, the buyer and the bank.

(a) The seller, Mr Goodman, is a party to the contract with the surveyor, but has suffered no direct loss from the overvaluation of the house. Should the need arise, however, the seller would have a contractual claim against the surveyor because there is a contract between them. The seller could, thus, rely on Article 1231-1 of the FCC to claim damages for breach of contract.

(b) The buyer, Mrs Fidel, and the bank are third parties to the contract. As such, they do not have a contractual claim against the surveyor. Case law provides for this situation, however, through the rules pertaining to tort law. Third parties have a claim under the general provision of Article 1240 of the FCC, which provides that any act that causes damage to another person obliges the person by whose fault it has occurred to repair it. The principle under French law is that any damage sustained as a result of a tort is recoverable,[28] even where it was unforeseeable,[29] as long as the damage was directly caused by the wrongful act.[30] In this situation, surveyors and other experts are liable to third parties for professional negligence, though a tort claim. Case law specifically holds that the claim is available both to the buyer, who has suffered a direct loss, and to the bank, who relied on the assessment of value upon granting the loan.[31] Additionally, according to the case law of the Cour de cassation, a third party to a contract may also invoke the improper performance of a contract as a ground for tort liability.[32] However, this solution is neither necessary nor relevant in this case because the court requires that there should be a direct causal relation between the improper contractual performance and the damage,[33] which would probably be somewhat overstretched with respect to the bank. It would be much easier, in the present case, to prove professional negligence of the surveyor and rely on regular tort liability.

---

28 Cass., civ. 2e, 19 nov. 2009, no 08-19380.

29 Under contract law, only the foreseeable damage would be recoverable unless the fault was intentional or of particular severity (Article 1231-3 FCC).

30 Cass., civ. 2e, 27 oct. 1975, nos 73-10318 and 73-14891.

31 Cass., civ. 1re, 12 janv. 1988, no 86-12756.

32 Cass., ass. plén., 6 oct. 2006, *Bootshop*, no 05-13255.

33 Cass., ass. plén., 13 janv. 2020, no 17-19963.

2.6. GERMANY

Sonja Meier

I. *Operative Rules*

Mrs Fidel and the bank will probably each be able to sue Mr Delmonte.

II. *Descriptive Formants*

Mr Delmonte is not liable in delict. A claim under §823 (1) BGB requires an infringement of a right of ownership or a similar right *in rem*. In the present case, Mrs Fidel and the bank have merely suffered pecuniary loss. A claim under §823 (2) BGB requires the violation of a statutory duty that is intended to protect specific persons, but such a statute does not exist here. §839a BGB provides for a claim for damages resulting from incorrect expert opinions, but the provision applies only to experts nominated by a court in legal proceedings.

Mrs Fidel and the bank will, therefore, have to base their claims for damages on §280 (1) BGB. This requires a *'Schuldverhältnis'* (obligational relationship) between the claimant and the defendant. There is no contract between Mr Delmonte and Mrs Fidel or the bank. However, it is generally accepted that liability under §280 (1) BGB can also arise where the parties are connected by a *'Sonderbeziehung'* (special relationship) which does not impose an obligation to perform but is able to generate duties to protect each other's pre-existing rights and interests. The main purpose of this concept is to supplement the protection afforded by the narrow law of delict.

In the course of the reform of the law of obligations in 2001, the concepts of protective duties, and of a *Sonderbeziehung* generating protective duties, were codified in §241 (2) and §311 (2)–(3) BGB. According to §241 (2) BGB, a *Schuldverhältnis* can generate duties to take care of the rights and interests of the other party. §311 (2) BGB states that a *Schuldverhältnis* generating only protective duties under §241 (2) BGB can arise between parties who are negotiating or preparing a contract, or who have other kinds of business relations. §311 (3) BGB extends the concept to certain third parties.

A *Sonderbeziehung* can be generated by a *'Vertrag mit Schutzwirkung für Dritte'* (contract with protective effects towards third parties).[34] The Federal Court and the majority of commentators use the concept of a *Vertrag mit Schutzwirkung für Dritte* in order to establish the liability of an expert towards third parties (i.e. persons who are not parties to the expert contract) in cases where the expert opinion is intended to be used by one or more third parties, and the expert knows that third parties will rely on the report as a basis for

[34] As to this concept, see Case 4, question 1.

making arrangements.[35] Where the expert has to assess the value of property, the protective ambit of the contract is extended to both the purchaser of the property[36] and the party who is financing the transaction.[37] According to the Federal Court, the promisee (in this case, Mr Goodman) has a vital interest in extending the protective ambit of the contract to third parties, since without any liability on the part of the expert, the report would be unreliable, the purchaser would not agree to pay the price calculated on the basis of the report, and the bank would not agree to provide a loan in order to finance the purchase.[38]

The use of the *Vertrag mit Schutzwirkung für Dritte* doctrine in expert liability cases has been criticised by some authors, who argue that the hypothetical intentions of the parties, and particularly the legitimate interest of the person commissioning the expert opinion in extending the protection to certain third parties, are mere fictions.

Some authors suggest focusing on the contract made by the injured third party, and applying §311 (3) BGB instead.[39] According to this provision, a third person who is not a party to the contract may have duties of protection towards a contract party, in particular where the third party claims to be particularly trustworthy and thereby significantly influences the contractual negotiations or the conclusion of the contract. In the present case, Mr Delmonte could be regarded as such a third person in relation to both Mrs Fidel's contract of sale and the bank's contract of loan. The major difference from using the *Vertrag mit Schutzwirkung für Dritte* is that the expert would be liable by operation of law, not by virtue of a contract. Therefore, liability cannot be excluded by the expert.

Others suggest applying the concept of '*Drittschadensliquidation*' (liquidation of a damage of a third party).[40] It is argued that a breach of contract by the expert will not lead to a loss for the person who commissioned the expert opinion, but instead for a third party relying on the report, so that there is a shift of loss which is characteristic of *Drittschadensliquidation*. Following this approach, Mr Goodman will have a contractual claim for damages against Mr Delmonte by which he can liquidate the loss of Mrs Fidel. Mrs Fidel, in turn, will have a contractual claim against Mr Goodman for the assignment of his claim against Mr Delmonte. It is not clear whether the same rules can be applied regarding the bank.

---

35 BGH *NJW* 1987, 1758; BGH *NJW-RR* 1989, 696; *BGHZ* 138, 257; P. Gottwald in *Münchener Kommentar zum BGB*, vol. 3 (9th ed., Beck 2022), §328, [218], [220]; S. Klumpp in *J. von Staudingers Kommentar zum Bürgerlichen Gesetzbuch*, vol. §§328–45 (Sellier – de Gruyter 2020), §328, [267]–[274].

36 *BGHZ* 127, 378.

37 BGH *JZ* 1985, 951; *BGHZ* 159, 1.

38 BGH *JZ* 1985, 951; *BGHZ* 127, 378.

39 D. Looschelders, *Schuldrecht AT* (21st ed., Vahlen 2023), §9, [24]; C.-W. Canaris, *JZ* 1995, 441; C.-W. Canaris, *JZ* 2001, 499 at 520.

40 J. Oechsler, *LMK* 2004, 178. As to *Drittschadensliquidation*, see Case 4, question 1 above.

2.7. ITALY

Claudia Amodio

I. Operative Rules

Mrs Fidel could arguably succeed in a tort action against Mr Delmonte, grounded on the general provision of Art. 2043 c.c. on tort liability for fault.

In addition to the tort action against Mr Delmonte, Mrs Fidel could also take a contractual action against the bank for non-compliance with the legal rules on consumer mortgage loans, which are based on provisions emanating from the EU.

Because of their own wrongdoings, the bank should not be able to take legal steps against Mr Delmonte.

II. Descriptive Formants

Mr Delmonte owes performance to Mr Goodman by virtue of their contract. However, this does not preclude Mrs Fidel from successfully using Art. 2043 c.c. in order to recover damages. Mrs Fidel will have to prove all the elements of the cause of action, including the defendant's negligent (or intentional) conduct.

The Italian Civil Code provides special rules for the ascertainment of the liability of those persons who, because of their profession, should possess special skills or expertise. According to Art. 1176 c.c., the standard model for the assessment of the professional's conduct cannot be the one that applies to the average man; that is, the diligence of a good *pater familias*.[41] The conduct expected from a professional must be evaluated more strictly, taking into account the professional activity to be carried out and the specific expertise that is usually expected in similar circumstances.[42]

Moreover, where the performance of a professional obligation involves solving technical problems of special difficulty, this might trigger the application of Art. 2236 c.c., which exempts professionals from liability whenever their conduct does not amount to fraud, malice or gross negligence.[43] It is likely, however, that in the present scenario the requirement for the application of Art. 2236 c.c. would not be met, as Mr Delmonte's obligation and activity do not seem to be characterised by 'a special difficulty'.

---

[41] M. Giorgianni, 'Buon padre di famiglia', *Novissimo digesto italiano* (Turin: UTET, 1958), II, p. 598.

[42] On the evolution of professional liability, outlined also through the analysis of evidentiary rules, see R. De Matteis, 'Le responsabilità dei professionisti' in V. Roppo and A.M. Benedetti (eds), *Trattato dei contratti*, vol. III, tome I, *Opere e Servizi* (Milan: Giuffrè, 2014).

[43] G. Visintini, *Trattato breve della responsabilità civile: fatti illeciti. Inadempimento, danno risarcibile* (Padua: CEDAM, 2005), p. 18.

Establishing evidence of the prerequisites of Mr Delmonte's liability (fault, unjust damage and a link between the two) may not be particularly problematic for Mrs Fidel.[44]

In addition to the tort action against Mr Delmonte, Mrs Fidel could also take a contractual action against the bank for non-compliance with two regulatory provisions on consumer mortgage loans. First, pursuant to Legislative Decree No. 72/2016, which implemented Directive 2014/17/EU (Mortgage Credit Directive), banks are required to seek an independent surveyor's advice in order to have an objective estimate of the value of the real estate given by the borrower as a warranty.[45] The bank did not comply with this obligation and relied on the evaluation of the seller's surveyor instead. Second, in the present case the bank finds itself in a situation of infringement of Legislative Decree No. 385/1993 (Testo Unico Bancario),[46] according to which the maximum amount for *'credito fondiario'* loans (that is, loans with a duration exceeding 18 months and secured by first-ranking mortgage) should not exceed 80 per cent of the value of the mortgaged assets.[47]

In light of this, one could argue that the bank should not be able to take legal steps against Mr Delmonte.

III. Meta-Legal Formants

The general provision of Art. 2043 c.c. is to be considered the default rule of the Italian system of civil liability whenever an existing contractual relationship would be impossible to establish. However, in recent years, Italian courts and scholars have displayed a remarkable tendency to maintain that, irrespective of the framework (contractual or non-contractual) in place, professional liability

---

44 Due to the broad formulation of Art. 2043 c.c., Italian courts generally tend to allocate the burden of damage suffered very much on the facts of the case. Compared to the French model, one finds in the concept of *'danno ingiusto'* (unjustified injury) an Italian peculiarity which has had a powerful effect on the development of case law, generally showing that identifying 'unjustified damage' is an evaluation inextricably associated with the assessment of the remaining requirements of liability.

45 The implementing measures are now contained in the Capo I-bis ('Credito immobiliare ai consumatori') of the Titolo VI ('Trasparenza delle condizioni contrattuali e dei rapporti con i clienti') of the Legislative Decree No. 385/1993 (Testo Unico Bancario). See, in particular, new Art. 120 *duodecies*. See F. Capriglione et al., *Commentario al Testo unico delle leggi in materia bancaria e creditizia* (Padua: CEDAM, 2018).

46 Namely, Art. 38, paragraph 2, of the Legislative Decree No. 385/1993 (Testo Unico Bancario) and delibera del Cicr 22-4-1995.

47 According to a recent *'revirement'* of the Corte di Cassazione, the breach of the 80% threshold rule should lead to the nullity of the *'credito fondiario'* loan, apart from the possibility of its conversion into another type of mortgage loan contract, less advantageous for the bank: see Cass., 13 July 2017, no. 17352, *Massimario Giustizia civile* (2017), confirmed by Cass., 16 March 2018, no. 6586, *DeJure Giuffrè*.

should be considered as liability for non-fulfilment of obligations, given the importance of the expectations arising from the professional status of one of the parties. Such a tendency, based on the theory of '*contatto sociale*' (social contact),[48] has thus expanded contractual liability beyond and despite the privity of contract.[49]

2.8. THE NETHERLANDS

Jan Biemans

I. *Operative Rules*

Assuming there is professional negligence on the part of Mr Delmonte, possibly Mr Goodman, the bank and/or Mrs Fidel can sue Mr Delmonte for damages.

II. *Descriptive Formants*

Mr Goodman is the client of Mr Delmonte. As such, it is clear that, in the relationship between Mr Goodman and Mr Delmonte, there has been a breach of contract (Articles 6:74 and 6:265 DCC) on the part of Mr Delmonte because of his professional negligence, which is a violation of his duty of care (Article 7:401 DCC). As the professional negligence is a given, it is clear that the duty of care as exercised by Mr Delmonte did not meet the standard that should be expected from a reasonably competent professional acting in similar conditions.[50]

---

48 C. Castronovo, 'Contatto sociale (fonte di obbligazione)', *Dig. disc. priv., sez. civ.* (Turin: UTET, 2010), agg. V, p. 346.

49 Cass., 27 January 1999, no. 589, *Corriere giuridico* (1999), p. 446, which is generally considered the first case law application of the '*contratto sociale*' doctrine, concerned the liability of a physician affiliated with a medical institution. The doctrine has subsequently been extended to a '*mediatore senza mandato*' (mediator without mandate) by Cass., 14 July 2009, no. 16382, *Vita notarile* (2009), p. 1446; then to a lawyer, in a case where an existing contractual relationship was impossible to establish (Cass., 23 March 2005, no. 6216, *Massimario Giustizia civile*, 4 (2005)); and finally, albeit *obiter*, to a notary (Cass., 23 October 2012, no. 14934, *Nuova giurisprudenza civile commentata*, I (2004), p. 112).

50 See e.g. Dutch Supreme Court, 29 May 1998, NJ 1999/287 (notary); Dutch Supreme Court, 14 December 2007, NJ 2008/8 (tax consultant), Dutch Supreme Court, 7 March 2003, NJ 2003/302 (lawyer); and Dutch Supreme Court, 10 January 2003, NJ 2003/375 (insurance intermediary). See also T.F.E. Tjong Tjin Tai, *Mr. C. Assers Handleiding tot de beoefening van het Nederlands Burgerlijk Recht. 7. Bijzondere overeenkomsten. Deel IV. Opdracht, incl. de geneeskundige behandelingsovereenkomst en de reisovereenkomst*, Deventer: Wolters Kluwer 2022, pp. 93, 95 and 200. See also P.H. Kramer, 'De zorgplicht van beroepsbeoefenaren jegens derden en de invloed van gebruiksbedingen en exoneraties in rapportages', *MvV* 2017/11, pp. 315–24.

Based on this, Mr Goodman could sue Mr Delmonte for damages. However, Mr Goodman would have to show that he has suffered loss in the first place. Although it is not unthinkable that he could suffer loss because of a claim against him by Mrs Fidel, Mr Goodman's loss is not apparent in this case.

The bank and/or Mrs Fidel could possibly sue Mr Delmonte on the basis of an unlawful act (Article 6:162 DCC).[51] An appraiser (a surveyor or real estate agent) who hands over a valuation report to their client has to vouch, within reasonable limits, for the correctness of the valuation report, the assumptions used therein, and the carefulness of the underlying research.[52] The appraiser not only a duty of care (based on contract) with regard to their client, but also, within limits, with regard to third parties. After all, third parties may also rely on the valuation report and the sales and execution values of the house mentioned therein. This is especially true with regard to banks, which rely on valuation reports for assessing the financing applications of buyers. The unlawful act would, thus, be bringing into circulation an incorrect valuation report, on which others – third parties – rely with regard to the value of the house. In order to claim damages, it would be necessary for the third parties to have suffered losses as a result of their reliance on the incorrect valuation report.

A valuation report may thus have a third-party effect.[53] Generally, professional negligence, as such, is not easily assumed. For example, it will not be assumed on the sole ground that there is a large difference between the estimated value and the real value of the house, as a valuation depends on many factors. In this case, however, the professional negligence is a given.

In this case, it would very much depend on the circumstances of the case whether it was foreseeable for Mr Delmonte that the bank and/or Mrs Fidel would rely on his valuation report. The requirement of foreseeability determines, in part, whether and in which amount damages can be claimed for pure economic loss (which includes loss suffered and lost profit, as per Article 6:96 (1) DCC), as compared, for example, with physical damage to property or people.[54] Thus, the question is whether Mr Delmonte knew or should reasonably have understood that his valuation report would be used by the parties for determining the sales price, and by the bank for assessing the financing application, and thus also knew or had to have known that any professional negligence by him would cause damage to the bank and/or Mrs Fidel (Article 6:98 DCC).

---

51 See e.g. Dutch Supreme Court, 9 September 2016, ECLI:NL:HR:2016:2044 (Art. 81 RO).

52 See Dutch Supreme Court, 9 October 2020, ECLI:NL:HR:2020:1592 (Art. 81 RO). See also E.J.A.M. van den Akker, *Beroepsaansprakelijkheid ten opzichte van derden*, The Hague: Boom Juridische uitgevers 2001, p. 74.

53 See e.g. District Court Zutphen, 20 January 2010, ECLI:NL:RBZUT:2010:BL0398, JOR 2010/358.

54 See C.H. Sieburgh, *Mr. C. Assers Handleiding tot de beoefening van het Nederlands Burgerlijk Recht. 6. Verbintenissenrecht. Deel II. De verbintenis in het algemeen, tweede gedeelte*, Deventer: Wolters Kluwer 2021, pp. 25 and 47.

III. Meta-Legal Formants

As, under certain circumstances, a valuation report may have third-party effect, valuation reports often contain a clause excluding or limiting the liability of the appraiser (an exoneration clause), not only in relation to their client, but also in relation to such third parties. The effect of such exoneration clauses is that neither the bank nor the other third party can hold the appraiser liable. In order to have accepted the exoneration clause, the third party relying on the valuation report reasonably needs to have understood that, by using the valuation report, they also accepted the exoneration clause.[55] Thus, not only the valuation report itself but also the exoneration clause therein may have third-party effect. In this case, however, there is no mention of such an exoneration clause.

2.9. POLAND

Dariusz Szostek

I. Operative Rules

Mr Goodman may seek compensation from Mr Delmonte. In general, the provisions of Polish law do not set out a possibility for Mrs Fidel to take any direct action against Mr Delmonte.[56]

II. Descriptive Formants

When concluding a contract for the valuation of real estate (preparing a real estate appraisal), the provisions of the PCC regarding the contract for a specific task (Arts. 627–46) apply, due to the characteristics of the document being prepared. According to Article 638 §2 PCC, 'if the orderer (the contracting party) was given a warranty for the work, the provisions on warranty in sale apply accordingly'.[57] Therefore, due to Mr Delmonte's defective performance of the contract concluded with Mr Goodman (the orderer), the provisions of the PCC regarding the warranty on sales – Articles 560, 561 and 568 – will apply.[58]

Polish regulations provide that a statement of price reduction may be made by a person in Mr Goodman's position. In that case, Mr Goodman can take legal

55 C.E. du Perron, *Overeenkomst en derden*, Deventer: Kluwer 1999, paras. 366–68.

56 The sale of an item (thing) by the seller does not cause a transfer to the buyer of the rights under the warranty for its physical defects.

57 W. Białończyk, 'Rękojmia za wady w umowie o roboty budowlane – cz. I', *Monitor Prawniczy* 2015, no. 6, p. 291.

58 D. Latawiec-Chara, 'Odpowiedzialność projektanta za wady projektu', *Nieruchomości* 2012, no. 10, p. 12.

action against the valuer. He may also terminate his agreement with the valuer, or call on them to rectify defects or provide a valuation which is correct. The basis for these activities is to obtain the right valuation.

The provisions provide a possibility for Mr Goodman to submit a statement on a price reduction, or to withdraw from the contract (Art. 560 §1 PCC),[59] or submit a request either for the item to be replaced with one free from defects, or for the defect to be removed (Art. 561 §1 PCC).[60] The valuation shall take into account the defectiveness of the item, as defined in the framework of non-compliance with the contract.

At the same time, Mr Goodman may seek compensation from Mr Delmonte before a civil or commercial court, by bringing an appropriate action[61] before the competent court. Mr Delmonte is obliged to repair the damage resulting from the non-performance or improper performance of the obligation,[62] which in the present case was the incorrect valuation of the real estate.

Moreover, in general, the provisions of Polish law do not provide a possibility for Mrs Fidel or the bank to take any direct action against Mr Delmonte to recover the losses incurred through the sale of the real estate for a lower price, because the sale of an item (thing) by the seller (Mr Goodman) does not cause the transfer to the buyer (Mrs Fidel) of the rights under the warranty for its physical defects.[63] However, the seller may transfer to the buyer the right to request a price reduction, the removal of the defect, or the provision of a thing free from defects.[64]

2.10. SCOTLAND

Lorna MacFarlane

I. Operative Rules

Mrs Fidel can sue Mr Delmonte for damages. *The bank likely cannot sue Mr Delmonte for damages.*

---

59 A. Kubiak-Cyrul, 'Komentarz do art. 560' in M. Załucki (ed), *Kodeks cywilny. Komentarz*, Warsaw 2019.

60 A. Brzozowski, 'Komentarz do art. 561' in K. Pietrzykowski (ed), *Kodeks cywilny. T II. Komentarz. Art. 450–1088. Przepisy wprowadzające*, Warsaw 2018.

61 The basis for liability is breach of (implied) warranty under Art. 638 §2 PCC.

62 J. Jezioro, 'Komentarz do art. 560' in E. Gniewek and P. Machnikowski (eds), *Kodeks cywilny. Komentarz*, Warsaw 2017.

63 M. Grochowski, 'Zbieg norm w zakresie rękojmi za wady rzeczy sprzedanej oraz błędu i podstępu', *Monitor Prawniczy* 2012, no. 19, p. 1048.

64 Resolution of the Supreme Court (Sąd Najwyższy, SN) of 5 May 2004, ref. file no. III CZP 96/03.

II. *Descriptive Formants*

In this case, Mr Delmonte has contracted with Mr Goodman only. Mr Goodman cannot claim against Mr Delmonte for breach of contract, because he has not suffered a loss. Neither Mrs Fidel nor the bank have recourse in contract, but both can consider suing Mr Delmonte for damages in delict.

The general principles of the law on negligent misstatement were developed in *Hedley Byrne & Co. Ltd v. Heller & Partners Ltd*,[65] an English case which has been applied in Scotland since *Martin v. Bell-Ingram*.[66] The exact parameters of the case have been subject to debate, but it is thought that 'the current view'[67] of its key principles is found in Lord Morris' judgment:

> if in a sphere in which a person is so placed, that others could reasonably rely upon his judgment or his skill or upon his ability to make careful enquiry, a person takes it upon himself to give information or advice to, or allows his information or advice to be passed on to, another person who, as he knows or should know, will place reliance upon it, then a duty of care will arise.[68]

In *Hedley Byrne*,[69] a bank produced a statement of its client's creditworthiness, which was relied upon by a firm of advertising agents which was considering entering into a contract with the client. The bank and advertising agents did not contract for the provision of the statement, which was provided free of charge. Nonetheless, it was found that the bank was liable for the agents' loss resulting from reliance on the statement, due to a sufficiently proximate 'special relationship' between the parties, such that it was reasonable to conclude that the bank knew that the agents would rely on its statement.[70]

In *Hedley Byrne*,[71] the statement was requested of the bank directly. However, professionals also owe a duty to third parties in respect of the performance of their duties. A recent Scottish case in the UK Supreme Court[72] found that a two-part test applies: it must have been reasonable for the third party to rely on the representation,[73] and the representor should have reasonably foreseen that the third party would do so.[74]

---

65 *Hedley Byrne & Co. Ltd v. Heller & Partners Ltd* [1964] AC 465.

66 *Martin v. Bell Ingram* 1986 SLT 575.

67 L.J. Powell and T. Stewart, *Jackson and Powell on Professional Liability*, 7th ed. (Sweet & Maxwell, London 2012), para. 17.028.

68 *Hedley Byrne & Co. Ltd v. Heller & Partners Ltd* [1964] AC 465, 503 and 514 per Lord Morris.

69 *Hedley Byrne & Co. Ltd v. Heller & Partners Ltd* [1964] AC 465.

70 Ibid. at 539 per Lord Pearce.

71 *Hedley Byrne & Co. Ltd v. Heller & Partners Ltd* [1964] AC 465.

72 *Steel and another v. NRAM Limited (formerly NRAM Plc)* [2018] UKSC 13.

73 Ibid. at paras. 32 and 35 per Lord Wilson.

74 Ibid. at paras. 19, 23 and 32 per Lord Wilson.

In the present case, it is reasonable for Mrs Fidel, as the purchaser of the house, to rely on the surveyor's report. Mr Delmonte ought to have foreseen that his report would be relied upon by Mrs Fidel as the purchaser of the property. Thus, the two-part test is satisfied, and Mrs Fidel can sue him for damages.

It is reasonable that the bank would rely on Mr Delmonte's assessment of the value of the house in determining whether to grant Mrs Fidel a security over the house. However, this is not necessarily foreseeable from the perspective of Mr Delmonte. In an English case decided by the House of Lords, *Smith v. Eric S Bush*,[75] a valuer was liable to a building society in respect of loss sustained by a mortgager due to reliance on his survey report. However, in that case, the mortgagor's building society had commissioned the valuation, and the valuer was consequently under a delictual duty of care to the building society to ensure that the report was accurate. The mortgagor thus had a sufficiently proximate relationship to the valuer.[76] In this case, the bank is further removed from Mr Delmonte than the mortgagor in *Smith v. Eric S Bush*:[77] there is nothing in the facts of the question to indicate that Mr Delmonte was or should have been aware of the loan arrangement. Additionally, the operation of *Hedley Byrne* liability requires that the relevant party must know the identity of the party on whom the loss has fallen, in order to owe a duty of care to that party.[78] In this case, therefore, the two-part test is not met in respect of the bank, and the bank cannot sue for damages.

III. Meta-Legal Formants

Lord Pearce observed in *Hedley Byrne*[79] that '[w]ords are more volatile than deeds. They travel fast and far afield. They are used without being expended.'[80] The courts have not, however, allowed liability to be extended to an unlimited class of individuals, and have limited the scope of liability in the manner described above, to prevent the courts from being 'inundated with claims'.[81] The case law, accordingly, reflects a balanced approach to upholding professional standards and protecting professionals from unlimited liability.

---

75 *Smith v. Eric S Bush* [1990] 1 AC 831.
76 Ibid. at 871 per Lord Jauncey.
77 *Smith v. Eric S Bush* [1990] 1 AC 831.
78 *Hedley Byrne & Co Ltd v. Heller & Partners Ltd* [1964] AC 465; L.J. Powell and T. Stewart, *Jackson and Powell on Professional Liability*, 7th ed. (Sweet & Maxwell, London 2012), para. 17.028.
79 *Hedley Byrne & Co Ltd v. Heller & Partners Ltd* [1964] AC 465.
80 Ibid. at 534 per Lord Pearce.
81 F. McManus and E. Russell, *Delict: A Comprehensive Guide to the Law in Scotland* (Dundee University Press, Dundee 2011), para. 3.2.

2.11. SLOVAKIA

Kristián Csach, Monika Jurčová, Peter Mészáros and Veronika Zoričáková

I. Operative Rules

1. In the contractual relationship between Mr Delmonte and Mr Goodman, Mr Delmonte is not liable for damages, as no loss was caused to Mr Goodman.
2. For aggrieved persons outside the contractual relationship between Mr Delmonte and Mr Goodman (Mrs Fidel and the bank), tortious claims against Mr Delmonte might arise, based on the breach of a statutory duty. A contractual claim based on a contract with protective effects upon third parties is also possible.

II. Descriptive Formants

In this case, Mr Delmonte will not be liable for damages to Mr Goodman for the breach of his contractual obligation to act with due diligence (see below for a more detailed interpretation of the content and nature of this obligation) because Mr Goodman did not incur any loss due to Mr Delmonte's gross negligence (on the contrary, Mr Goodman sold his property for more than its market value).

Mr Delmonte could be liable towards Mrs Fidel, and potentially also the bank (if it fails to recover the entire sum loaned to Mrs Fidel due to her insolvency). Although there is no relation of priority between the bank's claim against Mrs Fidel and the claim for damages against Mr Delmonte, the bank would need, firstly, to claim against Mrs Fidel, to ascertain the amount of damages attributable to Mr Delmonte. For the bank to be able to claim against Mr Delmonte, the insolvency of Mrs Fidel is not necessary. Nevertheless, it must be proven that Mrs Fidel is unable to pay the bank all residual debt, and that there is a causal link between this and Mr Delmonte's actions.

No special provision on liability for damages caused by incorrect information or advice is provided for by the SCC. No clear Slovak case law on the matter is known to the present authors, and therefore four general conditions of tortious liability according to section 420 SCC have to be tested:

(a) *Breach of duty.* The duties of the expert are extensively regulated in the Act no. 382/2004 Coll. on Experts, Interpreters and Translators and on Amendments to Certain Acts (the Expert Act). Although the Expert Act lacks an express requirement to act with professional care, this obligation may reliably be drawn from the purpose of its other statutory provisions.[82]

---

[82] J. Dankovčík and A. Rajničová Knapíková, *Zákon o znalcoch, tlmočníkoch a prekladateľoch. Komentár [Act on experts, interpreters and translators. Commentary]*, Bratislava: Wolters

It is advocated that the obligation of professional care exceeds the contractual framework of relations between a surveyor and their clients. The surveyor could reasonably assume that their client would use the opinion as a basis for determining the price of the property, for the purpose of its transfer, and therefore that the opinion's accuracy would be relied upon not only by the seller but also by the future buyer. The determining criterion for liability is, presumably, the legitimacy of the trust (reliance) in the accuracy of the expert's report.[83] However, the liability for trust is underdeveloped in Slovak civil doctrine, and there is no case law concerning professional liability in such situations. Mrs Fidel's claim is well founded, as her reliance is seemingly justified by the fact that she was presented with a valuation report prepared for the purposes of the transaction by a regulated expert surveyor. If the surveyor knew that a bank was also to rely on his expert opinion, it might be possible to consider the bank also to be entitled to damages. The case law seems to require the surveyor to have been aware of the identity of the third party, and that they might reasonably have foreseen that the rights of the third party would be affected.[84] As the issue of professional liability is settled neither by domestic doctrine nor the relevant case law, it may only be presumed that the liability of the expert in cases extending beyond the contractual framework (i.e. to a third party) may be established only if the third party, in all given circumstances, acted under the impression that the expert's opinion was reliable. It may only be presumed that these might be the criteria the court would consider when assessing such a case.

It is possible that Mrs Fidel might also have a contractual claim. Even though Slovak law has not yet fully acknowledged the notion of contracts with protective effects upon third parties, the SCC, in a judgment from 2020, established the requirements for a bank to be contractually liable towards third persons.[85] This would be the case, in exceptional circumstances, if the identity or the definition and protection of the third party must have

---

Kluwer, 2014, p. 128; K. Csach in K. Csach, T. Doležal, J. Husár, J. Suchoža and Ľ. Širicová, *Profesijná zodpovednosť' [Professional negligence]*, Košice: UPJŠ, 2011, pp. 271–72.

83 K. Csach in K. Csach, T. Doležal, J. Husár, J. Suchoža and Ľ. Širicová, *Profesijná zodpovednosť [Professional negligence]*, Košice: UPJŠ, 2011, p. 273.

84 Decision of the SSC file no. 7 Cdo 163/2020 dated 28.02.2020 (R 18/2022).

85 The SCC recently held a bank to be contractually liable towards third persons: Decision of the SSC file no. 7 Cdo 163/2020 dated 28.02.2020 (R 18/2022). Before that, the doctrine was rather critical of the extension of contractual protection towards third parties. Against the concept in Slovak law, while formulating exceptions, see K. Csach in K. Csach, T. Doležal, J. Husár, J. Suchoža and Ľ. Širicová, *Profesijná zodpovednosť [Professional negligence]*, Košice: UPJŠ, 2011, p. 147; rather unclear, and referring to the Czech case law, see A. Dulak in M. Števček, A. Dulak, J. Bajánková, M. Fečík, F. Sedlačko, M. Tomašovič et al., *Občiansky zákonník I, sect. 1–450. Komentár [Commentary on Civil Code I, ss. 1–450]*, Prague: C.H. Beck, 2015, p. 1337.

been known to the liable party, and the liable party could reasonably have foreseen that the rights of the third party may be affected by a breach of that obligation.

(b) *Damages and determination of their amount.* No per se limitation on compensation for pure economic loss is identifiable under Slovak law. In this case, damages can be determined as the difference between the aggrieved person's real state of assets and the one that would have occurred had the surveyor not acted negligently; that is, if he had duly taken the contamination and the state of the property market into account. Given the relatively short period between the preparation of the report and Mrs Fidel's sale of the property (about three months), it can be assumed that the sale price of €575,000 reflected the market conditions at the time of drawing up the report, and so it is reasonable to assume that damages of €120,000 would be calculated (on the basis of Mrs Fidel having paid €695,000 for the house).

(c) *Causation.* Damages must arise in a causal relation with the surveyor's breach of duty. There is nothing in the facts that indicate a breach of the causal link between the breach of duty and the loss.

(d) *Fault.* Lastly, the fault of the tortfeasor is the final requisite of a tortious claim. However, the SCC presumes the tortfeasor was at fault, so the aggrieved party does not have to prove his fault. The surveyor has the possibility to exonerate himself if he is able to prove that there was no fault on his side (not even unknowing negligence). With regard to the violation of the duty to act with due care, there is a certain overlap between breach of duty and fault, whereby a breach of the duty to maintain the required level of due care would also mean that the surveyor acted (at least) unknowingly negligently.[86]

III. Meta-Legal Formants

During the period before recodification of Czech civil law (when its tortious regulation was identical to the current Slovak law), the Supreme Court of the Czech Republic acknowledged the concept of the protective effect of the contract for a third party.[87] The Czech Supreme Court is also very influential in the Slovak legal system and, therefore, it might be useful to address this issue. According

---

86 K. Csach in K. Csach, T. Doležal, J. Husár, J. Suchoža and Ľ. Siricová, *Profesijná zodpovednosť [Professional negligence]*, Košice: UPJŠ, 2011, pp. 187–88.

87 See judgments of the Czech Supreme Court file no. 29 Odo 379/2001 dated 25.03.2003 and file no. 29 Odo 1673/2005 dated 20.12.2007. For a more comparative survey, see K. Csach, *Zodpovednosť znalcov v komparatívnom a kolíznoprávnom kontexte. Štúdia o zodpovednosti za škodu spôsobenú nesprávnou informáciou [Experts' Liability in comparative and conflict of laws context. Liability for damage caused by wrong interpretation]*, Košice: UPJŠ, 2009, pp. 61–66.

to the concept, a third party is entitled to claim damages based on breach of a contractual duty if the duty is also aimed at protecting them. However, the contours of this concept and the extent of the breach of the contractual obligation to third parties were not clearly defined by the Czech Supreme Court, and this protective effect has not yet been acknowledged by the Slovak courts. Given that Slovak liability regulation is identical to Czech regulation prior to recodification, it is possible that the concept of the protective effect of the contract will also be adopted by Slovak case law and doctrine. Recent developments underline the introduction of the concept of a contract with protective effects on third parties into Slovak law. In a judgment from 2020, the SSC established the requirements for a bank to be contractually liable towards third persons.[88] According to a later generalisation of the ruling in the process of its official publication in 2022,[89] the court considered two issues important. It held, firstly, that extending contractual liability to damage suffered by a third party is only acceptable if the identity or the definition and protection of the third party must have been known to the liable party at the time of conclusion of the contract. Secondly, a bank which, through a contract with their customer, has assumed the obligation to execute orders of the client to pay the obligations owed to that party by the client may be liable for damages caused to that person only if, when concluding the contract with the client, it could reasonably have foreseen that the rights of the third party may have been affected by a breach of that obligation.

However, in view of the issues discussed above, it is not necessary to adopt the protective effect of the contract in this particular case, as a remedy might in any event be available in tort.

2.12. SPAIN

Carles Vendrell Cervantes

I. *Operative Rules*

Mrs Fidel may sue Mr Delmonte for damages on the basis of non-contractual liability.

In theory, the bank might also sue Mr Delmonte for non-contractual liability, for lending too much without a sufficient security right (damages, for example,

88 Decision of the SSC file no. 7 Cdo 163/2020 dated 28.02.2020 (R 18/2022).

89 The official publication process in the collection of decisions of courts and opinions of the SCC is very important. A decision is published with a generalised statement (called a 'legal sentence') only if the publication and the generalised statement have been adopted by the collegium of judges in the respective branch of the SSC (civil, commercial or criminal). Therefore, the decisions published in the official collection are considered more important than ordinary judgments of the SSC.

in the case of foreclosure), albeit that in this case it would be questionable whether the bank would be entitled to compensation, as they could have carried out all the verifications they deemed appropriate in order to estimate the value of the house before lending.

II. Descriptive Formants

Mrs Fidel was not a party to the contract under which Mr Delmonte was appointed to assess the value of the house. Therefore, Mrs Fidel may only sue Mr Delmonte for damages by virtue of Article 1902 of the Spanish Civil Code, which regulates non-contractual liability. This article entails the obligation to repair damage caused by faulty or negligent acts or omissions.

Case law has established the requirements that have to be met in order for non-contractual liability to be due (decisions of the Supreme Court no. 448/1998 of 18 May, no. 9/2000 of 21 January and no. 479/2002 of 14 May). Thus, Mrs Fidel would have to prove the existence of: (1) an action (Mr Delmonte's assessment); (2) a loss (the excessive price paid by Mrs Fidel); (3) the casual link between the action and the harm (the purchase of the house at an excessive price, due to Mr Delmonte's assessment); and (4) Mr Delmonte's negligence (by overlooking the sharp decline in house prices in the neighbourhood and the heavy soil contamination mentioned in an inspection report).

Moreover, Mrs Fidel could claim for other damages that might derive from Mr Delmonte's negligence, such as the fees and taxes calculated using the value of the house as their basis. For instance, she could claim, where applicable: (1) the excess paid to the notary and the registry in relation to mortgage constitution expenses; (2) the excess in the fees paid to Mr Delmonte for the house assessment (if Mrs Fidel had to pay part of the fees); (3) the excessive amount paid for the insurance on the house; and (4) any costs incurred as a result of being unable to repay her loan.

In relation to the possibility of the bank suing Mr Delmonte for damages, it is worth noting that, according to Law 2/1981 regulating the mortgage market, if Mr Delmonte had been an employee of a company certified in accordance with the law, the bank would have been obliged to admit the valuation report submitted by the mortgage applicant, Mrs Fidel. However, assuming that Mr Delmonte is not such an employee, it is not very realistic to assume that the bank would have provided a loan to Mrs Fidel based only on Mr Delmonte's assessment. Moreover, as stated above, the bank could have carried out all the verifications it deemed appropriate. Furthermore, the bank would also have a claim against Mrs Fidel for the residual debt, which could exclude the existence of damage having been sustained by the bank.

2.13. SWEDEN

Oskar Mossberg

I. *Operative Rules*

Both the Bank and Mrs Fidel can sue Mr Delmonte.

II. *Descriptive Formants*

As Mr Goodman has suffered no losses, any action he brought would be unsuccessful.

The difference between market development and the soil contamination could, in principle, be of consequence in the assessment of the surveyor's potential negligence. Soil contamination is a factual issue that can be empirically assessed. In contrast, market development often involves prognoses, value judgments and subjective assessments. Therefore, when evaluating liability for negligence, a surveyor may be granted a wider margin of discretion regarding market development. However, as the case states that negligence is to be assumed, this is, however, of no consequence here.

The case resembles two HD cases: NJA 1987 p. 692 and NJA 2001 p. 878. These cases both concerned *'värderingsmans ansvar för oaktsamt intygande mot annan än kontraktspart'* (appraiser's liability for negligent statements towards persons other than contractual parties). According to these cases, an appraiser who has been negligent is liable towards non-contractual parties who have placed an objectively justified reliance on their appraisal and suffered damages as a result. The latter case sets limits on the principle from the former case, by stating that a disclaimer in the statement of appraisal can mean that reliance on the appraisal is not objectively justified. Even though there are similarities to contractual or quasi-contractual reasoning in these cases, they are tortious rather than being based on a rationale of contractual third-party effects. In the 1987 case, a financier (a credit institution, though not technically a bank) was awarded damages. Due to the existence of a disclaimer in the 2001 case, the appraiser was not held liable.[90]

Provided that: (a) there is negligence; (b) the bank and Mrs Fidel have, in fact, relied on the appraisal; and (c) that such reliance was objectively justified, both the bank and Mrs Fidel can invoke the principles from the cases to claim damages from Mr Delmonte (the three criteria listed above are taken from the aforementioned HD cases).

---

90 For analysis of these cases, see e.g. H. Andersson, *Ansvarsproblem i skadeståndsrätten*, Iustus, Uppsala 2013, pp. 263 ff., with extensive further references.

The fact that Mrs Fidel cannot repay the bank does not mean that she is not, in principle, legally required to do so. Therefore, she can be considered to have suffered a loss for which damages can be claimed. If the bank is awarded damages, these would cover the losses from Mrs Fidel's defaulted payments, and this should absolve her from the debt (otherwise the bank would be unjustly enriched).[91] If Mrs Fidel is awarded damages, this does not necessarily mean that the bank cannot sue, since the funds awarded to Mrs Fidel do not necessarily need to be funnelled to the bank (if she spends them otherwise, Mr Delmonte could, however, possibly object against the bank's suit on grounds of causality).

III. Meta-Legal Formants

The 1987 and 2001 HD cases should be seen in the light of the tortious statutory rule on pure economic loss in Chapter 2, Article 2 of Skadeståndslagen (the Act on Damages). This provision is weak, in the sense that negligence does not suffice as a basis for tortious liability. Instead, a criminal act is required for damages to be awarded for pure economic loss. However, the preparatory works for the Act on Damages state that this rule is not intended to be applied *a contrario*, meaning that the absence of a criminal act should not be taken to rule out damages being awarded. The legislator suggested that further principles on liability for pure economic loss were desirable, and handed the issue of further legal development over to the courts.[92] The courts have shown a somewhat reluctant attitude to awarding damages for pure economic losses outside the scope of the statute (several rationales have been mentioned for this, the 'floodgate' argument among them). This reluctance has been criticised, and there are some widely discussed cases where the HD has expanded the area of liability for pure economic loss – the aforementioned cases from 1987 and 2001 among them.[93]

---

91 On the relevance of an unjustified enrichment-based argument in the context of calculating compensation in tort, see H. Andersson, *Ersättningsproblem i skadeståndsrätten*, Iustus, Uppsala 2017, pp. 171 ff., 181 ff., 197 ff. Andersson covers all the relevant case law, and provides references to most of relevant scholarly work of the last century.

92 NJA II 1972 p. 609 – proposition 1972:5: Kungl. Maj:ts proposition med förslag till skadeståndslag m.m.

93 The main critical assessment is perhaps J. Kleineman, *Ren förmögenhetsskada: Särskilt vid vilseledande av annan än kontraktspart*, Juristförlaget, Stockholm 1987, which has had a big impact on the following discussion. Kleineman is critical of the aforementioned reluctance on several bases. In the present author's opinion, the most important of these is that the reluctance is characteristic of an unmotivated loyalty to the statutory provision in Ch. 2, Art. 2 of the Act on Damages. This provision was partly intended as a codification, and was never intended to bar claims for damages in cases of pure economic loss not caused by criminal acts. In Kleineman's view, the provision is an inadequate codification, as it missed important parts of the existing case law, thus giving the impression that the opportunities to claim compensation are more limited than they actually were before the enactment of the Act on Damages. The existence of the provision is also said to have led to a tendency to deny compensation in cases where there is no direct statutory support for doing so (outside the provision), contrary to the intention stated in the preparatory works.

3. COMPARATIVE REMARKS

Jan Biemans and Lorna Richardson

This case examines the legal consequences of third parties (C, as the buyer of a house, and D, as the bank financing the buyer) relying on a negligent valuation due to A's breach of contract with B in providing the valuation. The case seeks to identify any liability that A will have towards either C or D, or both, and the basis for that liability, whether contract, tort or some other means. The case also raises the issue of whether A will have any liability towards B, given that B is now better off, having received a higher price for the house than it was worth, as a result of A's negligent opinion.

Claim by Mr Goodman

In all of the systems surveyed, except one, Mr Goodman (B) cannot claim damages as a result of Mr Delmonte's (A's) negligent valuation. This is because he has not suffered any loss as a result of the breach of contract. In English law, Mr Goodman might successfully claim for breach of contract, but given that he has not suffered a loss, this would be for nominal damages only; such damages are a very small sum or token amount – often £1 – which is awarded purely to show that there has been a breach of contract.

It is only under Polish law that Mr Goodman would have a claim for damages against Mr Delmonte. This is on the basis of provisions of the Polish Civil Code, which stipulate that Mr Delmonte provided Mr Goodman with a warranty in relation to the condition of the house.

Claim by Mrs Fidel

In most legal systems surveyed (Belgium, Bulgaria, France, Germany, Italy, the Netherlands, Scotland, Slovakia, Spain and Sweden), Mrs Fidel would be able to claim damages against Mr Delmonte. In the majority of those systems (Belgium, Bulgaria, France, Italy,[94] the Netherlands, Scotland, Slovakia, Spain and Sweden), the claim would be extracontractual. It would be more difficult to succeed with the claim in some systems than in others. The Belgian reporters note that Mrs Fidel should have no difficulty in establishing her extracontractual claim, whereas in Bulgaria she may have some difficulty in doing so. In Bulgarian law, Mrs Fidel might have trouble proving the causal link between Mr Delmonte's

94 Although the Italian reporters noted a move away from classifying the claim as either contractual or extracontractual, and towards a claim for non-fulfilment of obligations, given the importance of the expectations that arise where one of the parties to the contract is a professional.

negligence and her loss. This is because some court decisions have recognised the practice, among surveyors, of giving high valuations in order to enable loan funding to be obtained, and also on the basis that Mrs Fidel could have obtained her own valuation. The Scottish reporter notes that Mrs Fidel would likely have a claim, suggesting that the matter is not beyond doubt. In a number of the legal systems where Mrs Fidel would have an extracontractual claim (Scotland, Slovakia and Sweden), its basis would be her reasonable reliance on Mr Delmonte's survey; in Scots law, Mr Delmonte must also have reasonably foreseen this reliance.

In German law, Mrs Fidel's claim would be based on a contract with protective effect for third parties; the valuation must have been intended for use by third parties, with Mr Delmonte having known that third parties would use the report to base decisions on the purchase of the house. In Dutch law, Mrs Fidel's claim would be based on the unlawful act of Mr Delmonte making a negligent valuation. Similarly to German law, in Dutch law the success of Mrs Fidel's claim would depend on whether or not it would have been foreseeable to Mr Delmonte that she would rely on his valuation for the purchase of the house.

In the Czech Republic, England and Poland, Mrs Fidel would have no claim for damages against Mr Delmonte. In Czech and English law, this is because there is no contract for the benefit of a third party on the facts of this case. The Czech reporter noted that any claim in delict would be uncertain, due to relatively new rules in the new Czech Civil Code and there being no established legal rules to define to whom Mr Delmonte might be liable outside of the contract. In English law, the reporter noted that there is case law in terms of which purchasers have successfully claimed damages in respect of negligent house valuations. However, in those cases, the valuations had been lender-commissioned rather than seller-commissioned. The line of cases has since been interpreted strictly, such that a claim in tort on the basis of those cases would be unlikely to succeed on the facts of Case 9. As noted above, Polish law would deal with the negligent valuation as a breach of warranty claim only. This warranty would not transfer from Mr Goodman to Mrs Fidel and, as such, Mrs Fidel would have no claim against Mr Delmonte.

Interestingly, the Italian reporters note that Mrs Fidel would also have a claim against the bank. This claim would be based on consumer mortgage legislation requiring the bank to obtain their own valuation of the house for lending purposes, as well as the loan-to-value ratio breaching the maximum limit.

Claim by the Bank

On this question, the position was finely balanced, with no clear majority either way. In seven systems (Belgium, France, Germany, the Netherlands, Slovakia,

Spain and Sweden), the bank is likely to have a claim; in six (Bulgaria, Czech Republic, England, Italy, Poland and Scotland), it is not.

In a majority of jurisdictions where a claim would be available to the bank (Belgium, France, Slovakia, Spain and Sweden), it would be on an extracontractual basis. In Slovak law, Mr Delmonte would have to have known that the bank would rely on his valuation, but this is unclear from the facts of this case.[95] In German law, the claim would, like Mrs Fidel's claim, be based on a contract with protective effect for third parties. The same comments made above regarding the intended use of the report, and Mr Delmonte's knowledge of this, also apply to the bank's claim. The Spanish reporter notes that successfully pursuing a claim will be more difficult for the bank than for Mrs Fidel, as the bank could have carried out its own verifications regarding the value of the house.

In the Czech Republic, England and Poland, the bank has no claim, for the same reasons that Mrs Fidel has no claim in those systems. As such, the comments made above in relation to that apply equally to the bank's position. In Bulgarian law, the bank would not be considered to be acting as a good merchant in using the seller's valuation to make a decision on funding Mrs Fidel's purchase, which would deny it a claim against Mr Delmonte. As noted above, the bank would be in breach of certain statutory obligations in Italian law relating to consumer mortgages, such that Mrs Fidel would have a claim against the bank. It is due to these breaches by the bank that it would be unable to succeed in a damages claim against Mr Delmonte in Italy. The Scottish reporter was of the view that, while it might have been reasonable for the bank to rely on Mr Delmonte's valuation, there is nothing in the facts of Case 9 that suggest that Mr Delmonte knew or ought to have known of such reliance. Accordingly, one of the two limbs needed for liability to be established in delict is absent, thus preventing a claim.

95 Indeed, it is on that basis that the Scottish reporter comes to the view that the bank have no claim against Mr Delmonte in Scots law.

CASE 10: SIMULATION

1. CASE

Tasman Ltd have entered into a contract to lease machines to Vinci Company. The lease contract states that Vinci have to pay a monthly rent of €2,000 for the machines. In reality, Vinci and Tasman have agreed that Vinci only have to pay €1,500. Tasman sell their assets, including the machines and the lease contract with Vinci, to Kepsky & Co. The lease is validly assigned. While neither Tasman nor Vinci make any inaccurate statements to Kepsky, neither of them inform Kepsky of the lower monthly rent. Based on the rent set out in the lease, Kepsky thinks it is worth buying the lease from Tasman. When Kepsky send out the first monthly invoice for €2,000 to Vinci after the sale, Vinci reply that they only have to pay €1,500.

Question

What do Vinci have to pay Kepsky?

2. DISCUSSIONS

2.1. BELGIUM

Siel Demeyere and Vincent Sagaert

I. Operative Rules

Vinci would likely have to pay €2,000 to Kepsky.

II. Descriptive Formants

Tasman and Vinci have agreed a different rent to that mentioned in their contract. This situation is addressed in Belgian law as a situation of *veinzing/simulation* (simulation). Simulation can relate to the existence of the agreement (e.g. sale where there is none), the sort of agreement (e.g. sale instead of gift), the identity of the contracting parties (in the case of *naamlening/prête-nom* (name lending)) or the content of the agreement.[1] In this case, the simulation concerns the content of the agreement, since the contract mentions a monthly rent of €2,000, while in reality only €1,500 must be paid. A third party to the contract can choose to rely on the contract (with the false amount) or the genuine agreement between the parties.[2] This is only possible where the third party acts in good faith, and has acted on the basis of the simulated agreement. Even though Kepsky would have become a contracting party by buying the lease from Tasman, Kepsky is a third party with regard to the simulation, since anyone who has not participated in, and is ignorant of, the simulation is a third party.[3] This entails that Kepsky can choose to claim either €1,500 or €2,000 in monthly rent; presumably they would choose the latter, as this is more beneficial to them. Between the original contracting parties, Tasman and Vinci, only their genuine agreement (monthly rent of €1,500) is valid and enforceable.[4]

2.2. BULGARIA

Petar Topurov

I. Operative Rules

Vinci must pay €2,000 to Kepsky.

II. Descriptive Formants

If the parties disguise the real agreement concluded between them with a seeming agreement, the rules that apply are those of the seeming agreement, provided the latter meets the requirements for being valid (Art. 17, paragraph 1 LOC). The disguise may also relate to separate clauses of the deal.[5] Rights acquired

1 W. Van Gerven and A. Van Oevelen, *Verbintenissenrecht*, Acco, Leuven 2015, 227; P. Van Ommeslaghe, *Traité de droit civil belge. II. Les obligations. Vol. 1*, Bruylant, Brussels 2013, 420, no. 266; P. Wéry, *Droit des obligations: Théorie générale du contrat*, I, Larcier, Brussels 2011, 877, no. 940.

2 Art. 5.39 BCC; S. Stijns, *Verbintenissenrecht. Leerboek 1*, die Keure, Bruges 2009–16, 253, no. 330; W. Van Gerven and A. Van Oevelen, *Verbintenissenrecht*, Acco, Leuven 2015, 227; P. Van Ommeslaghe, *Traité de droit civil belge. II. Les obligations. Vol. 1*, Bruylant, Brussels 2013, 440, no. 287; P. Wéry, *Droit des obligations: Théorie générale du contrat*, I, Larcier, Brussels 2011, 878, no. 944.

3 Cass. 11 December 1987, *Arr.Cass.* 1987–88, 481, *Pas.* 1988, 449, *RCJB* 1993, 49, comment D. Philippe.

4 Art. 5.39 BCC; Cass. 27 September 2012, no. C.11.0322.F, *Arr.Cass.* 2012, 2041; S. Stijns, *Verbintenissenrecht.* die Keure, Bruges 2009–16, 329; P. Van Ommeslaghe, *Traité de droit civil belge. II. Les obligations. Vol. 1*, Bruylant, Brussels 2013, 432, no. 281; P. Wéry, *Droit des obligations: Théorie générale du contrat*, I, Larcier, Brussels 2011, 878, no. 943.

5 M. Pavlova, *Civil Law. General Part*, Sophie-P, Sofia 2002, p. 548.

by third parties in good faith from the acquirer under the seeming agreement shall be retained, unless these are rights which relate to real estate acquired after registering in the property register a claim to reveal the differences between the parties' real agreement and the seeming agreement[6] (Art. 17, paragraph 2, LOC). In this specific case, the law regulates the primary means of acquiring rights,[7] and good faith is a matter of presumption until the contrary has been proved. Considering that Kepsky are acting in the capacity of a bona fide acquirer of the claims of Tasman Ltd under the lease agreement, Vinci have to pay €2,000. However, the lessee (Vinci) may be able to claim compensation from the transferor (Tasman). Vinci's right to file a claim for compensation from Tasman will depend on the specifics of the hypothetical agreement reached with Tasman about the rental amount. Possible grounds are any commitment from Tasman not to transfer the leased machines, and the failure to notify the purchaser about the agreement reached with the lessee about the rental amount.

2.3. CZECH REPUBLIC

Tomáš Richter

I. Operative Rules

Most likely, *Vinci must pay Kepsky €1,500* in monthly rent.

II. Descriptive Formants

The case turns on whether the lease agreement between Tasman and Vinci was validly amended so as to reduce the monthly rent, from the €2,000 which was

6 According to Art. 26 LOC, 'fictitious contracts are also null and void'.

7 M. Pavlova, *Civil Law. General Part*, Sophie-P, Sofia 2002, pp. 546, 548. The legal theory distinguishes the kinds of acquisition of rights according to the legal facts necessary for the acquisition: (a) original (primary) acquisition – in this case, the person who acquires the right becomes its holder regardless of its title previously being held by another person. An example of an original acquisition is a case in which a person becomes the owner of a property as a result of possession during a certain period of time without the same being transferred to them by the owner of the property. Another example is the bona fide acquisition of possession of moveable property by a person who is not the owner, but whose circumstance is not known by the person who established the possession of the property. In this case, it is necessary for the acquisition that there is no requirement for the participation of a notary; (b) derivative acquisition – the acquisition of the right is based on the previous ownership of a right by another person. An example of primary acquisition is the rule of Art. 78, paragraph 1 Ownership Act: 'Whoever has acquired for consideration the possession of a movable property or security to the bearer on a legal basis, even if not from the owner, but without knowledge of that fact, shall acquire the ownership. The same rule shall also apply to acquiring other real rights over a movable property.'

ostensibly agreed in the original (and presumably written) lease agreement, to €1,500, in respect of which the facts of the case stipulate that 'in reality, Vinci and Tasman *have agreed that* Vinci only have to pay €1,500' (emphasis added). The facts provide nothing about the form of this agreement, made 'in reality'. Since the law does not require the lease agreement to be in written form,[8] and since the facts stipulate nothing about the form of the lease agreement nor the form in which its amendments were agreed, it seems reasonable to conclude that the agreement made 'in reality' between Tasman and Vinci probably validly amended the lease agreement by reducing the monthly rent from €2,000 to €1,500. Under this assumption, Vinci would only have to pay €1,500 to Kepsky, as the validly agreed contractual amount of the lease. As reported in relation to Case 5 above, the key legal rule here is section 2221 CC, which provides that:

> (1) If the owner of the [rented] thing changes, the rights and obligations under the lease shall pass on to the new owner.
> (2) Where the lessor transfers ownership to the [rented] thing, the new owner is not bound by contractual provisions setting out the lessor's obligations which do not follow from the law. The rule [in the previous sentence] does not apply to contractual provisions which were known to the new owner.

Since the duty to pay rent follows from the law, as the lessee's most basic obligation (section 2201 CC), section 2221(2) does not grant Kepsky any real protection vis-à-vis Vinci here. Unless Vinci was somehow complicit with Tasman to defraud Kepsky, which the facts do not suggest at all, Czech law will not give Kepsky any other grounds to claim the difference from Vinci.

Whether Kepsky might have a claim against Tasman in this respect is not clear from the facts of the case, although it might indeed be so. The facts do stipulate that, 'while neither Tasman nor Vinci make any inaccurate statements to Kepsky, neither of them inform Kepsky of the lower monthly rent'. Whether this silence on the part of Tasman as seller/assignor might qualify as grounds for a claim which Kepsky could bring against Tasman cannot be assessed for want of factual details as regards the circumstances and contractual terms of the sale/assignment. Depending on those circumstances and terms, Kepsky might be able to avoid the transaction under section 583 CC, on the grounds of a mistake in a circumstance decisive to the transaction, and induced by Tasman. This might be so, in particular, if the Vinci lease was material to the overall value of the assets Tasman sold to Kepsky, and if Tasman made incomplete disclosure of the lease contract to Kepsky prior to the transaction.

---

8 M. Hulmák in M. Hulmák et al., *Občanský zákoník V, Závazkové právo, Obecná část (§1721–2054), První vydání*, C.H. Beck, Praha 2014, p. 223 at 90.

Alternatively, Kepsky might have a claim for monetary compensation against Tasman under section 584 CC, if the Vinci lease was not decisive to the transaction. But the analysis cannot meaningfully be conducted in the abstract, without stipulations as to the key terms of the asset deal between Tasman and Kepsky.

2.4. ENGLAND AND WALES

T.T. Arvind

I. Operative Rules

If the agreement to accept a lower rent varied the contract, it will bind Kepsky even if Kepsky had no notice. If it was a non-contractual promise, Kepsky may be temporarily estopped from raising the rent.

II. Descriptive Formants

Commentaries on assignment read the case law as reflecting a general principle that an assignee cannot recover more from the debtor than the assignor would have been entitled to.[9] The starting point, therefore, is that Kepsky, as an assignee, should not be in a better position than Tasman would have been. The precise outcome will, however, depend on whether the agreement lowering the rent is a contractual variation or a non-contractual promise. If it is a contractual variation or a 'collateral contract' that is entered into alongside the main contract to give a supplementary assurance or alter the parties' obligations, then it will bind Kepsky even if Kepsky did not have notice of it. Assignment, of its nature, relates to a chose in action (see Case 5 above). The classic definition of a chose in action is a personal right which can 'only be claimed or enforced by action'.[10] As this suggests, if a contractual right has been varied, only the actually extant right can be assigned, as only this can be claimed. The assignee, therefore, receives the assignment subject to all defects in, or claims in relation to, the assigned debt, even if the assignee took in good faith without knowledge of the existence of these defects or claims.[11] This is well established in the case law, which has held, for example, that a factor who purchased debts without knowing that they were subject to a rebate was, nevertheless, bound by the rebate.[12]

---

9 J. McGhee et al. (eds), *Snell's Equity*, 34th ed. (London: Sweet & Maxwell, 2019), para. 3-027.
10 *Torkington v. Magee* [1902] 2 KB 427, 430 (Channell J).
11 *Athenaeum Soc v. Pooley* (1853) 3 D&J 294.
12 *Bibby Factors Northwest Ltd v. HFD Ltd* [2015] EWCA Civ 1908, [2016] 1 Lloyd's Rep. 517.

The situation is, however, different if the agreement to lower the rent was not contractual, for example if it was not collateral to the main contract and no consideration was provided. A non-contractual promise to accept a lower rent creates only a defence of promissory estoppel, under which Vinci can argue that Tasman are 'estopped' (that is, legally precluded) from going back on their promise. This requires a clear and unambiguous promise relating to an existing legal right, on which the promisee has relied, and from which it would be inequitable to permit the promisor to resile.[13] It is not entirely clear whether promissory estoppel binds an assignee. An assignee takes the assignment subject to equities[14] and, as a recent treatise on the subject has argued,[15] promissory estoppel should, in principle, constitute such an equity. The case law on the subject is, however, less clear. Although courts in other common law jurisdictions, such as New Zealand, have held that assignees can be bound by an estoppel that originally arose against the assignor,[16] English courts have been reluctant to hold that promissory estoppel can follow an assignment. Where the issue has arisen, the case has typically been decided on some other ground, such as collateral contracts.[17] Accordingly, it is likely, but not wholly certain, that Kepsky will be bound by a non-contractual promise to accept a lower rent. Even if Kepsky are bound, however, promissory estoppel only suspends the legal right, and does not permanently extinguish or alter it. This means that Kepsky will be able to end the arrangement by giving Vinci a clear intimation of their intent to enforce compliance with the contractually stipulated rent.[18]

III. Meta-Legal Formants

The rule that a contractual variation binds a subsequent assignee of a contract, even if they act in good faith and without any knowledge of the variation, reflects a broader position that is very well established in English law. English law does not generally confer protection on a third party who purchases tangible or intangible goods or choses in action in good faith, without knowledge, and for valuable consideration. This rule has been controversial in its application to tangible goods (where a purchaser who unknowingly acquires stolen goods

---

13 *Central London Property Trust v. High Trees House* [1947] KB 130.

14 LPA, s. 136; see the discussion in Case 7, question 2.

15 M. Barnes, *The Law of Estoppel* (Oxford: Hart Publishing, 2020), paras. 2.253–2.256.

16 *Bay of Plenty Electricity Ltd v. Natural Gas Corporation Energy Ltd* [2002] 1 NZLR 173 (NZCA).

17 See e.g. *Brikom Investments Ltd v. Carr* [1979] 1 QB 467 (CA), where only one of the three judges hearing the case (Lord Denning) was prepared to decide that promissory estoppel could follow an assignment.

18 *Tool Metal Manufacturing Co. Ltd v. Tungsten Electric Co. Ltd* [1955] 1 WLR 761 (HL).

will not receive good title as against the true owner, even if the purchase was made in good faith). In relation to assignment of choses in action, however, the rule is generally uncontroversial, and is seen as reflecting the priority English law gives to protecting the interests of the debtor whose debt is being assigned.[19]

2.5. FRANCE

Sylvain Ravenne and Flora Vern

I. *Operative Rules*

Vinci have to pay €2,000 to Kepsky.

II. *Descriptive Formants*

Tasman and Vinci have concluded an apparent contract which states that Vinci have to pay a monthly rent of €2,000 for the machines. They have also concluded a secret or hidden contract, called a '*contre-lettre*' (counter-letter), by which they agreed that Vinci would only pay a monthly rent of €1,500.

Article 1201 of the FCC provides: 'Where the parties have concluded an apparent contract which conceals a secret contract, the latter (also called a "counter-letter") takes effect between the parties. It cannot be set up against third parties, though the latter may rely on it.'

The assignee of the apparent contract is regarded as a third party. Hence, Kepsky can rely on the apparent contract, and the counter-letter cannot be relied upon against Kepsky.

However, older case law provides that only a third party who is ignorant of the counter-letter, and therefore acts in good faith, can rely on the apparent contract for their own benefit.[20] Thus, the counter-letter could be relied upon against an assignee who knew of its existence prior to contracting with one of the parties, and was therefore in bad faith. If Kepsky had known about the counter-letter, Vinci would have been able to rely on it against them.

---

19 E. Peel (ed), *Treitel on the Law of Contract*, 14th ed. (London: Sweet & Maxwell, 2016), para. 15-067.

20 Cass., civ., 9 févr. 1848, *S.* 1848, 1, 481; Cass., req., 13 mars 1899, *S.* 1900, 1, 72; F. Terré, P. Simler, Y. Lequette and F. Chénedé, *Droit civil, les obligations*, 13th ed. (Paris: Dalloz, 2022), n° 739; H., L. & J. Mazeaud and F. Chabas, *Leçons de droit civil, Obligations, Théorie générale*, 9th ed. (Paris: Montchrestien, 1998), n° 822; C. Aubry and C. Rau, *Droit civil français*, 6th ed. by P. Esmein (Paris: Librairies techniques, 1958), t. XII, §756bis; M. Planiol and G. Ripert, *Traité pratique de droit civil français*, 2nd ed. by P. Esmein (Paris: LGDJ), t. VI, 1952, n° 337.

In this case, however, the assignees, Kepsky, were not informed of the counter-letter, which cannot be relied upon against them by Vinci. As a result, Vinci have to pay a monthly rent of €2,000 to Kepsky.

2.6. GERMANY

Sonja Meier

I. Operative Rules

Vinci will likely have to pay a monthly rent of €2,000 to Kepsky.

II. Descriptive Formants

According to §117 (1) BGB, contracts that are made for the sake of appearance only are void. If such a contract is concluded to conceal another contract, that underlying contract will, however, be valid if it is in accordance with the general law (§117 (2) BGB). Applying these rules to the present case, the lease contract for €2,000 will be void while the underlying agreement for €1,500 will be valid. It seems to follow that Kepsky will only acquire a claim for €1,500 per month.

However, according to §405 BGB, the debtor may not, as against the assignee, invoke the fact that the obligation was only entered into for the sake of appearance, if the obligor has issued an *'Urkunde über die Schuld'* (deed confirming the obligation), that *Urkunde* was presented to the assignee at the time of assignment, and the assignee had neither actual nor constructive knowledge of the fact that the obligation was only entered into for the sake of appearance. An *Urkunde über die Schuld* is generally understood to be a document by which the debtor has recorded the existence of the obligation, the purpose of which is to prove the existence of the obligation.[21] The lease contract fulfils these requirements. Assuming that it was presented to Kepsky at the time of assignment, and that Kepsky lacked both actual and constructive notice of the fact that the actual contract was for €1,500 only, Vinci will be liable to pay a monthly rent of €2,000.

---

21 E.-M. Kieninger in *Münchener Kommentar zum BGB*, vol. 3 (9th ed., Beck 2022), §405, [5]; J. Busche in *J. von Staudingers Kommentar zum Bürgerlichen Gesetzbuch*, vol. §§397–432 (Sellier – de Gruyter 2022), §405, [5]–[7].

2.7. ITALY

Pasquale Femia

I. Operative Rules

Vinci must pay €2,000 to Kepsky.

II. Descriptive Formants

The lower price can be characterised as 'relative simulation' (Art. 1414 c.c.).[22] A contract is simulated where the parties, despite appearing to intend to conclude a contract, do not actually want its effects. The simulation is 'absolute' where the parties want no contract at all; it is 'relative' when the parties agree that a different contract will take effect between them. A relative simulation may concern the type of contract, its object or its parties.

The pact not to declare the entire price is not enforceable against the assignee, who is a third party to this simulation agreement (under Art. 1415 c.c.),[23] unless the third party took part in the simulation agreement or had knowledge thereof,[24] in which case the assigned debtor must prove the third party's bad faith. Kepsky's good faith is presumed and fully protected until proven otherwise, placing the burden of proof on the other party to demonstrate Kepsky's bad faith. The simulation has no effect for the third party in good faith.

A difficult question is whether Vinci can recover from Tasman the loss of €500 per month (multiplied by the number of months in the entire lease period). The simulation agreement between Tasman and Vinci does not bind Tasman not to transfer the lease contract. However, Tasman's non-disclosure of the lower price to Kepsky may be characterised as a breach of an implied obligation constructed in the simulation agreement between Vinci and Tasman. Thus, Vinci can recover the loss from Tasman.

---

22 Art. 1414 c.c.: 'A simulated contract does not produce effects between the parties. If the parties intended to make a contract different from the simulated contract, the former is binding between them, provided that the requisites of form and substance are present' (tr. by S. Beltramo (ed), *Italian Civil Code and Complementary Legislation*, tr. in 1969 by M. Beltramo, G.E. Longo and J.H. Merryman (West, 2012), p. 302).

23 Art. 1415 c.c.: 'Simulation cannot be used as a defense by the contracting parties, by their successors in interest, or by the creditors of the simulating transferor, against third parties who, in good faith, have acquired rights from the apparent owner of the right, subject to the effects of transcription of a judicial petition concerning simulation. Third persons can plead simulation against the contracting parties, when it is prejudicial to their rights' (tr. by S. Beltramo (ed), *Italian Civil Code and Complementary Legislation*, tr. in 1969 by M. Beltramo, G.E. Longo and J.H. Merryman (West, 2012), p. 302).

24 Cass., 28 February 2013, no. 4986, *Massimario Giustizia civile* (2013).

2.8. THE NETHERLANDS

Jan Biemans

I. *Operative Rules*

Vinci have to pay €2,000 rent per month to Kepsky, as Kepsky can rely on a third-party protection.

II. *Descriptive Formants*

Although Tasman and Vinci have agreed to a rent of €1,500 per month, because Tasman and Vinci have led Kepsky to believe that the rent is €2,000 per month, and Kepsky did not know and should not have known about the actual rent of €1,500 per month, Vinci have to pay rent of €2,000 per month to Kepsky.

According to Article 3:36 DCC, where a person (in this case, Vinci), through its statements or behaviour, has created the impression that a certain legal relationship (in this case, a lease contract with a rent of €2,000 per month) exists or has come to an end, and a third party (Kepsky) has legally or physically acted in good faith because they assumed, and in the circumstances reasonably could assume, that this impression, although not directly addressed to them, was correct, then the person whose statements or behaviour is concerned cannot appeal towards this third party to the incorrectness of their assumption. Although there is no Dutch Supreme Court case law on this specific situation, the explanatory notes to Article 3:36 DCC give the example of a non-assignment clause to which two parties have agreed in a side letter, separate from the contract. If the creditor assigns the non-assignable claim, and both parties to the contract do not disclose to the buyer (the new creditor) the non-assignment clause, the debtor cannot rely on this clause to contest the validity of the assignment. The same holds true with regard to other defences the debtor may have: if the debtor and old creditor lead the new creditor to believe these defences do not exist, the debtor cannot utilise them against the new creditor after the transfer of the claim.[25] Similarly, it can be argued that Vinci cannot insist on the lower rent of €1,500 being payable to Kepsky if Vinci and Tasman have led Kepsky to believe that the actual rent is €2,000 per month.

III. *Meta-Legal Formants*

Alternatively, Kepsky could sue Tasman for breach of contract (Article 6:74 DCC), due to Tasman selling (among other things) a lease contract with a rental income

---

[25] See T.M., Parl. Gesch. Boek 6, p. 537, M.v.A. II, Parl. Gesch. Boek 6, pp. 543–45; M.v.A. II Inv., Parl. Gesch. Boek 3 (Inv. 3, 5 en 6), pp. 1134–35. See also, and for further reference, J.W.A. Biemans, *Rechtsgevolgen van stille cessie*, Deventer: Kluwer 2011, no. 567.

of €2,000 per month whose actual rental income turns out to be much lower. If the rental income is lower than promised, the goods delivered (the rental claims) are not in conformity with the sales contract (Article 7:17 DCC in conjunction with Article 7:47 DCC).[26]

2.9. POLAND

Agata Kozioł

I. *Operative Rules*

Vinci have to pay Kepsky the amount of €*1,500 as monthly rent.*

II. *Descriptive Formants*

According to Article 678 §1 PCC, in the case of transferring property in an asset that is the object of a lease, the purchaser enters into the lease relationship, thus replacing the previous owner of the good. By operation of the law itself *(ex lege)*, on the grounds of the above-mentioned provision, the party to the legal relationship is changed.[27] The purchaser becomes the subject of rights and obligations arising from the contract of lease that were previously vested in their predecessor, while the content of the lease relationship remains unchanged.[28]

The content of the lease relationship should be determined not only on the basis of the original (written?) contract between the previous owner and the lessee (in this case, Tasman and Vinci, respectively), but also taking into account any subsequent agreements between the parties to the lease contract, whether written or oral. The Polish regulation of lease contracts does not require written form for such a contract to be valid. The same applies to further agreements of the parties, modifying their rights and obligations. It could also be assumed, as it is not mentioned in the case details, that the parties (Tasman and Vinci) did not agree in the written contract that all changes to the contract would have to be in written form.

Upon the sale of an asset, the seller is obliged to inform the purchaser about all actual and legal relationships concerning the asset (Art. 546 §1 PCC).[29]

---

26 J.W.A. Biemans, *Rechtsgevolgen van stille cessie*, Deventer: Kluwer 2011, no. 658, 663–69.

27 P. Zakrzewski, 'Komentarz do art. 678' in M. Habdas and M. Fras (eds), *Kodeks cywilny. Komentarz. Tom IV. Zobowiązania. Część szczególna (art. 535–764⁹)*, Warsaw 2018, p. 446.

28 K. Pietrzykowski, 'Komentarz do art. 680 k.c.' in K. Pietrzykowski (ed), *Kodeks cywilny. Komentarz. Tom II. Art. 450–1088. Przepisy wprowadzające*, Warsaw 2017, p. 490.

29 A. Kozioł, 'Komentarz do art. 546' in M. Habdas and M. Fras (eds), *Kodeks cywilny. Komentarz. Tom IV. Zobowiązania. Część szczególna (art. 535–7649)*, Warsaw 2018, p. 53.

The obligation of the seller exists from the pre-contractual stage, and gives rise to liability of the seller on a general basis, as described in Articles 471 to 497 PCC.[30] This kind of liability is known as '*odpowiedzialność z tytułu niewykonania lub nienależytego wykonania zobowiązania*' (liability arising from the non-performance or improper performance of an obligation), and is commonly, but incorrectly, known as '*odpowiedzialność kontraktowa*' (contractual liability).

Information on the amount of monthly rent due to the owner of the assets sold could be seen as essential in Kepsky's decision-making process concerning the purchase. Kepsky may, therefore, sue Tasman for damages on the basis of Article 471 PCC, in the amount of €500 per month, as compensation for the expected sum of monthly rent. The good faith of the buyers (Kepsky) concerning the content of the loan agreement and the obligations of the lessees (Vinci) is legally irrelevant, and gives no grounds for any action towards Vinci.

2.10. SCOTLAND

Lorna MacFarlane

I. *Operative Rules*

Vinci have to pay Kepsky *€1,500* in monthly rent.

II. *Descriptive Formants*

Beginning with the contract between Tasman and Vinci, a contract for the lease of moveable property need not be in writing to be valid in Scots law.[31] An oral agreement as to the rent is, therefore, valid. The price is that on which the parties have reached consensus, and it would appear from the facts of the question that they intended for Vinci to pay the lower monthly rent. In other words, the clause in their contract concerning the rental price is formed through their verbal agreement rather than their written lease.

Assignment (known as assignation in Scots law)[32] is defined as follows: 'A right arising under a contract may be assigned by the creditor (cedent) to a third party (assignee) so as to give that third party a title to sue the debtor

30 Z. Banaszczyk, 'Komentarz do art. 546 k.c.' in K. Pietrzykowski (ed), *Kodeks cywilny. Komentarz. Tom II. Art. 450–1088. Przepisy wprowadzające*, Warsaw 2017, p. 282.

31 Requirements of Writing (Scotland) Act 1995, s. 1.

32 W.W. McBryde, *The Law of Contract in Scotland*, 3rd ed. (Thomson/W. Green, Edinburgh 2007), para. 12-05; R.G. Anderson, *Assignation* (Edinburgh Legal Education Trust, Edinburgh 2008), para. 1.01.

for performance of the right.'[33] Accordingly, assignment does not involve the formation of a new contract between the debtor (Vinci) and the third-party assignee (Kepsky).[34] Instead, Tasman's right to receive payment under the lease is assigned to Kepsky.

Tasman have a right to €1,500 in monthly payment. They cannot assign a right to any other value of rental payment, because they only have a right to €1,500. Vinci are, accordingly, bound to pay €1,500. Kepsky cannot claim a higher amount from Vinci. In terms of other potential remedies against Vinci, Kepsky cannot claim that Vinci have made a negligent misstatement as discussed in Case 10 above, because Vinci have not made a statement to Kepsky.

In terms of potential remedies against Tasman, the Scots law of error (developed in case law) provides that one party's unilateral error in contract makes a contract voidable if the error is known by the other party, who takes advantage of it.[35] In this situation, the error is that the rent is for €1,500 rather than €2,000. It is known by Tasman, who take advantage of the situation by failing to correct Kepsky's error. Describing the contract as 'voidable' means that it will remain in force until challenged by one of the parties to the contract.

III. Meta-Legal Formants

The debtor's consent to assignation is not required.[36] McBryde comments that:

> On the assumption that a right is freely assignable, the debtor has no control over when and to whom the debt may be assigned. Therefore, it would be unfair if the debtor could be prejudiced by an assignation by virtue of which the assignee acquired more rights against the debtor than the cedent had.[37]

---

33 H.L. MacQueen, *The Laws of Scotland: Stair Memorial Encyclopaedia: Obligations: Contract*, vol. 15 (LexisNexis/Law Society of Scotland, London/Edinburgh 1995), para. 855. See also R.G. Anderson, *Assignation* (Edinburgh Legal Education Trust, Edinburgh 2008), para. 1.04; W.W. McBryde, *The Law of Contract in Scotland*, 3rd ed. (Thomson/W. Green, Edinburgh 2007), para. 12-14; G. Lubbe 'Assignment' in H. MacQueen and R. Zimmermann (eds), *European Contract Law: Scots and South African Perspectives* (Edinburgh University Press, Edinburgh 2006), p. 307 at p. 310.

34 R.G. Anderson, *Assignation* (Edinburgh Legal Education Trust, Edinburgh 2008), para. 2.35: 'to speak of the assignation of *contracts* is inaccurate'. Anderson notes the historical confusion on this point at para. 1.04.

35 *Steuart's Trs v. Hart* (1875) 3 R 192 (for discussion, see W.M. Gloag, *The Law of Contract: A Treatise on the Principles of Contract in the Law of Scotland*, 2nd ed. (W. Green, Edinburgh 1929), p. 438).

36 R.G. Anderson, *Assignation* (Edinburgh Legal Education Trust, Edinburgh 2008), para. 1.03, citing J.D. Stair, *The Institutions of the Law of Scotland*, 3rd ed. (G. Hamilton and J. Balfour, Edinburgh 1759), para. 3.1.3.

37 W.W. McBryde, *The Law of Contract in Scotland*, 3rd ed. (Thomson/W. Green, Edinburgh 2007), para. 12-68.

Thus, Vinci are not required to consent to Tasman's right to payment being assigned to Kepsky. It would be illogical for Tasman to have the ability to effectively create a new right to a higher rental payment, in favour of Kepsky, without Vinci's consent.

2.11. SLOVAKIA

Kristián Csach, Monika Jurčová, Peter Mészáros and Veronika Zoričáková

I. *Operative Rules*

Vinci have to pay €1,500 per month to Kepsky. The claim is contractual in nature, as it arises from a valid dissimulated contract.

II. *Descriptive Formants*

The lease contract between Tasman and Vinci is a contract on rent, according to sections 663 ff. SCC, subject also to particular rules of special regulation, '*nájom hnuteľných vecí na podnikanie*' (lease of moveables intended for business activities), according to sections 721 ff. SCC, which is a subtype of rent. The SCommC does not regulate rental agreements, except for car rentals. Nonetheless, even civil law rental agreements concluded between professionals are considered as combined commercial contracts (s. 261(9) SCommC) and, therefore, the SCommC would also be applicable for general aspects of the obligation.

In order to identify the monthly rent which Vinci have to pay, it has to be ascertained, first, whether there was a valid lease contract between Tasman and Kepsky; second, if so, what its characteristics were; and third, whether the contract itself or particular rights or duties arising therefrom have been effectively transferred to Kepsky.

The arrangements between Tasman and Vinci indicate a simulation (covering up) of legal acts. According to section 41a(2) SCC:

> If a legal act is to cover up another legal act, this other legal act shall be valid if it corresponds to the will of participants and all its requirements are met. The invalidity of such legal act cannot be appealed to vis-à-vis a participant who considered it not to be covered up.

The written contract is a simulated lease contract which covers up the real agreement between Tasman and Vinci. In order to establish a cover-up or simulation of legal acts, it is sufficient that the price agreed upon in reality differs from the price stated in the written execution of the agreement.[38] Therefore, the written execution of the agreement is not valid, as it does not represent the true will of the parties. The hidden legal act (lease with lower rent) represents the true will of the parties. As a lease contract does not have to be executed in writing, the dissimulated contract with the monthly rent of €1,500 need not be in writing. Accordingly, the hidden contract is valid, as it fulfils both substantive and formal requirements (assuming that no other defect of the transaction has been identified).

This dissimulated agreement might have been transferred to Kepsky via the contract on sale of an enterprise according to section 476(1) SCommC (see Case 2 above), or via the contract on sale of the machinery. According to section 680 (2) SCC, the new owner of items which are leased is the legal successor of the previous owner regarding the lease contract – *'vstup nového vlastníka do nájmu'* (entry of the new owner into rent).

Therefore, Vinci is obliged to pay Kepsky only €1,500 per month.

However, an alternative result might be reached by taking into account the protective effects of section 41a (2), second sentence, of the SCC. Under this rule, the invalidity of such a simulated legal act cannot be appealed to vis-à-vis the participant who considered it not to be covered up. A participant who did not know of the true will of the other participant is protected. According to some sources, not only participants in the contract, but also third parties, are protected by this rule.[39] However, it seems the prevailing view is to the contrary, and only the (second) participant in the simulated legal act is protected (in cases of one-sided simulation).[40] According to the prevailing view, the protective rule should not be used to turn a two-sided simulation into a valid legal act. It is not clear, however, whether a legal successor of one of the parties is considered a third party to the simulated act or an actual contracting party protected by the rule. However, it might be argued that, if the transfer of lease occurred with the participation of three parties (with Vinci and Tasman acting in concert and hiding their true will), Kepsky might be considered as protected, even from the perspective of prevailing opinion regarding the application of protective mechanism on one-sided simulations only. Kepsky were a participant in the lease transfer arrangement

---

38 Constitutional Court of the Slovak Republic decision file no. IV. ÚS 340/2012 dated 22.11.2012.

39 J. Mitterpachová in M. Števček, A. Dulak, J. Bajánková, M. Fečík, F. Sedlačko, M. Tomašovič et al., *Občiansky zákonník I, sect. 1–450. Komentár [Commentary on Civil Code I, ss. 1–450]*, Prague: C.H. Beck, 2015, p. 306.

40 I. Fekete, *Občiansky zákonník, Komentár [Commentary on Civil Code I], sect. 1 – sect. 122*, Bratislava: Eurokódex, 2017, p. 413; P. Vojčík, *Občianske právo hmotné I [Substantive Civil Law]*, 4th ed., Košice: UPJŠ, 2014, p. 59.

and the terms of the lease contracts were not made clear to them. However, the lease might also have been transferred *ex lege* without any participation by Vinci, through a contract on the transfer of an enterprise according to section 476(1) SCommC (see Case 2 above), concluded between Tasman and Kepsky. If this were the case, the outcomes would depend on the interpretation of section 41a(2), second sentence, SCC.

Under the given circumstances, the requirements of a relevant mistake under section 49a SCC might be also considered to be met. The mistake must have been significant for Kepsky when entering into the contractual agreement, and the false fact must have been known to Tasman, as the other party to the contract. Kepsky may, therefore, apply for the *'relatívna neplatnosť'* (relative nullity) of the contract of sale of machinery, making it null.

Moreover, Kepsky may have a claim against Tasman under either liability for defects under the contract on the transfer of an enterprise, liability for defects according to the regulation on assignment of claims (s. 527(1) SCC), liability for defects *per analogiam* (in the event that the transfer of lease was in the form of a innominate contractual arrangement analogous to a sales contract) or *culpa in contrahendo* (liability for deceiving the counterparty). Furthermore, the characteristics of the rent could be an agreed condition within the contractual representations and warranties, and if these are not met, contractual claims could arise. The facts of the case do not, however, provide enough evidence to substantiate such claims.

2.12. SPAIN

Carles Vendrell Cervantes

I. Operative Rules

Vinci would only have to pay *€1,500 per month in rent* to Kepsky.

II. Descriptive Formants:

It is a fact that Vinci and Tasman have agreed that Vinci are only obliged to pay €1,500 in monthly rent, which means that the initial price has been validly changed. Even if the agreement to pay €1,500 instead of €2,000 has not been established in writing, it is safe to assume, since the general rule in Spain is that contracts 'are perfected by mere consent', that the contract has been validly modified by the parties. Vinci have the right to continue to pay €1,500 per month to the new owners of the machines, Kepsky, since this is what the contract has established.

However, since Kepsky bought the machines from Tasman assuming, under the terms of the written contract, that the lease was worth €2,000 per month, Kepsky have a right to take action against Tasman for contractual liability, as established in Article 1101 of the Spanish Civil Code, since Tasman failed to inform Kepsky of the change in the lease contract. The damage caused to Kepsky consists in the difference in value of the lease contract assigned by Tasman, because a lease with a monthly rent of €2,000 is more valuable than one with a monthly rent of €1,500. If the breach of contract attributable to Tasman is fundamental (which, in principle, should not be the case in the present scenario), Kepsky would also be entitled to terminate the contract (for the fundamental breach of an obligation, under Article 1124 of the Spanish Civil Code).

2.13. SWEDEN

Oskar Mossberg

I. Operative Rules

Vinci has to pay Kepsky €1,500 per month.

II. Descriptive Formants

The general principles of the law of obligations, as expressed in Article 27 of the Act on Debt Letters, apply here, which means that the assignee will not receive a better right against the debtor than the assignor had at the time of assignment. This relates to the actual right of the assignor, not the right according to any false statement, written or not. The rule is sometimes described in terms of it being impossible to *'godtrosförvärva enkla fordringar'* (acquire simple claims in good faith), entailing that the good faith of the assignee is not a factor in relation to the debtor. This can be contrasted with cases of moveable property and *'löpande skuldebrev'* (running debt letters), where an acquisition in good faith can void certain rights of, and objections by, a previous owner or debtor. A running debt letter is a kind of negotiable debt instrument, intended to be traded, and according to Articles 15 to 17 of the Act on Debt Letters, the debtor cannot make certain objections against a demand for payment from a new creditor; that is, the purchaser of the debt letter. This includes some grounds for invalidity of the debt letter, objections due to previous payments not made in accordance with a payment plan and not documented on the debt letter, and objections due to the legal relation pursuant to which the debt letter was issued (for example, that the goods for which the debt letter is payment are faulty). Such objections are not valid against a new creditor who has received the debt letter in good faith. This is, however, not directly relevant to the present case, as it does not involve a running debt letter.

Kepsky's loss of €500 in monthly rent would probably entail a *'rättsligt fel'* (legal fault), giving Kepsky a right of price reduction including repayment from Tasman, pursuant to Article 9 of the Act on Debt Letters and Articles 41, 37 and 38 of the Sale of Goods Act (Köplagen (the Purchase Act)). This applies even if there is no warranty or express statement from the assignor or debtor regarding the nominal value of the assigned claim.

III. Meta-Legal Formants

The rules of Swedish contract law are generally sorted by, and divided into, categories based on different types of contracts (contracts of sale, contracts of service, consumer contracts, contracts of assignment, etc.). Contracts regarding *'hyra av lös egendom'* (leasing of loose/non-real property) are generally taken to be a separate type of contract. There are some special rules concerning these, and during the 1990s a government-appointed investigative committee proposed further legislation.[41] However, this was never enacted, and there are no special rules concerning contracts of lease applicable to the current factual situation. Therefore, the general principles of the law of obligations, as expressed in Article 27 of the Act on Debt Letters, apply. On these principles, see Case 4 above.

3. COMPARATIVE REMARKS

Jan Biemans and Lorna Richardson

This case deals with third-party protection (if any) when one party relies in good faith on the inaccurate information of two other parties about the content of their agreement (simulation). The two contracting parties (A and B) make a third party (C) believe that B have to pay a certain amount of rent, which turns out, in reality, to be lower. A then sell the lease contract to C. The question is whether C can demand the higher amount of rent from B, or only the lower amount.

In the majority of the jurisdictions (Czech Republic, Poland, Scotland, Spain, Sweden, and most likely in England and Slovakia), the third party would not be protected against the secret agreement of the two parties, and so Kepsky would not be able to obtain the higher rent from Vinci. The acquirer of the lease contract would be bound by the terms the original parties had agreed upon,

---

41 See SOU 1994:120 – Finansiell leasing av lös egendom: Slutbetänkande av Leasingutredningen, and e.g. M. Möller, *Civilrätten vid finansiell leasing*, Iustus, Uppsala 1996.

even where that third party was unaware of the changes made to the contract. However, the buyer of the lease contract (Kepsky) could, in most of these jurisdictions (Poland, Slovakia, Spain, and perhaps in the Czech Republic), sue the seller of the lease contract (Tasman). In Poland, Kepsky's claim for damages against Tasman would be based on a provision of the Civil Code requiring a seller of an asset to inform the purchaser about all actual and legal relationships concerning the asset. In Spanish law, Kepsky's claim for damages would be on the basis of giving false statements about the content of the lease contract. In Sweden, it would be based on Tasman's legal fault, and would entitle Kepsky to a price reduction. In Slovakia (and possibly the Czech Republic), as well as damages being available, Kepsky may be able to claim nullity of the sale contract due to mistake. The contract may be voidable (valid until action is taken to annul the contract) in Scots law, due to Kepsky's error, which is known by Tasman and taken advantage of.

In the other jurisdictions (Belgium, Bulgaria, France, Italy and the Netherlands), the third party would be protected if they had, in good faith, depended on the apparent agreement of the two contracting parties. In Belgium and Italy, the amended contract between Tasman and Vinci will be a simulation which has no effect against Kepsky, who would be able to sue the lessee for the higher amount of rent. In France, the amended contract will be a counter-letter, which cannot be relied upon against Kepsky. The Bulgarian and Italian reporters note that Vinci would likely be able to make a claim against Tasman in relation to the additional €500 per month for the duration of the lease. This would be on the basis of a breach of an implied obligation in the simulated contract between Tasman and Vinci, in failing to disclose the lower rent to Kepsky (Italy), or a commitment not to transfer the leased machines or a failure to notify the purchaser of the lower rent (Bulgaria).

In Germany, Kepsky can seek the higher rent from Vinci. Assuming that the lease contract was presented to Kepsky at the time of the assignment, and that Kepsky did not have actual or constructive knowledge of the amended lease contract, Vinci cannot invoke the fact that the obligation with Tasman was entered into for the sake of appearance only. This is based on a provision of the Civil Code that applies where an *'Urkunde über die Schuld'* (a deed confirming the obligation) has been presented.

CASE 11: FRAUDULENT CONVEYANCE OF ASSETS BY A DEBTOR

1. CASE

One evening, Bernardo drinks too much at a party, drives back home, and crashes his car, damaging Carlos' house. Part of the house has to be rebuilt at significant cost. Bernardo is uninsured. He refuses to pay any compensation to Carlos. Carlos intends to sue Bernardo for damages. When Bernardo hears of this, he donates his house, which is worth a lot of money, to his niece, Maria. By doing so, Bernardo hopes that Carlos will see that it is not worth suing him, as he no longer has assets of value. Maria rents the house for free to Bernardo, helping him out.

Question

Assuming that Carlos is successful in his court case against Bernando, can Carlos take any action to ensure that Bernando's house is available as an asset against which he has recourse for his claim? If so, what action can be taken?

2. DISCUSSIONS

2.1. BELGIUM

Siel Demeyere and Vincent Sagaert

I. Operative Rules

Carlos can take action. He can raise an *actio Pauliana*.

II. Descriptive Formants

Where a debtor fraudulently organises their own insolvency, the creditor can raise a *pauliaanse vordering/action paulienne* (Paulian action or revocatory action),[1]

[1] Art. 5.243 BCC.

the effect of which is that the fraudulent act is not effective against the creditor (but remains valid as between the parties). This means that the creditor can ignore that such an act has taken place, and thus act as if the transferred property is still in the debtor's patrimony.[2] A successful *actio Pauliana* would, in this case, have the effect that Carlos can act as though Bernardo still owns his house, and can possibly also seize the house.

The conditions for the *actio Pauliana* are fourfold:[3]

(a) The creditor must have had a claim prior to the fraudulent act, also known as the anteriority condition. In this case, this condition has clearly been fulfilled, since Bernardo first damaged Carlos' house, giving rise to Carlos' claim, and only afterwards donated his own house.
(b) The disputed legal act has impoverished the debtor, or constitutes a disadvantage for the creditor's possibilities of redress. Here, Bernardo is clearly impoverished by donating his house, so this condition is fulfilled. The condition would have been fulfilled even if he had sold his house for good value, since a house is easier for a creditor to seize than money, which can be wired to foreign accounts or even hidden in the form of cash.
(c) The debtor has acted fraudulently; what this constitutes is interpreted extensively. The creditor need not prove that the debtor had the intention to disadvantage them: it suffices that the debtor knew, or should have known, that they would impoverish themselves (or disadvantage the creditor's possibilities for redress). The abnormal character of the legal act can be an indication.[4] This condition is, *in casu*, also met.
(d) The fourth condition only applies where the disputed legal act was an act *onder bezwarende titel/à titre onéreux* (for consideration), and not where the legal act was *om niet/à titre gratuit* (without consideration). This condition is not applicable in this case, since the disputed legal act is the donation of Bernardo's house to his niece. Where the fraudulent act was for consideration, the *actio Pauliana* will only succeed if the third party was (or should have been) aware of the debtor organising their insolvency through that act. This condition does not apply to acts without consideration, since the patrimonial situation of the third party – in this case, Bernardo's niece – would not be made worse than before by granting the *actio Pauliana*.

---

2 S. Stijns, *Verbintenissenrecht. Leerboek 1*, die Keure, Bruges 2009–16, 248, no. 325; W. Van Gerven and A. Van Oevelen, *Verbintenissenrecht*, Acco, Leuven 2015, 231; P. Wéry, *Droit des obligations: Théorie générale du contrat*, I, Larcier, Brussels 2011, 875, no. 937.

3 S. Stijns, *Verbintenissenrecht. Leerboek 1*, die Keure, Bruges 2009–16, 249, no. 327; W. Van Gerven and A. Van Oevelen, *Verbintenissenrecht*, Acco, Leuven 2015, 229–31; P. Wéry, *Droit des obligations: Théorie générale du contrat*, I, Larcier, Brussels 2011, 873, no. 936.

4 Art. 5.243 BCC; Cass. 15 March 1985, *RW*, 1985–86, 2609; Cass. 26 October 1989, *JLMB* 1990, 4; Liège 6 February 1996, *JLMB* 1996, 469.

If she had paid for the house, and the *actio Pauliana* was successful, the creditor could seize and sell the house. Bernardo's niece would then demand, from Bernardo, restitution of the purchase price, although he probably would not be able to return this to her. In such situations of a legal act for consideration, it is required that the third party – such as the niece, in this case – also knows about the fraudulent nature of the transaction.

Carlos can successfully submit an *actio Pauliana*, which will have the effect that, in relation to Carlos, the house will still be owned by Bernardo, and can serve as collateral for the payment of damages.

2.2. BULGARIA

Petar Topurov

I. Operative Rules

To ensure the satisfaction of his claims, Carlos can bring an action for annulment in accordance with Art. 135 LOC, whereby the donation made by Bernardo is declared invalid in relation to Carlos.

II. Descriptive Formants

According to Art. 135 LOC, the creditor may request that actions by which the debtor causes harm to the creditor are declared invalid, on condition that the debtor had knowledge of the harm to follow when they carried out those actions *(actio Pauliana)*. It is not necessary for the third person involved in the detrimental action to have been informed of the damage, where the action is gratuitous in nature,[5] as in this case, which involved donation.

If the claim is upheld, the transaction challenged is declared invalid. This invalidity is a relative one – it concerns only the relationship with the creditor – and also has effect *ex tunc*: from the moment of conclusion of the cancelled transaction. As a result, the house will be available as an asset against which Carlos has recourse for his claim. The nullity declared only favours the creditor who has exercised their right under Art. 135 LOC. The validity of the harm-causing transaction remains vis-à-vis the person with whom the debtor has contracted (here, Maria), but she must undergo enforcement by the creditor.[6] In this specific case, Maria will retain ownership of Bernardo's house, but Carlos

---

5 A. Kalaydzhiev, *Contractual Law. General part*, 5th ed., Sibi, Sofia 2010, p. 589.

6 Ibid., p. 591.

may try to sell it, via a bailiff, in the event that Bernardo does voluntarily pay compensation for the damage done to Carlos, should Carlos' claim based on Art. 135 LOC be upheld by the court.

2.3. CZECH REPUBLIC

Tomáš Richter

I. *Operative Rules*

Carlos *could sue Maria in order to have the donation avoided* and levy execution against Bernardo's house.

II. *Descriptive Formants*

Avoidance actions outside of insolvency are regulated by sections 589 ff. of the CC. The donation of Bernardo's house to his niece, Maria, would be a clear candidate for an avoidance action brought by Carlos, in order to have the donation declared ineffective pursuant to section 589(1) CC as a transaction hindering his enforceable claim against Bernardo. This is the sort of action referred to as *actio Pauliana* in other civil law systems, but this term is not used in Czech law. Carlos could sue Maria as a person who has obtained a direct benefit from the donation (section 594 CC). Prior to Carlos obtaining a final and enforceable judgment against Bernardo, Carlos could make a reservation with a notary, bailiff or court, towards Maria, and have it served on Maria under section 593 CC, thereby staying the time limit within which the avoidance action must be brought. Transactions which may be avoided are defined as the debtor's transactions which: (a) the debtor undertook in the past five years, with the intention to hinder his or her creditors, where such intention was known to the debtor's counterparty; (b) the debtor undertook in the past two years, with the intention to hinder his or her creditors, where such intention must have been known to the debtor's counterparty; or (c) resulted in the hindrance of the debtor's creditor in the past two years, as the result of a transaction with a person related to the debtor, or for his or her benefit, unless such person did not know, and did not need to know, at the time of the transaction, that the debtor intended to hinder his or her creditors (section 590(1) CC). The elements of intention and knowledge required under section 590 need not be present with respect to gratuitous transactions undertaken by the debtor in the past two years (section 591 CC).

If Carlos is successful, he will be able to obtain satisfaction of this claim against Bernardo from execution levied against the house (section 595 CC), in spite of the fact that the house is now owned by Maria.

2.4. ENGLAND AND WALES

T.T. Arvind

I. *Operative Rules*

Carlos will be able to bring an action under section 423 of the Insolvency Act 1986, on the basis that Bernardo's gift of his house to Maria was a transaction to defraud his creditors. The court has the power to restore the *status quo ante* and protect the victims of the fraud.

II. *Descriptive Formants*

The English courts have, since the sixteenth century, had a statutory power to intervene in transactions intended to defraud creditors. The power is currently contained in sections 423 to 425 of the Insolvency Act 1986. Despite its location in the Insolvency Act, the power is not confined to insolvent or bankrupt debtors, and can be exercised in relation to any transaction. Two conditions must be satisfied for the court to exercise its power. Firstly, the transaction must be at an undervalue; that is, it must either be for a significantly lower value than the value of the consideration that has been provided,[7] or be a gift,[8] or be entered into in consideration of marriage or civil partnership.[9] Secondly, the transaction must be entered into for the purpose of putting assets beyond the reach of a person who is making, or might make, a claim,[10] or for otherwise prejudicing their interests.[11] Any victim of the transaction may apply to the court for relief,[12] and the court has a broad discretion to restore the position to what it would have been had the transaction not been entered into,[13] or to otherwise protect the victims' interests.[14]

Cases have established that defrauding the creditors has to be a substantial purpose of the transaction. If the transferor entered into the transaction for some other purpose, it will not fall within section 423 of the Insolvency Act 1986, even if the transferor was aware that it would place the assets beyond the reach of their creditors.[15] That said, it does not have to be the sole or even a

7 Insolvency Act 1986, s. 423(1)(c).
8 Ibid., s. 423(1)(a).
9 Ibid., s. 423(1)(b).
10 Ibid., s. 423(3)(a).
11 Ibid., s. 423(3)(b).
12 Ibid., s. 424(1).
13 Ibid., s. 423(2)(a).
14 Ibid., s. 423(2)(b).
15 *JSC BTA Bank v. Ablyazov* [2018] EWCA Civ 1176, [2019] BCC 96.

dominant purpose. A dual-purpose transaction, where defrauding the creditors was one of several purposes, is also liable to be set aside under the section, if the other requirements are satisfied.[16] Given that the transfer in this case was a gift, and that it was made for the express purpose of discouraging Carlos' action, both ingredients of section 423 of the Insolvency Act 1986 are satisfied, and Carlos is likely to be able to have the gift set aside.

In addition, Carlos may also be able to argue that Bernardo retained a beneficial interest in the property notwithstanding its transfer to Maria, on the basis that a gift of property for no consideration gives rise to a 'presumption of resulting trust', such that the donor is presumed to have intended to retain beneficial ownership of the property despite transferring legal ownership.[17] The fact that Bernardo continues to live rent-free in the property will substantiate the presumption and make it harder to rebut. In such a case, Carlos may be able to have recourse to Bernardo's beneficial interest in the property for satisfying his claim.

2.5. FRANCE

Sylvain Ravenne and Flora Vern

I. *Operative Rules*

Carlos can take action to ensure that Bernardo's house is available to meet his claim, provided that Bernardo is effectively insolvent following the transfer of ownership. Carlos can seize the house in Maria's hands, by using the '*action Paulienne*' (Paulian claim).

II. *Descriptive Formants*

In this case, Bernardo is the debtor of a monetary obligation. Upon learning that his creditor, Carlos, intends to sue him, he donates his house to his niece, Maria, in order to (temporarily) dispose of the asset and fake insolvency. However, his niece has knowledge of the manoeuvre and lets him use the house for free. This situation can be characterised as a '*fraude Paulienne*' (Paulian fraud).

Under such circumstances, Article 1341-2 of the FCC protects the creditor, who may ignore the donation (in this case) and pretend that ownership of the house has not been transferred. This is known as '*inopposabilité*', meaning that

---

16 *Inland Revenue Commissioners v. Hashmi* [2002] EWCA Civ 981, [2002] BCC 943.

17 *Lavelle v. Lavelle* [2004] EWCA Civ 223, [2004] 2 FCR 418 [13]–[14].

the donation (or sale for a low price) has no effect with respect to the creditor, who can pretend it never happened. As a result, using *action Paulienne*, Carlos will be able to seize the house, even though it is now in Maria's hands, as if it still belonged to Bernardo.[18] Carlos will need to go to court and provide evidence that Bernardo fraudulently made himself insolvent before he can bypass the donation and seize the property. The nature and extent of the original claim will not be modified, meaning that Carlos can recover the amount of money he would normally get from establishing tort liability (in this case, the damage was caused by a motorised vehicle while driving under the influence); that is, recovery of all losses sustained (*'réparation intégrale'*).[19] Once Carlos has recovered his loss, any remaining claims will be settled between Bernardo and Maria, based on the donation or contract between them. In this case, so as not to cause undue harm to Maria, the Paulian claim will only succeed if, at the time of the claim, Bernardo is effectively insolvent and Carlos has no choice but to seize the transferred goods,[20] or if Bernardo were not insolvent but had, for instance, donated the house he previously agreed to sell to Carlos, thus fraudulently making himself unable to perform the contract.[21]

In a Paulian claim, the creditor sues the debtor (i.e. Carlos would sue Bernardo, in this case). Carlos must prove before the court that the debt existed, at least in principle, at the time of the donation. In this case, which arose from a tort, the fact that the damage occurred prior to the donation would be sufficient, even though the exact amount of damages had not yet been evaluated by a judge, and the debtor had not been required to pay them.[22] The creditor must also prove that the transfer of ownership was fraudulent before they can seize the property in the hands of the third party in order to recover the damages. Fraud does not require an actual intent to cause harm:[23] it suffices that the debtor had knowledge of the creditor's rights, and of the harm that would ensue from the debtor's resulting insolvency or inability to meet their obligations. Where the transfer of ownership occurs in exchange for a price (for example, in the context of a sale instead of a donation), collusion between the debtor and the third party is also required, according to Article 1341-2 of the FCC, which means that the creditor's claim only extends to persons who had actual knowledge of the fraud, and cannot be used to revoke subsequent property transfers (e.g. to good-faith third-party purchasers).[24] Where the fraud results from a donation, as in this case, the solution is more complex:

---

18 Cass., civ. 1re, 30 mai 2005, n° 02-13495; Cass., civ. 1re, 17 oct. 2012, n° 11-10786.

19 See Case 9 above.

20 Cass., civ. 1re, 31 mai 1978, n° 76-12891.

21 Cass., civ. 3e, 6 oct. 2004, n° 03-15392.

22 Cass., req., 15 nov. 1939, *JCP* 1939, II, 1252, *DH* 1940, 40; Cass., civ. 1re, 9 oct. 1990, n° 88-15.890.

23 Cass., civ. 1re, 29 mai 1985, n° 83-17329.

24 Cass., civ. 3e, 9 mars 1984, n° 91-20715.

if collusion existed between the debtor/donor and the donee, the creditor may claim the thing or its full monetary value, even if its ownership has been transferred to yet another person; on the other hand, if the donee had no knowledge of the fraud, the creditor may only claim the thing itself (in kind) or the value of the donee's actual enrichment, if the thing was destroyed or alienated.[25] This is meant to protect the good-faith donee from claims that would impoverish them.

In the current case, Maria had knowledge of the fraud and still owns the house, which can be seized by Carlos in payment of Bernardo's debt. Maria could also choose to pay the debt herself and be substituted in the creditor's rights (this is known as '*subrogation personnelle*').

2.6. GERMANY

Sonja Meier

I. *Operative Rules*

Carlos can challenge the transfer of property by way of legal action against Maria.

II. *Descriptive Formants*

A judgment ordering the payment of money can be executed by means of a forced sale of the judgment debtor's land (§866 ZPO). However, according to §17 (1) ZVG, a forced sale of land requires the debtor to be registered in the land register as owner. Assuming that Bernardo transferred title to the house (i.e. title to the land, since the house cannot be separated from the land (§§94, 946 BGB)) to Maria, a forced sale will prima facie be impossible, because Maria will be registered as owner of the land (§873 BGB). However, Carlos may be able to challenge the contract by which Bernardo transferred the property to Maria, using a statute called Anfechtungsgesetz (AnfG).

According to §1 AnfG, this requires, firstly, a transaction of a debtor that disadvantages their creditors. In the present case, the transfer of the land to Maria can be regarded as a transaction that disadvantages Carlos, since subsequently there are not enough assets left in Bernardo's name to satisfy Carlos' claim. It might be argued that the transfer is void according to §117 (1) BGB because it was made for the sake of appearance only. However, a court will likely not apply §117 BGB, since Bernardo's purpose of shielding his property from creditors could only be achieved through a genuine transfer of ownership. Even if the

25 Cass., civ. 1re, 19 avr. 1987, no 65-12060.

transfer were held to be void under §117 BGB, so that Maria could not acquire title to the land, it would still be regarded as a transaction disadvantaging the creditor, since it resulted in the registration of Maria in the land register, which, although not making Maria the owner of the property, impedes a forced sale for the benefit of Carlos.[26]

The second requirement is that execution of the judgment obtained by Carlos has been unsuccessful, or that it can be assumed that it will not lead to a satisfaction of his claim (§3 AnfG). This requirement will be met if Bernardo no longer has any assets of value after the transfer.

Thirdly, a specific reason for challenge is required. According to §4 (1) AnfG, the transaction can be challenged within four years if it was gratuitous. There is an exception in §4 (2) AnfG for ordinary gifts (for example, birthday or wedding presents) of a modest amount, which does not apply here. The contract transferring ownership to Maria is, therefore, open to challenge. Alternatively, the transfer may be challenged under §3 (1) AnfG, which requires an intention on the part of Bernardo to disadvantage his creditor and knowledge of this intention on part of the recipient, which will be assumed if she knew that there was the imminent danger of insolvency and that the transaction was of disadvantage to the creditors. If Bernardo can show such knowledge on the part of Maria, he will be able to challenge the transaction within a time limit of ten years.

Carlos will have to challenge the transaction by way of legal action against Maria (§13 AnfG). A successful challenge will not invalidate the transaction. According to §11 (1) AnfG, Maria will have to make the property available to Carlos, as far as necessary to satisfy his claim. This means that Maria will remain owner of the land but cannot prevent Carlos from arranging a forced sale. The land will be transferred to the purchaser, and the proceeds of the sale will go to Carlos to the extent of his unpaid claim.[27]

2.7. ITALY

Luca Ettore Perriello

I. *Operative Rules*

Carlos can take an action to set aside Bernardo's fraudulent donation and then have recourse against the house for his claim.

26 *RGZ* 50, 121; BGH *NJW* 1996, 3147 at 3148; A. Weinland in *Münchener Kommentar zum Anfechtungsgesetz* (2nd ed., Beck 2022), §1, [121].

27 *RGZ* 50, 121, 124; *RGZ* 56, 142; A. Weinland in *Münchener Kommentar zum Anfechtungsgesetz* (2nd ed., Beck 2022), §11, [40], [47].

II. *Descriptive Formants*

Under Italian law, a debtor is liable for the performance of their obligations with all their present and future assets (Art. 2740 c.c.). This goes by the name of '*responsabilità patrimoniale*' (patrimonial liability), while the action for the breach of this liability is the '*actio Pauliana*'. In the event that the debtor reduces this liability, the creditor can rely on several remedies, the most important being the '*azione revocatoria*' – the action to set aside the fraudulent transaction (Arts. 2901 ff. c.c.).

The law lays down a number of requirements for the action. Firstly, a credit must exist, which may consist in damages arising from tort, as in the case at hand, with Carlos claiming compensation for damages to his house caused by a car accident. The action sets aside '*atti di disposizione*'; that is, any transactions whereby the debtor adversely affects their patrimony, reducing their assets or increasing their liabilities. There is no doubt that a donation falls within this definition. The transaction in question must prejudice the creditor's position – it must cause *periculum damni* (Art. 2901, paragraph 1, c.c.). To this end, it is sufficient that the transaction makes it more difficult or costly for the creditor to obtain performance.[28] In the present case, this requirement is met by Bernardo no longer having assets of value left.

Specific requirements, then, concern the parties' intentions. It is necessary for the debtor to be aware that the transaction has been made to the detriment of the creditor; that is, that the debtor has *consilium fraudis* (Art. 2901, paragraph 1, no. 1, c.c.), such knowledge being presumed whenever a *periculum damni* is established.[29] Accordingly, by donating the property to his niece, Maria, and reducing his patrimonial liability, Bernardo was aware that this infringed Carlos' rights.

Where the transaction is made without consideration, it is sufficient that the debtor has knowledge of the prejudice to the creditor.[30] In the event of transactions made for payment, it is necessary that the third party, too, is aware of the prejudice (Art. 2901, paragraph 1, no. 2, c.c.). Thus, in the case at issue, the requirement is met by Bernardo knowing that the donation frustrates Carlos' rights. No such knowledge is required on the part of Maria, because she is the beneficiary of a donation; that is, a transaction made without consideration.

III. *Meta-Legal Formants*

There is broad consensus that the '*azione revocatoria*' does not affect the validity of the transaction, but only its effects vis-à-vis the creditor that has filed the action. The transaction remains valid and effective vis-à-vis anyone but the creditor

[28] Cass., 10 May 2016, no. 9461, *Guida al diritto* (2016), p. 82.
[29] L. Bigliazzi Geri, 'Revocatoria (azione)', *Enciclopedia giuridica* (Rome: Treccani, 1991), p. 2.
[30] Cass., 22 January 1999, no. 591, *Giustizia civile*, I (1999), p. 591.

who has brought the action to set it aside.[31] Accordingly, the property affected by the transaction does not transfer back to the debtor: it remains with the third party, but the creditor is entitled to have recourse thereto through separate executive proceedings (action to enforce their rights against the house) against the third party.

2.8. THE NETHERLANDS

Jan Biemans

I. *Operative Rules*

Carlos can nullify the donation on the grounds that it has disadvantaged him as a creditor *(actio Pauliana)*, and then take recourse on the house for his claim. The donation may even be void, if it was intended to harm Carlos' rights as a creditor.

II. *Descriptive Formants*

This case deals with a fraudulent conveyance disadvantaging creditors, to which the *actio Pauliana* applies.

It should be noted that the Dutch Supreme Court has ruled that, if an agreement is (solely) intended to disadvantage creditors, the contract is void on the ground that it violates public morality (Article 3:40 DCC).[32] For this, it is not necessary for the actual disadvantage to the creditors to be proven; the voidness of the contract is based on the intention itself. In the case decided by the Dutch Supreme Court, the intention to harm creditors was stated in the contract itself. In this case, Bernardo's intention also seems to be to disadvantage Carlos; if this can be proven, the contract will be void.

If the contract is not void, Carlos can nullify the donation on the grounds that it has disadvantaged him as a creditor *(actio Pauliana)*, and then take recourse on the house for his claim.

According to Article 3:45 (1) DCC,[33] if a debtor, although legally not obliged to do so, has performed a juridical act while they knew or should have known that the recovery rights of their creditors would be harmed as a result, then this juridical act is voidable on the ground of fraudulent conveyance.

---

31 U. Natoli, 'Azione revocatoria', *Enciclopedia del diritto* (Milan: Giuffrè, 1959), p. 889. In case law, see Cass., 22 July 2007, no. 11830, *Giustizia civile*, I (2008), p. 1771.

32 Dutch Supreme Court, 19 December 2014, ECLI:NL:HR:2014:3650, NJ 2015/190.

33 See C.H. Sieburgh, *Mr. C. Assers Handleiding tot de beoefening van het Nederlands Burgerlijk Recht. 6. Verbintenissenrecht. Deel III. Algemeen overeenkomstenrecht*, Deventer: Wolters Kluwer 2022, pp. 586 ff.

This ground for voidability may be invoked by every third person (creditor) whose recovery rights against the debtor have been harmed as a result of this juridical act, irrespective of whether their debt claim or right against the debtor came into existence before or after the moment the aforementioned juridical act was performed. The juridical act in this case would be the contract underlying the transfer (the contract of donation, as per Articles 7:175 ff. DCC), as Dutch property law uses the causal system of property transfer (Article 3:84 (1) DCC), and possibly also the juridical act of the transfer of the house itself, and thus the signed notarial act registered with the land registry (Article 3:89 DCC).

The grounds for voidability depend on whether or not the juridical act was performed gratuitously. A *non-gratuitously* performed juridical act is only voidable on the ground of fraudulent conveyance if the other party, with or towards whom the debtor has performed the act, also knew or ought to have known that it would harm the recovery rights of the debtor's creditors (Article 3:45 (2) DCC). Where a *gratuitously* performed juridical act has been nullified on the ground of fraudulent conveyance (for which the other party's knowledge is not required), then this nullification has no effect against the party that received the benefit from the debtor if they did not know or ought not to have known that this juridical act harmed the recovery rights of one or more creditors of the person who performed this act with or towards them, but only insofar as this party proves that it did not enjoy (or no longer enjoyed) any advantage from this juridical act at the moment the juridical act was nullified by an extrajudicial declaration of a creditor or the legal claim for a judicial nullification was filed in court. Thus, the nullification has no effect on a third party receiving a benefit in good faith, if and only if the party can prove that the benefit no longer exists at the moment of nullification. In this case, the nullification concerns a *gratuitously* performed juridical act. It cannot be said Maria does not enjoy any advantage from the donation at the moment of nullification, as she is the legal owner of the house. Based on the facts of the case, it is extremely likely, if not a given, that she knows that this juridical act not only harmed the recovery rights of Carlos, but was intended to do so.

In nullifying the donation, Carlos is assisted by some legal assumptions. First, if the juridical act that harmed the recovery rights of one or more creditors was performed no more than one year before its nullification, and the debtor had not legally committed itself before the start of that period to perform that act, then there is a legal presumption that the persons involved on both sides of the juridical act knew or should have known that the aforementioned recovery rights would be harmed as a result of the act, if the act (among other grounds) was performed by the debtor with certain closely connected persons. Such connected persons include the debtor's spouse, child or foster-child, father or mother, grandfather or grandmother, grandchild, brother or sister, or child of their brother or sister (Article 3:46 (3) (a) DCC). As Maria is Bernardo's niece, and thus a child of his brother or sister, Carlos could rely on this legal assumption.

Second, where the recovery rights of one or more creditors (in this case, Carlos) have been harmed by a juridical act that has been performed gratuitously by the debtor (Bernando) no more than one year before someone invoked this ground of voidability, then there is a legal presumption that the debtor knew or ought to have known that the aforementioned recovery rights would be harmed as a result of this juridical act (Article 3:47 DCC).

A creditor who nullifies a juridical act which is voidable on the ground of fraudulent conveyance is only able to nullify it on their own behalf, and not further than is necessary to undo the harm that it has inflicted on their recovery rights (Article 3:45 (4) DCC). Carlos can nullify the donation either through an extrajudicial declaration or a court's judgment (Article 3:47 DCC). The nullification has retroactive effect to the moment the juridical act was performed (Article 3:53 (1) DCC). Consequently, Carlos can take recourse on the house as far as necessary to fulfil his claim against Bernando.

Maria has rented the house for free to Bernardo, helping him out. Allowing someone else to use property for free is not considered a rental or lease agreement under Dutch law, which would require payment for such use, but is instead considered a loan. Although the *actio Pauliana* has a third-party protection clause, Bernardo, as the *mala fide* user of the house, is not protected against the nullification, for several reasons. According to Article 3:45 (5) DCC, where a third person has acquired a property right in or related to an asset which once formed the object of a voidable juridical act between other parties, which act has been nullified on the ground of fraudulent conveyance, then this property right will be respected, provided that the third person acted in good faith when they acquired it, and did not obtain it gratuitously. The nullification of a juridical act on the ground of fraudulent conveyance has no effect on a third person who has gratuitously acquired a property right in relation to such an asset, but only if this third person can prove that they did not enjoy any advantage from this juridical act at the moment the asset was claimed from them. Bernardo is not protected on the basis of this provision, as there is no lease agreement and so he has not acquired a property right (Article 7:226 DCC; see Case 5 above), he has not acted in good faith, and the loan of the house is gratuitous.

2.9. POLAND

Agata Kozioł

I. *Operative Rules*

Carlos *can successfully take action* to make Bernardo's house (donated to his niece, Maria) available as an asset against which he has recourse for his claim.

II. Descriptive Formants

Under Polish law, a creditor may take action against the legal act of a debtor that makes a creditor's claim against the debtor's asset ineffective due to the debtor's inability to pay.[34] Such an action is called *'ochrona wierzyciela w razie niewypłacalności dłużnika'* (creditor's protection against debtor's failure to pay), and is regulated in Articles 527–34 PCC.

This action, traditionally called *'skarga pauliańska'* (Paulian action), may only be taken outside of insolvency proceedings, and requires some prerequisites to be fulfilled. First of all, the debtor's inability to pay has to be the result of a legal act and not any other legal event (such as, for example, a court ruling distributing marital assets between divorced spouses). Secondly, the contested act must be harmful to creditors:[35] this means that it should result in the debtor's failure to pay, or worsen the debtor's inability to pay.[36] Thirdly, the creditor may take action against the legal act only where the debtor was aware that such an act would be harmful to creditors, and the third person was also aware[37] – or, acting with due diligence, should had been aware – of that fact.[38]

It should be noted that, under Article 527 §3 PCC, it will be presumed that a third person was aware that a debtor's legal act would be harmful to creditors, where the contested legal act brought benefits to a person with a close relationship to the debtor.[39] In addition, if, due to the contested legal act, a third party received benefits free of charge, the creditor may take action concerning the legal act even if the third person was unaware that the debtor knew the act would harm creditors, and could not have been aware of that fact, even if they had acted with due diligence (Art. 528 PCC).[40]

It is worth mentioning that the Paulian action protects creditors not only from legal acts causing the transfer of an asset from the debtor's property to

---

34 J. Naczyńska, 'Komentarz do art. 527' in M. Habdas and M. Fras (eds), *Kodeks cywilny. Komentarz. Tom III. Zobowiązania. Część ogólna (art. 353–534)*, Warsaw 2018, p. 1131; W. Popiołek, 'Komentarz do art. 527–534 k.c.' in K. Pietrzykowski (ed), *Kodeks cywilny. Komentarz. Tom II. Art. 450–1088. Przepisy wprowadzające*, Warsaw 2017, p. 213.

35 M. Jasińska, *Skarga pauliańska. Ochrona wierzyciela w razie niewypłacalności dłużnika*, Warsaw 2014, p. 19.

36 P. Machnikowski in E. Gniewek and P. Machnikowski (eds), *Kodeks cywilny. Komentarz*, Warsaw 2014, p. 1053; Z. Radwański and A. Olejniczak, *Zobowiązania – część ogólna*, Warsaw 2012, p. 32; L. Stecki in J. Winiarz (ed), *Kodeks cywilny z komentarzem, praca zbiorowa, t. I*, Warsaw 1989, p. 536.

37 M. Pyziak-Szafnicka, 'Ochrona wierzyciela w razie niewypłacalności dłużnika' in A. Olejniczak (ed), *System Prawa Prywatnego, T. 6*, Warsaw 2018, p. 1730.

38 But see P. Machnikowski in E. Gniewek and P. Machnikowski, *Kodeks cywilny. Komentarz*, Warsaw 2014, p. 1055.

39 W. Popiołek, Komentarz do art. 527–534 k.c.' in K. Pietrzykowski (ed), *Kodeks cywilny. Komentarz. Tom II. Art. 450–1088. Przepisy wprowadzające*, Warsaw 2017, p. 224.

40 L. Stecki in J. Winiarz (ed), *Kodeks cywilny. Komentarz*, Warsaw 2014, p. 538.

a third person, but also from legal acts preventing the transfer of an asset to the debtor's property.

The prerequisites for the admissibility of the Paulian action are not the object of broad interpretation; however, if the strictly interpreted prerequisites are fulfilled, they are the sole and sufficient grounds for such an action.[41] It must also be stressed that the action itself is directed towards the third person, and not towards the dishonest debtor.[42] In that way, the protected claim receives extended effectiveness, being enforceable not only between its parties.[43]

In the event that such an action is successfully taken, it results in the relative ineffectiveness of the contested legal act. It means that the effects of the contested legal act are legally inoperative towards the creditor (Art. 527 §1 PCC), and that the creditor may satisfy their claim (i.e. carry out execution) from assets transferred by the debtor to the third person, with priority over creditors of that third person (Art. 532 PCC).[44] The relative ineffectiveness does not lead to any kind of invalidity or nullity of the contested legal act towards any participant of civil relationships, including the dishonest debtor; the legal act is ineffective (legally inoperative) only towards the creditor protected by the Paulian action.

Case 11 also gives rise to considerations concerning apparent legal acts that are not made for real (with no real intent to engage in a legal relationship created by legal act, and sometimes to dissimulate another type of legal act). According to Article 83 PCC, a '*pozorna czynność prawna*' (an apparent legal act) requires the consent of a second party (the other party to the contract, or the person towards whom a unilateral legal act is directed) and is invalid. There is no need for any action to be taken, including on the grounds of Article 527 PCC, as the invalidity operates on the basis of the law itself *(ex lege)*.[45]

The facts of the present case do not give sufficient grounds to definitively conclude that the donation of Bernardo's house to Maria was an apparent legal action; it may only be supposed that there is a high probability that this is the case. The donation was made in the period directly preceding Carlos' decision to sue Bernardo for the damage he caused through his car accident, and Bernardo is still using the house free of charge, but those circumstances are insufficient to declare beyond any doubt that this legal act is an apparent one. Maria, as Bernardo's niece, could be the only member of Bernardo's close family, and thus his only heir, and therefore Bernardo's decision to transfer his property

41 See Court of Appeal of Katowice in judgment from 14.02.2008, V Aca 1/08.

42 W. Popiołek, 'Komentarz do art. 527–534 k.c.' in K. Pietrzykowski (ed), *Kodeks cywilny. Komentarz. Tom II. Art. 450–1088. Przepisy wprowadzające*, Warsaw 2017, p. 213.

43 See A. Kubas, 'Rozszerzona skuteczność wierzytelności', *SC* 1969, t. XIII–XIV.

44 M. Pyziak-Szafnicka, *Ochrona wierzyciela w razie niewypłacalności dłużnika*, Warsaw 1995, p. 162. See also R. Adamus, 'Kilka uwag o zasadzie pierwszeństwa zaspokojenia wierzyciela na podstawie art. 532 KC', *MoP* 2013, no. 15.

45 Ibid., p. 63.

to Maria, even if fraudulent towards his debtors, may be real rather than apparent. Moreover, the case does not clearly state whether Maria consented to an apparent legal action, which is a prerequisite of invalidity on the grounds of Article 58 PCC.

2.10. SCOTLAND

Lorna MacFarlane

I. Operative Rules

Carlos can seek to have Bernardo declared bankrupt ('sequestrated') and challenge the transfer of the property to Maria, as a 'gratuitous alienation'.

Variation: if Bernardo has not yet validly 'conveyed' (transferred) the house to Maria, Carlos can attempt to *'inhibit'* the property.

II. Descriptive Formants

Scots law does not allow the recovery of assets validly disposed of to third parties, in the course of a civil claim. If Bernardo has transferred the property to Maria such that she is now the legal owner of the house, Carlos cannot take any action against her.

Carlos should firstly seek to have Bernardo declared bankrupt (known as 'sequestration' in Scotland). Carlos is permitted to do so as a creditor under section 2(1)(b)(i) of the Bankruptcy (Scotland) Act 2016,[46] although he must provide Bernardo with a debt advice and information package before petitioning the court to sequestrate him.[47]

The transfer of the house to Maria is likely a 'gratuitous alienation'. According to section 98(2) of the Bankruptcy (Scotland) Act 2016, a creditor by virtue of a debt incurred on or before the date of sequestration can challenge an alienation. If the challenge is successful, the court can grant decree providing that the property should be restored to Bernardo's estate.[48] Any property restored is returned to the debtor's estate for the benefit of all creditors.[49]

The court would not grant the decree if Bernardo can show that the alienation was made for adequate consideration or as a 'conventional' gift, or that, at

---

[46] This assumes that the costs of rebuilding the damaged parts of the house amount to not less than £3,000 (approximately €3,500), in accordance with Bankruptcy (Scotland) Act 2016, s. 7(1).

[47] Bankruptcy (Scotland) Act 2016, s. 3(1). The package is defined in the Debt Arrangement and Attachment (Scotland) Act 2002, s. 10(5).

[48] Bankruptcy (Scotland) Act 2016, s. 98(5)(b).

[49] D.W. McKenzie Skene, *Bankruptcy* (W. Green/Thomson Reuters, Edinburgh 2018), para. 14.32.

the time of the transfer to Maria, his assets were greater than his liabilities.[50] It is unlikely that any of these exceptions would apply here. Maria did not pay for the house, and it is unlikely that the gift of a house would be treated as a conventional present. It appears that the house is Bernardo's only asset of value, and so, in light of his outstanding obligations in respect of the damage to Carlos' house, his assets would not have outweighed his liabilities, following the transfer.

If Bernardo is still the legal owner of the property and the donation has not been given legal effect, Carlos can seek to inhibit the property to prevent Bernardo from transferring ownership to Maria or otherwise disposing of the property. Inhibition is a type of diligence on a debtor's heritable property which prevents the disposal (by sale or otherwise) of the property.[51] In Carlos' case, it would be sensible to seek 'inhibition on the dependence' (i.e. inhibition granted once an action has been raised in one of Scotland's civil courts, but before final judgment).[52] This would prevent Bernardo from being able to transfer the property, pending the outcome of Carlos' case against him. Carlos can then seek to enforce the judgment against Bernardo.

If Carlos is unsuccessful in his attempts to have Bernardo declared bankrupt, and it is too late to inhibit the property, he could seek recompense in line with the Motor Insurers' Bureau's Uninsured Drivers' Agreement. According to this Agreement, which the Motor Insurers' Bureau (MIB) has agreed with the Secretary of State for Transport, the MIB will indemnify those who hold judgments against uninsured drivers for any damage caused by the driver.[53]

III. Meta-Legal Formants

In Scots law, diligence is not part of the law of contract, but of the enforcement of judgments. It is 'the set of procedures whereby an unsecured creditor who holds an unsatisfied decree for payment can enforce that decree against the assets of his debtor'.[54] In other words, Carlos has a right to payment, and the

---

50 Bankruptcy (Scotland) Act 2016, s. 98(6).

51 G.L. Gretton and G. Maher, *The Laws of Scotland: Stair Memorial Encyclopaedia: Diligence and Enforcement of Judgments*, vol. 8 (LexisNexis/Law Society of Scotland, London/Edinburgh 1991), para. 133.

52 Ibid., para 134.

53 The most recent document is the Motor Insurers' Bureau, 2015 Uninsured Drivers' Agreement England, Scotland, and Wales (applying to accidents on or after 1 August 2015) and Supplementary Agreement 2017, available at https://www.mib.org.uk/making-a-claim/claiming-against-an-uninsured-driver/uninsured-drivers-agreements/ (accessed 15 December 2019). The key provision is Art. 3(1): 'if a claimant has obtained an unsatisfied judgment against any person in a Court in Great Britain then MIB will pay the relevant sum to the claimant or will cause the same to be so paid'.

54 G.L. Gretton and G. Maher, *The Laws of Scotland: Stair Memorial Encyclopaedia: Diligence and Enforcement of Judgments*, vol. 8 (LexisNexis/Law Society of Scotland, London/Edinburgh 1995), para. 101.

law of diligence provides him with the tools to enforce his right. Inhibition is a type of diligence.[55]

The MIB's Uninsured Drivers' Agreement has been judicially recognised in England as being 'as important as any statute',[56] due to its protection of third parties from the consequences of dangerous driving.

2.11. SLOVAKIA

Kristián Csach, Monika Jurčová, Peter Mészáros and Veronika Zoričáková

I. *Operative Rules*

Carlos is entitled to file a petition to the court against Maria, to ensure that Carlos may satisfy his claim from Bernando's house. Carlos cannot raise an action directly against Bernardo, although Bernardo can take part in the action against Maria as an 'intervener' (a party that participates in an action because of their interest in the result).[57]

II. *Descriptive Formants*

The *actio Pauliana*, called *'odporovacia žaloba'* (contesting action or an action on avoidance) is regulated by sections 42a and 42b SCC. It serves to protect a creditor with an enforceable claim against a debtor who is trying to fraudulently transfer their property in order to evade the satisfaction of the creditor's claim.

The aim of the *actio Pauliana* is to make the donation contract[58] ineffective towards the creditor (Carlos), so that he can enforce and satisfy his claim from the house as an asset (within the enforcement of a judgment or other enforceable title). Even though the ownership of the house has been transferred (with *erga omnes* effects) by a contestable legal act, that transfer will, after a successful avoidance of that act, be considered ineffective with regard to the claimant (creditor of the transferor). The transfer is said to be ineffective *inter partes* (towards the creditor, Carlos). After successfully contesting the transfer, Carlos

55 Ibid.

56 *Hardy v. Motor Insurers' Bureau* [1964] 2 QB 745, 757 per Lord Denning.

57 SSC file no. 3 Cdo 61/2008 dated 30.07.2009 and file no. 3 Cdo 71/1998 dated 17.12.2001 (R 86/2003).

58 In general, not only the donation contract, but, under judicial practice, these legal acts as well: purchase contract, assumption of debt, assignment of a receivable, renunciation of an inheritance, renunciation of a gift, writing off a debt, etc. See the decision of the SSC file no. 5 Cdo 101/2017 dated 27.02.2020.

will be able to satisfy his claim (Bernardo being the debtor) from the property, which, although it belongs to Maria, is not considered to have been effectively transferred with regard to Carlos.

Carlos should file the petition for avoidance (contesting the transfer) within three years, to prevent the right from being precluded.[59]

Carlos' claim against Bernardo has to be enforceable in order to contest the transfer of the property. The interpretation of the *enforceable claim* requirement was not settled until very recently. According to the previous prevailing case law, the creditor's claim must be ready for enforcement; that is, it had to be adjudicated.[60] However, this opinion has been overruled by a recent decision of the Great Chamber of the Slovak Supreme Court.[61] It is now sufficient that the creditor has been able to bring the claim before the court at the time of raising the avoidance claim. In such a case, the avoidance proceeding would then be stayed until the proceeding between Carlos and Bernardo has been decided.[62]

An important factor is the family relationship between Bernardo and Maria. Maria is not a relative in a direct line of descent from Bernardo. If she was, Carlos would not be obliged to prove that she had knowledge about Bernardo's intention to curtail Carlos' claim. As Maria is Bernardo's niece, however, Carlos would have to prove either that Maria was *mala fidae* (aware of Bernardo's intention to curtail Carlos' claim) or should be considered a close person to Bernardo, under section 116 SCC, because an injury suffered by Bernardo would reasonably be felt by Maria as her own.[63]

2.12. SPAIN

Carles Vendrell Cervantes

I. *Operative Rules*

Carlos has the right to challenge the donation by means of a claim for rescission ('*acción rescisoria*' or '*acción pauliana*'), as established in Article 1291.3, together with Article 1111, of the Spanish Civil Code.

---

59 See the decision of the SSC file no. 3 Obdo 38/2020 dated 30.03.2020.

60 See the decision of the Constitutional Court file no. IV. ÚS 284/2010 dated 30.08.2010, PL. ÚS 39/2015 dated 01.07.2015. SSC file no. 6 Cdop 253/2012 dated 17.12.2013, file no. 5 Cdo 188/2010 dated 23.11.2011, file no. 5 Cdo 109/2018 dated 28.03.2019, file no. 6 Cdo 237/2017 dated 24.06.2020.

61 SSC file no. 1 V Cdo 1/2022 dated 17.05.2022 (R 2/2022).

62 M. Hlušák, 'Uznesenie veľkého senátu Najvyššieho súdu SR sp. zn. 1 V Cdo 1/2022 zo 17. 5. 2022, R 2/2022 (vymáhateľnosť pohľadávky ako predpoklad odporovateľnosti)', *Súkromné právo*, 6 (2022), pp. 216–20.

63 The report is part of the project APVV-17-0562.

II. Descriptive Formants

Carlos has the right to challenge the donation, since it was carried out in order to ensure that Bernardo would become insolvent vis-à-vis Carlos. This is what Spanish law calls a donation entered into 'in fraud of creditors' *(en fraude de acreedores)*. Other circumstances that could help establish that the rationale behind the donation was to commit a fraud against Carlos include the fact that Bernardo donated his house to his niece, who rents the house to him for free.

Alternatively, Article 643 of the Spanish Civil Code establishes that:

> in the absence of stipulation in respect of the payment of debts, the donee shall only be liable for those debts where the donation is made in fraud of creditors. The donation shall always be presumed to have been made in fraud of creditors when the donor has not reserved sufficient property to pay prior debts.

As per this article, Carlos could also take action against Maria, who is now the owner of the house as a consequence of the donation in fraud of Carlos' credit (i.e. the compensation due to Carlos for damages) against Bernardo. This reflects the interpretation of the Spanish Supreme Court in its decision no. 25/2004 of 30 January.

2.13. SWEDEN

Oskar Mossberg

I. Operative Rules

Other than applying to have Bernardo declared bankrupt, the issue is out of Carlos' hands, due to issues of executive enforcement primarily being handled by a government authority, and Carlos having no right *in rem* against Bernardo's property.

II. Descriptive Formants

According to Swedish law, this would be a problem mainly concerning *'utsökningsrätt'* (law of execution), which is the law of execution closely linked with the law of insolvency. In a technical sense, Carlos has no claim on Bernardo's particular assets. Carlos has a claim directed at Bernardo's person rather than against his property. In practice, Carlos would apply for an injunction to pay, and the matter would be administered by Kronofogdemyndigheten (the Enforcement Authority), a government debt enforcement authority which would handle the actual executive dealings.[64]

The most plausible recourse for Carlos would be to have Bernardo declared bankrupt, after which an administrator would seize control of Bernardo's estate. The administrator could then litigate *'en återvinningstalan'* (an action on recovery) regarding recovery to Bernardo's estate of property which the creditors have been deprived of through undervalued transactions.[65] According to Chapter 4, Article 6 of Konkurslagen (the Swedish Bankruptcy Act), *'gåvor'* (gifts) given within six months prior to the date when an application to have the debtor declared bankrupt was handed in to the court *'går åter'* (go back); that is, they are recovered to the estate. There are no further requirements.[66] This rule would apply to the present case, and would place both the bankruptcy administrator actually litigating the case, and Carlos, as creditor, in a favourable evidentiary position.

There is, however, another option. This is to litigate a case where a court would be asked to *'fastställa'* (determine) that the gift was not honestly intended, and that it was indeed a *'skentransaktion'* (false transaction). The circumstances can be taken to indicate that there was no real *'gåvoavsikt'* (gift intention or *animus donandi*) on the part of Bernardo, and that it was a sham transaction intended to deprive his creditors of a valuable asset.[67] Such a case could be brought outside of a bankruptcy proceeding, or as part of such a proceeding (in which case the issue would, in a sense, be out of Carlos' hands, as it would be up to the administrator to take action in court). The evidentiary position would be considered worse than in an action for recovery to the bankruptcy estate, if only because Carlos and/or the administrator would need to prove more facts (the intentions of the parties are less important in recovery cases, which are, in this sense, 'more objective').[68]

There are no Swedish rules of recovery (such as an *actio Pauliana*) applicable outside of insolvency proceedings.[69]

---

64 The authority's website has some information: https://www.kronofogden.se/en-GB/Omoss.html.

65 Generally on recovery in bankruptcy proceedings, see G. Lennander, *Återvinning i konkurs*, 3rd ed., Norstedts juridik, Stockholm 2010.

66 See H. Renman, *Återvinning enligt 4 kap. konkurslagen: En process of insolvensrättslig manual*, Norstedts juridik, Stockholm 2009, pp. 101 ff.

67 Generally on gifts and the criteria for a transaction to be considered a gift, see J. Hellner, R. Hager and A.H. Persson, *Speciell kontraktsrätt II: Kontraksrätt: 1 häftet. Särskilda avtal*, 6th ed., Wolters Kluwer, Stockholm 2015, pp. 278 ff., especially pp. 281–83, reporting on case law. See also the Supreme Court case NJA 2007 N 34 (N for the Notice Section of NJA, containing less precedentially important cases).

68 See G. Lennander, *Återvinning i konkurs*, 3rd ed., Norstedts juridik, Stockholm 2010, pp. 177 ff.

69 On issues of recovery outside of bankruptcy, see U. Göranson, *Återvinning utom konkurs: svenskt och rättsjämförande kring actio Pauliana, Anfechtung och fraudulent conveyances*, Norstedts juridik, Stockholm 1989.

III. Meta-Legal Formants

Issues of executive enforcement of debt are not part of Swedish contract law. Instead, they are considered part of public law and special procedural law. As such, their rules and principles are subject to legislative regimes and rationales other than those of contract law. As Carlos has no right *in rem* against Bernardo's property (he has no claim of ownership, no lien, etc.), he is, in general, subject to the financial risks associated with having a mere right *in persona*, including the risk of the debtor's insolvency and financially less than favourable transactions (bad business decisions etc.). Execution, or legal coercion of performance, is not considered something which should be administered by individuals: indeed, many actions which might be considered 'executive' are criminal when undertaken by private individuals. It is considered something best administered by government authorities and some officially designated individuals (such as lawyers appointed as bankruptcy administrators).

The introduction of rules of recovery outside of bankruptcy proceedings have been discussed in the scholarly literature.[70] Legislative interest in this has, however, been modest, and the practical need for such rules is probably considered limited.

3. COMPARATIVE REMARKS

Jan Biemans and Lorna Richardson

This case discusses the fraudulent conveyance of assets by a debtor in order to frustrate recourse to these assets by their creditor. The creditor has a claim for damages which the debtor cannot repay, and the conveyance is fraudulent because it is intended to harm the creditor; the debtor is trying to avoid a lawsuit by becoming void of assets. The conveyance is also fraudulent because the house has been donated to a family member and not sold for a realistic purchase price, while the debtor remains in the house, renting it from their relative.

The question is whether the creditor can undertake any action against such a fraudulent conveyance. Most jurisdictions (Belgium, Bulgaria, Czech Republic, France, Germany, Italy, the Netherlands, Poland, Slovakia and Spain) are familiar with the action which often goes by the name '*actio Pauliana*', although this term is not used in all jurisdictions. In England, an ordinary creditor can take court action to challenge a transaction intended to defraud creditors, and there is no need for the debtor to be insolvent, despite the relevant statutory

[70] See ibid.

provisions being contained in the Insolvency Act 1986. In Scotland and Sweden, the debtor would have to be declared bankrupt before the transfer can be challenged. In Scotland, the transfer would be challenged by the creditor, whereas in Sweden it would be the bankruptcy administrator.

Generally, the main requirements for invoking the *actio Pauliana* are, with several variations in the different jurisdictions, the following: (1) the creditor must have a claim against the debtor; (2) the disputed legal act must have impoverished the debtor, whether or not making them (practically) insolvent (French law requires the debtor to be effectively insolvent); (3) the debtor must have acted fraudulently; and (4) if the legal act was for consideration, the counterparty must have had, or ought to have had, knowledge of the fraud.

If the conditions are met, the *actio Pauliana* allows the creditor to nullify the donation and/or conveyance vis-à-vis himself (Belgium, Bulgaria, Czech Republic, France, Germany, Italy, the Netherlands, Poland, Slovakia and Spain). The effect is that the asset – in this case, the house – will be considered still to be in the patrimony of the debtor so far as the creditor is concerned, but not as between the parties to the fraudulent conveyance. This allows the creditor recourse to the house in seeking payment of the debt due to him. In Scots and Swedish law, and likely also in English law, a successful challenge will result in the house actually being returned to Bernardo's patrimony.

Some of the reporters noted alternative claims available to Carlos. In English law, Carlos might be able to argue that Bernardo has retained a beneficial interest in the house despite legal ownership having transferred to Maria. Carlos would be able to have recourse to this beneficial interest in satisfaction of his claim. In Spain, Carlos could take action against Maria, as owner of the house, instead of challenging the donation to her. In Sweden, Carlos would be able to raise an action asking the court to determine that Bernardo's gift was not honestly intended, but was a sham transaction intended to deprive his creditors of a valuable asset. However, this claim would be more difficult for Carlos to prove than seeking Bernardo's bankruptcy, as described above. In Dutch law, the donation to Maria may be void if it can be proved that Bernardo's intention was solely to harm his creditors, on the basis that such a transaction violates public morality.

PART III

CONCLUSIONS

CONCLUDING REMARKS

Jan Biemans and Lorna Richardson

1. INTRODUCTION

As noted in the Introduction to this volume, the topic of 'contracts and third parties' is extensive. Different jurisdictions deal with a variety of different legal situations within that broad umbrella term. The topic is not necessarily one that sits within one area of the law of obligations. As Professor Martín-Casals' chapter amply demonstrates, some legal systems use contract law, and others tort law, to deal with the protection of third parties. It is, therefore, hoped that this work will be of interest to scholars and students of contract and tort law alike.

The apparent lack of uniformity within European legal systems on 'contracts and third parties' was what prompted the idea for this work in the first place. Its aim is to provide some clarity on the approaches of the various legal systems considered in this work. While the case studies in this volume deal with a variety of situations where a contract between two parties impacts on a third party, there are some themes to be taken from the analysis of those situations. As discussed in the Introduction, these themes can be broken down into four main categories: (A) defining a third party's rights and obligations in a contract between two contractual parties (including exclusion or limitation of liability); and, related to this, (B) the *actio Pauliana*; (C) acquisition of contractual rights in the case of the transfer of property and assignment; and (D) relationships of principal and agent in the conclusion and performance of contracts. The present writers have come to the conclusion that, while there are many differences in the legal rules and principles governing 'contracts and third parties', and often differences in outcome for the parties involved, there is a small common core of rules in relation to 'contracts and third parties' among the jurisdictions represented in this volume. These are set out below.

2. CATEGORY A: THIRD PARTY'S RIGHTS AND OBLIGATIONS IN A CONTRACT

The first category of cases deals with the limits of defining the third party's rights and obligations in the contract between the two other (contractual) parties.

Those rights include not only third-party clauses granting benefits to a third party, but also clauses purporting to exclude or limit a third party's liability and (if possible) clauses imposing obligations on third parties. Cases 1, 3, 8 and 9 are part of this category. The category can be broken down into the following cases:

(1) The granting of third-party rights in a contract (Case 1).
(2) Exclusion or limitation of liability in a contract, in favour of a third party (Case 3).
(3) The possibility of imposing an obligation on a third party (Case 8).
(4) Third-party reliance on (statements made in) contracts (Case 9).

The common denominator of these cases is that there are two parties who have entered into a contract, and through that contract desire to influence the position of a third party, either in a positive or a negative way. This category investigates the limits of this. Cases 1, 3 and 8 are discussed together in section 2.1. below, and Case 9 in section 2.2.

Case 11, addressing the limits of contractual freedom when the position of a creditor (as a third party) is harmed by that freedom, also relates to this category. However, due to the specific nature of the *actio Pauliana*, this case will be dealt with separately below.

2.1. RIGHT IN FAVOUR OF THIRD PARTY

The right in favour of a third party might be considered the 'classic' third-party right, where the contracting parties – A and B – enter into a contract with a provision for the benefit of C, who is not a party to the contract. To what extent does C have a right that they may enforce should the right in their favour not be performed, or where performance is defective in some way?

In all of the legal systems considered in this work, it is possible for the parties to a contract to create an enforceable right in favour of someone who is not a party to the contract. Such a right is based on the intention of the contracting parties. As such, the parties' contract must be interpreted to determine their intention in relation to the third party. Another area of uniformity among the systems surveyed is that the third party needs to be identifiable by the time performance of the right in their favour is due, but that there is no need for the third party to be named in the contract. As such, a third party will obtain a right if they fall within a particular class, for example where they are a member of a group of companies or answer a particular description. In none of the jurisdictions within this volume does a right in favour of a third party have to be irrevocable, in order for it to be created. As such, the contracting parties can alter or revoke the right. There are, however, differences among the jurisdictions as to when the right to vary or revoke the third-party right comes to an end: in some jurisdictions,[1] the contracting parties can do so until the third party accepts the right; in others,[2] it is possible until the third party declares their intention to avail themselves of the right; or until the third party is informed of the right in their favour;[3] or until the third party has acted in reliance on the right.[4]

As well as being able to enforce a right in their favour, a third party has, in most jurisdictions considered in this volume,[5] a right to rely on a limitation of liability provision that is available to a contracting party, provided it is clear that the parties to the contract intend the third party to be able to rely on the clause. It would, for instance, be possible for a subcontractor to defend a claim by the employer on a limitation provision in the contract between the employer and main contractor, in the event that the subcontractor is sued by the employer. Allowing the third-party subcontractor to do this prevents a delictual claim from cutting across the contractual framework chosen by the parties to the transaction. It is worth observing that parties will price a contract on the basis of contractual exclusions and limitations of liability. Against that backdrop, it is difficult to justify allowing that framework to be undermined by the employer's delictual claim against the subcontractor where the employer would be unable to sue the main contractor for an amount in excess of the contractual limitation.

In all legal systems included in this work, the parties to the contract can only create a right in favour of the third party. In no jurisdictions are the contracting parties able to impose an obligation on the third party. However, in some jurisdictions,[6] the right in the third party's favour can be subject to conditions, which conditions become obligations when the third party chooses to exercise the right in their favour.

It may, therefore, be said that there is a common core among the jurisdictions in giving effect to the intention of the contracting parties where they choose to grant a right in favour of a third party. Here, we see a conflict between the principle of privity of contract and giving effect to the intentions of the parties, with the latter given precedence. The commercial and practical utility of being able to contract for the benefit of third parties is also important. This may be witnessed in situations such as companies within the same group or, indeed, in family situations where one family member enters into a contract from which they and others in their family benefit. The practical uses to which third-party rights can be put are facilitated by relatively flexible rules as to their creation: for instance, there is no need for the third party to be named in the contract, or

1 Belgium, the Netherlands and Spain. In England, the position is similar, with the third party communicating their assent to the term to the promisor.
2 Italy.
3 Scotland.
4 England and Scotland.
5 Belgium, England, Germany, the Netherlands, Poland, Scotland, Spain and Sweden.
6 France and the Netherlands.

even to exist at the time of contract formation. While privity of contract cedes to party intention in order to create a right for a third party, it is not possible to create an obligation or burden on a third party.

2.2. RELIANCE ON PROFESSIONAL STATEMENT BY THIRD PARTY

It is clear that, where a professional provides their opinion under a contract, they will be liable to the other party for breach of contract should that professional opinion be negligent, causing a loss to their counterparty. But what of the situation where a professional statement made is relied upon by someone other than the other party to the contract: does that third party have a claim where the statement is negligent? In most legal systems surveyed in this volume, the third party who has relied on a negligent valuation would have a claim. This claim would not be for breach of contract, but must be established on an extracontractual basis, such as tort. The third party will likely be successful in their claim where they have reasonably relied on the professional statement. Thus, while there is not uniformity on this issue among the jurisdictions, there is significant commonality.

3. CATEGORY B: *ACTIO PAULIANA*

In most legal systems included in this work, the *actio Pauliana* operates to protect a creditor from a debtor's fraudulent attempts to dissipate their assets to the creditor's detriment. While most systems provide the creditor with a remedy, not all jurisdictions use the terminology of the *actio Pauliana*.[7] Where the requirements of the action are met, the fraudulent transaction will have no effect vis-à-vis the creditor. As such, that creditor may act as though the asset is still within the debtor's patrimony. However, as between the debtor and the party to whom they have transferred the asset, the asset will belong to the latter. The *actio Pauliana* is dealt with in Case 11.

In a minority of legal systems,[8] the right to challenge the debtor's transfer only arises where the debtor is bankrupt. If the transfer is found to have been a fraudulent attempt to dissipate assets, the assets will be returned to the debtor's patrimony, in contrast with the position set out above whereby the property remains with the transferee/donee but can be utilised by the creditor for payment of the debt due to him.

---

[7] In Scotland and Sweden, the *actio Pauliana* is not recognised.

[8] Scotland and Sweden.

4. CATEGORY C: ACQUISITION OF CONTRACTUAL RIGHTS THROUGH TRANSFER OF PROPERTY AND/OR ASSIGNMENT

Category C essentially deals with the following question: if you transfer an asset (property, contract and/or contractual rights), what (in terms of the contractual relationship between the transferring party and their counterparty) will remain with the party transferring the asset, and what will pass on to the acquiring party? Cases 2, 5, 7 and 10 are part of this category, which can be broken down into the following cases:

(1) The owner of property has concluded long term contracts, which are linked to the property. The question is whether these contracts (or any contractual rights arising out of them) transfer with the property (Case 5).
(2) The owner of property transfers it. The property has suffered from some damage. That damage is linked to a contract between the former owner and its counterparty. The question is whether and how the new owner may profit from any rights arising out of that contract (Case 2).
(3) The owner of a claim (receivable) arising out of a contract transfers (assigns) the claims to a third party. The question is which contractual rights specifically transfer with the claim, and what the position of the counterparty (the debtor) is in relation to the new creditor (Cases 7 and 10).

Cases 2 and 5 are discussed in section 4.1. below, followed by a separate discussion of Cases 7 and 10.

4.1. TRANSFER OF PROPERTY

In this situation, A, the owner of a property, enters into a contract with B. B may have breached the contract and/or have contractual obligations outstanding when A sells the property to C. The question then is what rights does C, as the new owner, have against B. C is not a party to the contract with B, yet they are likely to have a significant interest in the performance of that contract, given that it relates to what is now their property. Indeed, in some cases the situation arises where A will have title to sue B for breach of contract, but A will have suffered no loss as a result of the breach, having transferred the property to C. C may be in the difficult position of having sustained a loss but having no contractual route available to sue B. What legal rules come into play to assist B, and are these rules contractual or tortious?

There were notable differences when dealing with the situation of A having title to sue B for breach of contract but having suffered no loss, with the loss suffered by C following a transaction between A and C. In some jurisdictions,[9] the claim for breach of contract passed to C along with ownership of the property concerned, and in these jurisdictions C received most protection. In other jurisdictions, a claim by C against B was possible, but was the subject of specific legal rules dealing with the situation rather than general principle;[10] or A could sue B to recover C's loss.[11] In the latter case, there was no imperative for A to sue on C's behalf and, as such, C was in a vulnerable position. It seems unlikely that A would entertain litigating against B, given the time, cost and risk involved in doing so, unless there was some benefit to A, for instance if A and C were members of the same group of companies.

There were also differences between the jurisdictions as to the effect on contracts relating to immoveable property when ownership of that property is transferred. In all jurisdictions, a lease of the property would pass and bind the new owner, demonstrating a uniform desire to protect the interests of the party utilising the property from a change in ownership. This was not, however, the case for other types of contract, in relation to which there was a divergence of outcomes. In the majority of jurisdictions,[12] a contract of insurance in relation to the building passed to the new owner, at least for an initial period of time following transfer of ownership. As such, the new owner would be protected by the existing insurance policy when they first became owner of the property. An even clearer divergence could be seen in relation to a contract for works on the immoveable property. In a minority of legal systems surveyed in this volume,[13] the contract for works would pass automatically by operation of law to the new owner; the rights under the contract for works are considered to be qualitative rights which follow the building, and so sit with the owner, whoever they may be. Where the contracts do not pass to the new owner by operation of law, it is open to the parties – the old and the new owner – to take steps to assign rights under those contracts to the new owner.

In this area, it is difficult to point to a common core of law among the jurisdictions reviewed in this volume. Protection of a tenant where immoveable property transfers to a new owner is the sole common theme from the case studies presented. Yet we take the view that there is much to be gleaned from this comparative work. In some systems, the disconnection between privity of contract/title to sue and loss has created problems.[14] Solutions developed in

---

[9] Belgium, France and the Netherlands.

[10] Bulgaria and Spain.

[11] Czech Republic, England and Scotland.

[12] Belgium, Bulgaria, France, Germany, the Netherlands, Spain and Sweden.

[13] Belgium, France and the Netherlands.

[14] This may be seen, for instance, in English law, where the issue has been referred to as a 'legal black hole', with the courts keen to find a workable solution for a person sustaining loss 'which under a rational legal system ought to be compensated by the person who has caused it': *Albacruz v. Albazero* [1977] AC 774 per Lord Diplock at 847.

some of the systems are imperfect in that the party who has suffered loss (C) has no right to take action against the party in breach of contract (B), but must instead rely on the party from whom they have purchased the property (A), who is B's counterparty. Yet there is no way in which C can force A to take such action. While privity of contract is undoubtedly a very important cornerstone of the law of contract, exceptions have been made – see the discussion in section 2.1. above in relation to the contract creating a right in favour of a third party. The preferable solution is that the claim passes to the new owner (C), who has suffered loss, to allow them to seek compensation for that loss from B.

4.2. ASSIGNMENT: ACCESSORY RIGHTS AND THE DEBTOR'S POSITION

A major topic in its own right, we have included assignment within this volume, given its significant commercial importance. It is also a situation where a third party to the contract, the assignee, becomes involved with the contract post-formation. Where a contract is assigned, the debtor must perform to the assignee rather than the cedent. The creditor in the obligation is substituted from A to C. To a large extent, the assignee steps into the cedent's shoes in terms of the contract. Thus, a contract between A and B becomes a contract between A and C, with the latter being a third party. Fundamental questions include what is it that is assigned? And what of the fact that the cedent and the debtor were in a contractual relationship prior to the assignment? Often a debtor has no say in whether or not their creditor assigns their interest in the contract to another person. The debtor may have had no advance knowledge of the creditor's intention to pass the contract on to the assignee, only finding out about it when the completed assignation has been notified to them. This raises the question of what rules come into play to protect their position?

In all of the legal systems considered in this volume, certain related claims pass to an assignee, as an accessory right, when a receivable is assigned. Case 7 provides the examples of the rights to interest on a loan, and any mortgage securing the loan, which pass along with the right to repayment of the loan. There are parallels here with the transfer of certain rights where property is transferred to a new owner, discussed in section 4.1. above. Clearly, the legal systems consider certain rights and/or claims so be so tied to the principal asset that they pass to the third-party buyer along with the principal asset. There are, however, quite significant differences among the jurisdictions as to what those accessory rights are.

In most of the legal systems considered in this volume,[15] the debtor's right of set-off against the initial creditor is preserved, and can be utilised against

[15] Bulgaria, Czech Republic, England, Germany, Italy, the Netherlands, Poland, Slovakia and Sweden.

the new creditor. Generally, the right to set-off only applies where the debtor's claim against the old creditor existed prior to the debtor being notified of the assignment, although in some jurisdictions debtors have the benefit of a more extensive right of set-off. Allowing the debtor to set off their claim against the new creditor seeks to ensure that the debtor is not disadvantaged by their initial counterparty's decision to transfer the contract to a third party.

In relation to assignment, there is less of a common core of legal rules than is observed with a contract in favour of a third party. One commonality is the transfer of accessory rights on the assignment of a receivable, but there are differences in detail.

4.3. ASSIGNMENT: SIMULATION

Simulation occurs where the apparent contract between the parties does not disclose the true 'secret' contract between them. The secret contract will have effect as between the parties themselves, but what of a third party who has relied on the apparent contract, such as an assignee? Interestingly, in most jurisdictions considered in this volume, the secret agreement also has effect against the third party. This may seem surprising, given the importance of good faith in most civilian jurisdictions. However, that does not mean that the third party is without a remedy. In most jurisdictions in which the third party is bound to the effect of the secret agreement, they will have a claim against the assignor for their loss, based on the difference between the secret agreement and the apparent agreement.

In some jurisdictions,[16] the third party is protected, in that they can rely on the apparent agreement where their reliance was in good faith and without knowledge of the secret agreement. Here, the secret agreement will have effect only between the parties to it, and not on any third party.

On this topic, there is something of a divergence between those systems which recognise the concept of simulation and those which do not.

5. CATEGORY D: RELATIONSHIPS OF PRINCIPAL AND (INDIRECT) AGENT IN THE CONCLUSION AND PERFORMANCE OF CONTRACTS

Like assignment, this topic might be considered a distinct area in its own right. It has been included in this survey given that it deals with a third party having a right in contract.

16 Belgium, Bulgaria, France, Germany, Italy and the Netherlands.

In agency/representation, the agent contracts with the third party, which, depending on the circumstances, may result in a legal relationship between the agent and third party, or between the principal and third party. The topic is also one of significant importance given the extent to which agents are utilised for the purpose of trading. It has been said that it is difficult to reconcile agency with privity of contract, but that it is permitted due to its practical utility and commercial convenience.[17] It is dealt with in Cases 4 and 6, where an indirect agent concludes a contract in its own name, but for the account of its principal. The underlying question is what happens to the rights and obligations arising out of this contract within the relationship between the principal and the agent.

In relation to this aspect of 'contracts and third parties', one can identify something of a civil law/common law divide, with Scots law (a mixed jurisdiction) falling on the common law side. In the case of indirect agency (where the third party knows that their counterparty is acting not on their own behalf, but on behalf of another (the principal), but does not know the identity of the principal), the contract is between the agent and the third party in civilian systems. In both English and Scots law, the contract is, in contrast, generally between the principal and the third party. In these jurisdictions, the contract is only between the agent and the third party where the third party believed the agent to have been acting on their own behalf in entering into the contract. In the civilian systems considered in this volume, it is only where the agent enters into the contract in the name of the principal that the contract has effect between the principal and third party.

Interestingly, in some civilian systems,[18] where the contractual effect is, as noted above, between the agent and the third party, the proprietary effects of the contract occur between the third party and the principal. As such, upon acquisition the third party passes ownership of the property to the principal, despite the third party's contract being with the indirect agent. In German law, while ownership passes to the agent, it is possible to agree before the transfer to him that the property will be transferred to the principal. When this is done, the property will pass from the patrimony of the third party to the principal when the property is transferred to the agent. In other jurisdictions, the agent must transfer, to the principal, property acquired for the benefit of the principal.

Within the civilian jurisdictions, there are differences in treatment where the indirect agent has become insolvent. In a minority of these systems,[19] the principal and third party can sue each other directly, should the agent become insolvent. In the others, such direct action will not arise on the agent's insolvency; instead, the third party will have to file a claim with the agent's

17 L. Macgregor, *The Law of Agency in Scotland*, W. Green: Edinburgh 2013, para. 12-30.
18 Belgium, Bulgaria, France, Spain and Sweden.
19 Bulgaria, the Netherlands and Spain.

insolvency administrator. This seems to lead to some strange results and an apparent imbalance in the operation of certain contracts, such as the property owner's ability to sue a tenant for rent in Case 4, despite the tenant being unable to sue for access to the property or continuation of the lease, where the agent has become insolvent.

Where an indirect agent holds property on behalf of their principal, there is a split in the jurisdictions as to whether or not the principal has a preferential claim on the agent's bankruptcy estate in relation to this property. It seems rather unfair on the principal that property that was intended for them, and was most likely bought using their funds, should end up in the indirect agent's insolvent estate for the benefit of all of the agent's creditors.

6. OVERVIEW

When looking at the four categories, it is striking that the outcomes in the different jurisdictions are most similar in Category A. All jurisdictions have quite similar approaches to granting third-party rights in third-party clauses, and also as to the impossibility of imposing obligations for the third party within such clauses.

Similarly, in Category B, almost all jurisdictions have the same approach to the limitation of contractual freedom when it comes to harming the creditor's rights. The only exceptions to the rule is that, in Scots and Swedish laws, creditors are only protected on the insolvency of the debtor.

Category C shows more differences between the legal systems. In all jurisdictions, the assignment of claims is possible. There are, however, differences in relation to which rights are transferred automatically by operation of law, and which rights are considered to be accessory rights or not. However, these differences appear to be relatively minor. More fundamental differences can be seen in the cases involving the transfer (by operation of law) of (long-term) contracts linked to property and/or contractual rights (to damages) related to property. As to the former the concept of contracts and/or contractual rights 'accessory' to property does not yet seem to have a place in most jurisdictions. In some jurisdictions, commercial law dominates outcomes. In the case of losses caused, much seems to be solved through tort law, rather than contract law, with some exceptions.

Category D probably shows the most differences between jurisdictions, as both cases relate to different systems of agency and property law, and often refer to specific rules of insolvency law. With respect to agency, English law and Scots law are especially different from the other jurisdictions. There are fundamental differences between all jurisdictions with respect to the transfer of tangible things, registered property, claims and money. Also, there seem to be great differences between the rights and obligations of the counterparty regarding the transfer of property to the principal in the event of insolvency of the agent, often leaving not the principal, but the counterparty, empty-handed.

7. CONCLUSION

Our survey of 'contracts and third parties' discloses that there is what may be termed a 'small common core' of European private law in this field. In many of the areas investigated, there was some divergence among the systems. The area in which there can be said to be a common position is in relation to the contract for the benefit of a third party. In all systems, the intentions of the contracting parties are given effect in the granting of an enforceable right to the third party. The utility of this legal device is increased by the flexibility surrounding its creation; that is, the fact that the third party need not be named, and that the contracting parties have the ability to vary or revoke the right once it has been created.

In relation to other areas considered by the case studies, the comparative analysis has proved very useful in identifying the legal positions across many European legal systems. This analysis may be of interest when it comes to developing national laws, where the law is thought to be in need of reform, or in providing inspiration when legal developments are required.

BIBLIOGRAPHY

BELGIUM

N. Carette, 'Het derdenbeding: wanneer heeft een beding de strekking van een derdenbeding naar Belgisch recht?' in I. Samoy (ed), *Derden in het contractenrecht* (Antwerp, Intersentia, 2009), pp. 81–128

N. Carette, *Derdenbeding* (Antwerp, Intersentia, 2011)

I. Claeys, *Samenhangende overeenkomsten en aansprakelijkheid* (Antwerp, Intersentia, 2003)

H. De Page, *Les incapables. Les obligations (première partie)*, II in *Traité élémentaire de droit civil belge* (Brussels, Bruylant, 1962–64)

H. De Page, *Traité élémentaire de droit civil belge* (Brussels, Bruylant, 1962–64), I and II

S. Demeyere, *Aansprakelijkheid van een contractant jegens derden* in *Instituut voor Verbintenissenrecht KU Leuven* (Bruges, die Keure, 2015)

E. Dirix, *Obligatoire verhoudingen tussen contractanten en derden* (Antwerp, Kluwer, 1984)

E. Dirix, 'De rechtsverhouding tussen principaal, commissionair en derde' in E. Dirix, P. Senaeve, W. Pintens and S. Stijns (eds), *Liber Amicorum Jacques Herbots* (Deurne, Kluwer, 2002), pp. 97–110

E. Dirix, 'Samenloop van aansprakelijkheid en allocatie van risico's' in I. Boone, I. Claeys and L. Lavrysen (eds), *Liber amicorum Hubert Bocken. Dare la Luce* (Bruges, die Keure, 2009), pp. 59–66

I. Durant, 'Tiers et biens en Belgique' in Bruylant and LB2V (eds), *Les tiers – Journées panaméennes* (Brussels, Bruylant, 2016), pp. 317–338

M. Fontaine, 'La transmission des obligations *de lege feranda*' in *La transmission des obligations* (Brussels, Bruylant, 1980), pp. 611–672

J.M. Herbots, 'L'affinage du principe de la transmission automatique des droits "propter rem" du maître de l'ouvrage à l'acquéreur de l'immeuble', *RCJB* (1992), pp. 512–549

R. Houben, *Schuldvergelijking* (Antwerp, Intersentia, 2010)

R. Jafferali, 'Tiers et contrat en Belgique' in Bruylant and LB2V (eds), *Les tiers – Journées panaméennes* (Brussels, Bruylant, 2016), pp. 55–70

R. Jansen, 'Overdracht van het verhuurde goed' in G.-L. Ballon, H. De Decker, V. Sagaert, E. Terryn, B. Tilleman and A.L. Verbeke (eds), *Contractuele clausules – Huur* (Antwerp, Intersentia, 2016), pp. 409–439

F. Laurent, *Principes de droit civil* (Brussels, Bruylant-Christophe, 1887)

V. Sagaert and S. Baeyens, 'De beëindiging van overeenkomsten in geval van insolventie van de partijen: loopt het insolventierecht uit de pas van het verbintenissenrecht?' in N. Carette and B. Weyts (eds), *Verantwoord aansprakelijkheidsrecht. Liber amicorum Aloïs Van Oevelen* (Antwerp, Intersentia, 2017)

V. Sagaert and E. Dewitte, 'Actuele ontwikkelingen inzake de derdenwerking van overeenkomsten' in *Themis Verbintenissenrecht* (Bruges, die Keure, 2012), pp. 131–159

I. Samoy, *Middellijke vertegenwoordiging: vertegenwoordiging herbekeken vanuit het optreden in eigen naam voor andermans rekening* (Antwerp, Intersentia, 2005)

I. Samoy and A. Maes, 'Over het beding dat de bevoegdheid verleent om een partijbeslissing te nemen en de vraag of de opname van objectieve criteria noodzakelijk is voor de geldigheid ervan', *TBBR* (2010), pp. 309–314

S. Stijns, 'Les contrats et les tiers' in P. Wéry (ed), *Le droit des obligations contractuelles et le bicentenaire du Code civil* (Bruges, die Keure, 2004), pp. 189–239

S. Stijns, *Verbintenissenrecht. Leerboek 1-2* (Bruges, die Keure, 2009-16)

S. Stijns and E. Verjans, 'Variaties op het begrip "derde" in het contractenrecht' in A. De Boeck, S. Stijns, R. Van Ransbeeck, F. Brandsma, N. Carette, D. Leroy, I. Samoy and E. Verjans (eds), *Positie van de derde in het privaat vermogensrecht* (Bruges, die Keure, 2012), pp. 19–66

M.E. Storme, 'Van Trust gespeend? Trusts en fiduciaire figuren in het Belgisch privaatrecht', *TPR* (1998), pp. 703–819

W. Van Gerven and A. Van Oevelen, *Verbintenissenrecht* (Leuven, Acco, 2015)

P. Van Ommeslaghe, *Traité de droit civil belge. II. Les obligations. Vol. 1* (Brussels, Bruylant, 2013)

P. Van Ommeslaghe, *Traité de droit civil belge. II. Les obligations. Vol. 2* (Brussels, Bruylant, 2013)

T. Vansweevelt and B. Weyts, *Handboek buitencontractueel aansprakelijkheidsrecht* (Antwerp, Intersentia, 2009)

P. Wéry, *Droit des obligations: Théorie générale du contrat* (Brussels, Larcier, 2011), I

P. Wéry, *Droit des obligations: Les sources des obligations extracontractuelles. Le régime général des obligations* (Brussels, Larcier, 2016), II

B. Weyts (ed), *Verantwoord aansprakelijkheidsrecht. Liber amicorum Aloïs Van Oevelen* (Antwerp, Intersentia, 2017)

V. Withofs, *Contractsoverdracht* (Bruges, die Keure, 2015)

BULGARIA

I. Apostolov, *Legal transactions affecting a foreign legal sphere* (Sofia, M. Staykov's printing house, 1937)

S. Bashov, 'Contract in favor of a third party. Concept and action', *Property and Law*, 10 (2016)

L. Dikov, *Civil Law Course. Contractual Law. General part*, Vol. 3 (Sofia, Royal printing House, 1934; phototype edition of 'St. Kliment Ohridski' University Publishing House, 2015)

O. Gerdzhikov, *Commercial Transactions* (Sofia, Work-and-Law Publishers, 2006)

P. Goleva, *Commercial Law. General part. Traders* (Sofia, Apis Publishing House, 2014)

P. Goleva, *Contractual Law* (Sofia, New Star, 2015)

G. Grigorov, *Insolvency* (Sofia, Sibi, 2017)

A. Ivanov, *Transfer of Receivables in Commercial Turnover* (Sofia, Sibi, 2010)

A. Kalaydzhiev, *Contractual Law. General part*, 5th ed. (Sofia, Sibi, 2010)

A. Kozhuharov, *Contractual Law. General concepts of contractual relationship*, new edition and supplements by Petko Petkov (Sofia, 'St. Kliment Ohridski' University Publishing House, Jurispress, 2002)

M. Malchev, *Destruction of Civil Law Transactions* (Sofia, Ciela, 2013)

M. Markov, *Contractual Law* (Sofia, Sibi, 2011)

N. Mevorah, D. Lidgi and L. Farhi, *Commentary on Law of Obligations and Contracts. Art. 1–333* (Sofia, Fotinov Cooperative Printing House, 1924)

K. Mitev, 'Exemption Clauses in Contracts and Third Parties', *Legal Studies*, 4 (2005)

K. Mitev, *Exemption Clauses in Contracts* (Sofia, Sibi, 2007)

B. Musseva, 'Is the autonomy of the will permissible in unlawful damage under Bulgarian private international law?', *Contemporary Law*, 6 (2003)

S. Popova, *Contractual relations in the construction* (Blagoevgrad, Southwestern University Publishing House, 2012)

M. Pavlova, *Civil Law. General Part* (Sofia, Sophie-P, 2002)

I. Ruschev, 'Acquiring rights under contract in favor of a third party' in *Research studies of the University of Russe*, 54(7) (2015)

A. Shopov, *Mistake as a ground for nullification of contracts* (Sofia, Sibi, 2013)

P. Topurov, 'Legal status of the contract in favor of a third party - Critical notes on the theory of direct emergence of rights' in *Compendium of reports from the VII National Conference of PhD students in legal studies* (Sofia, Institute on State and Legal Studies, 2017)

P. Topurov, 'Fulfilling a contract in favor of a third party' in H. Paunov (compilor) *Compendium Law - Traditions and Perspectives* (Sofia, Ciela, 2018)

I. Vassilev. 'Publicity of the entry under Bulgarian property law' in H. Paunov (compilor), *Law - Traditions and Perspectives* (Sofia, Ciela Norma, 2018)

T. Yossifova, *The commission contract* (Sofia, Sibi, 2006)

T. Yossifova, *Effect of the contract concerning persons* (Sofia, Sibi, 2019)

CZECH REPUBLIC

M. Hulmák et al., *Občanský zákoník V, Závazkové právo, Obecná část (§1721–2054), První vydání*, C.H. Beck, Praha, 2014

F. Melzer, P. Tégl et al., *Občanský zákoník, §2894–3081. Velký komentář. Svazek IX. První vydání*, Leges, Praha, 2018

J. Petrov, M. Výtisk, V. Beran et al., *Občanský zákoník. Komentář. 2. vydání*. C.H. Beck, Praha, 2019

F. Rouček and J. Sedláček, *Komentář k Československému obecnému zákoníku občanskému a občanské právo platné na Slovensku a v Podkarpatské Rusi. Díl čtvrtý (§859 až 1089)*. Nakladatelství V. Linhart, Praha, 1936 (reprint ASPI Publishing, Praha, 1998)

ENGLAND AND WALES

D. Chappell, *Understanding JCT Standard Building Contracts*, 10th ed. (Abingdon: Routledge, 2017)

M. Barnes, *The Law of Estoppel* (Oxford: Hart Publishing, 2020)
H. Beale (ed), *Chitty on Contracts*, 33rd ed., 2 vols (London: Sweet and Maxwell, 2019)
R. Derham, *The Law of Set-Off*, 4th ed. (Oxford: Oxford University Press, 2010)
F.E. Dowrick, 'The Relationship of Principal and Agent' (1954) 17 *Modern Law Review* 24
M. Furmston and G.J. Tolhurst, *Privity of Contract* (Oxford: Oxford University Press, 2015)
S. Goulding, 'Privity of estate and the enforcement of real covenants' (2007) 63 *Common Law World Review* 193
Law Commission, *Privity of Contract: Contracts for the Benefit of Third Parties* (Law Com No. 242, 1996)
K.M. Lewison et al. (eds), *Woodfall on Landlord and Tenant*, Release 120, 4 vols (London: Sweet and Maxwell, 2020)
J. McGhee et al (eds), *Snell's Equity*, 34th ed. (London: Sweet & Maxwell, 2019)
E. Peel (ed), *Treitel on the Law of Contract*, 14th ed. (London: Sweet & Maxwell: 2016)
J. Powell et al (eds), *Jackson & Powell on Professional Liability*, 8th ed. (London: Sweet & Maxwell, 2017)
G.J. Tolhurst, *The Assignment of Contractual Rights*, 2nd ed. (Oxford: Hart Publishing, 2016)
P.G. Watts and F.M.B. Reynolds (eds), *Bowstead & Reynolds on Agency*, 21st ed. (London: Sweet & Maxwell, 2017)

FRANCE

J.L. Aubert, É. Savaux and J. Flour, *Droit Civil. Les Obligations. L'Acte Juridique*, 17th ed. (Paris: Sirey, 2022)
C. Aubry and C. Rau, *Droit civil français*, 6th ed. by P. Esmein (Paris: Librairies techniques, 1952), t. V
C. Aubry and C. Rau, *Droit civil français*, 6th ed. by P. Esmein (Paris: Librairies techniques, 1958), t. XII
P. Delebecque and F. Collart-Dutilleul, *Contrats Civils & Commerciaux*, 12th ed. (Paris: Dalloz, 2023)
J. François, *Traité de droit civil, Les obligations. Régime général*, 4th ed. (Paris: Economica 2017), t. IV
J. Ghestin, C. Jamin and M. Billiau, *Traité de droit civil, les effets du contrat*, 3rd ed. (Paris: LGDJ, 2001)
M. Julienne, *Régime général des obligations*, 2nd ed. (Paris: LGDJ, 2018)
H., L. and J. Mazeaud and F. Chabas, *Leçons de droit civil, Obligations, Théorie générale*, 9th ed. (Paris: Montchrestien, 1998)
M. Planiol and G. Ripert, *Traité pratique de droit civil français*, 2nd ed. by P. Esmein (Paris: LGDJ, 1952), t. VI
M. Planiol and G. Ripert, *Traité pratique de droit civil français*, 2nd ed. by P. Esmein, J. Radouant and G. Gabolde (Paris: LGDJ, 1954), t. VII
F. Terré, P. Simler, Y. Lequette and F. Chénedé, *Droit civil, les obligations*, 13th ed. (Paris: Dalloz, 2022)

GERMANY

W. Bayer, *Der Vertrag zugunsten Dritter* (Mohr Siebeck 1995)
E. Braun and E. Bäuerle, *Insolvenzordnung* (9th ed., Beck 2022)
C.-W. Canaris, 'Schutzwirkungen zugunsten Dritter bei "Gegenläufigkeit" der Interessen', *JZ* 1995, 441
C.-W. Canaris, 'Die Reform des Rechts der Leistungsstörungen', *JZ* 2001, 499
P. Derleder and K. Bartels, 'Der Vermieterwechsel bei der Wohnraummiete', *JZ* 1997, 981
H. Dörner, *Dynamische Relativität* (Beck 1985)
C.T. Ebenroth, K. Boujong, D. Joost and L. Strohn, *Handelsgesetzbuch*, vol. 2 (5th ed., Vahlen 2024)
W. Hau and R. Poseck, *BeckOK BGB* (70th ed., Beck 2024)
K. Hopt, *Handelsgesetzbuch* (43rd ed., Beck 2024)
A. Lehmann-Richter, 'Mietvertrag zugunsten Dritter', *ZMR* 2010, 813
D. Looschelders, *Schuldrecht AT* (21st ed., Vahlen 2023)
Münchener Kommentar zum Anfechtungsgesetz (2nd ed., Beck 2022)
Münchener Kommentar zum Bürgerlichen Gesetzbuch (Beck), vol. 1 (9th ed., 2021), vol. 2 (9th ed., 2022), vol. 3 (9th ed., 2022), vol. 4 (8th ed., 2019), vol. 5 (9th ed., 2023), vol. 6 (9th ed., 2023), vol. 7 (9th ed., 2024), vol. 8 (9th ed., 2023), vol. 9 (9th ed., 2022)
Münchener Kommentar zum Handelsgesetzbuch, vol. 5 (5th ed., Beck 2021)
Münchener Kommentar zur Insolvenzordnung, vols 1 and 2 (4th ed., Beck 2019)
Münchener Kommentar zum Versicherungsvertragsgesetz, vol. 1 (3rd ed., Beck 2022)
J. Oechsler, 'Voraussetzungen eines Vertrages mit Schutzwirkungen zugunsten Dritter bei der Haftung für ein Wertgutachten, Anmerkung zu BGH, 20. 4. 2004 – X ZR 250/02', *LMK* 2004, 178
J. Petersen, *Der Dritte im Zivilrecht* (De Gruyter 2018)
Prölss/Martin, Versicherungsvertragsgesetz (31st ed., Beck 2021)
Soergel, Bürgerliches Gesetzbuch, vol. 5,3 (13th ed., Kohlhammer 2010)
J. von Staudingers Kommentar zum Bürgerlichen Gesetzbuch (Sellier – de Gruyter), vol. §§164–240 (2019), vol. §§249–254 (2021), vol. §§255–304 (2019), vol. §§328–345 (2020), vol. §§397–432 (2022), vol. §§488–490, 607–610 (2015), vol. §§557–580 a (2021), vol. §§631–650v (2019), vol. §823 A–D (2017), vol. §§985–1011 (2023)

THE NETHERLANDS

E.J.A.M. van den Akker, *Beroepsaansprakelijkheid ten opzichte van derden*, The Hague: Boom Juridische uitgevers 2001
S.C.J.J. Kortmann (in cooperation with J.S. Kortmann), *Mr. C. Assers Handleiding tot de beoefening van het Nederlands Burgerlijk Recht. 3. Deel III. Vermogensrecht algemeen. Volmacht en vertegenwoordiging*, Deventer: Wolters Kluwer 2017
S.C.J.J. Kortman, L.J.M. de Leede and H.O. Thunissen, *Mr. C. Assers Handleiding tot de beoefening van het Nederlands Burgerlijk Recht. 5. Deel III. Overeenkomst van opdracht, arbeidsovereenkomst, aaneming van werk*, Zwolle: W.E.J. Tjeenk Willink 1994

C.H. Sieburgh, *Mr. C. Assers Handleiding tot de beoefening van het Nederlands Burgerlijk Recht. 6. Verbintenissenrecht. Deel I. De verbintenis in het algemeen, eerste gedeelte*, Deventer: Wolters Kluwer 2020

C.H. Sieburgh, *Mr. C. Assers Handleiding tot de beoefening van het Nederlands Burgerlijk Recht. 6. Verbintenissenrecht. Deel II. De verbintenis in het algemeen, tweede gedeelte*, Deventer: Wolters Kluwer 2021

C.H. Sieburgh, *Mr. C. Assers Handleiding tot de beoefening van het Nederlands Burgerlijk Recht. 6. Verbintenissenrecht. Deel III. Algemeen overeenkomstenrecht*, Deventer: Wolters Kluwer 2022

T.F.E. Tjong Tjin Tai, *Mr. C. Assers Handleiding tot de beoefening van het Nederlands Burgerlijk Recht. 7. Bijzondere overeenkomsten. Deel IV. Opdracht, incl. de geneeskundige behandelingsovereenkomst en de reisovereenkomst*, Deventer: Wolters Kluwer 2022

J.W.A. Biemans, *Rechtsgevolgen van stille cessie*, Deventer: Kluwer 2011

T.E. Booms, *Aanvullen van subjectieve rechten*, Deventer: Wolters Kluwer 2019

N.E.D. Faber, *Verrekening*, Deventer: Kluwer 2005

P.H. Kramer, 'De zorgplicht van beroepsbeoefenaren jegens derden en de invloed van gebruiksbedingen en exoneraties in rapportages', *MvV* 2017/11, pp. 315–24

C.E. du Perron, *Overeenkomst en derden*, Deventer: Kluwer 1999

M.H.E. Rongen, *Cessie*, Deventer: Kluwer 2012

H.L.E. Verhagen and M.H.E. Rongen, *Cessie*, Deventer: Kluwer 2000

POLAND

R. Adamus, 'Kilka uwag o zasadzie pierwszeństwa zaspokojenia wierzyciela na podstawie art. 532 KC', *MoP* 2013, no. 15

Z. Banaszczyk, 'Komentarz do art. 546 k.c.' in K. Pietrzykowski (ed), *Kodeks cywilny. Komentarz. Tom II. Art. 450–1088. Przepisy wprowadzające*, Warsaw 2017

W. Białończyk, 'Rękojmia za wady w umowie o roboty budowlane – cz. I', *Monitor Prawniczy* 2015, no. 6

F. Błahuta in Z. Resich (ed), *Kodeks cywilny. Komentarz. Tom 2*, Warsaw 1972

Ł. Błaszczak and J. Kuźmicka-Sulikowska, 'Zbieg roszczeń ex contractu i ex delicto na tle art. 443 k.c. w ujęciu materialnoprawnym i procesowym', *TPP* 2013, no. 3

W. Borysiak in K. Osajda (ed), *Kodeks cywilny. Komentarz. Zobowiązania – część ogólna*, Warsaw 2017

A. Brzozowski, 'Komentarz do art. 561' in K. Pietrzykowski (ed), *Kodeks cywilny. T II. Komentarz. Art. 450–1088. Przepisy wprowadzające*, Warsaw 2018

W. Czachórski, 'Odpowiedzialność kontraktowa i jej stosunek do odpowiedzialności deliktowej wg k.c.', *NP* 1964, no. 10

W. Czachórski, *Zobowiązania. Zarys wykładu*, Warsaw 2002

J. Frąckowiak, *Komis w eksporcie według prawa polskiego*, Wrocław 1985

J. Frąckowiak, 'Umowa komisu' in J. Rajski (ed), *System Prawa Prywatnego*, vol. 7, Warsaw 2018

R. Golat, 'Skutki zbycia ubezpieczonej nieruchomości', *Nieruchomości* 2009, no. 2

Z. Gordon, 'Umowne klauzule egzoneracyjne w stosunkach obrotu uspołecznionego', *Acta Universitatis Lodziensis. Folia Iuridica* 1988, no. 34

M. Grochowski, 'Zbieg norm w zakresie rękojmi za wady rzeczy sprzedanej oraz błędu i podstępu', *Monitor Prawniczy* 2012, no. 19

E. Habryn-Chojnacka, 'Komentarz do art. 568' in M. Gutowski (ed), *Kodeks cywilny. Tom II. Komentarz. Art. 353–626*, Warsaw 2019

K. Haładyj and M. Tulibacka, 'Komentarz do art. 560' in K. Osajda (ed), *Kodeks cywilny. Komentarz*, Warsaw 2019

M. Jasińska, *Skarga pauliańska. Ochrona wierzyciela w razie niewypłacalności dłużnika*, Warsaw 2014

J. Jastrzębski, 'O umownych modyfikacjach podstawy odpoowiedzialności odszkodowawczej dłużnika', *KPP* 2007, no. 3

J. Jezioro, 'Komentarz do art. 560' in E. Gniewek and P. Machnikowski (eds), *Kodeks cywilny. Komentarz*, Warsaw 2017

J. Jezioro, 'Komentarz do art. 678' in E. Gniewek and P. Machnikowski (eds), *Kodeks cywilny. Komentarz*, Warsaw 2017

M. Kaliński, *Szkoda na mieniu i jej naprawienie*, Warsaw 2014

A. Kędzierska-Cieślak, *Komis, zagadnienia cywilnoprawne*, Warsaw 1973

K. Koch, 'Przejście uprawnień z tytułu rękojmi na kolejnego nabywcę rzeczy – glosa – III CZP 96/03', *Monitor Prawniczy* 2007, no. 3

W. Koczara and A. Brzoza, 'Przejście praw z umowy najmu nieruchomości w razie zbycia rzeczy najętej', *Nieruchomości* 2009, no. 2

J.M. Kondek, 'Komentarz do art. 823' in K. Osajda (ed), *Kodeks cywilny. Komentarz*, Warsaw 2019

G. Kozieł, 'Komentarz do art. 509' in A. Kidyba (ed), *Kodeks cywilny. Komentarz. Zobowiązania. Część ogólna. Tom III*, Warsaw 2014

A. Kozioł, 'Komentarz do art. 546', in M. Habdas and M. Fras (eds), *Kodeks cywilny. Komentarz. Tom IV. Zobowiązania. Część szczególna (art. 535–7649)*, Warsaw 2018

A. Kubas, 'Rozszerzona skuteczność wierzytelności', *SC* 1969, t. XIII–XIV

A. Kubas, *Umowa na rzecz osoby trzeciej*, Warsaw/Cracow 1976

A. Kubiak-Cyrul, 'Komentarz do art. 560' in M. Załucki (ed), *Kodeks cywilny. Komentarz*, Warsaw 2019

W. Kurowski, 'Komentarz do art. 509' in M. Habdas and M. Fras (eds), *Kodeks cywilny. Komentarz. Tom III. Zobowiązania. Część ogólna (art. 353–534)*, Warsaw 2018

D. Latawiec-Chara, 'Odpowiedzialność projektanta za wady projektu', *Nieruchomości* 2012, no. 10

P. Machnikowski in E. Gniewek and P. Machnikowski (eds), *Kodeks cywilny. Komentarz*, Warsaw 2014

J. Mojak, 'Komentarz do art. 509' in K. Pietrzykowski (ed), *Kodeks cywilny. T II. Komentarz. Art. 450–1088. Przepisy wprowadzające*, Warsaw 2018

J.P. Naworski, 'Terminy rękojmi za wady fizyczne – glosa – III CZP 39/02', *Monitor Prawniczy* 2004, no. 1

L. Ogiegło in K. Pietrzykowski (ed), *Kodeks cywilny. Komentarz. Tom II. Art. 450–1088*, Warsaw 2015

A. Ohanowicz, 'Zbieg norm w kodeksie cywilnym', *NP* 1966, no. 12

A. Ohanowicz and J. Górski, *Zarys prawa zobowiązań*, Warsaw 1970

A. Olejniczak in A. Kidyba (ed), *Kodeks cywilny. Komentarz. Tom III. Zobowiązania – część ogólna*, Warsaw 2014

T. Pajor, *Odpowiedzialność dłużnika za niewykonanie zobowiązania*, Warsaw 1982
M. Piekarski in Z. Resich (ed), *Kodeks cywilny. Komentarz. Tom 2*, Warsaw 1972
K. Pietrzykowski, 'Komentarz do art. 680 k.c.' in K. Pietrzykowski (ed), *Kodeks cywilny. Komentarz. Tom II. Art. 450–1088. Przepisy wprowadzające*, Warsaw 2017
J. Pokrzywniak, 'Klauzula zezwalająca na przeniesienie praw i obowiązków z umowy', *Monitor Prawniczy* 2004, no. 24
W. Popiołek, 'Komentarz do art. 527–534 k.c.' in K. Pietrzykowski (ed), *Kodeks cywilny. Komentarz. Tom II. Art. 450–1088. Przepisy wprowadzające*, Warsaw 2017
W. Popiołek in K. Pietrzykowski (ed), *Kodeks cywilny. Tom I. Komentarz. Art. 1–449*[10], Warsaw 2018
W. Popiołek in K. Pietrzykowski (ed), *Kodeks cywilny. Kom II. Komentarz. Art. 450–1088. Przepisy wprowadzające*, Warsaw 2018
M. Pyziak-Szafnicka, 'Ochrona wierzyciela w razie niewypłacalności dłużnika' in A. Olejniczak (ed), *System Prawa Prywatnego*, vol. 6, Warsaw 2018
M. Pyziak-Szafnicka, *Ochrona wierzyciela w razie niewypłacalności dłużnika*, Warsaw 1995
Z. Radwański in Z. Radwański (ed), *System prawa cywilnego. Tom III. Prawo zobowiązań – część ogólna*, Wrocław 1981
Z. Radwański and A. Olejniczak, *Zobowiązania – część ogólna*, Warsaw 2012
A. Rembieliński, 'Kontraktowa odpowiedzialność dłużnika za osoby trzecie w prawie cywilnym i w prawie obrotu uspołecznionego', *SPE* 1974, vol. XII
W. Robaczyński and P. Księżak, 'Niewykonanie lub nienależyte wykonanie zobowiązania jako czyn niedozwolony' in M. Nesterowicz (ed), *Czyny niedozwolone w prawie polskim i prawie porównawczym*, Warsaw 2012
K. Siwiec, 'Zmiana stron umowy najmu i dzierżawy w czasie obowiązywania umowy, cz. I', *Nieruchomości* 2013, no. 8
A. Śmieja, 'Umowna modyfikacja zasad odpowiedzialności kontraktowej', *Iust.* 2011, no. 3
A. Śmieja, 'O dopuszczalnych granicach umownej modyfikacji zasad i przesłanek odpowiedzialności odszkodowawczej' in W. Robaczyński (ed), *Czynić postęp w prawie. Księga jubileuszowa dedykowana Profesor Birucie Lewaszkiewicz Petrykowskiej*, Łódź 2017
A. Śmieja in A. Olejniczak (ed), *System prawa prywatnego. Tom 6. Prawo zobowiązań – część ogólna*, Warsaw 2018
L. Stecki in J. Winiarz (ed), *Kodeks cywilny z komentarzem, praca zbiorowa*, vol. I, Warsaw 1989
G. Stojek in M. Habdas and M. Fras (eds), *Kodeks cywilny. Komentarz. Tom III. Zobowiązania, Część ogólna (art. 353–534)*, Warsaw 2018
R. Strugała, 'Odpowiedzialność dłużnika w razie wykonywania zobowiązania przez osoby trzecie (art. 474 k.c.)', *PS* 2017, nos 11–12
A. Szpunar, 'Zbieg roszczeń odszkodowawczych', *Ruch PES* 1974, no. 1
A. Szpunar, 'Stosunki własnościowe przy komisie', *Rejent* 1994, no. 1.
W. Warkałło, 'Klauzule wyłączające odpowiedzialność za szkodę a ubezpieczenie odpowiedzialności cywilnej', *Ruch PES* 1974, no. 3
K. Zagrobelny, 'W sprawie szkody występującej pod postacią zwiększenia się pasywów poszkodowanego', *Acta Universitatis Wratislaviensis. Prawo* 2009, vol. CCCVIII

K. Zagrobelny, 'Komentarz do art. 512' in E. Gniewek and P. Machnikowski (eds), *Kodeks cywilny. Komentarz*, Warsaw 2016

P. Zakrzewski, 'Komentarz do art. 391' in M. Habdas and, M. Fras (eds), *Kodeks cywilny. Komentarz. Tom III. Zobowiązania. Część ogólna (art. 353–534)*, Warsaw 2018

P. Zakrzewski, 'Komentarz do art. 678' in M. Habdas and M. Fras (eds), *Kodeks cywilny. Komentarz. Tom IV. Zobowiązania. Część szczególna (art. 535–7649)*, Warsaw 2018.

F. Zoll, *Rękojmia. Odpowiedzialność sprzedawcy*, Warsaw 2018

K. Żok, 'Obniżenie ceny w świetle znowelizowanych przepisów o rękojmi', *Ius Novum* 2016, no. 4

SCOTLAND

R.G. Anderson and J.W.A. Biemans, 'Reform of Assignation in Security: Lessons from the Netherlands' (2012) 16(1) *Edinburgh Law Review* 24

R.G. Anderson, *Assignation* (Edinburgh Legal Education Trust, Edinburgh 2008)

R. Barnett, 'Squaring undisclosed agency law with contract theory' (1987) 75 *California Law Review* 1969

G.J. Bell, *Principles of the Law of Scotland*, 10th ed., vol. 1 (1889, reprinted by Law Society of Scotland, Butterworths, Edinburgh 1989)

G.J. Bell, *Commentaries on the Law of Scotland and on the Principles of Mercantile Jurisprudence*, 7th ed., vol. 1 (1870, reprinted by T&T Clark, Edinburgh 1990)

J.T. Cameron, '*Jus Quaesitum Tertio*: The True Meaning of Stair I.x.5' (1961) *Juridical Review* 103

B. Coote, 'The Performance Interest, Panatown, and the Problem of Loss' (2001) 117(Jan) *Law Quarterly Review* 81

J. Erskine, *An Institute of the Law of Scotland*, 8th ed. (Law Society of Scotland/Butterworths, Edinburgh 1871)

G. Fridman, 'Undisclosed Principals and the Sale of Goods' in D. Busch, L. Macgregor and P. Watts (eds), *Agency Law in Commercial Practice* (Oxford University Press, Oxford 2016) 70

K. Gerber, *Commercial Leases in Scotland*, 3rd ed. (W. Green, Edinburgh 2016)

W.M. Gloag, *The Law of Contract: A Treatise on the Principles of Contract in the Law of Scotland*, 2nd ed. (W. Green, Edinburgh 1929)

W.M. Gordon, *The Laws of Scotland: Stair Memorial Encyclopaedia: Donation*, reissue (LexisNexis/Law Society of Scotland, London/Edinburgh 2011)

G.L. Gretton and G. Maher, *The Laws of Scotland: Stair Memorial Encyclopaedia: Diligence and Enforcement of Judgments*, vol. 8 (LexisNexis/Law Society of Scotland, London/Edinburgh 1991)

G. Hawkes, 'Emerging from a Black Hole' (2003) 38 *Scots Law Times* 285

M. Hogg, *Promises and Contract Law: Comparative Perspectives* (CUP, Cambridge 2011)

M. Hogg, *Obligations*, 2nd ed. (Avizandum, Edinburgh 2006)

T. Hope, *Major Practicks* (Neill & Co, Edinburgh 1608–33)

G. Jackson, *The Laws of Scotland: Stair Memorial Encyclopaedia: Building Contracts*, reissue (LexisNexis/Law Society of Scotland, London/Edinburgh 2012)

G. Lubbe, 'Assignment' in H. MacQueen and R. Zimmermann (eds), *European Contract Law: Scots and South African Perspectives* (Edinburgh University Press, Edinburgh, 2006)
D.N. MacCormick, '*Jus Quaesitum Tertio*: *Stair v. Dunedin*' (1970) *Juridical Review* 228
L.J. Macgregor, *The Law of Agency in Scotland* (W. Green, Edinburgh 2013)
L.J. Macgregor, *The Laws of Scotland: Stair Memorial Encyclopaedia: Agency and Mandate*, reissue (LexisNexis/Law Society of Scotland, London/Edinburgh 2001)
L. MacFarlane, 'Black Holes and Revelations on the Transferred Loss Doctrine' (2015) 19(3) *Edinburgh Law Review* 388
H. MacQueen and Lord Eassie (eds), *Gloag and Henderson: The Law of Scotland*, 14th ed. (W. Green, Edinburgh 2017)
H. MacQueen and M. Hogg, 'Donation in Scots law' (2012) *Juridical Review* 1
H.L. MacQueen and J. Thomson, *Contract Law in Scotland*, 4th ed. (Bloomsbury Professional Limited, West Sussex 2016)
H.L. MacQueen, *The Laws of Scotland: Stair Memorial Encyclopaedia: Obligations: Contract*, vol. 15 (LexisNexis/Law Society of Scotland, London/ Edinburgh 1995)
A. Mason, 'Privity – A Rule in Search of Decent Burial?' in P. Kincaid (ed), *Privity: Private Justice of Public Regulation* (Ashgate, Dartmouth 2001)
W.W. McBryde, *The Law of Contract in Scotland*, 3rd ed. (Thomson/W. Green, Edinburgh 2007)
D.W. McKenzie Skene, *Bankruptcy* (W. Green/Thomson Reuters, Edinburgh 2018)
F. McManus and E. Russell, *Delict: A Comprehensive Guide to the Law in Scotland* (Dundee University Press, Dundee 2011)
G.C.H. Paton and J.G.S. Cameron, *The Law of Landlord and Tenant in Scotland* (W. Green, Edinburgh 1967)
C.G.H. Paton (ed), *Baron David Hume's Lectures, 1786–1822*, vol. II (The Stair Society, Edinburgh 1939–58)
J.J.H. Pearson, 'Agency' in A.D.M. Forte (ed), *Scots Commercial Law* (Butterworths, Edinburgh 1997)
L.J. Powell and T. Stewart, *Jackson and Powell on Professional Liability*, 7th ed. (Sweet & Maxwell, London 2012)
A. Rahmatian, 'The role of institutional writers in Scots law' (2018) 1 *Juridical Review* 42
K.G.C. Reid, *The Laws of Scotland: Stair Memorial Encyclopaedia: Property: Part 1 – General Law*, vol. 18 (LexisNexis/Law Society of Scotland, London/Edinburgh 1993)
R. Rennie, *Leases* (W. Green, Edinburgh, 2015)
Scottish Law Commission, *Report on Review of Contract Law: Formation, Interpretation, Remedies for Breach, and Penalty Clauses* (Scot Law Com No. 252, 2018)
Scottish Law Commission, *Report on Moveable Transactions Volume 1: Assignation of Claims* (Scot Law Com No. 249, 2017)
Scottish Law Commission, *Report on Third Party Rights* (Scot Law Com No. 245, 2016)
Scottish Law Commission, *Discussion Paper on Third Party Rights in Contract* (Scot Law Com DP No. 157, 2014)
Scottish Law Commission, *Memorandum on Constitution and Proof of Voluntary Obligations: Stipulations in Favour of Third Parties* (Memorandum No. 38, March 1977)
T.B. Smith, *Short Commentary on the Law of Scotland* (W. Green, Edinburgh 1962)

J.D. Stair, *The Institutions of the Law of Scotland*, 3rd ed. (G. Hamilton and J. Balfour, Edinburgh 1759)
P. Sutherland, 'Third-Party Contracts' in H. MacQueen and R. Zimmermann (eds), *European Contract Law: Scots and South African Perspectives* (Edinburgh University Press, Edinburgh 2006)
J. Thomson, 'Restitutionary and performance damages' (2001) 8 *Scots Law Times (News)* 71
G.H. Treitel, *The Law of Contract*, 9th ed. (Sweet & Maxwell, London 1995)
H. Unberath, 'Third party losses and black holes: another view' (1999) 115(Jul) *Law Quarterly* Review 535
D.M. Walker, *The Law of Contracts and Related Obligations in Scotland*, 3rd ed. (T & T Clark, London 1995)
I.N.D. Wallace, 'Third party damages: no legal black hole?' *Review* (1999) 115(Jul) *Law Quarterly* 394

SLOVAKIA

K. Csach, *Zodpovednosť znalcov v komparatívnom a kolíznoprávnom kontexte. Štúdia o zodpovednosti za škodu spôsobenú nesprávnou informáciou* [Experts' Liability in comparative and conflict of laws context. Liability for damage caused by wrong interpretation], Košice: UPJŠ, 2009
K. Csach, T. Doležal, J. Husár, J. Suchoža, Ľ. Širicová, *Profesijná zodpovednosť* [Professional negligence], Košice: UPJŠ, 2011
J. Dankovčík and A. Rajničová Knapíková, *Zákon o znalcoch, tlmočníkoch a prekladateľoch. Komentár* [Act on experts, interpreters and translators. Commentary], Bratislava: Wolters Kluwer, 2014
I. Fekete, *Občiansky zákonník, Komentár* [Commentary on Civil Code I], sect. 1 – sect. 122, Bratislava: Eurokódex, 2017
M. Hlušák, *Vymáhateľná alebo vykonateľná?*, http://www.lexforum.cz/571.
J. Husár, 'Správa cudzieho majetku' [Administration of assets belonging to others] in *Obchodné právo a jeho širšie kontexty*, Košice: UPJŠ, 2010
M. Jurčová and J. Zámožík, 'Ochrana majetkových záujmov komitenta v komisionárskej zmluve' [Protection of property interests according to the contract on commission], *Justičná revue*, vol. 62, 5 (2010)
P. Lukáčka, L. Dufalová and K. Lenhartová, *Zodpovednosť za vady diela* [Liability for defects of the work], Bratislava: Wolters Kluwer, 2016
M. Novotný, 'Vymáhanie cudzej pohľadávky vo vlastnom mene. (Niekoľko úvah nad rozhodnutím Najvyššieho súdu SR)' [Collection of claims belonging to other creditors (Some thoughts on a Supreme court Judgment)], *Právní rozhledy*, 23–24 (2016)
O. Ovečková et al., *Obchodný zákonník. Veľký komentár, vol. I* [Commentary on Commercial Code I], Bratislava: Wolters Kluwer, 2017
O. Ovečková et al., *Obchodný zákonník. Veľký komentár, vol. II* [Commentary on Commercial Code II], Bratislava: Wolters Kluwer, 2017
M. Patakyová et al., *Obchodný zákonník. Komentár* [Commentary on Commercial Code], 4th ed., Praha: C.H. Beck, 2013

M. Rušín, 'Schvaľovanie zmluvy o predaji (časti) podniku valným zhromaždením' [The approval of the contract on the transfer of enterprise by the shareholder assembly], *Súkromné právo*, 6–7 (2015)

M. Števček, A. Dulak, J. Bajánková, M. Fečík, F. Sedlačko, M. Tomašovič et al. *Občiansky zákonník I, sect. 1–450. Komentár* [Commentary on Civil Code I, sect. 1–450], Praha: C.H. Beck, 2015

M. Števček, A. Dulak, J. Bajánková, M. Fečík, F. Sedlačko, M. Tomašovič et al. *Občiansky zákonník II, sect. 451–880* [Commentary on Civil Code II, sect. 451–880], Praha: C.H. Beck, 2015.

J. Suchoža and J. Husár, *Obchodné právo a jeho širšie kontexty* [Commercial Law and its Broader Aspects], Košice: UPJŠ, 2010.

V. Trojčáková, 'Pričítanie škody spôsobenej pomocníkom; Zodpovednosť na pomedzí porušenia zmluvnej povinnosti a deliktu' [Attribution of damage caused by the assisting person, between contractual and tortious liability] in Z. Nevolná and D. Hlobíková (eds), *Porušenie zmluvných povinností v súkromnom práve a jeho následky*, Trnava: Právnická fakulta Trnavskej univerzity v Trnave, 2018

M. Valachovič, 'Zastupovanie vlastníkov pri správe bytového domu' [Representation of owners and the administration of the residental building], *Zlepšovák*, 4–5 (2018)

E. Valko and B. Jablonka, 'Zmluva o predaji podniku nepripúšťa dohodu o vylúčení niektorých práv a povinností (reakcia na článok)' [Transfer of enterprise does not allow any arrangement on exclusion of certain rights or liabilites (a reaction)], *Obchodné právo*, 8–9 (2004)

P. Vojčík, *Občianske právo hmotné I* [Substantive Civil Law], 4th ed., Košice: UPJŠ, 2014

P. Vojčík, *Občianske právo hmotné II* [Substantive Civil Law II], Košice: UPJŠ, 2006

SPAIN

A. Macía Morillo, 'El contrato o estipulación a favor de tercero a la luz del Derecho comparado y del moderno Derecho de contratos', *Anuario de Derecho Civil*, 2020, 559–634

A. Carrasco Perera, *Derecho Civil: Introducción. Fuentes. Derecho de la Persona. Derecho Subjetivo. Derecho de Propiedad* (5th ed., Tecnos 2016)

A. Carrasco Perera, *Derecho civil* (6th ed., Tecnos 2018)

A. Carrasco Perera, *Derecho de contratos* (3rd ed., Thomson-Aranzadi 2021)

B. Fernández Gregoraci, *La representación indirecta* (Thomson Civitas 2006)

B. Fernández Gregoraci, 'Representación indirecta. Artículo 1717 II CC: "cosas propias del mandante". Ámbito objetivo de aplicación y ¿responsabilidad del representante? (a propósito de las SSTS de 3 de enero de 2006 y 22 de abril de 2005)', *Anuario de Derecho Civil*, 2006, IV, 2035–2050

L. Díez-Picazo, *Fundamentos del Derecho Civil Patrimonial*, I (6th ed., Civitas, 2007)

L. Díez-Picazo and A. Gullón, *Sistema de derecho civil* (13th ed., Tecnos 2016)

N. Jansen and R. Zimmermann (eds), *Commentaries on European Contract Laws* (Oxford University Press 2019)

R. Sebastián Quetglas (coord.), *Fundamentos de derecho empresarial: Derecho Concursal* (3rd ed., Thomson Reuters 2018)

SWEDEN

AB92 – Allmänna bestämmelse för byggnads-, anläggnings- och installationsentreprenader, Svensk Byggtjänst och Föreningen Byggandets kontraktskommitté, BKK, 1992 (Standard contract terms for commercial building contracts)
AB04 – Allmänna bestämmelser för byggnads-, anläggnings- och installationsentreprenader, Svensk Byggtjänst och Föreningen Byggandets kontraktskommitté, BKK, 2004 (Standard contract terms for commercial building contracts)
A. Adlercreutz and L. Gorton, *Avtalsrätt I*, 13th ed., Juristförlaget i Lund, Lund 2011
H. Andersson, *Ansvarsproblem i skadeståndsrätten*, Iustus, Uppsala 2013
H. Andersson, *Ersättningsproblem i skadeståndsrätten*, Iustus, Uppsala 2017
E. Björkdahl, *Hyra av bostad och lokal*, 2nd ed., Iustus, Uppsala 2018
U. Göranson, *Återvinning utom konkurs: svenskt och rättsjämförande kring actio Pauliana, Anfechtung och fraudulent conveyances*, Norstedts, Stockholm 1989
K. Grönfors, *Avtalsgrundande rättsfakta*, Nerénius och Santerus förlag, Stockholm 2013
J. Hellner, R. Hager and A.H. Persson, *Speciell kontraktsrätt II: Kontraksrätt: 1 häftet. Särskilda avtal*, 6th ed., Wolters Kluwer, Stockholm 2015
J. Hellner, R. Hager and A.H. Persson, *Speciell kontraktsrätt II: Kontraksrätt: 2 häftet. Allmänna ämnen*, 6th ed., Wolters Kluwer, Stockholm 2016
J. Hellner and M. Radetzki, *Skadeståndsrätt*, 10th ed., Norstedts, Stockholm 2018
T. Håstad, *Sakrätt avseende lös egendom*, 6th ed., Norstedts, Stockholm 1996
S.O. Johansson, *Kommissionslagen: En kommentar*, Norstedts, Stockholm 2017
J. Kleineman, *Ren förmögenhetsskada: Särskilt vid vilseledande av annan än kontraktspart*, Juristförlaget, Stockholm 1987
J. Kleineman, 'Obehörig vinst och frågan om vårt behov av rättsliga tvångströjor', *TfR* 2013 pp. 531–549
O. Lando, M.-L. Holle, T. Håstad, B.-E. Konow, P. Møgelvang-Hansen, S. Nystén-Haarala, Á. Ólafsdóttir and L. Zackariasson, *Restatement of Nordic Contract Law*, Jurist- og Økonomforbundets forlag, Copenhagen 2016
G. Lennander, *Återvinning i konkurs*, 3rd ed., Norstedts juridik, Stockholm 2010
S. Lindskog, *Betalning: Om kongruent infriande av penningskulder och andra betalningsrättsliga frågor*, 2nd ed., Norstedts juridik, Stockholm 2018
C. Martinson, 'How Swedish Lawyers Think about "Ownership" and "Transfer of Ownership" – Are We Just Peculiar or Actually Ahead?' in W. Faber and B. Lurger (eds), *Rules for the Transfer of Movables: A Candidate for European Harmonisation or National Reforms?*, Sellier European Law Publishers, Munich 2008
O. Mossberg, *Avtalets räckvidd I: Om avtals tredjemansverkningar, särskilt vid tredjemansavtal och direktkrav*, Iustus förlag, Uppsala 2020
O. Mossberg, 'Spekulationer om implikationer: Om kommission och om vad NJA 2014 s. 760 egentligen innebär' in J. Samuelsson and L.M. Elvevold (eds), *Över gränsen*, Iustus, Uppsala 2024 (forthcoming)
J. Munukka, *Kontraktuell lojalitetsplikt*, Jure, Stockholm 2007
M. Möller, *Civilrätten vid finansiell leasing*, Iustus förlag, Uppsala 1996
R. Nordh, 'Bevisbörda och beviskrav i tvistemål', *Svensk juristtidning* 2012, pp. 781–799
H. Renman, *Återvinning enligt 4 kap. konkurslagen: En process of insolvensrättslig manual*, Norstedts juridik, Stockholm 2009

E. Runesson, 'Construction of Commercial Contracts in Nordic Law and the Rule of Prudence' in *The Nordic Contracts Act: Essays in Celebration of its One Hundredth Anniversary*, Djøf Publishing, Copenhagen 2015

M. Schultz, 'Nya argumentationslinjer i förmögenhetsrätten: Obehörig vinst rediviva', *SvJT* 2009, p. 946

G. Walin, *Förmånsrättslagen, lönegarantilagen m.m.: En kommentar*, 5th ed., Norstedts, Stockholm 2004

G. Walin, G. Millqvist and A.H. Persson, *Panträtt*, 3rd ed., Norstedts juridik, Stockholm, 2012

L. Zackariasson, *Borgenärsskydd och specialitet*, Iustus, Uppsala 2011

L. Zackariasson, 'Privity of Contract and Direct Claims' in T. Håstad (ed), *The Nordic Contracts Act: Essays in Celebration of its One Hundredth Anniversary*, Djøf Publishing, Copenhagen 2015

INDEX

www.ingramcontent.com/pod-product-compliance
Ingram Content Group UK Ltd.
Pitfield, Milton Keynes, MK11 3LW, UK
UKHW051905290926
8980IPUK00017B/1785

9 781839 705